SECRET MUSES

SECRET MUSES

THE LIFE OF
FREDERICK ASHTON

JULIE KAVANAGH

PANTHEON BOOKS
NEW YORK

Grateful acknowledgment is made to the following for permission to reprint
previously published material:

Yvonne and Rudolph Burckhardt: Excerpts from the writings of Edwin Denby,
which appear in the forthcoming book *The Edwin Denby Reader,* Yale University Press, 1997. Copyright © 1986 by Yvonne and Rudolph Burckhardt.
Reprinted by permission of Yvonne and Rudolph Burckhardt.

Arlene Croce: Excerpts from her articles appearing in *The New Yorker* from
1985 to 1991, and from her books, *Afterimages, Going to the Dance,* and *Sight
Lines.* Copyright © 1972, 1977, 1982 by Arlene Croce. All rights reserved.
Reprinted by permission of Arlene Croce.

Library of Congress Cataloging-in-Publication Data

Kavanagh, Julie.
  Secret muses : the life of Frederick Ashton / Julie Kavanagh.
    p.   cm.
  Includes bibliographical references and index.
  ISBN 0-67944269-3
  1. Ashton, Frederick, Sir, 1906– . 2. Choreographers—Great
Britain—Biography. I. Title.
GV1785.A8K38   1997
792.8′2′092—dc21
[B]   96-29525
                                         CIP

Random House Web Address: http://www.randomhouse.com

Printed in the United States of America
First American Edition
2   4   6   8   9   7   5   3   1

For Ross, Joe and Alfie

CONTENTS

SECRET MUSES

CHILD OF THE SUN
1863–1919

The curtains of a raised booth on stage were drawn aside and there she was, Anna Pavlova as the Fairy Doll, her deliberately slow, extra deep breaths making the sequins on her costume glint in the light. Set in a toy shop, *The Fairy Doll* required the ballerina to remain still until the toys came to life; yet even stationary, Pavlova danced – flickering her huge, kohl-smudged eyes and almost imperceptibly stirring her slender arms and fingers. The audience was silent with the suspense of waiting for her to perform, but the thirteen-year-old Peruvian boy who had whispered excitedly, 'Es ella? Es ella?' at the entrance of each female member of the company, felt cheated, and said so out loud: how ugly she looked with her pinkish wig and beaky nose, and how old. 'Espera¡' said the man sitting next to him. Wait. 'And he was right.' From the moment the ballerina descended the three steps on to the stage and began her variations – a delicate waltz, a sparkling, darting xylophone solo, and an adagio during which she balanced indefinitely in arabesque – the young Frederick Ashton's future was decided. Pavlova, he said years later, was the greatest theatrical genius he had ever seen. By today's standards, her technique was poor; she rarely executed more than two pirouettes, but they were done with such brio – 'a sort of *flurry*', in Ashton's phrase – that she gave the effect of at least half a dozen more. Pavlova's vibrant personality, the expressive play of every part of her body and the outpouring of ecstatic energy sent a charge through the auditorium, creating what one critic described as 'a kind of electrification of the air'. 'She was a spirit, a flame,' said Ashton. 'She wasn't human.' Like the fairy heroine in Stravinsky's allegory about Tchaikovsky, *Le Baiser de la fée*, Pavlova became Ashton's muse, imprinting a fateful kiss which lasted for the rest of his life. 'Seeing her at that stage was the end of me. She injected me with her poison and from the end of that evening I wanted to dance.'

This performance, a mixed bill of Pavlova classics, took place in 1917 at the Teatro Municipal in Lima, Peru, the city in which Frederick Ashton spent most of his childhood. He had motored to the theatre in a Marmon open tourer, a rare, prestigious American car, owned by an acquaintance of the family with whom he was then staying, the Watsons. His father's new job with a British commercial firm had taken George and Georgiana Ashton and their small daughter back to Guayaquil in Ecuador, where their four sons had been born. But owing to a yellow fever epidemic there, Frederick and his brothers were 'farmed out' to various friends in Lima: 'My mother was like a cat dispersing her kittens all over the place.' The Watsons lived in Miraflores (literally, 'look at the flowers'), which was then, as it is today, a pleasant suburb with English rose gardens, and bougainvillea and plumbago foaming over the walls. Guy Watson was the same age as Frederick, but, although they had now lived together for nearly three years, they were not close. Returning to the Calle Atahualpa after Pavlova's performance that evening, Ashton had given no indication that this was a turning point in his life. 'He was an interior type of child and there was little talk about anything like that between us.'

Except for Pavlova's plaintive signature piece, the Dying Swan solo, Guy remembered virtually nothing about her performance; the lasting impression for him was the Crusader costume worn in *Raymonda* by her partner, Alexander Volinine – 'For hours afterwards I was Volinine.' Ashton, on the other hand, 'hated Volinine', just as he had no interest in any of the men in Pavlova's company – 'I wanted to dance like *her*.' Images of Pavlova, such as her diagonal bourrées along a path marked out by roses, and all 'the carry-on' with her hands and eyes, never left him: every ballerina role he would go on to create was done so in the shadow of his muse. As Margot Fonteyn, the dancer who became his English muse, remarked towards the end of her life, 'I always felt that Fred was seeing Pavlova and that I wasn't living up to her by any means.'

Exiled from Russia by the Great War, Anna Pavlova was a missionary of classical dance, spending twenty years obsessively seeking new audiences throughout the world. It was in Lima that she had one of the greatest triumphs of her career; coming towards the end of a long, harrowing itinerary of North and South America, it had seemed like a city of light. Lima today, riven by economic collapse and terrorism, and shrouded in the mist the locals call 'neblina', is unsightly and threatening, but for the colonial expatriates in Frederick Ashton's time, it was another world. Jiron de la Union, where youths now stand with calculators peddling American dollars, was once the city's Bond Street: women bought their gloves from the French-owned Pygmalion, their hats from Oëchli, the Swiss milliner, or Crevanni, the Italian hatter, who also sold soaps and perfumes by Yardley and Roger et Gallet. Palatial colonial houses like the Torre Tagle, with its boxed-in Moorish wooden balconies – a reminder of the city's vice-regal occupation – were still privately owned, and the wealthier European women lived lives of Proustian splendour, importing lingerie from Paris, silk stockings from Liberty, and observing all the social niceties of the Edwardian era. Lima society made its own entertainment; there were dinner parties, recitals, amateur theatricals, balls at the Club, thé-dansants and soirées. In Peru, as Ashton said, 'people *danced*. You could tango before you could practically do anything else.' Although the theatre was rarely patronized, the crowds that filled the Teatro Municipal every night for a month, while Pavlova was in town, were ecstatically appreciative of everything they saw. For the Limeños, her season was the social event of the year. Rich patrons strove to outdo each other with ostentatious bouquets of flowers for favourite dancers, and the whole house wore evening dress, the European women competing with the glittering Latin Americans by decorating their silk Empire gowns with gilt embroidery, and adding diamond ornaments to their hair. Adrift from her normal Continental setting, the Italian Marchesa Casati appeared at Pavlova's farewell performance in cloth of gold, with a matching helmet decked with black ostrich feathers. As the final curtain fell, white pigeons were released from their cages, flying up towards the vast marble dome as flowers thrown from the gods rained on stage.

Frederick Ashton's adoration for Pavlova was not an adolescent infatuation, not a sexual frisson of the kind that the schoolboy Cecil Beaton had experienced at a performance in London, when she gathered up the wilting roses that he had thrown to her on stage. Ashton wanted to *be* Pavlova. It was an obsession. He found out at which hotel she was staying and waited for her to appear, watching the way she alighted from her carriage, draped in a stole of sable which fell to the ground, and walked away with her strange gliding gait. He hung, entranced, on accounts of her appearances off-stage. His mother met the ballerina twice during her month in Lima and, at a soirée at which Pavlova was guest of honour, Ashton heard how she had watched his eldest brother performing with great accomplishment on the dance floor. Nineteen years old, with black hair and blue eyes, Tony Ashton was exceptionally dashing, 'the most beautiful tango dancer you've ever seen'. Pavlova asked to be introduced to him and, during their conversation, invited him to join her company. 'He was horrified and absolutely shocked and refused point blank.' Even at this early stage, such chilling contempt provided Ashton with an inkling of the kind of opposition he would later face from his family. 'If my father had lived I wouldn't be here now.'

When Ashton was born in Guayaquil in September 1904, his father, George, was Vice-Consul at the British Embassy and also worked as manager of the Central and South American Cable Company. The family lived in Las Peñas, the diplomatic quarter overlooking the city's soupy brown river, but Frederick, the youngest of the four boys, retained no memories of their life in Guayaquil. His earliest impressions are of being in England at the age of two. Hearing news that her mother was dying, Georgiana (Georgie) Ashton had brought her children to Yaxley, the Suffolk village where she had grown up. Frederick and his four-year-old brother, Charlie, were christened in the church there, and later Georgie must have rented a house in Clifton, as Ashton remembered crossing over the suspension bridge – 'Sitting in a carriage and *hanging* on' – and a long street up a hill. His mother, he said, was a friend of the headmaster of Clifton Junior College, but although he maintained that the purpose of the visit was to settle his two elder brothers, Tony and Alex, at the school, the college have no record of their attendance. A nanny/governess was employed during the Clifton sojourn, a Miss Sutton-Flat. 'She was a *brute*. When I wet my bed she used to carry me over to the window and point at a policeman and say, "If you wet your bed tonight I'll hand you over to him." That used to frighten the life out of me. I was always a wetter and was absolutely terrified.' Ashton also recalled a visit to Madeira where they spent that winter because of Tony's delicate health. 'I remember the ox-carts and the cobbles because I was always falling down and bruising my knees.'

Soon after Georgie and the boys returned to South America, the family moved to Lima, renting an elegant bow-fronted terraced house in the Calle Washington, a side street off the fashionable Paseo Colón. A wide, handsome avenue, the Paseo had a long strip down the centre with palm trees, statues, benches and lush displays of tropical flowers, and at one end was a circular garden where the children would go to listen to the band that played twice a week. The British Legation was situated there and, although George had given up his post as Vice-Consul, Georgie, who loved entertaining, went out of her way to retain links with Lima's diplomatic corps, holding regular receptions to which several foreign ministers and their wives were invited. These evenings made a considerable impression on the young Ashton, who later romantically recalled how 'elegant ladies rather plump in slit skirts, enormous hats and tango shoes would all pour into our house, and the Chinese Minister would arrive with a Japanese wife and gradually empty the rooms because no one could stand his poppy scent'. For much of the time, however, the life of the close-knit British Colony was far from grand. Male society centred on the Phoenix Club, while weekly 'At Homes' were held by the wives. Mrs Ashton was one of a score of redoubtable exiles who had survived epidemics of plague and an early married life of sometimes appallingly primitive conditions. Dispensing tea and chatting about the Royal Family,

these women were all invincibly English, attaching a touching importance to any link with home – fading chintz, china knick-knacks, English
papers and periodicals, battered and out of date, which would be passed
from family to family until they fell apart. A remarkable woman of unfulfilled potential, Georgie Ashton was well liked by the other wives in
the community. She was spirited, witty and a good friend to anyone in
need of comfort. But she was a forceful personality and is mostly remembered as being extremely ambitious in matters of social status. When
she gave a reception for an English girl who came out to marry a young
colleague of George's in the cable company, Georgie completely took
over. 'It might have been her own wedding.'

If Georgie was fun and outgoing, her husband was the opposite – a
dark, introverted character with a melancholic streak which his son,
Frederick, felt he had inherited. As a child, he was always terrified of his
father. 'I don't know why now, except that he used to make me eat things
I couldn't manage . . . He was very strict indeed with me. I steered clear
of him as much as I could.' Although George Ashton had a soft spot for
Charlie, a delightful rogue, who would 'cheek him' and make him laugh,
he was implacably severe with his other sons. The older boys had to wear
smoking jackets for dinner and if anyone arrived late, there would not be
a place for him at table. In 1911, a longed-for daughter was born. 'Dear
little Edith' was adored and indulged by her father whom she resembled,
with her round, periwinkle-blue eyes. She was his lucky charm – just as
she became for Frederick years later – and George gave her a second
name, Gertrudis, after a Mexican silver mine in which he had invested a
lot of money. Edith used to say that she was the child of her parents' reconciliation, but relations between the incompatible George and Georgiana were to grow even more estranged. 'I don't think it was a very
happy marriage, although I didn't realize that at the time,' said Ashton.
'At night my mother would sit in the drawing room and my father would
sit in another room. That may have had a bit to do with Edwardian behaviour because of smoking – my father used to smoke pipes. But my
mother liked society and my father *hated* it.'

At every opportunity, George Ashton would escape to the walled garden on the outskirts of the city where he grew and propagated carna-
tions. 'He used to bring home a new variety with great delight,' said
Ashton. The garden was situated in the barriados, in the midst of a new
development of small houses which he had built for the poor. 'He was a
kind of hero there . . . All the people came out to greet him when he
walked past.' Although ruthlessly strict with his own sons, George was
well known in Lima as a philanthropist, scattering coins for the slum
children who loved him and always surrounded him, and, to the despair

of his wife, sheltering vagrants under their own roof. 'Any English beach-comber who told him a reasonable story was in the house before we knew it, dossing down.' His father, as Ashton said, was 'a mystery. An absolute mystery.' While Georgie often talked about her family and their Suffolk village, George never referred to his life in England. 'None of us knew anything about him at all. I used to ask my mother, but she didn't seem to know much either. She used to say that he had "some good blood in him". All I know is that he had a sister who was called Fanny – whether she was Ashton or not, I don't know – and she went to America.' Years later, while on a Royal Ballet tour, Ashton met Fanny's daughter, Daisy, in Santa Monica, but she appeared to know as little about the fam-ily background as he did. 'I know that as a boy my father sang in the choir at Wells Cathedral. That's the only thing I know.'*

In 1913 when Ashton was nine, a stepbrother, George's son from a previous marriage, arrived from England to live with the family. Al-though none of the brothers thought of questioning him at the time, it was John Ashton who was to throw light on at least one period of their father's past. John – or Stevens, as George called him, his first wife's maiden name – had not seen his father for twenty years. His mother had died when he was four years old and he had been left in the care of two maiden aunts who lived in Wells. George had sent a regular sum of money for his upkeep, but even so, John's well-being had been constantly on his conscience. Latterly, he had become increasingly worried that his son was wasting his time, articled to a broker for a pound a week, and had threatened to cut off the allowance in order to force him to make his own way. He wrote several letters to London firms trying to get John a better position and finally concluded that his son's prospects would im-prove only if he came to Lima – if nothing else, John could join the cable company as a bookkeeper for £15 per month and at least the move would allow him to escape the imminent war in Europe.

Although Frederick was at the time too young to remember, he had met John Ashton before, during his trip to England in 1906. Posing with Georgie and her sons for a group photograph, John, dressed in a three-piece suit and wing-collared shirt, looks conspicuously older than the other boys in their best sailor suits and ruched smocks – more like a young husband than a sibling. When he came to live at the Calle Wash-ington, he was still something of an alien, talking in a round Somerset ac-cent that his stepbrothers, who spoke mostly Spanish to each other, could not understand. Frederick did not particularly like John and said that his

---

*Even this was incorrect. George Ashton's name does not appear on the records at Wells.

mother felt much the same – 'she thought him rather common.' Evidently, however, Georgie, a keen card player, began to depend on John's company, as she would frequently turn up at his office in the middle of the afternoon and urge him to come home and join her in a game. 'He had to do what she wanted.' John came to admire his stepmother's strong character – 'She was so well educated and always said the right thing at the right time' – nevertheless, he left home as soon as he could, eventually marrying a Peruvian with whom he had three daughters. One daughter was so glamorous that, many years later, when her Uncle Frederico took her to dinner in London, 'everyone thought she was Sophia Loren'. Although Ashton and his stepbrother had never been close, it was when John brought his family to England in 1948 that he confided information about their father that would fascinate Ashton for the rest of his life. John told him that he had heard from the aunts who fostered him in England that George Ashton was the illegitimate son of the disgraced liberal politician, Sir Charles Wentworth Dilke.

The adultery scandal that shattered Dilke's career broke in the summer of 1885, the year that George Ashton, a twenty-one-year-old postal clerk, went to live in Wells, lodging in a cottage by the railway station belonging to two spinster sisters, Jane and Matilda Stevens. Jane, in particular, grew very fond of George and while her other two 'permanents' ate apart, the two of them would have meals together and he even began calling her 'mother'. Through Jane Stevens George met her niece, Elizabeth, a pretty girl from Wookey Hole, whom he began courting even though she was seven years his senior. Elizabeth Stevens had inherited a considerable amount of money from her father, a paper maker, who died before she was born, and when George proposed to her, 'the trouble began': Elizabeth's immediate family was suspicious of him, knowing nothing about his antecedents, and withheld their permission for the couple to marry. It was around this time that George told Jane and Matilda about the Dilke connection and they seem to have taken him at his word. When Sir Charles died in 1911, Matilda wrote and asked George whether this was the man about whom he had told her of his parentage. 'The answer,' he replied, 'is in the affirmative.'

It was, however, untrue. George's father was John Ashton, a cabinet maker, whose wife, Kezia, worked as a milliner and dressmaker in the village of Charmouth in Dorset. Although he did not admit it, Ashton had discovered his grandparents' identity for himself in 1954, when a friend of John's (Barbara Horstmann) had conducted a search on his behalf and sent him George Ashton's birth certificate. The myth proved more appealing than the truth. 'Fred had this obsession with the Dilkes and was always on at Jack about finding a connection.' Nor was he alone, it seems, in linking the Ashtons with the aristocracy. When *A Picture of Dorian Gray* was about to go to press, Oscar Wilde arrived by cab at his publishers with a last-minute correction. He had given a picture-framer in the book the name Ashton and it would not do. 'Ashton is a gentleman's name. And I've given it to a tradesman.'* In fact, the professions of both Ashton's paternal grandparents are extremely germane to his own. He himself was a master craftsman – 'His is the kind of technique that develops the instruments which steer vessels, that grinds microscopes and telescopes, that balances watches,' the choreographer Agnes de Mille has written. 'One finds a craft like Cellini's, like Fabergé's. Each dance and each phrase is set as a master goldsmith sets a gem.' Ashton often compared the choreographer's gift to that of an artisan and stressed the day-to-day routine of his profession: 'Every ballet that I do is a job . . . I'm like somebody who sets out with his implements to go and mend frozen pipes . . . There's too much talk of inspiration and all that kind of thing. I mean, all very well if the muse looks in.' (As usual, though, there is more than a touch of self-deprecation in Ashton's remark. Prosaic as it is, his plumber image is also tellingly symbolic: the freeing of pent-up water is a potent metaphor for the unleashing of inspiration – a classic example being the frozen pump in Seamus Heaney's poem, 'Rite of Spring'.) John Ashton, the son of a blacksmith, had spent six years lodging with a cabinet maker and learning his trade – the kind of apprenticeship Ashton himself sought when he studied in Paris under his mentor, Bronislava Nijinska. 'I believe that if young choreographers submitted to a master, they would learn a great deal. They would not have to copy, but they would learn an approach.' Ashton even inherited his grandmother's sartorial knack. By the age of ten he was fashioning gowns from bath towels and criticizing the hats Guy Watson's mother wore, until she finally relented and allowed him to choose them for her himself. His milliner's eye stayed with him all his life; he would often advise his courtier friends on their hats, for instance, telling The Queen Mother's lady-in-waiting, Ruth, Lady Fermoy, to have one that happened to suit her copied – 'and then *stick* to it.'

In 1958, when Roy Jenkins' biography of Sir Charles Dilke was published, Ashton and his siblings combed it for clues. 'I can find nothing in it that relates to Father,' wrote John Stevens. 'Nevertheless, Tony boy, there probably is a connection with Dilke somewhere.' Although both Ashton and his sister, Edith, eventually made direct enquiries of the Dilke family, no one they contacted had ever heard about the rumour. None the

---

*Changed to Hubbard, '[which] particularly smells of the tradesman'.

less, they remained reluctant to give up the idea. Like their father before them, they had noted one significant detail in the Dilke story – Ashton was the Christian name of Sir Charles's brother – and this was persuasive enough. 'I thought he must have given the name of Ashton to his bastard son . . . My father might have been the son of an aristocrat and a chambermaid for all I know.'

It is unlikely that Kezia Kenway, herself born out of wedlock (the child of a farm labourer's daughter), ever left Dorset to work in the Dilke employment in London. She was brought up in Wootton Fitzpaine, a vertiginously scenic hamlet above Charmouth, and when she married John Ashton in Charmouth's unprepossessing stone and flint church at the age of twenty-two, she was already working as a dressmaker in the village. George was the second of five children; his brothers, Frederick and William, were the originators of Ashton's first and second names (although, with characteristic affectation, Georgie had led him to believe that he was named after the Kaiser). The Ashtons, crammed into tiny Bay Tree Cottage at the bottom of the steep main turnpike road, were one of the poorest families in the village, but the neighbourhood of Charmouth, with its stupendous views of rolling, rich Dorset countryside, was an idyllic place for a child to grow up. The sea was only minutes away and as smooth as a lagoon, the 'sweet retired bay'* backed by cliffs with evocative names, such as Black Venn and Devil's Bellows. After school, the children could tear down Lower Sea Lane to swim or search for rocks imprinted with fossils, taking their finds to Robert Hunter, fossil collector, fisherman, bathing-machine proprietor and sometime smuggler. It was a close, convivial community which welcomed any excuse for a celebration – the laying of the school's foundation stone was enough to close the shops and bring out the flags and village band. All five Ashton children attended the village school for 1d per week, and it was not Wells Cathedral choir in which George sang, but Charmouth church choir, run by the organist, Clara Ann Pavey, a woman of Dickensian sweetness, who became something of a benefactress to George. She and Mr Pavey, the churchwarden, were responsible for selecting the Ashtons as beneficiaries of the Bullen Bread Charity, a trust fund which provided Charmouth's poor and infirm with bread rations at Christmas. The Ashtons were dependent on the charity for nearly ten years: an indication of the extent of the penury that had befallen them. In order to make a living, John Ash-

---

*Jane Austen's description in *Persuasion*.

ton had diversified into general carpentry, but even so, there were several other carpenters in the village who more or less monopolized the available work. When John became sick, the family was forced to rely on Kezia's small income and there were days when the children went hungry. George began spending more and more time at the Paveys' house, sitting in their kitchen eating meals provided by their cook, Bessie Churchill, whose kindness he never forgot. Their son, R. W. J. Pavey, Charmouth's chronicler, describes how, many years later, when George Ashton returned to the village as a prosperous businessman, he presented Bessie with the deeds of her cottage as a token of his gratitude.

A photograph of Clara Pavey's choir, c.1878, shows George and his brother, William, posing formally with the other singers who included the sons of the village blacksmith, baker, butcher and fisherman. Compared to William, a good-looking boy with slightly shifty eyes, George's demeanour is strikingly aggressive: frowning challengingly at the camera, with one thumb hooked in a pocket of his suit, he is by far the shortest in the group and yet looks like an adult in miniature. Only fifteen at the time, he was already helping to earn the family living. His father had died two years earlier at the age of thirty-eight, and George had started work as an errand boy. E. A. Vince's general supply stores had a drapery department on one side of the shop, and a grocery and post office on the other. Soon after George joined the business, a telegraph wire was installed – you could hear the needle ticking as you entered – which was to set him on course for his future career in cable communications. This period in the village shop proved formative all round; another of Vince's dealings was to serve as a valuer and 'umpire' in real-estate deals, a sideline which activated George's lifelong interest in property. By the age of nineteen he had left the village, moving to London to work in a branch of the Post Office, and when his mother died a year later, he went to Bristol, taking his younger brother, Frederick, with him. They both served as second clerks and telegraphists at the Post Office and, in 1885, George was transferred to Wells, where he began lodging with Jane and Matilda Stevens.

Although George had asked the two sisters to keep his secret, word of his 'good blood' may well have reached other members of the Stevens family, as, by July 1887, he and Elizabeth were married. George's only relative to attend the wedding was his younger sister, Frances (Fanny), who was one of the bridesmaids. When their son was born in June 1888, George named him after his father, John Ashton (presumably with his wife's knowledge – John Ashton is cited as his father on their marriage certificate). Among the godparents was Clara Pavey, with whom George had kept in close touch, writing frequently (as he continued to do when he emigrated to South America, from where he was to send the Paveys extravagant presents, including a llama-fur rug). Already there was reason for Clara to be proud of George: he had made a good marriage and, with his wife's legacy, he had begun investing in property, building two red-brick semi-detached houses in Portway, Wells, which he called Ashtonville and Ashton House (there is still an Ashton House at 29 Portway). Four years later, Elizabeth died of consumption. Her family still did not like George and wanted nothing more to do with him, and so, after mortgaging his property for £550, he went abroad for six months. Soon after his return, he rejoined the Post Office, taking up a position for a year in Wokingham, before moving to Sevenoaks in Kent. It was here that he first set eyes on Ashton's mother.

Georgie Fulcher had been staying with relatives in Sevenoaks when she came into the Post Office to send a telegram home announcing the time of her arrival. Although by no means a beauty, she was a vivacious young woman with a quick wit and merry smile. 'My father was taken by her, looked at the envelope to see what the address was, *wrote* . . . and my grandmother, who was anxious to get these three daughters married, invited him to stay. My grandmother was half French anyway, and so she was on to it all.' Twenty-three-year-old Georgie was at the time living with her parents and two sisters on a farm in Yaxley in Suffolk. Unlike George Ashton, she came from comfortable, secure stock as solidly rooted as a cedar. The Fulchers had farmed the land around Yaxley since Domesday, and Valley Farm had been in the family for 240 years. Thomas Fulcher, Georgie's grandfather, had run the farm and served as churchwarden at St Mary's, Yaxley – where generations of Fulchers were baptized, married and buried – just as an earlier Thomas Fulcher had done two centuries before him. Following the deaths of her grandparents in quick succession, Georgie and her family had recently moved into Valley Farm, a dairy farm of over 300 acres leased from Lord Henniker, whose great grandson still owns the land today. She had grown up at nearby Store House Farm (belonging to her grandmother), where her father had worked since his teens. Henry (Harry) Fulcher had been employed there as an apprentice steward when he had met Edith Mallandaine, a British Army captain's daughter brought up in Brittany, who taught French at the Abbey School in Bury St Edmunds, run by Anne Fulcher, Harry's sister. He and Edith married young and produced four children: a son, Thomas, and three daughters. Georgie was the plain one, tall, solidly built, with a masculine face and rather bulbous nose; May was pretty, with round flirtatious eyes; plump little Milly was the family pet. The girls were always close, but for much of their childhood they paired off with their cousins, the three Bullen sisters, who spent holidays at

Store House because their mother, Harry's sister Mary, had died. 'We loved going there to stay for we did exactly as we liked and it was liberty to us,' said Edith Bullen. These were carefree days. Harry Fulcher was a jolly soul, often singing to himself, and Georgie's mother, Edith, was also full of fun, organizing parties, plays and tableaux for the children in the holidays. A great friend was John Tillott (who married Edith Fulcher after Harry died), a neighbouring farmer with a large barn, in which the dances and entertainments were held. The barn's interior would be decorated to look like a rustic ballroom, its walls and beams covered with red flannel and swags of evergreen. After tea, the dancing would begin – polkas, waltzes and mazurkas, with pauses in between for refreshments of lemonade, oranges and apples laid out in the hall. When plays and concerts were given, the barn, well heated and matted, had a stage erected at one end, hung with authentically theatrical curtains. Half an hour before the performance began, there might be an overture played from behind the scenes, and often a musical interlude between the acts. Harry, John Tillott and Mr Willoughby, another neighbour, sang solos and the Fulcher sisters, all accomplished musicians, would play chamber pieces for piano (Georgie) and violin (May and Millie). Productions at the barn grew increasingly ambitious. One programme, put on twice in the same week, attracted more than 300 people, some of whom had to be turned away at the door. The performance was covered by the local press (who pronounced it to be 'amateur entertainment of a varied, pleasing, and highly-successful character') and profits were donated towards buying coal for the poor of Yaxley. Frequently, Georgie, anticipating her future son's predilection for droll cross-dressing, would act in the plays en travesti, appearing in the role of Spindle, for example ('A good little man, all heart'), in a sub-Restoration romp entitled *Princess Brighteyes; or, The Jealous Queen and The Talking Mirror*.

The sisters were given every encouragement to perform. A dancing class was held most mornings and they would all rehearse for weeks before a concert. Even querulous old Granny Fulcher, full of complaints and regrets, but with a 'very soft corner' for her grandchildren, would ask them to play to her when they went to tea at Valley Farm. With or without an audience, the girls were always playacting. 'Last night we had a private dance in our bedroom,' Edith Bullen reported in a letter to her father. 'Pie [Georgie] and Mary [Bullen] were the Masher gentlemen, they had tail coats made out of black jackets, shirt fronts and eye glasses made of wire and corked moustaches. May and I were the ladies and Milly the page in Tom's Eton jacket with bright buttons sewed on . . . May was Miss Olivia Lennox and I was Miss Amelia Eustace. Georgie was George Gregg Esq and Mary, Martin Freeman Esq.' This scenario predates by some fifty years the fancy-dress charades that Ashton would perform with Cecil Beaton and friends, as recorded in Beaton's spoof biography, *My Royal Past*, and it seems to have been carried out in much the same spirit. Georgie continued to arrange musical entertainments when she went to South America and, although she was never able to develop her artistic gifts, many of her enthusiasms resurfaced in her famous son. 'She had a great zest for life and any talent that I have comes out of her.'

For all the jollity of her early youth, Georgie's day-to-day existence was stiflingly insular. Although the village would always make token concessions to national events – locals celebrated the end of the South African War by raising the church flag and decorating their cottages – Yaxley society was circumscribed and parochial. St Mary's was the focus, its redecoration one of the most talked-about topics of the year. As both Georgie's parents had come from large families of eight siblings, mostly daughters, Yaxley at times seemed to be crawling with aunts. 'We girls spoke irreverently (and privately) of "the ant heap".' One or two were more popular than others; Aunt Jane, Fulcher daughter No. 5, was bright and cultured, a bonne viveuse whose fondness for travel would certainly have had some influence on her niece. On the whole, though, the Fulcher aunts were homely and set in their ways, whereas the Mallandaines were women of the world. 'I don't think there was very much cordiality between the two lots of ladies.' Another favourite was Aunt Alice Mallandaine, a good-natured woman who came to live in Yaxley after her parents had died. She was a great supporter of Georgie who tended to be unpopular with the adults, considered too mercurial and self-dramatizing. 'I can see your mother now,' Edith Bullen told Ashton, 'throwing a threepenny piece at one of them, which she had given her to make up for reducing her to angry tears.' When Georgie was sent as a boarder to the Abbey it seemed like a continuation of life at home; Aunt Anne, a forceful, ambitious character, was in charge, and various other aunts were employed by the school. Being another Fulcher teacher at the Abbey – and another spinster Fulcher at that – was the fate that Georgie must have seen in store for herself. While there had always been lots of boys around in her childhood (at one Christmas dance she and her sisters could not get to the lemonade because of the boys congregating under the mistletoe), ever since their brother, Tom, had left home and gone missing in Brazil, his friends had dwindled away. Most visitors to Yaxley tended to be female relations (like Georgie's Mallandaine grandmother, 'a rather massive and impassive figure with a big nose', known as Granny Mangle and who spent summers with the family). At one point, in order to pursue her musical training, Georgie had been sent away to study, but this departure was short-lived. 'The man she was studying with tried to seduce her and my grandmother got her back immediately. Back to the farm.'

Then, George Ashton arrived on the scene. Short, stocky, with bulbous eyes and a dubious past, he may not have been the most attractive proposition, but at least he offered the chance of escape to another life. 'It was really rather a question of "anything to get away from Suffolk".' George told the Paveys that he had fallen in love with a general's daughter and that the general would agree to the marriage only if the couple went abroad. This was, of course, another fabrication. The only military man in the immediate family was John Mallandaine, Georgie's grandfather, who, while never a general, had served with the Royal Rifle Corps, but even he had been dead for six years. For all that, the proviso may well have been made by Harry and Edith Fulcher who, according to Ashton, gave their blessing to the couple because they hoped that if Georgie went to South America, she might somehow trace her lost brother. So, assuring his fiancée that he would send for her when he had made good, George left the country. His son, John, who had been living with him in Sevenoaks, was escorted by his governess to Wells under the pretext that he was going to spend his fifth birthday with his great aunts. Then, as far as he was concerned, his father simply disappeared. Neither he nor the Stevens sisters knew anything of George's whereabouts until six months later, when Jane received a letter from the Central and South American Cable Company in Peru appointing her as John's guardian. George eventually wrote himself to tell them that he was living in South America and engaged to be married. Two years later he was transferred to Guayaquil and Georgie left Suffolk to join him.

Built on a swamp, Guayaquil was (and still is) one of the ugliest and unhealthiest backwaters of the world, its chokingly humid 100-degree heat an incubator of plague and disease. When Georgie arrived, the centre was in the process of being modernized, but the old part of the city was squalid and tumble-down. As soon as you stepped off the main thoroughfares, the side streets were grass-grown and puddled with stagnant water nurturing the mosquitoes which were a constant menace. At first, the couple lived on the Maleçon, the site of George's office in a good part of town. George was becoming increasingly prosperous. He had been promoted to manager of the cable company; he was branching out into Guayaquil's thriving import–export business, specializing in the coffee trade; later, he went on to try his luck prospecting for oil in the petroleum fields around the Santa Elena Peninsula. For expatriates in South America, this was a time of great opportunity and even greater risk; shifting from one scheme to another, Englishmen were taking over derelict rice-farms in the coastal valleys or tapping wild rubber in the high Montana forests, and their attempts to wring a livelihood out of this unknown territory often imposed a great strain on their wives. Demoralized by the hazards and discomforts of living in rotting ranch houses without sanitation or running water, many a woman would persuade her husband to give up his lone venture and return to a safe city job with one of the big companies. Georgie was determined to be more stoical and supportive.

> How many men who have occupations in out of the way places where little or no English is spoken, have been obliged to throw up their appointments simply because their women folk were not able, or perhaps were not willing to adapt themselves to the conditions, surroundings & language of the people into whose midst they had been thrown, in other words, did not make the best of things.

Her remark appears in an article entitled 'When in Rome', one of several pieces of journalism written over thirty years later when she was living in considerably reduced circumstances in London and trying to earn extra money. She goes on to suggest that new brides should adopt a tolerant attitude towards the foreign race – and especially towards native servants, the main cause of discontent.

> It is no good reviling people, especially domestics, for not doing things they have never seen, nor learned how to do . . . Patience, much patience, more patience . . . , coupled with a little tact and a great deal of philosophy is the advice I would give to anyone who contemplates living anywhere out of Europe.

Nevertheless, her own powers of endurance were constantly being tested to the limit. Accompanying her husband to an oil region in the Sierra, Georgie visited a primitive hot spring hydro, hardly able to believe its 'abomination of desolation and solitude'. The only accommodation on this bleak landscape of sand and scrub was a split cane shack with no electricity, the only signs of habitation 'a lean donkey or two, an emaciated dog, perhaps a goat, untidy, draggled, fish-fed hens . . . half-naked children and mess and filth of all kinds'. Associating peasant workers with the dairy maids and farm-hands of her Suffolk childhood, she was appalled at the extremes of poverty she saw in Ecuador, the 'mean, hideous, and squalid hovels, wherein reside the poorest natives'. The Andean people in their traditional costumes – the women in bowler hats and bright plumply layered skirts, the men in gaily coloured ponchos and high-crowned panama felt hats – may have looked picturesque, she said, but were in reality 'unutterably filthy and revolting'.

Not long after their marriage, which had taken place at the British Consulate in November 1895, George suffered a near-fatal attack of yellow fever and it was Georgie – 'She was a heroine' – who nursed him back to life. To begin with, 'Mr Ashton', as she always called him, was devoted to her, buying her emeralds and anything she wanted. Even later in their marriage when their lack of shared interests had driven them apart, relatives say that he seemed 'very soft and nice' with his wife. While George was serving as Vice-Consul and earning a good living, their life was as comfortable as it was possible to be in Guayaquil – 'the pest-hole of South America', as he put it. On the mud flats of the river Guayas with the water only a few feet away, the Ashtons had built an imposing two-storey house on stilts, Villa Antonio, named after St Anthony, the family saint.* Their first child, Edward Anthony Fulcher Ashton, arrived in October 1898 and the other boys followed at regular, two-year intervals: George Alexander Hawkes; Charles Henry Kenway; and, on 17 September 1904, Frederick William Mallandaine. 'You were the dregs,' Georgie later told him, explaining why he was 'so puny'. He may not have been the daughter his parents had wanted, but Frederick was a bonny, cherubic baby, whom his mother nicknamed 'Freddles' and would dress in frocks and broderie anglaise blouses – a display of maternal coddling that did not last long. With her strict Edwardian manners, Georgie was a distant figure to her sons. As Frederick later recalled, 'My mother was marvellous, but you couldn't go and throw your arms round her. I remember her once saying to me, "Don't be mawkish." I didn't know what she meant. She wasn't really hard; it was the attitude then that children didn't do that sort of thing.' All the same, his parents' undemonstrative natures and the lack of any tenderness in Ashton's childhood left a vacuum that lasted for the rest of his life. Even at the height of his career, he continued to crave reassurance both in his professional and private life. Love became the motive force of so many of his ballets; the yearning, extravagant romanticism that defines them inherited – however inconceivable it might seem – from his father.

Around the time of Frederick's birth, George Ashton became besotted with the daughter of his immediate superior, the British Minister and Consul General in Lima and Quito, Nelthorpe Beauclerk. Separated for long periods from his wife, Beauclerk would take twenty-one-year-old Violet with him on his travels. She was a fanciful young girl who, as a child, prepared herself for the venturesome life for which she believed she was destined, by sleeping on the floor 'so as to become hardy'. The years she spent in South America with her father are chronicled in *The Book of*

*The association began in Guayaquil just before the Ashtons' first child was born. 'My mother made a vow to St Anthony that if he found the key of her house or her diamond brooch or something, she'd call her first son Anthony, which she did. Whenever I lose anything I light a candle to him. Always.'

Talbot, a memoir of her husband, the explorer Talbot Clifton. Writing in the third person and in romantic-novel style, she describes how, before she met her husband, she had lost her heart in an Ecuadorian jungle to a man she hardly knew. 'The vision she had of him was in a tangle of sunlight, and he had a share in the wonder she felt at the glory of the forest.' The man, it would appear, was George Ashton. A few pages later, Violet names Ashton as the owner of a 'young and wanton' horse she loved to ride. Twice thrown, she had laughed and mounted again, and her account of herself riding side-saddle, pressed against the neck of the pacing horse, is rendered with such cinematic vividness and suppressed eroticism that one can well imagine the stirring effect this spirited young creature had on her middle-aged admirer. His response to her departure was correspondingly melodramatic. When Violet returned to Lima with her father, George Ashton, overcome with emotion, went out and shot the horse she had ridden so that no one could ever take her place.

Talbot Clifton, Violet's 'lodestar', arrived in Guayaquil in January 1906 and it was George Ashton who sealed their fate. 'In Ecuador he will hear a man talking about Violet, and because of what is said, he will sail onwards to Peru'. When George escorted Clifton from the docks to his hotel, there was anarchy in the streets of the city, with gunfire sending people running in all directions and the sound of shots continuing throughout the night. The liberal revolutionary Eloy Alfaro had displaced as President Leonidas Plaza Gutiérrez, his bitter rival, and, for fear of his life, General Plaza had bolted to an English vessel, his soldiers stripped of their uniforms and rifles. By the morning the streets were strewn with dead men and horses and all business was at a standstill. Talbot Clifton's diary records the aftermath.

> Sunday 21 January 1906. The revolution at an end. 150 killed, 450 wounded . . . I had breakfast with Ashton and his wife. A deadly dull hole this place. Have an appointment with Ashton to see the late chief of police about a vessel for the Cocos. The chief is in hiding at the American consul's. We would have been shot if we had attempted to go near his vessel today.
> Monday 22 January. Went for a walk, and after dinner took flute to the Ashtons. Mrs Ashton accompanied me. Heat very oppressive today. Hope to get away by end of month.

The revolution in Guayaquil was followed by a series of earthquakes, one of which was violent enough to set the bells ringing in the steeples. 'The people had rushed into the street and, falling on their knees, had cried out: "Jesús! Maria!" and signed their breasts with the cross.' Although George Ashton believed himself to be a timid man, his sense of duty to the stranger in his city had made him cross the street to the hotel where Talbot Clifton was staying. 'He swayed in at the bedroom door. Sitting up in bed, wrapped in a barbaric many-coloured gown, Talbot was playing the flute.' One evening, sitting and smoking his pipe in his living room, George talked at length to Clifton about Violet Beauclerk. In her memoir she describes how Ashton had then risen from his chair and, turning away to look out over the river, remarked nostalgically, 'Perhaps there is your hidden treasure. Anyway, go to Peru and see.' A year later, Violet and Clifton were married.

During a yellow-fever epidemic that broke out around this time, the Ashton children were entrusted to the care of an English nun who ran a convent in the Andes – a refuge known to Violet Beauclerk, who writes of the Madonna lilies which the English mother superior would send to her in Lima from an enclosed garden. Cut into a shelf of the mountain, the school was built high above a village in the Cordillera where the air was cold and pure, an exhilarating contrast to steamy, disease-ridden Guayaquil. Having decided that the city was no place to bring up children – 'Six months of it would make a living corpse of anybody' – George resigned as Vice-Consul and (after selling his property in Wells for £825 to his successor at the Embassy) took up the position of manager of Central and South American Cables in Lima. In 1907, soon after Georgie's return from England with the boys, the family joined him there.

It was in Lima that the young Frederick Ashton came into his own. He later told Cecil Beaton that he considered he had lived all his adult life on investments from boyhood; and, although it was not until his early twenties that Ashton even contemplated making ballets, as a child he instinctively stored choreographic images for the future. On Sunday afternoon walks with his nurse, he loved to watch modish Peruvian women promenading up and down the Paseo Colón in their open carriages, and in years to come would imitate the way they tilted their chins to reveal to perfection the line of their lovely throats. He noted the graceful hand-gestures of an old sewing-woman as she turned her wheel, and would study the photogenic movements and attitudes of a disdainful beauty who fascinated him, the Brazilian ambassador's wife, whose reputation was based on the fact that she had once danced with the Kaiser. The romance that certain Edwardian icons held for Ashton in his youth (Pavlova being the epitome) remained with him for the rest of his life – even the plotless *Birthday Offering*, choreographed in 1956, is endowed with 'the airs and graces of his mother's generation'. Peru, with its 'particular interweaving of lightness, sombreness and ritual', formed Ashton's personality and permeates his art. 'From the songs of his half-Inca nurse he imbibed a love of melancholy which still mingles, characteristically for a Latin, with his wit and gaiety.'

Ashton adored his nurse and even in old age remembered 'the most terribly melancholy songs' that she would sing to him. She took him with her to Mass at Lima Cathedral, and to watch religious processions, the feast day of Santa Rosa de Lima being their favourite. 'That was a great day, very crowded and full of pilgrimages.' Also of great fascination for children was the saint's little house in Lima where, lying in her cradle as a baby, she had appeared to her simple Spanish parents in the shape of a white rose. In the garden was the well in which she had thrown away the key to the iron girdle she wore clamped round her waist as one of many penances she inflicted on herself. In Lima Cathedral Ashton's nurse would point out the glass coffin where a breathing, lifelike replica of Santa Rosa lay in white robes crowned with thorny roses. 'I was disgusted years later to find an almost identical figure at Mme Tussaud's; the Sleeping Beauty.' Another feast day Ashton loved was that of St Peter. 'He [the saint in effigy] would have himself transported out in a boat to fish . . . and would return to proceed through the flower-scattered streets with the fish flopping against his baroque carved robes.' El Señor do los Milagros, a procession conducted predominantly by Lima's Roman Catholic black population, was remembered by Ashton when he collaborated with the composer Virgil Thomson on *Four Saints in Three Acts*, Gertrude Stein's opera written for an all-black cast. Commemorating the miracles performed by the poor black saint from Angola whose name is not even known, a brotherhood of twenty-four men would lift on to their shoulders in two distinct movements the immense platform bearing the solid-silver statue of the saint. Old and young, well dressed and in rags, the devotees wearing mostly purple, with purple lipstick for the women, would inch their way through the streets to dirge-like music and drums – two steps forward, one step back – a ritualized walk that Ashton adapted for the Thomson–Stein opera. 'He does know what it is to be a Peruvian,' wrote Stein in *Everybody's Autobiography*, 'and that made it possible for him to do what he did with *Four Saints* – to make a religious procession sway and slowly disappear without moving.'

In Lima, Ashton loved dressing up and entertaining his friends with imitations of the processions. He spent a lot of time with the children of the Elguera family, who owned the row of houses in the Calle Washington where the Ashtons lived. It was not Manuco Elguera or his brother, Januacho, with whom he was close, but their sister, the lovely Leonor, known as 'Panchita', who was, he later said, the only girl he ever really loved. 'When I told her I thought she would burst out laughing, but she didn't.' As a child, Freddie Ashton was considered special; he liked play-

ing with dolls 'but not in a motherly way, more as if they were mari-
onettes'. He was sweet and gentle, rather pretty for a boy – 'not rough
like the rest of us,' said Dorothy Escolme who recalls being told not to
tease him, even though he was a little older than she was. Both children
went to Elsie Bedwell's ballet class and appeared together in a production
of *Snow White and the Seven Dwarfs* at the Colón Theatre: Dorothy was
a flower and Freddie Ashton one of the dwarfs – his stage début, although it was not until he had seen Pavlova that he began to take ballet
seriously. Attended mostly by girls, Mrs Bedwell's classes consisted of
vague steps, skipping and highland flings – 'really awfully childish' – and
her charity shows were mounted less as entertainment than as part of the
war effort to collect money for the Red Cross, being performed in much
the same spirit as the rolling of bandages that went on after school.

Like many of the children in the British Colony, Ashton attended a
small school held in the house of two Scottish spinster sisters, Winnie and
Ethel Gilzean. Sweet-natured, attractive, with beautiful handwriting,
Winnie Gilzean taught him – 'God knows. Nothing. I was utterly un-
teachable all my life. I could only learn what I was interested in.' All he
could recollect was being ticked off for not being attentive enough and
Miss Gilzean reading Mrs Molesworth stories to him after class. When
he was eight, soon after Edith was born, he and his brother, Charlie, were
sent to Lima's Dominican school, La Recoleta.

> There were two grand schools – the Dominicans and the Jesuits –
> a kind of Eton and Harrow – and it depended which one the
> President's son was at as to which was considered grander. School
> with the Dominicans was very tough: every boy sneaked on every-
> one else. During class someone would put up his hand and say,
> 'Frederico Ashton is doing something or other,' and the priest
> would come over and grab you, push you onto your knees and
> make you put your hands in the air, and you had to stay kneeling
> like that. They were quite brutal. We used to do our lessons in
> French, and during the breaks we had to talk in French. A priest
> used to go around and if he heard anyone speaking Spanish, he'd
> hand him the marble. Whoever had the marble at the end of the
> break would be punished. I learnt nothing. Except I learnt how to
> assist at Mass.

Ashton's sense of awe and drama was first cultivated in Lima's great
Cathedral, where he served as a favourite acolyte of the Archbishop, specially chosen, he claimed, because he was blond. Amid the dark splendour of the elaborately carved cedar and mahogany choir-stalls, he

would hold the salver on which the Archbishop's jewels were placed while he changed his vestments, a ceremony that taught Ashton 'to time things rightly and to make effects at leisure, and the proper times for climaxes and the whole rightful measure of things and the ecstasy of ritual'. Although he was not then aware of being of any particular religious denomination, he entered into the spirit of the services 'as if I were a Catholic', and for the rest of his life retained traces of his Roman Catholic upbringing – steeping himself during the Second World War in the writings of the Spanish mystics, and lighting a candle in the Brompton Oratory each time he began a new ballet. Having spent a great deal of his childhood in church, he was even prepared for his first communion.

> In those days you had to have a great ribbon attached to your robes, so I went to my mother and asked for some money. 'What for?' she said. 'To get a ribbon for my confirmation.' Well, she blew up and she rushed to the Father Superior and put a stop to the whole thing. She was very friendly with the Father Superior because she spoke perfect French, being of Huguenot descent.

To Georgie, the appeal of La Recoleta would have been its social cachet, combined with its provision of French tuition (Ashton was trilingual by the time he left). Hoping to see their sons embark on careers in the diplomatic service, the Ashtons realized that foreign languages would be of vital importance to them. The two elder boys were sent to the German School in Lima and both did in fact go on to work for the British government: Alex taking up the post, once held by his father, of Vice-Consul in Guayaquil, and Tony working as HM Consul General in La Paz, Bolivia (he was later awarded an OBE and CBE for his wartime work and his services to the Crown). The brother Ashton liked most was Charlie: 'The most interesting of us in a way. He had the sense to buy up Ecuadorian and Peruvian silver and baroque paintings and his house in Quito was apparently like a museum. He had tremendous charm and wit and was marvellously entertaining. He married one of the most beautiful women I've ever seen in my life. She was an Ecuadorian – a glorious beauty.'

It was Charlie who, with reluctance, would eventually pay for Ashton's first ballet classes in England; even so, Ashton maintained that his brothers were, to all intents and purposes, 'utter strangers' to him. 'I had no feeling about them and they cared nothing about me. Only when I became well known did they show any interest.' As yet unaware of his ambition to dance, the Ashton boys were embarrassed by Frederick's femininity, and would tease and even punch him. Tony could be especially disparaging: apologizing to a mother in the British Colony who had hoped that Tony would marry her daughter, he remarked, 'Oh I'm so sorry, but if you show Freddie all those lovely hair ribbons she has, *he* might marry her.' All the same, if Ashton's own claim is to be believed, his brothers' derision did not prevent them from participating in some form of exploratory sexual play with him, even though he cannot have been more than ten years old at the time. 'I was buggered by all my brothers,' he told his old friend, Billy Chappell, over drinks one night during the late 1980s. Their conversation had begun with a discussion of masturbation (Chappell: 'I did nothing else between the ages of twelve and twenty.' Ashton: 'The first time it happened I didn't know what on earth had happened. I thought I'd burst something.') Then, with remarkable insouciance, Ashton went on to describe how the sexual experiments with his brothers, which they regarded as a kind of risqué game, had been abruptly terminated when one of them, prevented from 'going first', had sneaked on the others as revenge. Horrified by what they saw, their parents threatened to send the offender to sea, but settled for making him stand on a chair for the rest of the day with his hands behind his back. 'I was let off because I was the victim,' Ashton added. Far from being traumatized, he claimed to have 'rather enjoyed it' with Charlie, always the most companionable of his brothers. (He later repeated the story to an acquaintance, Nicholas Haslam, who was taken aback not so much by the disclosure itself, as by the matter-of-fact way in which Ashton delivered it.)

Ashton's future sexual inclinations were clearly defined as a child. He was attracted by pretty girls, once asking a pupil of Elsie Bedwell's to be his sweetheart – 'Somehow coming from Fred it was slightly astonishing' – and, as he admitted, his infatuation for Leonor Elguera struck deep. They would play at being husband and wife and one day were discovered in bed together. Leonor's mother was told and went rushing upstairs, only to find that the pair had rolled on to the floor and were still entwined. At other times, however, enacting a marriage ceremony on his own, Frederick would play the bride, sashaying down an imaginary aisle with a broom-handle groom, in much the same way as his Cinderella would later waltz in the kitchen with her broom, making believe that it was the prince of her dreams. Assuming a female role came more naturally to Ashton. He later confessed to a friend that he spent his first years of puberty yearning after a handsome, hearty friend of Tony's who was always surrounded by beautiful women. 'I remember Fred saying that it was his dream to have gone to the Café de Paris with him, wearing a black velvet dress.'

Frederick's effeminacy and finicky ways were a constant irritant to his father, who made his displeasure quite plain. Daunting and hard-driving,

George Ashton would never have condoned an artistic career for his son, for, quite apart from the social shame involved, his philosophy was that nothing was worth doing unless there was money in it. He had made good on his own and expected his boys to do the same. 'It is all rot that you have too little experience to start up on your own,' he wrote to John Ashton before his son's arrival in Lima. 'I only wish I had the same chance when I was young. I would have made a name for myself by this time.' But circumstances were to release Frederick from George's stern vigilance. When, in 1914, his parents returned to Guayaquil with Edith, and the ten-year-old Ashton moved in with the Watsons, it was virtually the last he ever saw of his father. His mother, who loved Lima, made frequent return visits to the city, but as it turned out they spent very little time together. George would send money for his wife's passage home, but she stayed on regardless. 'She had someone there. Even as a child I saw that.' John Ashton later confided to a friend in England that his stepmother had had an affair with the family doctor. 'He was terribly ashamed even after all these years and said to me, "Don't you ever let on to Fred." ' But Ashton would have been fascinated, not shocked. 'If my mother had lived, I would have asked her about her lovers.'

For the rest of Ashton's childhood, Guy Watson's mother became his surrogate parent. She was exceptionally kind to him and he grew to love her, remembering her fondly as 'such a very dear woman'. Described as 'the spitting image of Queen Mary and rather a grande dame – much more so than Mrs Ashton' – Mrs Watson loved to entertain, holding Thursday afternoon 'At Homes' at which and she and a neighbour, Mrs Ruddock, would play duets. Genteel but stout-hearted women, they had lived through harrowing times together in the first years of their respective marriages. Their husbands, attempting to make their fortunes in the coffee rush, had ventured into dangerous territory in Chanchamayo, and there Mrs Watson had delivered a still-born baby and Mr Ruddock been shot through the neck by an arrow. When the business failed, both couples forfeited everything they had and Mrs Watson was forced to take her three children back to her family in England. After living a bachelor existence for four years, her husband eventually went to work for the English firm, Duncan Fox, and the Watsons, reunited once more, settled for a suburban life in Miraflores.

Number 18 Calle Atahualpa was a typical single-storey Spanish villa with a long narrow veranda, tall railings between it and the street, and flower-beds on either side of the path. As there was no spare bedroom for Frederick, he was put up in a small room leading off the lounge at the front of the house. 'We'd never met before, and suddenly, there was Freddie in the playroom,' said Guy Watson. 'From that moment on we lived in each other's pockets.' Ashton immediately joined Guy at the school he was attending in Lima, run by a retired Army chaplain, Canon Nichol. It had been established for the children of the English Colony and was housed on the premises of the Protestant Church of the Good Shepherd, in the centre of the city. Not in the least ecclesiastical-looking, it was an ordinary house with one spacious room fitted to look like a small, plain English country church. Canon Nichol, a chubby bachelor, besides running his school, acted as the local padre. Although he would address all his pupils, male and female, in an abrupt public-school bark – Frederick was suddenly 'Ashton, F.' – he was a popular, respected figure, whose idea of discipline was to send a wayward child to sit alone in the carpentry workshop 'to calm down and think over one's sins'. Ashton, who would have appreciated the fact that 'not a jot of sport' was taught at the school, appears to have been quite happy there, even though he was an occasional target for bullying, on one occasion being pushed into a barrel of soot in the kitchen-garden by Dolly Pflücker, a precociously clever older girl. Canon Nichol's syllabus covered most subjects – according to Guy Watson, he was 'a marvellous teacher in general knowledge' – although Guy, a potential scholar and great favourite of the vicar, benefited far more from his tuition than Ashton did, leaving with a report which he claimed could have earned him a place in almost any school in England. 'Freddie couldn't have got that piece of paper in a month of Sundays. He didn't take to any traditional subjects, his mind was turned to other things.'

To reach the English School, the boys would travel by a horse-drawn local tram to the outskirts of Lima and from there change to the big inter-urban tram. 'Everything was done on the trot,' said Guy, especially on the return journey when they would run from the tram stop in Miraflores, 'hell for leather down to the sea.' The steep track from the terminus at the top of the cliffs zigzagged sharply, eased here and there with rough-hewn steps, and was roofed over its entire length with bamboo. 'We ran a bit, four steps: jumped them. Ran again, four steps: jumped them.' On each side of the path were wild geraniums, morning-glory, nasturtiums and ferns which grew beside the little streams seaming the cliff. These flowed into a fresh-water pool behind a row of bathing-huts, where everyone rinsed off the salt water after bathing. Slimy wooden steps covered in mussels and seaweed led down to the water, the heavy Pacific rollers often making ordinary swimming impossible. Peruvians love the sea and Ashton remembered 'nuns in long trousers, every part of them covered, hanging on to a rope like vultures and being bashed about by the huge breakers . . . priests fat and floating like porpoises, with

pursed lips and their tonsures showing above the waves.' Women and elderly people would hire Mestizo men to take them into the water waist-
deep and lift them over the waves. These were the bañadores – fishermen
by profession who wore ragged, rolled-up trousers and torn singlets 'displaying mahogany bodies of immense power, with forearm muscles like
whipcord to the touch. They needed all their strength to withstand the
drag of the undertow as they lifted some twelve-stone female high
enough to keep her face clear of a crashing breaker.'

Although one imagines Ashton dreaming of being wafted over the
waves by a sinewy bañador, he was in fact a strong and intrepid swimmer. About 150 yards offshore were a couple of crates sunk with heavy
stones and linked by a rope leading to the beach. In rough weather the
boys would haul themselves along the rope to the crates, which gave
them the lift-off to surf in. 'The main thing was surfing, really. We'd have
short boards and use the rope to go back out again, or else we'd swim
sideways through these huge breakers.' December to March were the
school holidays. At the start of the season, the beach would be covered
with sea-urchins, the crunching of which was a popular seaside sport for
children, and by the end the boys' espadrilles would have disintegrated
like blotting paper. Virtually the whole summer was spent on the beach;
they would rise with the Watson's cook at 6 a.m. when she went off to
market, and be in and out of the water for the rest of the day. On the
journey home they used to climb up a little ravine to some sandhills at the
top of the cliff where they hunted for scorpions and spotted the occasional snake. They often dropped in at the house of the poet and essayist,
Ricardo Palma, 'an old, old gentleman' who was very fond of children
and a repository of local history and stories (as a young man he had been
shown the remains of La Perricholi's* gilt and painted coach which she
had given to the Descalzos Padres after her sudden repentance). If they
saw the ice-merchant – El raspadillero – they would always stop. He was
a wizened little Chinaman, with black-rimmed fingernails, who came
round with a handcart, blowing a loud horn. For a few cents he would
shave slivers of ice off a large block into his hand and cram them into a
glass, adding with a quill dropper whatever flavour of fruit syrup you
chose from the sticky bottles displayed in the cart.

In winter, when the tram stopped after school in the church square,
the boys would dash across the road to an Oriental grocer-cum-baker
and each chose their own loaf for tea. 'Then we'd run off to the corner

---

*The Mestiza actress and dancer Micaela Villegas, mistress of the Viceroy and
heroine of Offenbach's operetta, whom in 1949 Ashton considered making the
subject of a ballet.

where my cat would be waiting and the three of us would run down the street together back to the Calle Atahualpa.' If Mrs Watson gave them money to pay the bill at the grocer, they would haggle on her behalf and use the change to buy themselves sweets or 'come y calla' – a Viennese-type tart so fluffy that its name, 'eat and be quiet', explained itself. Other goodies could be bought from hawkers who came to the door, like the turrónero* and the biscochero with their wooden trays resting on a vine ring on their heads. Every religious festival brought further delicacies, such as rosquitas on Santa Rosa de Lima day – little rings of twisted pastry, lardy-textured and covered with poppy seeds – and during Lent you could get pan de dulce, a sweet roll representing a nail of the Cross, with five almonds down the middle for the Five Wounds.

Three days before Lent was carnival time. Decorated floats paraded the streets to conflicting brass bands, and rooftops and windows were crowded with people shouting and throwing flowers. At night there were fancy-dress parties and firework displays staged by Lima's Chinese community. For six weeks in advance, Guy and Frederick would make lists of chores they could do to earn money and with the cash buy water balloons. Carnival licensed you to drench anyone you met until noon, and children everywhere were up at dawn with slings and pouches filled with balloon bombs, while their parents kept open house all day.

The mess was indescribable: friends, acquaintances and perfect strangers rushing in with buckets or moulting bouquets: everyone dishevelled and sick with hysterical laughter. Water slopped around all morning.

Near the Watsons' house was a high wall with a convenient step behind it. 'We would wait for the first unwary person who came along and quite literally tip a bucket of water over them and roar with laughter.'

Ashton's Miraflores childhood – nostalgically remembered by him as a time of 'sunshine and beautiful bathing, sometimes in and out of the water from morn to moonrise, having our last dip as the huge moon rose in the black sky' – were some of the happiest years of his life. 'I would gladly have them all over again,' he later told Mrs Watson. It was a period that coincided almost exactly with the Great War, which, when the Germans defeated the British in the Battle of Coronel, fought off the coast of Chile in November 1914, appeared to be coming their way. But the only hostility that affected the two English boys was the jeering of

---

*Turrón were trellises of pastry glazed with sugar-cane syrup and covered with sprinkles, and biscocho a cross between a bun and a cake.

some German children who lived in the colony across the harbour. 'A couple of months later the British caught and sank the lot, so we got our own back and jeered across at them.' Oblivious to external events, Freddie and Guy lived in a world of their own invention, whether mucking about in a pile of sand at the back of the President's summer residence, smoking out a wasp's nest in the Watsons' sunbaked back yard, or playing for hours in a boat constructed from wooden boxes, with a flat deck propped up on beer barrels and a mast and sails acquired from Guy's mother. 'We travelled all over the world in it.' Years later, when the curtain went up on the second act of Ashton's *Ondine*, the shipboard scene, Guy Watson 'at once remembered our boat'. Together they manufactured a couple of effective implements for pinching grapes from the garden next door: one long bamboo with a scissor contraption on the end cut the bunches, while another with a cage tied to it would catch them. 'It wasn't that I was leading Freddie on, we quite literally never did anything separately.' The boys would sneak out Mr Watson's rackets – 'far too heavy for us' – and half-heartedly knock a ball about at Miraflores tennis club. 'We were much more interested in what we did afterwards.' Alongside the club was the local cinema and, as there were always ladders round the courts, they would each put one up and peer in through the eaves at Pearl White, perhaps, queen of the silent serials, in the latest *Exploits of Elaine*. At the end of the month when the films were shown at the Teatro Municipal, the boys would buy seats in the gods with the result that, by the time they saw Pavlova perform, they were both familiar with the theatre.

Some days they would wander off further afield to Estancia Santa Cruz, a big pond on the way to Lima, or to Huaca Juliana, an Inca burial ground. At that period, there were vineyards and fields between the city and the suburbs; Huaca Juliana, which still exists today as a fenced-off conservation area amid solid urban sprawl, was then a lonely and beautiful place next to a small lake matted with blue water-hyacinths. Around the grassy mound itself you could find bits of ancient shard or cloth, or even make a wicket of leg-bones to be bowled at with a skull. The boys would clamber into the tunnel entrance and light fires to ward off the ghosts that were rumoured to skulk inside. There was also a Huaca Juliana 'witch' – one of Lima's many derelicts to whom George Ashton had given money. But the boys' favourite outing of all was a train ride to Chosica, a popular resort in the Andean foothills. A friend of Mrs Watson, General Morkill, the Head of the Peruvian Corporation, would invite the two of them to leave after school on a Friday evening and they would spend the night on the train, sleeping in their own coach at Chosica. At 4 a.m., they used to wake themselves up in order to stand on the platform and watch the milk train leave for Lima, sliding silently down the mountain powered by gravity alone. One summer they spent a fortnight at a hacienda on the coast with a friend from the English School, Stuart Wood. At Callao, they were put on a ship – 'there we were, on our own, having a two-day coastal cruise' – embarking at Pacasmayo where the family owned a cotton ranch. 'The first morning a horse was brought round with a sort of mattress flung over it; Stuart got on first, Freddie second and me third and off we trotted to the beach.' A few days later, they were each given a horse of their own and went camping in the hills – 'the three of us and a gun.' They were determined to shoot something and spent so long stalking a deer that, when they did not return home, Stuart's father had to come out in search of them. Guy Watson claims that Ashton was as game for adventure as he was, but also admits that the Woods made sure that Freddie was given the tamest pony on the farm. Even this he found difficult to control; returning to the hacienda, Guy heard a wail for help from behind, 'I'm going amongst the beehives!'

For all their easy camaraderie, there was a side of Ashton that Guy never saw. He did not know, for instance, that the friend with whom he had spent the day surfing was at bathtime performing imitations to amuse his mother, creating a gown for himself out of her towels. Unlike Guy, who years later did not even remember her, he was enthralled by the stylishness of their neighbour in the Calle Atahualpa, Mrs Robert Pflücker (mother of their schoolmate, Dolly). Her house, with its cool, North European interior and imported Maples wallpaper, had an enormous, light living room panelled in pale grey, with french windows opening on to a terrace, beyond which stretched Mrs Pflückers's parterres and English rose garden. Invited to tea on one occasion when his mother came to Lima, Ashton spent the time arranging and rearranging the cushions, the lilacs with the blue, until in exasperation Mrs Pflücker exclaimed, 'Darling, why don't you go into the garden and play like other little boys.' Much as he enjoyed his boisterous pursuits with Guy Watson, he kept the feminine side of his nature well-hidden from him, and even more rigidly repressed were the increasingly intense romantic yearnings he was experiencing towards members of his own sex. 'I never got any inkling of that in him, I saw no trace of it at all,' said Watson who was 'staggered' when he later learnt of an adolescent infatuation that Ashton had for a boy at their school. Ashton insisted that Guy 'was never a friend' and certainly their opposing priorities on the night they saw Pavlova perform confirm the distance between them. Guy Watson, as he himself admitted, had no idea, until he was told many years later, about the impact Pavlova had had on his closest companion. And, whereas Ashton had accepted the Marmon car they travelled in as nothing more than a means of getting to and from the theatre, Guy was so exhilarated

by the prospect of the journey home that he could hardly wait for the performance to end. However, the two boys seemed destined to be together
for several years to come, both bound for the same English boarding
school, Dover College, which Guy would take to 'like a duck to water',
but which succeeded in twisting Ashton – 'the free, uninhibited child of
the sun' – into a chilblained, miserably displaced public schoolboy.

CHAPTER TWO

PLAY UP, PLAY UP

1919–1924

As soon as peace was declared in Europe, it was decided between the two mothers that Frederick and Guy, having spent so much time in each other's company, should go to public school in England. 'It was to have been Clifton,' said Ashton, 'but the onrush of people sending their children to school after the war was so great that there wasn't room, they couldn't get me in.' The headmaster, an acquaintance of Georgie's, suggested the less competitive Dover College, which, having been accommodated by Leamington College for the duration of the war, was reopening in September and had space for a larger intake of boys. On the strength of his recommendation, both boys were accepted. 'Because, you see, I would never have been able to pass any entrance exam. I didn't know the rudiments of anything, or even how to learn.'

In the early summer of 1919, the fourteen-year-old Ashton set sail from the port of Callao with Guy and Mrs Watson. It was the last he would ever see of Peru. The three-week journey to England on *The Mexico*, 'an awful old steamer pulled out of retirement to ship English people home', was, in itself, something of an adventure, but the boys took it all in their stride. Peace in Europe was celebrated on board with a day-long jamboree of deck sports, but just as vivid were memories of the steaming salt baths run by the bath steward every night – 'with a tin basin of fresh water to get the soap off' – and being patted on the head by the bull-fighter, Juan Belmonte, who joined the ship mid-voyage.

The remaining months before the Michaelmas term began were spent on a farm in the Dales behind Newcastle, where Mr Watson had relatives. 'On the first night Freddie ate too much cream and was as sick as a dog.' With train services disrupted by the 1919 North Yorkshire coal strike, the boys' arrival at school was delayed by two weeks. When, at last, the big day came, they spotted on the station platform one other lone Dover College pupil, also wearing a conspicuously crisp uniform –

college cap, striped grey flannel trousers, black jacket, tell-tale new boys' Eton collar (obligatory until you reached the age of fifteen, which Ashton was about to do). Guy Watson distinctly remembered 'the poor chap's mother saying, "Go on then, speak to them," and his reply, "No, I couldn't possibly. They're in First Class."' As it turned out, William Redman, a scholarship boy, was bound for the same house, St Martin's, an attractive Georgian building which accommodated around forty boarders, almost all of them new to the school. 'It should have been money for jam for us but when we walked in a fortnight late, all the others struck us as terribly knowledgeable,' said Guy Watson. 'They seemed to have been there for ever.' Ashton recalled being 'terribly ill-treated' at first, but the harshness probably amounted to little more than the usual public-school austerities and humiliations. New boys – 'the lowest form of animal life' – were treated like slaves and subjected to an uncompromising series of initiation rites, including being made to stand on a ledge above an ancient fireplace, singing 'God Save the King' to the tune of 'Onward Christian Soldiers'. After about a week, the boys were individually summoned to the head of the house and examined on school colours and customs: who was allowed to put hands in their pockets (only prefects; everyone else's had to be stitched up); who was permitted to venture on to the grass close and when (out of bounds to all pupils apart from prefects, except on Sunday afternoons in summer), and so on.

Frederick and Guy's first rugger match was another ordeal. Although they were both strong swimmers, and could ride and play tennis after a fashion, neither had had any experience of the English sports field. Watson, who made a far better show of disguising his ineptitude, remembers being locked in a scrum and seeing Ashton 'teetering on the side wondering what on earth to do and not daring to laugh'. There was some comfort in braving the jungle law together. Dover prided itself on the fact that almost all the boys had a room of their own – 'about 800 c. ft as in a hotel', boasts the prospectus. 'Of this every boy has *undisturbed* possession, *intrusion being impossible*.' But, said Watson, 'Mater had somehow managed to acquire the only double room in the school for Freddie and me.' This was a mixed blessing as far as Ashton was concerned. He, more than anyone, would have appreciated the privacy of his own room, but at least Guy Watson's presence provided a consolatory link with home. In contrast to the freedom they had been used to in Lima, the compulsions and physical discomfort of their new life were appalling. The St Martin's housemaster, the Revd Punton-Smith, with his sleek black hair, was 'a beast', remarked Watson. 'He really was a nasty piece of work. He starved us. There was never enough bread and we were always hungry.' Situated in a hollow on the outskirts of the town, the College was a dank, raw place in winter and, although amazed by his first fall of snow, Ashton suffered dreadfully from the cold. None of the bedrooms was heated and, even on a frosty night, a prefect would come round after lights-out to make sure the window was open. In the morning, before the boys could wash they had to break the ice that had formed on the jug of water; in the evenings, they did their prep wearing coats, woollen scarves and fur-lined gloves. Oddly enough, however, although one imagines them swopping tales of misery, Guy Watson claimed that they hardly ever talked to each other when they went to bed. 'We both just lay there shivering.'

Initially as lonely and homesick as Ashton, Guy – destined to become one of Dover's Great Men – very soon began to settle in. 'I passed exams, I was good at sport. I was alright, but Freddie was all wrong.' Almost comically out of his depth, Ashton admitted that he was 'Good at nothing. Absolutely nothing. When the teacher said, "Turn to page 54 in your geometry textbook," I said, "What's geometry?"' He got through, he said, only by cheating and cribbing from other people. A boy called Kenneth Mayle would solve maths problems for him in return for a share of his tuck. The only time he shone was during Saturday-afternoon dancing classes – an optional extra, considered by Guy Watson to be 'an abominable waste of time'. Equipped with the appropriate footwear, a dozen or so 'Gentlemen', as they were addressed by the teacher and her young female assistant, would attend the local dance academy to learn the rudiments of the waltz, foxtrot, tango, and one-step, boys dancing with boys. 'Everybody wanted to dance with me because I could follow,' said Ashton. 'So I had a lovely time. There was a special boy I danced with and we would be dragged out to show the others. I adored that.'

If Ashton's prowess on the dance floor had extended to the sports field, his academic inadequacy would have mattered much less. 'The whole essence of Dover was games, with a smattering of what was necessary on the scholastic side,' remarked one contemporary. 'If you succeeded at sport, you really felt you were someone and were *made* to feel someone,' remarked another. Although a small school, Dover was riding high on its games tradition: 'We were playing against Merchant Taylors and Mill Hill and *beating* 'em.' With a brilliant athlete as headmaster – W. S. 'Piggy' Lee, a triple blue at Oxford – it was inevitable that the sporting achievements of the school took priority: rugby and football in winter; hockey and athletics in the spring; cricket, tennis and fives in summer; with boxing and fencing available as optional extras. For Ashton, 'It was all quite hopeless. We played cricket every summer and I made eleven runs in all that time, five of which I made in one inning.'

Another misery to be endured was OTC drill. In those days, Dover was considered a first-rate preparation for a career in the Army and Navy; the Cadet Corps, which embraced the whole school, was highly respected and had even won the Ashburton Shield. After fifth form, there were special classes, known as Army I and Army II, in which interested candidates were coached for Woolwich and Sandhurst (the College had an unusually high rate of success of admissions to both). To Ashton, who lacked any sense of patriotism towards a country in which he felt a foreigner, and who did not intend ever to take up arms to defend it, the compulsory training sessions were not only bewildering, they were thoroughly disagreeable – all the shouting, marching and standing about, the scratchy uniform and tourniquet-tight puttees, handling heavy, unmanageable rifles, and fixing bayonets with frozen fingers. Short of physical disability, however, there was no escaping it. 'How he stuck public school life, I don't know,' said Fergus Mason, a fellow pupil. 'To a sensitive boy like him, the regimentation, the company whether you liked it or not, having nobody to talk to about the things nearest to his heart – the ballet, the theatre – must have been absolute hell. He very sensibly kept quiet.'

Ashton was neither popular nor unpopular among his year, and was remembered mostly as a modest, reserved boy, neat in appearance, but not overtly effeminate. 'There was no teasing of him. Even as a schoolboy, Ashton appeared oblivious to the hoi polloi and was a boy of destiny. Although he appeared somewhat ethereal, he had a dignity and a strength about him.' Ashton maintained that, initially, his strong Spanish accent distanced him even further from his peers – 'I used to say "non" and "nossir" [no, Sir] to the teacher' – but he must have lost it quickly, as his contemporaries recall no trace of accent. 'It never dawned on me that he wasn't English, born and bred,' said Fergus Mason, whose memory is of 'a slim, personable lad, hair well brushed, tie properly tied. His clothes fitted, he looked well dressed – that's what impressed me about him – but it didn't extend to dandyism, which it couldn't have done. Things like coloured handkerchiefs were taboo.' Although, like everyone else, Ashton grumbled about school rules and constraints, he never allowed his true desperation to show. 'I used to write my mother very pathetic letters. I remember that when she came down to see the Headmaster at one stage she told me that I was being "mawkish" . . . There wasn't this idea of knowing and sympathizing with your children and I would never have dared to tell my father about school or complain to him. He wouldn't have listened.'

Ashton's schooldays, he always said, were the unhappiest period of his life. Isolated and undervalued, he became increasingly withdrawn, treating his time at Dover 'as something ghastly that had to be gone through', just as another 'artsy crafty sort of chap', the poet, Richard Aldington, had done a few years before. If Ashton is Dover's most famous Old Boy, Aldington is its most infamous. Leader of the Imagist Movement, youngest of a group of writers which included Ezra Pound, Wyndham Lewis, T. S. Eliot and D. H. Lawrence, his autobiographical 'jazz novel', *Death of a Hero*, satirizes the school (renamed Dullborough) with undisguised contempt and bitterness. With a similarly poor games record and resistance to conform to the type of 'thoroughly manly fellow', whom the College aimed to produce, Aldington spent much of his time silently defying the system, reciting to himself Keats's 'Ode to a Nightingale' – 'as a kind of inner Declaration of Independence.'

> They worried him, they bullied him, they frightened him with cock-and-bull yarns about Smut and noses dropping off; but they didn't get him . . . They didn't get at the inside vitality.

With no one whom he could talk to openly, Aldington's only refuge was to be found in books and the paintings that he studied during his holidays. 'They were his interpreters of the mystery, the defenders of the inner vitality which he was fighting unconsciously to save.'

Ashton was more fortunate. Not long after his arrival, he was able to reveal his enthusiasms to an English master, who would become a friend as well as a spiritual ally. A. S. Dixon was an inspired teacher, much liked by everyone. 'Alf was the star,' said Old Dovorian, Andrew Man, 'the pick of the masters at the College who tried to instil into us youngsters an understanding of art in all its forms as a counter to the worship of games and all who excelled at them.' 'Oh, he could teach,' said Fergus Mason. 'He had that supreme virtue of stimulating his pupils' interest and encouraging them to find out things for themselves.' A Mr Chips character who wore a small moustache, Dixon taught Latin, German, Scripture and cricket, but English was his subject – more than that, his vocation – and he was fierce about any corruption of the language. 'He hated slipshod, slovenly speech – split infinitives, unrelated participles, the use of particular words,' said Mason. 'Ashton spoke English, grammatical English well, and Alf would have taken a favourable view of that.'

Dixon was in charge of the sixth-form library, which was kept under lock and key. Ashton's first contact with the master would have been when he opened the room twice a week to the rest of the school. Softly spoken, with a quiet sense of humour, he was the only master who took a personal interest in the boys. Slowly, he began to instil a degree of confidence in Ashton, more or less resigned to his role as college 'wet', by drawing him out of himself, and awakening in him a love of English poetry.

Dixon was a great proselytizer when it came to literature. His own form was the middle fifth and, without fail, when addressing a class of new boys, he would say, 'Everyone in this form *must* take out a library book.' He would then add, dryly, 'You don't have to read it.' 'Alf was a bit of a cynic, a bit of a philosopher, someone who played his cards very close to his chest,' said Andrew Man, 'quite an intellectual and someone you couldn't fail to respect. A Harold Macmillan type.' Dixon was a strict disciplinarian, but not a bully. He would take the boys as they came, but set high standards and expected high returns. When his form took School Certificate, he promised to present a bound volume of each boy's choice to anyone who passed with credit. 'As it happened he had to dish out about half a dozen. No one else ever did that.' Dixon took trouble with his pupils and they did their best to keep in his good books – 'Your day was made if he gave you high marks.' Dixon admired the urbane and entertaining *Times* columnist, E. V. Lucas – an authority on anything, from Florentine pictures to London clubs – and he would get the boys to read his essays to show them how it should be done. He was better at teaching those who enjoyed his classes; Ashton, gazing out of the window and dreaming, did not appear to be one of them. Yet the master saw some potential and took him under his wing, inviting him to tea in his rooms on Sundays, along with a handful of the brighter boys. Although Dixon was regarded as 'very much a bachelor', there was no question of any sexual element behind his interest in pupils he favoured; on the contrary, he already had his eye on the matron of St Martin's – 'A sweetie. Round and twinkly like the Queen Mother' – whom he eventually married. He instinctively understood Ashton's temperament, and was as encouraging and supportive at Dover as he would be many years later when, conscripted into the services, Ashton found himself thrust once again into a nightmarish recapitulation of public-school conditions. 'A C.O. can make life hell for those he dislikes, even more perhaps than an H.M., and of course you would be easy prey for such a man.'

Dixon could talk about art and literature, and even appeared to share Ashton's taste for Edwardian beauties. He was, as Guy Watson said, 'the only chap who got through to Freddie'. Other privileged boys, in whom he showed an interest, were rather overawed, finding him a little cutting at times and a difficult man to get to know. With Ashton, there developed a mutual fondness and admiration that, in the end, was to become more one-sided. The retired master, a pensioner living on Dover's seafront, followed his ex-pupil's progress over the next forty years with touching delight, keeping a photograph of him – '1922 vintage' – on his bookcase and another, clipped from the *Dancing Times*, in his wallet. Even though Ashton never made the effort to visit him in Dover and disregarded Dixon's hopes for a reunion – 'Cannot we ever meet in this world or would it be a mistake?' – he continued to send postcards from all over the world and even the occasional food parcel of tinned luxuries from America. Dixon educated Ashton virtually single-handedly, and, even at the height of his eminence, the choreographer never forgot his debt.

With the arrival of a new housemaster, the jovial Douglas (Tusky) Munns, who replaced the Revd Punton-Smith in 1922, Ashton's daily routine had become slightly more bearable. If nothing else, the food improved at once. Although he would never come to terms with the 'ghastly English climate' – in Lima, it had rained so seldom that hardly anyone owned an umbrella – when the sun shone, mellowing the flinty grey walls, it was hard not to admire the beauty of Dover's setting. Built in the 1870s, on the ruins of an old priory, and still retaining its fourteenth-century gateway and thirteenth-century chapel, the college was, as one contemporary remarked, 'a very ancient and noble place in which to grow up – I can't imagine it not rubbing off on him'. The realities of school life, however, continued to be oppressive. Fagging loomed large throughout Ashton's first year. Each new boy was assigned to a prefect for whom he performed the usual menial tasks, ranging from cleaning his rugger boots to warming the seat of a freezing outside lavatory. 'We all went through it,' said Fergus Mason, 'but the duties were not arduous, nor did they last long.' More unpopular was the 'fag call', which disrupted any degree of privacy that might be enjoyed in one's 'bunk' (a desk of one's own in the prep room, where family photographs and a few personal belongings could be kept). Hearing the summons of a foot pounding on the floor above, every fag would have to dash upstairs at high speed, and the last breathless boy to arrive was selected for the job. Having spent much of his childhood 'on the trot', Ashton was usually exempt – 'the one thing I could do was run' – although he would have suffered, along with everyone else, the routine beatings inflicted by prefects for minor misdemeanours, such as forgetting to turn off the light above one's bunk. School prefects beat with their canes and house prefects with a specially prepared tennis shoe, which was considered to be marginally preferable. But even though the system was rigid and barbaric, it was not abused. Tusky Munns knew exactly what was going on and, despite his blimpish morning rollcall – 'Abson, Allcard, Ashton,' etc. – ran a relatively relaxed and happy house.

Throughout his time at Dover, apart from benefiting from Alf Dixon's erudition, Ashton's only intellectual sustenance were the theatres, concerts and museums he went to during his holidays in London. Over a period of ten days, he would see twelve to fifteen plays – a binge achieved against considerable opposition. Reluctant to inflict her son on the Watsons' relatives for longer than necessary, Georgie Ashton had arranged for Frederick to be 'billeted' each summer with an old school friend from Bury St Edmunds, Maud Lawson, who had a flat in Argyll Mansions, Chelsea. Although kind and well meaning, Aunt Maud was spinsterishly over-protective, with no idea of how to treat a teenage boy. Believing that Ashton's obsessive appetite for culture was unhealthy for someone of his age, every evening she would try to persuade him to stay at home.

> I can't tell you what an awful time I had. I was fourteen [*sic*] and there I was with this middle-aged lady and her *mother* in Chelsea. She would lock the door every night and I'd be stuck with them, having to play Bezique. If I went to see a show, she waited up for me until I came back. So I had to come back by 10.30 in order for her to lock the door.

Ashton went everywhere alone, and to escape from the stiflingly tiny flat he would take the number 19 bus as far as Putney and back again to the end of the route.

> That was my diversion. It was as hard as that – I had no fun at all. And then she used to take me on holidays, renting cottages somewhere or other like Exmoor. A horse was hired for me which would arrive in the morning. I'd get on the horse with a pack of sandwiches and go off all over Exmoor by myself. And see nobody.

One holiday was spent in France with Georgie's sister, May, who, as Ashton put it, had 'gone native' and returned to Brittany, home of the Mallandaines. 'My aunt didn't want me in the house so she put me into a kind of pension. She kept an eye on me and I'd go and have meals with her occasionally. I was very lonely. I was always lonely, somehow. Isolated and living with old ladies.'

It was equally as lonely at Dover. Not even Guy Watson, who 'couldn't get back to school soon enough', would ask him what he had done in his holidays. 'Looking back I find that quite astonishing,' said Watson, explaining that they lived entirely different lives. 'We got up in the morning, rushed downstairs and came nowhere near each other until we went to bed.' Eventually, however, Ashton began to make a niche for himself and even found a handful of like-minded friends. 'A new boy was a new boy for about a term, perhaps two,' said Fergus Mason, 'then you got the idea and after that if you were an oddball of any sort, it didn't matter. The chances were you would discover others like you.' Peter Fielding-Ould was one. Well groomed, charming and exceptionally good-looking, Fielding-Ould was a Londoner, the son of an aristocratic mother and a father who was a vicar of 'some very grand West End church'. To the boys, he was 'Sophistication with a capital S', 'an embryo man about town', who seemed to have been everywhere and done everything. Despite being two years younger than Ashton, he was much more self-confident and an unashamed exhibitionist, dressing up at every opportunity. At bathtime (recalling Ashton's antics for Mrs Watson), he would entertain the boys in his house by doing a striptease with a bath-towel, but he escaped a ragging because he was unaffected and was able to laugh at himself. He and Ashton became instant allies. 'They were both on the arty side of things and both detested sport, so naturally they were thrown together.' Members of the same junior rugby league, they decided to start an 'anti-game'. 'We met at half-time and used to put mud on our knees to look as though we'd been tackled. "Did you touch the ball?" "No. Did you?" And another time. "Did you touch the ball?" "Yes, but I had to because it was thrown at me." "Well, why didn't you *drop* it?"'

Fielding-Ould was as avid a theatre-goer as Ashton, and became a welcome and entertaining companion during the holidays. 'When I went with him we were in the dress circle or stalls, whereas I had been going for 1/3d in the gallery.' At school, they began to establish themselves as leading lights in the school plays, usually competing for the star female role. The wealthy Mrs Fielding-Ould would lend them her dresses to use as costumes and the two boys, anticipating the stagey tussles of Ashton and Robert Helpmann as the Ugly Sisters, used to bicker over which one they wanted to wear. In Pinero's *The Magistrate*, Fielding-Ould played Agatha Poskett to Ashton's Charlotte Verrinder, but although, of the two sisters, Agatha is the more central role, it was Ashton who carried off the acclaim, *The Dovorian*'s reviewer presciently highlighting the future dancer's mimetic flair.

> Charlotte deserves much praise for the way in which she carried on for quite long periods, without a sentence to help her. Her changes of expression and her actions were well worth watching and the incident of the play which comes back now with the greatest vividness is the disconcerting plate of lemons and arm attached and Charlotte's amazement, horror and supreme collapse.

Thanks mostly to Alf Dixon's influence, the standard of drama at Dover was high – high enough for the town, which was much smarter in those days, to attend school plays in evening dress. 'I would say that drama was the first of the arts to emerge from the stigma of cissiness,' said Timothy Cobb, a subsequent headmaster. There was no school theatre, but the choice of plays, performed on a raised platform in the refectory, was ambitious. Ashton was to have appeared as Lydia Languish in *The Rivals*, a production that was later cancelled for some reason, but won further praise in *The Dovorian* for his portrayal of the imperious and crotchety Mrs Sykes in E. M. Fotheringham's *A Cash Concern*. This was his first experience of performing a bosomy English dowager, a role he would later develop into a well-honed party piece. In a coincidental nod to Ashton's milliner grandmother, Fotheringham's *Play for Seven Boys* is set in a hat shop – or, rather, in the morning room of Mrs Sykes's London house where, in her absence, her own hats are displayed for sale as part of a money-making ruse dreamed up by her son (played in drag by Redman, the boy whom Ashton and Watson had spotted at Charing Cross on their first day). The play unfolds with an abundance of jokes and innuendoes intended to appeal to schoolboy humour, while Mrs Sykes's indignant, rapidly accelerating tirade provided Ashton with much scope for pantomime ad lib – voice rising to a falsetto, exaggerated fanning with a handkerchief, etc. Once again, *The Dovorian* approved: 'Mrs Sykes was excellent – in every way the nervous affected, highly-strung mother. Her acting was admirable.'

Under the camp, extrovert influence of Peter Fielding-Ould – 'Give him a wig and some sort of frock and he was happy' – Ashton himself became notably more effervescent. He could be seen strolling round the Close on summer evenings, with Fielding-Ould and two or three others, 'obviously entertaining them with his conversation and witticism'. William Wallis, the star of the school choir, was another kindred spirit. 'He had one of the most beautiful treble voices I've ever heard,' said Fergus Mason. 'While it lasted there was nobody else in his class.' Wallis was also unsporty – tall, self-consciously pretty and the source of much attention from the older boys. To Ashton, however, he was simply a close friend. His own inamorato was 'Rosie' Parr (so called because of his fresh complexion), a scrum-half and school prefect. Rosie was the younger of the Parr brothers (both sporting heroes), slim, superbly fit, with black hair, a lovely smile and soft Irish brogue. 'I was madly in love,' said Ashton. 'I used to *languish* at him, but nothing . . . *Never* anything else.' He mildly embarrassed Fergus Mason one day by producing a snapshot of Rosie from his wallet and saying, '*Look!*' even though it came as no great surprise. Fledgling liaisons abounded at Dover – 'Ask anybody' – usually lasting until the adored one's voice had broken or he started to shave. Anything beyond a minor crush would have been trounced very quickly, but, on the whole, although there were several sermons about 'Purity' which most of the boys only half-understood, the management turned a blind eye to schoolboy crushes. 'As long as it didn't go *too* far. I remember the headmaster saying once, "You know, boys can be very sentimental."' At Dover they called it 'chasing' and any boy prepared to be chased was called a 'chase-me'. 'I was a "chase-me" which was *ghastly*,' said Ashton, whose sexual inclinations at Dover set a precedent for the future. 'Fred always despised anyone who was in love with him,' remarked one of his oldest friends, Barbara Ker-Seymer, an observation confirmed by Ashton himself. 'There were people who were in love with me whom I hated, because I was very romantic, you see, and had the Greek point of view about the Ideal One.' Even though he was describing his schoolboy inclinations, Ashton's preference for the role of pursuer over that of the pursued was one that stayed with him for the rest of his life.

His encounters at Dover were as often physical as platonic. 'Rubbidubs but no buggering,' Ashton maintained – a ritual frequently carried out with an anonymous expedience akin to adult homosexual 'cottaging'. 'There were others around who one didn't necessarily like, but they were randy and they came to you because you were available. One boy I had sex with never addressed a word to me during, after, before or anything. I knew what he was after, he knew what he was after, and once it was over, that was it.' Assignations usually took place in the music rooms behind the fives courts, which could not be seen from the headmaster's house. There were four of these claustrophobic little chambers, smelling of illicit cigarette smoke, each with an ancient piano, only one of which was in tune. The handful of Dover's musical boys would make it their business to know when this was available and race to get there first – among them, Fergus Mason. Although Mason was a country boy who had never been to a London show, or, indeed, any production other than *Peter Pan*, he loved nothing more than sitting at the piano, picking out the dance tunes of the day – melodies such as 'Tea for Two', 'I Want to be Happy', 'Yes, We Have No Bananas' – which he had heard on gramophone records or at parties he had been to in the holidays. If Ashton were passing within earshot and heard a song he liked, he would always drop in. 'He'd say something like, "Have you seen the show?" which of course I hadn't. And sometimes somebody else like Wallis would amble in and he and Ashton would natter away quite happily between themselves.' It was the first time that Mason noticed Ashton come alive. He was not a boy known to smile much, but, in the company of someone with whom he felt at ease, Ashton suddenly became vibrantly enthusiastic and amusing, intriguing Mason with his conversation.

> Ashton opened my eyes to the existence of a world of which I knew nothing. I was three years younger and so innocent, whereas he'd been to every show in London, or so it seemed. But he never talked down to me. I used to ask him to describe to me what went on – the nuts and bolts of a theatre. Who compiled it? Was it the author or a backer? What's the difference between a stage manager and a producer? And he would give me straight answers. He was very patient. He explained. Even at school, he knew.

Their common ground, Mason said, was music. But although Ashton gave the impression of knowing more about the subject, he never learnt to play an instrument at school. The reason for this is a mystery. His mother, as a talented pianist, would surely have promoted it; and while music was not actively encouraged at Dover, it was at least tolerated, giving artistic boys the chance to make a reputation for themselves – if only by playing in the school jazz band. As a choreographer, Ashton was intuitively musical to the point of genius, but his lack of any technical knowledge left him with feelings of inferiority about his work which he never entirely overcame. It also left him vulnerable to criticism. George Balanchine, formally trained as a musician, was always disparaging about the fact that Ashton could not read a score, which was the reason, according to his lieutenant, Lincoln Kirstein, that he did not take Ashton's ballets more seriously. 'I tried to learn the piano,' said Ashton, 'but I couldn't. I could never concentrate, you see.'

Yet if Ashton did not involve himself in any musical activity at Dover, he went out of his way to seek the company of musical boys. Reginald Palmer was the school's most accomplished pianist, envied by Fergus Mason for 'his apparent ease of execution, accuracy and above all his remarkable sight-reading. Prop any piece of music in front of him, one glance and off he went'. A year older than Ashton, Palmer was more of a young man than a schoolboy, mature not only in appearance but in his manner and conversation. He became Ashton's greatest friend at Dover, and although Palmer left school a year earlier, they remained in close touch, going to plays and concerts together in London. Palmer, who was also a balletomane and took the *Dancing Times* regularly, may well have been the only boy to whom Ashton confided his ambition to dance. In fact, it was he who would later point out an advertisement in the magazine which set Ashton on course for his career.

*   *   *

During the Easter holidays of 1921, Ashton saw a series of matinées in London that had almost as profound an effect on him as Pavlova's performance in Lima. To half-empty houses, Isadora Duncan, the great revolutionary of twentieth-century dance, gave a week of recitals at the Prince of Wales Theatre, to which Ashton returned several times.

> I didn't think I'd like it, but I was completely captivated. I suppose she was rather blowsy about that time – I remember she had red hair – and the first impact of her gave me a bit of a shock, but that soon passed . . . She wasn't really the old camp that everyone makes her out now, she was very serious, and an immensely strong personality that came right across the footlights and held the audience and compelled them completely.

Duncan was forty-four years old by then, and so heavy that she shook with fat, but was still capable of dancing an entire symphony with undimmed stamina and charisma. She would perform a programme of Wagner on one afternoon, and a programme of Chopin, Schubert or Liszt on another, the music played by her young lover at the time, the pianist Walter Rummel, whom she called her 'Archangel'. Ashton described the atmosphere in the theatre as almost like a nightclub: Rummel would play various pieces while Duncan remained on-stage seeing to her next costume and, between solos, she would talk to the audience, introducing George Bernard Shaw, who happened to be there, or inviting a famous tenor up on stage to sing while she danced. 'And she talked a good deal about what great artists she and her pianist were.'

One of the most powerful pieces Ashton saw was a solo to Chopin's 'Funeral March', during which, swathed in a huge cloak, Duncan faced the audience and simply stayed quite still. 'You'd think, "My goodness, how much longer is she going to stand there?" Then slowly she would open the cloak and she had a whole armful of lilies inside.' Not only had the loss of all three of Duncan's children charged the dance with enormous personal resonance; she was also able to make the audience experience her grief for themselves, stopping their breathing and keeping them hanging with her in the stillness 'on that one note which you musicians mark in your scores with a fermata meaning you can hold it as long as you like'. From watching Duse and Ellen Terry, she had learnt that the true expression of tragedy lies not in an actress raging on stage, but in remaining mute and immobile. This was a device that Ashton would adapt and develop for himself with increasing mastery, his 1946 ballet, *Sym-*

phonic Variations, being the crowning example of how stasis can reverberate with such intensity that it touches the transcendental.

In complete contrast to Duncan's tragic impact was a childlike, frolicsome side, seen most engagingly in her series of Brahms waltzes in which, lying on an imaginary beach playing at knucklebones, or walking slowly forward scattering rose petals, she demonstrated how to achieve a potent theatrical effect with the utmost simplicity of means. (The memory remained so vivid to Ashton that over fifty years later he was able to recreate the dances to perfection in *Five Brahms Waltzes in the Manner of Isadora Duncan*, a homage to her genius brilliantly rendered by Lynn Seymour.) Even though the seventeen-year-old schoolboy was not so smitten by Duncan as to be unaware of a 'certain amount of galumphing around' in her performance (it was, he admitted, a bad age at which to see an ageing fat woman half-naked under flimsy chiffon tunics), rather than being embarrassed by the way she would remove her drapes one after the other as she danced, like 'a kind of intellectual strip teaser', he marvelled at her grace, plasticity of movement and quality of repose. Like his visions of Pavlova, Duncan's dancing stayed with him for the rest of his life, infiltrating his classicism and helping him to arrive at a style of his own. But it was Duncan's musicality that impressed Ashton most: 'I suppose she was the first person to interpret music. Others danced it.' Her illustrative, subjective approach was one with which he could identify; like Duncan, he responded to a music heard inwardly, music that was, in her description, 'an expression of something out of another, profounder world'.

Resuming his autodidactic regime every holiday, Ashton went to exhibitions, concerts, musicals, plays, and never missed a ballet performance. He discovered the ballet bookshop in Charing Cross Road*, run for fifty-five years by the dance writer, publisher and translator, Cyril Beaumont. Subconsciously, Ashton was storing away his impressions of a period that was particularly rich and stimulating for the dance. At the Coliseum he saw Loie Fuller, icon of the Symbolist poets, whose strangely impersonal, metaphorical solos were considered emblems of a still vibrant aesthetic (it was her Fire Dance that inspired Yeats's 'Byzantium'). He saw the arrestingly innovative troupe, the Ballets Suédois, whose production of *The Foolish Virgins* may even have sown the seed of his own *The Wise Virgins* choreographed during the Second World War. On one of his holidays to France he saw the belle époque beauty, Cléo de Mérode, partnered by a nineteen-year-old English dancer, Rupert Doone,

---

*A dance book shop still exists, located in nearby Cecil Court and owned by the bookseller and publisher David Leonard.

whose precocious achievement spurred his own ambitions even more. Yet by far the most formative influence was the Ballets Russes's 1921 production of *The Sleeping Princess*. Hoping for a long-running West End hit, Diaghilev had brought to London a staging of Imperial splendour, commissioning designs by Bakst and casting in the central role three of the most brilliant exponents of Russian classicism: Vera Trefilova, Olga Spessivtzeva and Lubov Egorova. In their dancing, Ashton witnessed for the first time true classical purity, with no exaggeration of ports de bras or mannerist interpretation, while the ballet itself taught him more about construction, form and climax, he claimed, than any other choreographic experience of his life. He noted Petipa's decrescendos of atmosphere; the way the mime scenes were placed, like recitative in opera, or a prosaic passage in an epic poem, 'to rest the Spectator and the Eye', as he later put it; and he saw how a simple gesture, when powerfully performed, could be as thrilling and eloquent as any passage of dance. Although it proved a financial disaster for the Ballets Russes (Diaghilev fled England with £500 in his pocket borrowed from the mother of a dancer), *The Sleeping Princess* was Ashton's creative primer. Even as a master of his art, he would return to the ballet again and again, as if to a refresher course in choreography. 'If I educated myself, it was because I was interested. At school as I was interested in nothing except English Literature, that's all I ever learnt.'

In the late summer of 1921, George and Georgie Ashton came to England to bring the ten-year-old Edith to boarding school, and to settle Frederick's future. Edith was no problem. She was a pretty, clever, outgoing girl, who not only excelled at sport but proved to be an exceptionally gifted pianist, winning the Silver Challenge Shield at the Brighton Festival and reaching concert standard by the time she left school. 'Ish', as she was called (because of the 'sh' in Ashton), settled in almost immediately at Micklefield, a secondary school for girls, and was loved by everyone. 'She was always smiling and jolly,' said a fellow pupil. 'I never saw her cross or bored.' Her brother, on the other hand, despite Alf Dixon's nurturing and the name he had made for himself on stage, still felt that he was 'looked upon as a sort of hopeless character'. Apart from being efficient in English and French, he had learnt 'a bit of geography, a bit of scripture and that was all' – certainly not enough to move up to the sixth form and meet the standards required for Higher School Certificate. After a session with the headmaster, Ashton's parents decided that it was time for him to leave. 'Piggy' Lee – otherwise aptly known as 'the Oiler' – was charming and polite enough, but made it clear that the only boys who really interested him were those likely to bring credit to his school – boys like Guy Watson, 'a joy to his teachers', who would stay on at Dover gaining one distinction after another for two more years. But what was Ashton to do next? His inability to pass exams ruled out the career in the diplomatic service that Georgie had had in mind for him; likewise, university was out of the question. Eventually, through the intervention of Maud Lawson, whose brother was a partner in a Fenchurch Street firm of import–export merchants, a job as an office boy was found for him for thirty shillings per week.

The sense of release that engulfed Ashton as the term drew to a close culminated at chapel service on his last evening at Dover. It was an intensely emotional occasion, as Alf Dixon reminded him years later when he was trying to persuade him to revisit the College and, as an incentive, quoted a stanza of the hymn that was sung.

> When to the scenes of your boyhood returning
> Backward your footsteps shall wander alone
> Bright be your hopes and strong be your yearnings
> When you remember the days that are gone

However, the sentiment was lost on Ashton, who, once he had left Dover, wanted nothing more to do with it. In 1971, when the college was engaged in its Centenary Appeal, Jeffrey Archer, an ex-teacher, received no answer to his letter asking the choreographer either to give money or lend his name to their fund-raising efforts. Similarly, during the week of centenary celebrations when *The Tales of Beatrix Potter* happened to be running at the local cinema and the headmaster took the whole school to see it, Ashton never replied to Timothy Cobb's letter telling him how much everyone had enjoyed it. He did, however, respond to a St Martin's House pupil who had written about his plans to start an arts magazine. 'In my philistine days,' said Ashton, 'the Arts were very much neglected – I would even go as far as to say looked down upon. All that mattered were games, so things must have changed very radically if you are able to find a public, so to speak, for this amongst the boys.' Ashton's unhappiness at school is well known, but, like George Orwell's vengeful depiction in *Such, Such Were the Joys* of the physical and mental abuse he suffered as a boarder, it is not a complete picture. Philistinism was rife at Dover, but no more so than at many other public schools of the period. In fact, in the field of drama it was probably ahead of its time. However intensely Ashton disliked his schooldays, they were not the 'absolute desert' he described. And yet, this was the version which he, like Orwell, came to believe.

Ashton's exhilaration at leaving Dover was tempered by trepidation at what lay ahead. 'Frankly, it was more shattering to be pushed into the City than almost anything else that ever happened to me.' To begin with, however, life as an office boy at William Menzies & Co, was not that bad: 'I rather enjoyed the filing and licking the stamps.' He was cheery towards his fellow juniors, and made no secret of his real ambition, quite confident that one day he would succeed. 'So well do I remember you telling me that ballet was the most wonderful thing in the world, as you used to dance your way round the office,' an ex-colleague recalled. Although Ashton was still living in Argyll Mansions, Maud Lawson seemed more aware now of how grim the set-up was for him and during one school holiday had taken him off to Florence – a revelation to the culturally voracious teenager. Now, hoping that his prospects at Menzies might improve if he polished his languages, she proposed to send him to France, where, 'because she was very anti-Catholic', he was to stay with a Calvinist priest and his family.

> They said I'd be the only English boy and I would have plenty of opportunity to talk French, but when I arrived, there were three other English boys there and I didn't speak a word of French. One of them was so racy and randy that he used to go off to the brothels. He was only seventeen or whatever we were. We used to get bicycles and stay out all day, cycling all over the place.

All the same, Aunt Maud's good intentions paid off because Ashton was soon promoted to junior foreign correspondent, which meant having to translate any business letter that arrived, in whatever language it happened to be. 'The manager would bring me letters in Arabic and I'd say, "But I don't speak Arabic," and he'd say, "But you speak Spanish. And there's a dictionary over there."' Ashton carried out his duties competently, but with clenched teeth: 'I must say I still don't know how I stood it in the City. It was all terribly restricted and frustrated and closed up.' Early in the New Year, he received news that threatened to trap him in his job indefinitely: his father was dead (he did not learn until several years later that it was a suicide), and his mother was already making plans to join him in London. Ashton's immediate reaction was not one of grief for his father, who had always been a stranger to him, but anxiety at having his mother on his hands.

> What else was she to do? She had two children here, all her other children were grown up and all over the place. What alternative had she but to come to England? By that time she'd lost contact

with people in Lima. There had been a world war and she'd been friends with a lot of Germans and French people. What was she to do? She wouldn't want to have stayed in a horrible place like Guayaquil, she couldn't go up to Quito – she couldn't stand the height. She had intimate friends here, girls she was at school with, that she came back and saw a great deal of. After all, she was English and had her sisters here.

By this time, in order to have more space, Ashton had moved to Croydon, where he commuted to and from the City, lodging with friends of Georgie's who owned a large house 'with a tennis court and all that'. Gibson Pacy was a wealthy banker and he and his wife, May, were very sweet to Ashton, but having briefly enjoyed being the ward of this kindly elderly couple, he suddenly found himself thrust overnight into adulthood, responsible for the next twenty years for the welfare of his mother.

Georgie had left Guayaquil as soon as she could. 'She almost ran away,' said Charlie Ashton's grandson, Carlos. 'She took her jewels and left everything else behind.' Her sudden flight from a Catholic country can be explained by the stigma attached to suicide, which is considered a mortal sin, but it may also have been compounded by guilt. If George had found out about his wife's lover in Lima, could the disgrace of cuckoldry have been reason enough for him to take his own life? George Ashton had already demonstrated his volatile, impetuous nature when he shot his own horse in a fit of passion over Violet Beauclerk. He was a romantic, a fantasist, who, without a creative outlet into which to channel his visions, had fictionalized his own life. This duplicity eventually took its toll. According to a letter Georgie wrote to John Ashton explaining his father's death, the melancholia from which George suffered throughout their marriage had become pathologically severe over the past year. Beyond that, the subject was never discussed in the family, and George's death remained as much of an enigma as his past life. Ashton always assumed that his father had committed suicide 'because his business went wrong', but this was far from the case: at the time of his death, George Ashton's professional reputation was thriving.

In 1916, when the British commercial firm Milne, Williamson opened a branch in Guayaquil, George had been appointed manager of the company, and although his period of stewardship was not a financial success, he was considered, at a tough time in a tough place, to be laying good foundations for the firm's later prosperity. As a businessman he was known for his astute, straightforward and honest nature. His signature was one of the most prestigious in the city, offering a guarantee of security and trust, and he was respected enough for the Ecuadorian President, Dr José Luis Tamayo, the firm's ex-lawyer, to grant him an interview in George's own office. When Milne, Williamson became an Ecuadorian company, George remained in charge, and later, when Sociedad Comercial Anglo-Ecuatoriana Limitada became sub-agents for a new company, Anglo-Ecuadorian Oilfields, it was he who pioneered the drilling for oil on the Santa Elena Peninsula. In addition to this, he was described at the time as having 'vast connections with banking, trade and local commercial services'. One association was with the family firm, Casa Carlos Ashton, run by his sons Charles and Alex, and specializing in the export of cocoa and coffee. As senior consultant, George was largely responsible for its success and financial solvency, and, by 1924, business was at its peak. 'My grandfather was very important,' said John Ashton's daughter, Elsie. 'He had money, a good situation, a good house. Nobody could imagine that he was going to kill himself.'

On the morning of 14 January 1924, George Ashton arrived, as usual, at his office on the Malecón, immediately devoting himself to the work on his desk. None of his employees noticed any change in him – on the contrary, everything seemed perfectly normal. A little before eleven, he spoke on the telephone to a colleague and later dealt with his correspondence, answered cables that had come in overnight, examined some false gems he had bought on the street and finally studied the end-of-year accounts. He then left his desk and went down to the vaults. A few minutes later, a shot was heard and Charlie Ashton, working in an office upstairs, went to investigate. His father was lying on the floor with his head blown off.

The following day, George Ashton's obituary, accompanied by a large, ornately bordered photograph, made front-page news in El Telegrafo, the newspaper at which he had been chairman of the board. In extravagantly reverent prose, the article laments the loss of one of the city's most distinguished gentleman, its homage deflated somewhat by the repeated misspelling, 'Sn Dn Geo Asthon'. Nevertheless, whoever was responsible for the obituary appears to have known George Ashton well, pointing out that although his death remained surrounded in mystery, 'nobody should think that it was motivated by anything other than profound disillusion and disenchantment caused by menial and petty miseries which life sometimes offers to high spirits who fly to regions of ideals and only death can surpass'.

There is mention in El Telegrafo of the 'fortune' that George Ashton left in legacy to his children, but as most of his funds had been invested in property, there was little available cash – so little, in fact, that Georgie had to apply to the British authorities for her repatriation expenses. It is unlikely that her husband's oil interests would have been much of a meal-ticket in 1924; even though Anglo-Ecuadorian Oilfields was the only operator of any significance on the coast, the company had had little time to become established in George's lifetime. One of his grandsons claimed that he had 'owned three oil rigs', but this is overstating the case; George would have had no more than a minor concession in AEO's three Santa Elena rigs and, of these, only one had given encouraging results.* Characteristically, George used most of his money to buy property, including no less than eight houses in the Andean market town of Riobamba, which he left in Charlie and Alex's names. Georgie, it appears, was much less well provided for. 'As a widow in South America, she would have been on her own,' said Wallis Hunt. 'There was no pension scheme until the mid-thirties. There may have been some land here and there, a few shares, but one way or another it turns to dust by the time you try to bring it home.'

Georgie had arrived in Liverpool on the SS *Cedric* at the end of February and, although she claimed that she was unable to refund her repatriation allowance, she must have received some form of support from her sons in South America, as she and Frederick lived quite comfortably at first. They had moved into the Alwin Court Hotel in Gloucester Road, which Ashton described as 'very nice with good food, although it was full of old ladies – the manager's wife used to take me to the theatre'. Georgie spent her first months in England renewing connections with relatives and old friends, including a Mrs Caesar Hawkins, a Naval officer's widow, who owned The Vache in Chalfont St Giles: a vast, mainly eighteenth-century manor house, surrounded by eighty acres of parkland. Described by the writer, Nicholas Lawford, as 'a rare treasure in increasingly vulgarized metroland', it was, Ashton said, his first visit to a grand English house. To accommodate Edith in the school holidays, he and Georgie then took a three-bedroom flat in West Bolton Gardens. This must have come as a relief to Edith. She used to dread the weeks she had to spend in Middleton-on-Sea with her Aunt Sidney and her Uncle Wilf, who was always making a pass at her. They considered Ashton to be a potentially bad influence, and so would not allow Edith to see him, and it was only during these holidays in London that they had the chance to get to know each other for the first time. They went to the theatre and

---

*As Wallis Hunt points out in *Heirs of Great Adventure*, his chronicle of the history of the Balfour, Williamson group, it took another year before production reached 12,000 tons – less than the parent company, Lobitos Oilfields, produced in a month.

ballet together, and Edith, hanging on his every word, began to have ambitions of her own to dance (she had beautifully formed dancer's feet and
had been trained as a gymnast at school), but Georgie would not hear of
it. 'She wanted me to be a pianist.' Edith had been devastated by George's
death, as she had been very close to her father. For her brother, however,
it had been a liberation. It was at this time that Ashton began to take ballet lessons.

The advertisement which Reginald Palmer had clipped out of the
Dancing Times was for classes with Léonide Massine, the charismatic
dancer and choreographer made famous by Diaghilev. As a performer,
Massine had always lacked technical skill, but compensated for this
with an extraordinary stage presence and sense of showmanship. He
was, in Edwin Denby's description, 'an encyclopedia of ballet, character,
speciality, period, and even formulas from modern German dancing' –
an eclecticism which could not fail to infiltrate the imagination of a
young choreographer in embryo. Having recently fallen out with Diaghilev, Massine had formed a small touring company with his Ballets
Russes colleague, Lydia Lopokova, and was now based in London
where he had opened a one-room studio off Oxford Street. Responding
to his offer of a trial lesson, Ashton wrote to Massine after first talking
over the idea with Cyril Beaumont and his wife. Hearing how this particular teacher had come to his notice, Mrs Beaumont had exclaimed,
'You looked in the *Dancing Times*? Goodness, you might as well have
looked into the telephone directory.' And she was right. By the early
1920s, dance in England was booming, and reflecting this were the fast-
expanding pages of advertisements and personal columns of the *Dancing
Times*, in which, cashing in on the growing opportunities for dancers,
literally anyone with a notion to do so could declare themselves to be ex-
perts in the field.

> 'Just think of it!!!' Read an advertisement for the Park Lane Danc-
> ing School and Galleries in 1922, 'One Year's Training, and you
> are ready to take your place as prominent people in the Dancing
> World. With a Diploma bearing the signatures of the universally
> famous Mme. Lydia Kyasht and Mr Henry Cooper, you should get
> a post anywhere in the world, or set up as a Teacher for your-
> self . . . '

Ashton often remarked that he was remarkably lucky to have fallen
into safe hands. 'Somehow I just hit on the right one. I might have hit on
a Miss Mavis Someone or other.' But this was unlikely. Not only had he
seen enough first-rate performances by now to discern real professional-

ism for himself, he had had good counsel all along. It was Mrs Beaumont, he later reminded her husband, who had encouraged him to go to Massine in the first place.

In reply to his letter, Massine instructed Ashton to appear at his audition in soft slippers and pyjamas. 'With my rigid upbringing, I didn't think that was right at all. So I wore cricket flannels and a shirt.' Massine remembered a young man arriving at his studio one day, 'somewhat informally attired in shirt and shorts', anxious to know whether he would make a dancer. 'I asked him to demonstrate a few steps, and finding that he had the basic qualifications I enrolled him in the school.' As Diaghilev's protégé, Massine was himself a product of what Richard Buckle called 'one of the most sensational feats of "talent-spotting" in history'. In Ashton, he would have noted unusually high insteps, essential for achieving perfect line, a natural flexibility of the torso, but little else. At twenty, Ashton had long passed the ideal age to train as a professional, but at least he had the advantage of his sex. While the dance explosion had brought with it a striking change in the social status of the dancer – 'Suddenly, the "ballet girl" had become respectable' – ballet as a career for a man was still socially and morally taboo. Of Massine's dozen or so pupils almost all were 'rather arty girls' and he was therefore all too ready to take on a young male student willing to flout convention. 'I got away with murder . . . If I had to do it now I don't think I'd get far.'

Because Ashton was still working in the City, he was restricted to having one lesson per week, which he realized was a waste of time. Every Saturday afternoon, Massine would demonstrate an exercise in front of the mirror and wait for Ashton to copy him. 'I didn't know what I was doing . . . I drove him crazy.' Often Massine would sit with a chair-back between his legs, beating time with two drum-sticks and, when exasperated, would sometimes strike the chair so violently that he would break his stick and fling it away in fury. With his intense black eyes boring into a recalcitrant pupil – Byzantine eyes, Diaghilev called them – Massine could be a formidable figure. But not only was Ashton unruffled by the maestro's temper, his determination to achieve his ambition to be 'the world's greatest dancer' made him audacious enough even to challenge Massine's methods. 'I used to say to him afterwards, "This is all very well, but when are you going to teach me to dance?"' 'In three years' time,' was the reply, a prospect Ashton found totally unacceptable. 'I was in despair. I didn't like that at all.'

Private lessons with Massine were costing him one guinea per week, leaving him with nine shillings on which to live. 'I could never pay for anything, not even my washing. I never had a penny.' Georgie, to whom Ashton had not dared confess that he was learning to dance, could not understand why he had no money, although she was pleased that his prospects at William Menzies seemed to be improving. However, as someone who 'hadn't a clue about mathematics – I couldn't add without my fingers', additional responsibility in the firm was the last thing Ashton wanted.

> When I did my first bit of business I lost the firm a thousand pounds so that I was called before these distinguished old boys who were reprimanding me for carelessness and everything else and I suddenly turned round and said to them, 'Well, gentlemen, the money is lost. What are you going to do to retrieve it?' They all practically blew me out of the door, and that was it.

The strain of being out of his depth at work, and having to keep up the subterfuge at home, proved too much. Ashton began to get 'terribly thin and really worried' and finally, in desperation, staged a nervous breakdown, taking to his bed and refusing to get up. An elderly Scottish doctor was summoned. He 'must have been a wise old bird' because he told Ashton there was nothing physically wrong with him, but asked what was, in fact, troubling him.

> So I told him about my dancing lessons and he told my mother unless I was allowed to do ballet I might end in the loony-bin. That frightened her and then she thought she'd better concede.

It was around this time that Charlie Ashton came to London for a couple of months with his wife and baby son. Although he had married very young, almost immediately after leaving college, his parents considered that he had made an excellent match. Maria Saenz, a voluptuous beauty with wavy black hair and creamy skin, was a descendant of the famous Manuela Saenz, the fiery mistress of Simon Bolivar, liberator of South America. Her family was aristocratic and extremely wealthy, presenting the couple with one of the grandest colonial houses in Quito as a wedding present. Maria, who was like a pampered nineteenth-century heroine, habitually carrying a parasol and, even in a motor car, shielding her face from the sun, fascinated Ashton from the moment they met. 'My sister-in-law was so lazy she used to insist that her Indian nurse should sleep on a sofa at the end of the bed so that if she dropped her handkerchief it would be picked up.' Although Ashton said his family were 'outraged' when they found out about his dancing lessons, Charlie, who had always been fond of his younger brother, proposed a compromise, offering to pay for Frederick's tuition on condition that he never

went into a chorus. 'So I said, "Yes, of course." But if I'd had the op-
portunity to go into a chorus I would have done so. For the money.'
After that, Ashton was allowed to leave William Menzies and study with
Massine every day.

Classes became progressively more inspiring, especially when barre
practice was over. Massine would stand in the centre of the studio
demonstrating a series of arm movements, which the students watched
intently before performing them for themselves. As a dedicated pupil of
the great teacher Enrico Cecchetti (Cecchetti and his wife even came on
holiday to Italy with Diaghilev and Massine so that Léonide could continue his daily practice), Massine was a brilliant exponent of the eight set
exercises formulated by Cecchetti to achieve graceful carriage of the arms,
pliability of the torso and co-ordination of movement with the head. Described by Ashton as 'the most wonderful port de bras that exists', their
ultimate objective in developing the use of the upper body is to help a
dancer to master épaulement. The principle of twisting opposition in the
upper body, épaulement – once likened to 'the continuous tension of a
garland wound around a turning column' – was to prove the key to the
movement idiom of Ashton's choreography.

For some of his students, Massine was not an ideal teacher – 'He had
such an individual style himself, he was difficult to copy' – but it was precisely this eccentricity that Ashton began to assimilate in his own movements, Massine's 'breaking of the classical line and his funny little quirky
ways. He was a marvellous demi-caractère dancer and not being a classical dancer myself he was somebody I could take from.' Although Ashton
claimed that the classes did 'not directly' teach him anything about
choreography, Massine's influence was to pervade much of his early
work.

Unwilling to become a father-confessor figure to his pupils, as Cecchetti had been, Massine did not develop much of a personal rapport
with Ashton, who found him very aloof – 'You couldn't get anywhere
near.' His school friend, Reginald Palmer, would often wait for him after
class in a nearby Lyon's Corner House, but, on the whole, these were
lonely days. One morning, however, he noticed the arrival of a new student who, with his foxy features, was not particularly good-looking, but
who generated an infectious energy and sense of fun. At the end of one
class, after executing an exuberant double tour en l'air, fourteen-year-old
Walter Gore found himself seized by the hand and dragged to the middle
of the room by Ashton, who instructed him to perform the step again in
front of Massine. Ballet technique came easily to Gore, but as the fifth
generation of a family of actors (he had grown up on the road with his
parents' Portable Theatre company), he remained unconvinced about

taking up dance as a career. Methodically, Ashton began persuading him to change his mind.

> So the days went by, taking milk after class with Fred and promising to go to class the next day. I think we gave each other courage. I know he would implore me to be there, or he wouldn't go, and each day I pledged myself afresh over a glass of milk.

Ashton was immediately attracted to Gore. However, although the six-year age difference inevitably cast him in the role of a 'chase-me', the infatuation was one-sided, and so it remained even years later when Gore, by this time the object of romantic obsession for Ashton, became the choreographer's first male muse. Not that there was much scope for amorous activity, with Ashton's mother in the next room. He claimed, though, that, despite Georgie's watchfulness, he was able to retain a modicum of independence. 'By sleeping in other people's beds, that's how. I never stayed out all night. She always had her light on, waiting up for me. The moment I came in, she'd turn it off. But she'd have been lying there *vigilante.*'

One day, he came home after class to find Georgie looking white with despair. 'We're ruined,' she said dramatically. Casa Carlos Ashton had gone into liquidation and there was to be no further financial support from Charlie, most of whose money had been squandered on foreign travel, gambling, Ecuadorian art, cars, and mink coats collected by Maria. Although George Ashton's shares in Anglo-Ecuadorian Oil had greatly increased their value owing to a spectacular advance in petroleum production over the past year, because no one had ever claimed them, the shares had gone to the Ecuadorian government. There were still several of George's properties that could have been sold, but Charlie and Alex had taken so little interest in their father's business affairs that, apparently, they 'just forgot' about the Riobamba houses. Tony, who was just beginning his career with a British commercial firm, was not able to help out financially at the time (although, much later, he sent regular payments and food parcels to his mother). For Ashton and Georgie, there was no option but to move immediately to less expensive premises. This meant settling for not much more than a cupboard in Earls Court for Frederick, and a larger room for Georgie, where they both lived, cooked and ate. Edith would either have to squeeze in with them in the holidays or be 'farmed out' again to relatives. The day the removal van came to West Bolton Gardens, Ashton was in such a state of desperation about how he was going to be able to continue his ballet tuition that he stayed in bed until the men had taken away everything in his room. Later, he dragged himself over to Earls Court Square, somewhat shamefaced, to find his mother sitting among the packing cases, answering letters as though she had lived there for years. They were 'down to nothing', as Ashton said, and although Georgie would continue to face poverty with unfailing resilience, she would never again have a life of her own. 'It was *awful* for her. In the end, you see, she just lived for me.'

CHAPTER THREE

A MAD BRIGHT YOUNG THING
1924–1928

One by one, Georgie's good connections dropped away. Faced with genuine adversity, she was unwilling to accept any invitations as she would be unable to return the hospitality – not that she would have dreamt of inviting anyone of importance to their lodgings in dismal Earls Court. She and Ashton could easily have had more spacious accommodation if they had moved out to the suburbs, but even when their financial circumstances had reached their lowest ebb, Georgie refused to leave central London. 'She was always very snooty about the fact that one of my schoolfriends lived in Tooting Bec.' Instead, she did her best to make life as cheerful as possible with what they had. 'She was sweet in a way, poor thing, because I'd come back one day and she'd have moved all the furniture and say, "We've gone to the seaside." ' Nevertheless, his mother's dependence on him was increasingly oppressive. 'I used to feel guilty if I left her alone all the time . . . Her whole existence had been South America, and although she had a few friends here, she had no life.'

Initially, Georgie had gone out of her way to maintain links with Peru and Ecuador, joining the Lyceum Club in Piccadilly which had recently inaugurated a South American section (she was among several hostesses assisting the Marchioness of Aberdeen with a reception to launch the new affiliation), but by this time she saw little of anyone, except Maud Lawson and Milly, Georgie's sister, with whom she could relax and remember happier days. 'I'd arrive home and find my aunt sitting in a chair smoking a Craven A and my mother sitting on the floor – for some reason she always sat on the floor. Milly was a big woman and I'd see her absolutely *shaking* with laughter at some reminiscence or goodness knows what.' Most of Georgie's time was spent on her own, waiting for Ashton to come home, occasionally occupying herself by writing articles which she hoped would bring in a few extra pounds.

The Overseas League, to which Georgie belonged, published a monthly journal with contributions from its members on subjects such as 'Life on a Jamaican "Pen" or Farm', or 'In Praise of Indian Servants'. They were typical expatriate musings that Georgie, drawing mostly on her experiences in Ecuador, attempted to emulate. Under her pseudonym of Anthony Sant, she submitted several short pieces which, although platitudinous and weakly epigrammatic in tone, are interesting as barely disguised confessions of her own state of mind at the time. 'Possessions: What Becomes of Them' warns of the folly of placing too much value on material things, but ends poignantly by lamenting her decision to leave behind all her own belongings.

> If ever again one should make a home, there will be no mementos of good old times to comfort one, when life is no longer active but reminiscent. Well – It can't be helped, but I'll miss my 'Things'.

'The Hen That Hatches Ducks by One of Them' is a baleful little allegory comparing the pangs of separation felt by a hen watching the ducklings she has hatched swim far out into the pond away from her care, 'certainly in no way needing her', with a mother's despair and loneliness at losing her sons to the world. When the editor of *Overseas* accepted one of her articles, Georgie was so delighted that she wrote asking for several extra copies of the magazine, but 'The Light that Does not Fail', her touching memorial to George, did not appear in the issue for which it was scheduled or in any other that followed. She and Ashton were able to keep going for a while on the money she had obtained by pawning her emeralds, and with the small sum given to her by Milly. All the same, it was a hard life compared with that which Georgie had been used to, while for Ashton it was a determining factor in shaping the man he was to become. The reputation for meanness he later acquired was a direct result of these early years of poverty; even at the height of prosperity, he would still *feel* poor.

At least he no longer had to pay for his ballet classes. Massine had by now given up his London studio in order to rejoin the Ballets Russes, and sent Ashton to a fellow disciple of Cecchetti, the Polish-born teacher, Marie Rambert. For the last four years, Rambert had been sharing a studio in Bedford Gardens with a sculptress, whose tall figures covered with damp cloths were pushed into a corner when the ballet students arrived. Ashton had already taken classes with Rambert on and off throughout 1924, when Massine was away working with the Comte Etienne de Beaumont in Paris, but he did not feel that she had much to offer him. Although she had a thorough grounding in the Cecchetti method, Rambert had come late to classical ballet and, appearing only in the corps of the Ballets Russes, had not gone on to distinguish herself as a dancer. 'Rambert was a terrible dancer,' said Ashton. 'She was a kind of joke among all the other teachers; she had the most terrible feet and couldn't even get up on her pointes. Everybody knew she couldn't dance, so nobody really respected her.'

At first, Rambert was not entirely convinced about Ashton either. She could see that he was extremely gifted and that even when he made mistakes, his untrained movements had a grace of their own, but he lacked strength and technique, and had little idea of traditional barre work and even less of centre practice. The main point at issue, however, was his lack of any musical training. Musical theory was second nature to Rambert. Her early training by Emile Jaques-Dalcroze had given her such a command of eurythmics that Diaghilev had engaged her to help Nijinsky count out the rhythmic complexities for *Le Sacre du printemps* (the Ballets Russes dancers used to call her 'Rythmitchka' – the rhythmic one). But although it was clear that Ashton had an instinctive musicality, Rambert was irritated by his apparent inattentiveness; he could not pick up the combination of steps she had set and could not keep time. 'Later I realised that as he was himself creative, the music probably suggested to him subconsciously much more beautiful enchaînements than the purely educational ones which I combined.' Coming from Massine, where a famous ballerina like Lydia Lopokova might be alongside him on the barre, Ashton found lessons with Rambert amateurish and uninspiring. 'It was frightfully boring. She didn't have a piano. She used to whistle all the way through things and I absolutely hated it, hated her class.' He would steal off whenever he could to Margaret Craske, an outstanding teacher of classical ballet, who had made it her vocation to transmit the Cecchetti legacy both in her West Street studio and in the manuals she was then writing with Cyril Beaumont. For basic technique and simplicity of style, Craske was unbeatable; but seeking to combine the discipline of the Cecchetti method with a freer, more spontaneous approach, Ashton took classes with the retired Diaghilev dancer Serafina Astafieva, an amusingly eccentric character with a flour-white face and charcoaled eyes, who would demonstrate wonderfully lyrical adagios wearing an ancient chiffon evening dress and frayed satin high-heeled shoes, a stick in one hand, a long cigarette holder in the other. 'Fred wouldn't have got technique from Astafieva. She would have taught him how to dance.' When the great Nikolay Legat, premier danseur at the Mariinsky Theatre in St Petersburg, who succeeded Cecchetti as Diaghilev's ballet master, opened a school in London in 1926, Ashton rushed to join the galaxy of ex-Ballets Russes stars who frequented his classes. But Marie Rambert, determined to hold on to her only male pupil, especially one in whom she sensed 'the born artist', tracked him down. 'She would haul me back again, haul me back again.' He finally stayed with her, not out of loyalty, but because he could not afford to do otherwise. Sympathizing with his financial difficulties, Rambert had offered to take him on for nothing. 'That's why I kept coming back to her and eventually I became acclimatized, when I got to know her better.'

They soon became friends. Rambert found Ashton amusing, intelligent, and charming, while he was surprised by how entertaining she could be. She was one of the wittiest women in London – 'Margot Asquith used to steal her remarks all the time' – and despite his low regard for her as a classical teacher, Ashton was increasingly aware of the intellectual stimulus that she could offer. A highly cultivated woman, quintilingual and well read in European literature, 'Mim', as she was known (her real name was Myriam Ramberg), began systematically to cultivate Ashton, guiding his reading, taking him to the theatre and ballet and inviting him for meals at her home in Campden Hill. She was married to the dramatist, translator and critic Ashley Dukes, a friend and collaborator of T. S. Eliot and W. H. Auden, who was himself highly esteemed at the time. Dukes's latest play, *The Man with the Load of Mischief*, which was running at the Haymarket, had been both a critical and commercial triumph. From the proceeds he would later buy the freehold of a large church hall in Ladbroke Grove which he divided into a studio for Rambert and a tiny theatre for them both. It was the Mercury – 'this shoebox, this Punch and Judy show' – in which Eliot's *Murder in the Cathedral* received its first London staging, and in which, as a result of the slight but charming, well-crafted early choreographic attempts of the young Frederick Ashton, English ballet was born.

In addition to his writing, Dukes was London editor of *Theatre Arts Monthly*, the American periodical that regularly published the essays of ballet historian and critic André Levinson, and had devoted an entire issue to dance. Yet Dukes claimed to be a serious balletophobe. The Rambert-trained choreographer, Agnes de Mille, has described how he would wander into the studio after a conference with Auden and stand in the door, beaming, in 'a kind of effulgent dislike'. 'I must say I do hate all forms of dancing,' he would announce before leaving. Fortified by self-importance, Dukes regarded his wife's profession as little more than a time-killing Victorian hobby, like needlework or acrostics, although, for all his amused condescension, it was Rambert's school that paid the bills. Many of her pupils were what Ashton called 'middle-class ladies', the daughters of well-to-do parents, like Diana Gould (now Lady Menuhin, Yehudi Menuhin's wife), who was so young when she began her studies that she and her sister would arrive with their Scottish nanny. Although Ashton was far and away her favourite student, Madame took a personal interest in them all. 'We were very close. It was all much more intimate in those days because there were so few of us.'

When the Ballets Russes were in London, Rambert went every night of the season, taking one of her pupils with her. 'She had absolute entrée,' said Ashton. 'Diaghilev always gave her seats.' The avant-garde repertory that Diaghilev brought to London during the last era of the Ballets Russes had alienated even the company's most faithful devotees. To Ashton, however, new works like *Le Train bleu*, with its Cocteau libretto, Milhaud score, Picasso curtain and Chanel costumes, were thrilling expressions of the new age. He went to Nijinska's ballet 'expecting to see someone wearing a dress with a long blue train' and, instead, encountered 1920s flappers, athletes, tarts and gigolos disporting themselves on a Riviera beach (the ballet's title referred to the Blue Train that sped smart Parisians to their newly discovered summer playground). 'Lifestyle modernism' was a genre Nijinska had inaugurated in *Les Biches*, a fragrantly wanton depiction of Cocteau's world, made all the more piquant by its evanescent atmosphere of irony and sexual equivocation. It struck Ashton, who went to its London première in October 1925, as a revelation. 'I thought it was the most wonderful thing I'd ever seen. The chic, the elegance, the complete evocation of what life was like at that time was staggering to me. And then later when I saw *Les Noces*, I realised what a great choreographic genius Nijinska was.'

However exciting he found the Diaghilev ballets, he continued to derive inspiration from more traditional forms of dance, particularly as personified by Pavlova, who came frequently to London during the early 1920s. Now in her mid-forties, out of sympathy with Diaghilev's novelties, she had continued to play safe, reluctant to lose an audience that had paid to see her signature works. Pavlova's repertory of popular kitsch, the light, gay fragments with their second-rate, hummable scores, compared unfavourably with the daring experiments of the Ballets Russes, but, to Ashton, the trite material was beside the point. For Pavlova, ballet meant *dancing* and, as far as he was concerned, her artistry was undiminished. Far more analytical now than when he had first seen the ballerina in Lima, he studied not only her unique, vibrant movements and the gradations of emotion she conveyed, but what she did in between: how she ran, how she approached her partner and how she took her curtain calls – in themselves, performances of outstanding grace, theatricality and surprise, often taking longer than the solo she had just danced. Far from being old-fashioned, he considered Pavlova to be as much of an innovator as Nijinska; in their own way, both women were instrumental in showing him how to personalize the classical idiom and to make it live.

In September 1925, when Pavlova was appearing at Covent Garden, Ashton summoned the courage to apply to join her company. The ballet master, Pianovsky, auditioned him, but he performed badly and was turned down. Fortunately, as it turned out. Pavlova was widely known for eclipsing her partners – no one since Mikhail Mordkin had emerged with an enhanced reputation – but, more crucially, as Ashton still had no thoughts of choreographing at the time, it is questionable whether, without Rambert's goading, he would ever have progressed from dancing to making dance. He was left with his memories of Pavlova, memories which he claimed kept him going when he could not find work as a performer, 'and when my mother and I had no money'. Much as an adolescent of today might pin pictures of football heroes or pop stars to his bedroom wall, Ashton began clipping and pasting a collage of photographs of his idol on to two panels of a wooden screen: Pavlova at home in her garden at Ivy House, Pavlova in her dressing room, Pavlova's foot, image after image of Pavlova as the Dying Swan. On the reverse, he stuck photographs of Ballets Russes stars: Vera Nemchinova in *Les Biches*, Lydia Lopokova in *The Good-Humoured Ladies*, Vaslav Nijinsky and Tamara Karsavina in *Le Spectre de la Rose* . . . names that had the aura of an incantation to him and his Rambert colleagues. 'This was the fabric of our lives,' remarked Diana Gould, 'the background against which we worked, the inspiration which drove us to emulate that which we yet knew to be unattainable.' But, although they all dreamt of an Elysian future in which they would perform alongside their deities, in reality theirs was a world of 'bus tickets and banana skins', their mornings beginning in a cold, cramped changing room, shuddering into practice clothes still clammy from the day before. Spaced along the barre in the studio, its walls beaded with damp, were the students – modest, dogged girls, with rosy, virginal complexions and long, tapering figures. Slighter than any was Ashton, his bare, skinny legs clad in black shorts and white socks, his adolescently spotty face so concave that his mother used to say it looked as if two profiles had been pressed together. Darting between them was fiendish, foxy little Madame Rambert, wheedling, cajoling, pushing, pulling, poking. 'Now and then she would stamp her foot and literally howl with distaste. "Frrrrrreddie, pull in your great bottom. You flaunt your bottom like a banner."' Ashton, who held Rambert responsible for the large flat bottom he was developing (just as a couple of the girls blamed her exercises for grafting jodhpur-shaped musculature on their legs), did not take kindly to Rambert's notorious candour, and many years later was still taking his revenge. 'Fred used to vilify Mim,' said a mutual friend. 'She had the knack of hitting on your weakest spot; told you truths you didn't want to hear.'

Ashton's longed-for professional début proved no more uplifting than the daily grind in Notting Hill Gate. His first public performance took place on the end of the Palace Pier in Brighton on 10 April 1925 (Good Friday) in one of H. Bernhardt's Popular Concerts. 'In those days the agents used to book some well-known music hall act for top of the bill and any old thing was dragged on beforehand, including me.' Fred Ashton, as he was billed, appeared in Item 4, a 'Fandango', a dance of South American origin which should have come naturally to him, but according to Doris Sonne, who had arranged the piece, Ashton was 'jolly bad and couldn't keep time', although he had distinct flair and style. He remembered nothing about the occasion, 'Except horror. We got paid nothing. We were given our railway fare and half a crown to have lunch and that was it.' That same summer, he appeared in various danced 'prologues' to silent films at the Shepherd's Bush Pavilion. 'We did pretty numbers to make some sort of entertainment. In a much lesser way we were doing what the Rockettes did.' Cast in one show as Captain Hook and, in another, made to lead on a donkey, Ashton was paid £3 10s per week for up to three performances each day. Life had fallen well short of his expectations, but change was close at hand.

At lunch one day in Campden Hill, Mim Rambert introduced Ashton to a Polish painter friend, Sophie Fedorovitch, whom he had seen before when she came to sketch the dancers in class, and whose appearance had made a great impression on him at the time. 'She was the first woman I had seen who wore her hair cut very short, and she dressed in a very singular way – she was a garçonne type, with a marvellously beautiful choirboy's face.' Although Fedorovitch was eleven years older than Ashton, they found themselves so drawn to each other that, when they left Rambert's house, they decided to continue their lunch round the corner at the Express Dairy. Apart from her being a wonderfully sympathetic listener, he found that Sophie, in her gruff, laconic way, was full of fun. She painted scenery on occasion for the Ballets Russes; Sophie was 'in with all the Diaghilev people', and told some wonderful stories, yet at the same time seemed incapable of pettiness, guile or gossip. He later learnt that she had been through the Russian Revolution and had not had an easy life, forced to collect driftwood from the River Neva in order to survive the St Petersburg winter. As she was extremely reluctant to talk about herself, it was only much later, through the reminiscences of friends (collected in a book of tributes edited by her friend Simon Fleet and privately printed after her death), that Ashton was eventually able to piece together her past.

Living in Moscow at the time of the Revolution, Sophie had escaped via St Petersburg to London, where she fell in with a group of artists which included Augustus John. John and Dorelia McNeill kept open-house at their Chelsea studio, and it was probably at one of their buffet suppers that Sophie first met Iris Tree, the lively, liberated daughter of actor-manager, Sir Herbert Beerbohm Tree. A playmate of Diana Cooper and Nancy Cunard (their friendship was once described by Janet Flanner as a kind of Mayfair troika of elegance, intelligence and daring), Iris became a great devotee of Sophie's and, later, a catalyst in Ashton's own life. In Paris, where Sophie had gone to seek fresh inspiration for her work, she and Iris shared an attic flat on the Quai d'Orléans. She began driving a taxi at night to earn enough money to paint by day. 'At midnight in her peaked cap and gauntlet gloves,' wrote Iris Tree, 'this tiny, brave creature would dare the ruffian streets, driving old roués to their assignations in Montmartre.' However, night driving proved unlucrative and too much of a strain, so after selling her taxi and spending some time in the Gurdjieff Institute at Fontainebleau, Sophie returned to London.

When Ashton was introduced to her, she was living in far greater hardship than he was, lodging in a single room on the Embankment with a broken window-pane and no bed. 'She slept in one of those chairs that go back.' Fanatically independent, Sophie always declined any offer of financial help, but, to a certain extent, her frugality was self-imposed. Having survived the Russian Revolution and been conditioned by Gurdjieff's rigorously ascetic disciplines, Sophie, as Ashton said, 'didn't give a rap for comfort and frippery'. Even years later, when well able to afford to travel overnight in a wagon-lit, she preferred to spend the night in a train corridor, sitting on her suitcase, dozing. Yet, however wilfully stinting she was with herself, Sophie was always immensely giving towards others. With Ashton, her generosity knew no bounds; as he often acknowledged, the greatest luck he ever had was meeting her.

Between them, they must have had saved some money because, at Sophie's suggestion, they went to Paris for a few days. Paris was where everyone was going, where everything was happening – a vertiginous period when writers, painters, musicians, dancers, exiles from Communist Russia and Prohibition America all converged on the city at the same time – and Sophie wanted Ashton to get a taste of it for himself. 'She was educating me. Enlarging my scope. She even arranged for me to have make-up lessons while I was there.' They stayed in a cheap, old-fashioned hotel near the Odéon, and, at the first opportunity, joined the excited throng at the Théâtre des Champs-Elysées queuing to see Josephine

Baker in the *La Revue Négre*, the most fashionable theatrical experience since the advent of the Ballets Russes.

La Revue Négre was Ashton's first exposure to American jazz, the new music that, in Baker's unforgettably electric performance, appeared to have been created by the dance itself. 'The rhythmic spurt comes from her, with her frenzied flutterings and reckless dislocated movements,' wrote André Levinson. 'She seems to dictate to the spellbound drummer, to the saxophonist who leans lovingly towards her with the pulsating language of the blues.' The Cubist angles and undulant curves of Baker's beautiful brown limbs were an inspiration to Ashton, although she did not affect his choreography as directly as Pavlova and Isadora had done. It was more her lack of inhibition and what Nancy Cunard called her 'wildfire syncopation and whirlwind hot rhythm' that influenced him, seen years later not only in his jazz choreography of the 1930s, but also in the fast, abandoned lissomness of his performance of the Dago in *Façade*.

Almost as exhilarating to Ashton was his first taste of Parisian café society. On the terraces of the Dôme and the Select in Montparnasse, the Café Flore and Deux Magots in Saint-Germain, Ashton was introduced by Sophie to a group of Polish and Russian artist friends, among them Michel Larionov and his mistress, Natalia Gontcharova. As Nijinska's collaborator on *Les Noces* and designer of the new production of *The Firebird* for Diaghilev, Gontcharova was a figure of such eminence and glamour to Ashton that her gentle, self-effacing manner took him completely by surprise.

> Gontcharova was wonderful: like a nun, very quiet, serious, very reserved and he was the reverse. He was the alert one . . . A charming man. He did all the talking and was full of ideas and fantasies.

Back in London, Ashton found himself spending almost all his time with Sophie and her circle, drawn first by one friend then another into the vortex of 1920s society. Olivia Wyndham, 'really the instigator of the Bright Young Things', was Ashton's key to a raffish other life, giving him his first glimpse of the group Cecil Beaton called 'the illuminati'. Olivia had the most romantically aristocratic pedigree of anyone Ashton had ever encountered; her aunts on her father's side were Sargent's Three Graces – the Wyndham sisters Pamela Glenconner, Mary Wemyss and Madeline Adeane – while on her mother's side was Sheila, Duchess of Westminster, and Daisy, Princess of Pless. But like Allanah Harper, also a charter member of the coterie, Olivia had broken away from the débutante world and made a niche for herself among the high-bohemia of

Chelsea and Bloomsbury. Her friends were smart young socialites, such as David Plunkett Greene, Elizabeth Ponsonby and Stephen Tennant, her cousin. She also belonged to what an acquaintance described as a school of lesbians. 'Olivia was head girl. She was their goddess. They were all mad about her like the girls round Sappho on Lesbos.' With cocktails laced with absinthe, cocaine inhaled as nonchalantly as nicotine, and any available bed orgiastically writhing with bodies, Olivia's parties grew more infamous by the year. A typical one which she co-hosted with Stephen Tennant in 1928 was recorded by Edith Olivier in her journal.

> Two tiny rooms and two hundred guests at least – an extraordinary scene. Dazed drunken faces slowly rotating in a room tightly packed and where dancing was really impossible. A mixture of fancy and ordinary dress. Upstairs people lay talking in heaps on the floor as there were no seats . . . Stephen in huge gold earrings, as a sailor, wearing a succession of different coloured blouses. Oliver Messel, marvellously painted as a Chinese mask.

And yet, however wholeheartedly she participated in the fashionable dissipations of the time, Olivia remained far more than a fast party girl. As her half-brother, Francis Wyndham, has written in the short story she inspired,* she always showed extreme sensitivity to the sufferings of other creatures, animal as well as human. 'She was deeply upset by any manifestation of exclusion, of selectivity, of judgment – anything even faintly implying discrimination.' Olivia had a rare gift for fitting into any world and she expected others to do the same. When Ashton first met her, the parties she gave were not so much wild as eccentrically cosmopolitan, grouping together Communist refugees with London's beau monde. 'Olivia had extraordinary ideas about mixing everybody – like the Duke of Windsor, Mrs Patrick Campbell and all of us,' said Ashton. 'Of course, nobody mixed at all.'

During the General Strike of May 1926, when innumerable society figures helped to keep essential services running (Lady Louis Mountbatten operated the switchboard of the *Daily Express*, and Lady Diana Cooper sat up all night folding an abbreviated version of *The Times*), Olivia's tendency to side with the underdog meant she was far more likely to have been supporting the miners. She persuaded Ashton to help her deliver pamphlets on the Great West Road, a task to which he submitted more out of a sense of obligation to Olivia than empathy towards any political cause. 'She was always paying for me because she knew I had no

*'Ursula' in *Mrs Henderson and Other Stories*.

money.' Olivia's kindness to her fellow beings told on her face, her sweetness of expression suggesting 'an eagerness to please and the assumption of a similar generosity in other people'. Although she had inherited her Wyndham grandmother's serene grey, heavy-lidded eyes and refined nose, she was by no means a beauty. Her pleasant, rather lardy face, unkempt brown hair and sturdy figure gave the impression of an intelligent, responsible English-county sort. At the same time, however, countering the governessy demeanour, was a subversive, irrepressibly frivolous flip-side.

After delivering their pamphlets, Olivia and Ashton walked through the eerily still, blacked-out London streets to have supper at the Gargoyle Club in Soho, owned by her cousin, David Tennant. With its dark-blue Moorish ballroom on one floor (the mirrored mosaic walls designed by a Club member, Henri Matisse), and, on the floor above, a contrasting country-house atmosphere, with a huge open fireplace on which steaks were spitting, the Gargoyle attracted an eclectic membership recruited from society and every branch of the arts. Tallulah Bankhead, Noël Coward, Adele Astaire and virtually all London's young party set were regulars, as was the Prince of Wales, who was often seen cutting a rug on the dance floor. 'I adored it,' said Ashton. 'There was a band and you could have supper and dance. And there were always people one knew there.' Among them was Lady Dean Paul, otherwise known as Irene Poldowski, the pianist and composer, who regularly played and sang her own songs – 'The Caledonian Market Suite', 'Midnight Blues' and an especially popular number called 'Those Cud-Cud-Cuddle Blues'. 'A magpie spectre' with hair half-white and half-black, Lady Dean Paul was a champion of talented young artists like Noël Coward, whom she proclaimed to be the Congreve of modern times, and she took a great shine to Ashton. He found her eccentric, witty and sharp, and he liked her daughter, Brenda, another Gargoyle habituée, just as much. With her wavy bob, dark dissolute eyes, scarlet mouth and pencil-slim figure, Brenda Dean Paul was the personification of a 1920s girl, her whole person aglow with an aura of forbidden pleasures (over the next decade she would become notorious for her drug addiction). A wonderful dancer, with such natural rhythm that Florence Mills of *Blackbirds* fame told her that she could have been born in Harlem, Brenda would grab Ashton to partner her in a hilariously abandoned Charleston. Daughter of the baronet, Sir Aubrey Dean Paul, now separated from his wife, she was launched from an early age into her mother's world of parties, travel and music. Melba, Sir Henry Wood and George Gershwin came to their house, Arthur Rubinstein played their piano. Whenever Lady Dean Paul was engaged to perform at some grand musical evening, Brenda always accompanied her. Mother and daughter were as close as sisters, and, when Ashton first met them, they were living together in a large studio with blue varnished walls, tall windows, a grand piano and brilliantly coloured divans flanking the walls. On the long oak refectory table were paper patterns and various fabrics: in addition to her musical career, Lady Dean Paul, subject most of her life to fluctuating financial circumstances, had taken up dressmaking (among her grand customers was the Prince of Wales, whom she supplied with monogrammed pyjamas). By the late autumn of 1926, money was so tight that the Dean Pauls had to let their studio go and move into furnished accommodations. Brenda, who had fallen in love and wanted to escape the dominating influence of her mother, asked Ashton to help her find lodgings of her own. After traipsing from one place to another, each one having fallen through, he suggested as tactfully as he could that she might have more luck if she took off her false eyelashes. 'It worked.'

Their friendship began to wane as Brenda's drug addiction took hold. Unlike Olivia, who, through Brenda's 'persuasively poised example', had begun experimenting with cocaine and would eventually also fall victim to heroin, Ashton remained unaffected by her influence. His thin, pallid face may have looked like an addict's (Tallulah Bankhead once came up to him at the Gargoyle and said, 'Tell me, darling, where do you get it?'), but he was too self-motivated and hard-working to succumb to anything that might debilitate him. Often, when he visited Brenda, she would still be in bed and he would watch in morbid fascination as, from time to time, she rolled down the blankets and injected her thigh with a full syringe.

Witty and well mannered, Ashton was the ideal escort for a modern girl. Although his appearance was that of a languid exquisite – 'one of Beau Brummel's retinue. All he needed was high stock and an eye glass' – Ashton was not so conspicuously effeminate (like Stephen Tennant with his gold-dusted marcel finger-wave) as to provoke parental disapproval. Olivia frequently took him home to meet her father, Colonel Guy Wyndham. She had spent much of her life at Clouds, the great house in Wiltshire that her grandparents had built as a shrine to Pre-Raphaelite art and decorative beauty, but by the time Ashton met her, Clouds had become an expensive white elephant (rented out by her uncle, Dick Wyndham, who could not afford its upkeep), and Olivia's father had taken a summer place in Littlehampton. As he was a keen tennis player, she used to plead with Ashton to 'Give Daddy a good game, but don't beat him' – a request with which he willingly obliged. He was rather intimidated by the Colonel, 'an Edwardian gentleman with strict codes', who had once reprimanded him for leaning across the table in a restaurant and touching the arm of a 'Viscountess Whatnot' in order to ask her to repeat a remark he had not heard. Later, when Ashton and Wyndham met in the gentlemen's lavatory, the Colonel turned to him and said, 'You're a very nice boy, but I think you must learn that one doesn't touch ladies in public.'

Through Olivia, Ashton met two of the Edwardian era's most celebrated icons, Ada Leverson and Mrs Patrick Campbell, both of whom were related to her. In 1923, Olivia's father had married Olivia's young friend, Violet Leverson, the daughter of Ada Leverson, Oscar Wilde's faithful 'Sphinx'. 'An intriguing survivor from the faded *Yellow Book* past', Ada would sometimes stay at the Wyndham's house in Lowndes Street, where Olivia was still living. Although grown very deaf and clothed from neck to ankles in shiny black satin, she seemed to carry an atmosphere of festivity around her. 'She loved popular tunes and would be "mad about" some contemporary hit.' Not surprisingly, young people were instinctively drawn to her, especially Olivia, who shared Ada's spontaneous sense of the ridiculous and a tendency to collapse into uncontrollable fits of the giggles. Often when Ashton brought Olivia home, they would find a note on the hall table which read, 'Come up and see me *whatever* time you get in.'

Olivia's connection with Mrs Patrick Campbell was through a cousin, the actress's husband, George Cornwallis-West. Once a protégé of Mrs Percy Wyndham, the ageing star had become something of a liability to the family, regularly appearing at Lowndes Street to ask Olivia's father for help. When Ashton first met her, Lady Dean Paul was also there, smoking her seven-inch-long cigars, and the two dowagers, both having seen better days, addressed each other throughout the evening as 'My Harlot' and 'My Whore'. In characteristically imperious form, the actress who had always maintained an equivocal attitude towards Shakespeare, recited a favourite phrase, 'the foul womb of night' (from the Prologue to Act IV of *Henry V*), declaring, '*That's* what made him great, not "To be or not to be" which is a question anyone could ask.' Ashton sat in silence, feeling very young and unsure, his gaucheness malevolently played on by Mrs Pat. Addressing him in a booming voice, she said, 'You're a very nice boy. I'd like to give you a present.' After searching in her bag, casting aside various objects with a theatrical flourish, including the Craven A cigarette packet in which she kept her Pekinese lapdog's chopped meat, she produced a lipstick which she held out for Ashton to take. 'She was sending me up. She was catty alright.' On another occasion, when he and Olivia went to see her latest play, an unmemorable farce called *What Might Happen*, he derived some consolation from the fact that he was not the only target of her unwavering rudeness. Taking exception to one member of the cast and showing no interest in the production as a whole, she went out of her way to sabotage the performance. 'We were sitting in the pit and couldn't hear a word she said, so we found seats in the front row where everyone was shouting out, "SPEAK UP!" And later, in the middle of her leading man's long speech, she said to him loud enough for us all to hear, "Can't you see how you're boring them?"'

Most of the time, however, the company Ashton kept was young, fun and fashionably louche – an English equivalent, in fact, of the modish, sexually equivocal milieu of *Les Biches*. 'Just as people are called fag-hags now, I used to be escort to a host of lesbians.' One was Madge Garland, a friend of both Olivia and Sophie, whom Ashton had met independently at a dance hall in Notting Hill Gate. 'We used to go on Friday nights,' said Madge Garland. 'Fred was a delightful young man who danced extremely well. He told me he wanted to be a professional dancer and I told him I wanted to be a journalist.' At that time, Madge lived and worked with Dorothy (Dody) Todd, the formidably gifted editor of British *Vogue*. 'A fat little woman, full of energy, full of genius, I should say,' Rebecca West has written. 'Good editors are rarer than good writers and she was a great editor. Madge Garland [the fashion editor] was her equal.' By persuading many of the literary figures of the day to write for her, Dody Todd had turned *Vogue* into the most literary journal of its kind. While it never entirely shed its veneer of frivolity (Virginia Woolf wrote of 'whoring' and selling her soul to Todd), the magazine retained a dazzling collection of star writers, including Bloomsbury luminaries as regular contributors, and Aldous Huxley (succeeded by the young Raymond Mortimer) as literary and drama critic.

> Together these women changed *Vogue* from just another fashion paper to being the best of fashion papers and a guide to the modern movement in the arts. They helped Roger Fry in firmly planting the Post-Impressionists in English soil and they brought us all the good news about Picasso and Matisse and Derain and Bonnard and Proust and Jean Cocteau and Raymond Radiguet and Louis Jouvet and Arletty and the gorgeous young Jean Marais. They also gave young writers a firmer foundation than they might have had by commissioning them to write articles on intelligent subjects at fair prices. There never was such a paper.

At home, too, Todd and Garland gathered together a young and gifted group; their parties held at their studio in Chelsea were among the best of the decade. Bloomsbury came out in force and, although Ashton never entered further than the periphery of their world, by virtue of being entertaining, he more than held his own. At a Bottle Party at Royal Hospital Road in December 1926, the twenty-two-year-old photographer, Cecil Beaton, watched transfixed as Ashton carried out a series of impersonations of various ballet dancers and an uncannily accurate imitation of Queen Alexandra, 'conjuring up the entire aura of this Parma violet scented old Royal harridan'. At exactly the same age and stage in their careers, the two young men had been launched simultaneously into this brilliant intellectual world, where the talk 'was not of Mr Baldwin and unemployment but of "Les Six", D. H. Lawrence, Lydia Lopokova's marriage to Maynard Keynes, and Lady Ottoline's contretemps with Siegfried Sassoon'. Admitting that his appetite was uncurbed for closer acquaintance with Bloomsbury's glamorous free-spirits, Beaton envied Ashton's audacity to perform in front of them, although, privately, he felt that Ashton's display had gone too far – 'the sort of thing one is ashamed of and only does in one's bedroom in front of large mirrors when one is rather excited and worked up.'

Being a protégé of Todd and Garland would over-inflate almost anyone's confidence. To Ashton, they were the sovereigns of the modern age, their taste and judgement impressive enough to convince even the lofty Virginia Woolf, who relied on them both to chose her clothes for her. Madge, an intellectual devotee of haute couture, encouraged Ashton's interest in women's fashion and was pleasingly responsive to his comments on her appearance. Slender and lovely, the embodiment of 1920s elegance, she was a living fashion plate, her tailored silk suits and perfectly chosen hats prompting Aldous Huxley to ask, 'Are you dressed like that because you are on *Vogue*, or are you on *Vogue* because you are dressed like that?' A foil to her coy, Marie Laurençin femininity was the alarmingly butch Dody Todd – short, stout, Eton-cropped, double-breasted and bow-tied. Theirs was a ménage even Bloomsbury found 'incredibly louche'; the extreme contrast of their visual impact was something that Ashton would obliquely caricature in his first ballet.

A Tragedy of Fashion, Ashton's own version of lifestyle modernism, was acclaimed by Madge Garland as 'a brilliant evocation of the period, reflecting not only the physical appearance, but the whole tonality of my youth'. It came about through an idea suggested to Marie Rambert by Ashley Dukes when they were on holiday in Normandy. Dukes, who was reading Madame de Sévigné's *Letters*, recounted her anecdote about Vatel, the Prince de Condé's chef, who committed suicide during the King's visit to Chantilly because not enough fish had been delivered for the banquet the next day and he feared his reputation would be ruined. Dukes felt that the tragi-comic tale would make an ideal ballet, but Rambert was less sure, considering that, after Massine's witty supper-table scene in *Les Femmes de bonne humeur*, they should stay clear of food. Rather than a cook, the hero became a couturier, Monsieur Duchic, who, distraught at the failure of his latest creation, stabs himself with his scissors. As Duchic, Rambert cast Ashton, still her only male dancer, and had thought of appointing her pupil Frances James as choreographer, until, one day in the studio, Ashton demonstrated a few movements that so impressed Rambert as evidence of the true choreographer's gift for transposing character into dance, that she insisted he undertake the whole ballet. With typical lack of confidence, Ashton demurred, but not for long. He began talking excitedly of a collaboration on a Ballets Russes scale, suggesting that they commission a score from Poulenc or Auric, designs from Chanel . . . until Rambert brought him down to earth. Not only was there no money for such grandiose schemes; for a first effort, it was far wiser to use existing music and a professional stage designer, not a dressmaker (choosing Chanel for *Le Train bleu* had been Diaghilev's one mistake, she felt). Instead, she proposed Sophie Fedorovitch, who, inspired by Burnacini's soft pleating which she had seen illustrated in Ashley Dukes's copy of the *Monumenta Scenica*, had designed some ravishingly feminine costumes for Frances James's ballet *Les Nénuphars*. Despite her own careless appearance, Sophie had a real feeling for ethereal fabrics on the stage – her costumes *danced*. In her lofty indifference to comfort, there was, as Iris Tree has written, a concealed sybarite. 'I am sure she wore fine white silk under her sober habit; she loved champagne, delicious tastes and fragrances and beautiful clothes on other women.' Ashton was enchanted by the preliminary sketches Sophie showed him; although little more than impressions, they revealed a sophisticated simplicity reminiscent of the restricted palette of Christian Bérard, and were also perfectly adapted for movement. From the very beginning, Sophie understood that ballet is an art of suggestion rather than of full statement, and could create nuances of mood by the humblest means. 'She will successfully suggest a forest with one conifer, all Venice with a mooring stick,' her friend, Simon Fleet, has written. She and Ashton began to work together in the evenings in her little studio on the Embankment, embarking on the long, close creative partnership that would prove, along with that of Fonteyn, the most important of his career.

Finding suitable music was more of a problem. After making many suggestions, none of which Ashton liked, Rambert came up with a set of piano pieces by the English composer Eugene Goossens, Diaghilev's favourite conductor at the time, who had made his name by conducting the London première of *Le Sacre du printemps*. Influenced by the French

Impressionists, with playful dissonant reminders of Stravinsky, Goossens' compositions were tuneful enough to inspire Noël Coward's jaunty line, 'My heart just loosens when I'm listening to Mr Goossens'. Yet Ashton felt that Rambert's choice of *Kaleidoscope*, despite being aptly modern and witty, was not suitably danceable for a ballet score. Hoping to change his mind, Rambert, who was to appear in the ballet as Monsieur Duchic's assistant, went away and worked out a sequence of her own to the music. 'Fred became interested in my tentative sketch and began to alter the movements so successfully that he turned it into an excellent dance. From then on he went straight ahead.'

Fortuitously, Marie Rambert then met the impresario Nigel Playfair, who was looking for a new piece to add to his revue, *Riverside Nights*. 'When he heard that we were doing a ballet to a synopsis by Ashley he became very interested, as Ashley's name was at that time on everybody's lips.' Nigel Playfair had an established reputation for presenting neglected classics and experimental productions at the Lyric Theatre, Hammersmith, which otherwise would have had little chance of a West End staging. Considered by some playgoers to be one of the most enjoyably versatile revues ever produced, *Riverside Nights* was in itself a pot-pourri of old and new. Among the highlights were Elsa Lanchester, wearing a short ballet dress with bare legs, high heels and a top hat, who caused a sensation by singing innuendo-filled, forgotten Victorian songs in pastiche music-hall style; the innovative creative dancer Penelope Spencer performing a startlingly original solo enacting Lord Berners' 'Funeral March for the death of a rich aunt'; and A. P. Herbert's burlesque of Chekhov, which included a send-up of Mrs Patrick Campbell. Such wit and sophistication was a challenge to follow, but nevertheless, *A Tragedy of Fashion* (given the subtitle *The Scarlet Scissors* by A. P. Herbert), the last item on the programme, certainly made its mark.

Monsieur Duchic and Orchidée, his Maîtresse de Maison, open the ballet. Ashton was the epitome of a 1920s dandy, with a huffy, sashaying walk, his theatrical mannerisms clearly derived from Massine; Marie Rambert, dressed 'in a sort of lesbian-like fashion', smoking a cigar and striding around giving orders, a veiled send-up of Dody Todd. A pair of wealthy customers arrive in the salon, the Viscount and Viscountess Viscosa (Viscosa was a jokey alias for the wealthy balletomane, Samuel Courtauld, leading producer of viscose yarn*). The Viscount and his wife are shown two of Duchic's former creations by his house models, Désir du Cygne (Elizabeth Vincent), wearing a frothy white confection, and

---

*A product much in the news that spring, with London's first Artificial Silk Exhibition and an extensive supplement on the subject published in *The Times*.

Rose d'Ispahan* (Frances James), delectable in pearl-buttoned pink satin, the enormous bow at the back of her dress lingeringly displayed as she entered with her back to the audience and bourréed along the back-cloth. Rose d'Ispahan was inspired by the 'pearl-hung and silken' Madge Garland, who as Rebecca West said, could have been a model – 'That was me,' Garland confirmed. 'Fred more or less based her on me' – but her dance was also Ashton's homage to Nijinska, recreating the chic hauteur, exaggerated épaulement and stylized, angular strut of *Les Biches*' girl in blue.

Although, in choreographic terms, this solo was the ballet's pièce de résistance,† Duchic's latest creation, a mannish gold and brown evening suit, was given to his Maîtresse de Maison to wear. With her own simple stylish clothes and shingled hair, Rambert was an elegant woman – 'six inches taller and she would have epitomized those chic, flat-chested, Eton-cropped women with a pearl at the lobe of each ear who filled the pages of *Vogue*' – but she was coquettish by nature, with none of her character's overt masculinity. It was far more likely to have been the sexual deviancy signalled by Orchidée's appearance, than the cartwheels, splits and belly turns which the original scenario required her to perform, that scandalized the customers into withdrawing from the salon.‡ Reinforcing the point was an in-joke which only the balletomanes in the audience can have picked up: Orchidée was the name of a dancer in Loie Fuller's troupe where lesbianism was rife.

After Duchic has stabbed himself in shame, the two mannequins return to dance a lament over his body, their 'most realistic convulsions' to a 5/4 dirge, causing much mirth among the audience. The absurdity of the conclusion was Ashton's nod to his source, a tale coloured with macabre, farcical humour and irony (in Madame de Sévigné's account, it took three attempts by Vatel to stab himself, and, as he lay dead, load upon load of fresh fish began arriving at Chantilly from contractors round the country). *A Tragedy of Fashion* made no claim to be more than a light concoction, but, in its small way, it was a considerable success, with none of the gaucheness or sentimentality common to many first artistic attempts. It was also remarkably attuned to the times, its esoteric jokes and contemporary references anticipating the witty collaborations

---

*A poem by Leconte de Lisle, set to music by Gabriel Fauré.
†It was later revived as a divertissement entitled *Mannequin Dance*, and performed by the precociously alluring Diana Gould, whose impersonation of the snooty expressions of shop dummies made it all the more effective.
‡According to Rambert, Nigel Playfair had insisted that she turn cartwheels in the ballet – a trick for which she was famous.

that Ashton and Lord Berners would produce ten years later. 'That's not ballet,' the dancer Maude Lloyd, newly arrived from South Africa, remembers thinking when she was taken to see it. And although Ashton's neoclassicism was, as he admitted, 'enormously derivative', it nevertheless showed a definite spark of originality. 'You can't expect it to be perfect straight away, but . . . if there's a personal and individual style which comes across, a person's signature, even if it's quite faint – then that's all right.' Among his admirers in the audience were two people destined to play major roles in his life: Ninette de Valois, who rushed backstage afterwards to congratulate him, and the young David Webster, who wrote Ashton his first fan letter and took him out to lunch. De Valois, who would one day become director of the Royal Ballet, had just founded her own school in London, the Academy of Choreographic Art, while David Webster, then a Liverpool businessman, eventually became general administrator of the Royal Opera House, the cradle of English ballet after the war.

A Tragedy of Fashion had been sold on Ashley Dukes's name, but Ashton's choreography was nevertheless singled out for its wit, elegance and imagination. He appeared in the next issue of Vogue looking like a Lepape silhouette in Duchic's soigné dinner-jacket, face in profile, arms elegantly folded, one leg relaxing across the other, his dancing described as 'a perfect expression of the spirit of that whimsical ballet'. Ashton thought he was made, especially after hearing that Eugene Goossens had brought Diaghilev to see it, not once but twice. 'I thought the offers would come pouring in. But nothing happened.' Although Diaghilev had let it be known that he had come primarily to see the singular satirical Elsa Lanchester, he was polite to Ashton all the same and, as a result of A Tragedy of Fashion, asked him to audition for his company. This was the opportunity Ashton had been waiting for, but the strain of anticipation proved too much.

> I felt so inadequate that I couldn't do it. I remember walking round and round the Lyceum Theatre and I couldn't go in because I was in a most terrible state. Knowing the standard of his company I felt I would have been hopeless, though afterwards I regretted not going very much. My mother asked me what he'd said and I made something up, something to tell her because I was ashamed of myself.

It was, Ashton said, the only genuinely weak moment in his life. Things deteriorated further. Not only was he lacking offers, but, after about six weeks, Playfair dropped the ballet from the revue as it was proving too costly to retain four dancers for such a short piece. Ashton's salary, which had been £15 per week, was now reduced to nothing. 'We were living in one room and my mother kept saying, "Oh well, you've tried it and you're not getting anywhere so now you must go back to the City and get a job."'

A similar fate had befallen Edith who, after leaving school, had been forced to abandon the idea of a career as a concert pianist so that she could contribute to the family income. It had been a considerable sacrifice. Inheriting her mother's long slender fingers, Edith had shown such talent at Micklefield that Myra Hess, who gave a concert there, had encouraged her to pursue her studies. Now, however, she played only socially, and worked a nine-to-five day as a secretary in the typing pool at the Foreign Office. Although he was the more egotistical and driven of the two, Ashton, nevertheless, felt under enormous pressure to follow suit. It was Sophie who came to his rescue, talking his mother into letting him continue to dance by persuading a friend to give Georgie a regular sum of money. Ashton's benefactor was one Captain Mordaunt Goodliffe, an exceedingly handsome former officer in the Hussars, known to his friends as 'Beau'. When she was driving a taxi in Paris, Sophie had taken him home from his club on several occasions and one night spotted him in the street, obviously very drunk. She stopped to pick him up, took him back and put him to bed. 'Nothing about money or anything, and he was so amazed and touched by this that he was determined to find her.' By coincidence, Goodliffe, who was interested in contemporary art, saw Sophie in a Montparnasse gallery that was exhibiting her paintings and after some initial resistance on her part, their lifelong romance began.

The Captain, as she called him, was a great womanizer, accustomed to being adored and pandered to, and yet he was completely captivated by this strange, waifish creature, who was always putting him in his place in her low rumbling voice. 'He had a beautiful French mistress whom I met,' said Ashton. 'She told me, "It's terrible because I have nothing with which I can fight her: she doesn't dress, or do anything like that. For the first time in my life I have no weapons."' To her friends, the match between Sophie and her upstanding guardee – 'like a joke captain', with his rolled umbrella and obsession with his regiment – was extraordinarily incongruous. 'It was a very strange love-life, I don't know what it consisted of,' said Ashton, who never discussed Goodliffe with Sophie. 'If anyone asked her about her private life, she used to say, "Don't be personal."' The Captain set Sophie up in a charming little house in Bury Walk which her friends called 'the Gothic Box'. Generous and good-humoured, he had no objection to supporting her struggling friend and colleague, Ashton. Sophie began spending a great deal of time at Goodliffe's retreat on the northernmost coast of Norfolk – a haunting, bleak landscape which Ashton also grew to love, its infinite vistas of unchanging space helping to inspire their greatest collaboration, *Symphonic Variations*. Yet, despite her new role of mistress, Sophie always retained her freedom, living independently in London, where rarely, if ever, was the Captain part of her social life.

She and Ashton had infiltrated a new set, a group of art-school students, one of whom, William (Billy) Chappell, remained a close friend for over sixty years. Marie Rambert, who had been introduced to Chappell through a mutual acquaintance, had brought him backstage, hoping to entice him into the profession. She was eager to procure another male dancer, and Chappell, although he had 'never lifted a foot, except to do the Charleston', had a natural dancer's physique and the theatre in his blood (his mother was an actress, his fifteen-year-old sister a hard-working West End chorine). Rambert had already auditioned him and persuaded him to take early-morning barres with her at the studio before the first pupils arrived, but Chappell rather resented this bustling little person firing instructions at him and forcing his limbs into ballet positions he had never heard of. 'It was absolutely dotty, the whole thing. I rushed away and didn't go near her, but she wouldn't give up. She wouldn't leave me alone, and in the end she caught me.' Seeing Ashton in his dressing room in a Harlequin costume and full stage make-up finally won Chappell over. He studied with grave interest the dancer's matte and glowing skin, his exaggerated insect eyes and curving, polished garnet lips. 'This, all this, was much more what I expected of the ballet. Perhaps I would, after all, go back to classes.'

Ashton was delighted to have some male support. 'He was so overpowered by all Mim's well-brought-up, glorious girls that he'd have put up with almost anybody.' Finding Ashton the height of sophistication – 'he knew everybody and was in with a lot of very doubtful bohemian folk' – Chappell was rather nervous of him at first, and his wariness was increased by the fact that Ashton had 'lurked about' outside the studio, cornered him when he came out, and lectured him about the terrible things that would happen to him if he became a dancer. 'Men, *old* men, will be after you and think you're to be had,' Ashton said ominously – a warning motivated less out of avuncular concern than as a way of investigating Chappell's sexual inclinations. With his fine-toned muscles, beautifully sculpted face and large turquoise eyes, he was an extremely attractive seventeen-year-old, although, in those days, he was as yet unaware of his allure. His bemused grin and the lack of any encouraging signals took effect: Ashton, he said, 'gave up after a bit and became perfectly ordinary'.

As the only two youths among Rambert's students, it was natural that they should gravitate towards each other, and it was not long before their friends became friends too. A tight little group was formed: Ashton, Sophie, Olivia, Chappell and his two colleagues from art school, Barbara Ker-Seymer and Edward Burra. The youngest students at the Chelsea Polytechnic, Chappell and Burra, thirteen and sixteen respectively, had automatically sought each other out and later struck up an acquaintance with Barbara when they discovered that she too was a movie fan. 'That was the great bond.' They became inseparable. 'We spoke the same language, we liked the same artists, we liked the same books. We were cinema-mad and great ballet fans. We would queue for five hours for Ballets Russes tickets in the gallery. We were what you might call birds of a feather and yet we all came from different nests.'

Barbara Ker-Seymer came from what Chappell described as 'grand stock': her paternal grandmother, Gertrude Ker-Seymer, wrote racing novels and was a friend of Edward VII; her other grandmother, Carolyn Creyke, the subject of a biography by Macdonald Hastings, was painted by Gustave Doré and lived in a Park Lane house renowned for its magnificent frontage decorated with caryatids. But Barbara's father, an impulsive, romantic figure, had squandered the family income on gambling debts, and, at that time, she was living with her mother in West Kensington. Chappell, who, like Ashton, lived in furnished rooms in Earls Court with his mother and sister, had always been poor. His father had walked out on his mother when he was very small, leaving her to bring up the children single-handedly. Burra, by contrast, was extremely well-off; the first time Chappell visited him at Springfield, the family home in Rye, he felt like one of the Treasure Seekers in the Nesbit books: 'I suddenly found myself in a house full of servants with wonderful gardens. It was bliss, absolute bliss, and really coloured the rest of my childhood.'

Among the three, it was always tacitly accepted that Burra was the star turn. Even then, his gifts were obvious. He drew with a strength and purity of line more than exceptional, and his friends were always aware that he was different. 'We had absolutely no doubt about it,' said Chappell. 'And you could tell from the way the masters reacted to his work that he was somebody special.' 'There were a lot of serious students at the Poly doing rather dreary paintings,' said Barbara. 'Billy and I were at the stage of doing crinolined medieval ladies and knights jousting and I remember Edward doing a picture of two hideous old crones hitting each other with carpet beaters.' The trio remained just as close after they had left art school, chronicling each other's every move in an extraordinary correspondence spanning over fifty years.*

When Chappell introduced his two chums to Ashton, they took to each other with equal enthusiasm. 'We instinctively knew that we had absolutely everything in common – the same taste and behaviour and everything else'. Ashton even began to adopt a 'sort of drawly' approximation of their group voice, which in Burra's delivery was exaggerated into the world-weary tones of a middle-aged Edwardian tart. They used to meet at the Samovar in St Martin's Lane, or the Tea Kettle in Rupert Street, the favourite haunt of chorus boys and girls, including Honor, Chappell's sister, 'talking nonsense by the hour'. 'What we liked to do was sit in tearooms and gossip about our friends and run them down,' said Barbara. To survive in their circle you had to be quick, cynical and self-mocking. However serious you felt about your work, you could never admit it, the point being never to show your feelings and to make a joke of everything. 'I don't know why we were so frivolous,' said Barbara. 'People were like that then. It was the fashion. But Fred was much more serious and dedicated.' Less adept at disguising his aspirations, Ashton soon became a prime target for Burra's notorious nicknames – a favourite weapon for the deflation of any over-grandiose ideas – and was known alternatively as La Princesse Vinaigrette and Madame Megalomania (Meggy for short). 'Edward could be very malicious in a funny way,' said Barbara. 'He loved Fred and admired him enormously. It was just his way.'

Although Barbara was equally known for her destructive wit, she and Ashton established a tender rapport when they first met.

> For some reason we used to go on Saturday mornings on the tube to Shepherd's Bush where there was an open-air swimming bath with grey water and lots of dead leaves. We'd have a swim and splash each other for a bit and then get the tube back. Fred would bring me all the way to my house in West Kensington and then go all the way back to his own place in Earls Court. He had the most beautiful manners.

When she said goodbye to Ashton, they would have such long kissing sessions on the doorstep that Mrs Ker-Seymer used to call out anxiously, 'Are you coming up now, dear?' But, even though Barbara was appealing in a boyish, fashionably flat-chested way, Ashton was only half-heartedly

---

*Burra's lively, gossipy letters – all the more zany for their satirical illustrations, lack of punctuation and phonetic spelling – were collected by Chappell in *Well, dearie!*, published in 1985.

playing the sort of youthful courting games that he felt was expected of him. After Barbara had left home to share a flat with an art-school friend, he would come up to her room, but to do no more than listen to her collection of records, winding up the gramophone over and over again to play his favourite tune, 'Laugh and sing, make love the thing'. What attracted Barbara to Ashton was the brilliance of his company. A generation of young men had been lost in the First World War – there were so few, in fact, that hostesses, desperate to find partners for their daughters' dances, often sent invitations to complete strangers at smart clubs – and all the suitable bachelors Barbara knew were a conservative, cloddish lot.

> We called normal men 'He-men'. They were a special brand that you don't see nowadays, unless you watch old black and white films. They had moustaches and were interested in cricket and thought it cissy to like art. It worried me terribly because I didn't think I'd ever be able to get married. I couldn't stand any one of them.

By the mid-1920s, however, a new camaraderie of youth had begun to take place, creating an independence, tolerance and equality between the sexes. 'Now-a-days so many boys are *girlish* without being effeminate,' Edith Olivier wrote to a friend. 'It's the sort of boy which has grown up since the war.' Ashton was in this category, popular with young women such as Barbara and Olivia because they felt they could talk to him in the unguarded way that they could to each other. 'With the young men we knew, our mothers would say, "Don't you think so & so is being rather familiar?" if he took your arm. But of course we all took each other's arms and kissed each other. When you're a dancer, there's no difference between the sexes. And the same with artists, we were the same.'

Barbara was about to take homosexuality one stage further. Through Ashton, she had got to know Olivia Wyndham, who seduced her the first time they met. 'They seem *very* friendly,' a friend remarked to Burra. 'Oh yes, ses I – bosoms, my dear.' Barbara had moved into Olivia's maisonette above the post office at 19 King's Road, but there was nothing domestic about their ménage. Wantonly promiscuous, Olivia was unstoppable. 'She had no taste at all. Sometimes a great butch lady would arrive at the door and Olivia would send me up to cower in the dark while she showed our empty bedroom to the irate visitor.' At King's Road parties, when Olivia was not disappearing with one person after another, male or female, she was playing pander, 'dragging people upstairs and putting them on top of each other'. This was how Ashton was set up with a fetching young hustler known as Pip. 'Fred had his way with him and they went on so long that he said he almost fainted.' Their first encounter developed into what Ashton's friends called 'a wild affair', but not one of them approved of the match. The boy, although good-looking with blondish-red hair, appeared to have no other merits at all: he 'went with everybody'; he was 'a cocktease'; 'a glamorous male tart'; and, years later, Ashton ruefully admitted that Pip had been 'attractive but unfaithful, like all the rest'. But he instinctively favoured the role of yearning chaser over adored chase-me. Following naturally from his schoolboy infatuations, Ashton's sexual rite of passage had been an easy transition, with none of the soul-searching or guilt afflicting many other young men attracted to others of their own gender. Homosexuality may have been illegal in Britain, but in Ashton's world it was virtually the rule, a symptom of the 'excessively perverse', sophisticated new code of social manners. 'How tempting and dangerous, beautiful and wicked, gloriously anarchic and strange, Life appeared,' remarked Billy Chappell. Except for Edward Burra, 'who wasn't anything' (when asked if he had ever had an erection, he admitted only to a very *slight* one while watching a Mae West film), almost everyone in Ashton's group was either androgynous or bisexual. 'If you weren't,' said Chappell, 'you made an attempt to be.'

The year immediately preceding the Wall Street crash, 1928, was a period when there seemed to be a party every night, the wilder and sillier the better. Parties had become a mania, a stunt, with young hosts and hostesses competing to find the next amusing theme, their guests going to extraordinary lengths to enter into the spirit. At Norman Hartnell's Circus Party, Lady Dean Paul appeared as a Lyon's Nippy in fuzzy black wig and enormous bow, chocolate tray and steel pince-nez; Brenda as a champion lady wrestler in tights and stuffing; and Olivia as a snake charmer, with real serpents twisted round her arms and neck. Too lazy to make much of an effort, Ashton tended to play things down. At an End-of-the-World Party, for which funereal black-bordered invitations instructed guests to 'dress as you would wish to meet your Maker', he wore a black straw boater and veil.

> Fred never bothered about a costume. He always wore a boater, and used to pin ribbons all over his suit and drape himself with bits and pieces and be perfectly respectably dressed underneath it all. His favourite flowers were gardenias and he'd fill his pockets with them so that they overflowed and floated about on his suit. He'd

go in an ordinary suit and then sort of trim it up. He had a frightfully ingenious eye for that kind of thing.

As the decade drew to a close, parties, by this time lacking in originality and amusement, grew more frequent and more debauched; entrance was assured, even if you did not know the host and hostess, by
bringing a bottle. 'Of course, as a result of the mix of different drinks,
everyone got wildly drunk,' said Chappell, who received the following
account from Burra.

Well old sport Miss Wyndham gave a cocktail party last Friday
and everybody was there the Kings Road & Sloane sq were lined
with plainclothes detectives to guard Lady Dean Pauls priceless diamond ankle watch & the princess Haines pearls were the sinecure
of all eyes till the eyes saw double which was very soon. from what
I hear in my radio grammes they all went down like ninepins and
it was suspected that aphrodisiac had been added to the cocktails . . .

Not surprisingly, these Dionysiac revels frequently turned violent.
'There was a bit of a brawl at last Tuesday's party,' Burra went on. 'Miss
Olivia Wyndham . . . was layed out everyone rushed & held the combat-
tants back and the language ma chere fidone nothing has been heard like
it since the general strike.' 'Only one fight,' Evelyn Waugh remarked
about another of Olivia's parties, held on a Thames steamer. 'It was not
enough of an orgy. Masses of little lesbian tarts and joyboys.' Although a
regular joyboy at them all, Ashton was incongruously restrained. 'I don't
think Fred ever got drunk or disorderly,' said Barbara. 'I don't remember
him being outrageous in any way. He never really let go.' Ashton's
mother was less sure, and it was around this time that she told him about
George's suicide. 'When she thought I was behaving like a mad bright
young thing, she told me in order to make me more serious.' 'She obviously thought he was in a queer set which indeed he was,' said Neil
(Bunny) Roger, an Oxford graduate renowned on the party circuit for his
flawless looks and lily complexion. 'But I don't think that Fred was really
wild. I never saw him lying in a corner being had by a negro or
Charlestoning on the table like Clara Bow. He would be more likely to be
sitting on the sidelines with Billy making witty strictures about people.'
According to Roger, Ashton's most outré behaviour at this time was a
masturbatory encounter with a melon, an experience said to be of un-
paralleled sensuality. But having successfully completed the experiment,
Ashton was left with having to dispose of the evidence, a task inflated

into a tale of epic elaboration by his circle. One recounted how he stole out into the night to Chelsea Bridge and dropped it into the river; another that he threw it out the window, unaware that it had landed on a ledge and had been recovered the next day by his mother. Delighted by her find, which appeared to have dropped out of the sky like a gift from the gods, Georgie then produced the delicacy as a surprise treat for their supper.

Misconstruing the basis of Ashton's friendship with Chappell, Georgie was anxious about their frequent and lengthy meetings. 'She couldn't understand how I could stay up till two o'clock talking to Billy. You know how, when you're young, you have so much to say. "Well, what could you *possibly* talk about till then?" she'd ask.' Ashton would never lose his reluctance to stop talking and go to bed – the reason he found it 'agony' to get up in the morning. Every day, without fail, Sophie used to telephone him to wake him up, often with a follow-up call to be sure. In addition to this, the dancer Maude Lloyd, who lodged in nearby Redcliffe Gardens with Billy and his mother, would call in for him on her way to Notting Hill. 'Mrs Ashton used to say, "He's still in bed," and I'd say, "Fred, I can't wait any longer," and he would shout out, "*Please,* wait for me, wait for me!" He really was very conscientious about his work. He wouldn't miss a class and worked very hard at his technique.'

Since *A Tragedy of Fashion* Ashton, while continuing to study at Rambert's studio, had been performing when and where he could, appearing in places such as Littlehampton and Bournemouth with Flora Fairbairns's Mayfair Dancers, and touring the provinces with a travelling opera troupe who mounted occasional one-act ballets. In June 1927, when Marie Rambert was asked to produce dances for the Purcell Opera Company's revival of *The Fairy Queen*, she entrusted Ashton with the key dances, an undertaking that proved he had a genuine feeling for period, and an innate understanding of the gravity and gaiety of Purcell's music. The choreography was delightfully inventive. In the Swans' dance, a trio of girls was arranged with softly linked arms in painterly, harmonious lines, while the Echo duet provided a visual equivalent of the musical conceit by having Diana Gould, then the smaller of the two dancers, mimic the movements Maude Lloyd was making further downstage.* A month later, Rambert presented three short Ashton pieces at a teachers' matinée performance: a pas de deux to the music of Fritz Kreisler (the Austrian-born violinist and composer); an *Argentine Dance*, in which he appeared with the soloist Eleanora Marra; and a *Suite de danses* to music from Mozart's *Les Petits riens*, which he performed with Rambert

---

*This was an idea Ashton went on to develop to even greater effect using three dancers in Constant Lambert's 1946 production of the opera.

herself. Ashton's inspiration for the Mozart piece had been Yvonne Printemps's acclaimed performance as the young Mozart at the Gaiety Theatre the previous year. He had been captivated by the star, spending all his money on tickets to see her again and again. She was an appealing spaniel-eyed performer, whose acting John Gielgud has compared to that of Gertrude Lawrence, both of whom shared 'something of the same inimitable brand of impish sentimental comedy'. Ashton's appearance in *Les Petits riens* in a powdered wig, lace jabot, black knee-breeches and buckled shoes, was an exact impersonation of Printemps's Mozart, while his choreography paid tribute to her youthful interpretation by bringing out the grace, wit and gaiety of the score.

In the early summer of 1928, Ashton and Chappell were both employed as dancers with the Royal Opera at Covent Garden, the regular income the season guaranteed undercut somewhat by the meagreness of its amount. Ashton was delegated by the dancers to negotiate a more realistic fee on their behalf, and he held out for £5 per week, only to discover, when their pay packets arrived, that the management had thought he had meant £5 per performance. 'We absolutely reeled.' But not even this unexpected bonus was enough to make the dancers commit themselves to their roles. Taking advantage of the unvigilant, haphazard efforts of Belgian choreographer François Ambroisiny, they either improvised or sent the whole thing up – for example, painting their faces into demonic distortions in *Armide*, where they emerged from beneath the soprano's feet as apparitions from the Underworld. 'I remember taking my stick of black and making my face like a corkscrew, then another time a long stream of tears – nobody objected at all.' The overpowering smell of perspiration coming from the singers, who for some reason wore their costumes over their street-clothes, was another running joke. In the Hall of Songs scene in *Tannhäuser*, where the dancers appeared in tiers behind the chorus, one gave the word, 'Now move!' at a given moment and they all moved up one rung. 'Nobody noticed, and then we'd say, "Now!" and go up to the next one, until we ended up on the top tier with a great gap between us and the singers.'

Aware how anxious Ashton was to continue his creative work, Rambert had arranged for him to produce a short interlude for Ashley Dukes's adaptation of Lion Feuchtwanger's novel, *Jew Süss*. As it turned out, the play was postponed until the following year, but the ballet, *Leda and the Swan*, took place all the same and was given its first performance in June 1928 at a reception to celebrate the opening of Rambert's new premises in Ladbroke Road. The piece, which used the music of the Blessed Spirits from Gluck's *Orfeo*, featured Diana Gould as Leda and Ashton as the god-swan. Far from evoking the aggressive perpetrator of

Yeats's sonnet, a symbol of power and phallic strength, Ashton, resplendent in a white-feather toque and carried in by two male Naiads (Billy Chappell and Harold Turner, Rambert's new recruit), seemed more of an Odette-like vision of femininity and grace. He was playing Pavlova, his fantasy role, and, with his exquisitely arched feet, slender legs and lyrical movements, he more than brought it off. 'Fred would have been a beautiful female dancer,' said Diana Gould, who described how, between rehearsals, they would often reverse roles to amuse themselves. Ashton would borrow her pointe shoes, playing the ballerina, and Gould partnered him – 'I always loved codding.' In Ashton's version of *Leda and the Swan*, the myth was transposed into a pretty pastoral, its violence subdued into tenderness and charm. The shudder of coition was delicately stylized by the fluttering hands of the nymphs who screened the couple, the soft lines of their grouping inspired by Botticelli who also influenced Billy Chappell's designs. Like several of Ashton's early ballets, *Leda* was, in a sense, an animated painting, and, while it still showed signs of Massine's influence (Arnold Haskell compared it to *Zephyr and Flora*), the piece had moments of great original beauty, especially the romantic pas de deux, a crowning point of almost every subsequent Ashton work. It was, as Haskell said, truly classical in feeling – 'a Greek ballet without any of the inanities of pseudo-classicism' – and Rambert was delighted with it. 'It became Mim's showpiece,' said Billy Chappell. 'We did it everywhere. There was no grand charity matinée at which we weren't doing *Leda*.'

One day, when Rambert was half-way through teaching class, she suddenly noticed Ashton go 'as white as a sheep', as her small daughter later put it. Entering the studio at that moment was Diaghilev – imposing, aristocratic, dressed in black – accompanied by his secretary, Boris Kochno. Because the impresario had shown an interest in Diana Gould, Rambert had invited him to come and see her dance. After watching the rest of class, Diaghilev then asked to see something new; hoping to persuade him of Ashton's merits as well, Rambert told the two dancers to perform the duet from *Leda and the Swan*. Once again, Diaghilev appeared to admire Ashton's ballet, but later dismissed Ashton, the dancer, to Rambert as 'plain' – a rejection that turned out to be a blessing in disguise. Not only was Diaghilev dead by the following year, but, as it happened, Ashton had already made plans of his own. With £5 borrowed from Sophie, he had recently gone to Paris and been accepted by Nijinska for a troupe she was assembling with the backing of Ida Rubinstein, the wealthy dilettante. When Diaghilev asked Ashton what he was up to – 'Not because he wanted to engage me or anything' – his response to hearing about the rival company was a sardonic smile: 'Hmmm,' was all he said. With designs commissioned from Benois and new scores from Ravel, Poulenc and Stravinsky, the Rubinstein enterprise must have seemed like a provocative challenge to Diaghilev. For Ashton, however, it was a godsend, proving to be the most formative period of his career. 'It *created* him so to speak,' said Billy Chappell. 'Everything he went on to do grew out of that time.'

CHAPTER FOUR

MENTORS AND MUSES
1928–1931

4 Rue de Ruisseau, Paris 18e

My very dear Mim,

I hope you won't consider that you have had to wait a long time for this letter but if so it is only that I might have the more to say to you. Life is very strange here or so it still seems to me & I never realised before how really far Paris is removed from London, as a town it is more beautiful but for everything else give me London. From a work point of view Paris is undoubtedly better no distractions & no friends, but rather lonely at times & though in my heart of hearts I am not liking life here I feel as though I had known no other, so concentrated is it on one purpose & there seems no other existence outside the 'village' life of the Salle Jeffroy.* The Company is very large & the competition very keen indeed, but I am by no means the worst dancer & I think that though Nijinska has no especial reason for liking me from the point of view of work or life she is not entirely negative to me & that is already something in so big a company. Nijinska is a wonderful woman more wonderful than I had ever imagined, her efficiency is overwhelming & her knowledge & vitality something quite superhuman & inspiring. She gives a brilliant class, very difficult & never dull & in doing it one realises over & over again that the best system of dance training is obviously Checcetti [*sic*] (I can't spell his name, disgrace!) her arms are I should say entirely based on his & her bar [*sic*] is the same except that she introduces various sorts of developes before the petit battement which one afterwards does in the centre & she very seldom makes us do rond de jambes en l'air. Nearly all her steps in the centre are jumping, she

*The church hall in the Ave Jeffroy where the company rehearsed.

demonstrates the whole time & smokes incessantly her own jump is wonderful & gives one some idea of what Nijinski's jump was like in quality. She is a beautiful dancer & a dancer above all her ugliness. We have two groups for classes & they take place alternate weeks at 9 am & 10 am after them we rehearse till lunch & then back at 3 or 4 till dinner & then back at 9 or 10 till 11.30 or 12 pm. Generally one doesn't rehearse more than twice a day sometimes 3 as she takes people in groups till the ballet is finished & then calls full rehearsal. Rubinstein never appears, she has been once to look on only & has now gone away for a holiday. But *I* have been going 3 times a day as I have been understudying. She [Nijinska] has finished one ballet [*La Princess Cygne*] & as would be my luck it is Russian rather Childrens Tales-fire-bird Noces like people pile themselves on each other but we do real vigourous dancing 6 men. The music is by Rimsky-Korserkoff [*sic*]. The second she has just begun [*La Bien-Aimée*] is rather Carnival-like [*sic – Le Carnaval*] & romantic & is by Shubert [*sic* and Liszt]. I haven't done anything in that yet but understudy in the corner. Massine arrives on the 1st September I hope he will be kind to me. For I am being very diffident & feel really of no count as a dancer as yet & I fully realise what a wonderful experience it is. I think better than Diaghileff because of the lessons. I also realise how little strength I have, what a meagre physique I have. I get thinner instead of fatter or more muscular & how hard & long one must work to be anything as a dancer & how the years do tell in it. I also again realise how much worse I should be without your excellent teaching & grounding as I see I have more finish than most people & I hope God will give me muscles in time. I am more ambitious than ever & I long & pray that I will succeed, but life is hard & there is so much against one one thinks. I must stop now I am tired, if there is anything you would like to know please ask me as I may have not told you something you would like to know. Well dear Mim, I think of you a lot & wish you were here many things would amuse you as they do me, & I am constantly more than grateful to you for making it possible for me to enter this Company. My love to you from your Fred.

Ashton's letter to Marie Rambert was written shortly after he had started rehearsals with the Ida Rubinstein Company on 1 August 1928. At first, he lived in the heart of the apache quarter in Montmartre in a flat belonging to the composer Lennox Berkeley, who, at that time, was studying in Paris with Nadia Boulanger. With Berkeley away most of the month at his parents' house in the South of France, Ashton had the place to himself, but he was miserable there; it was gloomy, damp and run down, and, after being used to living with his mother, he would have preferred some company. At times, he felt so homesick that he would go and chat to the concierge, 'an extraordinary old creature with a riddled face' (Edward Burra's description), with whom he sat up one night during an alarmingly violent summer storm. Burra and Billy Chappell had passed through Paris to see Ashton on their way back from a holiday in Toulon. But when they went to find him at the Rue de Ruisseau, they discovered that he had moved to the Hotel St George in the Rue Bonaparte where he had taken an attic room a steep climb up an unlit staircase to the sixth floor. Ashton shared a lavatory and bathed in the bidet (he had burst into tears when Sophie had told him that he would never be able to afford a proper bath every day on a salary of 1,000 francs per month). He was naturally thrilled to see his friends. Although he was popular with other members of the company, who found him polite, serious and hardworking, he complained to Burra and Chappell that he had no one to talk to – 'They're all Poles and Lithuanians and Russians and Czechs.' With his gift for languages, Ashton had already picked up enough Russian to communicate with a couple of the dancers he liked, and his French was fluent; nevertheless, he was so anxious to have an English companion that he spent most of the week bullying Chappell, still 'lazy and dreamy' from Toulon, to audition for Nijinska.

> He nagged and nagged at me until finally I agreed. I thought she'd never take me because I was hopeless – I was so untaught at that period and really wasn't any good. But I went along and made a terrible exhibition of myself and the next thing I knew I was in. It didn't really matter that I was no good as she was determined to have me for Fred's sake. She liked him so much that she was prepared to overlook my faults just to please him.

In his letter to Rambert, Ashton plays down Nijinska's regard for him, but in fact she had already spotted his potential and was, Chappell maintains, 'devoted to him from the word go'. 'She saw that he had the temptation to become someone in his life,' said the dancer Roman Jasinsky. 'He was a good worker. A smart boy I would say. He was interested in everything and watched Nijinska very carefully.' Realizing how little he still knew about his art, Ashton had apprenticed himself to Nijinska 'just like students did with Michelangelo and Raphael'. He observed her continually: how she could revitalize the classical line simply by bending an elbow or flexing a wrist; how she physically manipulated a dancer's body into positions that were more supple and extreme than any he had seen before; how she made the narrative clear, and manipulated a crowd of dancers, not realistically, but as a human assemblage, an impersonal architectural configuration in space. 'The thing that a choreographer really needs is an eye,' Ashton once said. 'He has to do his training through his eye. It's not a thing you can teach, any more than you can teach people the rudiments of music and turn them into composers. I think that if someone has the desire to express himself in this way he should work under other choreographers. That's the only way I can see it happening.' Nijinska had been pleased by Ashton's intense scrutiny. According to her daughter, Irina, who often sat with him on the floor of the studio, waiting for her mother to take her home, he was the only dancer whom she allowed into a rehearsal in which he was not involved. 'My mother found him very talented. She admired him very much.' 'Nijinska loved Fred,' said Billy Chappell, 'and she used to talk to him a great deal herself. She was the biggest influence on his career, setting him off into all sorts of things that were not pure classicism but were eccentric and beautiful and unusual. He watched her all the time and she was aware that he was watching her and she liked it.'

Ashton could not have had a more formidably accomplished mentor. 'If I had a daughter,' Diaghilev once remarked of Nijinska, 'I would like one with such gifts.' She had been trained as a dancer, at the Imperial School in St Petersburg, by the three great teachers – Cecchetti, Legat and Fokine – and coached during the summer holidays by her astoundingly gifted brother, Nijinsky, whose revolutionary first ballet, *L'Après-midi d'un faune*, had been moulded upon her during their evenings spent at home. Between 1911 and 1913, while Nijinsky's fame continued to soar, she emerged as a prized soloist in the Ballets Russes while, at the same time, assisting her brother in the creation of *Jeux* and *Le Sacre du printemps*, groundbreaking works whose stylistic distortions she later absorbed into her unique form of ballet modernism. Leaving Diaghilev in 1914, Nijinska eventually opened a studio in Kiev, the main purpose of which was to train dancers for a company to be formed by her brother, but although it lasted no more than two years, the École de Mouvement was the turning point in Nijinska's artistic development. Concerned that the teaching of classical ballet had not kept pace with twentieth-century advances in choreography – 'Even the Ballets Russes, whose accomplishments are universally acknowledged, did not create a school to parallel its innovations in the theatre' – Nijinska set out to devise a system of her own to provide dancers with the necessary training to work with modernists such as Nijinsky and herself. The school became a centre for experimentation, its manifesto was not to deny the past – destroying the basis of the existing school – but rather to renew and enrich the classical legacy. Under its aegis, Nijinska emerged from the shadow cast by her brother to create the first ballets that bore her choreographic signature and established her as the leading exponent of neoclassical choreography.

Returning to the Ballets Russes in 1921, the year her brother was committed to a mental institution in Vienna, Nijinska served Diaghilev as principal dancer and choreographer, creating within four years nearly a dozen works, including her two masterpieces, *Les Noces* and *Les Biches*. Having once again resigned from the Ballets Russes, in 1928 she was in Buenos Aires, working for the Colón Ballet, when she received the invitation to become artistic director and ballet mistress of Ida Rubinstein's new company. She readily accepted the offer, as it not only allowed her to be reunited with her two children, who were living in Paris with their grandmother, but also provided her with unlimited resources to advance her choreographic career. She was to create a new repertory almost single-handedly (of the nine new works planned for the first season, all were Nijinska's, apart from two by Massine), which meant that she was working under tremendous pressure, with no break between finishing one ballet and starting another. 'She used to churn them out because she had to,' said Ashton. Economizing on time, Nijinska often tried out ideas for ballets during morning class and made it compulsory for every member of the company to attend. Even though these classes were extremely hard work – at two hours, they were double the length of those he had been used to in London – they were as much of an inspiration for Ashton as Nijinska's choreography.

> Her classes were fascinating. They were never the same. She'd decide to do everything in waltz rhythm one day or everything in Spanish rhythm or syncopated rhythm. She brought the music to class, all worked out. But the pianist didn't sit going tum, tum, tum, she came with her tomes and would one day do a whole class of Chopin with the most wonderful adages, another day a whole class of Bach, another day there'd be a whole class of nothing but tangos.

Continuing the regime she had established in the École de Mouvement, Nijinska's classes, while modelled on Cecchetti methods, incorporated her own theory of movement, developing and embellishing the old school. Ashton passionately shared her belief that classical ballet should provide the basis and structure for new choreography: his own poetic (briefly outlined in a letter to the critic, James Monahan, in the 1950s) is directly inherited from her. 'My obsession is the classical dance, the drama latent in it & the possibility of extending its line to contemporary rhythm & thought without breaking the line or resorting to the grotesque.' Just as influential was Nijinska's emphasis on épaulement, the enhanced expression of the torso, head and arms, which became the defining characteristic in Ashton's own choreography. 'There was always tremendous mobility in the whole body, you weren't allowed to be stiff. And even when you jumped you had to use épaulement. She wouldn't allow you just to jump up and down.'

In addition to developing plastique, Nijinska's classes were designed to build stamina. Having been trained by her brother to work at an accelerated tempo at the barre to increase her strength, she expected similar standards from her dancers and could be extremely severe. (Even the company's male star, Anatole Vilzak, has admitted to being intimidated by her.) At rehearsals, everyone had to perform at full steam and repeat a sequence dozens of times until it was perfect. Faced with young, inexperienced dancers recruited from all over the world, Nijinska was forced to adopt Draconian methods to instil into them some sort of stylistic homogeneity within a short space of time. 'She just had to whip us into some kind of shape,' said Ashton. 'You were at it all the time.' Discipline was rigid: newspapers and knitting were banned from the studio, dancers were not allowed to lean on the barre, but between steps had to stand as if they were ready to perform. Nijinska herself, waving her habitual cigarette in its long holder like the hostess in *Les Biches*, the role she created, was an awe-inspiring presence. Despite the silence in the studio, dancers would strain to catch her directions issued in a low grumbling mixture of French, Polish or Russian, and no one complained if they were burnt by falling ash as she corrected them, or scratched by her infamously long fingernails. Ashton, however, was undaunted by Nijinska. 'I remember once going to her because I was practically crippled. I couldn't move at all because her work was so difficult that my calves were completely seized up and so I asked if I could be let off rehearsals. And she said no – "C'est parce que vous n'avez pas l'habitude de travailler, ça passera." ' And yet, for all her tyrannical demands, in other ways Nijinska showed a motherly regard for Ashton. Concerned that he was so thin, she insisted that he take ten minutes off during rehearsal each morning to drink a pint of milk at a dairy opposite the studio in the Avenue Hoche. 'But of course working the way we did, my dear, it was a waste of time.' And when Ashton confessed to her how lonely he was, she was genuinely sympathetic, telling him that if he brought an English-speaking friend to her who could dance, she would take him on.

Nijinska was not only flattered by Ashton's attention to her work, she valued him as a dancer. Although he would always have to fight the fact that he did not have an ideal physique, his technique improved so significantly under Nijinska's tuition that soon she was able to cast him in lead corps de ballet roles. As someone who, as Margot Fonteyn often remarked, did not seem to have any bones at all, the choreographer's lissom movements came easily to him. Not only that, but like Nijinska herself, he had beautifully arched, fast feet and natural ballon. 'He could get off the ground,' said Billy Chappell. 'He bounced like a ball. It was a lovely jump, very light and neat.' Ashton also won Nijinska's favour by the speed at which he learnt an enchaînement; on one occasion, when he was the only dancer to get it right, she made him stand in front of the class – 'before Lichine and Shabelevsky and all the others.' Billy Chappell, on the other hand, who was always making mistakes, 'suffered dreadfully' from Nijinska's quick temper. 'She didn't like me and used to shout at me sometimes. *Terribly*. One day during a rehearsal she threw all the music at me. I was so bad that it annoyed Fred in the end because he felt I was letting him down.'

Irritation, compounded by exhaustion, was having a corrosive effect on their friendship. 'We are all in the pink rehearsing till 12 midnight daily so you may imagine our tempers are a little off,' Burra reported to Barbara Ker-Seymer. 'Instead of Faith hope & charity its vinegar vitriol & acrimony.' The two dancers were sharing not only a room, but a large double bed, which was all that was available at the price they could afford. 'So we used to put a bolster down the middle, and Fred would say in a furious voice in the morning, "Your *foot* was over my side. Would you keep to your side of the bed please."' The Hotel St Brieuc, at 72 Boulevard Montparnasse, was at the time run by a Normandy family with six children: 'They all had square heads and looked exactly the same.' The kindly Madame Euzenat all but adopted Ashton and Chappell, sending them off each morning with a kiss on both cheeks, straightening their collars and smoothing their hair. Equally fond of them was the hotel maid, a plump, jolly character, who took them on a Sunday outing to Versailles. Mostly, however, Ashton and Chappell were too exhausted and too badly paid to do much with their free time. 'We were so poor. Everything had to be worked out: if you had breakfast for five francs, you could only have lunch for eight francs including the tip, and dinner for ten francs perhaps. It was as tight as that. Sometimes we went without dinner and just had a ham sandwich.' Sophie tried to help Ashton augment his income by arranging for him to give English lessons to a Polish friend of hers, but knowing as little as he did about the rudiments of English grammar, this was not a success.

As a treat, he and Chappell would occasionally eat at the St Brieuc's restaurant, which specialized in creamy Normandy cuisine, but, on the whole, they depended on friends passing through Paris to take them out for a meal, or took advantage of the generosity of colleagues. Although Joyce Berry, as a fellow member of the corps, earned as little as he did, she often paid for Ashton because she liked him so much. 'Oh, he was lovely. He wasn't grand like he is now.' Birger (Billy) Bartholin, a Danish dancer living in Montparnasse, would also obligingly pick up the bill. He was a genial young man, whose family regularly sent him money from Copenhagen, and was highly amused and not at all put out by Ashton's mock-insolent retorts to his invitation to tea at the Magasins Réunis: 'I'll only come if you pay.' 'He thought Fred was a miracle of wit even though Fred used to bully him unmercifully as he always did when he had some-one he liked absolutely under his thumb,' said Chappell. Edward Burra would also subsidize an occasional meal. The artist had joined them at the St Brieuc, spending his days working on companion portraits of his two friends. 'If it ends as it's begun, my dear,' Burra wrote to Barbara Ker-Seymer about his oil painting of Ashton,

> It will be a triumph for Artiste & model its so like yet lovely Fred-dies delighted Ive given him such a daintie bouche & huge grey eyes like a gazelles oh its lovely. so we are going to call it 'Portrait of a dancer' Yes says Freddie everyone will come up and say oh I wonder *who* it is? Dolin I suppose . . .

Ashton, however, must have changed his mind about the painting, and complained to Burra that it made him look disagreeable. 'So Edward happily painted it out. He slapped black paint all over the canvas,' said Chappell. 'It was done at a time when we weren't speaking, and when-ever I was in the room a bitter look would come over Fred's face which Edward carefully put on the canvas. But Fred was very foolish. It was a marvellous painting.'*

With Sophie Fedorovitch also in Paris, renting a studio across the Boulevard Montparnasse, it was almost like old times. Whenever Ashton and Chappell were able to escape the rehearsal studio, they would all go to the cinema to see melodramatic silent films, or else head for the ho-mosexual bars in the Rue de Lappe, the regulars – tough, middle-aged

*Later regretting his rashness, Ashton became convinced that a Burra owned by Barbara Ker-Seymer – 'The Hand', depicting the artist's hand holding a ciga-rette – was concealing his own portrait. Every time he saw it hanging in her kitchen, he would half-seriously nag her to remove the top layer of paint to see if he was underneath.

navvies, affectionately dancing with one another – providing colourful material for Burra.

> On Sunday me & Billy danced a beautiful tango my dear you should have seen it and as for Freddie he was surrounded by doubtful Spaniards who terrified him into paying for all there drinks they also took all Sophies cigarettes when she was doing a can can with Billy. Everyone pretended to think she was a man dressed up & kept saying ah monsieur monsieur as for the matelots such buttocks ma chere and the lesbiennes so long drawn out.

More than anything, they liked sitting in a Left Bank café. Although La Coupole was few doors away from the St Brieuc, it was not yet fashionable, considered more of a workman's zinc-bar. They preferred the new, small and aptly named Select, which was frequented by the Cocteau set, a Russian contingent, and various English painters, including Nina Hamnett, Cedric Morris and Robert Medley, whose lover, the dancer Rupert Doone, was also a member of Ida Rubinstein's company. Ashton should have had much in common with Doone, whom he had seen partnering the veteran ballerina, Cléo de Mérode, when he went to France as a schoolboy; in fact, the two dancers were always arguing. 'There was tremendous jealousy on both sides,' said Robert Medley. 'Freddie, who was only in the corps, was envious of Rupert's position as soloist and Rupert was very ambitious and wanted to be a choreographer.'* Doone had been a protégé of Cocteau's at the age of nineteen, and was famously difficult, living close to the nerve and quick to burst out in uncontrollable storms, especially if he felt in some way threatened, as he did with Ashton. 'Rupert was frightfully superior and rather resented me. He once said to me, "You really ought to stop doing choreography, you have no talent at all." Going on and on at me through a whole evening. And I said to him: "I don't care what you say, I'm still going to keep trying."' Their mutual antipathy, which reached such a pitch on one occasion that Ashton feared they would be thrown off a bus for shouting so loudly, even extended to their friends. 'We met Rupert Doone the other day,' Burra told Barbara. 'My dear the look he gave me would have mopped up Niagara falls.'

With its reputation as 'a great queer haunt' (according to Billy Chap-

*In 1930, Doone in fact gave up a career exclusively devoted to dance and, after apprenticing himself to Tyrone Guthrie, formed a project which became known as the Group Theatre, and counted W. H. Auden among its collaborators.

pell), the Select was becoming a cruising ground for predatory older men, several of whom would go to the café after attending a performance, hoping to befriend the ballet boys.

'We were always considered fair game by these terrible old pussies who sat there eyeing everybody,' said Chappell. 'One took a fancy to me and would turn up at the St Brieuc with vast bouquets of roses which I'd toss to one side with my washing. Fred used to get very embarrassed because I'd forbid him to leave the room and I used to get embarrassed, and had to say to Madame Euzenat, you must not let that gentleman in any more. So she didn't.'

Because they were known to share a double bed, most people in the company assumed that Ashton and Chappell were having an affair, and those who knew better found their set-up very droll. When Sophie arrived at the St Brieuc one morning and saw them still in bed sipping their morning chocolate, she burst out laughing and said, 'Och, you look like two old cocottes!' Invariably together, they made an odd couple: Ashton conservatively dressed in a neat double-breasted suit, collar, tie and trilby; Chappell 'looking very fanciful and Montparnassian'. Although their domestic arrangement was hardly conducive to romance, Chappell was in constant demand. His current conquest was a devoted, handsome, but humourless Scandinavian, who was the source of much satire between Ashton and Burra. 'You wouldn't believe the Norwegian realy is twee,' wrote Burra. 'He kept looking at Nettie with such melting looks . . . when he left he said, "Goonight . . . boy" (long look & hand-press) old Vinaigrette & me had a laugh I can tell you.' Although Ashton's work took priority, part of him longed for the sort of amatory success enjoyed by Chappell – 'undisputed queen of the Select Bar' – and he became peevishly critical of his friend. 'Freddie gets bitterer and bitterer every minute,' Burra reported. 'Last night at supper how the girls did snip at each other realy if Fred & Billy are going to share a room on tour for the sake of economy it will be no economy as after 10 minutes they'll be clawing off the taps of the wash basin to ram up each others bums.'

Fortunately, tensions were defused by a new addition to their circle: Arthur Mahoney, an American dancer who had recently joined Rubinstein's company and quickly endeared himself to everyone. He was not only wonderful looking – blue-eyed, with striking Native American features, and a virile, muscular physique – but he possessed an intriguingly adventurous past. Mahoney, a choirboy at St Paul's Cathedral in Boston, had run away from home when his voice broke, and had gone West to be a cowboy. Some time later, browsing through magazines in a drugstore, he came across a picture of Nijinsky, which spurred him into changing his career. He had proved a natural dancer – stylish, rhythmical and tremendously versatile – and often joined Ashton and Chappell in impromptu revues staged for their own entertainment. Burra called the trio 'the Mahoney Sisters'.

Arthur & Billie open in pullman porter suits and Freddie comes on later whilst their singing the hot number and does his german Jazz dressed in an ostrich feather tail a diamonte bust boddice & top hat holding an imitation tin saxophone . . . also an oriental number to Allahs holiday & the great Ashton chinese number (in a 2nd hand chinese kimono) to Limehouse blues he's so funny Ime sure if he designed dreadful costumes for himself & did it all deadly seriously and not pulling bewitching faces he would make mints of money.

Ashton loved Mahoney – 'a sweet, adorable man' – and Burra was even more enchanted, savouring every detail of the 'Ammerican's' dress and behaviour: his large diamond ring, voluminous raglan overcoat, with huge mother-of-pearl buttons and 'vagabond' hats . . . 'Realy if I was Billy I should cultivate such a treasure.'

However, any advances by Chappell would have been firmly rebuffed. Mahoney was a dedicated womanizer – 'kind of a bad boy', said Thalia Mara, the dancer he eventually married. With the prospect of a company tour ahead, Chappell was beginning to regret the decision he had made to share digs with Mahoney rather than Ashton; as Burra merrily pointed out, 'There wont be any room for Mistress Chappell my dear as Arthur likes no less than 3 girls a night if possible so C will have to put up a little pied a terre in one of the drawers.' Tales of Mahoney's crazy philandering became a favourite topic of conversation. There was the anecdote (passed on by Burra) of how Mahoney had solved the problem of a persistent erection. 'It simply *wouldn't* stay down so my dear I just opened the window & let it fall on it. Jesus Christ that brought it down says Artie.' And the saga of a mysterious boil that had appeared on Mahoney's wrist: 'Of course on showing it to the hotel keeper [she] burst into shrieks of laughter and said HA HA c'est mal d'amour (knowing what went on up in Arties room, a special tax of 40 francs having been put on Art's bill for wear and tear of mattress).' But what astonished Ashton about Mahoney was not so much his sexual exploits as his brazen behaviour towards Nijinska. 'She would fly at him because he was always late for class. He was fucked-out. "Aw shut up!" he used to say. He was the only one who *dared* to speak to her like that. But she adored him.'

*   *   *

Finally, in November, after almost four months of round-the-clock re-hearsals, Les Ballets de Mme Ida Rubinstein presented its first season at the Paris Opéra. In the opening programme, Ashton appeared in all three Nijinska ballets: in the Carnival scene in *La Bien-Aimée*; as one of the four winds and as a faun in *Les Noces de Psyche et de l'Amour*; and as one of a group of male dancers supporting Ida Rubinstein in Ravel's *Bolero*, which had been written especially for her. Of all Nijinska's works for the company, *Bolero*, fast, exciting and charged with passion, is con-sidered to have integrated the talents of its collaborators most success-fully. The set, by Alexandre Benois, was designed to look like a Spanish tavern, and, as the music began, Rubinstein, dressed as a Goya-esque Spanish dancer, leapt on to a huge low table, lit by an overhead lamp, and started to sway seductively, gradually accelerating her tempo as she was urged on by the rhythmic beating fists and clapping of the encircling male spectators. Ashton and his colleagues had first performed this scene with Rubinstein in her own studio at home, where they had been summoned because she did not attend company rehearsals. (Even Proust's friend the Duchess de Clermont Tonnerre, who later wrote a libretto for one of Rubinstein's productions,* was expected to pay court. 'Madame Rubin-stein doesn't come to one, one has to go to her,' she told Ashton when they met a few years later.) The dancers were instructed to wear clean white shirts and clean socks, and when they arrived at Rubinstein's house in the Place des Etats-Unis, an elegant mansion with interiors designed by Bakst, they were shown into a dressing room and each handed a bottle of eau-de-Cologne. 'We knew that she didn't like the smell of sweat. So we *soused* ourselves and wore our clean shirts, and after it was all over a footman came round with petits fours.'

To members of her company, Rubinstein was an enigmatic character, gracious and very grand, whom they had seen only when she swept into the studio to watch rehearsals. She was tall and slim, with dark russet hair and heavy-lidded eyes, and, countering the fashion at the time, she always wore a long dress with a hat and gloves, but never any jewellery. 'Her hats were like gilt trelliswork wastepaper baskets with these huge green roses hanging down from the side and she had more fur on one of her coats to make two fur coats for an ordinary sized person.' Struck not only by her style and dignity, but also by her immaculate manners, Ash-ton was surprised to discover that Rubinstein knew the name and na-tionality of every dancer, whom she always greeted in her or his own

---

**Diane de Poitiers.*

language. And yet, despite this human touch, she remained remote from them all. 'We had the feeling of being a company run by an Electress of some Palatinate for her own amusement.'

The orphaned daughter of a wealthy Jewish family from St Petersburg, Ida Rubinstein had created a sensation when she appeared in the title role of Cleopatra and as Zobeida in *Scheherazade* in Diaghilev's seasons of 1909 and 1910. She was not a trained dancer but a mime, renowned for her natural elegance of movement and her dark beauty. 'All Diaghilev had her do was lie on a couch and then she probably stood up and made a few gestures,' said Ashton. When Rubinstein's technical limitations proved too marked, she left to pursue her own career, using her large inheritance and brilliant connections to commission works from such notable artists as Leon Bakst, Michel Fokine, and André Gide, as vehicles for herself, the most famous being *The Martyrdom of St Sebastian* in 1911. Financed by a wealthy lover, she formed her own company in 1928, once again surrounding herself with only the first rate. In addition to *Bolero*, Ravel's *La Valse* was created expressly for Rubinstein, and so was Stravinsky's *Baiser de la fée*. Both composers often attended rehearsals, either playing the piano or conducting (Ashton remembered Stravinsky on one occasion performing with great dynamism, chanting, 'I-da-hache! Et-da-hache!') Although Rubinstein's limited talents as an artist prevented her from reaching the heights achieved by her collaborators, she was determined to be a star, insisting for instance that her name be the only one to appear in bold type in the programme. She must, however, have been aware of her weaknesses, and, as Ashton pointed out, feared 'the cold scrutiny of her hard-working company'. She always worked in private with Nijinska and in general rehearsals walked through her roles, 'white-gloved and richly clad'.

The company would see Ida Rubinstein dance only at the first performance – an extraordinarily deflating experience for them all. By now in her early forties, she was still a striking, statuesque presence on stage, but the classical roles in which she determinedly appeared cruelly highlighted her technical defects. 'Once she was on her pointes she couldn't get off them,' said Ashton. 'She couldn't relevé or do any of those things. She was hopeless, really. Once she got up she staggered around. She was awful, awful.' After months spent working to perfect Nijinska's choreography, he found it demoralizing, to say the least, to see Rubinstein make a mockery of it all. *Bolero*, Ashton said, could have been wonderful 'were it not for her in the middle. But all the work we did building up for her entrances would sag right down. *On* would come this poor old thing and everything would collapse.' Rubinstein's biographer, Lynn Garafola, argues that contemporary reviews of the dancer in *Bolero* are highly complimentary, and that the languid, serpentine movements of her upper body had a certain mesmerizing quality. However, Osbert Sitwell, reviewing Rubinstein's performance during a London season in 1931, clearly disliked what he saw.

> It is enraging to see so much money lavished on productions that are simply spoilt by the presence in them of Madame Rubinstein . . . for example, in *Bolero*, where she dances on the table, the effect was that an amateur, upon whom the spotlight had happened to fall, had strolled into the middle of a performance of professionals, and, quite unashamed, had insisted on playing the chief part.

If Rubinstein had been content to supply the money, assuming the role of impresario, and occasionally appearing in something suitable, it would have been fine, said Ashton. 'But she was in *every* ballet.' Young and inexperienced as he was, Ashton was disenchanted by the duplicity of geniuses such as Stravinsky and Ravel, who would go backstage expressly to praise Rubinstein's performance, 'usually talking vaguely about the beauty of her gesture which was all they could find to say', while Rubinstein would murmur, 'Vous trouvez?' Even Nijinska said to the dancers one day, 'Madame Rubinstein peut faire tout sauf la virtuosité.' Needless to say, Ida Rubinstein's parodic attempts at classical ballet became a rich source of amusement for Ashton and his friends. 'As for bonny old Ida!' quipped Burra. 'Oh Fi Madame will have to have a special arrangement of invisible ropes to keep her for more than 3 seconds on her battered points. Billie says she's just like Beatrice Lillie in her famous skit on Les Sylphides.' Ashton would reduce the company to fits of laughter by imitating Rubinstein's sick-ostrich posture as she tottered around the stage, with curiously hunched shoulders and spread, bent knees, throwing back her head, fluttering her eyes, and making little moues with her mouth. 'Because she always got so nervous,' said Chappell, 'whenever her back was to the audience, she'd roll her tongue round her mouth and lick her lips all the time because her mouth dried up. Then she'd switch on a gushing smile again as she faced the front. Fred did it brilliantly.'*

It was mystifying to Ashton why Rubinstein should establish a lavish company only to torment herself with stage-fright, her panic compounded by the grandness of the venues in which they appeared. 'She was offered the chance of a London season, but as she couldn't get Covent Garden she wouldn't come.' At the beginning of 1929, the company left

*Thirty years later, Ashton was still dining out on Ida Rubinstein imitations – as Gore Vidal describes in *Palimpsest*, his memoirs.

Paris for a four-month tour of Europe. As Burra noted with glee, 'Ma chere about 6 goods Trains will be required to travel the scenery as it is all real staircases & real columns and real marble and real gilt & everything real but poor old Ida.' When her nerves got the better of her, Rubinstein would cancel an engagement without warning, leaving the dancers stranded. 'We'd be dumped in a cheap hotel near by and given enough to pay for lodgings until Madame decided she could go on again. When we went to Monte Carlo, for a whole week we weren't paid at all.' Earning an average of £3 10s per week, the dancers were forced to live on a shoe-string, deliberately staying in bed until lunchtime so they need pay only for breakfast.

Yet for Ashton, 'this crazy, half-starved tour' was rewarding in other ways. Seeing Vienna in the snow, Naples in the spring, performing in the great opera houses of Europe, rehearsing in the same rooms in Monte Carlo where so many Diaghilev ballets had been created, made a deep and lasting impression. During the months they were together on the road, Chappell became aware of what he called 'a kind of unconsciously crusading spirit' in his friend.

> Where I was driven into a kind of childish hysteria by the lyrical sunshine of Naples and spring in the South of France, and by looking all ways at once saw nothing, this same lyrical sunshine was for him making shapes of the shadows and bringing out the patterns of trees and the unexpected gesture of people, all of which his mind was seizing and savouring and taking in to the smallest detail, to bring out later when the moment arose.

Ashton kept his eyes open continually, trawling for the future. He bought several musical scores in Paris, including Debussy's 'Valse romantique', 'Moria-Blues' by Roland-Manuel (an extract from an obscure ballet called *Le Tournoi Singulier*) and, more significantly, Satie's 'Gymnopédies', music he eventually used for his ballet *Monotones*, in 1965. In May 1929, when the company returned to Paris for a season at the opera house, news came that Nijinska had resigned. As artistic director, her powers had been limited: not only did Ida Rubinstein make all the final decisions, but, in consigning the visual aesthetic of every production to Alexandre Benois, Rubinstein implicitly rejected an experimental approach. The main problem, however, had been the constraint of having to make Rubinstein the centrepiece of every ballet. This had proved creatively inhibiting not only to Nijinska but also to Massine, and had recently become a cause of friction between the two choreographers.* If Nijinska was no longer head of the company, Ashton felt there was no reason to stay, especially as Marie Rambert was urging him to come back to choreograph a new ballet. His apprenticeship had reached a natural conclusion and now he was impatient to return home.

Although Ashton did not see Nijinska again for many years, he did not forget her, frequently maintaining that it was through her that he had learnt his craft. 'I learnt far more from Nijinska than I ever did from Massine.' During the mid-1960s when he was director of the Royal Ballet and concerned that Nijinska's reputation had fallen into decline, he invited her to London to mount *Les Noces* and *Les Biches* for the Royal Ballet, considering it to be a way of repaying the debt he owed. Both ballets were triumphantly received, re-establishing Nijinska's place in dance history. 'She was so sweet when she came to London, she said, "It was such a pity I couldn't get to know any of you, but I was working so hard I didn't have time to really preoccupy myself with the company." She told me how touched she'd been by the way I used to watch her and she embraced me and said, "Tu es mon fils."'

The ballet that Marie Rambert wanted Ashton to choreograph was *Mars and Venus*, to be performed as an interlude in Ashley Dukes's long-awaited adaptation of *Jew Süss*. The actor Matheson Lang, having himself in mind for the title role, had bought the dramatic rights to Lion Feuchtwanger's best-selling romance – a baggy monster of a novel, with a multitude of characters, incidents and scenes – and commissioned Dukes to write a much simplified original play on the main theme of the rise and fall of the wealthy Josef Süss Oppenheimer, the power behind the ducal throne of Wurttemberg. The ballet, based on Ovid's tale of seduction, was to take place in the second act during a fancy-dress ball, setting the mood for the following scene in which the Duke has returned from his victorious campaign and foists his attentions on the Jew's innocent daughter – his 'Hebrew Venus' – with tragic results. Rambert had already chosen the music (Scarlatti sonatas, orchestrated by Constant Lambert), and devised a synopsis consisting of three short episodes: the arraying of Venus by her nymphs, the entrance of Mars, and his disarming and se-

*Edward Burra elaborates: 'Massine cunningly arranged a ballet so that Ida needn't go on her battered old points & just appear in lively poses. Ida was furious & said Madame Nijinska shall do the choreography instead so M says allright & promptly arranged a terribly difficult ballet poor old I couldnt even crumble through & now ma cherie a terrible scandale has burst as Massine has left for Ammerica [*sic*] with all Aurics music and is now arranging dainty prologues at the Roxy theatre.'

duction by Venus. Harold Turner, Rambert's only virtuoso dancer, would make a convincingly virile hero, Pearl Argyle, who was to become, in Ashton's estimation, the most beautiful woman of her generation, was the obvious choice for Venus.

Nineteen years old, and so shy and unconscious of her great beauty that she would blush whenever Ashton spoke to her, Argyle was the choreographer's first English muse. As the ballet begins, she is seen in profile, her arm raised in an arc in front of her face as if gazing at her reflection – the mirror of Venus – her two attendants swaying her languorously to and fro, and embellishing her movements. Their pas de trois, with tendrilly, interweaving arms, is another of Ashton's homages to Botticelli's *Primavera*, a study of Three Graces in motion, its soft, slow lyricism contrasted with a witty diagonal jumping sequence, in which their port de bras continue to waft independently from their legs. Considering that *Mars and Venus* was the first ballet Ashton created after returning from Paris, Nijinska's influence is surprisingly muted. It can be seen in the supple fluidity of the women's arms and upper back (Arnold Haskell commented that this was the ballet in which Pearl Argyle first overcame her defects of reserve and rigidity), and in the way Ashton has linked his painterly groupings with continuous, living movement, breathing life into pauses and transitions. But these are also the hallmarks of Pavlova's dancing, her romantic imprint just as pervasive here as in every Ashton work to come. What is so remarkable about *Mars and Venus* is how soon and how smoothly the choreographer assimilated outside influences into a style entirely his own. Although a youthful work, the ballet demonstrates not only how well defined his poetic identity already was, but also presents several ideas in embryo that he went on to develop (the stylized martial conceits in Harold Turner's solo prefiguring those given to the female amazons in his 1952 *Sylvia*; the delightful sequence with silver ropes, Ashton's first ribbon-dance, a simple sketch for the far more intricate ribbon-play in *La Fille mal gardée*). And when Mars and Venus dance together, their arms entwining and framing each other's faces, you see exactly the sort of human tenderness characteristic of all Ashton's great love pas de deux. The way a bravura 'fishdive' melts into a gentle rocking embrace is evidence enough that the choreographer was already instinctively extending the formal classical pas de deux into a metaphor for the act of love.

After an out-of-town run, *Jew Süss* opened on 29 July 1929 at the Duke of York's theatre. Expectation was immense: Matheson Lang was a star, a magnificent character actor with a stupendous bass voice, but it was a complete unknown, the twenty-two-year-old Peggy Ashcroft, playing the Jew's daughter, Naemi, who dominated the stage that night by sheer talent and by the haunting serenity of her stage presence. The play itself was well liked, but Ashton's ballet received short shrift with only one review and a hostile one at that, its critic responsible for the inaccurate remark often quoted by Rambert, 'What a pity dramatic authors have wives, and those wives meddle in ballet.' It was revived at the Lyric the following year, considerably reworked, with Billy Chappell replacing Harold Turner. In *Punch*'s view, it had been improved beyond recognition. 'Mr Ashton is to be warmly congratulated. This little gem could have been presented on any of the great evenings we have known and have had no reason to blush for itself.'

Confident all along of his ballet's merit and untroubled by his first bad notice, Ashton was in irrepressibly high spirits. When *Jew Süss* was playing at the Duke of York's, where it ran for several months, he kept an eye on it while performing across the street at the Coliseum with Anton Dolin's company on a twice-nightly music-hall bill. Ashton played the Barman in *Rhapsody in Blue* and, as Dolin, its choreographer, had given little thought to the role, he took the liberty of changing the steps and generally drawing attention to himself, at one point jumping up spectacularly on to the top of the bar. When one of Dolin's friends asked him who the barman was, Ashton was promptly told to modify his antics. Instead, he put on a show backstage, entertaining the corps de ballet girls with a zany repertoire of imitations, borrowing a *Sylphides* costume to impersonate Ida Rubinstein taking an arabesque and dropping her false teeth, and appearing as Queen Victoria in a black kimono, with a powder puff on top of his head – an act he spun out to twenty minutes.

At parties, too, Ashton obligingly provided impromptu cabarets. He and Billy Chappell were regulars at the celebrated Great Ormond Street gatherings of Cedric Morris and his lover, Arthur Lett Haines ('You'd see everybody there you could possibly think of – Virginia Woolf, Vanessa Bell, and endless Stracheys'), and as the evening wore on, a space would be cleared and guests would sit down to watch the pair perform the Charleston and the exhibition Black Bottom, a deadpan double-act that Ashton was soon to rework as the Popular Song in *Façade*. As much the party girl as ever, Tallulah Bankhead, who had returned to London to appear in *Lady of the Camellias* at the Garrick, was delighted by their act. 'She thought we were dear little things and called us over and said, "You must come and see my play, I'll leave tickets for you at the stage door."' When the time came, Chappell wanted to buy a bouquet of flowers for the star, but Ashton insisted they should first wait to see if she had left their tickets. 'And do you know she *remembered*! I've never got over that. We went round to her dressing room afterwards and she couldn't have been sweeter.'

*   *   *

Although Ashton's party days were by no means over, they were put in check by one of the most intensive and varied work periods of his career. Marie Rambert frequently maintained that, without her prodding, he would never have stirred himself to create another ballet, but this oda-lisque image, although accurate up to a point, is hard to reconcile with the sort of dedication he had shown in Paris. Rambert was, indeed, mid-wife to many of his early works – she was, as Chappell said, 'a very spe-cial kind of creator; a creator of creativity' – but Ashton's first significant ballet, one which proved to be a classic, was created independently of Rambert. It was the result of an idea suggested by the composer Constant Lambert. An extraordinarily gifted twenty-three-year-old, Lambert had been an admirer of Ashton's since he conducted a charity matinée of *Leda and the Swan*, after which he talked enthusiastically to Rambert about her new discovery. To Ashton, his approbation meant a great deal. One of two English composers to be commissioned by Diaghilev (responsible for the score of Nijinska's *Roméo et Juliette*), Lambert was already a leading figure in the intellectual and social life of London, lionized by the Sitwells and a key member of their inner circle, renowned for his wit and brilliant conversation. There was also the hard-drinking, nightclub Lam-bert, inhabiting cheap dives till four in the morning, part of the set that gathered at the Eynsford cottage of the composer Philip Heseltine (alias Peter Warlock) for riotous weekends devoted to the pub. Defeated by the convivial pressures, Ashton was reluctant to become part of this particu-lar world, but the two young men were profoundly compatible, never-theless, equally passionate about their work and yet frivolous at the same time. 'Fred adored him,' said Billy Chappell. 'Constant was a very lov-able man – so lively and funny and daft and wild.' Formidably intelligent, too. Ninette de Valois would later speak of him as 'our only hope of an English Diaghilev'. Right from the start of their association, Ashton was sufficiently impressed to allow Lambert to take his musical education in hand, steering him towards arcane enthusiasms, unjustly neglected com-posers, and contemporaries such as Peter Warlock, whose *Capriol Suite* was the score that Lambert persuaded him would make a first-rate ballet.

In 1925 Cyril Beaumont had issued an English translation of the *Or-chésographie* of 1588 (Thoinot Arbeau's celebrated treatise on dancing, written as a dialogue with his pupil, Capriol), using Warlock, a recog-nized authority on the period, to transcribe the music examples into modern notation. Inspired by the Elizabethan melodies, Warlock then wrote six movements for piano (later orchestrated) which, while repro-ducing the old tunes and basic structures, were no mere arrangement or

pastiche. In the same way, Ashton's interpretation would not be a reconstruction of sixteenth-century dances, but a free and exuberant evocation
carried out in an amusing, original and personal style.

Eager to absorb the spirit of Elizabethan life, Ashton saturated himself in the period, reading Shakespeare's sonnets and deriving movement
ideas from paintings such as the well-known portrait of Queen Elizabeth
lifted in a Volta 'with her feet dangling in the air'. He spent the best part
of two days at Knole, the great house given by Queen Elizabeth to
Thomas Sackville, the ancestor of Vita Sackville-West. Ashton had persuaded a wealthy young South American friend, Harry Bright, whom he
had known slightly at La Recoleta, to drive him to Sevenoaks and pay for
a night in a local inn. Ashton, said Bright, was 'very struck by the whole
thing', but impressions he carried away with him of 'galleries hung with
gothic tapestries, great state bedrooms preserved with their ancient fur-
nishings, gildings and velvets, four-posters of silver and flamingo satin
towering to the ceiling . . .' were absorbed and then virtually eliminated
in the ballet itself.

Rambert's tiny Mercury Theatre laid down strict terms of its own.
With a stage eighteen-feet square, and no room in the wings into which
scenery could be slid, ballets had to be intimate rather than awe-
inspiring, mounted with the economy that was by now characteristic of
her productions. 'She was relentless about pennies, ha-pence even,' remarked Agnes de Mille. 'Costumes were let out, material redyed, coats
turned, scenery painted over . . . She had to do this; it was carry on this
way or quit.' Billy Chappell was put in charge of the set and costumes,
and the assignment launched him as a gifted stage designer. Pre-empting
any of his over-ambitious ideas, Rambert marched Chappell off to John
Barker's basement, where they bought beige linen at sixpence a yard and
pink linen at two shillings and sixpence. The total cost of the production
was £5. The Mercury was a challenging school for choreographers,
dancers and designers; with the audience so close that you could almost
see the colour of their eyes, it was difficult to create any sense of illusion.
Yet it taught Ashton vital lessons that never left him, lessons such as how
to make even the smallest gesture resonate with meaning.

The Elizabethan setting of *Capriol Suite* could hardly be more mini-
mal, the inspiration of Knole abstracted to a suggestion of topiary and
two benches on which the dancers, waiting their turn to perform, are
frozen in silhouette like garden statuary. The titles for the six sections and
some movement ideas are taken from descriptions Ashton found in the
Orchésographie, but his debt to his source stops there; 'Basse dance', for
example, the folksy opening duet for a couple waving white handkerchiefs, derives from a display of English national dancing which he had

seen at the Albert Hall. 'Pavanne' is the heart of the piece, a pas de trois in which a woman is courted by two suitors (Pearl Argyle, Harold Turner and Ashton), one with a poem on a scroll, the other with a rose. Their deadpan decorum and the exaggerated stateliness of their movements is faintly sent up by Argyle's graceful pelvic thrust and by the men's droll walk, an explicitly comic version of which Ashton gave to the chickens in *La Fille mal gardée* nearly thirty years later. Although it is a plotless piece, there are fleeting seconds of drama in this love triangle told through movement alone, the emotional content being so oblique that it is hardly there at all. A sudden retiré with turned-up toes, as the two men stand looking at each other, takes on a combative note, and, when Argyle and Turner move away together, Ashton turns with one hand on his forehead in a classic image of a jilted suitor, before joining the couple in a formulaic Elizabethan pose.

'Tordion', a slower version of a galliard, is another ceremonial dance for two swaying couples, but with very little movement, save for extravagant use of the upper body and arms, lending a tender lyricism to the stilted period formations. 'Mattachins', originally a pyrrhic dance, said to have been invented to amuse the infant Jupiter by the noise the performers made by striking swords against their shields, is turned into a characteristic piece of bucolic Ashtonian nonsense, like the rustics' number in *The Dream*, or the roly-poly vegetables in *Pas de légumes*. Alternate pairs of four men perform entrechats with flexed feet, roll across each other's backs with tantrum-kicking legs, or bottom-shuffle along the stage with pistoning elbows – all put in a classical context and done at top speed. The jaunty 'Pieds en l'air' duet is an Elizabethan precursor of Ashton's 1952 Neapolitan Dance; while 'Bransles', the finale, brings on the ensemble and shapes them into a human wagon, a wheel, a rippling chain – the sort of playful conceits that Ashton would re-use time and again. Brimming with his hallmarks, *Capriol Suite* was a blueprint for the future. Yet for all its idiosyncrasy, it was also totally in tune with Warlock's music – a visualization of its melodic invention, contrapuntal lucidity and jeu d'esprit. The ballet made an enormous impression, its vitality and freshness lasting far longer than Ashton could ever have envisaged. 'It had such a perfume about it, it transported you at once,' remarked ex-Rambert dancer Elisabeth Schooling, responsible for mounting Rambert's March 1983 revival. 'Fred was a man of genius even then.'

The critic, Arnold Haskell, whose balletomania began with the Diaghilev company and who had been nurturing a passionate enthusiasm for Marie Rambert's dancers, and for Ashton's work in particular, went as far as to call *Capriol Suite* a masterpiece. Haskell told Ashton that Pavlova had sat behind him at one performance and been so impressed by the ballet that she had asked him to tell her about the choreographer. Ashton was so excited that he wrote to the ballerina immediately, saying he would like to hear her opinion in person. A reply arrived from Pavlova's husband, Victor Dandré, inviting him to tea at Ivy House, their house in Hampstead. When Ashton arrived 'in fear and trembling', he was shown by Dandré into an elegant drawing room, with high lead-paned windows overlooking the croquet lawn. While they were talking, he became aware that he was being observed through a gap in the curtains screening a glass-panelled door. Pavlova then entered the room slowly, still studying him carefully, and exclaimed, 'Ach, so young!' Tea appeared, and Ashton was mesmerized by the ceremony and grace with which Pavlova measured spoonfuls from numerous little pots of jam into her cup. But he was also struck by how old she looked, with white, parchment-dry skin and workaday hands which he could not associate with the delicate gestures he had seen on stage. Conversation flowed easily and Ashton, animated with the confidence of youth, suggested to Pavlova that she might visit the Rambert studio to see more of his work. She could not, she replied, because she was about to go on tour. 'But, with great impetuosity, I said, "What time is your train? You could come on your way to the train." She was rather taken aback, but she did it.' To his colleagues' amazement, Pavlova arrived in the middle of class – 'it was as though a spiritual effigy of the Dance had suddenly materialized' – and having watched *Leda and the Swan* and a few other extracts, she spoke most encouragingly to Ashton before departing for the Continent.

> After that I didn't see her again until the last matinée that she gave in England. I went to the theatre and asked to see her at the stage door. But the doorman said, 'No, she doesn't see anyone after performances.' So I asked to see someone else I knew in the company. He let me in and of course I went straight to Pavlova's dressing room. Imagine the cheek! I banged on the door and Dandré let me in and I remember saying to myself, 'Notice her make-up.' 'Notice all the things about her.' But she had a scar, a sort of hole, on her breastbone – I think she'd stabbed herself during a ballet and the dagger hadn't folded – and my mind was riveted on this curious blemish and I never noticed anything about her except that. But she took my hand in hers – she was very sympathetic – and she said, 'You have a great future; it will come slowly, but it will come,' and that was the last I ever saw of her. She'd said that she would re-organize her company when she came back from the tour in Europe. She'd said that she'd take me in. Only she never came back.

On the journey from the Midi there was an accident on the line and all the passengers were made to leave the train; in a cold, damp dawn, Anna Pavlova contracted pneumonia and died within two weeks, on 23 January 1931. But Ashton's great future was already assured. Arnold Haskell had embarked on a scheme that would not only give countenance to new Ashton ballets, forging several of his most important creative partnerships, but would also prove to be a first step towards the eventual formation of the Royal Ballet itself.

Arnold Haskell had evolved a plan over lunch one day with the editor of the *Dancing Times*, P. J. S. Richardson (alias the ubiquitous 'Sitter Out'), whereby ballet in Britain could be made to perpetuate the principles on which Diaghilev had run the Ballets Russes, as a fusion of dance, music and decor. The aim was to organize the production of new works, which would be presented on a Sunday night and a Monday afternoon in a West End Theatre, three or four times a year; a nucleus of dancers would be drawn from Marie Rambert's troupe, and from Ninette de Valois' Vic-Wells Ballet, recently installed with a ballet school at Sadler's Wells. After writing to a number of people who they thought would be interested, Haskell and Richardson arranged an inaugural dinner at the Metropole Hotel on 16 February 1930, an impressive gathering of Britain's leading dancers, composers and painters, most of whom pledged their support. The chairman was Edwin Evans, the only music critic in the country with a practical knowledge of the ballet and one who had been closely associated with Diaghilev. A silver-bearded, genial character, whose natural bonhomie made him a popular member of the committee, Evans had come up with the idea of naming the society after the first French modern ballerina, Anne-Marie de Cupis – La Camargo. Having been enchanted by *Capriol Suite*, he was already a keen champion of Ashton, and, having reminded the committee about Lambert's ballet *Pomona* (staged in South America with choreography by Nijinska, but never seen in England), Evans invited Ashton to provide a new version for the first programme. Camargo's key players, however, were not its pioneers, Haskell and Richardson, but a triumvirate comprising Constant Lambert, enlisted as resident conductor, Lydia Lopokova, choreographic advisor, and the dancer's husband, the eminent economist, Maynard Keynes, who took over the role of treasurer. The general committee has been described as Diaghilevian in concept – 'It functioned as a collective catalyst – determining not only when, where and what should be presented but also which composers, designers and choreographers should be invited to work as a collaborative team' – but, in fact, it was Lopokova who had the real impresarial power. During the year in which the society met on a regular basis, she held splinter-group gatherings at home, day-long Sunday lunches, at which Ashton, Lambert, Ninette de Valois and Edwin Evans were regulars. Camargo committee procedures have been well documented and preserved, but far more fascinating are the unofficial minutes, mixed with snippets of gossipy conversation, recorded in the correspondence between Lydia Lopokova and Maynard Keynes.

During term time when Keynes was in Cambridge teaching at King's College, Lydia was installed at 46 Gordon Square, the house her husband had once shared with Vanessa Bell. But although the dancer's presence technically affiliated her with Bloomsbury, she was ostracized by the Group. 'They were beastly to her,' said Ashton. 'They resented her I think because when she moved in she cleared them all out.' A more plausible objection was that Lydia subverted serious conversation with Keynes. 'They say you can only talk to Maynard now in words of one syllable,' protested Virginia Woolf. Vanessa Bell was particularly resentful towards Lydia for reducing one of the great minds of the century to simply another fool of love. Her cartoon of the ballerina taking a curtain call is a malicious caricature, showing the dished Maynard Keynes goggling at his wife, hat in one hand, flowers in the other like a besotted fan. Things had not always been this way. When the popularity of the Ballets Russes was at its height, Lopokova had been the talk of London, her effervescent individuality as the Lilac Fairy in *The Sleeping Princess* eclipsing the decorous performances of the great Mariinsky ballerinas in the lead role. Everyone wanted to meet her. 'It's impossible for anyone nowadays to realize how famous she was,' said Ashton. 'She was the darling of the public.' Taken backstage by Lady Ottoline Morrell, Duncan Grant had been charmed by her vivacious manner and singular appearance: small blue eyes, pale plump cheeks and a curious beaky nose, her hair very fair, fluffed up and gathered into a low bun. Lopokova was high-spirited, ingenuous and altogether delightful, her Russian pronunciation and quaint expressions only adding to her comic gift. Vanessa Bell had also been captivated by Lydia at first, but grew disenchanted as soon as Keynes announced that he intended to marry her. As a mistress on the stage, Lydia was a colourful addition to Bloomsbury and could be tolerated, even enjoyed, but not as a wife.

Outside Bloomsbury, however, as Keynes's biographer, Robert Skidelsky, points out, there is unanimous testimony to her intelligence, although it was purely intuitive, not trained. Her roots were in the ballet, but she was curious about other worlds and eager to learn. Keynes was enchanted by his wife, whose letters to him bear witness to her mercurial chatter, genuine appreciation of life and inventive use of English – both a form of coquetry and a genuine passion for the language. They were a devoted pair and, to the astonishment of their friends, they were also sexually compatible. Keynes was known as a voracious homosexual, yet Lopokova's early letters are full of expressions of sexual endearment. Her husband's involvement in Camargo was a demonstration of love almost as palpable as the theatre in Cambridge he would later build especially for her. He saw the venture primarily as an opportunity to provide a second ballet career for Lydia, and was unfailingly supportive and optimistic, even though its timing coincided with a world-wide economic collapse. An added attraction was that it brought him in proximity to a new circle of attractive youths to whom he was clearly still susceptible. Ashton and Chappell were individually invited to stay with Keynes at King's, where he made a habit of wandering into the room while they were taking a bath. And when for the first time they went to supper with Keynes and Lydia in Gordon Square, their host took them out on to the balcony, ostensibly to explain which Bloomsbury figure lived where, but then pounced, giving them both 'terrible great smacking kisses'. It was hard not to recoil. Although distinguished-looking in a donnish way, as an ageing roué Keynes was most unattractive – 'a gorged seal', in Virginia Woolf's description – 'double chin, ledge of red lip, little eyes, sensual, brutal, unimaginative.' 'We were absolutely horrified, but we didn't like to say, "Don't do that,"' said Chappell. 'And there was Madame, twiddling her thumbs inside. When we appeared she made a typically wonderful remark: "Have some more *Bols*," she said to Maynard.' Keynes was a worshipper of creative artists, as well as being genuinely stagestruck. He was fascinated by the ballet and had a high regard for Ashton because, as Chappell put it, 'Maynard wanted to further Lydia's career and Fred was quite clearly the one to do it.'

Ashton got on extremely well with Keynes, although he was always slightly in awe of him. 'One felt he was a great man and all that.' Keynes was wonderful company: his conversation was quick, animated, highly informed, and 'as exciting as fiction' – the latest gossip about Continental statesmen, their mistresses, their neuroses, their political manoeuvres, as well as financial talk of the latest movements of the exchanges, budgetary positions, all related to theoretical doctrine. Uncondescending towards his dancer guests, Keynes would mix them with clever young men from Cambridge, such as George 'Dadie' Rylands and Douglas Davidson (who were renting rooms from Vanessa Bell at 37 Gordon Square), and friends such as Joan Robinson, the first great woman economist, whom Ashton particularly liked. 'Whenever we went there,' said Chappell, 'we were always landed with a group of intellectuals and Fred and I hardly opened our mouths, but Maynard thought it quite right that we should meet and converse with them.'

It was always easier and livelier in Lydia's sole company, and Ashton would usually stay on, sitting in a comfortable armchair, chatting until six or seven in the evening. Her Sunday salon was held in the first-floor drawing room of number 46 where, at a small table, she would produce makeshift meals of heavy Russian fare. Other habitués were Vera Bowen, a choreographer and producer of plays; Boris Anrep, the mosaicist; and Madame Zanfretta ('Zannie'), once a great beauty and famous Italian mime, whom Ashton encouraged to talk about her days on the Empire stage. Ashton and Lydia also began to meet frequently on their own; she would telephone at the last minute to ask him to dinner, or they would go to a film or a show together. He loved being with her, she was such fun and laughed constantly – 'laughter of a gaiety you'd never believe.' One night, when they got a taxi, the driver refused to let him pay the fare: 'To hear that lady laugh has done me more good than anything.'

Ashton grew extremely fond of Lydia. She was loyal and kind, and went out of her way to make friends with his mother, inviting 'Mrs Ashton', as she always called her, to tea at Gordon Square and encouraging her to reminisce. Despite her own lustrous career, Lydia had no conceit and was exceptionally generous towards other dancers. She was anxious to help Tamara Karsavina, the great Mariinsky ballerina, now living in London in considerable financial difficulties. When Lydia went to visit her one day, she stopped at the gate to rummage in her bag until she found her hat and put it on. When Karsavina, who had been watching her from the window, asked why she had bothered to wear it, Lydia replied, 'Out of respect for you.' Later, when Ashton enquired how their meeting had gone, Lydia snorted, 'Och! It was hopeless. Tamara has English pride, Russian pride and *false* pride.' Like a child, she always spoke her mind, regardless of the circumstances. Ashton went with her and Keynes one night to see the Russian ballerina Alice Nikitina in *Le Spectre de la Rose*, and when she appeared on stage, Lydia's voice rang out all over the theatre, 'Maynard, look at her mouth – it's indecent! It looks as if it belongs somewhere else.' 'She was utterly frank,' said Ashton. 'It wasn't affectation but in some kind of way she knew how to make an effect. One of the ways of amusing you was to make you laugh by saying exactly what she thought, even if it might be embarrassing or hurtful.' Ashton found Lydia's candour less funny when it was directed towards him. As Camargo's choreographic advisor, it fell to her to tell Ashton that he could not expect leading roles in their productions, that his future lay in choreography, not dancing.*

---

*25 May 1930: 'About Fred Ashton,' she reported to Keynes, 'he longs to dance himself . . . but *Pomona* should and must have Pat [Anton Dolin] . . . or Mim's best pupil [Harold Turner] who dances with Karsavina. Fred is intelligent and sensitive so you see it is all delicate.'

If Ashton felt rebuffed, he was soon consoled by the fact that none other than Karsavina had chosen him as her partner during the Rambert Dancers' season at the Lyric. Nigel Playfair had insisted that, for box-office reasons, they must engage a star and suggested Karsavina. Needing the money and keen to take an active part in the developing fortunes of the young British ballet, she agreed not only to perform but to stage two Fokine ballets that she had helped to create, *Les Sylphides* and *Le Carnaval*. As one of the great ballerinas of her generation, Karsavina was, to Ashton, a goddess – luminously beautiful and intelligent; 'the Duse of the dance'. Just to be near her was an honour, and a lesson in artistry and behaviour, and the young dancers crowded the wings nightly to watch her. Knowing that she had danced with Nijinsky, Ashton was at first terrified by the thought of partnering her, but she was infinitely gracious, patient and encouraging towards him, while at the same time demanding his absolute dedication and understanding of the technicalities of the roles. 'They were days of inspiration and absorption on my part . . . I drenched myself in her presence – I learnt the meaning of gesture, "nuance," the drama of movement inherent in the dance.'

Ashton's performance in *Les Sylphides* marked his début as a danseur noble. Although he lacked strength and technique, the elegance of his bearing and his romantic nature were well suited to the lyrical, poetic atmosphere of the ballet. He was a sensitive, considerate partner, using his instinct for line to enhance that of the ballerina. His choreographic intelligence, however, also proved a hindrance. 'The feeling that he is introspective, watching and criticising himself,' wrote Arnold Haskell, 'deprives one of the thrill that a seemingly more spontaneous and purely physical performance can give.' As if determined to prove his worth on stage, Ashton arranged two new numbers for the Lyric programmes, casting himself in both: *Saudade do Brésil*, a fiery, Massine-like solo, and a duet in which he danced with Marie Rambert, *Mazurka des Hussars*. But when the Camargo Society gave its opening programme at the Cambridge Theatre that autumn, Lopokova was proved right: it was as a choreographer that Ashton would be regarded seriously from that time onwards. It was unanimously agreed that *Pomona*, his most ambitious work to date, more than justified Camargo's existence, although the rest of the evening left much to be desired. It included a historically interesting, but dull extract from the long-forgotten ballet from the opera *Robert le Diable*, and various divertissements, among which was Penelope Spencer's tedious and unfunny skit on a visit to the dentist, the combined effect of which reduced Cyril Beaumont to a 'state of profound depression'. The critic of the *Nation and Athenaeum* reproved the committee for underestimating public taste, adding, 'It was noticeable that the audience reserved its enthusiasm for the ballet which deserved it.'

Taking his cue from Constant Lambert's contemporary musical treatment of old forms, such as the passacaglia and rigadoon, Ashton had produced a modern conception of a mythological theme – the story of the wooing of Pomona, goddess of fruits, by Vertumnus in disguise – without any sacrifice of classical feeling. Much of the ballet's success was owing to the presence of two outstanding dancers in the lead roles: Diaghilev's star, Anton Dolin, and the American ballerina Anna Ludmila, whom Ashton had admired since they had performed together in Ida Rubinstein's company. Dolin and Ludmila were not only already established as partners; at around this time, they were briefly engaged to one another and made a stunningly glamorous couple. In a photograph by Dorothy Wilding, Dolin, stripped to the waist, shadows Ludmila, touching her arm. The sexual frisson between them was something which Ashton would exploit to great effect in the ballet.

As Dolin's partner, Ludmila had taken over Vera Nemtchinova's roles, and the contrast of types was so striking that she had been found lacking. Nemtchinova, creator of the androgynous Blue Girl in *Les Biches*, was a classical purist, cool and precise; Ludmila was an emotional dancer, voluptuous and temperamental. For the first time, *Pomona* showed the real Ludmila – not a sylph, or a goddess, but a modern young woman. She was a beautiful American blonde, with what Arnold Haskell called 'Elinor Glyn's vague "It"': the look of a Hollywood actress or a Follies girl, combined with intelligence and artistic integrity. Ludmila translated sex appeal into terms of ballet and Ashton made full use of this, building the role around her personality. He also brought the best out of Dolin, in whom Cyril Beaumont had noticed an unusual sense of restraint. 'I have always regarded Mr Dolin as a first-rate dancer and nothing more . . . but came away charmed.' Dolin barely mentions *Pomona* in his memoirs, probably because Ludmila carried off most of the acclaim. He may not have liked being made to appear faintly ludicrous in one of Vertumnus's disguises when, veiled and gowned as 'a lady of uncertain age', he attempts to comfort Pomona, an episode he was inclined to overdo. 'How much was due to his wig and veil suddenly going awry I do not know,' commented the *Dancing Times*. The dancer Wendy Toye remembers Dolin being quite funny, 'Whether we just thought it was camp, I don't know.' But his strong solo work was highly praised, as was his pas de deux with Ludmila to Lambert's soft Siciliana, described by one critic as 'glorious'.

Pomona marked a significant progress in Ashton's choreography. His beautiful melting dances for Ludmila and her nymphs, and the shapes and patterns of their groupings, showed an increasing sense of design; his movements were more adventurously musical, including one striking contrapuntal effect when he moved the corps de ballet behind the principals in different rhythms. The ballet's Nijinska-inspired modernism divided the critics: Haskell praised the inventiveness with which Ashton used the new movements, without once resorting to distortion; Beaumont disliked the angular movements which he felt did not suit a mythological love story. But, despite this quibble, it was clear that the ballet, with its first-rate contemporary score, and evocative designs by John Banting, had successfully fulfilled Camargo's aims. 'We were able for half an hour to forget that Diaghileff was dead,' remarked the *Nation and Athenaeum*.

Lydia Lopokova, who took to the stage that night and proclaimed, not strictly accurately, that the occasion marked the birth of British ballet, was at the time collaborating with Ashton on a programme in which, as she put it, 'I use my tongue more than my legs.' *A Masque of Poetry and Music: 'Beauty, Truth and Rarity'* was to be staged at the Arts Theatre Club in December 1930, with a cast of Cambridge's most fetching undergraduates, including Dadie Rylands, producer of the show, and the young Michael Redgrave. First discussions of the programme had taken place in the summer, when Ashton and Constant Lambert, the musical director and conductor of the piece, visited Lydia at Tilton, the Keyneses' farmhouse under Firle Beacon on the South Downs.

> We arrived on the Friday, and Constant who loved his drinks, found nothing but water. Then Saturday came and Maynard arrived, and with him was a full symphony of wonderful wines from Cambridge. He told us about the pedigree of each, and the ensuing evening was one of great gaiety and laughter. On Sunday it was back to water, and Constant went off to the pub, which was a long way away, saying he must go for a walk.

Subsequent meetings occurred over the next few months at Gordon Square, but, by now, Lydia had been prevailed upon to raid Keynes's cellar. (Aware of her husband's parsimony, she always confessed – 'Forgive me for an extra luxury but I did offer a bottle of port, as all the fellows were in a mood for it.') As the wine flowed, the project in hand took a frivolous turn. Ashton and Lambert proposed that one of the items should comprise Keynes and Lytton Strachey sitting on armchairs by a fire, 'repeating the dialogue of Tilton on free trade, Lytton's voice gradually disappearing'. Another idea put forward was a skit on the 'happy marriage' between Vita Sackville-West and Harold Nicolson. When, finally, they got down to serious work, Ashton, although nervous of Lopokova at first – 'I was just a beginner' – found her receptive and unalarming. She was not temperamental, although she could be forgetful, and, like many Russian dancers, was musically not very exact. But she did everything with such intensity and was so game, lively and funny, that he found her a joy to work with. She was over forty by this time, and not the most technically expert of dancers – she had always been too small, round and pert to make a classical ballerina – but she had great charm and in roles requiring verve, character and humour, she was unbeatable. Together, she and Ashton worked out poses for the first item on the programme, Shakespeare's *A Lover's Complaint*, to be presented in a series of tableaux by miming and recitation, Lopokova playing the Afflicted Fancy to Rylands' Poet. Although she had performed as an actress in America, many people, including John Gielgud, maintained that she was defeated by the English language, her Russian vowels and iambic delivery of Shakespeare proving too distracting. Isaiah Berlin, who saw Lopokova perform Nora in Ibsen's *The Doll's House*, found 'the whole thing acutely embarrassing'; but, in a less challenging speaking role such as this, she was most beguiling.

Follow Your Saint: The Passionate Pavane, with costumes by Billy Chappell and, as music, a Peter Warlock transcription of a John Dowland score, was highly reminiscent of the Pavanne in *Capriol Suite* – 'except much more exquisite and languorous,' said Chappell. 'It was a very romantic, glamorous, dreamy piece, arriving naturally out of *Capriol* and yet it was a development.' The dance was primarily a showcase for Lopokova who, as Ninette de Valois pointed out, had three expressive instruments at her command: her face, with its neat curly mouth and doll-wide eyes; her beautifully arched feet; and her delicate, shell-like hands, which had once caught Picasso's eye. (Among his sketches of Lydia on blotting paper are several studies of her hands, showing her crooking her fingers in an idiosyncratic way, which Ashton and Turner both imitated in the ballet.) Following her performance as the Lady in an excerpt from Milton's *Comus*, and after another Milton piece, an all-male debate between Satan and his Infernal Peers, Lopokova appeared with Ashton and Harold Turner in *Dances on a Scotch Theme*, with music by William Boyce – a lively balleticized Highland fling, intended as a tribute to Duncan Grant's portrait of her in a kilt – 'like a Scotch whirlwind so much activity and not only in the legs, everywhere' – painted during her season with Massine's troupe at Covent Garden. She was pleased with Ashton's efforts on her behalf. 'Fred brings me out as a ballerina,' she told Keynes. 'It looks most difficult for me, but it is the two men that work hard.' As it turned out, however, the choreographer did not do as well by Lopokova as she and Keynes might have hoped. Whereas her exuberant individuality had been paramount in helping Massine to define his vividly theatrical, demi-caractère style, she never really sparked off Ashton to the same extent; her importance to him was as a friend and mentor, rather than as a muse. In Arnold Haskell's view, Lopokova failed conspicuously in English ballet, 'for the good reason that the choreography assigned to her was insufficient in complexity to extend a dancer of such wide experience'. But Ashton was not entirely to blame. Of late, the ballerina's comedy, which had once been so light and subtle, had become laboured and over-coy; not only that, but, as de Valois pointed out, the kind of exhilarating impact she made by the projection of her personality was now a thing of the past. 'Today, we do not meet such individual performers as Lydia in the ballet . . . Personalities have become discreetly submerged, and are dedicated to the relationship of the part to the whole.'

Ten days after the first performance of the *Masque*, Ashton staged a new piece for Rambert, *A Florentine Picture*, with music by Corelli, inspired by an exhibition of Italian art that at the time was attracting a multitude of visitors to Burlington House. Rather than attempt to reconstruct any particular paintings, Ashton had conceived the ballet more in the spirit of Florentine art as a series of moving pictures, the dancers melting from one tableau to another – a device he had borrowed from Massine, described by Edwin Denby as an inexhaustible pictorial arranger. Marie Rambert was cast as a fifteenth-century Madonna – 'Mim loved her role so much, rocking the infant Jesus and pressing it to her breast' – and surrounding her was a group of Florentine angels, including Pearl Argyle, her fine-boned beauty the epitome of 'an exquisite Botticelli angel', as Ashton often said. The main focus of the exhibition was, in fact, Botticelli, whose *Birth of Venus* was among a dozen of his paintings on display, once again providing the stimulus for Ashton's movements and for Billy Chappell's costumes. The artist is a great poet of line, creating fantastic arabesques and slow and continuous dance-rhythms for his figures – a master for any choreographer. Even Balanchine, while maintaining that he did not get ideas from looking at paintings, acknowledged the genius of Botticelli, whose most famous painting Diaghilev had urged him to study when they had been in Florence. 'Diaghilev led me to the Uffizi Gallery, sat me in front of Botticelli's *La Primavera*, and said, "Look at it." Then he went off with Lifar and Kochno to lunch.' Hungry and irritated at the time, Balanchine nevertheless admitted that the image stayed with him for life. Equally stirred, Ashton reacted more obsessively, copying Botticelli's postures and trying to create what he called 'a fresh, spring-like morning of the world atmosphere'.

Now that I am older I rather despise this form of creation, but it is certainly an absorbing way of working, for it necessitates the study of a whole period of painting and of manners and this gives the plastic richness and diversity to the pattern of the dance.

A Florentine Picture was enjoyed by the public and the critics, but disliked by the dancers, who called it 'Flossie' and resented it as 'an endurance of standing and slowly moving and looking ethereal'. It did not, however, diminish their admiration for Ashton, for whom they had nothing but respect. One colleague after another praised the way he never lost his temper, and was always calm and perfectly charming. 'Fred was an *angel* to work for,' said Maude Lloyd. 'We never questioned anything, we did what he said and more. We were interpretative dancers who seemed to be able to understand what was needed and were very open to ideas. Maybe it was because we were so close. As contemporaries we were less in awe than we might have been with someone forty years older.' Like Nijinska, Ashton demanded high standards and exceptional flexibility of the body; if a dancer did not move luxuriantly enough, he would go over and pull her physically into a position. He could also be gently tactile when he was composing. Maude Lloyd remembered how 'he would hold one's hand and walk round chafing one's cuticle'. The process of creation was never tortuous for Ashton as it was for Antony Tudor, who was just beginning a parallel career as a choreographer in Rambert's company; ideas and steps flowed easily. 'Once he got going you couldn't stop him,' said Billy Chappell. 'He'd play the music and it would pour out of him.'

Although they still had a long way to go, the Rambert dancers were fine material on which to build, particularly Pearl Argyle and Maude Lloyd, regarded by their doting young colleagues as the Garbo and Dietrich of the company. There was also the stately Diana Gould; Prudence Hyman, vital and mischievous; Andrée Howard, charming and very musical; and Harold Turner, a fine virtuoso. After the success of their season at the Lyric, it seemed a waste to scatter this gifted band of dancers and allow their enthusiastic public to disperse. It was Ashton who persuaded Rambert to expand her school into a permanent production group, his almost immediate success as a choreographer giving her the necessary confidence to do so. They founded what they called the Ballet Club, based in the Mercury Theatre, but the opening season survived only through the invincible optimism of Ashley Dukes. The first night had been completely sold out, but numbers dropped considerably after that, and the theatre was almost empty until the policy was changed from presenting seasons of ballet to single, regular performances on Sundays, Thursdays and occasional matinées. Then, suddenly, the Ballet Club became fashionable. Dukes had made it an elegant and congenial place in which to be, with tapestry curtains, a remarkable collection of nine-teenth-century Romantic ballet prints, and a bar renowned for its fine wines (stocked from the sales he frequented as wine buyer for the Garrick Club). 'He enjoyed bringing the masculine arts of good writing and ap-preciation of good wine, good food and good talk into the more delicate world of ballet,' said Mary Clarke. By the end of 1932, membership had increased from 700 to 1,700, and although the theatre seated only 150 people, they comprised a lustrous rollcall of names from society and the arts – among them, Anthony Asquith, Lord Berners, Arthur Bliss, Lady Violet Bonham Carter, C. B. Cochran, Lady Colefax, Lady Diana Cooper, Douglas Cooper, Lady Cunard, Lady Juliet Duff, Jacob Epstein, Edwin Evans, Rupert Hart-Davis, J. M. Keynes, Lydia Lopokova, Oliver Messel and Viola Tree.

The Ballet Club opened on 16 February 1931 with two new works: *Le Boxing*, a 'sporting sketch' by Susan Salaman, and Ashton's *La Péri*, cre-ated as a vehicle to launch the twenty-year-old Alicia Markova in England. A child prodigy, known as the Baby Pavlova, Markova's career had been abruptly halted by the death of Diaghilev. The impresario had had great plans for her – she would have been his next prima ballerina – and for four years she had worked under his protective eye. He Russianized her name from Marks to Markova, put Stravinsky in charge of her musical education, allowed her to dance the Swan Queen at the age of fourteen, flanked by Danilova and de Valois, and had even promised her *Giselle*, in which she was to alternate with the legendary Spessivtzeva. In England, however, Markova's future looked bleak. She was not established as a ballerina, and, even if she had been, there were no major companies to nurture and challenge her. And with her strangely undeveloped body, she lacked the commercial appeal to be lured into revues or musical-comedies. After dancing with the foremost ballet company in the world, in half the capitals of Europe, Markova found herself back in Golders Green with her widowed mother and sisters, baking, dressmaking and thinking her life was over.

One day, a letter arrived from someone signing himself Fred Ashton, asking if she would consider appearing with him in a production of Dryden's *Marriage à la Mode*, for which he was providing the dances. They arranged to meet at Hammersmith Tube station, and, when Markova asked how she should identify him, Ashton replied, 'I'll know *you*.' He had seen her perform on many occasions during the Diaghilev season at the Princes Theatre, marvelling at her poise and serenity, her instinct for phrasing and her weightless descents. He was also attracted by her likeness to Pavlova, both dancers possessing the same fragility, rapidity, delicacy and lightness – the illusion of moving without preparation. Ashton was surprised by the alacrity with which Markova had accepted the Lyric engagement, but, after a grim year, she was only too happy to seize a chance to work again. It was a well-judged decision. *Marriage à la Mode* was pronounced Playfair's best production since *The Beggar's Opera*, and Ashton's 'delightful little fantasia upon the theme of young love' was considered by the critic of *Punch* to be a very fine, and not merely promising, piece of work.

By this time, Ashton had suggested to Marie Rambert that Markova be taken on at the Ballet Club as guest ballerina and almost immediately he started working with her on *La Péri*. The supernatural creature who, in Persian mythology, holds the flower of immortality, was one of Pavlova's roles, danced to the same Dukas score that Ashton had chosen, but the ballerina was not his only inspiration. Struck by the oriental contours of Markova's features, Ashton wanted to create a ballet with an Eastern flavour, and found the stimulus he was looking for at the International Exhibition of Persian Art currently on show at Burlington House. Decorative rather than representational, its effects achieved through abstract qualities of line, contour, colour, form, mass and movement, it was a tradition that, to Ashton, seemed to crave dance treatment. He took Markova with him to study the pictures and they came away planning exotic make-ups and devising strange, semi-oriental movements. To evoke the stiff, stylized groupings Ashton had seen at Burlington House, he borrowed an idea from Nijinska's *Les Noces*, architecturally massing a corps of six girls, attendants on the Peri, into abstract constructivist pyramids. He took the role of Iskender, the Prince, playing it forcefully to highlight the delicately reticent, otherworldly character of the Peri, modelled on Markova's own ethereality. It was clear to the ballerina that Ashton had made a profound study of her work, and knew both her strengths and her limitations – the latter of which she had learnt to disguise brilliantly. Edwin Denby, who has defined Markova's qualities more eloquently than anyone else, would later describe the way she could hide the weakness of a développé by throwing her leg up in a flash with a half-bent knee, and yet watching her, all you were aware of was the adagio motion immediately afterwards, the 'slow dreamy extension of the beautiful instep', the diminuendo effect of a port de bras finished a few counts later, the softening forward droop of her shoulders at the end of a phrase.

There is no other dancer whose movement is so perfectly centered . . . who diminishes the stress so precisely as it travels out-

ward along the arms and legs. It is this that gives her dancing figure its incomparable clarity, its delicacy and its repose. It is this,
too, that makes her dance rhythm so clear to the eye and so full of
variety.

Working with Markova was an education in itself, and Ashton benefited not only from what Denby called her 'superlative dance intelligence', but also from her experience. 'Fred was able to use me. I'd say, "I
don't think you can have that step." "Why not?" "Well, because Massine
or Balanchine has already done it." ' Theirs was a genuine collaboration
and they also began to work as a team outside Rambert's studio. Whenever Ashton was asked to provide a new ballet, he would suggest to the
management that it should be mounted on Markova. He chose her, for
example, for a run at the Regal cinema, Marble Arch, which was combining films with spectacular shows in the style of the Roxy in New York.
Sharing the bill with *Outward Bound*, a successful Warner Brothers film
starring Leslie Howard and Douglas Fairbanks Junior as ghosts on a ship
bound for Purgatory, Markova made her entrance descending from the
flies in a crescent moon, then danced a lyrical pas de deux with Billy
Chappell to the 'Dance of the Hours' music. 'Lumping about' in the
background was a corps of thirty-two girls from the Regal Ballet. 'We did
anything to make money,' said Chappell. 'We did the most humiliating
things because we couldn't live otherwise.' The stage management was a
shambles; Chappell and Markova were supposed to meet in the middle of
the stage, but were dazzled by spotlights and walked right past each
other. The show was so successful, however, that, as engagement after engagement followed at the Regal, Markova was able to repay Ashton the
debt she owed him by insisting that he be rehired as choreographer. In return, he provided her with a challenging repertory that she could call her
own. 'Every ballet he conceived gave me a chance of attempting to conquer a new world.' And whereas she had been criticized on occasion for
lacking in personality, Ashton displayed aspects of Markova that took
everyone by surprise, and nowhere more triumphantly than in his next
ballet.

The first time Ashton heard a recital of *Façade*, a novel entertainment
combining the poems of Edith Sitwell with the music of William Walton,
was probably at a repeat performance at the Chenil Galleries in Chelsea
in 1926, when Constant Lambert replaced the poet as the narrator. The
evening was a success, unlike the mishandled first public performance at
the Aeolian Hall three years earlier, when consternation over Edith's

barely audible declamation of her verse through a 'Sengerphone' had made the Sitwells notorious overnight. *Façade* uses the texture of words – assonance, dissonance, rhythm and repetition – to approximate the character of various dance measures; but it was Walton's music, rather than the poems themselves, that had enchanted Ashton, its wit and modernity seeming, he said, to fit the mood of his youth. 'I wanted to do it and I did do it.' Constant Lambert made the first approach to the composer and, although Walton was not a great admirer of classical ballet, Ashton's enthusiasm for the project won him round. They worked together adapting seven numbers for a ballet, but without any collaboration from Edith Sitwell, who had disassociated herself from the project, even insisting that her name should not appear on the programme. 'She didn't want anything to do with it but when it was a success she changed her mind.'

Ballet had once been a source of inspiration to all three Sitwells, its metaphorical impact and the fantasy and beauty of its imagery a major element in shaping their personal styles. Since the death of Diaghilev, however, Osbert's activity on the dance scene had diminished, and Edith, who had never been totally engaged by it in the first place, was heard to remark, 'To tell you the truth, my dear, ballet bores the pants off me.' Only Sacheverell showed a genuine interest in the emerging British ballet (considerably fuelled when he fell in love with Pearl Argyle), but, once Constant Lambert had persuaded Osbert that Ashton was worth his attention, the choreographer found himself in the enviable position of being a new Sitwell protégé. Osbert, the most dynamic member of the trio, was, as Ashton said, the reigning sovereign at that time. 'Sachie was just his brother.' Osbert was squirearchical, a poetic satirist of some distinction, polemicist and editor of the influential magazine *Art and Letters*; Sacheverell was languid, elegant, and uncertain, a natural connoisseur, pursuing a self-appointed role as a patron and impresario of the arts, but reluctant to involve himself in the japes, literary feuds and public rows that invigorated Edith and Osbert. By the time Ashton came to know the Sitwells, their reputation had been temporarily eclipsed by the gritty, proletarian intellectual climate of the early 1930s. The backlash, which began with the publication of Wyndham Lewis's *The Apes of God* satirizing the trio as sham aristocratic amateurs trading on their social position, grew more savage as the decade wore on. Quick to take umbrage, Edith was often on the defensive – as Ashton discovered to his cost, when he was invited by Osbert to stay at Renishaw, the Sitwell family seat, for a weekend.

A long, low, sombre crenellated house, lying in the mining district of Derbyshire, Renishaw Hall is fabled for its sinister, melancholy atmosphere, and the aggressive nature of its ghosts. One night, Ashton nervously ventured out of his room and headed for the bathroom along 'twenty miles' of winding passages. He was carrying a candle, as there was no electric light in the house, and saw a shimmeringly lit, white-gowned figure making towards him. It was Edith Sitwell, who quickly disappeared. When they met formally, he found her just as intimidating: immensely tall, with long oval features, an abnormally high forehead and no eyebrows. Throughout the weekend, she was 'simply dreadful' to him, he said, staring down her long hawkish nose at him and conspicuously snubbing him.

It was terrifying. When I first spoke to her she said, 'I only allow people to call me Edith if I've given them permission.' It was really alarming and got so uncomfortable that Osbert finally spoke to her. On the Monday when I was leaving, she said, 'I'd like to have a word with you.' She took me into Osbert's study – it was just like going before a headmistress – and said, 'Why wasn't I given a credit for *Façade*?' And I said, 'Well, I was told by Constant that you didn't want anything to do with it, but of *course* I would prefer to have your name added to the programme. It would add great lustre to the whole thing.' She seemed pleased and said, 'I'll give you a copy of my poems,' and gave me a dedicated copy. From then on we put in the programme: freely adapted to music originally written as a setting to poems by Edith Sitwell. That settled the matter. Then it was peace for ever more and we became great friends.

Ashton's *Façade* was not the first ballet to the Walton score; Gunther Hess had staged it for a German chamber dance group in the small town of Hagen in Westphalia, its scenario described at length in the *Dancing Times*. But, apart from a couple of details in common, Ashton's version was entirely his own – a perfect match for the mood, wit and rhythms of the poetry and music, preserving a Sitwellian sense of fantasy and fun, while, at the same time, adding a personal, totally new dimension. Beginning with a lively 'Scotch Rhapsody', the ballet is a humorous divertissement, satirizing various kinds of folk, social and theatrical dance. 'Jodelling Song', which played on the Alpine setting of the poem, is a piece of sheer Ashtonian nonsense, which presented Lydia Lopokova as a Milkmaid, with Ashton, Billy Chappell and Walter Gore as Mountaineers. When her suitors metamorphosed into an ingenious human cow, with udders made by the fingers of one, the swishing tail by the arm of another, Lopokova attacked her task with such a sense of commitment, said Ashton, that 'one almost felt that the milk really was beginning to squirt out between her fingers'. The 'Polka' came next and invariably stopped the show. The initial joke was that the audience should see Alicia Markova posed like the figure painted at the back of John Armstrong's cheery set and, as she prepared to dance, her skirt dropped off. To gasps from the audience, she stepped out of it and breezily performed in her bloomers: 'It was the first striptease in ballet.' 'The incongruity of a classically flawless Markova in a cheeky straw hat, removing her short skirt to dance a skittish rag polka, was in itself almost a discovery,' wrote Arnold Haskell. 'It *made* Alicia,' said Billy Chappell. 'It gave her a new lease of life from being just a classical dancer.' Although there are jokes galore throughout *Façade*, much of its humour derives naturally from the movements themselves, such as Markova's 'fall-over' step, which all the comedians used, or the insouciant double tour en l'air with which she ended her solo – a male tour de force that few subsequent performers have been able to repeat.

'Valse', for a quartet of dancers, parodied 'those groups of girls that there used to be at that time, the Hoffman Girls and all that sort of thing'* 'Popular Song', created for Walter Gore and Billy Chappell, is Ashton's version of a soft-shoe double act, inspired by the deadpan nonchalance of Jack Buchanan, the silliness of some of the steps, such as an upside-down scissoring of legs and saucy shimmy, made all the more amusing by the blankness of the performers' expressions. 'Tango Pasodoble' again featured Lopokova, this time as a débutante ingénue, all virginal white lace and blue ribbons, attempting to follow the lead of a rakish boulevardier, played by Ashton. His pomaded Dago was a blatant caricature of Massine, who had partnered Lopokova in their famous cancan in *Boutique Fantasque*, crimped, curled and dapper to an exaggerated degree, although, in fact, it was Lopokova who was criticized for overdoing things, playing for easy laughs and debasing the comedy.

Ashton knew that he had allowed Lopokova too much latitude as the Débutante, and, when *Façade* was taken into the repertory of the Ballet Club, he gave the role to Markova, whose instinctive sense of restraint gratifyingly redressed the balance. He was pleased, though, with the work as a whole. 'I'm very fond of *Façade* because I think it seems to me to be a complete entity in itself. It's successful in what I set out to do – which was a parody of dances at that time.' 'It's a piece of genius,' remarked Wendy Toye. 'The comedy is so light.' Indeed, it is the unforced effect of *Façade* – the throw-away ease of Markova's Polka; the laid-back drollness of the Popular Song – that accounts for much of its achieve-

---

* When it was redesigned in 1935 with the girls wearing pink tulle and long white gloves, it became more a pastiche of Balanchine's 1932 ballroom ballet, *Cotillion*.

ment. But such levity is elusive and, although *Façade* remains popular with audiences, its appearances are increasingly rare, and its humour too often vulgarized into a travesty of what Ashton intended.

In biographical terms, the Popular Song is the most interesting number in the ballet: a clever composite, mimicking the real-life characters of its two players – lazy, lackadaisical Chappell; happy-go-lucky Gore – as well as the double act Ashton and Chappell performed at fashionable London parties. At the same time, its obliquely homoerotic aspect – recalling the Sapphic couple in *Les Biches*, also identically dressed and drolly synchronized – shows a certain amount of wishful thinking on Ashton's part. By this time, he had become seriously infatuated with Walter Gore, on whom he had had his eye since they were pupils together at Massine's studio. 'Fred was absolutely dotty about Wally for quite a long while,' said Chappell. Although he gave the impression of being resolutely heterosexual, Gore's indifference only fanned Ashton's ardour – 'You can't leave this room until you've kissed me,' he said on one occasion – but Gore stood his ground. 'A terrible fight used to go on. Wally would never give in. I don't *think*. But he loved Fred, he doted on him. He loved him as a *person* and got on very well with him and it used to upset him really that he couldn't bring himself to go to bed with Fred.'

Since leaving Massine, after a promising start in revue, Gore's career had declined. He was, as he put it, 'getting nowhere fast', until Ashton intervened. The choreographer first cast him opposite Markova in *Marriage à la Mode*, in which he was highly praised, and was also responsible for persuading Marie Rambert to invite him to join her company. Ashton took charge of Gore from his first day at Ladbroke Grove, spotting the nervous new arrival at the door, taking him by the arm and marching him up to Rambert, watching him change and guiding him through the unfamiliar routine. But it did not take the dancer long to endear himself to his young colleagues, who were impressed by his theatrical experience and charmed by his puckish personality. 'Everybody loved Wally,' said Wendy Toye. 'All the girls were mad about him. And all the boys. He was the world's rogue – a *feller* – and in ballet that's rare. There was something so boyish about him. Like Woizikovsky, he was very male but still very graceful.'

Ashton's romantic interest in Gore was no secret in the company and it was much resented by Harold Turner, whose roles Gore began to learn. When the choreographer chose Gore for a new ballet in which Turner felt he would be more suited, he threw a chair at Ashton. Shortly afterwards, he announced that he was leaving Rambert to dance with the Vic-Wells company. It was Gore who took over his roles. 'Don't worry', remarked Chappell. 'Fred wouldn't use someone who couldn't do it and Wally could do it *all*.' Although not as accomplished a virtuoso as Turner, Gore was an exciting performer, a marvellous interpretative artist, with the authority on stage and quirky mannerisms of an English Massine. 'He was magnetic, with exceptional range,' Clement Crisp has written, 'and he was one of the most musical dancers I have known – to see him dance was to see the music.' 'Whenever you watched him perform you thought he was improvising,' said the dancer David Poole. 'You were never aware of the machine at work, it just happened. And when he walked it was with a swinging, jazzy cool. The kind of thing Twyla Tharp does now, breaking the classical mould, was all there with Wally.' Although Gore's brilliance at contemporary dance provided Ashton with the impetus he needed to take him in a new choreographic direction, his main importance as a creative catalyst was his position as an object of obsessive unfulfilled desire. Ashton's romantic yearnings for Gore marked the beginning of a lifelong pattern in which his own sufferings in love would be filtered into his work. With him, as with many artists, the poetry was in the pain, his ballets containing encoded subtexts of melancholy. But all this was in the future. At present, Ashton, as his friends point out, was a happy person and only too happy to be in love. Besides, he simply did not have time to brood.

Ashton did not use Gore in his next ballet, to Erik Satie's *Mercure*, the major new work at the Lyric, Hammersmith. He cast himself as the messenger of the gods – just as Massine had done in his 1924 version – and chose Billy Chappell to dance Apollo. (Gore later took over Ashton's role.) *Mercury* was intended mostly as a showcase for Karsavina, who created the part of Venus, giving Ashton a chance to deify this 'sacred figure' and arrange his choreography to show her off to greatest advantage. The original Massine version, with its Picasso designs, had been a provocative exercise in modernism: a 'cubist production' that enraged a group of Dadaists, who burst into Picasso's box on the first night and harangued him until the police were called. Ashton's ballet, by contrast, although described by one of the dancers as 'full of very interesting things we'd never done before', was yet another homage to Botticelli, with Maude Lloyd, Prudence Hyman and Elisabeth Schooling as the Three Graces, and Karsavina as Venus rising from a human sea of lifting, undulating arms and legs. 'It is the Adriatic,' Rambert told Agnes de Mille, who happened to wander into the studio; 'It is *Mercure* by Ashton.' 'And by God, it was the Adriatic.'

Once again, the new ballet divided the two leading dance critics. Haskell called it in many ways Ashton's finest achievement: witty, subtle and revealing a deep understanding of the spirit of French art. 'It is a perfect interpretation of Satie's music, flippant, laughing at itself, but often and in the least expected places, strangely beautiful.' Beaumont, on the other hand, who disliked the music in the first place, was positively tetchy with displeasure.

> Intended to be very modern, it only succeeded in being very dull. There was not so much dancing in it as poses and arm movements, which seemed to be designed to fill out the music rather than express it. Mr Ashton's choreography suffers from three weaknesses: 1) insufficient groundwork of pure dance interest, 2) over-elaboration of gesture and port de bras, which tends to be fussy and irritating, 3) an insatiable desire to be amusing in the strictly fashionable sense of the word. When he can overcome these drawbacks he will produce something of importance.

But Beaumont's hostility would not have cut that deeply with Ashton, whose colleagues had made him feel 'the apex of everything', 'the hero of Notting Hill'. These were halcyon days, remembered with nostalgia by them all. 'Fred and I often talked about how we used to laugh so much in those days,' said Maude Lloyd. 'We'd sit around the stove in the studio chatting, and always seemed to be giggling and fooling around. Nobody had any money, but it didn't seem to worry us, we had no fears and lived from day to day.' The dancers spent most of their time together, eating lunch at the Express Dairy in Notting Hill Gate where Ashton, because he was so thin, would insist on having a meat pie which cost one and threepence – a great extravagance to the others who would settle for a poached egg for sixpence and a cup of 'milk and a dash'. Ashton would often spend weekends with a coterie of Rambert girls staying either with Andrée Howard's parents, who took a cottage by the sea every summer, or with the choreographer Susan Salaman's family, who lived near Horsham in a beautiful old house in enormous grounds, full of paintings and interesting people. The Salamans, who were artists themselves, were friends of Augustus John and several actors, including Alec Guinness, who later married their daughter, Merula. The food was wonderful, with a great baron of beef for Sunday lunch. 'We used to stuff ourselves every weekend. Fred would always say, "Can I have a piece with the *fat* on it?" He was so thin and as he was partnering Karsavina in those days, he had to be quite strong.' Ashton spent a couple of weekends at Rambert's and Ashley Dukes's little cottage at Dymchurch in Kent. He loved the simple life – bathing, paddling, having picnics – and was always happy to amuse their two daughters who loved him and called him 'Fled'. 'He would dive with the children's tyre, part his hair under water, emerge with the tyre round his head, two fingers of his right hand pointing upwards, call out "St Luke" and disappear under water.'

Yet Ashton, as he himself said, was never 'stuck in just one world' and always kept a life for himself outside the ballet. He was still as thick with his circle of friends from the 1920s. For the past few years, Olivia Wyndham had been working as a society photographer, employing Barbara Ker-Seymer as her assistant and general dogsbody. Even though Olivia was baffled by the technical aspects, and too wild and aimless to be a serious professional, by exploiting her connections and relying on Barbara to cover for her, she was able to run quite a successful business. 'We used to go to parties and I would have to hold the camera because Olivia would get dead drunk. I'd help her into a car with the cameras and get her home and put her to bed and sit up all night developing her photographs.' Then, one day, Olivia announced that she was going to New York for a month and wanted Barbara to carry on the business in her absence. She never came back. She had fallen in love with a black American actress, Edna Thomas, 'a very calming, nice motherly woman', who helped her overcome her addiction to heroin and alcohol, and remained with her for the rest of her life. Alarmed by finding herself suddenly having to pose as a professional photographer, Barbara immediately called on her friends for support.

> Fred and Billy and everybody I could think of. They were delighted and brought their costumes and made up their faces, and I had a very good time because they were very good models. Then I said, 'But supposing I have to do a fashion photograph, I don't know how to.' And Fred said, 'Oh, I'll show you.' And he pulled down the black velvet curtain, draped it round himself and picked up a tatty old goatskin rug from the fireplace and draped it round his shoulders. And I said, 'You haven't got a hat, Fred.' So he picked up a paper bag that had had buns in it for tea and put it on his head. He looked very chic and glamorous. He really had great flair. I made it into a postcard and sent it to all my friends, captioned 'Famous Beauty Series No 3', and said, Now I'm a fashion photographer.

Although she never really took her work seriously, Barbara Ker-Seymer was to emerge as one of the foremost women photographers of her generation – 'a sharply radical portraitist of a new English avant-garde.' She opened her own studio in Bond Street, a thirty-shillings-per-week room above Asprey's, which was decorated by the painter John

Banting. 'It was a marvellous play-ground. Anybody at a loose end would come in, they knew the door was always open – I had to keep it open in case any customers appeared.' Although Ker-Seymer continued to perpetuate a spirit of frivolous amateurism in her studio, simply by photographing her friends – Ashton, Burra, Chappell, Nancy Cunard, Brian Howard, Julia Strachey – she became the chronicler of a London Bohemia which was soon to disintegrate. She was, as her friend and colleague Paul Tanqueray put it, 'this marvellous photographer who wasn't famous which she should have been'. Her portraits were stylish, witty and ahead of their time, rejecting all the artifices of studio photography – the retoucher's brush, the soft-focus lens – although she could flatter when she wanted to. Ashton was delighted with her first serious studies of him, posed, with heavy Vaseline-lidded eyes, in costume against a tapestry background.

That summer, he and the group went on holiday to Toulon in the South of France. Unlike Cassis, the neighbouring seaside town which had been discovered by Bloomsbury, Toulon had not yet become smart and was a sailors' port – an important part of its attraction. At Constant Lambert's suggestion, they stayed in the Hotel du Port et des Négociants situated on the waterfront. It was far from luxurious, a double room costing the equivalent of about four shillings per day, but it had attractive iron balconies, from which to watch the boats and the action on the Rade, and it was conveniently placed for the paddle-steamer to the beach. The English contingent made quite a party. In addition to Ashton, Barbara, Burra and Chappell, there was Sophie Fedorovitch and another designer friend, Beatrice (Bumble) Dawson; Irene Hodgkins (Hodge), a pretty painter and model, who had also been to Chelsea art school; Bunny Roger, the famous Oxford beauty; Marty Mann, an American woman journalist, who was Barbara's current lover; and the infamous Brian Howard, another Oxford celebrity. Although not part of the set – initially, at any rate – the writer Anthony Powell was already in Toulon when they arrived. He had intended to work hard on his new novel, but, in the event, undertook little more than a few pages of revision. 'That was because of the company found at the hotel.' Of great fascination to them all was the fact that Cocteau and his entourage were fellow guests, although they did not emerge until sundown, spending their days smoking opium in shuttered rooms. 'We kept thinking what a delicious smell there was on the stairs and boxes kept arriving covered with Chinese lettering but we were too innocent at first to know what was going on,' said Barbara. Having heard that she was a photographer, Cocteau came to see her one evening with a mask he had bought in the market and asked her to take a portrait of him with it. 'He was very good and easy. He loved being photographed.' At his suggestion, she went to his room the next day to photograph him smoking opium, but with no lights and no flash on her old-fashioned Baby Box camera, she knew she was wasting her time. 'They were all lying on the floor unconscious with the blinds drawn and a little Arab boy was making pipes. Cocteau had a very obstreperous monkey that kept trying to get inside my camera, and so I crept away. Nobody noticed.'

Burra also spent most of his time cloistered in the hotel. He had chosen a gloomy back bedroom overlooking the tramlines and worked throughout the day painting with the canvas on the back of a chair, or drawing on a large sheet of paper overhanging a small table. When he reappeared in the evening to meet his friends, he looked, in Powell's description, 'like a prisoner just brought out into the sunlight after years of confinement in a pitch-dark subterranean dungeon'. Everyone else went to the beach, catching the ferry after breakfast to a long empty crescent of white sand known as Les Sablettes. Sunbathing was the rage and taken very seriously. Keeping his distance from the others, Ashton used to sit propped against a wall reading *War and Peace*, determined to get to the end. Only Bunny Roger sought the shade of a beach umbrella. 'It was very crafty of him,' said Billy Chappell. 'Everybody else was black and he was *so* white he looked absolutely magical.' At night, when the Rade became a catwalk, the sight of Roger sashaying along to meet his friends would stop people dead in their tracks. 'Ed [Burra] loved that,' said Chappell. 'He loved anyone who made what he called "a stylish sensation".'

They would all dress up in the evenings and rendezvous at a café, either Raymond's Bar overlooking the Place de Puget in the town (its crumbling eighteenth-century fountain of entwined dolphins smothered in rampant greenery, the inspiration behind Ashton and Burra's first collaboration), or the Café de la Rade, the haunt of Cocteau and his lover, Jean Desbordes. Although the English group did not attempt to make friends with the French – 'They were a generation older than us' – they never kept their eyes off them. There was an amusing scene one night when Brian Howard, keen to parade a pretty German boy he had discovered in Munich in front of Cocteau, suddenly leapt to his feet.

> This glorious creature . . . [had] got himself up in what he thought were his best clothes, a most unbecoming, very cheap business suit, and his golden locks were smarmed down to his head . . . [Brian] forcibly dragged him off down the Rade. For the rest of his stay he was not allowed to be seen except covered from top to toe in a black leather bicycling suit, or full Tyrolean regalia. Very odd in Toulon, in the blazing Mediterranean sun!

Being continually in a gang proved too much on occasion and there were numerous squabbles – 'absolute screaming rows we had' – usually about something trivial like food.

We used to have supper in a brasserie where you could get a mace-doine of vegetables for something like sixpence, but Fred had much grander ideas. He believed in feeding himself correctly and would insist on having a steak so he didn't lose strength. Billy was very particular about our finances and would say it was nonsense and that he couldn't have it. Once when we were sitting in a café on the water front Fred gave Billy's chair a great kick and it *teetered* on the edge of the harbour wall. Everybody took sides over this, but Fred got his steak because the friend I was with wanted steak too. So he and she and I went off.

Ashton wasn't spoken to by the rest of the group for about two days and Chappell, who was sharing a double bed with him as usual, slept on the floor. Mostly, however, they had a very good time. Everyone was sailor-mad and wore striped T-shirts and bought death's-head tin rings from the sailor shops, wearing three on each hand,* or pressing them on to their belts as insignias. After dinner, they went to seedy little boîtes frequented by French sailors, using the girls as decoys. One night, Ashton danced with a beautiful sailor who made a pass at him, but he was too nervous to take things further. 'I didn't know whether I'd have to pay him or not.'

The ballet Ashton created immediately after his return to London had a nautical theme – it took place on the steam yacht 'Old Vic' off Cowes, and featured such incidents as lifebelt drills, deck flirtations, callisthenics and symptoms of mal de mer – but the potency of Toulon as an inspiration was still to come. *Regatta*, with hornpipey music by Gavin Gordon and designs by Billy Chappell, was disappointingly slight, but, as David Vaughan remarks, had a significance that went beyond the ballet itself: it was Ashton's first work for the Vic-Wells Ballet, his future company. By now, he was so much in demand as a choreographer that the pressures of work were making him 'very neurothic', as Lydia Lopokova put it. When he announced that he felt unable to carry out his next Camargo commitment, she wrote in a state of great indignation to Keynes.

*Burra himself wears one in his painting, *The Hand*.

A Bomb-shell. Fred under influence of Mim is behaving disgracefully, he refuses to do [Constant Lambert's] *Rio-Grande* for the first programme, suggested by him, as he has too much to do for Mim, but it is absolutely nonsense, he must do it. I feel I cannot speak on the telephone to Fred, I am disgusted yet I know he is a nice boy, & it is a matter of influence, the Jewess dominates him at present.

First, Ninette de Valois undertook to reason with him, promising to provide him with dancers and a studio, then Lopokova herself 'had it out' with Ashton, until he finally capitulated and agreed to go ahead with *Rio Grande* for double the money – £20, rather than £10. 'Fred and I left great friends & kissed as usual. We knew beforehand he couldn't say "No" to me, poor Fred.'

Ashton's immediate project was a twelve-minute piece for the Ballet Club based on Tennyson's poem *The Lady of Shalott*, using a selection of piano variations by Sibelius. The story is not an easy one to transfer to the stage, but Ashton caught the episodic, pictorial spirit of the poem by composing the work in short sections including a dance for the reapers and two young lovers, although he focused mainly on the falling of the curse. As a device for the mirror in which the Lady is condemned to watch the shadows of the world, Ashton used a gauze stretched across the front of the stage, with Pearl Argyle as the Lady on one side and Maude Lloyd as her Reflection on the other, their movements gracefully synchronized. Ashton appeared as Lancelot, not attempting to impersonate Tennyson's dazzling young god, but playing him as a crusader, who one observer said looked like St Joan, but Billy Chappell said looked 'simply Joan without the saint'. The *Dancing Times* was not at all impressed by Ashton's solo, performed with a spearlike lance, and compared it to 'the "Greek" section of the Solo Competition'. The ballet was ecstatically received, none the less, with even the difficult-to-please Cyril Beaumont conceding that *The Lady of Shalott* was 'quite the best ballet Mr Ashton has so far given us'. A snippet of film which exists of the final scene is evidence enough of an exceptional achievement, both choreographically and on the part of Pearl Argyle, who, as Haskell said, rose to heights in this ballet of which nobody had thought her capable. Her final solo is a dance of death, in which the movements of a drowning body – rolling and rippling in the water, buffeted by waves – are enacted with startling, unballetic abandon. There is a touch of Isadora in the Lady's supplicating arms and surrender to gravity, as well as of Pavlova, in her broken Dying Swan arms. But the main impact of the dance is its remarkable modernity, looking forward not only to the inelegant emotionalism of Kenneth MacMillan, but even to the bare-footed mood dramas of Mark Morris. It was, everyone agreed, a remarkable piece of dance theatre – 'most beautiful, touching', remarked Lopokova. And, as an example of 'pure Ashton', with little evidence of late-Diaghilev influence, it was also the first truly English romantic ballet.

A fortnight later, *Rio Grande* was premièred as planned in the first programme of Camargo's second season. It was probably Lydia Lopokova who drew Ashton's attention to the score, as it was one she had admired for some time. 'I have bought Rio Grande by Lambert, nobody else does,' she told Keynes in February 1930. 'Even the salesman called it "complex music" but it is not, only influenced by moderns, Stravinsky, de Falla . . . It has real beauty in spite of influences and for a young man [is] indeed a remarkable achievement.' Today, *Rio Grande*, a mere quarter of an hour of music for chorus and orchestra, is considered to be a masterpiece, equalling Milhaud's *La Creation du Monde* as a classic of transfigured jazz. It takes its title from a poem by Sacheverell Sitwell, the words of which supply a choral background, but the music transforms rather than serves the text, and the ballet made an even more radical departure. Originally called *A Day in a Southern Port*, its setting is not Sitwell's hushed Brazilian town, but a cosmopolitan dockside inhabited by tarts, sailors, stevedores, stokers and loiterers. It was Ashton's *Les Matelots*, a homage to the sailor cult and a fanciful re-creation of life in Toulon, with Lydia Lopokova as the Queen of the Port, Walter Gore as her Sailor, and Alicia Markova and Billy Chappell as an olive-skinned Creole Girl and Boy. Designed by Edward Burra, who based his backcloth on the Place de Puget's dolphin fountain, adding a buxom nude of his own, the ballet was, as Chappell said, 'like a Burra painting come to life'. It was too shocking for some. Cyril Beaumont protested that Ashton had reduced the poem to 'an orgy of sailors and their doxies, very suitable for the Folies-Bergère, but hardly calculated to raise the status of dancers in this country', while the critic of *The Times* was aghast at the choreographer's 'crude travesty' of Lambert's music.

Even Ashton had cold feet at the dress rehearsal, suggesting in apparent seriousness that they should use the reverse, unpainted side of the cloth, until Lopokova reminded him that this would be too much of an insult to the artist. Burra's backcloth was felt to be not only distractingly lewd, but too colourful and busy for a stage design – 'It always happens when you take a talented young man from outside the theatre,' remarked Keynes. Burra's costumes were just as uncompromising. Outraged by the sight of bare thighs, skin-tight bodices and what Lopokova described as a 'big flower sticking out in a little place', several mothers took their young daughters out of the ballet. But the first-night reception was more enthusiastic than anyone dared hope, and only two women in the audience walked out. 'The household stirred by RG will probably dance all night,' remarked Lopokova.

Again criticized for overacting, the ballerina, a soubrette not a siren, was badly miscast as the lead whore and Ashton knew it. Originally he had had Anna Ludmila in mind for the role, with Errol Addison to star opposite her, but hearing that Addison had refused the part, Ludmila disloyally followed suit and, at the last minute, Lopokova agreed to fill in. 'Fred says "I have done for you what you asked now you must do something for me." I cannot refuse although I resist.' Keynes was disappointed with her role – 'your obscenity is not redeemed by poetry, which is a great task to accomplish' – but the problem lay in Lopokova's interpretation, not in the choreography. Markova, by contrast, was highly praised for her subtle portrayal of a wanton young girl: 'Because of her perfect restraint [she] has caught the mood to perfection, sailed as near as vulgarity as possible.' Enlivened by a musical-comedy skit which she performed with the languid, beachcombing Billy Chappell, *Rio Grande* was considered to be 'very much Markova's ballet', but, in fact, Ashton had reserved the plum part for Walter Gore. As a virile, athletic, happy-go-lucky sailor, Gore was made for his role and embodied Lambert's jazzy, musing, technically brilliant piano solo in movements of thrilling complexity and exuberance. 'Fred put every single trick and twist and turn in it to show Wally off,' said Chappell.

There is a photograph of the *Rio Grande* collaborators on the opening night, with Lopokova in costume posing with Lambert, Burra and Ashton, his eyes cast down, his hand on the shoulder of Walter Gore, who is kneeling puckishly at his feet. His plaintive expression and proprietorial hand appears again in an autobiographical collage that Ashton made around this time on additional panels of his Pavlova screen. Among the many photographs of his dancers is a cameo-shaped portrait of Gore, behind which the choreographer has pasted himself nestling intimately close. Ashton was as smitten as ever by Gore, despite the fact that it was a romance which, as a colleague put it, 'dear Wally took not a great deal of notice of. He couldn't really have cared less.' But even if the dancer had felt inclined to reciprocate Ashton's feelings, they would have made an incompatible match. Their lives were so different: Ashton was very social and loved to stay up late; Gore was the opposite, withdrawn, moody and private. 'If there was a reception given for us, Walter would be missing,' said Markova. By now, Ashton had resigned himself to yearning – 'Once Fred got attached to someone he'd put up with not being allowed near them. As long as he could *see* them' – but, nevertheless, he could be unexpectedly predatory with other attractive quarry. Humphrey Spender, younger brother of Stephen Spender, the poet, was sitting on the top of an open bus, returning home after one of Barbara Ker-Seymer's parties, when a young man next to him asked him where he was going. 'Back home,' he answered, to which Ashton replied, 'I'm coming too.' Spender's flat in Upper Montague Street was often used, he said, by 'people who were mother-bound like Fred', and, once there, Ashton wasted no time in launching his attack. Spender was compliant enough – 'In those days I rather liked the idea of being what he and his friends described as "a cup of tea"' – and, although he found the experience not at all to his taste, it had an emboldening effect on Ashton. In August 1931, Barbara Ker-Seymer wrote delightedly to Burra, 'Freddie has grown a moustache!!! & has gone to make a final try for Walter Gore who is staying with Mim at Dimchurch [*sic*]. I wonder if the moustache will win where Freddie himself failed.' It did not. Billy Chappell, however, fared somewhat better. It was during the Manchester run of the musical-comedy *Helen* at the end of the year that Chappell and Gore, who were both employed as dancers, found themselves sharing a double bed in unheated digs. 'Our room was a refrigerator with an icy oilcloth on the floor and the only way we could keep warm was to wrap ourselves round each other.' The inevitable took place and, although Ashton never found out about his friends' betrayal – 'I wouldn't have dreamt of telling him and neither would Wally' – he had, in a way, already intuited it by insinuatingly coupling them together in *Façade*.

A few weeks later, Lydia Lopokova broke the news to Keynes that Alicia Markova had declared her love to Ashton, 'but Fred is not ready'. All the same, the revelation created a flurry of excitement, with Lydia summoning his mother to lunch to discuss this and other suitable matches. 'We decided that Alicia or Prudence wouldn't do for Fred's mistress, but Pearl or Andrée might.' Markova insists that, at the time, she was too intent on her career to take an emotional relationship seriously, and yet she admits that she found Ashton very attractive – handsome, elegant and beautifully mannered. 'I loved him but not in a physical way. I was more like another sister' – a remark greeted with some scepticism by Ashton's friends. 'She hoped she might get him in the end,' said Billy Chappell. Romantically, Ashton was in a state of limbo, achieving nothing with Gore and no longer feeling creatively stirred by him. Confiding in Lopokova, he confessed that 'he used to be very jealous and that gave him spice, now under wise influences he is less so, but his spice is gone, so what is a fellow to do?' As things turned out, Ashton was able to provide the answer for himself. Feeling that it might, after all, be time to contemplate a liaison with someone of the opposite sex, he and Barbara, promising to compare notes, each undertook to indulge in what amounted to a Tiresian experiment, an attempt at heterosexuality, whatever the outcome might be.

CHAPTER FIVE

TELL ENGLAND

1931–1935

Ashton's next Camargo commission, *The Lord of Burleigh*, was planned at one of Lydia Lopokova's Sunday lunches. Discussions about the plot, cast and choreography were mixed with the latest ballet intrigues and typical Lydia-isms, such as her announcement that a female monkey hides her genitals from unfamiliar males with one hand. 'Evans knew why Venus de Milo had that famous position,' she told Keynes. Edwin Evans had arranged a sequence of Mendelssohn pieces for the ballet, and devised a scenario which brought together various characters from Tennyson's poems, 'whom the poet has neglected to introduce to each other'. Some were paired, like the eponymous hero, disguised as a landscape painter, who woos a lowly village maiden, Katie Willows of 'The Brook'; others, like Mariana, were left unattached. Ashton was careful to bring out the music's contrasting juxtapositions of mood, his daringly halting choreography for Maude Lloyd as the melancholy Mariana, a striking antithesis to the blithe lightness of Alicia Markova who danced Katie Willows. But the ballet was not popular with the critics, most of whom complained that the slender narrative, with its echoes of *Giselle*, disappeared completely as the ballet went on, and that its length was out of all proportion to its dramatic interest. The 'endless' array of dances reminded Cyril Beaumont of a conjurer pulling out yard upon yard of paper ribbon, while Lopokova, who wanted the work to be cut in half, came backstage to see Ashton afterwards exclaiming, 'Oh Freddie, I *loved* the first three days.'

The dancers felt that Ashton was not inspired, 'giving us little bits and pieces like something he might do for a gala', but *The Lord of Burleigh* was exactly that: a pièce d'occasion, presented at Lady Wimborne's 'Midnight Ballet Party', a charity performance given at the Carlton Theatre before the Prince of Wales. Expected to produce something suitable for the event, Ashton could hardly have risked the impact of a ballet like *Rio*

Grande, which had shocked several society ladies, including Christabel Aberconway. The première was predominantly a society gathering, with a photocall held the day before at Wimborne House, débutantes serving as programme sellers on the night and dancing on stage after the performance until the early hours. Unlike Ashton's 1968 Edwardian ballet, *Enigma Variations*, a masterpiece of period atmosphere and dramatic nuance, *The Lord of Burleigh* was little more than a pleasant divertissement, a modish parade of George Sheringham's elegant costumes. Ashton himself made no great claims for the work. 'It was quite an interesting idea to bring all those Tennyson characters to life, but in those days I was really only interested in making beautiful dances and I did not go into it as deeply as I should have done.' Nevertheless, the ballet had its supporters, one of whom, Margot Asquith, told Ashton at the party how much she admired his work and asked him if there was anyone to whom she could introduce him. 'I said I'd like to meet Reinhardt, and she said, "No good to you at all." "Well, Cochran, then." And she said, "I'll bring him to see you next Sunday."'

Margot Asquith, widow of the prime minister, was already well known to Ashton as her son, Anthony (Puffin) Asquith, the film director, was a great devotee of the Ballet Club and had often brought her to performances there. 'She used to come because she adored her son. I once said to her, "Do you know any angels?" and she said, "Only my Puff."' Asquith was slender and attractive, with a gentle, humorous, dreamy nature, and had always been a good friend to the company. During the summer of 1931, when he made *Dance Pretty Lady*, a film about a ballet dancer working in the London music-halls of the Edwardian era, he cast several of the Rambert girls in the corps and chose Ashton to arrange the dance sequences. For the scene in which the heroine falls in love at first sight with an aristocratic young artist in the audience, Ashton created a charmingly lyrical *Les Sylphides* pastiche, and for an earlier sequence arranged a patriotic music-hall number. 'We were like Edwardian chorus girls, high-heeled boots, tight busts and showing lots of leg,' said Maude Lloyd.

Margot Asquith watched the filming, shot at night at the old Metropolitan music-hall in the Edgware Road, and, when she and Ashton met on subsequent occasions, they grew to like one another more and more. She would invite him to dinner at her pretty little house in Bedford Square, where, although money had been tight since her husband's death, she still entertained in style. 'I had the luck to be thrown into this different world. I fitted in. It was no effort – I was well brought up and had good manners.' Many people were dismayed by Lady Asquith's formidably mannish appearance and reputation for speaking her mind, but Ashton found her most winning and loved to re-enact her more notorious moments, such as her interruption mid-performance of a German diseuse who had announced, 'Now I'll sing you three songs by Kurt Weill with lyrics by Bertolt Brecht.' 'Oh no you won't,' Lady Asquith had retorted, 'we're all going down to supper.' Ashton described how he was once in a taxi with her, struggling to light a cigarette between her Mr Punch nose and chin, when suddenly she grabbed his gold Fulco di Verdura lighter and flung it out of the window, remarking, 'Matches are much better.' Yet, however rude and dictatorial she could be towards others, with Ashton she was always kind, going out of her way to promote him by bringing parties of friends to see his work. One Sunday night, true to her word, she arrived at the Ballet Club with Charles B. Cochran.

At the time, Cochran was working on a new Jerome Kern musical, *The Cat and the Fiddle*. It is a complicated love story, concerned mainly with an affair between a young American jazz composer (Peggy Wood) and a highbrow Romanian musician (Francis Lederer), who composes a new operetta blending both their styles. When Cochran met Ashton at the Mercury, he told him that they were having great difficulty with the operetta, a show-within-the-show, entitled *The Passionate Pilgrim*, and asked him if he would like to come to a rehearsal to try to make it work.

So of course I said yes, and went along the next day to the Palace Theatre. I had to do the scene with Alice Delysia who was a great star. She was being Pierrot. I arrived and there she was with her furs and pearls and she took one look at me as if to say, 'Cockie must have gone mad. Who *is* this chit of a boy?' But I started to work on it to the music and by degrees she became interested and took off her coat and then took off more things and she ended up on the floor. Then she said, 'Now we must stop because I have a performance tonight, but come up to my room and we'll have some champagne.' And so then I knew I'd won.

At the dress rehearsal, Cochran's manager reminded Ashton that they had not yet discussed a fee and asked him how much he would like. Accustomed to receiving a pound per minute for his ballets from Rambert, but feeling that Cochran could afford a good deal more – 'After all, I'd saved the bloody show' – Ashton asked if £15 would be all right. The man said he would let him know and Ashton watched as he went up to the impresario sitting in the front row of the stalls with Jerome Kern and saw them all roar with laughter. 'I was in a panic thinking I'd asked far too much, but he came back and told me, "Mr Cochran says not fifteen but fifty."' After a try-out in Manchester, *The Cat and the Fiddle* opened at the Palace Theatre, London, on 4 March 1932, and was greeted by the critics as an enchanting show that ended all too soon. Alice Delysia was effusively praised for the delicacy of her singing and miming, one reviewer calling her 'truly superb'. At the end of the run, as a token acknowledging Ashton's contribution to her success, she sent him her Norman Hartnell pierrot costume, which he later wore to fancy-dress parties.

Clearly pleased with the choreographer's work, Cochran immediately engaged him to stage dances for his next production, *Magic Nights*, the new late-night 'Song and Dance Show' in the Grill Room of the Trocadero. A Trocadero cabaret comprised a miniature revue of half a dozen musical numbers, interspersed with acrobats and dancing, and could run for as long as a year. Ashton compared it to a prison sentence, because, as a performer, he had to stay until the show ended every night. Abuzz with adrenalin from the rousing finale, and too late for the last bus, he would often walk through the deserted streets at one or two in the morning with Billy Chappell, also engaged that season as a Trocadero dancer, to Chappell's digs in Redcliffe Square. 'Fred would say, "Now walk to Earls Court with me," and still nattering we'd get there and then walk back again to Redcliffe Square. He'd always want to wake up my sister, Honor, to make a pot of tea for him and read the leaves in his cup.'

Among Ashton's contributions to *Magic Nights* was a tango for Pearl Argyle and a rumba for Eve, the dancer and contortionist. Later in the run, he appeared with Eve in a duet called *The Bell Boys Stampede*, in which, identically dressed, they imitated the black bellhop boys from *Dover Street to Dixie*. He also choreographed a beguiling, if incongruously classical number called *An 1805 Impression* for Pearl Argyle cast as Madame Récamier (he took the role of her Suitor).* Appearing as a chorus of Friends were six of Mr Cochran's Young Ladies, grouped like bonneted Botticelli Graces, with harmoniously aligned arms and interlaced fingers. Few of the chorus girls and leading ladies with whom Ashton worked were trained dancers, but they were elegant and attractive, and he soon learnt to tailor his choreography to suit their abilities. 'Some of them were very beautiful and could put over a number but when it came to doing steps they had no idea *what* to do.' His experience in commercial theatre proved a valuable discipline – just as it had been for Balanchine and Massine, who had both worked for Cochran in the 1930s – forcing him to meet a deadline, to rework a number on the spot during an orchestra rehearsal, and to hold a restless audience's attention. 'You

---

An 1805 Impression went into the repertory the following year under the title *Récamier*, with Antony Tudor taking over from Ashton.

had to be adaptable, and you had to deliver the goods.' Marie Rambert worried that Ashton's taste would be corrupted by working in revue, but he insisted otherwise. And, in the meantime, he would like to eat.

Feeling undervalued by Rambert as a dancer, Ashton complained to Lydia Lopokova that he had nothing in which to appear except *Façade*. 'He would like to do *Gisel* [*sic*] I couldn't allow it, but Ninette and I asked him to prepare a good part for himself in the new ballet. Poor Fred, he does not want to see his defects & he wants to be "a star". However, after long silence & tea & polite conversation, he said "after the battle is lost I turn my mind to something fresh".' Which he did. Ashton's next project – effectively an inter-racial marriage between classical ballet and black jazz dancing – was a genre that no one on either side of the Atlantic had attempted before.

The cult of the black performer in Europe had begun in 1926 with the arrival of the *Blackbirds* company, whose bittersweet jazz rhythms influenced a generation of English composers, including Constant Lambert, the best of whose work owed a profound debt to the group. *Blackbirds* parties became de rigueur and it was suddenly thought daringly chic to invite black people to your party. Barbara Ker-Seymer described an occasion when Olivia Wyndham 'set on' Nancy Cunard's black lover and made him dance with her. 'Nancy came up and drew her long red nails down Olivia's face.'

In 1930s London, one man epitomized New York's Harlem Renaissance, bringing writhing, figure-of-eight hip movements, elastic jazz rhythms and intricate tap techniques to the West End stage. As a teenager, Buddy Bradley, among the best young dancers in Harlem, had worked his way up from being an elevator boy by day and a chorus boy by night, to running the most successful show-dance studio in New York. He was a born teacher and the stars turned up in force – Mae West, Pat Rooney, Jack Donahue, Lucille Ball, Eleanor Powell, Paul Draper, Clifton Webb, Fred Astaire and his sister, Adele, who so loved what she called Bradley's 'dirty steps' that, when she was given a solo dance in a Ziegfeld show, she went to Bradley, rather than to her brother, for a routine. Throughout the late 1920s and early 1930s, although he was seldom credited, Bradley created dance routines for many of the Broadway musicals, but never choreographed a 'white' show as long as he remained in the United States. Well paid, but well known only within showbusiness circles, he received no public recognition until, in 1933, Cochran hired him to choreograph the London production of *Evergreen* – the first time a black person had been in charge of a white show and had received credit in the programme. He stayed on in London, working for Cochran, and Ashton met him during the making of *Magic Nights*, for which Bradley had staged the tap finale, a routine that Ashton, who was among the performers, admitted having to fake. Aware that Bradley had a lot to offer him and beginning to contemplate the idea of a collaboration, Ashton invited him to the Ballet Club one Sunday night to show Bradley the kind of work he was doing. Bradley liked what he saw and the two men agreed to try to blend their styles.

Bradley was, by now, running a dancing school in the West End and the record permanently on the turntable was 'Six Bells Stampede' by Spike Hughes, a double-bass player who had recently been signed up by Decca. Bradley played the piece to Ashton, who was impressed enough to suggest that they ask Hughes to write a ballet for the next Camargo programme, persuading the apprehensive young composer that 'something very like A New Art Form' would result from the three-way match. Conferences took place late at night in Bradley's small flat off Leicester Square. The Ashton–Bradley side of the partnership worked smoothly, but Hughes felt somewhat out of his depth, his composing, until now, having been a 'largely last-minute affair thought up and completed for the deadline demanded by the next Decca recording session'. Not only had Hughes not given the music for the ballet any serious thought, he had failed to write a single note. In desperation, he produced five pieces which had already been recorded, consisting of the whole of 'Six Bells Stampede', plus various other short pieces and the finale from his 'Harlem Symphony'. This seemed to satisfy his collaborators, who had wanted an elegiac opening and an upbeat ending for their story, a slight affair concerning the departure of a young black man from his two sweethearts, who soon find solace in the company of a couple of sailors just landed on the island. The ballet's tropical setting, 'somewhere off the coast of Florida', led Constant Lambert to come up with the title *Coral Gables*, or, alternatively, *Pink Palms*; the Firbankian *Sorrow in Sunlight* was another idea put forward, until finally *High Yellow* met everyone's approval. Slang to describe someone who is of mixed race, it was the obvious choice for a cross-breed of black and white dance styles.*

The question of who should design the ballet was decided by Maynard Keynes. Originally Ashton had Jacob Epstein in mind, but was persuaded to use Vanessa Bell, then at the height of her reputation and

---

*Hughes credits the idea to a friend of his, but, in fact, the title had already been used for a number Bradley created for Clifton Webb in *The Little Show*. Webb played a 'high-yaller' pimp and Bradley devised the whole scene for him, using Earl Tucker's Snake Hips dance. It caused a sensation.

renowned for her sensuous, exuberant style. Her decor was a standard tropical beach scene, with palm trees and sailing-boats on the sea, painted 'as bright as possible with every sort of colour', she told Roger Fry. She and Ashton got to know each other quite well during this period as she also painted his portrait – '*Lost*, alas' – and although, at first, he found her a mixture of 'kind and terrifying', he soon attuned himself to her sharp, mocking humour. Billy Chappell, who also worked with Vanessa Bell designing the costumes for *High Yellow*, was less equivocal: 'She was a darling angel. A terribly sweet person – much nicer to us than Virginia.'

The ballet opens in a blaze of sunlight with a domestic scene of 'Mammy' busy at the washtub as her son Bambu prepares to take his leave and bids his two lovers (Alicia Markova and Doris Sonne) farewell. Everyone applauded when Markova, who had been privately coached in jazz dancing for six weeks by Buddy Bradley, came on looking like Carmen Miranda. 'From then on,' wrote Cyril Beaumont, 'it was what is known in the current vernacular as "snaky hips" repeated ad nauseam.' Opinion varied as to whether anyone else in the ballet brought off the new style as successfully as Markova. Several reviewers remained uneasy at seeing highly trained dancers consciously impersonating black show dancers: 'naturally they lack something of the simplicity, the large movement and the abandon of the true negro.' Beaumont was critical of Ashton as Bambu, the two-timing son, who he said 'remained a white man despite his make-up, and was far too self-conscious and absorbed with the fascinations of "snaky hips" to be convincing'. The *New Statesman and Nation*, on the other hand, pronounced Bambu 'superb'. Walter Gore excelled as one of the sailors, dancing with easy, fluent movements, as did the young soloist, Doris Sonne. 'I have never seen a European capture the very essence of the true jazz spirit so completely.' As a choreographic collaboration, Bradley's hand was more conspicuous than Ashton's, whose influence was apparent mostly in the ballet's harmonious groupings. 'For once Ashton has kept his sophistication in the background – unfortunately perhaps, for I find that the material has not been sufficiently balletised,' wrote Arnold Haskell.

Despite being conceived as a novel experiment, *High Yellow* caused more of a stir than Ashton intended, shocking Lady Cunard and upsetting Olga Spessivtzeva, who did not want it to appear on the same programme as her 'beloved *Swan Lake*'. The *Dancing Times* was unpleasantly patronizing about what it dubbed a 'darkey' ballet, saying it belonged in a revue and not on a Camargo programme. 'It was a matter of absolute impossibility to teach a company of ballet dancers the necessary nigger steps and movements in the sort of time at the disposal of the producers.' But although its impact was short-lived (with only a few sub-sequent performances), *High Yellow* proved a valuable touchstone as far as Ashton was concerned, a practice run in a new dance vernacular that he would go on to 'balleticise' with much greater finesse.

A fortnight after its première, on a warm mid-June day in 1932, he (and most of the cast) attended the wedding of his sister, Edith, as bonny and petite in her clingy cream-satin gown as any of the dancers there. Ashton gave her away – 'They looked like fifteen-year-olds,' said Maude Lloyd – to Trevor Richards, then working as a bus driver with London General County Services. Although the bridegroom came from a good family (his elder brother was a QC), Georgie Ashton had hoped for a bet-ter match for Edith, perhaps with one of the junior diplomats with whom she worked as a secretary. For a time, she had been besotted with a col-league in the department, Frank Roberts, who had taken her to a Chali-apin performance and whom she had taken to watch her brother dance, but Roberts was sent abroad and they did not see each other again. Des-perate to get away, to escape from under her mother's oppressive eye, she rushed into a marriage with Trevor Richards, a handsome, gentle young man, with a rather weak nature and a tendency to drink too much. They opened a club together, 'Steve's', off Sloane Square (so-called because that was Edith's nickname at the time), but even though she regularly played the piano in the evenings, Ashton rarely went there, it was not his sort of place. He adored Edith, and relied on her affection and support: 'At every important moment of Fred's life Edith was there. He couldn't have a first night without her. She was his lucky charm.' Socially, however, they led relatively separate lives during this period, Ashton perhaps believing that his set was too fast to accommodate a little sister. His 1930s milieu was one in which, as the Cole Porter song had it, 'Anything Goes'. At the Al-bert Hall's annual Chelsea Arts Club Ball, everyone wore outrageous cos-tumes (Billy Chappell and Barbara Ker-Seymer made a point of dressing identically), and 'things could get very louche' behind the drawn curtains of Bunny Roger's box on the first tier. 'There'd be an amazed waitress standing at the back.' Ashton himself was always impeccably behaved, a wry observer rather than a participant at any orgiastic scene. Spotting a minor playwright performing fellatio on a major playwright in a corner of a typical theatrical party, Ashton quipped to Bunny Roger, 'Look! There's K— trying to suck some talent out of E— .'

With three new projects to complete before Christmas, Ashton was much in demand, dividing his time between the Ballet Club, the Camargo Society and the commercial theatre. In October, his latest piece for Rambert, *Foyer de danse*, to Lord Berners' score 'Luna Park', was premièred at the Mercury Theatre to great acclaim. Set in the practice room of a large opera house, it is a ballet about ballet, taking its inspiration from Degas, whose paintings are re-created by a group of coryphées in long white ballet-dresses preparing for class, arranging one another's hair, kneeling to tie a shoe-ribbon, stretching at the barre. The ballet was also a homage to Nijinska, a stylized re-creation of her classes in Paris, with their extravagant use of épaulement accompanying even the simplest barre exercises, and with wonderfully choreographed enchaînements. Ashton danced the Maestro, fussy and dapper in a yellow waistcoat, blue tailcoat and trousers, bustling around, prodding his pupils with his stick – a composite caricature of Cecchetti and Massine, which also flaunted his own fleet footwork in a bouncy display of sissonnes and entrechats. Markova was cast as a Cléo de Mérode-style étoile of the Opera, glinting with diamonds and so obsessed with her reflection that, to the delight of the audience, she nonchalantly performed the highly technical steps with her mind only half-focused, until a cloaked admirer arrived to lure her away from class, flirting with a few corps girls in the process. The short film that exists of *Foyer de danse* is soundless and incomplete, but, even so, it is clear that the ballet was a delight. It is lively, amusing and evocative, not only of its period, but of the backstage world of ballet at any time, capturing the strange, swans-out-of-water gracelessness of dancers waiting to perform. Horace Horsnell called it 'the dearest little pastiche imaginable . . . The bevy of coryphées – period peaches every one, and Degas models to the life.'

Ashton recycled the same idea in *A Kiss in Spring*, the new Stoll production at the Alhambra, allowing the audience to glimpse a cluster of dancers standing in the wings. His ballet, which starred Markova and Harold Turner – 'the joy and idols of the evening' – took place in the final scene and was said by more than one leading London paper to have saved a dismal show. His next commercial venture, *Ballyhoo* with Hermione Baddeley, was another team effort with Buddy Bradley, and had great style: Pearl Argyle, 'the prima ballerina of *Ballyhoo*', looked wonderful in her black and white piano-key choker; the *Observer*'s comment that the revue was 'Smart stuff, indeed' was said mostly in tribute to Ashton's inventive touch.

The chic of 1930s society, pronounced by *Vogue* as the most glamorous decade of the century, was reflected in his most popular work for Rambert, *Les Masques*: a flawless little piece, urbane, witty and intrinsically of its time. It had the sophistication of a late-Diaghilev collaboration and Ashton used an existing score, Poulenc's 'Trio for Oboe, Bassoon and Piano', and designs by Sophie Fedorovitch. Described by the dancer Elisabeth Schooling as having the atmosphere of a Chelsea Arts Club Ball – 'where people were in sort of disguise and nobody ended up with whom they arrived' – *Les Masques* drew on the lifestyle of Ashton's world, sublimating its social and sexual manners into an oblique, decorous episode charged with intrigue and innuendo. The ballet told of a Personage (Ashton) who goes to a masked ball with his Lady Friend (Alicia Markova), but finds himself irresistibly drawn to a woman (Pearl Argyle), who, at the final unmasking, turns out to be his wife. Hinted at by his black lips and tightly curled black hair, was the fact that the lover with whom Argyle arrived (Walter Gore) was black. Gore's jazzy, sinuous movements suggested to David Vaughan Edith Sitwell's line so redolent of the 1930s, 'allegro Negro cocktail-shaker', while the rest of the choreography throughout the ballet was unusually slinky and subdued, with gestures sharply stylized and hands held flat. Pearl Argyle's languorous dancing was contrasted with the flashier style of Markova, whose beautiful insteps were displayed in a motif of a spiky, point-heel walk. 'Once again the dimensions of the Mercury forced Ashton into understatement. There was not a wasted movement in *Les Masques*.' A dance for three girls in grey consisted mostly of walking and elegant swooping movements; their function being to provide a kind of chorus miming a commentary behind their fans on the interplay of emotions on stage (crescendoing into stylized melodrama at one point, when Ashton slaps Markova's face three times after remonstrating with her for behaving indelicately with Gore).

The inspiration behind the neoclassical steps and the general atmosphere of veiled wantonness was Nijinska's *Les Biches*, which also used a Poulenc score. Both were ballets in which, as the composer said of *Biches*, you may see nothing at all, or into which you may read the worst. However, Ashton was, by now, so in command of his art that Nijinska's influence, while still clearly discernible, had been alchemized into a style that was unquestionably his own. This was his first ballet to make a feature of what subsequently came to be known as the Fred Step. Borrowed from Pavlova's famous *Gavotte*, it refers to a short sequence of simple steps,* given endless variations of tempo and style in later works, by which time it had taken on a talismanic significance for him. (Always superstitious, he believed that a ballet made without it 'would never arrive'.) In *Les Masques*, two Young Girls in black link arms with Ashton and perform a stately Fred Step, their white-gloved hands bent at sharp art-deco angles from the elbows.

---

*The Fred Step (in David Vaughan's definition) consists of posé en arabesque, coupé dessous, small développé à la seconde, pas de bourrée dessous, pas de chat.

Made by the couturier Matilda Etches, with accessories by Beatrice Dawson, the ballet's costumes were exquisite. Pearl Argyle wore black and white accordion pleating; Markova, a white frothy tiered ball-gown, with a train that she could gather up while dancing. She carried a transparent mica muff and visible through her hat was a white gardenia in her hair. Fedorovitch's cinematic black and white set was also a work of art, suggesting, with its two curtained opera boxes on each side of the stage, a diminutive version of an Arts Club Ball. She made a central feature of the Mercury's flight of steps at the back of the stage, concealing its banisters with silver foil and adding a column which, like the curved boxes, was made from white-painted corrugated iron.

Les Masques was a miniature masterpiece, an inspired fusion of scenery, steps and music. Poulenc was enchanted when he saw it, and he and Ashton became 'sort of friends'. (In a later production, he came to play the piano at a rehearsal.)* The ballet has not survived, however, and a recent attempt by American dance scholars to reconstruct it proved unsatisfactory. It belongs fundamentally to its decade, dependent for its effect on dancers with an intuitive sense of period: 'Fred never explained anything to us, we *felt* what he wanted.' Even during his lifetime, Ashton would not consider the idea of reviving it. 'You couldn't do it now, it wouldn't work. You couldn't achieve that elegance today. We were a perfect cast – Markova, Wally Gore, Pearl Argyle with her beauty . . . We were just acting being ourselves.'

A month later, Ashton was engaged as choreographer on the new André Charlot revue, *How D'You Do*, starring Douglas Byng and Frances Day. Casting Walter Gore as her partner, he used Day, dressed like a Valkyrie, in a medieval ballet, 'The Legend of Berenice', a role for which she was clearly unsuited. As the *Dancing Times* commented, he was clearly trying to make bricks without straw. Not only was Day's dancing ability limited, the image she cultivated was incongruously lighthearted, flirtatious and plaintively coy. As far as Ashton was concerned, the show was memorable only for the fact that it brought to his notice a fetching natural blonde, Iris March, who appeared in a saucy little number called 'The Lady in the Bath'.

One Sunday night at the end of May, Lydia Lopokova wrote to Keynes about the lunch she had had that day with Ninette de Valois, Constant Lambert and his wife, Florence.

---

*Poulenc wanted Ashton to use his ballet score *Les Animaux modèles*. 'I liked the music but disliked the idea.'

F was invited also, but he was away, & the gossip is that he is experiencing with a woman. Of course I asked who? No answer except that F's taste or liking would be something of Lady Cunard's type or a chorus girl, he would be bored by good girls.

The gossip was well founded. It had begun with a conversation between Ashton and Barbara Ker-Seymer earlier that year. 'I remember saying to Fred, "I really think it's time you had an affair with a woman," and he said, "Well, I think it's high time you had an affair with a man." So one night we made a pact.' When it came to finding a suitable candidate, Ashton was spoilt for choice.

In the commercial theatre all the girls were very alluring, charming, wanting to . . . And it was one of Mr Cochran's Young Ladies who first seduced me. She was frightfully attractive and I said to her, 'Well I'd like to try.' And she said, 'I'll only try with you on one condition, if you promise me that I'm the first.' 'What are you worrying about,' I said. 'You'll *see* whether I'm the first one or not.'

When Barbara rang Ashton the next morning to ask him how it had gone, he claimed that it had been 'terrible' and that he would never do it again. 'He asked me how I'd got on and I said, "Wonderful, I'm never going back." But actually, Fred's was a lovely girl and after that, having broken the ice, he was able to relax.' Looking back years later, Ashton could hardly recall the experience, although he denied that it had been unpleasant for him in any way. 'It was once or twice with the chorus girl and that was that. She wasn't trying to make a great affair of it and nor was I.'

The identity of the girl in question is not certain. Billy Chappell claimed that it was Aimée Gillespie, whom Ashton had worked with several times and who took over Pearl Argyle's role in the revue, *Magic Nights*. Barbara Ker-Seymer said, with equal conviction, that it was Iris March. Certainly, it was Iris with whom Ashton liked to be seen at that time: 'He seemed to want the world to know that he had a lady lover,' she said. He brought her home for supper one evening to meet his mother in their small flat in Clarges Street, Mayfair. He took her to stay with Cecil Beaton in Wiltshire, where they went over to see David Herbert at Wilton. On another occasion, Buster Tonge, a balding wealthy fan of Ashton's, sent his car and chauffeur to collect them for a weekend at Branches, his family seat near Newmarket. The weather was glorious, and they spent their two days sunbathing and posing for Tonge's camera, Iris provocatively screening herself behind a giant gunnera leaf, Ashton imitating Nijinsky in *L'Après-midi d'un faune*, posing sideways in striped Edwardian bathing trunks, a scarf and a toque. 'Fred was always such fun,' said Iris, who found him physically attractive too, 'very racé, with a sort of grace and a beauty without being handsome'. She sensed that at the time he was fighting his tendency towards homosexuality. 'Fred was at a stage when his sexuality could have gone either way – although as far as I know, there was nobody male in his life. He wasn't *fretting* about anyone. But if I'd thought about it (I was so young, only nineteen or something), I don't think that I was convinced that he was a practising homosexual.' She was at what she called 'the butterfly stage' of her life, and regarded Ashton as just one of several young suitors who would take her out to dinner and take her dancing. 'We'd flirt and laugh together, get silly and have a few kisses – things like that. We were good friends but I never felt that he was in love with me or anything.'

In July, the choreographer again teamed up with Buddy Bradley on *After Dark*, a slick satirical revue at the Vaudeville Theatre, which starred Nelson Keys. The two ballets Ashton produced were pronounced 'pretentious rather than entertaining' by the *Sunday Times*, but the importance of *After Dark* was not the show itself, but its opening-night party. It was at the rented Chelsea house of the New York art dealer, Kirk Askew, and his wife, Constance – celebrated saloniers on both sides of the Atlantic – that Lincoln Kirstein made 'a headlong onslaught' on George Balanchine about his dreams of establishing an American ballet academy and company. And it was here that Ashton first encountered the Kansas City-born composer and critic, Virgil Thomson, who was responsible for launching him in New York.

Throughout the 1920s, Thomson had been living in Paris, sending back to the United States sonatas, songs, quartets and symphonies, and, most important of all, an opera to a libretto by his friend Gertrude Stein, *Four Saints in Three Acts*. A small, vivacious man, with a pale face, clipped voice and 'a will power that became evident within thirty seconds of meeting him', Thomson spotted in Ashton a potential collaborator and spent much of the evening proselytizing about *Four Saints*. Since 1927, when he completed the opera, he had been performing it in its entirety for his friends in a succession of New York drawing rooms, banging away at a piano and taking all the parts himself, singing arias, recitatives, choruses and stage directions in his thin, piercing tenor voice – a performance lasting close to two hours. Ashton, however, was spared the full treatment; Thomson merely 'talked about the thing' with great enthusiasm and encouraged him to respond. 'I said I think you

should do this and do the other – just casually,' but whatever Ashton suggested convinced Thomson that he was completely in tune with what he
was trying to achieve. 'Fred and I understood each other thoroughly
about the choreographic direction of opera, which was a matter very
much on my mind in those days.' Ashton's South American upbringing
was preparation enough for an understanding of the Catholic, baroque,
ecstatic background of Stein's opera (based on her two favourite Spanish
saints, St Teresa of Avila and St Ignatius Loyola). Thomson realized this
and, even though he had never seen an Ashton ballet, he found himself
asking the choreographer, 'Can you imagine staging my opera?' 'Oh yes,
and with delight,' was Ashton's reply.

Over the next few months, their friendship flourished, Thomson attributing to Ashton 'a stunning intellect' and lots of imagination. They
saw each other in Paris in the late summer when Ashton was passing
through with Barbara Ker-Seymer en route to the South of France.
Thomson took him to dinner with his neighbour, the Scottish soprano
Mary Garden, and they spent a long afternoon together, during which
Thomson took Ashton to see a men's clothing store, Le Fashionable,
where the shop-window mannequins, dressed in outlandishly cut, snazzy
tweed suits, were all modelled on contemporary celebrities such as
Cocteau and Lifar. The following day, Ashton set off for the Riviera with
Barbara and her new suitor, Humphrey Pease, who was in the process of
trying to persuade her to marry him (which, eventually, she did). Undeterred by the idea that he might be intruding – even to the point of camping on the floor of their sleeper – Ashton had invited himself along. 'Fred
was at a loose end, so he came too. He knew that once he got there he'd
find plenty of people he knew, which he did.' All three stayed in a noisy
little commercial hotel near the bus station in Antibes and spent their
days at Eden Roc. 'There was no beach or anything and the sea was
filthy – full of French letters and dead cats. You sat on the rocks in the
boiling sun and drank cocktails.' They joined an attractive young London set which included Cochran's 'English Rose', Joan Clarkson, and
Ashton went out of his way to look smart, wearing a jaunty white yacht-
ing cap, short shorts and a shirt knotted Joan Crawford-style. The photographer, Paul Tanqueray, was there and took an immediate liking to
Ashton – 'He was *so* relaxed and easy' – filming him one afternoon at
Juan les Pins gliding along in a pedalo boat. Buster Tonge was staying at
the Hotel du Cap and took Ashton under his wing. 'In those days we all
regarded him as a dear little boy who needed looking after.' Among
Tonge's party was an apprentice trainer from Newmarket to whom Ashton took a great shine. (Barbara photographed them jokily posing on a
bed in one of the rooms at the Hotel du Cap.) Her art-dealer friend,

Arthur Jeffress, was also in Antibes and drove them around in his convertible.

> We were motoring along and Fred and I had a row – we were always having rows. Fred said, 'I'm getting out.' He had his hand on the handle of the door and I told Arthur to stop the car at once because I was afraid that he was going to jump out while it was moving. But Fred then *had* to get out so as not to lose face. We drove off and Fred claimed later that he had to walk all the way back to Antibes because I'd thrown him out of the car. We saw him that night at a club, sitting all by himself, and sent the waiter over to ask if he'd like to join us for a drink. The waiter came back and told us, 'The gentleman says thank you, but he's not thirsty.'

This particular argument had started when Ashton reproved Barbara for behaving disgracefully towards Humphrey Pease, to whom she would refer as 'The Trembling Stick'; like children who had grown up together and knew each other too well, they fought as much as they had fun.* Ashton's friends used to say that he had folies de grandeur, citing, among other things, his increasingly protracted and indulgent first-night curtain calls – 'Madame's sweeping bowings & scrapings & kissings of the hand', as Barbara Ker-Seymer put it to Burra, contrasting his exhibitionism with the embarrassed humility of Sophie Fedorovitch, who would take her calls 'white as a sheet, bobbing nervously to right & left, & trying to escape'. Then there was the occasion when they had all gone to Rules restaurant after a performance. 'We ordered toasted cheese and coffee (at Rules!) and when it was Fred's turn he chose champagne and caviar.' Billy Chappell made a point of deflating the slightest sign of self-aggrandizement in Ashton – 'he was very good at squashing Fred in those days' – and even better was a young dancer from Melbourne, Robert Helpmann, who, although he had only recently joined the Vic-Wells, had already become notorious for his cutting wit.

Arriving with a letter of introduction from the actress Margaret Rawlings, Helpmann had made a striking first impression, looking like a joke Australian in a jaunty hat – 'it practically had corks bobbing from it' – an over-large gangsterish coat and red Russian boots. De Valois claimed she could tell immediately that Helpmann had something special, staring into his large, protruding eyes and famously remarking, 'I could do something with that face.' In her log-book she wrote, 'On the credit side: talented,

---

* After the Juan les Pins holiday, Ashton and Barbara were never as close, and she rather dropped out of his life once the 1930s were over.

enthusiastic, extremely intelligent, great facility and vitality, witty, cute as
a monkey . . . On the debit side: academically technically weak, lacking
in concentration; too fond of a good time and too busy having it.' All of
which was true. Helpmann was as committed a performer socially as he
was on stage. At two in the morning in Manchester he might be seen with
Constant Lambert, declaiming the entire balcony scene of *Romeo and
Juliet* from the first-floor gallery of the Midlands Hotel. Recognizing in
Lambert, Ashton and Chappell kindred spirits with a similar sense of humour, Helpmann attached himself to them from the start, becoming so
inseparable from the two dancers in particular, that Lambert used to call
them the Three Bears. They never stopped entertaining each other and
everyone else, killing time on chilly station platforms while on company
tours by inventing new tableaux vivants (a photograph records the trio
posing feyly with linked arms: the Three Bears metamorphosed into the
Three Graces). Helpmann was the most extroverted of the trio; Chappell,
content to be an observer: 'Bobby was noisier and nastier than Fred. He
took all the limelight, but every now and then Fred would put in a sharp
and pungent word.'

Realizing the potential of this impudent young newcomer with theatrical flair, de Valois gave him a major assignment almost immediately,
the role of Satan in *Job*, which he performed with such panache that Ashton decided to test him out in *Les Rendezvous*, his first important ballet
for Vic-Wells. He cast him in a fast and taxing pas de trois, full of beats
and controlled landings, later described by Arlene Croce as 'the ultimate
instep dance . . . the most difficult-to-sustain number in the ballet'. Choreographed mainly as a showpiece for Markova, *Les Rendezvous* was
Ashton's most technical work to date. He also had at his disposal the Polish virtuoso Stanislas Idzikowsky, who had danced for Pavlova and Diaghilev. 'Idzikowsky was a great male dancer,' said Ashton. 'I didn't like
him, but he was. He was a freak, a freak out of Nijinsky. He was the size
of Nijinsky; he could do everything *he* could, but he wasn't Nijinsky. But
from the point of view of execution, he was remarkable.'

Les Rendezvous – as even the self-deprecating choreographer conceded – is 'a frightfully good ballet'. One of four works that survive from
the 1930s, it is of seminal importance in the Ashton canon: his first substantial classical composition and an exultant statement of his idiosyncratic approach to academic ballet. For the first time, Ashton explored
different ways of organizing stage space, using the corps to form geometric floor patterns – concentric circles, double avenues, entrances at different angles. The ballet comprises a suite of lighthearted classical dances

arranged round a gathering of friends in a park (the setting was designed, with a Regency flavour, by Billy Chappell). Two young girls, dressed like débutantes in beribboned party dresses and with flowers in their hair, interrupt their entrance of jetés across the stage to stop and exchange pecked kisses; two more follow, then the rest of the ensemble, among whom there are little flutters of recognition as well as hints of friction. Ashton's classicism, as Alastair Macaulay has remarked, is intensely social. '*Les Rendezvous* is an old-world ballet coloured by a certain nostalgia. Its social graces . . . hint at a bygone, nineteenth-century world. Its locale is a place of flirtation.' Markova and Idzikowsky are the lead couple and it is their party; they greet their young guests who celebrate their first pas de deux with a charmingly eccentric sequence of stylized applause marking time to the music. The exuberance of their dancing is infectious and soon Markova's flying cabrioles are being echoed by all the girls, contrapuntally swung in the air by their beaux.

The model for *Les Rendezvous* was Balanchine's *Cotillon*, the prototype of romantic party ballets, which had been made the previous year, but its manners are intrinsically English and the whole work sings with Ashton's personal style. Filigree details abound: wrists flourish, fingers fly to shoulders, arms and upper back are constantly alive. But it is in the ballerina's principal variation that, as Arlene Croce points out, we see Ashton's vision of female classical style most clearly defined. 'The choreography is full of unexpected and contradictory details. She pirouettes to a stop, then immediately whirls to a different stop . . . we notice crisp épaulé address, elaborately shaped arms.' It is a delightfully feminine style, with lavish renversé turns positioned so that the audience never loses sight of the ballerina's face; conversational arms move as freely as long, flowing ribbons, enlivened with elements of surprise, such as a quirky, hiccupy motif of the shoulders. Once again, Ashton revealed a new side to Markova, who added gaiety, warmth and wit to her familiar virtuosity, and looked entrancing in her grey dress with clusters of large red roses on either side of her smooth head. 'No one who saw her will ever forget her exit at the end of her brilliant solo, head jauntily tilted, shoulders and arms delicately lifted, her narrow feet exquisitely placed.'

The première was 'an uproarious success' and the very next day, on 6 December 1933, Ashton set sail for New York, 'sent for' by Virgil Thomson to stage and choreograph *Four Saints in Three Acts*, which had finally found a producer. A. Everett (Chick) Austin, director of the Wadsworth Athenaeum in Hartford, Connecticut, was to present the opera in the small theatre he was building into a new wing of the museum. The world première of *Four Saints* would be its inaugural presentation, coinciding with the Avery Wing's opening show: the first Picasso retrospective ever to be held in America. Thomson had already put the director John Houseman in charge of the production, but sensing that Houseman's gifts were organizational rather than imaginative, he felt that a choreographer was needed to provide a stylistic unity to the piece, 'not only for the dance-numbers', he told Gertrude Stein, 'but for the whole show, so that all the movements will be regulated to the music, measure by measure, and all our complicated stage-action made into a controllable spectacle.' What Thomson and Stein had in mind was 'something other than opera', a collaboration along the lines of Picasso, Satie and Cocteau's *Parade*, which had been not so much a ballet as an inspired fusion of music, movement and images. 'I don't really want them to act. I want them to be moved,' he had told Houseman in their first interview. The choreographer he originally had in mind was either Balanchine or Agnes de Mille, but, as neither was free at the time, Thomson 'wished in front of Chick and to the Askews' that there was a way of getting Ashton over to the States.

> He had never directed opera, but he understood *Four Saints*. We could pay his fare third class, and the Askew household could provide a bed. If he were willing to work free, like the rest, Constance would send a telegram inviting him. So it was sent; and he did accept; and he arrived on December 12.

Claiming to have been 'bombarded with cables' from New York, Ashton had rung Maynard Keynes to seek his advice about the offer (his main worry being how, with no money coming in, he was going to keep his mother). But Keynes must have convinced him of the folly of missing such an opportunity, because Ashton set sail immediately for New York, travelling steerage on the *Ile de France* 'with all the immigrants right down under the water'. It was a miserably rough passage, his discomfort barely mitigated by the fact that a fellow *Four Saints* collaborator was on board: Maurice Grosser, whose role it was to translate the fleeting, random meanings of Gertrude Stein's text into a sequence of actions on stage. Grosser had come up with what he described as a 'dance scenario' to be fulfilled 'at the discretion of the choreographer', but, although the two men made contact on board, they left it at that, feeling too queasy to contemplate any serious exchange of ideas. The waves were so mountainous towards the end of the voyage that the tiny area of third-class deck was covered over and the passengers confined to their cabins. On the last day, when Ashton finally emerged from the hull, the cutting sub-zero air quite took his breath away. Just as overwhelming was his first sighting of the famous New York skyline silhouetted across the water, a view so intoxicating that, as he confessed to Lydia Lopokova, he 'half-expected orchids and newspaper men' to greet his arrival.

The reality was considerably more low-key. At the Askews' high brownstone on East 61st Street, he was accommodated in a twin-bedded guest room which the novelist Elizabeth Bowen had just vacated, and which Virgil Thomson would occasionally share. That and the $10 per week pocket money he received during rehearsal were his only remuneration, but, however stretched he was financially, he was elated by everything the city had to offer. 'New York in 1934 was *marvellous* – Harlem, the parties, all the jazz.' Culturally, the place was booming – Broadway was at its zenith, Martha Graham was performing at the Guild Theatre (Ashton would sit in the cheapest seats to see her), and although Prohibition was in force, New York social life flourished, fuelled by bootleg gin and vodka concocted in bathtubs. Every night except when dining out, the Askews had guests and held regular Sunday afternoon 'At Homes' in the large drawing room overlooking a garden. Theirs was the group which came to exert a dominant influence on the modern movement of the time, comprising museum directors Alfred Barr and Jere Abbott; the future architect Philip Johnson; poets e. e. cummings and Lincoln Kirstein; musicians Aaron Copland and, later, the young Leonard Bernstein; photographers George Platt Lynes, George Hoynigen-Huhne and Lee Miller; stage directors Joseph Losey and John Houseman; painters Pavel Tchelitchew and Florine Stettheimer. Virgil Thomson had chosen Stettheimer, one of four daughters of a distinguished New York family, to design *Four Saints* – the earliest instance of an artist of repute working for the American stage. Ashton described her as the most refined and delicate woman he had ever met: 'She was tiny and frail and yet at the same time capable of doing these terrific paintings with great passion and observation.'

Edward Burra and Sophie Fedorovitch were also living in New York, having anticipated Ashton by two months, and both were habitués of the Askews' salon. Burra was in his element there, finding inspiration in sleazy hot-dog stands, luncheonettes, Jewish delis and uptown dives lit by red electric bulbs which made white intruders look like corpses. 'Theres so much talent at the partys here that its more like non stop Variety,' he told Billy Chappell. 'If only Fred could come here he would adore it Ime certain if he doesnt come hes crazy despite the broad Atlantic.' The minute Ashton did arrive, Burra and Sophie took him on the town, accompanied on one occasion by the Duchesse de Clermont Tonnerre, another Askews regular.

We visited a few hot spots one in the village which was camp lovely my dear a monster rose up in an old red wig with a bit of spinach hanging off the back and sang 'they call me red head brick top carrot tops and strawberry garden but *I* dont care (scream) my favorite number then we went to the Savoy and then to Hot Cha . . . La Paloma Clermont Tonerre at once asked for une veille Kentucky darkie song which flung the whole place in an uproar then we went to a underground grave yard called the log cabin my favorite resort in which a terrifying negro midget with a mouthful of gold teeth sang a repertoire of dirty songs Madame was delighted.

Ashton spent many an evening in the large, dark Harlem apartment where Burra was staying, recklessly walking back in the small hours to the Askews' house midtown. It belonged to the black actress, Edna Thomas, a woman of remarkable dignity, warmth and presence, who lived there in an unusual ménage with her husband, Lloyd Thomas, a charming good-for-nothing, and her lover, Ashton's great friend Olivia Wyndham. 'They were a trio,' said the singer Elizabeth Welch. 'Lloyd just accepted it.' Ever since Olivia had fallen in love with Edna and bolted to New York – an exploit considered by her friends to be 'so extraordinary that it almost transcended scandal' – she had become quaintly conventional, giving up drink and drugs, and adopting the genteel ways of an English county wife, offering guests Earl Grey tea, cucumber sandwiches and Gentleman's Relish. 'Harlem was a strange setting for Olivia,' remarked David Herbert, describing a Christmas party at which she had stood beside the Christmas tree handing out presents to small black children 'exactly as though she had been doing it at Clouds'. At the same time, oblivious to the subtle shades of social distinction in Harlem, Olivia's undiscriminating nature had proved trying to Edna, who had spent years struggling to establish a sophisticated salon. As a character remarks in the short story Olivia's half-brother, Francis Wyndham, wrote about her, 'If she had her way, my dear, she'd fill the place with the sweepings of the Harlem streets: drug fiends, pimps, prostitutes of *both* sexes . . . she gives the unfortunate impression of liking *anybody* just so long as they're black.' But Olivia had found the perfect outlet for her crusading instincts in the black American cause and for her English friends she had acquired a reputation comparable to that of Carl Van Vechten, the writer and photographer, as the undisputed authority on uptown night-life. 'Olivia is such a figure in Harlem society you cant conceive', exclaimed Burra. 'She seems to know all the neighbourhood.'

Through Edna and Olivia, Ashton was introduced to the élite of Harlem, two of whom became closely involved with *Four Saints in Three Acts*. Eddie Perry, described by Ashton as 'a kind of black ADC, so to speak, who came everywhere with me as a kind of liaison officer', was a young Van Vechten protégé, elegant, slender and softly spoken, who helped the collaborators scout for singers and dancers. The cabaret singer Jimmy Daniels, 'as popular with white people as with black', was another invaluable guide. 'Anybody who wanted to come to Harlem, Jimmy brought them there,' said Elizabeth Welch, who had a double-act with him at one time. 'He had the touch. He knew English people and people from café society.' Ashton had already met Daniels in England when Olivia had been living with Barbara Ker-Seymer (Barbara photographed the two young men performing a mock revue turn together). He was an attractive, charming person, with great style, a Europhile at heart, affecting Anglicisms in his speech such as 'been' rather than 'bin'. 'He was a rather superior type and rather grand,' David Herbert has written. 'A gentleman in every sense of the word.' When Ashton was in New York, Daniels was host and entertainer at the Hot-Cha, 'kind of a secret club', as the singer, Bobby Short, put it. 'It was a dive but an elegant dive,' said Elizabeth Welch. 'Noël and Tallulah used to go. It was ermine and pearls go to Harlem.' Although Daniels was not a very good singer, he had a small, touching voice and marvellous diction. 'Sometimes it was no more than a whisper and yet it had a thrilling and strangely sexual quality which made everyone fall in love with him,' said Virgil Thomson, who claimed that it was the impeccable enunciation of Daniels' 'speech-in-song' that had made up his mind to have his opera performed by black people.*

As virtually no ballet schools existed in the United States at that time, Ashton would go to the Savoy Ballroom with Perry or Daniels as a way of auditioning dancers for the opera. They used to 'pick out boys there who danced the Lindy Hop, or whatever it was at that time, marvellously, and ask them if they'd like to come and do it . . . at first they thought we were pulling their legs.' Situated on Lenox Avenue, between 140th and 141st Streets, the Savoy was *the* dance palace in Harlem, filled every night with hundreds of young couples dancing with a rhythm, speed and complexity that onlookers could scarcely believe. These were not professionals but lively, athletic young people, who worked in offices and shops in the daytime and, at night, got intoxicated on nothing more than the music. The spectacle was Dionysian to watch; the bands seemed to be swinging faster every night, and all the best dancers could follow

---

*Carl Van Vechten, however, ascribes this decision to another occasion, maintaining that it was during an intermission of Hall Johnson's revivalist lay, *Run Little Chillun!*, that Thomson had turned and said, 'I am going to have *Four Saints* played by negroes. They alone possess the dignity and the poise, the lack of self-consciousness that proper interpretation of opera demands.'

them in new and startling ways. Carl Van Vechten describes one such scene in his novel *Parties*.

> This dancing was exalted, uplifting, dangerously exciting to the mere observer . . . Each dancer gave as serious an attention to his beautiful vocation as if he were in training for some great good game . . . Wilder and wilder the couples became in their abandon, individuals separating from one from the other to indulge in breath-taking displays of virtuosity and improvisation, and then joining again in double daring.

Tuesday's '400 Club', reserved for dancers at reduced prices, was the night to see the best performances: no crowds, plenty of floor space and the finest Lindy Hoppers out in force. Eventually, Ashton was able to select three girls with a knowledge of what he called extremely elementary '*fancy* dancing', and three youths: a swimmer, an amateur prize-fighter and a basketball player. 'None of them was trained, but naturally like all Negro people they were very plastic and knew how to move, so it was a question of adapting.' The Lindy Hop was not an erotic dance – the couples barely touched each other – but was more what Van Vechten describes as 'a kind of terpsichorean megalomania'. To Ashton, however, the Savoy's slender girls, with their natural chic, and virile young partners, were intensely arousing and, according to John Houseman, he had several romances with black dancers in Harlem, 'which he enjoyed and was very funny about'. It is a claim confirmed by Billy Chappell – 'Fred always had a feeling for the dinge, dear' – and, indirectly, by a photograph taken by George Platt-Lynes. In it, Ashton poses in a formal suit 'looking like a bank clerk' while harmoniously grouped at his feet are three black male dancers, each completely naked.

Rehearsals for *Four Saints* took place in the basement of St Philip's Episcopal Church on 137th Street – 'an old Harlem ballet club that used to be a church so its quite dear old Notting hill all over again', declared Burra. Thomson took the vocal rehearsals himself, keeping the tempi firm and the words clear, while Ashton choreographed the action standing centre-stage and moving the singers round him. At first, Stein's text, with its jumbled meanings and violated syntax, baffled the performers – 'I thought, my God I'll never learn those crazy words, but as I began they became the most singable words I'd ever heard,' said Beatrice Godfrey (then Robinson-Wayne), who played St Theresa, a plain middle-aged woman with a celestial voice 'and all the things Virgil was looking for –

the clear speech and the rapt, simple, dedicated quality of a Saint'. Thomson was delighted with his cast, who sang with grace and conviction, but Ashton's experience was not nearly as felicitous, the main problem being the short memory span of the performers.

> One would get a whole scene set, and then one would come to lunch-time, and I'd say, Let's do it once more to make sure, and they would do it, and they would do it perfectly, and then come back after lunch, and I'd say, Now we'll go through Scene 2, and they'd never heard of Scene 2, and I'd have to start all over again, and so it was a terrible test for me, I had no assistant or anything, I had to remember everything all the time because they always forgot, which made it frightfully exhausting.

Eager to please, the cast were alarmed and flustered by Ashton's outbursts of impatience and despondence: 'If you didn't do it right this awful scowl came over his face,' said Dorothy Bronson, one of the singers. Gertrude Stein's biographer claimed Thomson saw to it that 'young Freddy was kept away from rehearsals', but her account conflicts with Thomson's own avowal that Ashton was 'a godsend', both to Houseman and himself. Singularly responsible for the whole production's style of movement, Ashton had proved infinitely resourceful and imaginative, orchestrating the synchronized movements of a chorus of saints as they swayed to the music, raising their arms and moving them in sweeping arcs. In the continuous flow of loosely curved groupings around St Ignatius, Ashton's compositions once again reflected borrowings from pictorial art, the baroque swirls and rhythm of the lines all part of a single curving unity. One formation was believed by the critic, Stark Young, to be directly influenced by the Giotto frescoes in Santa Croce. 'In another scene Goya has given the key, and in another El Greco.'

Everyone in the cast, however 'pug-nosed and pigeon-toed', was choreographically placed by Ashton, who even gave instructions on facial expressions and mannerisms. 'He was very good at it but this face of mine just wouldn't change,' remarked Beatrice Godfrey. At first, the soprano found the choreographer's cues difficult to follow: his speech was florid, his inflections so English that he was hard to understand. Gradually, however, Ashton won everyone over – he was funny, dandyish, adorable and quite unlike anyone they had ever known. 'You *had* to like Freddie,' said Tommy Anderson (St Giuseppe). 'He was a strange little one, always playing and flitting around from place to place.' 'Today what the term would be for . . . well some of us would have taken him for that,' remarked Dorothy Bronson. 'He was a little effeminate with his steps – that little walk he'd put on.'

Ashton reached an understanding with his cast, and particularly with his untrained dancers, when he finally realized that it had been a mistake to expect them to copy him exactly. He would, instead, allow the performers their own interpretation of a pose or gesture, which they could do easily and naturally, drawing on their own tradition of vernacular dance. 'They would do something quite different but full of the beauty of their own skinny plasticity . . . they were never gawky, and though strange, always harmonious.' Ashton's movements, like Florine Stettheimer's costumes, were designed to display the black dancers' youthful ebullience, as well as their sexual allure. In the first act, the girls wore short skirts and halter-neck tops exposing a bare midriff and shoulder; their male companions, just as striking in shiny blousing shorts, bare chests and bright bandannas. Even as angels in Act II, the girls were decidedly sexy in white semi-transparent tunics, through which their brown limbs and bare feet could be glimpsed (an effect, Thomson had felt obliged to assure Stein, not aimed at titillation, but at keeping the texture of the stage as light as possible). Not that the erotic element was intrusive: the dancers' natural restraint, defined by Ashton as 'a kind of delicacy that was very touching', kept any vulgarity in check, as did the choreographer's sense of humour. In a spirit of joke-jock, the athletic young men held musclemen poses, and in an interlude structured on the idea of little angels learning to fly, the three scantily clad girls assumed Earl Tucker's snake hips posture, bending from their waist, hands hanging down and letting rip, with hips undulating, swinging, rocking, legs rolling, arms making converging circles out in front, feet scooting across the floor in sideways Charleston skids. The effect was hypnotic – imbued with all the dance-floor tricks and, at the same time, voluptuous and whimsical.

What Ashton called the opera's 'beautiful leisure' contrasted with the energy and hot rhythms of the dance. The first act was marked by the stillness of a sustained series of tableaux in which the lifting of a hand or a raised eyebrow was given intense dramatic weight. Towards the end of the opera, he devised a four-minute-long procession which, although it gave the illusion of movement, was remarkable for the fact that the ensemble did little more than sway and take an occasional step. Reflecting the sombre gravity of Catholic processions he had watched as a boy in Lima, the spectacle, as Ashton said, was not operatic but ritualistic, not balletic but ceremonial: 'I did *Four Saints* well . . . I say this though I made it, because I am devout and the Negroes are devout and I am plastic and they are plastic.' It was, as he said, the strangest and most beautiful production, and both Stein and Thomson agreed that its success was in large part owing to his skill and inspiration. Although his approach was not self-consciously modernist, his medium – as much an art of suggestion as Stein's symbolist wordplay – automatically put Ashton in accord with his avant-garde collaborators. The responsibility of overseeing the entire show, however, had taken a personal toll.

Travelling by bus with the company in Arctic temperatures, Ashton arrived at the dress rehearsal in Hartford on Friday, 3 February 1934, to become immediately embroiled in two emotional scenes. The first was a classic conflict between conductor and choreographer over the placing of performers on the stage. Alexander Smallens, the musical director, was a bully, whose shouting drove Ashton to breaking point. Stopping long enough to retaliate, 'I have worked with Sir Thomas Beecham! A genius! And he never spoke to me as you have!' Ashton left the theatre in tears. But, as it was fifteen below zero outside, he returned almost immediately and the rehearsal continued, although 'the whole thing was chaos', Ashton said, as the performers reverted to their old ways and forgot everything he had ever taught them.

> I was so tired by then, I came up on to the stage to give them my notes, and I started on the notes and I just burst into tears. And I remember one lady coming up to me and saying, Don't worry, Mr Ashton, we made [Rouben] Mamoulian [the film director] and we'll make you. And then an extraordinary thing, the first night came and a miracle took place, they seemed to remember everything, they did it all marvellously, with their wonderful vitality, you know, and the fact that they had an audience and the audience were with it, made all the difference.

On 7 and 8 February, the New Haven Railroad added extra parlour cars to its afternoon train for the New York socialites, the press and members of the international art world travelling to Hartford to honour the opening of the wing. The audience had arrived for the première anticipating something special, but were totally unprepared for the extraordinary beauty that the first curtain disclosed, and which intensified as the performance went on. It was, as Lincoln Kirstein said, 'a wonderful vision'. Brilliantly evoking the tinselly effect of Catholic iconography, with its painted plaster, gilding and artificial flowers, Florine Stettheimer's designs were astonishing enough in themselves. With trees made out of feathers and a background of crinkled sky-blue cellophane set in white lace borders, the set looked like a valentine against which was contrasted the royal red-velvet costumes and brown skins of the performers. The audience's response was ecstatic; even hard-boiled and worldly connoisseurs were in tears by the end. The art critic Henry McBride saw the show four times – 'Thinking it over in cold blood, I can't conceive how Virgil dared to do what he did,' he wrote to Gertrude Stein. 'The incessant inventions in choreography supplied by Freddy Ashton seemed like some baroque dream of the eighteenth century (only far more finished and perfect than the eighteenth century itself could have dreamed of).' Carl Van Vechten also sent a breathless report to Stein.

> *Four Saints*, in our vivid theatrical parlance, is a knockout and a wow . . . I haven't seen a crowd more excited since *Sacre du printemps*. The difference was that they were pleasurably excited. The Negroes are divine, like el Grecos, more Spanish, more Saints, more opera singers in their dignity and *simplicity* and extraordinary plastic line than *any* white singers could ever be . . . Frederick Ashton's rhythmic staging was inspired and so were Florine's costumes and sets.

Four Saints made such an impact that the Broadway producer Harry Moses, throwing caution to the winds, announced a New York opening a fortnight later at the 44th Street Theater, one of the largest musical-comedy houses on Broadway. For six months, the show was named at least once a week in every New York paper; there were constant editorials, cartoons, and jokes about it (Macy's department store advertised its autumn collection as Four Suits in Three Acts). On the night of the New York opening, the streets were icy and there was a taxi strike, but everybody came: George Gershwin and Toscanini, Cecil Beaton escorting Tilly Losch, Robert Benchley with Dorothy Parker. Intoxicated by his success – 'Americans make you *feel* it when you've done something well' – Ashton sent his mother a telegram consisting of only two words: 'TELL ENGLAND.'

Feeling that he had never been adequately appreciated at home, Ashton began thinking seriously about moving to New York: 'I'd enjoyed it so much there. Here, when you do a good ballet you don't know whether it's a success or failure. In America either they all rush at you or rush away from you.' But although Gertrude Stein was now famous to everyone as the Mama of Dada, neither Ashton nor Virgil Thomson had received any worthwhile offers as a result of the publicity generated by *Four Saints*. Anxious to do the right thing, he consulted John Martin, dance critic of the *New York Times*, and a great champion of the opera. Martin advised him against staying. 'He said, "You're a classicist, there's no room for you here." And it was true that at the time there was no ballet in America, only Martha Graham.' But this was not strictly the case. Balanchine was already in New York, having the previous year, at Lincoln Kirstein's invitation, formed the School of American Ballet to provide dancers for a new company. The American Ballet made its New York début in 1935, by which time Ashton was too entrenched in helping to establish a national dance of his own in England. 'I said I'd come back. But in America when you're out of sight, you're out of mind.'

Ashton had, by now, begun to feel very homesick. Burra and Sophie, who had attended the Hartford première, had since returned to London, and he 'suddenly got terribly nostalgic for an English spring'. On 22 March 1934, after the show had closed at the 44th Street Theater but before it reopened at the Empire, Ashton returned to England, touched by the fact that most of the cast of *Four Saints* lined the quay to see him off. (He used to mimic the sniffy expressions of his fellow passengers, aggrieved at such a conspicuous display of black friends.) It was the last voyage of the SS *Berengaria*, flagship of the Cunard fleet, and this time Ashton had paid a supplement out of his own pocket to spare himself a third-class crossing. Also on board was Jimmy Daniels' lover, Kenneth Macpherson, a rich young Scottish cineaste, 'sweet and rather vague', whom Ashton had met in England through Barbara Ker-Seymer.* When the crossing grew rough and Ashton was again very seasick, Macpherson offered him something that would make him feel better. 'He told me to sniff it and almost immediately my heart started pounding and I got into a terrible state and told him he had to call the ship's doctor, which of course was the last thing he wanted.' Ashton claimed that Macpherson had given him heroin (although his description of his symptoms suggest that the drug was more likely to have been a stimulant, such as cocaine). He told Barbara Ker-Seymer that he had to be 'practically carried off the boat', but, if so, he had clearly composed himself by the time he was met at the station by his mother and by Marie Rambert, who described the occasion in her memoirs. 'We felt elated by his success but he himself was very modest about it. However, we laughed a lot in the old shaking taxi.'

Ashton's friends were amazed by the change in him. They had never seen him so euphoric, and swopped stories of his outlandish behaviour – how he had danced for four hours without stopping at a party, or performed an hilarious pas de deux with a chair, singing out his favourite number, 'I just can't take it, baby, loving you the way I do'. Having always preferred tea to alcohol in the past, he had also started drinking recklessly, ordering Horse's Necks at the Café Royal, then sending them back because they were not strong enough. 'He was stirred up. New York

*In the 1920s, Macpherson had become entrenched in the romantic alliance between the poet, H.D., and her heiress friend, 'Bryher' (Winifred Ellerman), by having an affair with the former and marrying the latter – a friendly, profitable arrangement, which made him very rich.

stirs you up.' Even after vowing never to touch drugs again, Ashton went to dinner with Kenneth Macpherson one night and insisted on trying once more.

> I said, 'I can't think that was the right reaction,' so he gave me some more and I was even *worse*. I said, 'You must open all the windows because I don't want to die in your house and for my soul not to fly out.' I was rambling like that. So they opened the windows and when they came back I said, 'But you haven't opened the one at the top.' Then I said, 'I'm not going to die in your house,' and insisted on leaving. But I couldn't walk. Fortunately there was someone else there, so they marched me round and then they both got into bed with me because I was shaking so much. They lay there trying to warm me up.

By the end of April, Ashton's soaring spirits had come crashing down: the lack of stimulation and attention in London, after a period of such acclaim, had proved too much to bear. Lydia Lopokova had Sunday lunch with his mother and Constant Lambert, and reported to Keynes: 'Fred is in a state of lethargy, having no work and reaction from American cocktails. What can we do for him?' Her immediate stratagem – pleading with 'Mrs Cockie'* to get her husband to give Ashton work – indirectly paid off, although only eight months later. Not even the prospect of a new Rambert assignment scheduled for the summer seemed to motivate him. 'I'm afraid our Ashton has grown too big for the little Ballet Club and nothing smaller than the Chiswick Empire will do now. Times Square gets them,' Burra commented, snidely.

In June 1934, Ashton's first Liszt ballet, *Mephisto Valse*, was premièred at the Ballet Club. Although Sacheverell Sitwell's biography of Liszt had appeared two months earlier, it was, in fact, Constant Lambert who was behind Ashton's interest in the composer. For some time, the two men had been meeting regularly on Saturday afternoons for Lambert to play and discuss Liszt's music.

> At the end of the Twenties no one wanted Romantic, emotionally charged music, everything was Bach, Mozart, Poulenc, simplicity of orchestration, Stravinsky and all that. Constant felt that Liszt's music wasn't properly appreciated and started to speak out for it. He would talk about Liszt as one of the innovators of new music

*Mrs C. B. Cochran.

of that period and about the influence he had had on Wagner. People didn't agree with him, of course, but he had a very positive point of view.

As a ballet for Markova, Lambert had suggested Liszt's first *Mephisto Waltz*, a study in sombre Romanticism encapsulated by the choreographer in an emotionally stirring chamber piece focusing on Marguerite, Faust (Walter Gore) and Mephistopheles (Ashton). Ashton underlined the darkening atmosphere by enclosing the action with a corps of three couples, their self-absorption and indifference an effective foil to the melodrama being played out on stage. Ashton also contrasted the high passion of the music with affecting moments of stillness: for example, when Mephistopheles brings Faust and Marguerite face to face, they stand motionless looking into one another's eyes, while the couples dance behind them. Lasting only eleven minutes, *Mephisto Waltz* was, as David Vaughan has said, 'a perfect Romantic ballet in miniature', its simplicity and austerity enhanced by Sophie Fedorovitch's perfectly judged designs. As much of an influence on Ashton as Lambert at the time, her method of scrupulous elimination profoundly influenced his own purging of the dance to its essence. It was to her alone that he would defer in matters of taste – 'She proved my instincts' – although he admitted that he could, on occasion, be irritated by what Beaton called her 'farouche directness', the way that, in her mumbling gruff voice, she would always tell him the truth.

> She used to say to me: 'Oh you must change that bit there.' And I used to get furious about it and say, 'There's no *must*, Sophie,' and then she would go on and on, 'But you must change . . . ' She always had to get in the last 'must'. And I'd go to bed and think, 'Ah well, she's right.'

At the end of July, Ashton went to stay with Lydia at Tilton, still feeling so gloomy about his prospects that she offered 'B&B till better times'. His depression lasted until November, compounded by feelings of paranoia that Ninette de Valois, motivated by jealousy, was preventing him from choreographing a new ballet to Walton's *Belshazzar's Feast*, as it was a score that she had wanted to use herself.

> He has no work to do, looks with horror into the future, yet hopes for *Balthazar* [sic] and £100 . . . We must work [de Valois] the other way and tell her how noble she is in encouraging Fred. I have learned English politicks . . .

Lydia continued to worry about Ashton, who had developed an abscess on his arm and had taken to his bed in a state of gloom. 'Mrs A told me privately that they have sold their last security & it is simply awful. I said I'll talk to you about the Camargo money so that he could do a ballet at once for Sadler's Wells . . . Fred if he gets no work, he might die.' Keynes was sympathetic, but only up to a point, 'I am very sorry for Fred – but I don't know what more we can do for him. He just lacks that fighting power which the wicked world requires.' Ashton was relying on Lopokova to do his fighting for him, which he knew she was very good at. It was thanks to her intervention that Ashton was engaged to provide the dancing for a new film, *Escape Me Never*, starring Elisabeth Bergner, the great Viennese actress. Keynes wrote to congratulate Lydia, 'You have certainly saved his life.' Cochran was not involved with the film itself, but earlier that year had produced Margaret Kennedy's *Escape Me Never* as a highly successful play which had launched Elizabeth Bergner in England and made her a star. The director of the film was Paul Czinner, the actress's husband (who, in the 1950s, would collaborate with Ashton on the film *Ondine*), and the music was by William Walton. Although Ashton liked working with 'the Bergners' and had great fun with them, *Escape Me Never* was not a project that either he or the composer took very seriously. 'When they asked Willy and F to compose something a la Massin,' remarked Lopokova, 'W whispered to F, "What they want is bad Russian ballet, let's do it."' However, just to be working again was enough to restore Ashton's spirits, although Burra was right: he was finding the Ballet Club constricting and longed to get away. Colluding with de Valois, Lopokova was a prime influence in persuading him that it was time for him to move on: 'I believe Mim's atmosphere is destructive,' she told Keynes. 'It has no grandeur of view.'

Ever since de Valois had set up her Academy of Choreographic Art in 1926, she and Rambert had been rivals. Rambert, in fact, was so struck by the professionalism of de Valois' enterprise that it almost broke her nerve. 'She was terrified of Ninette in a kind of way,' said Ashton. 'Ninette was much more practical; she had a proper theatre and she could pay us. Rambert also had vision, but she wouldn't take risks.' Rambert had never wanted to expand, preferring to keep a small company with whom she could feel she had personal contact. 'She used to walk us all to the bus, holding Fred's arm and talking all the way,' said Maude Lloyd. De Valois was scathing about Rambert's familial approach.

A marvellously intelligent woman but a born amateur because she couldn't dance herself . . . She could give them an intellectual break-down rather like a critic would do, but she did not have the touch I was able to give. She hadn't got that background. She'd never done it. *Dalcroze*, you see.*

For a time, the two women shared the best dancers, especially the male dancers who were in short supply; but, throughout the seasons, there was, as Agnes de Mille said, 'a royal scrimmage between them for talent'. One by one, Rambert lost members of her company to Sadler's Wells. 'Mim let go, however bitterly, because egocentric as she was, she never stood in the way of a young artist's progress.' This was the reason she had let Ashton go – 'although she minded to the point of desperation' – and he knew that she could not criticize him for being disloyal. 'She couldn't give me the scope. To her credit she understood that. She couldn't even give me £10 a week.' Ashton had a lot more sympathy for Rambert as a person than he did for de Valois, whom he found dictatorial and lacking in taste: 'Rambert was much more cosmopolitan, as I was.' But as an ex-Diaghilev soloist and a respected choreographer, de Valois was far better equipped to advise him on his craft. She also had Constant Lambert as her musical director – 'the backbone of everything to do with ballet at that time.' Ashton was as keen to go to Sadler's Wells as de Valois was to have him, even though she did not take his dancing seriously. 'It was the choreographic side we were all desperately interested in.'

De Valois told Ashton that she would take him on as soon as the Financial Committee gave the go-ahead. Meanwhile, he occupied his time with any commercial offers that came his way, including *Jill, Darling!*, a light, bright musical-comedy by Vivian Ellis. The title role was played by Frances Day, for whom Ashton choreographed a swooning little number, 'I'm Dancing with a Ghost', in which, at her insistence, he also partnered her. 'Frances Day was no dancer. I can still see Freddie lying there full-length in the stalls gangway *exhausted*,' said Ellis. At Christmas, pining for better days, Ashton sent to Virgil Thomson a bunch of rosemary 'for remembrance', with a snapshot of himself. 'By the look on my face I was obviously thinking of the beauties of *Four Saints* . . . what became of *Medea* and Florine's ballet? I often think of our triumph last winter and get very nostalgic indeed.'

His romantically plaintive mood filtered into his next ballet, *Valentine's Eve*, which, as one observer put it, was simply about characters in a room – 'the only thing like it was *Cotillon*.' The score was

*Emile Jaques-Dalcroze, the Swiss-born teacher, who developed a system of music training through movement called 'gymnastique rhythmique'.

Ravel's 'Valses nobles et sentimentales', and Ashton used every shade and variation of the waltz to express the different personalities of his young protagonists and their different attitudes to love: the noble waltz of the poet, who gives a keepsake of a heart to the coquette; her gay and flippant waltz, as she gives it to her next partner, and he to his, until, having circled the ballroom, it reaches the sentimental young girl, who attempts to give it to the poet whom she loves. 'He recognises it. He is broken-hearted, as he traces it from dancer to dancer, and throws it at the feet of the heartless one. His fellows laugh. They are men of the world.' Ashton's appearance as the love-lorn Constant emphasized the fact that the role is a self-caricature; *Valentine's Eve*, a history in disguise of an unrequited love story of his own. Walter Gore, who 'always had a different woman on the go,' is the model for Phryne, the callous flirt; but in the ballet the genders were changed and the part performed with graceful vivacity by Pearl Argyle (Gore appearing among her suitors). *Valentine's Eve* was one of the most beautiful things ever shown by the Ballet Rambert, in Mary Clarke's view, its atmosphere of amorous intrigue heightened by Sophie Fedorovitch's exquisite designs. Her costumes and decor stylishly suggestive of an Edwardian conservatory with gauze screens and silhouettes of ferns so enchanted the *Observer* critic that, instead of writing a notice, he wanted to fashion his own Valentine re-creating Fedorovitch's colours, 'pink and plum . . . with rosebuds, and lace framing a tender motto'. *Valentine's Eve* made such an impression, with its music, dancing and decor fused into a single, almost indistinguishable element, that the *Dancing Times* hailed it as 'the best English ballet we have seen'.

With no contract as yet forthcoming from de Valois, Ashton was still having to 'pot-boil with [his] left hand', as Constant Lambert put it. Cochran wanted him to do Trocadero 'whimsicalities', but he was pleased to say that, at the moment, he was engaged. He was working with Jack Buchanan on *The Flying Trapeze* (in which the Alhambra Theatre was transformed into the interior of a Paris circus of the 1860s), but Ashton claimed that he ended up doing most of the work. 'Fred, darling, finish the scene for me,' Buchanan would entreat. Ashton's main contribution was the creation of a remarkably convincing tightrope ballet for Pearl Argyle and Hugh Laing, a dancer with a reputation for enjoying dangerous physical stunts. The pas de deux took place on a black-painted platform eight feet above the stage: 'The stage was in darkness except for a spotlight on the two dancers: one of the things Laing had to do was to run the length of this platform, of which he could not see the edge, carrying Argyle in an arm's-length lift.' But for all its elaborate effects, the show proved to be Buchanan's first failure in London for over ten years. In July, Ashton appeared with Tilly Losch in *Cochran's Mammoth Cabaret*; in August, he provided several numbers for the new George Black revue, *Round About Regent Street*. By now, however, he was so desperate to involve himself in something serious that Ninette de Valois was able to persuade him to go to Dublin to talk to Yeats about directing plays for the Abbey.

> We were very low on money just then. I knew I couldn't take Fred in for another year and I wanted to find him some regular work, so I said, 'Look, Fred, you *could* go to Dublin and do some productions there for W.B.' I thought he could revive the *Plays for Dancers* that I'd done, but although Yeats was very interested in Fred, I don't think he did very much.

Ashton had already met Yeats in the late 1920s through Edmund Dulac, who had been very supportive to the Mercury Theatre in its early days. 'Yeats took a fancy to me for some extraordinary reason and every time he came to London he used to ask me to dinner – tremendously highbrow dinners at l'Escargot.' In the latter half of 1935, Yeats had sought his help. He had been having an affair with a twenty-seven-year-old poet and actress, Margot Ruddock, and wanted Ashton to rehearse her. 'I brought her to Dulac the painter and Ashton the creator and producer of ballets, subtle technical minds with a instinctive knowledge of the next step in whatever art they discussed.' Margot Ruddock, Yeats felt, had the potential to be a great actress. Not only did she possess a quality, rare on stage, of intellectual passion; with her lovely contralto voice, he saw that she might also make an excellent speaker of his own verse. She was an extremely attractive young woman, with large dewy eyes, whom Ashton found 'frightfully serious and anxious to get on'. Despite being handicapped by professional mannerisms – what Yeats called 'all the professional elocutionists bag of tricks' – she improved so significantly in rehearsal that Yeats subsequently asked Ashton to advise him on his own spoken delivery.

At that time, the poet was in his late sixties – 'a beautiful man with a wonderful head' – and had recently returned with new vigour to writing poetry, attributing this to a rejuvenating operation, which he believed had revived his creative literary power and sexual desire. He told Ashton, 'Whatever they say about me, I will die an old but passionate man.' He would summon the choreographer to various addresses in London – 'He used to stay all over the place' – and Ashton would listen to Yeats recite his poetry. 'I'd say – can you imagine my insolence – "But why can't you read them naturally? Why do you put on that portentous voice?" And he would start again, "Is that better?"' Ashton admitted that he would be 'bored stiff' and impatient to join his friends at the Blue Lantern in Ham Yard, a popular club which had a dance floor and Hugh (Hetty) Wade playing the piano. And when Yeats asked him to produce his *Plays for Dancers* in Lady Londonderry's drawing room, the choreographer turned him down. 'I said, "No, I don't like doing things in drawing rooms. I want to work in the theatre." But he went on and on and on. He courted me a lot.'

Ashton agreed to go to Ireland to meet Yeats, but only after he had taken a holiday with friends who had rented a house on the south-west coast of Scotland. Vera Greig, an elegant married woman, loved to encourage talented young people and had taken a great interest in Ashton since watching him in class one day at Ladbroke Grove. Her two daughters were Rambert pupils, one of whom, Diane, had developed 'a mad crush' on him, but it was Vera to whom Ashton was drawn, seeing in her the kind of refined Edwardian beauty that he had admired since childhood. He was intrigued to discover that she was related by marriage to Violet Beauclerk, the spirited young girl his father had passionately loved in Ecuador (her first husband had been Violet's brother). 'My mother was a very romantic figure for him, and he was always interested in her clothes,' said Diana Chauvin de Précourt. Ashton would go to the Greigs' house for tea and for summer picnics in the Thames Valley, often accompanied by Edith. 'Mrs Ashton could be very forceful and Fred and Edith had quite a hard time with her. They came to my mother as a refuge. She understood their aspirations.'

Vera Greig and her husband had taken a house at Airds, Appin, for the summer. It was not grand, but had a large garden, with a patch of shore suitable for bathing. Ashton had a very good time there: the surrounding countryside was breathtaking, the company young and fun, and there were lots of enjoyable excursions to places such as Lismore and Glencoe. During his stay, there was a dramatic rescue by Prince George Galitzine, the undergraduate tutor of Vera Greig's stepson, who swam nearly a mile and a half out to sea to the aid of a friend whose light aircraft had crashed in Wigtown Bay (an act for which he was awarded the Royal Humane Society medal for gallantry).*

Ashton went straight from Scotland to meet Yeats, catching the ferry from Stranraer to Larne, where Yeats's wife met him at the docks. 'He sent his psychic wife to see me. To sense whether I was right.' He spent

---

*Galitzine's connection to Ashton was through his mother, Princess Galitzine, an avid supporter of the Ballet Club.

the first evening alone with Yeats at his house in Rathfarnham, outside Dublin. Yeats had wanted to discuss a play about Parnell, which Ashton said was by George Moore, but which Yeats's biographer, Roy Foster, believes was probably W. R. Fearon's *Parnell of Avondale*, or a revival of Lennox Robinson's *The Lost Leader*. Knowing nothing about politics, let alone Irish politics, Ashton found it hard to express any interest in the idea, but, whatever objection he made – such as 'I'm not a theatre director, I'm a choreographer' – Yeats saw only as an advantage, in that he had long disliked the predominance of realistic drama at the Abbey and was anxious to resuscitate declining standards. The following day, a meeting was arranged with Lennox Robinson, producer and senior dramatist at the Abbey, who asked Ashton which plays he would like to see performed at the Abbey. When Ashton half-jokingly replied, '*La Dame aux Camélias*,' his frivolity shocked Robinson, a complex character, 'drunk, repressively gay and married', whose interest lay in hard-hitting plays about Irish life and politics. 'Aesthetically we were poles apart,' said Ashton. 'I hated him and he hated me.' Mostly because of Robinson's hostility towards him, Ashton could not wait to get away. When a contract from the Abbey arrived by post, he returned it unhesitatingly with a refusal.

It was just as well. Major changes were taking place in the London dance world, brought about by Markova's announcement that she was leaving the Vic-Wells to form her own company with Anton Dolin. The two stars tried hard to persuade Ashton to join them, but he refused. Markova, he felt, had let him down badly earlier that year, when he had wanted to use her not only for the lead in *Valentine's Eve*, but also for revivals of several other ballets for a season at Sadler's Wells.

'Oh no, I can't,' she said. 'Not after *Giselle*.' [Prissy, mock-refined impersonation.] She'd become frightfully grand and thought she couldn't stoop to do my little things. We were having dinner at the Café Royal and I don't know if under my breath I said, 'Fuck you, that's the end,' but that's what it was. It was the end. Her utter pretension . . . I cut her out of my life. If that's the sort of person you are – *out!* Then when she left Sadler's Wells and wanted me to join her, I thought, 'No. You let me down and I'm not coming with you.' I didn't say that, but Ninette heard they were after me and thought, 'This is dangerous; I'm losing Markova and I'm losing Fred.' So she *immediately* offered me a contract.

At the time, Antony Tudor, who had fallen out with Rambert, was also hoping to join Sadler's Wells as a choreographer. He was on the verge of producing his masterpiece, *Jardin aux lilas* (première at the Ballet Club in January 1936), but, because he was as yet relatively unproven and was not a classical choreographer, de Valois turned him down in favour of Ashton. 'I don't know what her reasons were – perhaps that I was more prolific and worked more easily.' De Valois says that she chose Ashton because he was senior to Tudor – 'He'd been at it much longer' – and, although she would have liked to have kept them both, she could not afford to. Tudor, however, believed to the end of his life that de Valois had never had any faith in him, a view shared by Agnes de Mille: 'Her great mistake was in thinking Tudor had no talent at all.'

Ashton took up his new post as resident choreographer in September 1935, contracted to produce three ballets a year for a salary of £10 per week. The pressing question was: who was going to succeed Markova? In those days, the audience went to Sadler's Wells not so much to see the ballets but to see the ballerina: Markova carried the repertoire almost single-handedly. To please Ashton, de Valois had taken Pearl Argyle into the company, but, although she had one or two successes in roles he created for her, Argyle proved to be out of her element in a large theatre. 'When she later danced the Swan Queen in *Swan Lake* her performance was miniature to the point of invisibility,' wrote P. W. Manchester.

There was one young dancer, however, on whom de Valois had been keeping a sharp eye ever since she had joined the school. Not yet sixteen, Peggy Hookham, with blue-black hair and lovely proportions, was already making a definite impression in small roles, winning an ovation, for example, when she danced alongside Markova in *The Lord of Burleigh* as Katie Willows's friend, Lilian. 'It was obvious that something wonderful and beautiful had come into our midst,' de Valois has written. 'Elegance . . . was discernible, even beneath the careless breadth of adolescent movement. Children are generally either gauche or graceful. Miss Hookham was both.' By the autumn of 1934, Margot Fontes, as she now called herself (Fontes was her half-Brazilian mother's maiden name, later modulated to Fonteyn), had worked with Ashton on a new quartet which he had added to *Les Rendezvous*. But, as it is now widely known, this first attempt at working together had been more confrontation than collaboration.

> There is almost no way of describing adequately the incredible zest of Ashton when he was choreographing. After listening to a few bars of music he would fling himself into some swoops and twists and dives, his movements just flowing out of the music, apparently spontaneously. Then he would stop and say, 'What did I do? Now you do it.' I was flabbergasted by these extraordinary inventions . . . We four little girls tried to repeat what Ashton had

shown us, but I could never manage without losing my balance and nearly toppling over. That evening I complained to my mother: 'Frederick Ashton is absolutely mad; his steps are impossible.' He in turn complained to de Valois about me.

Finding her obstinate and unmalleable, Ashton did not have nearly as much faith in Fonteyn as did de Valois. Lopokova was also unpersuaded. 'If you are not convinced about Margot Fontaine [sic], then beyond doubt you are right,' Keynes told her. Nevertheless, when Markova refused to perform her role of the Creole Girl in *Rio Grande* that spring, Ashton had no choice but to give it to Fonteyn. 'She was the only one there. The one who had the extra substance.' Although the role did not demand a great deal of technique, it was an unlikely début for so young and inexperienced a dancer, requiring artistry, life and characterization. But with her round face, frizzy hair and hips provocatively thrust forward in a baubled, half-transparent costume, Fonteyn made an effective child prostitute, her dark-eyed, sallow-skinned South American looks allowing her to slip effortlessly into the atmosphere of the ballet. The *Dancing Times* presciently recorded her appearance as 'the most notable event of the past few weeks'. After that, Ashton began systematically giving Fonteyn the key Markova roles: the Polka in *Façade*; the lead in *Les Rendezvous*, in which he '*worked* at her to make her have a success. There was a certain amount of connivance,' he chuckled. And indeed, to begin with, Fonteyn's promotion was motivated as much by revenge as by necessity.

> If Markova hadn't been so utterly stupid, if she had stuck by me, she would in the end have had the place Fonteyn did. She never had the same kind of cachet that Margot had. But she was idiotic. She lost out.

Markova continued trying to win Ashton round in the hope that he would join her, but he was adamant: 'I'm like an old elephant, I don't forget.' A time would come when he would take the initiative and break the feud, telephoning Markova to tell her that they had been silent long enough, but for the next few years he indulged his animosity, remarking to the ballerina before she left Vic-Wells, 'I'm going to take Margot and make her much greater than you *ever* were.'

CHAPTER SIX

Two Terpsichores
1935–1936

W hen Ninette de Valois suggested to Ashton that he should give Margot Fonteyn the lead romantic role in his next ballet, Stravinsky's *Baiser de la fée*, he agreed, although he continued to claim not to see anything in her. Based on Hans Christian Andersen's *The Ice Maiden*, this was Ashton's first important creation for the young dancer, 'Although nobody thought at the time that Margot was going to be my muse.' Once again, early rehearsals were marked by a clash of wills which de Valois observed, but without much concern. 'Frankly, I think a little antagonism is rather a good thing.' Having been accustomed to working with Markova, Ashton felt 'set back' by the fact that Fonteyn was not nearly as technically proficient, and frustrated that he was unable to mould her as precisely as he had wanted. She was still mulishly resisting him, complaining that he never seemed satisfied at rehearsals, 'always urging me on to an unattainable standard and complaining about my soft feet – "Margot's pats of butter", he called them.' Feeling that he needed confirmation of her potential, Ashton sought the opinion of Karsavina, who told him that Fonteyn was very gifted and exceptionally musical, but had no understanding of épaulement. 'From tomorrow,' he said, 'I will ensure that she does.' But attempts to instil the kind of lushness of movement in Fonteyn that he had learnt from Nijinska only increased Ashton's demands upon her. 'I got very cross with her at times and went on and on at her relentlessly.' Finally, the dancer burst into tears, flung her arms around his neck, and the problem was resolved.

Ashton had loved the score of *Baiser de la fée*, Stravinsky's homage to Tchaikovsky, ever since he had danced in its original staging in Paris. It had not been a success – Nijinska's choreography left Stravinsky 'cold', and was dismissed by Diaghilev as 'still born' – but Ashton thought that the production had been doomed by Ida Rubinstein appearing as the Fairy, and was convinced that the role would be ideally suited to Pearl

Argyle, whose remote lunar beauty would make a striking contrast to the softer, rounder movements of the very young Fonteyn. He was right. The Ice Maiden proved to be Argyle's most successful creation at the Wells, allowing her the opportunity to reveal more fully her purity of line and control, while a striking make-up gave her an air of authority which she did not normally possess. But there were more deep-rooted difficulties with the ballet. Having borrowed the greater part of his melodic material from Tchaikovsky, Stravinsky's music is uncharacteristically derivative, the structure of his narrative almost unstageable at times, particularly the over-long epilogue. And yet, although Ashton's version reflects the un-evenness of the score, he did manage to overcome *Baiser*'s problematic ending.

The ballet begins dramatically with the storm that threatens the safety of the new-born baby, which is conveyed by movement alone: by the Martha Graham-style swaying of the mother's torso and by the swirling of the Spirits of the Tempest, effectively clad in Sophie Fedorovitch's grey-green draperies. The second tableau, in which the child, now a young man at the height of his good fortune, dances with his betrothed, goes on much too long, mainly consisting of pastiche peasant dances which only emphasized the tedium. 'Where I fell down – where I think everybody falls down – was in the village scene, because I didn't break it up enough,' said Ashton, who also attributed the failure of this section to the perversity of Stravinsky's instrumentation – 'what sounds on the pi-ano like a robust rustic dance proves to be very sparsely orchestrated.'

The third tableau, which takes place in the bridal chamber, is the high-light of the ballet. Ashton cleverly exploited Harold Turner's virtuosity in the role of the Bridegroom, pairing him with Fonteyn for a tender adagio, which crescendoed into a full-scale Petipa-style pas de deux. Fonteyn per-formed her simple, Cecchetti-based solo with an easy grace, her poise and beautiful elaboration of port de bras more than justifying Ashton's in-tense coaching, and proving beyond all doubt, the *Dancing Times* wrote, that she had true ballerina quality. *Baiser de la fée* ended as arrestingly as it had begun, with the corps seen behind a gauze curtain in Nijinska-type architectural groupings, and with Turner carrying Argyle in slow, floating lifts until, finally, she is borne along a line of dancers and into a beam of light, as though into Eternity.

In Stravinsky's allegory, the Fairy is Tchaikovsky's muse, imprinting her magical kiss on him at birth and claiming him at the height of his powers. To a lesser degree, the story also had symbolical implications for Ashton, its conflict of allegiances echoing the duality in his own sexual identity at the time. There was a sixteen-year-old dancer in the company – like the innocent young bride or the romantic ingénue in *Valentine's Eve* – who had given her heart to Ashton and had been rejected. With her fresh complexion and brown hair cut in a Christopher Robin bob, Rose Paget could have passed for a child, and Ashton treated her like one, standing in the wings, pulling chewing-gum to make her laugh. But she was desperately infatuated with him, and used to lurk at the back of the dress circle when she was not dancing, '*hoping*' to bump into him. 'Freddie had some kind of charm. Every time you passed him backstage or in the corridor, you felt something.' At five feet eight inches, she was too tall to go far in her profession and had to make do with small corps de ballet roles, first at the Mercury and then at Sadler's Wells (her move coincided with Ashton's new appointment).

It was while she was with Rambert that Rose had proposed to him. Her father, the Marquess of Anglesey, had given her a generous allowance and she tried to convince Ashton that marriage could be a mutually agreeable arrangement. 'Fred was still not making money. I thought it would be a good idea for him. I absolutely understood that we'd have our own rooms. I was a virgin but not at all innocent. I understood quite a lot about life.' Ashton refused to take her seriously – 'He said, "Don't be so stupid, Rose. You've got to marry a rich man and have affairs with dukes."' Yet he continued to see a lot of the young dancer, taking her out to dinner at cheap Italian restaurants and afterwards putting her on a bus home. The first time she took him to meet her parents at their house in Queensgate, she felt very apprehensive, thinking that they would disapprove of her going out with someone so much older, but, at first sight, Ashton and Lady Anglesey were charmed by each other. Marjorie Anglesey was the daughter of the Duke of Rutland, and a great beauty, with deep-set dark brown eyes and a pure white streak in her auburn hair. Many people thought her more striking than her famously beautiful younger sister, the blonde, blue-eyed Lady Diana Cooper. And, like Diana, she had a passion for the theatre, having spent much of her youth in Herbert Beerbohm Tree's dressing room. 'She and Freddie adored each other,' said Rose, who realized that Ashton took her seriously as a friend because he had fallen in love with her family. He was determined to dampen Rose's ardour, nevertheless, and when she was sent to finishing school in Paris he returned her impassioned letters, after first having corrected her spelling.

Rose did not know that, throughout the making of *Baiser de la fée*, Ashton was falling under the spell of a seventeen-year-old boy – 'an absolutely magical creature', in Lincoln Kirstein's description – who was to exert a hold on him until the day he died. Michael Somes had arrived from the West Country for an audition at Sadler's Wells school at the end of 1934, encouraged by Karsavina, who had seen him dance at a school display and been impressed by his musicality, good looks and unusually high jump. He was a wonderfully handsome youth, with dark hair, a beautifully planed and chiselled face, and a rather supercilious public-school manner, a result of holding his head back and looking down his nose. 'Michael was Fred's Ideal,' said Kirstein, 'the personification of a young Englishman, very refined, with enormous charm – a throwback to *Brideshead*, if you like.' Somes was wry, intelligent and worked very hard, noticeably keeping his distance from the rest of the company when they were relaxing and laughing about trivial things. According to a colleague, he became 'totally bound up with Fred' during this period, Ashton having begun to court him assiduously by assuming the role of mentor. Writing to the choreographer on New Year's Eve, Somes thanked him for the 'lovely present' and for all his help, advice and kindness, 'which I have missed *very* much since you have been away'.

Ashton had been in Manchester over Christmas, working on the new Cochran revue, *Follow the Sun*. His main contribution was an Edwardian cameo, *The First Shoot*, which had a libretto by Osbert Sitwell, music by William Walton and designs by Cecil Beaton (who would work with Ashton on a much grander scale the following year). Claire Luce starred as the lovely aristocrat accidentally shot during a shooting party, and six of Mr Cochran's Young Ladies, including Winston Churchill's daughter Sarah, rhythmically strutted around in Beaton's authentic-looking pheasant costumes. Although amusing enough, the ballet was not much liked by the public and was loathed by the pheasants, who revenged themselves by secretly renaming it *Swallow the Fun*.

In the revue's opening number, there appeared a very tall, glamorous showgirl with wonderful legs, to whom Ashton took a great shine during the Manchester run. Elizabeth Corcoran, a major-general's daughter, was fun and uninhibitedly flirtatious: 'Elizabeth popped in and out of bed with anybody so it was natural that she would with Fred,' said her first cousin Gerald Corcoran,* on whom Ashton had also been quite keen at one time. Throughout this period, Ashton's sexuality was swinging both ways with the regularity of a metronome, his attraction to Michael Somes not yet consuming enough to preclude a series of brief encounters. In February, when the Vic-Wells opened Maynard Keynes's new Arts Theatre in Cambridge, Ashton met Colin Harding, an undergraduate in his final year. He was a small, dapper little person, with a delicately boned face, who appeared en travesti in Footlights Revues. 'Freddie made no secret of his yearnings, but I don't think it ever went further,' said a fellow student, Neville Blackburne. The unattainable was then, as

*Edward Burra's London dealer.

it continued to be for Ashton, the only enduring attraction. It was much the same for Constant Lambert, 'always looking for The Ideal One', and *Apparitions*, their next collaboration, would reflect this, filtering their own predilections into a Gothic tale of unrequited romantic love.

Keen to sponsor a new production with the remaining funds held by the Camargo Society, Maynard Keynes had asked Lambert to come up with an idea for a ballet for Ashton. In September 1936, he wrote to Keynes that he had found the ideal subject: an essay in the High Romantic style based on Berlioz's *Symphonie fantastique*. Lambert had made some changes to the libretto, substituting in place of Berlioz's composer, a poet in search of a beautiful woman in a ball dress who appears to him in three macabre, opium-induced dreams. Gothic ballets were very much in vogue at the time: in April 1934, de Valois choreographed *The Haunted Ballroom*, a fantasy about a doomed man danced to death in his own ballroom by a host of threatening apparitions; in the summer of 1936, Massine produced his own *Symphonie fantastique* at Covent Garden. But rather than using the Berlioz score, as Massine had done, Lambert considered that the Mephistophelean atmosphere of *Apparitions* would be best served by Liszt, whose pianistic style was defined by melodramatic crescendos, frenzied glissandi, blurring and clouding of harmonies. He had already begun to arrange a dramatically cohesive score from fragments of the late piano works, and now it remained for him only to persuade Ashton to bring the project to fruition.

> My dear Fred,
> I was up in London last night and pursued you from theatre to theatre like a symbolist foot chasing a courtesan and equally in vain. My object was to bore you with my new idea for a ballet. I quite agree that we should have at least one new ballet that is not drawn from the repertoire of another company and I think that a Liszt ballet by you would be the ideal thing. My idea for it will sound a little odd put down on paper – principally because I have conceived it more from the visual and aural point of view . . . I want as far as possible to use only unknown pieces mostly from the latest period though I may allow you Valse Oubliée and Consolation as a sop to your feelings.
> The genre is 1830 romanticism of the fruitiest type plus a leavening of surrealism. Though not entirely original (it derives slightly from *Bien Aimée*, *Errante* and *Mephisto Waltz*) I think the conception as a whole will come quite freshly to the audience.

It will be a longish affair: 3 big scenes with a prologue and epilogue . . . a super-Gothic poets study, the 3 scenes respectively a ballroom with a Polish accent, a snow clad plain and a brothel. I think it will suit very well the style you developed in *Valentine's Eve* and *Mephisto* (actually my two favourite ballets of yours).

For that reason I think Sophie might be the best person for the decor if she can be juicy enough. The ball scene and brothel scene want to be as like Constantin Guys as possible – the rest should be a little more fantastic.

The man's part will suit Bobby very well and the woman's part will be ideal for either Spessiva or Fonteyn (whom to my great surprise you don't seem to appreciate at her true level. Though obviously immature at the moment she is to my mind the only post-Diaghileff dancer with of course the exception of Toumanova, to have that indefinable quality of poetry in her work.)

You may of course not like the idea at all. But if you do I hope we will be able to spend some time on it going though the pieces again and again and really moulding the ballet into shape. All the Wells ballets suffer not only from being put on too quickly but from being too cut and dried. The best Diaghileff ballets were always the result of a long and close collaboration between the artists . . .

Ashton was easily won over. He and Lambert had been wanting to create another Liszt ballet together for some time. '*Apparitions* grew from an equal appreciation of Liszt. We had been through all the music we liked long before – I was just as much pushing Liszt as he was.' The libretto, Ashton said, 'was all Constant who at that time was falling in love with Margot. It was much more him than me.' But with the image of Michael Somes never far from his thoughts, the ballet's theme had personal resonance for him too.

The question of who should design *Apparitions* was answered by Maynard Keynes. Sophie Fedorovitch was vetoed – presumably because her style was considered too restrained for the genre – and so was Pavel Tchelitchew, Lambert's alternative, because he was too expensive. Cecil Beaton was the final choice, an apt compromise, as his work, at the time, was heavily influenced by the French neo-Romantics. Beaton's use of shadows projected on to white screens (the outline of chandeliers, music-stands and a 'cello in the ballroom scene'), was an idea he had borrowed from Tchelitchew; while his gradations of colour, and preference for mauve, were derived from Christian Bérard's palette. There were no doubts about who should play the Byronic protagonist. Having already displayed his histrionic gifts to great effect in *The Haunted Ballroom*,

Robert Helpmann was the obvious candidate for a role which called more for mime than for dancing, and depended on an artist with a vivid sense of theatre. Capable of timing a gesture or an expression to perfection, Helpmann had only to walk on stage to draw all eyes to him. He dominated the whole ballet, seeming to move in another dimension from the rest of the dancers – 'his opiate-induced visions, transfigured from scene to scene as his hallucinations deepened.' In the first tableau, set in the ballroom, he moved as in a dream among the gyrating dancers, while the alluring image of Fonteyn in a ball-dress elusively beckoned and evaded him. The use Ashton made of the corps de ballet in this section was far in advance of anything he had done before; their delicate groupings, entrances and exits, arranged with drama and imagination. The remaining two tableaux were nightmarish set pieces and included a brilliantly executed funeral cortège, which drew once again on Ashton's memories of religious processions. The ballet ended where it began: in the poet's study. Waking in despair, he kills himself. The woman who, until now, had been a figment of his dreams, enters, and she and her sinister hooded companions bear him away.

The final rehearsal was chaotic, mainly because the ball-gowns (made by Karinska, the favourite costumier of Bérard and Balanchine) were nowhere near completed. Everyone was very tense, and, as Lambert wrote to Beaton, 'The atmosphere was dead . . . One felt the awful weight of middle-brow opinion against the whole thing.' Beaton was to take the production photographs and, in the taxi which Ashton shared with Fonteyn to Beaton's studio, he began to tell her about all the qualities that he felt were missing from her interpretation. He had designed his choreography for a woman of elegance and sophistication, using, for the first time, many of his signature motifs: melting backbends displaying a long expanse of throat, emotional, silent movie-star flutterings of hands to cheeks. But the role, a prototype of his later romantic heroines like Marguerite Gautier or Natalia Petrovna was, as Fonteyn admitted, 'hardly one I could adequately fill at the age of sixteen'. Ashton tried his best to guide her, impersonating Pavlova and Karsavina by re-creating their expressions, the use of their eyes, their theatricality and unorthodox freedom of gesture, but the ballerina he saw on stage at the final rehearsal remained 'a sincere, simple girl, with no guile and no affectation'. Ashton's criticism was too much for Fonteyn, who had by now developed a crush on him and was feeling over-emotional enough, sitting next to him at such close range. She burst into tears, knowing for certain that she was going to fail him, and went home 'desperately afraid of the fiasco to come'. The next night, however, by what she describes as 'some alchemy of despair', she discovered that she had matured just enough to meet the demands of the ballet.

Apparitions was a triumph: 'a great collaboration and everyone agrees it knocks spots off any ballet since *Cotillon*', wrote Lambert. Fonteyn was applauded as the epitome of romantic glamour, Helpmann was praised to the hilt, and Ashton was commended for avoiding melodrama, and responding brilliantly and with extraordinary sensibility to an unfamiliar epoch.

> Ashton has made it live. He has conceived it as a romantic and not as a modern looking back upon a quaint period . . . I have in the past often doubted Ashton's ability to come to grips with real problems and have deplored his enormous facility for the creation of amusing trifles. I have obviously been wrong.

Although the ballet had been conceived principally as a vehicle for Helpmann, its great surprise was that it launched Fonteyn as an artist of equal stature. Her technique was still immature, but her interpretation had a lyricism, sensitivity and serenity which seemed to set her apart from other dancers. It was a performance imbued with what Lambert had presciently described to Ashton as 'that indefinable quality of poetry', its significance stretching far beyond this particular work. 'In her,' Haskell wrote, 'Ashton has undoubtedly found someone who can evoke and reveal the deeper sides of his art.'

If 1936 was the year which cemented Ashton's creative partnership with Fonteyn, it also brought another woman into his life, an unsung muse whose influence would prove just as formative, in its own oblique way. He first saw her on the lawn at Ashcombe, Cecil Beaton's house in Wiltshire. On a Sunday morning in May 1936, she was walking up and down, with her head bent in thought. He watched her from his bedroom window: a hesitant gazelle, with blue-black hair and large, plaintive eyes. 'She seemed an extraordinary creature; so elegant and sort of sad.' Her name was Alice von Hofmannsthal, and, although her husband, Raimund, was with her (the son of the poet, Hugo von Hofmannsthal), Ashton did not discover until later that she was married. That afternoon, Beaton took photographs of them all in the garden, and afterwards they went for drinks with Lady Juliet Duff at Bulbridge, opposite the Wilton estate. Ashton recalled that 'all the grand Wiltshire people were there, like Daphne Weymouth who, I remember, had butterflies in her hair'. Although the other guests did not notice any particular rapport between Ashton and Alice, they must themselves have felt it, because when Beaton told him that Lady Weymouth would give him a lift back, he protested: 'No, I don't want to be driven by her, she frightens me. I'm not used to that kind of assurance. I'd like Alice to take me.' Clearly, however, Alice was equally drawn to Ashton. A few days later, he received a telephone call from Iris Tree, who had been persuaded to act as go-between, and invited Ashton to dinner at the von Hofmannsthals' house in London, where she and her second husband, the handsome Count Friedrich Ledebur, were staying. Ashton must have known that Alice was rich because he used to quote a remark that Eva Curie, who was among the Beaton house-party, had made during the weekend: 'Elle est tellement riche, mais ses gestes sont pauvres.' But he had no idea of the extent of Alice's fortune until he dined at her house that night.

Iris Tree had given him the address: Hanover Lodge, Regent's Park, but after wandering up and down Park Road, peering at the names of the red-brick mansion blocks, he had to stop a passer-by to ask the way. As directed, he turned into the park and walked along the Outer Circle, through wrought-iron gates and down the drive to the entrance of a magnificent Regency villa. Posted at the open doors were two footmen: one took his 'threadbare' coat, the other led him into the drawing room with a triple set of french windows overlooking a sunken garden. Hanover Lodge was a great deal more imposing when Alice owned it than it is today, its views of the canal and park now obstructed by the London Mosque, as well as by five neo-Nash houses recently built on what used to be the rose garden and tennis courts. The house Ashton knew had four acres of grounds and was one-storey higher, a Lutyens addition that has since been demolished. Alice ran Hanover Lodge like an ancestral estate, employing at least a dozen servants, including a personal maid, a seamstress, Dean the butler, and an internationally renowned chef, Vassily (Basil) Yourtchenko, who had served as an apprentice in the kitchen of the Grand Duke Vladimir and escaped the Revolution with Alice's first husband, Prince Serge Obolensky. It impressed Ashton that, when the Obolenskys divorced, it was Alice who kept the chef; Basil's imperial Russian cuisine – a typical hors d'oeuvre was tomato shells filled with caviar, topped with poached eggs and hot hollandaise – proved crucial in Alice's strategy of seduction. During dinner that night, Ashton turned to Iris and, in a whisper, asked her who Alice really was. 'She told me and that was how it all began.'

Alice von Hofmannsthal was born an Astor (although there are doubts about that), the daughter of John Jacob IV and Ava Willing, a celebrated Newport belle. She was ten when her father died, drowned on the *Titanic*, leaving her $5 million, held in trust until she reached twenty-one. Her life had been a classic poor-little-rich-girl tale. Her mother had no time for Alice, or for her brother, Vincent, and the siblings were never close. Even when their father was alive, it had been an unhappy family. Ava made a cold, selfish wife and ruthlessly dominated tall, shy, shambling John Jacob. Society saw the best of her: with her dark, dancing eyes, tiny waist and full bosom, she was witty and flirtatious, and used her beauty to licence her wayward behaviour. No one was in the least surprised by the rumours zigzagging between London, Newport and New York that Alice was not John Jacob's daughter. 'I'd always heard about it,' remarked the writer Nicholas Lawford. 'Emerald Cunard and Chips Channon assured me it was true. Alice didn't look remotely like Vincent.' But the idea that Alice might not be an Astor did not worry her in the least, claimed Iris Tree's son, Ivan Moffat: 'If anything she was counter-snobbish.' It was the total lack of warmth from Ava that affected her, inflicting upon her, for life, a sense of emotional insecurity which corroded all her relationships. As one of her friends observed, 'The key to Alice is her mother.'

While Vincent was at boarding school, Ava would trail Alice between America and Europe, travelling wherever her whim took her. It was a Jamesian life of lavish opportunity and immense culture but devoid of affection. After Ava's divorce from Astor (adultery was cited, but the papers are sealed) she brought her daughter to live permanently in England, where she soon remarried. To Ava, her second husband, Baron Ribblesdale, was definitely a catch. Former lord-in-waiting to Queen Victoria and a famous ladies' man and sportsman, he was nicknamed 'the Ancestor' by the Prince of Wales because of his patrician good looks, which were captured, riding crop in hand, by Sargent in the portrait now owned by the Tate. After his first wife died, he moved into the Cavendish Hotel, where he was fussed over by its celebrated Cockney proprietress, Rosa Lewis. However, by the time he met Ava, she found she had married a melancholy soul, content to lead what he called a pot-au-feu life in the country, reading the classics aloud to his far from docile new wife. In Ava's increasingly frequent absence, he sought the company of Alice, who, although grateful for the attention, felt stranded and more alone than ever. But her life was soon to change.

As a diversion, Ava had begun ambitious marriage plans for Alice. Two English aristocrats, an American and a rich Spaniard, were among the beaux on whom she set her sights. But in her quiet, characteristically stubborn way, Alice sabotaged her mother's plans by falling in love with a man *she* was determined to marry: Serge Obolensky, a cavalry officer with the tall, suave good looks of a romantic hero. This 'impoverished Russian Prince' (his description) had been married before to the daughter of the Czar,* but it was his lack of means, not his status as a divorcé, to which Ava objected. To begin with, the affair had to be conducted in secret with the help of friends. The couple eventually married in the sum-

---

*Princess Catherine, daughter of Alexander II.

mer of 1924, the year after Alice reached twenty-one. They settled in England, where Alice bought Hanover Lodge, and soon afterwards their son Ivan was born. (Chips Channon, who had played matchmaker to the Obolenskys and was having dinner at Hanover Lodge that night, was one of Ivan's godparents, in company with the Grand Duchess Helen and William Waldorf Astor.)

Prince and Princess Obolensky continued their lustrous lifestyle, golfing in Cannes, skiing in St Moritz, gambling in Monte Carlo, party-going in Paris and Venice. When they entertained during the London season, guests would sit down to a great feast, prepared by Basil, in the long panelled Regency dining room, and then the dancing would start. By day, there would be tennis and tea parties in the garden; midsummer was spent in Newport; the autumn and Christmas in Rhinebeck, outside New York, where Alice had built a grey-stone manor house on 100 acres of Astor estate given to her by Vincent. This uncharacteristic display of generosity towards his sister – a token of his approval of her marriage to Obolensky, whom he liked and admired – was something he would soon regret. After only a year, Serge and even the shy, tentative Alice began to spice their life of leisure, first with flirtations and then with more serious infidelities. By 1931, she had fallen in love again and was demanding a divorce.

The man Alice wanted to marry was Raimund von Hofmannsthal. He had arrived in America, speaking no English, at the age of nineteen, appearing as an extra in Max Reinhardt's production of *The Miracle*, with Diana Cooper as the Madonna and Iris Tree as the Nun. Overcome by Diana Cooper's mythical beauty, Raimund had become her devoted Rosenkavalier, chauffeuring the two women across the continent. 'He was court official at Diana's court,' remarks Isaiah Berlin. 'That's what formed him in a way.' Knowing her marriage to Serge was over, Alice willingly agreed to bolt with Raimund to Berlin; but before the divorce came through, their daughter, Sylvia, was born – a child that Serge (mostly in deference to Vincent) would publicly claim to be his. English society took Raimund for a foreign bounder, but those who knew him well admired his extraordinary capacity for enhancing other people's lives. He had what Lord David Cecil called an 'exquisite Rococo spirit of pleasure', an intense and infectious appreciation of beauty and hedonistic pleasures. He was a true child of the 1920s, whose vision of life was profoundly coloured by the poetry and personality of his father. Like Serge, Raimund cheerfully admitted to not owning a dime, but Alice didn't care – she loved his romantic extravagance, and, for a time, he made her happier than she had been, or was to be, in her life. However, an important component of Raimund's 'incandescent aesthetic feeling', so eloquently hymned by his friends, was a relish for beautiful women.

'He knew more about women than anyone else,' says Isaiah Berlin. 'He was a great flatterer but of tremendous skill.' Raimund and Alice had not been married more than a year or so before he began his private pursuit of pleasure. There were a number of distractions about which Alice could not help but know as he was never very discreet. Poppet John, Augustus John's pretty daughter, remembers him trying to seduce her, despite the fact that Alice was in a nearby room. He was surprised when she refused, asking incredulously: 'Vy not? Vy von't you?' listing all the women who 'vould'. One was a wanton, self-destructive American beauty called Angelica Welldon, whom Alice had discovered in bed with Raimund when they were staying at the Gladstone Hotel in New York. Her marriage was disintegrating into farce, as she was well aware, and Ashton appeared in her life at exactly the moment she most needed comfort and diversion.

Alice was immediately charmed by him, by his elegant, self-effacing manner and by his company. He made her laugh, which few people could, and his sexual ambivalence only added to the attraction. 'She was always determined to get her own way about something difficult,' said a mutual friend. 'She was determined to have a love affair with Fred; and that was very difficult.' For all his heterosexual ventures of the past few years, Ashton was now seriously infatuated with Michael Somes. Alice knew that, but was undeterred. From the beginning, she was the pursuer, casting him in his fantasy role of fin-de-siècle mistress, sending him flowers, giving him expensive trinkets and taking him to grand parties. On formal occasions, she and Raimund would appear as a couple (arriving together after dinner, for example, at Chips Channon's soirée for the King and Mrs Simpson), but Alice began to use Ashton as her escort with increasing frequency.

She took him to dine at Emerald Cunard's salon in Grosvenor Square, where the company was brilliant and the conversation inevitably returned to the possibility of a royal marriage (their hostess was a close friend of Edward VIII and Wallis Simpson).

> I sat there and didn't say a word. I was absolutely terrified and tongue-tied: suddenly to be plonked into society like that. I cursed Alice afterwards and begged her not to take me anywhere like that again. But she was always doing it to me. You must remember that society in those days was tremendously assured – hostesses like Lady Cunard expected one to contribute. It's not like now when people are more used to meeting undesirable boyfriends.

To a certain extent, Ashton's self-portrait is misleading. Not only had he long been initiated into society through his friendships with Olivia

Wyndham, Margot Asquith and the Angleseys, but it is hardly likely that Emerald Cunard, with her gift for collecting and mixing new people – quite apart from her interest in the ballet – would have seen him as the gauche outsider he describes. It is certainly true that dancers in the mid-1930s did not have the cachet of twenty years before, when Diaghilev's troupe were the toast of London. Unconventional as she was, Lady Ribblesdale was said by Ashton to have exclaimed to a friend: 'My daughter has gone mad and fallen in love with a ballet dancer.' But like Noël Coward, Ashton soon discovered that the passport to upper-class life was an ability to make people laugh. As Diana Cooper put it, 'He was proper fun – quite apart from his art, which again, we thought frightfully good.' Also, unlike the hilarious but socially hazardous Bobby Helpmann, he knew how to behave. The persona he had begun to cultivate of 'a middle-class boy at sea in such grand surroundings' was more than a little calculated: he knew that it amused people and it made him appear unthrusting. As he often said, 'I fitted in because I never tried to be one of them.'

As soon as Ashton felt that he had arrived 'under my own steam, as it were, and not as Alice's boyfriend', he was able to thrive in her milieu. He even became a confidant of Lady Cunard, an insomniac, who used to ring him at three in the morning to talk. 'And once when we met she cried to me about Sir Thomas Beecham whom she loved. She used to blacken her eyes and I remember great black tears pouring down her face' – an image he would remorselessly impersonate in his imitation of a heartbroken dowager. However, beneath his increasing confidence there was a genuine sense of awe at his new surroundings. Loelia Westminster confirmed how shy he was when they first met at Hanover Lodge. 'We made friends from the word go. He didn't know anybody and I felt very lost too, and that's why we chummed up together.' It is hard to associate shyness with Loelia Ponsonby, as she was in the 1920s – one of the original Bright Young Things and inventor of the Bottle Party – but, brought up to be reserved and repressed, she insists that she and Ashton saw each other as allies, and would sit together in a corner at Hanover Lodge, chattering like débutantes about fashion and jewellery. Ashton confided to her that he had expected more perks from Alice – she remembered that he particularly wanted a gold cigarette case, which eventually he was given – but this open display of venality was probably his way of putting himself in parodic competition with the Duchess, who at the time was being showered with diamonds by Bendor, England's richest duke. It was precisely the feeling that people were saying he was 'out for the dibs', as he put it, that made Ashton uneasy about his relationship with Alice. 'I was too poor, I couldn't cope with it. I couldn't be among them earning £5 a week at Sadler's Wells.'

Alice, who was always happiest in the company of artists and writers, did everything she could to put him at his ease. At the end of June, she took him to spend a week with Lord Berners at Faringdon, where Osbert Sitwell, Michael Duff and Dali and his wife were fellow guests. He had met Berners while working on *Riverside Nights* in the 1920s, and came to know him better through Constant Lambert, but it was only after this occasion that they became good friends and began to meet almost every other week. It was at Faringdon, away from the scrutiny of Alice's husband and Ashton's vigilant and ailing mother, that their relationship was consummated, although for him, the shadow of Michael Somes was ever present. Alice knew she had what a confidante called 'an off-stage rival', but refused to acknowledge the truth. 'I was utterly frank with her,' said Ashton. 'I told her about the whole thing, but she said, "No, no, you're not really queer."' Certainly, he had no difficulty 'obliging' Alice, as he put it, boasting to friends that they made love at least once a day. In later years, he attributed his bisexual prowess to the audacity of youth: 'When I was young I could have done it with anything. *Anything*. I could have fucked a duck. If you're a young person you can *do* it – it's no trouble. Alice was very nice to me and I said to myself: "Well, what does it cost you, dear?"' But this sexual return of favours was not as cynical as it sounds. Although he was not really physically attracted to Alice, he was captivated by her elegance and felt a genuine affection for her. 'She didn't like flattery and she knew Fred's admiration for her was sincere,' said Ivan Moffat. On the other hand, there was also a child-like, grasping side to Ashton, which he expected Alice to indulge. 'When I went anywhere in those days a Rolls-Royce would appear at the house; there would be a footman with a ticket; and I'd be shown to a reserved seat on the train.' Which is exactly what happened five days after his return from Faringdon, when Ashton set off for Austria at Alice's invitation.

Every summer, she would rent from Eleonora von Mendelssohn, a great-niece of the composer, one half of Schloss Kammer, a fourteenth-century castle on the Attersee in the Salzkammergut. An exile from Nazi Germany, Eleonora, named after her godmother, was an aspiring actress and a talented musician. Noël Coward and Max Reinhardt were among the guests she invited to Kammer, but on the whole, life in Eleonora's part of the castle was not particularly social. The von Hofmannsthals, on the other hand, made sure there was always a convivial toing and froing of friends from England: Loelia Westminster, Diana Gage, Gerald Berners, Cecil Beaton and David Herbert were especially welcome. As Kammer was only thirty miles from Salzburg, nights would often be spent at the Festspiele, while lazy days were spent in, on, or around the lake. The extravagant hospitality at Kammer was a great lure to visiting celebrities: Dietrich arrived for the day one summer, and a surprise supper was given for Toscanini with whom Eleonora von Mendelssohn was infatuated, despite the thirty-three-year age gap. On this and other occasions, the long narrow lake was used to magical effect: on a barge floating a quarter of a mile from the shore was a formally laid dining table, a footman behind each chair; on a second barge was an orchestra playing Strauss waltzes; and erupting from a third would be dazzling galaxies of fireworks. At exactly the appointed time, a motorboat would emerge from the darkness, bringing coffee from the castle.

As a contrast to the grandeur, there would be rustic picnics in the hills. Diana Gage watched Lord Berners toil along with rivulets of orange sweat trickling from his dyed hair. For all the surface gaiety, however, Kammer is mostly remembered for its dark, troubled atmosphere. 'It was most uncomfortable,' says Loelia Westminster. 'Everyone was miserable there – certainly I was. Half the time people weren't speaking to each other.' 'It has a strong personality, ruthless, fantastic and sometimes sinister,' wrote Cecil Beaton, who was there that August, until his holiday was cut short by news of his father's death. He was an avid chronicler of the intrigues at Kammer, and found it 'stimulating and strangely sympathetic'. He does not single out the Ashton–Alice liaison, but remarks how the atmosphere improved after the departure of Rex Whistler and Rose Paget's two beautiful sisters, Elizabeth and Caroline, 'all of whom were in love with someone else and were all violently jealous'. The Duke and Duchess of Kent were also among the guests but were oblivious to the 'forlorn sighing couples', whom Beaton describes as 'longing to explain their tragedies of jealousy, envy and indiscretion', but springing to attention to make conversation with the Kents, 'who stayed for too long and would never go to their rooms'.

When the Mistral-like Föhn wind blew, it seemed to fan the emotional fever of the place and Raimund would shut himself away in his room. He was neither jealous by nature, nor one to keep double standards, and yet, according to Daphne Weymouth, he was openly hostile towards Ashton. 'People noticed it very much. Simply because he wasn't a great hater.' The following year, when Raimund himself fell in love ('That's what straightened it out'), he came to appreciate the good value of Ashton's company and his friends were struck by how much he 'adored Freddie'.

For all the glamour of that summer, Ashton was glad to get back to his own life and, especially, to get back to work. At the end of September, he went to discuss the music and libretto of a new ballet with the critic Edward Sackville-West at Knole (deriving considerable satisfaction from the fact that he was now a guest at the sumptuous Elizabethan manor, whereas six years earlier, researching *Capriol Suite*, he had been only a tourist). For the score, Sackville-West had suggested a tone poem by Delius: *Nocturne: Paris (Song of a Great City)*, a piece which Lambert, although a prominent champion of Delius, had tried unsuccessfully to persuade Ashton not to use – at that time, the suitability of symphonic music for ballet was particularly controversial. The score is a personal evocation by the composer of the city he knew and loved, but wishing to avoid association with a specific place, the collaborators decided to call the ballet simply *Nocturne*. Sophie Fedorovitch designed the ballet, providing only a hint of the locale, the courtyard entrance to a Parisian dance hall.* 'She throws a nosegay of sweet peas into a Baudelaire gutter band, pulls out of it a classical column, a dark blue velvet sky, a cloak, and dresses that must be the heart's desire of every girl for her first ball.'

The ballet's libretto has always been accredited to Sackville-West, but, in fact, it was Ashton's idea. It is a simple story about a young man loved by two women, one rich, one poor. A standard ballet theme, as in *Giselle*, but what the dancers did not know was that *Nocturne* drew on aspects of Ashton's own life.

He may have been emotionally in thrall to Michael Somes, but Alice had captivated him with her subtle beauty and her style. Her Boldini-esque refinement was imaginatively, if not physically, stirring for him, and, in *Nocturne*, he enshrined it in the character of the Rich Girl. June Brae, 'who was Alice', danced the part without any idea of whom it was modelled on, and yet, with her dark hair swept up and her Worth-inspired ballgown, she portrayed exactly the kind of Edwardian sophistication caught by Beaton in his alluring study of Alice wearing couture evening dress. But whereas the relationship was creatively fruitful for Ashton, with *Nocturne* drawing on the romantic dichotomy that he himself was experiencing, it was an unhappy situation for Alice: 'It was miserable for her,' said their mutual friend Doris Langley Moore. 'Fred used her, frankly. Alice was very rich and very much in love.' At this point, as Lydia Lopokova gossiped to Maynard Keynes, Ashton had 'taken from her only shirts'. But they were silk shirts, given to him in Gatsby-like quantities. Ashton, however, seemed perfectly willing to indict himself with any charge of opportunism, claiming that the roué in *Nocturne* was a self-caricature: 'Bobby was the cad, who was me.'

Premièred at Sadler's Wells on 10 November 1936, *Nocturne* was declared a 'triumph' by the *Dancing Times*, and even Adrian Stokes, who still had reservations about Ashton's importance, admitted in his *Specta-*

---

*In the 1944 revival, the 'bal' posters decorating the pillars on one side of the stage were removed, as Ashton wanted to give the impression of a scene set outside a private house.

tor review that, judged by the highest (i.e., Ballets Russes) standards, the new work was 'good'. Stokes wrote effusively about the choreography for the poor Flower Girl, which captured Margot Fonteyn's own vulnerable appeal, as in her arabesque with arms curved over drooping head, her whole body straining forward at a distorted angle to enact her despair. Ashton won praise all round for his deft orchestration of Revellers and Masquers who, ebbing and flowing to and from the ballroom, intrude with sardonic gaiety on the sad little episode being played out that night.

The young woman whose heart is breaking with unrequited love is usually the subjective figure in Ashton's ballets. This time, however, he identified with the roving hero (danced by Helpmann), but cast himself as an authorial character: the charismatic, black-cloaked Spectator, who opens and closes the ballet. To one anonymous critic, he was like 'Baudelaire himself'. Arnold Haskell considered Ashton's portrayal of this mysterious outsider who takes pity on the spurned Flower Girl to be his finest role. And *Nocturne*, he felt, was the 'first of his sophisticated ballets to have depth and show a really serious confrontation with his material'.

It was agreed that the ballet's significance lay in its atmosphere, in the choreographer's distillation of the hazy, valedictory mood of the music. Beecham called the tone poem an 'audacious experiment (the greatest yet made) in musical impressionism', and both Ashton and Sophie Fedorovitch found a visual equivalent to the music's dissolving colours and indefinite melodies by creating the dream-like illusion of 'faintly blurred edges' with 'everything a little misty'. The score's outbursts of wild hilarity were embodied by the grotesque and colourful figures of the masquers. To Mary Clarke it was 'one of the most successful uses of existing music in all ballet'.

Antony Tudor, the acknowledged master of atmospherically charged ballets, considered *Nocturne* to have been influenced by his *Jardin aux lilas*, which had been first shown by Ballet Rambert at the beginning of the year. 'I know Fred wanted to be like me at one time (I got that from Marie Rambert). He wanted very much to do a ballet that would convey an emotional atmosphere to the audience. Thank God that he didn't.' Tudor's facetious remark was half-serious and illustrates the rivalry that existed between the two men throughout their careers. Although, to a certain extent, they influenced each other at this period – Tudor's psychological use of gesture filtered into *Nocturne*, and the sophisticated, social milieu of *Les Masques* influenced *Jardin aux lilas* – as choreographers and as personalities they were complete opposites. Tudor regarded Ashton and his work as 'chic and flippant'; while Ashton thought Tudor too serious. 'I used to say: what is Antony doing these days – another *depth* charge?' The hieratic, reclusive Tudor possessed none of Ashton's social aplomb; always inhibited by his lowly background, he was reluctant to mix with the beau monde of the Ballet Club and avoided Ashton's company. 'I never even had lunch with him,' said Tudor. 'He was the last person I would have talked to about my work: he wouldn't have been interested in my ideas and I wouldn't have been in his.' Their obvious dislike for each other makes all the more absurd the persistent rumour that, at one stage, they had been lovers, a rumour which astonished Ashton when it reached him. '*Ugh!* [theatrical shimmy]. I found him *desperately* unattractive. I couldn't have touched Tudor if he'd been scented in myrrh.'

The critics made no mention of any Tudor borrowings in *Nocturne*, and June Brae, who danced in both this and *Jardin aux lilas*, was not struck by a marked similarity between the works. The ballet remained fairly constantly in the repertory after its first night, but in subsequent casts, according to Mary Clarke, only Pamela May as the Rich Girl captured the ballet's original spirit. Alice must have thought so too, as she lent the dancer a pair of diamond earrings to wear on stage which May nervously secured to her ears with cotton.

As Alice fell more deeply in love with Ashton, she began to submerge herself in his world. She brought large groups of her friends to his ballets and would invite the performers to join them for supper at Hanover Lodge, after which all the guests would 'dance about like lunatics'. Alternating lavish parties with intimate dinners at the Ivy, Alice homed in on those closest to Ashton: 'She was a great magician in that she got everybody that Fred liked round her,' said Billy Chappell. 'She brought us all into the picture, it was very well done.' Either out of curiosity or because she was anxious to please Ashton, Alice even included Michael Somes at Hanover Lodge suppers. 'He fitted in by being quiet.' Her main object was, of course, the pursuit of Ashton, but the romance of the ballet was a potent part of her infatuation. She loved to watch rehearsals and her appearance in the studio was intriguing to the company, who regarded her at first as some kind of rare, paradisal bird, although she soon became one of them. She was immensely cultivated and knowledgeable about the arts; and with her slight frame, quaint, turned-out walk, and insteps as eloquently arched as Pavlova's, she easily passed for a dancer herself. Ashton's theatrical hours suited Alice perfectly, as she, too, had difficulty getting up in the morning and came to life at night. He loved recounting stories, such as the way she would be still in bed when luncheon guests were announced, would summon Gilbert, the chauffeur, to bring the Rolls-Royce to the back door, finish her make-up in the car, and be driven to the front entrance, where she would rush in apologizing, as if she had only just arrived. For all her grandeur, however, her character was defined as much by what her American friend Leo Lerman described as 'a really magnificent disorder'. It was this unassuming side, as much as her generosity, that endeared her to Ashton's circle. 'She is nice, simple and complicated and a little sad,' Lydia Lopokova wrote to Keynes, after Ashton had brought her to a Sunday lunch for the first time.

His best friends became hers: in particular, Billy Chappell, Bobby Helpmann, Constant Lambert and Sophie Fedorovitch. For them all – but, in essence, for Ashton – she provided 'a scene well set and excellent company', as Lady Gregory had done for Yeats. Hanover Lodge became something of a Coole Park for him and later he would make a pocket of it his home. There, he was introduced to the kind of rarefied living that filtered into his ballets and was applauded as his famous grasp of period and manners. No one could claim to have bestowed on the choreographer a sense of taste – he was born with his unerring eye – but it was Alice, like Sophie before her, who helped him to focus it. For all the pleasures, however, there would be a price to pay for both of them. Alice was not to be a creative ally for Ashton, like Lady Gregory, or a distant, selfless benefactress like Tchaikovsky's Madame von Meck. She was too much in love. As the years went by, her commitment to Ashton and to his life began to alarm him. Her obsession, although flattering at first, now manifested itself as an almost pathological possessiveness, against which he found himself cruelly retaliating.

CHAPTER SEVEN

ALICE, GERTRUDE AND ALICE
1936–1937

At the end of November, Ashton, Alice and Bobby Helpmann spent the weekend with Sacheverell Sitwell at Weston Hall in Northamptonshire. Cosseting Ashton as usual, Alice – or rather, Gilbert, her chauffeur – collected his bags from home, picked him up from the Old Vic and drove the three of them to the Sitwells' pretty, Gothicized seventeenth-century house. Weekends at Weston were not grand, but extremely comfortable – a haven of log fires, good books, feasting and conversation. It was a relief for Ashton to escape the claustrophobic atmosphere of the flat he and his mother now shared in Guilford Place. He had created an attractive room for himself – white-painted, with a blue carpet and furnished with Caledonian Market antiques – but the house was small and its outlook depressing: 'opposite huge good English lavarotories [sic] it looked an institution' (Lopokova's description). More importantly, Georgie had become a considerable burden to him. Her health was failing rapidly and, although she still kept in touch with her South American family and the occasional diplomat friend, she saw almost no one in London, often lunching alone at the Half Moon café in Curzon Street. Now that their financial outlook had become more secure, she no longer wrote short stories, but occupied herself by listening to the wireless and transcribing sadly revealing aphorisms: 'One must *accept* life, and not "put up" with it . . . ' and 'Peace only exists in families where one or other of the couple makes *all* the mutual concessions . . . ' With her son away for Christmas, staging numbers for the new Cochran revue in Manchester, Georgie's feeling of isolation was especially acute. On the other hand, there was the cheering prospect of an immediate windfall: Ashton was to earn £300 for collaborating on the new show and receive a £5 royalty for each week of the run. It was his most lucrative commission to date. 'Hy-ho! My boy!' Lopokova exclaimed when she heard.

Home and Beauty, grandiloquently subtitled *C. B. Cochran's Coronation Revue*, in fact coincided with the Abdication. With a libretto by A. P. Herbert, it was designed and staged around the theme of an elegant house party. Binnie Hale and Nelson Keys were the stars, and the Young Ladies (who included Ashton's old flame Iris March) hardly danced at all, but made glamorous Ziegfeld-like appearances. In scenes such as 'Dressing for Dinner', 'The Tapestry Room' and 'Seeing the Estate', Ashton's recent sorties to great houses helped him to establish an authentic atmosphere, although he was given little opportunity to exercise his choreographic skills. It was precisely the lack of dancing that drew the most complaints from the critics. The high spot of the evening was declared by the *New Statesman and Nation* to be the number, 'I like a nice cup of tea in the morning'. The revue transferred to London early in the New Year, where it received much the same tepid reception.

In January, Ashton spent the weekend in Wiltshire at Dumbleton Hall, the family home of Joan Eyres-Monsell,* the beautiful daughter of the First Lord of the Admiralty, Sir Bolton Monsell. 'When I was a deb, longing to meet some people I thought interesting, Bumble Dawson asked me for a drink with Freddie, Bobbie and Sophie. I stayed on mesmerized, and finally they took me out to dinner. After that we all became great friends.' To be invited to Dumbleton, 'you had to be very jolly and young', according to Wilhelmine (Billa) Cresswell, who was there that weekend. Ashton, of course, was both. 'Everyone knew Freddie by then and wanted him to stay.' John Betjeman, a friend of Graham Eyres-Monsell, Joan's brother, was another popular guest, and wrote two jocular poems about the house. Gerald Berners, who was among the Dumbleton party on this occasion, collected Ashton at Didcot station and they drove to Evesham for what turned out to be a wild weekend with everyone drunk, ragging about and flinging a lot of clothes around. Billa Cresswell did a striptease and swung from a vast bronze candelabra (a stunt of which Ashton drolly reminded her when they were both in their eighties and she, the widow of the distinguished economist Sir Roy Harrod, was engaged in campaigning with Prince Charles to restore Norfolk churches).

Back in London, Ashton went straight into rehearsals of *Harlequin in the Street*, a good-humoured trifle commissioned by Maynard Keynes as a curtain-raiser to the Cambridge Arts Theatre production of *Le Misanthrope*. André Derain designed both the play and the ballet, chose the Couperin music (arranged by Lambert) and wrote the scenario. Since the early 1920s, Commedia del Arte characters had figured prominently in

*Now, Mrs Patrick Leigh Fermor.

the work of Derain and his contemporaries, inspiring one of his greatest paintings, *Arlequin et Pierrot*, in which the two figures cradle stringless instruments. (The artist might even have been alluding to this meditation on silence when, in the ballet, he has his moralistic Harlequin silence a trio of gossips.) The piece is peopled with stock types such as a bourgeois gentilhomme and an ancient marquis, whom the former rescues after Harlequin has puckishly upset his sedan chair.

Keynes was concerned at first that, in Derain's conception, there was 'too much business and too little dancing' and Ashton agreed, putting this right by turning Harlequin into a virtuoso (danced by Stanley Judson), who ends the piece on a crescendo of multiple pirouettes. Yet, despite his reservations, Ashton realized the importance of the collaboration – the first time he had worked with one of Diaghilev's artists. 'He says Derain is remarkable to give him the scenario, he now appreciates it very much,' Lopokova wrote to Keynes. After a hefty lunch of Irish stew with Ashton, she watched a rehearsal, finding the ballet 'very nice, pleasing', but it was her own performance in the Molière play as Célimène which charmed the critics. Raymond Mortimer, while enthusing in the *Spectator* about the improvement of her vocal range and expressive physique – 'her whole body talks' – did not consider Ashton in top form, maintaining that Derain's imaginative costumes and background of a French town were the ballet's most distinguished features. After the London run, in which the sixteen-year-old virtuoso Alan Carter took over as the Harlequin, Keynes gave the sets and costumes to the Vic-Wells as a gift. Eighteen months later, a longer version with a new scenario by Lambert entered the repertory and received much more enthusiastic notices.

Between completing work on *Harlequin in the Street* and beginning to choreograph his new ballet, Ashton was coerced by Marie Rambert into dancing in Ballet Rambert's season at the Duchess Theatre. 'Mim wants to own Fred,' Lopokova remarked to Keynes. '[She is] tiresome about it.' He was also having to help produce funds for a new work which Lilian Baylis claimed was proving too expensive. (According to Lopokova, he procured £10 from Claire Luce 'for the good of the cause'.) The ballet was *Les Patineurs*, an Ashton classic, which was originally to have been choreographed by de Valois.

> We'd done a matinée and in those days at Sadler's Wells every dressingroom had a piano. I heard Constant playing this music to Ninette and I burst in on them and said: 'That's not for you, it's for me.' At that time, Constant wanted me to do *The Rake's Progress* and so I said to Ninette, '*You* do *The Rake's Progress* and I'll do this.' She was delighted; it was much more up her street.

De Valois agreed that she was 'much keener on the Hogarth', which was of no interest to Ashton.

> So we said, 'Let's change over.' It was quite an obvious choice. One was a divertissement which is what he adored and the other was a narrative ballet, which I always like. We were equally worried about doing the other one and so made the change just like that.*

The initial work on *Les Patineurs* was carried out by Constant Lambert, who derived the idea for it from an old programme advertising the Paul Taglioni ballet *Les Plaisirs de l'hiver; ou, Les Patineurs*, a spirited divertissement with a winter lakeside setting, consisting of skaters dancing in groups and alone. (Preserved among Ashton's papers, the programme is inscribed in Lambert's hand 'With the maledictions of the "Old Master"'. The stage machinery for this production, given at Her Majesty's Theatre in 1849, was carried out by a Mr Sloman, whose name Lambert underlined to call attention to the joke.) Impressed with the success of Taglioni's 'Ice Ballet' and about to produce his opera *Le Prophète*, Meyerbeer had invited Taglioni to recreate a *Pas de Patineurs* for the new project. And it was from *Le Prophète* that Lambert took four numbers for the Wells version, as well as four from another Meyerbeer opera, *L'Etoile du Nord*. The result is a score so melodic that most of the audience is smiling after the first few bars. Ashton gives in unabashedly to the barrel-organ beat, marking time to the emphatic waltz rhythm with the dancers' gliding motif of chassée, hop, hop. He knew little about skating, other than the filmed championships he had seen on Movietone News broadcasts, but he asked Elisabeth Miller, who used to go to the Westminster Ice Rink on Sundays, to demonstrate some typical movements which he then adapted for the stage. There was nothing new about fusing classical ballet with a sporting idiom: Nijinsky's *Jeux*, and the three *Sporting Sketches* Susan Salaman made for Rambert (*Le Rugby*, *Le Cricket*, *Le Boxing*), had successfully expressed the essence of the game in pure dance. Skating ballets themselves were a genre of sorts – *Skating Rink* was a popular item in the repertory of the Ballets Suédois – but only Ashton's work has endured. One of his most popular works, it is a paradigm of an Ashton ballet, perfectly crafted, with a complex structure be-

---

*It could not, however, have been the simultaneous swap they both describe, as de Valois had choreographed *Rake's Progress* eighteen months earlier. When Ashton was rehearsing *Patineurs*, she would have begun planning *Checkmate*, which was premièred four months later.

neath the effervescent surface. And only he could have pulled off creating a blithe evocation of a Victorian skating party at a time when Londoners had recently had their eyes opened to the work of Picasso (whose first British exhibition was running at Tooth's Gallery).

Ashton's main aim was to reveal the virtuosity of the burgeoning English ballet. This was a vintage year for Sadler's Wells, a wonderfully productive period confirming, as Clive Barnes wrote, 'that the initiative in modern ballet was passing from the post-Diaghilev Ballets Russes into the lusty infant hands of British ballet'. The previous summer, the stars of Colonel de Basil's Ballets Russes season at Covent Garden had been idolized for their technical prowess – particularly Toumanova, for her fast pirouettes, and Lichine, for his powerful elevation and astonishing spins. Ashton made *Les Patineurs* as a direct challenge to the Russians: the Blue Boy's nonchalant shrug, which became an Ashton trademark, is here meant to be cockily provocative, placed after a quotation of brisés volés from the Blue Bird solo in *Aurora's Wedding* (brought to London by the Russians), during which the Blue Boy repeats the gesture elatedly, over and over again. In this role, Harold Turner was able to rival any of the Russian virtuosi;* while the fouetté sequence for Mary Honer, instantly followed by Elizabeth Miller's manège of posé and attitude turns, brought the house down – not only the speed and polish of their spins, but also the lightning arm movements co-ordinated with them. 'It was so much more complicated then than it has become,' Ashton used to complain in his eighties, also maintaining that the illusion of skating was not as effective among the corps as it used to be. 'Those boys! They do it so badly now. They do a chassée without a plié. I'd like to put a hot poker up each ass to get them moving.' In the original cast, he singled out Michael Somes, one of the pas de huit boys, by showing off his high-arching jetés. Harold Turner, who resented this deflection of the limelight, walked out of the studio when he first saw Somes rehearsing: 'He felt *he* should have been given those jumps,' remarked a colleague. 'Fred gave Michael a tiny moment which everyone noticed and said, "Ah-hah! that's who will be the next one,"' said Billy Chappell. 'Sure enough he was.' And in more ways than one.

Although Ashton had set out to create a showpiece, what makes *Les Patineurs* so much more than an approximation of Russian bravura is his 'rebrightening' (in Edith Sitwell's term) of academic steps. Rather than inhibiting the space and movements, the skating theme triggered a rush of

---

*Not even Baryshnikov, who performed the Green Skater, as the role is known in America, could manage the butterfly jumps; he replaced them with flying splits in the air.

exultantly inventive choreography, coloured by some playful conceits. The human sleigh is one example (later reworked as a farm cart in *La Fille mal gardée*); as are the little trip-ups of the two girls in brown, which Ashton newly mints as ballet steps. The depiction of skating through dance proves to be much wittier than the easy laughs Ashton scores with various dancers' boomps-a-daisies on the ice. The choreography can be amusingly self-reflexive. When the Blue Boy flings himself into a gymnastic sequence of 'butterflies' – legs scissoring, while his body flips and hovers in mid-air above the stage – his bravado is aimed not only at the Ballets Russes, but also parodies the Girl in White who has just been horizontally upended with great charm by her partner. This romantic couple – Fonteyn and Helpmann in the original cast – weave lyrically in and out of the hectic action, providing a balmy change of pace. As P. W. Manchester noted at the time, it was a 'stroke of genius' on Ashton's part, showing him completely in command of his craft. He was rewarded by a standing ovation on the first night, followed by unanimous critical acclaim.

Almost immediately, Ashton turned his mind to his next project: *A Wedding Bouquet*, based on the Gertrude Stein play *They Must. Be Wedded. To Their Wife*. The first planning meeting took place over lunch with de Valois, Lambert and Gerald Berners, who was to be both composer and designer of the ballet. The libretto was a collaboration effected in an atmosphere of great gaiety over several weekends at Faringdon, Berners' Palladian-style house in Oxfordshire. 'Gertrude Stein wasn't involved,' said Ashton. 'I had no thing with her, any more than I did with *Four Saints*. We did *Wedding Bouquet* between us: Gerald and Constant and I.'

Life at Faringdon was extremely enjoyable – mostly because of the company, a cosmopolitan mix of artists and aristocrats. 'He didn't like ordinary people and he didn't like people just because they were grand,' said Ashton. 'They had to have something.' Bores, dubbed Dry Blankets, were never asked back. The food was famously good: classic French and very rich. Ashton remembered how Penelope Betjeman would come into the drawing room before dinner and ask: 'Gerald, what's the *pud*?' Some meals were unique, including the one in which all three courses were as pink as the dyed fan-tail pigeons outside. Like everyone else, Ashton was amused by the silly side of Faringdon – the No-Dogs-Allowed notice hung at dog's-eye level; or the pornographic books which guests found on their bedside tables, disguised as leather-bound classics – but he remained sceptical about how authentically cranky Berners in fact was.

'Being in a privileged position and having money, he could assume eccentricity, but I always thought that it was put-on.' Certainly, like his autobiographical persona, Lord Fitzcricket, Berners knew that a little eccentric publicity would help further his artistic pursuits. 'He was too sane,' as Ashton remarked, 'he knew what he was doing, what he was at.' Berners was far too professional to be the gifted amateur his reputation claimed – the 'fluffy mixture of a great many talents without any basis of work or application', as he was condescendingly described by that real candyfloss confectioner, Beverley Nichols. While recognizing that Berners' talents were light, Ashton strongly commended his theatrical know-how and his serious approach to work. 'He was very good at constructing a ballet. He could do a very good pas de deux in rather a Tchaikovsky/Delibes way. And he understood about lengths . . . If I said, "That's too long," he would cut it. With Benjamin Britten, every note was sacred . . . Gerald was much more realistic.'

In the mornings at Faringdon, when everyone else remained in bed, Berners would be at the piano. The previous summer, he had been to stay with Gertrude Stein in France, where he had derived the idea for his washy pastel backcloth from a colonial American rug given to her by Sherwood Anderson. But the Corot-esque scene contains other allusions, including the view of Faringdon House from across the lake, and the shimmering, mirrored image of Schloss Kammer seen from the von Hofmannsthals' barge on the Attersee. By the time Ashton and Lambert came in on the project, Berners had completed most of the score, but, according to Ashton, it was Lambert who was largely responsible for the arrangement of the spoken word with the music. 'Gerald didn't do all that. Constant was an enormous help to him.' The collaborators drew on only a fraction of Stein's 'play' – in effect, a collection of phrases divided into erratically shifting scenes – although clues to character and ideas for movement are sometimes taken from lines not incorporated in the choral text. Fragments of coherence, such as 'Julia is known as forlorn' and 'Josephine may not attend. A wedding', are elaborated into a fairly conventional scenario: a provincial French wedding party at the beginning of the century. There is even a plot of sorts, centred on a Bridegroom (a comic version of the roué in *Nocturne*), his dippy bride and his rejected mistress, the love-lorn Julia. Then there is Josephine, for whom Ashton creates a jokey drunk scene, choreographically translating Stein's description 'She chooses her air' as an episode in which Josephine, vertiginously balanced on a table, steps off into the void. Julia's dog Pépé, modelled on Stein's own Mexican terrier, originates from the phrase, 'Little dogs resemble little girls' – a part traditionally danced by one of the smallest girls in the company.

As in so many other Ashton ballets, the characters of the dancers helped to define their roles. Even their costume designs are drawn, by Berners, as caricatures of the performers themselves. The bridegroom, Bobby Helpmann, was given his first opportunity to be funny on stage. Those who remember his performance insist that he really was outrageously amusing, delighting the audience, and making the dancers 'corpse' helplessly with his antics and hissed verbal asides, while maintaining an illusion of deadpan decorum. (Arnold Haskell commented that Helpmann never overdid his quest for a laugh.) The prettily plump Mary Honer was also wonderfully funny as the Bride – *too* funny, in the view of Helpmann, who felt upstaged by her. 'I think Bobby saw her as a rival,' remarked a colleague. 'He kept trying to put her off, telling her how frightful she was.' Although technically more accomplished than Fonteyn, Honer had been considered capable but unremarkable, until Ashton brought out a hitherto unexposed, enchanting gift for comedy.

As the 'unknown' Guy, a handsome wedding guest, Michael Somes was favoured with an eye-catching series of tours en l'air; while Ninette de Valois appeared in a self-caricature as Webster, the finger-wagging, officious maid. The character who owed least to the personality of the original dancer, Margot Fonteyn, was poor demented Julia. But then again, raking and fanning out her long, loose black hair, the dancer seemed to be sending up her own recent début in *Giselle*. (In the programme, Lambert calls Julia a 'modern Giselle'.) One of many indelible moments in Fonteyn's performance was when she clung desperately to the Bridegroom's leg – a comic literalization of Stein's phrase 'attached jealousy'. But several critics found the tragic undercurrent disquieting. A. V. Coton complained that Julia 'toppled the farce into the abyss of reality, from which the rest of the cast were unable to rescue the work'.

The reason the cameo jarred was because Ashton had allowed a piece of emotional biography to come dangerously close to his art. There is usually an element of self-identification in his distraught, love-struck women; in this case, he created his portrait of Julia as a parody of Alice. She, too, had bewitching black hair – Tchelitchew painted it hanging long and straight – and, although she was too unconfident to be vain, Alice was engrossed by her hair, using lipsalve to slick down stray wisps and getting Katie, her maid, to brush it with an exotic potion. 'You mustn't tell any one about it,' she once told Beaton, who watched her at her dressing table. 'It's got a drug in it – morphine or something – and its wonderful for the hair.' Yet only Ashton was fully aware of the extent to which Alice had a much greater affiliation with Julia: when Alice fell in love, she, too, became plangently, stiflingly insecure.

Lately, Alice had begun to arrive unannounced at rehearsals, which

Ashton resented as a threat to his freedom. '*He* liked being the possessive one, the one in charge,' said Billy Chappell. 'He was a great chaser and very good at it.' The more cornered Ashton felt by Alice, the more resolutely he set his sights on the elusive Michael Somes. Sensing his reticence, Alice turned to his friends as a way of discovering more about him. Chappell found himself 'continually summoned' to see her at Hanover Lodge. 'She went out of her way to charm me because she saw me as a kind of leaker, but I was under instructions from Fred not to tell her anything and was terribly good at evading her.' Chappell would arrive for lunch or dinner and be shown into the drawing room by Dean, the butler, and given a drink. Then he would have another drink and eventually be taken upstairs to where Alice was in bed. 'We'd have an absolutely exquisite meal on a tray and we'd talk. She'd say things like: "Well, have you seen Fred lately? What's he been doing?" It was difficult not to be disloyal to Fred and not to give Alice too much hope. You had to be very careful or you'd be in trouble with everybody.'

By this time, Alice desperately wanted to marry Ashton, and it was while he was involved with *A Wedding Bouquet* that she proposed to him, offering him half her fortune. 'I liked her too much to accept,' said Ashton. 'And besides, I had another side to my life.' He could have resorted to marriage as a shield of respectability, but, instinctively, he knew that being kept by Alice would jeopardize his career: 'Imagine me and my laziness, surrounded by valets and footmen – I'd never have done another thing in my life.' He had heard how she had tried to prevent her previous husbands from working. She could never understand why Raimund wanted a job. What was the point? She had more than enough money for them both. Ashton realized, too, that Alice was attracted by the fact that he was unattainable. 'If I'd married her, she'd soon have been bored by me.' Her friend Gore Vidal confirmed that Ashton's handling of the relationship was consciously tactical. 'He was an intuitive man, he knew she was emotionally masochistic and behaved accordingly. He saw that was what she wanted. The fact that she could make life materially pleasing suited both of them.'

The caricature of Alice as the sad, spurned Julia in *A Wedding Bouquet* is a prescient portrayal of her life as it turned out, rather than a complete picture of her at the time – Alice's real tragedy was to come. All the same, her anxiety about Ashton's feelings was now oppressing them both. At the first *Wedding Bouquet* weekend at Faringdon, even though she was also there enjoying the fun, she had a way of making her unhappiness almost tangible to those around her. 'She spread a kind of gloom,' said Isaiah Berlin. 'Cyril Connolly used to say she was like the upas tree under which everything dies.'

Creating *A Wedding Bouquet* gave Ashton the chance to make light of his own situation by debunking marriage and a good deal else in the process. Without the jokes, the wedding celebrated on stage would be a sorry tale of a bride too stupid to realize that she has pledged herself to an indifferent cad. The underlying cynicism sums up Berners' views on marriage which he had satirized before in his story 'Percy Wallingford' (chronicling the character-eroding effect of a 'perfect fool of a wife' upon an old Etonian, a figure of homoerotic allure, who is driven to murder as his only escape). But, of the three collaborators, Lambert had most reason to feel sceptical about conjugal shackles: he was now deeply in love with Fonteyn and, by the following year, he and his wife Florence would be irreparably estranged. As Gertrude Stein observed about *A Wedding Bouquet*, 'It is very sad but everybody has to laugh.' It also reflected Berners' own personality. Beneath the frivolity and fun, he was a melancholic (soon to turn to psychoanalysis) who used mockery to distance himself from his emotions.

The mood of the time was to send up anything remotely serious, and high-mindedness was particularly open to ridicule. The humourlessly evangelical lesbianism of Radclyffe Hall is mercilessly guyed in Berners' naughty novelette about schoolgirl crushes, *The Girls of Radcliffe Hall*, written under the pseudonym Adela Quebec. It, too, is a gallery of caricatures of his friends and acquaintances, including Cecil Beaton as Cecily Seymour (though there may also have been a touch of Ashton in Cecily, whose brilliant extemporizations, parodies of music-hall turns and solo dancing won her the admiration of the whole school). *A Wedding Bouquet* reflects this spirit of burlesque. Classical ballet is lampooned again in a tug-of-war duet, a travesty of the grand pas de deux which seals Aurora's marriage in *The Sleeping Beauty*. The final tableau, in which the whole cast poses for a photograph, is modelled on Berners' painting of Chips Channon's wedding group. Pépé the dog joins in at the last minute, cocking a leg in attitude – a literal piss-taking of the pose of the dancer reclining on the floor in *Les Sylphides*, as well as a reminder of the embarrassing poodles in Massine's *Boutique fantasque*.

Gertrude Stein was, of course, a prime target for parody. Ten years earlier, in his unpublished notebooks, Berners had written several pastiches of her writing which Diana Mosley claims that he thought 'absolute rubbish'. He certainly allowed himself considerable licence with Stein's play, conventionalizing her whimsical style of punctuation, traducing her repetitions, adding characters' names, and iconoclastically imposing old-fashioned tunes on her avant-garde text. Ashton was slightly less irreverent. He liked the jingle chime of Stein's idiom and often used her phrase from *A Wedding Bouquet* in conversation – for example,

'That would make a dog uneasy' if the weather were unseasonably warm. He particularly liked the theatrical opportunities implicit in Stein's writing, directing a singer in *Four Saints* to deliver the line, 'Please be coming to see me', in an insinuating, Mae West tone. But in the ballet, Ashton, like Berners, undermines Stein's status as high-priestess of modernism by producing steadfastly legible and conventional choreography. Rather than creating a balletic equivalent of Steinese, he prefers to follow Berners' traditional rhythms, responding to the cosy inevitability of what he calls his 'governess waltzes' by creating dance-hall pastiches of his own.

Arlene Croce would later criticize the spirit of *A Wedding Bouquet* as being all wrong for Gertrude Stein: 'the effect is incongruous, like tying ribbons on an elephant.' But Stein has not been as conclusively 'conscripted' as Croce maintains. The ballet's frivolity is just a façade, its levels of satire and suppressed despair making it a much more subversive piece of work than the brittle period toy she describes. The whimsy is still there: Ashton has mirrored Stein's mundane diction in his classroom-style enchaînements; just as, musically, Berners has found an equivalent to her device of reiteration by making his phrases seem to stumble and go back on themselves, 'as if the last word had heard the next word and the next word had heard not the last word but the next word', as Stein put it. The author certainly did not feel overridden. Before the first night, she discussed with Alice B. Toklas whether or not Ashton was a genius: 'Being one it is natural that I should think a great deal about that thing in anyone.' Seeing *A Wedding Bouquet* certainly did nothing to make her change her mind. She was delighted and excited by the première, particularly by the warmth of the acclaim. 'I liked everything they did to the ballet,' she enthused in *Everybody's Autobiography*. Stein's only reservation, Ashton said, was that the words could not be clearly heard above the orchestra. When the ballet was revived during the war, a narrator – first Lambert, then Helpmann – replaced the chorus to save money. Stein preferred the change, but Ashton did not. He felt the more lucid enunciation of the text distracted from the dance. 'Bobby was always drawing attention to himself.'

Helpmann's arch delivery brought out similarities in the ballet to *Façade*. Not only does *A Wedding Bouquet* contain a Waltonesque tango and a waltz, but the lilting rhythms of the narrative has, in Arlene Croce's phrase, 'an inescapably English, Sitwellian ring'. Ashton would certainly have discussed the ballet with Edith Sitwell – who also used words in inconsequential abstract patterns, for their rhythm rather than their meaning – as he had been seeing a great deal of her at the time. Although she had long forgotten the slight she had felt over the choreographer's appropriation of *Façade*, he remained nervous in her presence. Alice helped to break the ice. Edith counted her as one of her greatest friends, and admired her beauty and style: 'like a Persian miniature, very racée, with a look of really tremendous breeding, unusual in Americans, and enormously rich'. She would have appreciated Alice's patronage of her beloved Pavel Tchelitchew, who had drawn a series of eight charcoal studies of Alice, as well as his huge, surreal oil painting of her looking like a sibyl, with an egg suspended above her head: 'It's where she keeps her money,' Tchelitchew explained. Since Alice had come into Ashton's life, his acquaintance with Edith Sitwell had deepened into a new intimacy. In April, shortly before the première of *A Wedding Bouquet*, she heard news of his brother Tony's imprisonment in Bolivia, and sent a letter commiserating with the 'dreadful anxiety' he and his family were going through. 'I hope that our government will take steps to put a stop to your anxiety at *once*.' Tony Ashton was the representative of a firm which distributed arms to Bolivia (then at war with Paraguay). The Peruvians had issued an embargo to prevent a consignment of guns from reaching their destination, and, consequently, a law suit was filed by Bolivia. Tony and a colleague were put in jail until the British Government did indeed intervene, and they were found not guilty and released. The 'closed corporation' of Edith Sitwell and her brothers made her especially solicitous towards Ashton at this time, but her anxiety on his behalf was misplaced. So firmly had he distanced himself from his South American family that only the potential slur on his name would have concerned him.

Ashton was now included among Edith Sitwell's court of admirers whom she entertained at the Sesame Club in Grosvenor Street – or, rather, it was Ashton who entertained her, usually in tandem with Bobby Helpmann. 'She used to *adore* us doing imitations. Tears would pour down her face. She was a tremendous giggler and loved fun.' Natasha Spender remembers an occasion in the Sesame Club when Edith urged a group of them (including Stephen Spender) to try to clamber up the chimney breast, 'as if they were Beryl de Zoete climbing a mountain'. The eccentric, uninhibited partner of Arthur Waley, de Zoete was the butt of many jokes, bringing out a spiteful streak in Edith, who disapproved of her morals. Ashton liked her, however, and was rather ashamed of his disloyalty.

Over the next couple of years, Gertrude Stein would bombard Ashton with projects for the future. She hoped to interest Lincoln Kirstein in producing *A Wedding Bouquet* in New York; she wanted Ashton to direct a 'play simply as a play' and sent him *Daniel Webster*, which he enjoyed and would like to have staged. 'I'd have had everyone being terribly courtly and talking absolute nonsense.' She sent him an annotated manuscript of her play *Listen to Me*; and she wanted him to produce another play, *Superstitions*, as 'half ballet and half theatre', with designs by Cecil Beaton. The following year, Ashton was to have been involved in *Doctor Faustus Lights the Lights*, a three-act opera based on Stein's modern spoof of the Faust legend, in which the characters talk in American vernacular. The composer was Lord Berners, but the outbreak of war curtailed the project and he never completed the score.

Ashton was tremendously encouraged by Stein's regard, although he was confident that he had made a good job of *A Wedding Bouquet*. 'I think it is odd how any of those characters might have fitted into your countryside without spoiling it, before I had seen or felt its character', he wrote to her. Thanking her for 'the wonderful things' she said about him in *Everybody's Autobiography*, he ends the letter with a crescendo of unprecedented self-assurance: 'I love you feeling that way about me as I feel that it is true too.' (Always the parodist, he may just have been imitating Stein's open expression of her own gigantic egotism.) A friendship founded on mutual flattery quickly developed into genuine affection. Stein was reluctant to part from her new circle of friends from the ballet, which now also included Bobby Helpmann and Billy Chappell. Before she left, she made all three promise to come to France for a holiday with her and Alice B. Toklas.

Ashton spent the early part of the summer on tour with the company, starting with a short season in Bournemouth. As their digs, he, Billy Chappell and Bobby Helpmann had chosen the Solent Cliffs, a temperance hotel, because it was cheap, comfortable and overlooked the sea. These days, the trio always shared a room (with Chappell inevitably assigned a child's bed or the sofa), and would be awake most of the night, dressing up in sheets and shrieking with laughter. One morning, there was a tap on the door and one of the nice elderly chambermaids called out, 'It's ten to ten, ladies.' They all thought this hilarious and it became a catchphrase if ever anyone was late.

Despite the first hints of commitment in two letters Ashton had received from Michael Somes, there was no getting away from the fact that the dancer was now deeply involved with a young Vic-Wells soloist, Pamela May. A cool, attractive blonde, she had made a great impression when she was partnered by Somes in *Les Sylphides*, and the pair made almost as much of an impact off-stage, strolling hand-in-hand like mannequins along Bournemouth's promenade. Ashton hardly attempted to hide his jealousy when Somes, preferring to be with May, turned down his invitations to dinner, and, if they went out together as a threesome, he was a conspicuous outsider. In June, the Vic-Wells performed at the Arts Theatre in Cambridge, exactly a year since Ashton's last trip there. With late-night parties, picnics on the river, and doting undergraduates sitting in his dressing room to watch him make up, the summer of 1936 had been a carefree, idyllic time for Ashton, as Noel Annan reminded him in a letter written many years later. 'Were not those Cambridge days perpetual sunshine of glorious youth? With endless laughter & fun & drink & delicate romances of no duration. I think of them as some of the happiest times & Lydia's champagne laughter.' But Ashton spent much of the current season in a state of despair, tortured with longing for Michael Somes. Alan Carter remembers seeing the dancer canoodling in a punt with Pamela May while Ashton sat with them, glumly looking on. 'I suppose he felt it was better to be with someone in a rotten situation than not to be with them at all. But there was a curious element of sado-masochism apparent in both Michael and Fred.'

The role of the suffering lover was one which Ashton embraced for life – as he said, 'I never once pulled it off. I was always the loser.' But self-knowledge was little comfort to him at the time. During the few days the company spent in Cambridge, the atmosphere was charged with sexual electricity. It was on one of these nights that Margot Fonteyn fell in love at first sight with Roberto (Tito) Arias, whose Latin good looks and off-hand manner left her 'quivering'. But the sight of the young in one another's arms only served to heighten Ashton's sense of exclusion, particularly when the company moved to Paris, a city even more conducive to romance.

The Vic-Wells had been invited to perform at the Théâtre des Champs-Elysées, where Ashton had appeared with Ida Rubinstein eight years earlier. They were to represent their country at the International Exhibition of Industry and Art – a great accolade for British dance. Their arrival in Paris, however, proved something of an anticlimax. On the first evening, the dancers, hurrying out to scan the café billboards and corner kiosks for posters announcing their season, found that advance publicity for 'Le Vic-Wells Ballet du Sadler's Wells Théâtre de Londres' comprised two small handbills on the back wall of the twee, tucked-away British Pavilion. Neither the première of de Valois' *Checkmate* nor the new productions of *Les Patineurs* and *Nocturne* attracted much attention. The influential critics were not invited to the first night and the house remained less than half full for the rest of the week. Although the French President and British Ambassador attended the opening, there was neither the usual celebratory party nor any other gesture of hospitality that week, until the indefatigable hostess Lady Mendl stepped in and invited the whole company for tea in the gardens of the Villa Trianon. Playing swing songs on the terrace, with its backdrop of Versailles, was the most popular band in Paris, the Hot Club Quintet de France, led by Django

Reinhardt and Stephane Grappelli, and it was not long before the dancers, led by Fonteyn, were 'stomping' on the topiary-edged lawns below.

Most of the company was staying just off the Champs-Elysées, at the Hotel Lord Byron, where Ashton and Billy Chappell had connecting rooms, even though Alice was in town. It was early June and Paris was looking radiant, but Ashton was disinclined to be enticed into a private tryst with Alice and sought refuge in numbers. Sophie Fedorovitch was there, too, and the friends went everywhere in a pack, staying up all night and dancing in the boîtes and bars. One afternoon, they went to what Chappell described as 'a queer tea dance', with Bobby Helpmann's mother in tow. 'It was all frightfully respectable: a middle-aged man would come up and say to Sophie or Alice: "Would you allow me, Miss, to ask this gentleman to dance?" Bobby's mother was horrified by it all but we fell about laughing.'

There was a manic edge to the fun. Intoxicated by Paris and the prospect of the holidays ahead, everyone was 'gaily hysterical', as Chappell put it – their mood even more highly charged by the politically explosive atmosphere in the city that summer. A right-wing terrorist group, Les Cagoulards, had chosen Exhibition time to stage a series of incidents, and there had been clashes between agitators and gendarmes among the pavement cafés of the Champs-Elysées. Such aggression was infectious: 'At five in the morning', Chappell has written, 'Freddy Ashton and I might have been seen busily hitting one another in the Place Pigalle followed by each of us haughtily taking separate taxis back to the same hotel.' This latest rift in their affectionately irascible friendship had been triggered by Ashton's cavalier attitude towards the eighteen-year-old Rose Paget, who was at a finishing school in Paris and still hopelessly infatuated with him. The three of them had been out dancing and it was after Ashton had bundled Rose into a taxi, rather than escorting her home, that the protective Chappell swiped him in rage. The next morning, he was woken by a rueful voice crying out, 'Mrs Chappell, you *struck* me!' and, true to form, they both collapsed in giggles.

The emotional crossfire in Ashton's life was now as volatile as the Cagoulards' bullets ricocheting round the Place de la Concorde. Alice may have welcomed the Restoration complexity of the situation – Chappell thought 'it added to the attraction on her part' – but Rose was too young and too innocent to relish such sport. She did not know that Alice was in Paris, but certainly saw her as a threat, challenging Ashton by saying, 'If you marry Alice, I'll *kill* her.' But he had no intention of marrying anyone, wanting instead to 'carry on within limits, as it suits him', as Lopokova informed Keynes. He returned to London to find himself as much in demand professionally as romantically. The Ballets Russes, now headed by Colonel de Basil, with Massine as choreographer, had invited him to rechoreograph *The Triumph of Neptune* (originally staged by Balanchine). Lord Berners, who had cut down the score to twenty minutes with three scenes, wrote, begging Ashton to agree, adding a postscript, 'Massine situation O.K.' Gossiping to Keynes, however, Lopokova disclosed the contrary: Massine had, in fact, been duplicitous, obstructing Ashton's involvement in the ballet. 'He tells Fred, "My best pupil, I am proud of you, I'll do anything for you at Sadler's Wells." Ha-ha! De Basil says, "I always wanted you to create the new ballet, but Massine did not allow it, Ha-ha!"' Ashton was also being courted by René Blum, de Basil's former partner, who wanted him to make a ballet entitled *Epsom* for his Monte Carlo company, with décor by Raoul Dufy. He returned to France on 13 June, presumably to discuss the idea; but, even though both works were advertised in the dance press with Ashton as choreographer, he did neither. He was talked out of the idea of leaving Sadler's Wells by a persuasive letter from Constant Lambert.

My dear Fred,

I have been thinking a lot about your offers from de Basil and Massine and speaking quite objectively without any old school tie feeling, I think you would be a fool to take either. You must surely realise that they are only after you because you are in a stronger position than they. Think of the coming year. Massine will be taking all that time to form his company and de Basil will be in want of a really good choreographer. You on the other hand have your own theatre behind you with organisation and a growing reputation and if you produce two really striking ballets you will at the end of the year be in a far stronger position than either. Massine obviously only wants you to prevent de Basil from presenting a rival. You don't seriously imagine that you would get a 'fair deal' from him do you? Think what happened to Nijinska. Another thing to remember is *Massine has never yet succeeded on his own*. Mark my words. As you know I have an occasional gift of prophecy.

Like most dancers he needs an artistic framework and that after all is what you get at the Wells in spite of its many deficiencies. I quite realise that the schoolroom atmosphere must irritate you even more than it does me but that is really only a minor point. You have much more there than de Basil could give you at the moment. At the same time I think it would be better to go to de Basil than to Massine. You would after all be their star choreographer and have a really big company even though they wouldn't as yet be familiar with your style. But don't go there and work with your left hand. That would be fatal. Don't do your equivalent of Cent Baisers. Think how the people who know only that have underestimated Nijinska. People remember one failure or even one modified succes-d'estime far more than half-a-dozen successes. If I were you even if you want to go to de Basil eventually I should certainly stay at the Wells another year, after which your position will be ever stronger. After all even if you hate doing revues it is better to pot-boil with your left-hand than to do a second-rate ballet.

Excuse this long lecture but it comes from the heart. If it seems disconnected that is because two people are trying to describe the plot of the last Marx brothers film to me.
Yours ever
Uncle Constant.

It appeared to Ashton that almost everyone he knew was laying claim to his loyalty – even his mother, whose possessiveness, Lopokova believed, bordered on infatuation. 'Fred's mama is more and more tiresome, and wants to share everything with him, even junket.' Like Rose Paget, Georgie saw Alice as a rival and made this quite clear to her son. 'She didn't want me to marry because she knew she would lose me,' Ashton said. 'Although Alice was a millionairess and if I'd married her it would be supposedly wonderful for me in the eyes of the world, my mother used to say, "She's not sincere." She didn't dislike Alice, but she was wary of Rose Paget too.' Lopokova suggested that the answer might be for Ashton to set up his mother in a separate, modern flat, which he could now afford to do, but the idea came to nothing and they continued to live together until her death. That summer, Ashton offered Georgie the grand sum of £75 to take herself on holiday, which at first she martyrishly refused to do, even though he would soon be going abroad for nearly a month. A frank pep talk by Lopokova persuaded her to change her mind, and she agreed to go to Brittany for a week to stay with her sister.

Before Ashton could leave, he had to complete work on a new revue, *Floodlight*, written and composed by Beverley Nichols, with Buddy Bradley again sharing the dance routines. The production was beset with problems – including the fact that the director, Dennis Freeman, was a cocaine addict and would fail to turn up for rehearsals. The show was overlong (nearly three hours), over budget and memorable only for its launching of Frances Day 'into something quite special', in the view of her co-star, John Mills. The whole enterprise – culminating with Day's trilling and miming of the Wordsworthian number 'Dancing with the Daffodils' – was, by most accounts, insufferably cloying. 'Oh dinkums and pinkums! . . . Aw, shucks!' cringed the *Tatler*'s reviewer.

By 13 July, Ashton was free at last to escape from unrewarding commissions and the constrictions of Guilford Place. Already at Kammer, Alice had left behind Gilbert and the Rolls to convey Billy Chappell, Bobby Helpmann and him to Bilignin to visit Gertrude Stein, on condition that Ashton then join her in Austria. The summer retreat Stein shared with Alice B. Toklas was in the Ain countryside outside Belley, with spectacular views across a poplared valley to the shadowy Alpes Maritimes. The solid seventeenth-century manor had a large terraced garden, its vistas bisected by gravel pathways and ivy-clad parapets. At five each morning, Toklas would already be pottering about in her cretonne smock, a large basket on her arm and a cigarette wobbling between her lips. She used to gather vegetables from the kitchen garden for the day's meals and pick old English roses from box-edged beds, which she then arranged beautifully, 'like esoteric still-lives', in Cecil Beaton's phrase. While Toklas stayed at home preparing an exquisite lunch, Gertrude Stein took their three guests into Aix-les-Bains to shop. The greengrocer's she favoured was owned by a Madame Balmain, who ran a sideline in lingerie, and whose son, Pierre, became the couturier.

Stein's sepulchral features and close-cropped grey hair always made Ashton think of 'an old bishop', but he was not in the least intimidated by her, and neither were his two friends. 'People thought she was a wild, mad, affected old thing,' said Billy Chappell, 'but in fact she was very straightforward and sweet and terribly cosy.' Ashton found the snug familiarity of the Stein–Toklas ménage most amusing.

They called each other Lovey and Pussy. Alice was Pussy and would say, 'Don't forget, Lovey, to bring the cream.'

'No, I won't, I promise,' said Gertrude.

Of course, the moment we got back Alice used to say, 'Well, Lovey, did you bring the cream?'

'Oh God, I forgot,' Gertrude would say and then whisper to me, 'I forgot it on purpose. I like it much better without.'

Making the most of having Gilbert at their disposal, they would motor about the Ain countryside and be taken by their hostesses to call on grand neighbours who spoke perfect English and never went to Paris because they considered it too vulgar. Occasionally there were outings further afield. One day, Stein suggested that they should all go to an early morning Mass at a beautiful chapel in the region to hear the Gregorian chant. She was fascinated by ecclesiastical ritual and often drew Ashton out on the subject, encouraging him to talk about Peruvian processions he had seen 'when a young boy in a monastery'. As soon as they arrived, they were shown round by a fat little monk, who was obviously tickled by the motley group which had alighted from a white Rolls-Royce. 'He was so full of fun and so lively that he could hardly stay still,' said Chappell. They slipped into the church just as the service was starting, but the moment the wailing liturgy began, all three dancers were seized by uncontrollable fou de rire, which Stein tried to quell by making Helpmann move to a pew a couple of rows ahead – a stratagem that failed the minute the other two saw his shoulders begin to shake. There was more smothered laughter on the way back, at the behaviour of Basket, Stein's huge, lewd-looking poodle, a companion to *A Wedding Bouquet*'s Pépé. 'He was a dear dog,' remarked Chappell, 'but had this horrible habit of getting round your knee. Especially when you were in the car and he was pushed up against you and felt he had to do something about it. Of course that made us hysterical but we could hardly say to Gertrude, "Your dog is trying to seduce us."' Hearing more snorts in the back of the car, Stein turned round and drawled, '*Well*, I thought only *girls* giggled.'

'You saw from our giggles how happy and at ease we were', Ashton later wrote to Toklas, thanking her for the holiday, but she and Stein had also had fun and photographed the trio's antics with a thirty-five-franc camera bought to record the visit. Bobby Helpmann sang tirelessly for his supper, dressing up as an Arab woman for a photograph and, during a visit to the Abbaye d'Hautecombe, impersonating Mme Recamier by puffing out his hair and reclining on a couch in the Royal Apartments. He and Ashton saved their best imitation, a parody of 'les mesdames Americaines', for after they had left, Helpmann posing as Alice B. Toklas with pursed lips, a beribboned hat and a faraway expression, clutching the arm of marmoreal-faced, heavy-lidded 'Stein', who wore a tweed coat, pull-down cap and carried a man's umbrella.

At the end of their week in France, Helpmann and Chappell went by train to Dubrovnik, a fashionable resort that year, while Ashton was conveyed in style across the Swiss border to the Attersee. The sight of the Schloss reflected in the lake was just as exhilarating on a return visit. But, although the scene was idyllic, with the midsummer sun gilding the half-naked young bodies lounging on the shore, the atmosphere of the place was darker than ever. Nazism – rife in Salzburg – was now closing in on the castle. 'People used to come by and practically spit on the place,' Ashton said. Raimund was half-Jewish on his mother's side, and unsmiling locals who had rowed out to watch the latest festivities on the lake would stare at the flamboyant aristocrat with silent resentment, refusing to return his greetings. Then one night on a hillside two miles away, a fire broke out, its flames dividing to form the four right-angles of a swastika. 'It was probably directed at us,' said Iris Tree's son, Ivan Moffat, who was nineteen at the time. Raimund also took it as a sign of hostility and, with valedictory sadness, remarked to Ivan's stepfather, fellow Austrian Friedrich Ledebur, 'This will be our last summer in Austria.' And it was. It was also the last year of his marriage to Alice.

Raimund was now extravagantly and openly in love with Lady Elizabeth Paget, one of Rose's four sisters* – 'Imagine poor Alice coming up against another Paget girl,' said Ashton. Dark-haired, with silvery pale skin and her mother's deep-set brown eyes, Liz Paget was considered to be the most beautiful girl in England. When Ashton arrived at the castle, Liz had just celebrated her twentieth birthday and it was the spectacle orchestrated for her by Raimund that had drawn the surly onlookers on to the lake that evening like moths to the light: the bathing raft, illuminated with eight flaming torches, had been her birthday cake. It had been towed out at dusk, the podium for a formally laid dining table, strewn with white flowers. Alice was not among the party that drifted out to the raft in the long, red-sailed barge; she had stayed behind in the castle, playing bezique with Dr Kommer, equerry to Diana Cooper (who was also at Kammer that summer), and known as the Cat. It was an uncharacteristic display of self-preservation on Alice's part, for the Plattboot's cargo was heavy with star-crossed lovers: nineteen-year-old Ivan Moffat was silently besotted with the wayward Angelica Welldon, whose eyes were fixed on Raimund, who could see no one but Liz.

Alice's restraint collapsed with the arrival of Ashton and he found himself rowing out on to the lake, with her in tears, while, in another boat in the distance, Raimund could be seen with Liz. After a fortnight at Kammer, Ashton could not take any more and escaped with Alice to Venice, where Bobby Helpmann and Billy Chappell were spending a weekend, staying on the Lido in a 'ghastly modern hotel', while Alice and Ashton were settled into a small, elegant pensione in Venice itself. When they met, the two dancers found Ashton in a foul humour: 'You look absolutely terrible!' he snapped, when he saw how relaxed and tanned they were. 'It's no good thinking you look good, you look all dried out and burnt.' Alice had taken him shopping to buy an expensive dressing gown, but he was impossible to please, behaving like a petulant gigolo, even to the point of staging fainting fits. 'I think he was worn out,' said Chappell. Ashton had complained that Alice was 'insatiable'. (Years later, when he met her friend, George Dix, whom he mistakenly understood to be a potential suitor, he described the weekend in Venice and warned him, 'If you have any intention of marrying her, you'll have to be the strongest man in the world.') But it is far more likely that Ashton, increasingly ob-

*She became his second wife.

sessed with Michael Somes, was finding it much harder to consummate their relationship. There was also another, more serious cause for his distress, one that he did not want to confide to his friends at the time. Alice had told him that she was carrying his child. Ashton's reaction was to be 'quite ruthless' and insist that she must terminate the pregnancy, giving as his reason the old adage, 'I felt she was cornering me into marrying her.' Later, when Billy Chappell heard about it, he, too, believed that Alice was trying to ensnare Ashton. 'But if it was a trick, it was an unwise one to play on Fred because it made him very cross.'

Ashton went back to Kammer with Alice, but brought along Chappell and Helpmann for moral support. Raimund disliked them both on sight, finding their leopard-skin trunks and theatrical antics in the water in poor taste. 'He thought they were trash,' remarked Ashton. 'As we all were.' But the pair were oblivious to any antipathy and loved every minute they spent there, 'goggle-eyed' at everyone's behaviour and at the traffic of grandees. A dance was given for the Duke and Duchess of Kent; Mrs Simpson arrived for lunch and tucked into two helpings of écrevisses and liver sausage; Margot Oxford appeared dressed for a garden party, took one look at the guests, most of whom were wearing bathing suits, or dirndls and lederhosen, and said, 'I see you're all in fancy dress.' She refused to allow Dean, the butler, to remove her luggage from the car and snapped rudely at Alice, 'I'm not a duck – I'll go to the hotel.' She later reappeared in a more relaxed frame of mind and, when Iris Tree broke a strap of her bathing suit, hoisted up her skirt, revealing long fitted knickers, and removed a safety pin from a neat row down one side. 'I never move without them,' she said.

To please Ashton, Alice had invited his sister, Edith, to Kammer, as well as Constant Lambert, who arrived with his wife, Florence, and their baby son. But the Lamberts only contributed to the mounting tensions. From the moment of their arrival, Florence had caused trouble, initiating one row after another with Constant and creating a terrible scene about a lost opal earring which, when found by Alice, she threw into the lake. It was joined by her wedding ring after she discovered that Alice had lent Lambert and Fonteyn the gate cottage of Hanover Lodge as a love nest. Unable to bear any more, Raimund physically threw Florence out, picking her up and depositing her outside the front door with her luggage. Before she flounced off, she retaliated, by 'rudely exhibiting her behind'.

Constant remained at Kammer to work on *Horoscope*, the score of the new ballet he was composing for Ashton, but the choreographer, desperate to get away, was not in the mood for work. Alice begged him to stay – at least until the Kents' ball – but he was adamant. He was sitting in the car ready to go, when he remembered that he did not have his passport. 'I said to Gilbert, the chauffeur, "Have *you* got it?" But he hadn't. It had been left at the Austrian frontier *deliberately* by Alice to get me to stay.' So he stayed, and, as a result, formed a lasting friendship with Princess Marina, Duchess of Kent, whose beauty and elegance entranced him. He was very reticent towards her at first, but found that she, too, was shy, and he felt that she appreciated the fact he did not 'grab the opportunity to court favour'. Yet not even his first genuine friendship with royalty was solace enough. Ashton was seized by one of his 'spasms' and rushed to a clinic. 'It appears that the nerves of my stomach are in a terrible condition,' he wrote from Kammer to Alice B. Toklas. It was not only the 'boisterousness in the air' which had brought on his condition; the real cause, as he admitted, cut much deeper. 'I suppose it is all the result of a hard winter on my nerves and emotions; cold winter months of hankering after the wrong person.' Michael Somes was the cure he craved, not the 'pills and drops' that were administered to him in Austria, but his love-sickness was soon to be assuaged. Not only would the coming year reward him with glimpses of the intimacy for which he yearned, but, on his return to London, he was able to give vent to his covert feelings in *Horoscope*, a ballet encoded with a cobweb of real-life allegiances, as intricate as those between the lovers on Kammer's long barge.

CHAPTER EIGHT

LOVE IS NOT A BAD THING TO PUSH

1937–1939

Ashton's summer holiday at Kammer was followed by a tour of the north of England. While the company performed in Leeds, he and Bobby Helpmann stayed at Renishaw with Edith Sitwell, who, deeply affected by the terminal illness of a great friend, was glad of entertaining distraction. She had written to Ashton to say how much she was looking forward to hearing about their 'adventures with Gertrude and Alice among the edelweiss', and she longed for a repetition of one of their impromptu performances at the Sesame Club, which she said had been one of the most enjoyable evenings of her life. On this occasion, Ashton had brought new subtleties to his well-practised imitations of Nijinska and Ida Rubinstein, which Sitwell recalls in a glowing critical appraisal:

> I think on the whole, the Nijinska episode was my favourite. Osbert is right in saying it has a peculiar Daumier-like quality – something sinister in its atmosphere. I am also deeply attached to the lilies and languors of Ida Rubinstein, the phosphorescent glamour of her. Helpmann's lighter, vocal number, is very great, and I am afraid would be a subversive force among stage-struck young women. And Hamlet is perfection. Indeed, *everything* is . . . You will both have an awful time of it at Renishaw, – so be prepared.

News of the jollities in Derbyshire reached Alice, who wrote a postcard to Ashton from Austria saying how pleased she was that he was in a good mood and back at work. She, meanwhile, was absorbed by a distraction of her own. It was the end of the summer, Raimund had gone to Switzerland and Kammer was nearly deserted. Ivan Moffat was one of the last guests to leave. He had intended to drive to Munich and Prague with an American friend, but, when their car broke down, they returned to the castle. 'Perhaps tactlessly, as there was Alice and Jamie Hamilton not at all pleased to see us. We didn't know that they were having an affair.'

Hamish (Jamie) Hamilton, the publisher, was a quiet, distinctive-looking thirty-eight-year-old man, with a wry sense of humour. He masked insecurity about his provincial Scottish roots with a pose of great sophistication, but, in fact, he was easily impressed by glamour and yearned after the sort of life to which Alice could give him access. She was no more than toying with Hamilton, but her indifference only stimulated his interest. 'It made him frantic,' commented a friend. 'He was like a little Scottie running round a greyhound.' Alice's affair with Hamilton continued in England, although she remained in love with Ashton and saw him whenever she could, usually in the company of friends. They continued to spend weekends together at Faringdon and at Weston Hall, but Bobby Helpmann would accompany them to provide light relief. As far as Ashton was concerned, his romance with Alice was over: Michael Somes now had total possession of his heart. 'It was an obsession,' he said. 'I bored everyone by talking incessantly about him.' He was pursuing the dancer with Alice-like relentlessness, but that was the way he wanted it. 'He liked being the one in charge,' said Billy Chappell. 'And when he set his mind on someone, there was no holding him back.'

A gift of a watch, the promise of roles, and Ashton's unremitting devotion began to take effect. Hints of submission appear in the letters Somes wrote to Ashton around this time and chart their deepening commitment. Other dancers, such as Alan Carter, watched with interest. 'The motives behind Michael's behaviour were not clear to us. Fred was very persuasive and Michael was very ambitious, but there was more to it than that. I suppose that Michael saw a Diaghilev quality in Ashton and that was very glamorous.' But if there was an element of self-interest on Somes's part, it was something that Ashton understood and even condoned.

Why shouldn't you? Massine who was as normal as can be, *he* gave way to Diaghilev. He did it because it was going to help his career. If you're a young person it's perfectly sensible – what does it cost you? People make such a fuss about it . . . I remember saying to one of Massine's mistresses, 'What did he think about going to bed with Diaghilev?' and she said, 'Oh it was rather like going to bed with a nice fat old lady.' Michael was never queer in any way. He liked me because he appreciated what I was doing for him, but I wasn't doing it only for him I was doing it for myself because there was nothing better.

Ashton was ready to prove his point. Disregarding muttered allegations of sexual favouritism and the tantrums of Harold Turner – 'It was awful for poor wretched Harold,' said Chappell, 'we all saw that' – he took Somes out of the corps de ballet and gave him a leading role in *Horoscope*. The section of *Les Patineurs* based round the dancer's impressive jump had already signalled his potential, but Ashton was offering Michael Somes the ultimate challenge: an opportunity to be the new partner for Margot Fonteyn. Personal considerations apart, the choreographer was forced to look ahead. Helpmann was just beginning his transition into the theatre (when *Horoscope* was in progress, he was appearing as Oberon to Vivien Leigh's Titania at the Old Vic), and, although Somes was technically unpolished and at the time lacked the assurance as a partner he would later acquire, he had something much rarer: the charisma and stature of a romantic lead. As one colleague remarked, 'When Michael was on stage, you couldn't take your eyes off him.' Somes, as Ashton realized, could prove the ideal foil to Fonteyn.

> He looked *wonderful* behind Margot – a hundred times better than Bobby Helpmann did. When Michael and Margot presented themselves on stage they looked a wonderful couple. I'm not saying that he was the greatest dancer in the world – he wasn't – but he was perfectly efficient at what he did. Michael did great turns in the air, he was very musical . . . a beautiful creature – so why not? Who else was there? Harold Turner, who was a virtuoso, but small . . . Who else? *John Field?* Michael was a better dancer than Helpmann and the only premier danseur with nobility on stage.

Ashton was far too professional to promote a dancer without talent, however intense his infatuation. 'You mustn't let it blind you,' he used to say. Somes's glamour as a performer was all part of his allure. 'Fred wouldn't have used him if he'd been too raw,' confirmed Billy Chappell. 'And he'd have lost interest if Michael hadn't progressed the way he did.' Realizing he had to prove his worth, Somes had already embarked on a self-imposed regime of improvement, writing out the daily classes from memory, and practising special exercises he had been given by Alexander Volinine, one of Pavlova's premier danseurs, whose classes he had attended when the company had been in Paris. Volinine had been struck by Somes's rapid development and told him that he had achieved in two weeks what would usually take a dancer two years. But only Ashton could make him a star.

> I was very taken with him – I'm not saying I wasn't. Look at the history of the Diaghilev ballet. Because Diaghilev was taken by Nijinsky, Diaghilev was taken by Massine, Diaghilev was taken by

Lifar . . . isn't that good enough? Diaghilev made Nijinsky into a
worldwide figure. Nijinsky goes, Diaghilev takes Massine, a beautiful man, a great personality, puts the right material round him,
makes a great thing of him. He goes, then there was Dolin: pretty,
lovely boy. Gets Nijinska to do the right things for him. He goes,
along comes Lifar. They fitted the bill, they attracted the audiences,
there was nothing wrong in it. And what about Balanchine and his
company? All the girls . . . It lifts the whole thing. An element of
love is not a bad thing to push.

It was not only Ashton's infatuation for Somes that was to 'lift the
whole thing'; Constant Lambert's passion for Margot Fonteyn was beginning to transform a uniquely gifted young dancer into a sophisticated
prima ballerina – the persona Ashton had in mind when he made *Apparitions* for her. While the choreographer was moulding Fonteyn as a
dancer, the composer moulded her life. During the making of *Horoscope*,
she began responding seriously to Lambert's advances, knowing that her
infatuation for Tito Arias was one-sided. By now, the circumstances for a
romance with Lambert were far more propitious. Since his divorce pro-
ceedings had been initiated, he had been living alone in the gate cottage
of 'Hangover Lodge', as he called it, and even Fonteyn's mother's vigilance – so uncompromising during the company's trip to Paris – had
eased off a little. Initially, the ballerina looked to Lambert to give her the
education she lacked. Desdemona-like, she would devour his conversation as he sat with her for hours in the studio, going through his score,
and talking about literature, music and art. She had always been eager to
learn. Her best friend, Pamela May, who had been taught at school to
memorize passages of Shakespeare by heart, remembers how irritated
Fonteyn used to be if she ever came out with a quotation. 'How do you
know that?' she would say, while glaring at her mother for failing her in
this respect.

It was during this period that a colleague, Annabel Farjeon, spotted
Fonteyn on the top of a number 19 bus, engrossed in a volume of Proust.
'Constant gave it to me to read,' she said. She loved to discuss books with
Lambert, but knew she was not capable of equal debate: 'He was on an
intellectual level that was way over my head.' She never overcame a
sense of inferiority about her intelligence, as she admitted years later in a
letter to Ashton. 'From way back during the war when I did not write because I thought my stupid letters would bore you, I still have a silly hidden complex that no one is good enough to invite to dine with you and
you would have a miserable evening with me.' The orthodoxy, stipulated
most stringently by Balanchine, is that ballerinas should dance and not

analyze their roles. Fonteyn was not clever, but she was sharp and could pass acerbic judgements on other performers. She was also quick to assimilate new steps, which won her Ashton's esteem, but it was her malleability and humility which made her his muse. He could not work with a dancer who resisted him, and Fonteyn's increasing dependence on Ashton and on Lambert was fundamental to their art. To both men, watching her respond sensitively and acquiescently to the nuances of the tempi, she appeared to be the spirit of music made visible.

Horoscope was Lambert's declaration of love for Fonteyn who, in response, danced the role of the Young Girl with a new aura of confidence noted across the footlights. 'Today . . . there is something triumphant about her dancing,' commented Arnold Haskell. Lambert dedicated his score to Fonteyn and in it he confessed his strengths and his weaknesses. Edmund Dulac's cover design of the printed work is an illustration of Lambert's birth chart. And it is this interplay of his own astrological symbols on which he based his scenario:

> When people are born they have the sun in one sign of the Zodiac, the moon in another. This ballet takes for its theme a man who has the sun in Leo and the moon in Gemini, and a woman who also has the moon in Gemini but whose sun is in Virgo. The two opposed signs of Leo and Virgo, the one energetic and full-blooded, the other timid and sensitive, struggle to keep the man and woman apart. It is by their mutual sign, the Gemini, that they are brought together and by the moon that they are finally united.

Yet, even though the ballet contained a cryptic account of the composer's relationship with Fonteyn ('Not strictly accurate,' said Ashton, 'as Margot is a Taurus, and she was made a Virgo which is my sign.'), it was predominantly about Lambert himself. He was born on the cusp of Leo and Virgo, and considered this to be the explanation for the contrasting extremes in his personality. Cecil Gray's definition of the blend of opposites in Lambert is well known: 'A fin-de-siècle Frenchman with morbid faisandés tastes, and a bluff and hearty roast-beef-and-Yorkshire Englishman; Baudelaire and Henry Fielding combined, Purcell and Erik Satie, Ronald Firbank and Winston Churchill (to whom he bears an uncanny physical resemblance . . .)' This duality in Lambert's nature extends to his music, where, as Gray observes, the influence of the French school competes with the English for ascendance. The result is not merely a combination of the two elements, but a unity: a Hegelian reconciliation of opposites, allegorically enacted by the dancers in the ballet when the two lovers are united by the moon.

The nine sections of music epitomize Lambert's versatility and eclecticism. They include an energetic, rhythmic passage for the Followers of Leo in the syncopated style of *Rio Grande*, a limpid saraband for the followers of Virgo, and a popular waltz for the Gemini. The result, as champions of Lambert contend, is not mixture of styles but a fusion. A. V. Coton, on the other hand, dismissed the score as a work of 'minor grading' which inhibited Ashton's imagination. He was quite wrong. With designs by Sophie Fedorovitch, *Horoscope* followed *A Wedding Bouquet* as an enormously successful collaboration of friends. 'Grouping, characterisation, melody and rhythm, colours, lighting are all brilliantly integrated,' wrote the *Bystander*'s reviewer. Arnold Haskell considered it to be a venture of such importance that it could serve as an example to the Russians, whose standards had seriously declined. 'With *Horoscope*, ballet, now truly indigenous in England, reaches a splendid maturity. It is no chauvinistic cry to add that both in creation and in creative method, in the Diaghileff sense, it leads the ballet world today.'

Horoscope contained some of Ashton's most original and forward-looking choreography to date. Although short-lived (it was 'lost' during the Second World War and has never been reconstructed), many of its steps and formations have reappeared in more recent works. The choreographer's response to both the music and its subject was ingenious, particularly the way in which he used the dancers to impersonate astrological figures. Alan Carter and Richard Ellis as the Gemini twins looked glued together after practising for hours in front of the mirror to achieve perfect synchronization of line and timing. And for the Moon, he used Pamela May's harmoniously round port de bras to create endless variations of crescents and circles. Tranquilly beautiful and aloof, May made a deep impression in the role, subordinating emotion, like a Balanchine dancer, to purity of line. The pas de trois, in which the Moon was partnered by a Gemini twin on each side, was developed by Ashton three decades later in the serenely abstract *Monotones*. Indeed, when Richard Ellis first saw the 'Trois Gymnopédies', he exclaimed, 'That's Pamela, Alan and me!'

Unsurprisingly, Ashton's most inspired choreography was for Michael Somes. Casting him as the Young Man whose birthsign was Leo, he defined the aggression in the role by drawing on his qualities as a dancer, as well as his personality. Somes's celebrated ballon generated the springy leonine movements, while the dancer's emphatic musicality – the ability to be always absolutely on top of the beat – was used by Ashton to dramatic effect. This abrupt rhythmicality combined with the dancer's virile presence and attack was extremely exciting to watch – so much so that Margot Fonteyn, embodying the contrasting attributes of lyricism and timidity, was almost eclipsed by him. 'Dance like a god!' Ashton had written in a note delivered to his dressing room on the first night, and Somes had not let him down. The audience roared their approval (the ballet received more than twenty curtain calls), and all the critics, including the exacting Coton, agreed that this was a remarkable début.

Contributing to the power of the dancer's performance was an element of suppressed violence and arrogance which Ashton immediately captured in the opening stance as Somes stood isolated against a tableau of male Followers, his chin defiantly raised and his arms held in a defensive demi-second position, with fists clenched. Even at this impressionable age, he was 'difficult', to use his own euphemism for his notorious rages. Rehearsals had been fraught – 'It was all frightfully complicated,' Ashton admitted – and the atmosphere was still electric when *Horoscope* transferred to the stage. 'You could just feel those tensions,' said Alan Carter. 'The ballet had a very het-up feeling about it.'

Somes's romance with Pamela May was coming to an end. She had been seeing a student friend of Tito Arias', whom she had met on the last tour of Cambridge; and, by the following summer, at a memorable twenty-first party that she and June Brae shared in King's Parade, it was obvious that she was in love. The triptych of friends all went on to marry the undergraduates who joined their celebrations that night: Brae became Mrs David Bredin; Fonteyn, Mrs Tito Arias; and May, 'to Fred's delight', Mrs Paignton Cowen. (There was to be a further connection when Charles Gordon, in whose rooms the birthday party was held, became May's second husband.)

Somes resented having a rival for May's affections, but more unsettling was the dilemma within himself about his sexual identity. 'Michael was a very mixed-up boy in those days,' commented the dancer Joy Newton. His disquiet manifested itself in dark moods and irascible outbursts which took their toll on Ashton's nerves. 'I think Fred was more upset by Michael's moods than I was,' said May. 'He took it more to heart.' About a fortnight before the première of *Horoscope*, there was a confrontation during which Ashton, realizing the hopelessness of the situation, threatened to go abroad. Alice's ex-husband, Serge Obolensky, was reorganizing the Monte Carlo Ballets Russes with a group of American and Russian performers. Fokine was to be resident choreographer and Ashton had also been approached. A letter from Somes induced him to stay. Full of veneration and self-recrimination, it was an obsequious avowal of his dependence and gratitude.

The reviews of *Horoscope* had celebrated the arrival of one who (in

Coton's words) 'cannot fail to become, with adequate guidance during the next year or so, the greatest English male dancer of this century'. But Somes knew that his continuing success lay in Ashton's hands alone. For the next few months, their see-sawing balance of power over each other settled into an equilibrium which, as the dancer's letters reveal, was acceptable to them both. Each knew, however, that the closeness and peace of mind they achieved that summer could not last.

Drained by the emotional complications of *Horoscope* following a remarkable span of unremitting creativity, Ashton produced work of only minor significance over the next year. For a Royal Gala held in May 1938, to raise money for extensions to the Sadler's Wells Theatre (making possible the revival of *The Sleeping Princess*, the dance event of the winter), he created a fifteen-minute piece to a 'voluptuous' new score by Lennox Berkeley. With its neoclassical music, choreography, and design (by Chappell), *The Judgement of Paris* was no more than a pièce d'occasion, which, like Ninette de Valois' *Le Roi Nu*, provided a showcase for the 'divinnely fair' but overlooked Pearl Argyle. Her role as Venus was shared by Margot Fonteyn, whom the *Bystander* found to be 'a warmer, more human goddess'.*

After the gala, a party was given by Alice at Hanover Lodge, where Benjamin Britten was among the guests. Encouraged by Tchelitchew, the composer was anxious to acquire Alice as a patron. But even though, on a return visit, he played her some of his songs, she did not respond in the way he had hoped, despite the fact that Ashton, still the focus of her attention, was then showing an interest in Britten's work. The following month, the choreographer discussed with Britten the idea of making a ballet of his 'Frank Bridge Variations', but this and various other projects came to nothing. They did not work together until 1947, when Ashton directed *Albert Herring* at Glyndebourne.

That summer, remembering his ordeal of the previous year, Ashton turned down Alice's invitation to accompany her to Venice. Instead, he spent his holidays at a hotel in Shaldon, South Devon, choosing the West Country because it brought him nearer to Somes, who was staying with his parents in Cornwall. The dancer's letters over this period – signed 'Rooney', short for Mickey Rooney, Ashton's nickname for him – are teasingly familiar. He makes a running joke of mock-confessions of infi-

---

*Perhaps conceding to the ascendance of the younger dancer, Argyle did not remain with the Vic-Wells much longer. She left the company to marry a German film producer and live in Hollywood.

delity with farm-hands and milkmaids, calculated to fuel Ashton's insecurity, but always ending with the assurance that avuncular types are more to his liking.

At the end of August, Ashton and Bobby Helpmann spent a few days in Oxfordshire with Gerald Berners. Given the unconventional set-up at Faringdon, it is surprising that Ashton did not take Somes with him. But, even among his immediate circle, he maintained an acute sense of propriety about his personal life and expected others to do the same. When the young Private Secretary, Nicholas Lawford, turned up at one of Chips Channon's parties with an attractive young man in battledress, Ashton took him aside and lectured him on 'how to behave in public and yet be happy in private'. No one, on the other hand, raised an eyebrow at Bobby Helpmann's appearance at the party in drag, impersonating a minor European princess, in a hat made out of silk stockings. Ashton was perfectly aware, of course, that in the witty milieu of Faringdon, Helpmann would always be a more welcome guest than the beautiful, brooding Somes.

Alice should have been among Berners' guests that weekend, but was delayed in Switzerland. She sent a note of apology to Ashton and asked him to be sure to give her all the dates and addresses of the forthcoming tour to Manchester, Dublin and Cardiff, so that she could join him on the road. The day after she got back from her holiday, she and Raimund, soon to be divorced, had a sentimental last dinner together at Hanover Lodge. Cecil Beaton envisaged the Coward-like scene: 'They toasted each other and laughed and Raimund gave his last command for a bottle of champagne.' Dean, the butler, left at the same time as Raimund, and was replaced by a new butler, also called Dean. 'A new saga begins with a new Dean.'

Although Alice and Jamie Hamilton were now considered a couple, it was Ashton who accompanied her for a late summer weekend at Ashcombe, Cecil Beaton's house in Wiltshire. While she was characteristically quiet, their host describes Ashton as being 'extraordinarily eccentric, ridiculous and full of fantasy'. On his way to have a bath, Ashton appeared before them in a dressing gown, and a turban fashioned from Alice's scarves, fastened with a jewelled brooch. And as the night wore on, he entertained his audience with 'brilliant, spontaneous imitations, each a choreographic gem in itself'. The non-stop costume balls frequented by Ashton and his set in the 1920s – 'Go Tropical. Go Greek. Go Sailor. Go suitably dressed to celebrate the End of the World' – had long abated, but Ashcombe incited a spirit of gaiety and masquerade. Guests came to the house, as Beaton has written, expecting 'to exchange reality for a complete escape into the realm of fantasy'. They were encouraged to bring either fancy costumes (the actress, Ruth Gordon, arrived with her entire wardrobe from *The Country Wife*), or to raid the dressing-up chest. 'It was astounding how the same masks and remnants of tattered tinsel could be made to clothe a nun, a Casino de Paris chorus girl, a St. Sebastian or Queen Elizabeth.' Yet, despite the Saturday evening routine of charades, cross-dressing and audaciously inventive impersonations, Beaton was amazed by Ashton's deft, professional performance that night. 'His sure hands created improvised effects from whatever his eye lighted upon with the certitude that only an artist can possess.' With a coal-scuttle lid, Ashton created a picture hat, a coolie hat, a garden basket in which an Edwardian lady gathered flowers. But most impressive of all was his cameo of a Sarah Bernhardt tour de force, in which she enacted a dramatic scene while simultaneously arranging an elaborate bouquet of flowers. 'Her back to the public but head turned towards the arc lights, she selected each bloom, placed it with careful precision until the arrangement was finished, then stepped back with grandiose gesture to admire the effect.'*

On Sunday, the four friends went to lunch with Napier Allington at Crichel, where they found the atmosphere extremely uncongenial, with backgammonites glued to their boards, 'and those that were polite were only pleased to see us as relief from Randolph Churchill and the monotony of their family'. Tea back at Ashcombe was much more fun: David Cecil and Mary Pakenham arrived, and they all laughed and gossiped continually. Sunday evening was quiet, with Beaton scrap-cutting, Alice drawing, and Ivan Moffat and Ashton looking at an early draft and drawings for *My Royal Past*, and offering 'a few good pointers'.

The memoirs of Baroness von Bülop, 'as told to Cecil Beaton', were intended to parody the fatuous reminiscences of royalties like Queen Marie of Romania, whose book Beaton had been reading at that time. The joke was not new – Mary Dunn had published *Lady Addle Remembers*, the first of her three spoofs, two years earlier – but *My Royal Past* was a far more ambitious and stylish affair. For Beaton, it proved to be a trial run for photographing the real thing, which he was to do for the first time in 1939, the year of the book's publication. (His portrait of the heavily bejewelled, white-gloved Princess Paul of Yugoslavia, seated

---

*Bernhardt's original performance was one that Ashton imagined rather than witnessed. As a schoolboy in his Easter holidays, he may have seen her last London appearance in 1921. But not only was her role that season en travesti; her leg had been amputated by that time, and she did everything sitting down. It was the *idea* of Bernhardt – as great a theatrical personality as Pavlova – that Ashton was instinctively able to re-create.

against a backcloth of classical arches, could have been taken straight from the pages of *My Royal Past*; as could his assignment two days later, when he had the 'great thrill' of returning to Buckingham Palace to photograph the Queen.)

Beaton had hoped to use Ashton as his model for the Baroness, but the choreographer preferred to appear in less conspicuous roles, such as the Grand Duchess Marie-Petroushka, which he played to perfection. (Ashton would boast that the Duke of Kent told him he looked the most authentic of them all.) With his wasp waist, long pearled throat and graceful carriage, he did, indeed, look genuinely aristocratic, with none of the pantomime dame characteristics of his definitive drag act, the shy Ugly Sister in his ballet *Cinderella*. Many of the photographs for the book were taken in the studio of an Edwardian society photographer well equipped with period backdrops, but 'The arrival of King Boris at Klosterhoven 1899', the best known tableau, was posed in the drawing room and panelled dining room at Hanover Lodge. Sitting in the front row of one version of the picture, with the Whistleresque, shell-festooned double doors in the background, are Ashton as the Margravine of Kulp-Kronstadt, Gerald Berners as King Boris, and Alice as Princess Schnorr-Partenkirchen.

Far from being put out at seeing the man she loved in the guise of a society beauty, Alice, who loved theatricality, enjoyed playing the part of métteuse en scene. She kept a trunk of Lady Ribblesdale's discarded finery, and, on a similar occasion in the 1950s, when Beaton, Ashton and Michael Duff were staying with her in America, she insisted that they enact an Edwardian tea party, appearing respectively as Queen Alexandra, Queen Victoria and Queen Mary. A friend of Alice's daughter, Romana, witnessed the whole performance. 'Tennessee Williams was also there and couldn't believe what he was seeing. I remember him saying to my father, "I don't think Alice should allow that sort of thing in front of the children."'

Ashton needed little persuasion to channel his creativity into frivolous digressions, as his professional life at that time was not in the least demanding. In October, he arranged the Venusberg Scene for a Sadler's Wells production of the opera *Tannhäuser*. Although his dance for the Three Graces was predictably Botticelli-like, Charles Reading, the designer, recalls that Ashton did come up with 'some pretty novel things'. He had recently been inspired by the famous Louis Jouvet version of *Ondine* in Paris, with Pavel Tchelitchew's décor and costumes. For *Tannhäuser*, he lifted one of its most innovative effects, the creation of atmospheric images, such as a vision of a waterfall, by the use of backlighting and colour film. He also went one step further, mixing fantasy with reality, by having a genuine waterfall on stage, through which the dancers appeared. 'At the dress rehearsal,' remembers Reading, 'the girls kept hopping round the side so as not to get wet. The orchestra were at full tilt until Fred, from the stalls, shouted out, "*Wet* yourselves girls! *Wet* yourselves!" and every musician just collapsed.'

With its watery grotto, and corps of nymphs and dryads, the opera ballet was a sketch for Ashton's own *Ondine*, choreographed twenty years later. He discussed with Tchelitchew the idea of a one-act version of this ballet, but, while the collaboration was never undertaken, they did make other plans to work together and remained good friends. It was during 1938 that Tchelitchew created his silverpoint drawings of Ashton, exaggerating his Sitwellian profile and large melancholic eyes to conform to the neo-Romantic tradition.

A few days after *Tannhäuser*, Sadler's Wells showed the revived and extended *Harlequin in the Street*. It was a slight but popular piece in the Massine vein, reviving memories of *The Good-Humoured Ladies* and Fokine's *Le Carnaval*. Michael Somes, incongruously bewigged, powdered and patched like a Congreve suitor, was cast as the handsome lover opposite June Brae's La Superbe. But, on this occasion, sixteen-year-old Alan Carter as Harlequin stole most of the acclaim. His clean, easy technique encouraged Ashton to experiment again with virtuosic choreography, resulting in a lively display of bouncing batterie and nimble footwork – an effective contrast to the couple's terre-à-terre formality. Ashton himself excelled at these steps, and there may even have been an element of wishful self-identification with the teasing outsider, who disrupts the lovers' rendezvous, and steals and rewrites their billets-doux: Somes was beginning to set his sights on another of the company's gifted young girls.

Harlequin in the Street was, as A. H. Franks wrote at the time, 'polished, highly entertaining – and insignificant'. But, if it fuelled mounting criticism of Ashton as a lightweight, content to follow a well-established formula, its high spirits were at least an antidote to the tensions Ashton faced at home. Not only had his sister's marriage to Trevor Richards reached the point of collapse, but their mother was now virtually an invalid. The faster Georgie's health deteriorated, the more self-pitying and bitter she became, nursing resentful criticisms of Edith and her brother. The company's tour of the north gave Ashton a chance to escape, but a long, reproachful letter caught up with him in Liverpool. While repeatedly apologizing for being 'such an old worry' and 'a tiresome old ma', Georgie's tone is martyred and accusatory, calculated to needle Ashton's conscience. The characteristic aphorisms are more naggingly censorious than ever. 'Personal happiness is a wonderful possession, but it can only be got by personal unselfishness . . . Concessions have to be made on *both* sides. Sometimes if you made an effort to be more normal. Getting up earlier, not wasting your lovely young life between the sheets . . .' She goes on to outline the inventory of anxieties that are eroding her 'thoroughly jagged nerves': income tax, medical expenses, and a paranoid suspicion that her son and daughter are 'concocting impossible plans for my welfare . . . to relieve yourselves of the feeling of neglect'. Ashton's attitude towards his mother was not irreproachable. He knew she dreaded another lonely Christmas; but, rather than making an effort to be with her, or to take her away 'to get a change', as she would have liked, he buried his guilt and spent the holiday with the Angleseys in Wales, in the opulent surroundings of Plas Newydd. Georgie's loneliness and her dependence on Ashton were never more oppressive. As she admitted in her letter, 'Life hangs on you.' But, although he may not have allowed her to compromise his independence, he remained devoted to her and tried hard to make her empty routine more comfortable. He encouraged Gilbert, Alice's chauffeur, to take her for drives; arranged for a companion-housekeeper to visit her in the afternoons and evenings, and, in perhaps the most expansive gesture of his life, rented their first house, which he was '*just* able' to do, for £10 per week.

Number 24 Wharton Street, EC1, a nineteenth-century end-of-terrace house, with a striking classical pediment and Regency ironwork, was owned by the Lloyd Baker estate. Now a conservation area, this villagey district of Clerkenwell, a short walk from Sadler's Wells, was then just beginning to be gentrified. Olive Lloyd Baker preferred to rent her properties to writers and theatrical people: consequently, everybody knew everyone else. Several dancers were tenants, including Ninette de Valois, Robert Helpmann and Michael Somes, whose parents took a flat in Wharton Street. Number 24, comprising a basement and three floors, was baronial in comparison to what Ashton and his mother had been accustomed. He converted the top storey into a light studio bedroom for himself, and furnished the whole house with Alice's cast-off black and gold Regency pieces, and with antiques foraged from Saturday-morning trips to the Caledonian Road. There was even a pretty Victorian-style spare bedroom, intended as a refuge for Edith. Having married to get away from her mother, she was now forced to return to the same constricting ménage. The Edwardian code of conduct that Georgie prescribed – 'I wish Edith could see that by sacrificing her will a little to her duty she would be happier, even with Trevor' – was unrealistic in the face of the couple's incompatibility and Richards' drinking problem. Their marriage was long past saving – a fact that was to be the major strain on Georgie's nerves. 'She was frightfully upset when my sister got divorced. In her day you married *really* for better or for worse.'

Even after the move to Wharton Street, Ashton spent little time at home. He went to Faringdon for several weekends, accompanying Alice there for Easter, where they joined a jolly group that included Constant Lambert, Mary Lygon and Joan Eyres-Monsell. This time, however, he had the excuse of starting work on a new collaboration with Berners. Interspersed with photo-sessions on *My Royal Past* at Hanover Lodge were meetings to discuss their new ballet, *Cupid and Psyche*, which Berners had devised as a burlesque of the classical tale. The designer of the one-act work was Gertrude Stein's protégé, Francis Rose, who, at the time, was being talked about as a rival to the brilliant Christian (Bébé) Bérard. Rose had just mounted his first retrospective show in London, and he had been one of the sitters for Beaton's book. The second edition carries a picture of him in an Edwardian dress and picture hat laden with roses – presumably alluding to the Stein motto which he inspired, 'A Rose is a Rose is a Rose'. He also wears a stagey moustache, making the photograph look ludicrously defaced, and it was in exactly this camp, graffiti-like spirit that *Cupid and Psyche* was created. 'A good deal of quiet fun is got out of dressing Olympian personages correctly but oddly,' reported one newspaper article.

As with *A Wedding Bouquet*, much sport was derived from the making of the ballet. Berners gave Francis Rose a studio and a room in his London house, and their planning took place during belle époque dinners served by liveried footmen. This time, however, the emphasis was on the social, rather than the professional, and even the dissolute Rose noted that 'it was difficult to get Gerald to conform to the hard work of the theatre'. Berners viewed the designer's creations as interpreted by Ira Belline (Stravinsky's niece) 'with much amusement', but the costumes that were put on display for their friends (Lady Diana Cooper, Lady Cunard and Lady Elizabeth Paget were among those allowed a preview) were not fit for performance. The hats of the Tanagra figures might, as the *Bystander* remarked, 'have caused a sensation in Bond Street', but wings dropped off Zephyrs and wigs were made top-heavy. The scenario had been Berners' idea, but the sly humour and irony that distinguished *A Wedding Bouquet* were entirely missing from the new work. Most of the jokes were stale by the time they reached the stage. As one member of the cast remarked, 'It looked as if they'd all got drunk and hashed something together.'

The ballet started seriously enough, with two Tanagras – students from the Old Vic drama school – declaiming Pater's translation of the Apuleius tale. In a strong solo inspired by Nijinsky's faun, Michael Somes as Pan piped and danced in sideways angles, until Psyche appeared, the seventeen-year-old Julia Farron. She and another newcomer, Frank Staff as Cupid, danced several lyrical pas de deux – 'Very Fred, couru-ing forwards and backwards' – but the vulgarity of the finale obliterated the ballet's highlights. 'The last scene was a real disaster,' said Farron. 'Even at my young age I could see that. They got into something they couldn't get out of and it became desperate.' Mistaking mock-heroic for farce, Jupiter and Juno were portrayed as a couple of lushes, staggering and hiccuping about the stage. Venus (probably in imitation of the whore-goddesses in Tudor's *Judgement of Paris*) was 'a mixture of a courtesan and an insolent young dowager', or, as Mary Clarke saw her, 'a shop-soiled floozie'. There was a dance featuring Psyche's two 'ugly sisters', which was 'neither funny enough nor sufficiently sinister' to rate as a forerunner of Ashton's celebrated double act.* Sensing trouble, Lambert took to the bottle. Rose commented that 'There were quarrels and at the end . . . Lord Berners was nearly forced to conduct *Cupid and Psyche* on the first night, but Constant Lambert regained his health sufficiently to appear.' The dress rehearsal had been a fiasco: only half the costumes were ready, and Cupid, who was meant to fly above the stage, swung about uncontrollably, knocking Julia Farron to the ground. When the ballet met with loud boos on its first night, Francis Rose left for Paris in a cloud of snuff and Floris. He never went on to fulfil his promise; his weaknesses, which included a destructive addiction to alcohol and 'rough trade', outweighed his talent, and his career as a theatre designer never went any further.

Cupid and Psyche was to have been the two young leading dancers' great chance, but, as Mary Clarke pointed out, its failure would not have been felt so keenly had they been more experienced artists.

Ashton had shown an interest in Farron from the beginning. He persuaded her to change her name from Joyce to Julia, 'after the character in *Wedding Bouquet*, although I thought it made me sound like an old aunt'. Her extreme youth and fey beauty gave her an air of appealing vulnerability. As Rose remarked, 'She was a Juliet and a Psyche in one.' Inevitably, Michael Somes, who as Pan had to hold and protect her, found himself increasingly smitten. 'She was so lovely, little Julia,' he said, still tender after all the years. Somes used to coach Farron in the role after hours. 'He taught me a lot' – she smiled wryly – 'about all sorts of things.'

If Ashton was wary of their rapport, he showed no sign of vindictiveness towards Farron. 'I think he knew there was no future in it and I was always aware that Fred was there.' Indeed, Ashton went out of his way to be solicitous to Julia, offering to escort her to the first-night party. 'Alice will lend you a dress,' he told her, 'and my mother will alter it for you.' The dress was ravishing: different shades of blue-silk net, gathered

---

*A more likely influence is Fokine's *Cendrillon*, which had been performed in London by the Monte Carlo Ballet the previous summer.

tightly at the waist and smelling wonderfully of Alice's perfume (she was always especially generous to the current sweetheart of Michael Somes). After the performance, Ashton collected Farron and added the finishing touches to her hair before driving to Berners' house for what must have seemed more like a wake than a celebration.

With one or two exceptions, the critics pronounced *Cupid and Psyche* to be a complete failure, and it received only three performances. The spring of 1939 was no time for silliness – in particular, the caricature of goose-stepping fascists (as in the last scene). George Bernard Shaw, who was in the audience on the first night, took Ashton aside and told him, 'You've made the same mistake I once did, you've been frivolous about serious people.' The cult of frivolity had backfired on Ashton and his world (*My Royal Past* would also sink like a stone when it was published at the end of the year, and would not be reprinted until 1960). The dilettante era was over and external circumstances were forcing maturity upon Ashton, whether he liked it or not.

Just two days after the première of Ashton's new ballet, his mother was dead. Although she had been ill for a long time, the end nevertheless came as a great shock. He knew that he had been neglectful towards her and his guilt increased over the years. 'You were always a much more thoughtful and sweet son than I,' he assured Billy Chappell after his own mother's death. '*You* need have *no* remorse and I mean it.' Ashton soon found himself missing Georgie's company. For all the problems of living with her, it suited him to be fussed over and to play the role of the reliant child. All his life he would seek friendships with women, and with men, too, who would take care of him. He admired his mother as 'a woman of enormous potential which she never had the opportunity to fulfil'. From her, he inherited his single-mindedness, his sharp wit and much more. 'I am sure that a great deal of your talent came from her,' Sacheverell Sitwell wrote to him on hearing the news.

Ashton was deluged with letters of condolence from his twin spheres of society and dance. Diaghilev's English star, Lydia Sokolova, who was something of a medium, claimed to have received a message from Mrs Ashton, and wrote to him, 'she hardly knows the passing has happened'. Ashton was susceptible to clairvoyancy and might have taken some comfort from this, as the extent of his mourning over Georgie's death took him by surprise. He would find a limited release in his next ballet for the Wells, but not even this was cathartic enough. His grief was a wound that would never heal, he warned Chappell in darkly rhetorical terms. 'Time will lessen it, but from now onwards you will always walk with the conscience of death and the image of death graven on your soul with its startling immobility.'

For Ashton, the loss of his mother seemed to be 'the end of youth and irresponsibility and a facing up to a maturer and less carefree life', a remark he made to Cecil Beaton before he knew about the global catastrophe in store. But there would be consolations. Unlike Gerald Berners, who, as Ashton said, never really recovered from the war ('it was the loss of his world and everything he liked – frivolity and a light touch towards everything'), he himself experienced a contradictory triumph. Rather than eroding his achievements, the war years marked a new beginning, infusing his work with power and depth, and heralding Ashton's coming of age as a choreographer.

CHAPTER NINE

BANG GOES
THE WHOLE CONCERN
1939–1941

Ashton's immediate plans were overturned by his mother's death. He was due to go to the South of France to begin work on his first commission for a foreign company, the Ballets Russes de Monte Carlo. Massine, its new artistic director, had invited him to choreograph *Le Diable s'amuse*, based on the life of Paganini. Anxious not to jeopardize this opportunity, Ashton wrote immediately to Ninette de Valois, breaking the news of his bereavement and asking what she thought he should do. Her advice was characteristically sound.

> Ask them for a few days respite if you feel that such a thing would make any difference. But don't decide to do anything further than that. For one thing, to regard it from a practical point of view, you would have to return a sum of money that you can ill afford to send back. Secondly, one's feelings are not reliable when under an emotional shock – please don't be rash.

He also received a reassuring letter from Alicia Markova, who was now a member of the Ballets Russes and, therefore, able to gauge the situation. She reported that Massine, who had sent a telegram of condolence, was being 'sweet and understanding', and seemed happy for Ashton to postpone his arrival until the end of May, when the company would be in Paris.

> That will give you about three weeks to recover and strengthen yourself darling, then I think it would be a good idea for you to join us for a change of people and surroundings and help you forget a little of your loss ... so take heart dearest Fred and don't worry as I am here and will help and guide you if you want me to.

Ashton was, indeed, relying on Markova's assistance, and begged her to come to all the rehearsals, even the ones in which she was not involved. The scale of the assignment, a forty-five-minute ballet, demanding spectacular crowd scenes, was intimidating enough, quite apart from the prospect of working for a new company under the exacting eye of its maestro and his first mentor. Ashton appears to have been third choice for *Le Diable s'amuse*, which Massine had originally wanted to undertake himself. Balanchine was the next candidate and, by the time Ashton became involved, the work had already been planned, with costumes by Eugene Berman and a complicated scenario by Vincenzo Tommasini, who had also arranged the music on themes by Paganini. Casting was left to the choreographer, which is where Markova, who knew the company, was able to help.

For the part of the young girl who, at the devil's conjuring, abandons her fiancé and falls in love with a beggar, Ashton chose Alexandra Danilova, the company's prima ballerina and a dazzling exponent of the Petrograd style. In 1924, she had left Russia with Balanchine, her lover, and soon afterwards became one of Diaghilev's leading dancers. It would have been less daunting for Ashton to have created the role on Markova, but, ambitious to widen his experience, he made her second cast and looked to Danilova to 'show him another approach'. Ashton was in awe of her Russian training and, after rehearsals were over, he would ask her to perform the Petipa variations for him as a private tutorial in the classical tradition. Accustomed to working with Balanchine, who was so secure about his art that he never asked a question of anyone, Danilova was struck by the element of uncertainty in Ashton's method. 'I thought he was a little bit more simple than Fokine or Balanchine. He wasn't as strong in his ideas. You could see he wondered if like this or like this would be better.' Ashton's lack of confidence was exacerbated by language differences, which meant that it was difficult for him to establish immediate contact with the performers. The émigré dancers were very much a clique, and rehearsals were conducted in Russian. 'We understood just enough to get by,' said the American ballerina Rosella Hightower. There was noticeable competition between the nationalities, and, in particular, an element of friendly rivalry between the company's two divas. 'I am Russian. I dance *strong*,' Danilova announced at a rehearsal, after watching Markova's effortlessly lyrical interpretation of their role. 'Choura being the elder, treated Alicia like a little girl', observed Hightower. (When Ashton passed on the story to Fonteyn, it had a profound influence on her: 'From that day on, I danced strong with every bit of energy I could muster.')

Danilova, Massine once said, was like champagne on the stage. She had powerful sex appeal and the most famous legs in ballet. Ashton brought out her femininity and coquetry in a sensuously yielding pas de deux, a dream sequence which ends with the ballerina being swung round in soft spirals until the couple melt together on the floor. Her partner, playing the poor young lover, was Frederic Franklin, whose performances in the Markova–Dolin company had been admired by Ashton in London. The devil was danced by Marc Platoff, an American, who was given a striking, jazzy solo. In both men, Ashton found the kind of snake-hips plasticity and versatility he had not encountered since Walter Gore, and which he clearly enjoyed exploiting. Startlingly original was Franklin's acrobatic solo, with its rubber-legged kneeling walk, skids and reckless dives.

The choreography took its cue from Tommasini's jaunty score, and was full of high-spirits and innovation, with little sign of the emotional strain Ashton was under at the time. The steps seemed like 'discoveries', as Edwin Denby wrote, reminiscent of 'the kind of awkward and inspired dancing that young people do when they come back from their first thrilling ballet evening and dance the whole ballet they have seen in their own room in a kind of trance'. Another admirer of the ballet's spontaneity was Matisse, then designing *Rouge et Noir* for Massine, who used to watch rehearsals. Ashton thought the elderly gentleman who offered him little patisseries during breaks was 'probably some old White Russian duke or something', until, one day, the old man said to him, 'Monsieur, je vous admire beaucoup, votre chorégraphie se déroule comme une chaîne.' Ashton thought this was a marvellous remark and asked Danilova who the old man was. 'Don't you know? That is Matisse.' She shrugged, accustomed from her Ballets Russes days to working among artistic deities. But Ashton was far from blasé: 'Thank God I *didn't* know, because I wouldn't have been able to do anything.'

When he finished the ballet, after only two weeks of rehearsals, the company gave him a spontaneous ovation. Although he had confided his misgivings and inhibitions in letters to Michael Somes, he had nevertheless done an outstanding job. A major incentive was the fact that the ballet was to be shown in New York: 'Fred loved America so much and this was going to be the opportunity for him to return,' said Markova. But *Devil's Holiday*, as it was renamed, was not to be the unqualified success of *Four Saints*. Although it had staunch defenders in Denby and Walter Terry, the influential *New York Times* notice by John Martin was hostile and condescending. 'A extremely weak effort,' he concluded, like a tetchy schoolmaster. As a result, *Devil's Holiday* had only a few performances in America – 'something I never understood,' said Rosella Hightower, 'as it was a delightful ballet: very gay and always interesting' – and was 'unfairly treated' by the company, according to Markova, under-rehearsed and staged with inadequate lighting. 'I am afraid you had a very bad deal here . . . ' she wrote to Ashton. 'If only we could show them *Façade, Rendezvous* and Degas [*Foyer de danse*] as they really should be presented, you would have enormous success here.'

Had Ashton been able to stage *Devil's Holiday* himself, things might have been different; but not only was he unable to get to New York for the première, he never saw his ballet performed at all. It was not staged in France and its Covent Garden opening scheduled for September was cancelled, along with the company's season. He must have known that its fate was precarious. Since April, it had been obvious that war was imminent (the reason that the première had been scheduled for New York). One night, Ashton went for a walk with Markova, Danilova and Franklin past the Moulin Rouge, where they saw sumptuously bejewelled women and their escorts boarding landaus lined up to take them to the midnight races. 'Look children,' he remarked, 'we may never see this again.' When he returned to England, however, he was still expecting to supervise final rehearsals at the Royal Opera House.

In August, he and Bobby Helpmann decided to take a holiday together in fashionable Cassis-sur-Mer, then travel on to the Isle of Wight. Before leaving, Ashton spent a few days with Michael Somes and his parents in Taunton. The dancer had dutifully written to Ashton in Paris every few days, encouraging and admonishing him throughout the making of *Le Diable s'amuse*. As soon as Ashton returned to Wharton Street he rang Somes, who seemed gratifyingly keen to see him, suggesting either that Ashton should come to Somerset or that he should join him on the Isle of Wight. Ashton then invited him and his parents to Cassis – being together with Michael's family was better than not being together at all – but the Someses, nervous of travelling in the current political climate, declined his invitation and spent their summer holiday closer to home.

At the end of the month, the company began its annual tour of the provinces. For the dancers, this often meant arriving in a town without knowing where they were going to spend the night, humping suitcases around the local digs until a room was found. When settled, everybody then went out looking for their friends, walking up and down the streets whistling *Swan Lake* and waiting for windows to open. Manchester, where the landladies were famous for their stinginess, was usually the low point.

(Once, when a couple of dancers were checking out, they were presented with a bill on which was itemized: 'Cruet – 1 shilling.'

'What's this?' Dick Ellis asked the rotund character barring the door.

'I have to charge for your salt and pepper,' she self-righteously replied.)

Over the years, however, some grew quite fond of these landladies, who looked forward to their arrival and plied them with huge high teas in front of the fire. In Liverpool, Ashton's motherly landlady knew how anxious he was about the increasingly alarming news and tried to protect him from it. 'Oh, it's terrible,' she would say to the others, 'but don't tell Mr Ashton.' And to him she would croon soothingly, 'There's not going to be no war, no there's not going to be no war.'

After Manchester came Leeds. On Sunday, 3 September, as the train pulled into the station, the company chattering and leaning out of the windows as usual, Billy Chappell saw a sour-faced porter walking alongside the train repetitively intoning, 'War's been declared,' like a stuck gramophone needle. Stunned groups of dancers huddled together on the platform, not knowing what to do. Ashton was silent, and not even Lambert or Helpmann managed to be flippant about the situation. Eventually, one of them suggested telephoning their friend, Doris Langley Moore, in Harrogate, ten miles away, to ask her how many of the company she would be prepared to accommodate. She agreed to have Ashton, Chappell and Helpmann, and she and her young butler set to work moving beds into her 'Museum', a large attic space, where she stored her celebrated collection of costumes.

Doris Langley Moore, later to become the biographer of Byron and E. Nesbit, was also the author of several novels and handbooks on domesticity, love affairs and fashion. Ashton and Chappell had known her since their early Rambert days. She had been introduced into their set by Edward Burra and became a good friend to them all. Ashton called Doris his 'oracle', as she told fortunes and would 'prophesize' about his ballets. 'Fred used to ask, "What do your voices say?" And I'd tell him, "Very good, if you don't do this or that."' She frequently sat in on dress rehearsals, conferring with Ashton's long-standing advisor, Sophie Fedorovitch. Doris was a fashion historian, with an extensive and valuable collection of antique costumes, and had decisive views on ballet design; but, unlike Sophie, she was a slave to fashion, frequently appearing in one of her latest acquisitions. 'I used to dread what Doris was going to wear,' said Ashton. 'It always had to be so extraordinarily eye-catching.' With her slightly stooping posture and strong, equine face, she was no beauty, which meant that her sartorial excesses – described, with particular relish, by Burra – were easy targets.

I must say, I can see no difference between Doris hats modern style & a vast mausoleum jam pot cake swathed in gauze with 2 giant hatpins with large tin plates for heads. One of her moderns for country wear (but not teas) was a white & black transparent straw poke bonnet tied under the chin with black velvet ribbon and 2 black velvet mariposas negras de mal augurio on each side!

Soon after they had met, Ashton and Doris became very close. When she came to London, they would have dinner after the ballet and Ashton would walk her back to her club in Grosvenor Place. Often they were so engrossed in each other's company that she would follow him back to Earls Court, only to zigzag back again with him automatically to Grosvenor Place. 'You could have lovely personal talks with Fred. He was always very very truthful, very open and in a way, quite modest.' Once a year, they met for tea and caviar at Appenrodt's in Piccadilly, where, needless to say, Doris always paid the bill. She came from a wealthy South African Jewish family, the Langley-Levys, and she and her sister, June, had married prosperous brothers in the Yorkshire wool trade. Doris and her dull but congenial husband settled in Harrogate, where they had bought a large turreted Victorian villa. Ashton always enjoyed staying there, because, as an authority on hospitality (co-author with June of *The Pleasure of Your Company*, a guide to entertaining, stylishly illustrated by Billy Chappell), Doris knew how to make life extremely comfortable. Mr Moore was never much in evidence, but he was always welcoming towards his wife's theatrical guests, even though, as Chappell says, 'he must have thought us all completely daft'.

When the friends sat down for dinner on the night of 3 September, their humour, albeit jittery and forced, had returned, although the conversation never strayed from the calamity ahead. Doris had chosen the main bathroom as a shelter, which was the most exposed room in the house. That night, an air-raid warning sounded and Ashton rushed around waking people; everyone obediently filed into the bathroom, where they sat drinking large brandies. Then they noticed that their hostess was missing. 'Didn't you wake Doris?' they all asked Ashton. 'Oh, I didn't like to,' he replied. 'She always sleeps so badly.' The siren, a false alarm, signalled the start of the Phoney War when, for the next seven months, the expected apocalypse never arrived. But, to Ashton and the dancers, it seemed like the beginning of the end. Just as English ballet was being taken seriously, it was confronted by imminent extinction. Conscription would not only destroy individual careers, it would precipitate the collapse of everything they had achieved. The following day, most of the company returned to London and dispersed until further notice: the Home Office had closed all the theatres. Ashton was to have travelled back to London that Monday to meet the Ballets Russes, but, with their season cancelled, Massine and his dancers left for America, where they remained for the duration of the war. After spending a few days in Harrogate, rather than returning to Wharton Street, Ashton evacuated himself – along with Chappell, Helpmann, and the hordes of expectant mothers and children leaving the city – to the Isle of Wight, where they stayed with Bobby Helpmann's 'formidable' aunt.

Ashton might have escaped the war altogether, had it not been for a twist of fate that, in effect, dictated the outcome of English ballet history. On 5 September, Richard Pleasant, who, with the ballerina Lucia Chase, was planning the inception of a new American company, wrote to Ashton from New York:

> Through Miss Rutherton and Mr Richardson of the *Dancing Times*, I have had some communication with you about the possibility of your coming to New York to mount ballets for Ballet Theatre . . . I am interested in having your work represented in our repertoire. At the time I first heard from Miss Rutherton you were not available at all. Now, with the declaration of war over last weekend, I don't know whether it will be totally impossible for you to leave the country or if by chance it might make you more available. We plan a great permanent organization in which there will be definitely a place for a person of your attainments.

Ashton never received the invitation; the envelope was wrongly addressed to 24 Harton Street and stamped 'Return to Sender'. Similar letters were dispatched the same day to Andrée Howard and Antony Tudor – a second approach to Tudor, according to Agnes de Mille. Earlier the directors had sought her advice on which English choreographers they should contact. 'I said, "Now wait, Freddie won't come, or if he does he'll stay for just one season, because his heart and soul is sold to Sadler's Wells. He'll never stand by you, but Tudor is free."'

De Mille was right about Ashton. Even if he had received Ballet Theatre's offer in time, it is unlikely that he would have accepted. 'He was as patriotic to his company as he was to his country,' said Michael Somes. Tudor, on the other hand, felt no such obligations. Having fallen out with Marie Rambert and been turned down as a choreographer for the Vic-Wells by de Valois, he was a free agent. Nor did he share Ashton's sense of national duty. If de Mille is correct, Tudor did not respond to Ballet Theatre's original offer until after the outbreak of war, when he sent a wire agreeing to join them. Following the example of Auden and Isherwood, Britten and Pears, he and Hugh Laing left England for New

York in October 1939. Tudor's defection – like that of Andrée Howard, Anton Dolin and Alicia Markova, who also (in Somes's phrase) 'buggered off to America' – was considered cowardly and irresponsible by the English dance establishment. When he returned to England in 1946 with his company, he was conspicuously snubbed in the Crush Bar of the Opera House. He was not pardoned by the English ballet establishment until 1967, when Ashton, at the helm of the Royal Ballet, commissioned him to choreograph a new ballet, the Zen-mystical *Shadowplay*.

On 7 September, which should have been the first night of *Devil's Holiday*, Michael Somes sent a telegram of commiseration to Ashton in Harrogate, following it up that evening with a letter posted to the Isle of Wight to await his arrival. At home with his parents, Somes was feeling isolated and depressed, even though he realized that the sensitive Ashton, with his ulcerous stomach, would be suffering more acutely. In a second letter sent c/o Mrs Helpmann, he makes a promise not to enlist, news Ashton would have welcomed were it not for the fact that Somes went on to say he could no longer continue the intimate side of their relationship.*

Michael Somes's infatuation for Julia Farron was growing by the day. When war broke out, she too had gone to live in Somerset, Somes having helped her mother to move out of their London house. 'Mummy Farron', as she was known by the company, travelled on the tours at that time as chaperone, occasional wardrobe mistress and extra. She was popular with them all, particularly with Somes, who had his reasons for being scrupulously attentive. Accompanying Mrs Farron, the dancer went to London for a couple of days. Returning to Sadler's Wells to collect his belongings, he found that, along with all the other dancers' personal possessions, they had been bundled into a dark corner. Walking morosely on to the stage, he did a final double tour en l'air before leaving the theatre, perhaps for good. Then came news from Ashton. The choreographer, with Constant Lambert, planned to reassemble what he could of a quickly diminishing company and take it on tour. Alice had agreed to provide most of the backing.† There was to be no orchestra; only two pianos, played by Lambert and the rehearsal pianist, Hilda Gaunt. All the dancers, whether principals or members of the corps de ballet, would be paid the same rate of £5 per week, to be increased if box-office takings were high. Somes was euphoric.

---

*'I'm afraid, dear F, it's *no* good – I have a pretty certain & shrewd idea I shall never be happy that way now. But don't you worry, I'm glad to have made *you* happy for a little while.'
†Kenneth Clark also takes credit for this: cf. his autobiography, *The Other Half*.

Oh I was *so* excited I nearly *died* my precious work, & all that I loved so – a glimmer of light & the thought of seeing you again if only for 2 weeks & we could be together & talk about our particular case, instead of being isolated down here, with everybody mocking. I would go if it were only *10/-* a week & I had to sleep in the *street*. You know how much my work meant to me, as it did to you, & a few of us – once *that* was gone, & that awful disbanding, I had no further use for life.

Suspecting that Ashton, however carefully he concealed it, might have been offended by his rebuff, Somes made a point of reassuring the choreographer that his letters still meant a lot to him – 'I have brought them away with me in a little tin box' – and that he was happy they were soon to spend some time together.*

Ninette de Valois did not involve herself in the new scheme, feeling impelled to 'do an awful lot of work at home'. Her husband was a doctor whose partner had been conscripted and, consequently, her help was needed to run their medical practice. There was also the ballet school to keep going. 'It was like a little concert party. I let them do it on their own, there was no point in me going.' All the same, her biographer's claim that de Valois 'gave the company a lead throughout the whole course of the war', is scathingly challenged by Ashton. 'Ninette – *wonderful* Ninette – said that a woman's place is in the home and she went away and disappeared. She absolutely abandoned us. But that's never written about. When Ninette saw it was going to work she came back and took the whole thing in her hands again.'

At the end of September, the Vic-Wells dancers regrouped under Ashton's direction and began a tour of indeterminate length. 'Oh, what sore muscles and bruised toes we had as we went straight into performances without practising a step for fourteen days,' Fonteyn remembered. The schedule was gruelling, with six evening shows and three matinées in each town, engagements in military camps proving especially hard, because soldiers would walk out mid-performance, banging their seats and cursing loudly. Travel in wartime was depressing, too, with trains cancelled or delayed, and carriages often unlit and unheated. There was no food available, and what was on offer back at their digs was frequently inedible: congealed wedges of dried-egg-powder omelettes had to be se-

---

*These letters no longer exist. Somes, who told the author, 'They'll go with me to the grave', destroyed Ashton's love letters to him before he died.

cretly incinerated in the fire, or smuggled out to the nearest pig bin. One landlady offered a munificent choice of toasted cheese, Welsh rarebit or cheese 'a grottin'. Theatres rarely had the luxury of hot water, without which it was almost impossible for the girls to scrub off the 'wet white' after a performance of *Swan Lake*. Bedrooms at their lodgings were only a few degrees warmer than outside; the lavatory was either a shed in the garden, or situated at the end of a terrace and shared by all the families in the row. But the company, all seasoned troupers, were well practised at keeping up morale. 'We were so pleased to be doing something, to be back at work,' said Pamela May. 'There was a certain natural reaction to the outbreak of war – we all had our different thoughts about it. But basically we were as mad as ever.' Bobby Helpmann was soon up to his old tricks. On one occasion, when their train emerged from a tunnel, while gazing nonchalantly out of the window, he sat waiting for someone to notice that he was exposing himself. This became known as his 'duck in flight' act. At their lodgings, he was even more outrageous. A turn begged for by Constant Lambert was Helpmann in the role of a wanton Edwardian maid. Lying naked on a bed, with his private parts tucked between his legs and a dollop of KY jelly on his 'pudenda', he would call out to the composer in a grating cockney drawl: 'I'm ready for you, master.'

Ashton and Lambert found another, more edifying way to relieve the tedium of touring in discussing new creations, including *Dante Sonata*. Ashton came up with the theme of Dante's *Inferno*, and Lambert chose Liszt's 'Fantaisie, quasi sonate: d'après une lecture de Dante', an impressionistic distillation of the first two books of the *Divine Comedy*, which, in itself, provided a simple synopsis. The ballet was clearly inspired by the outbreak of war, but the collaborators wanted to discourage too literal a reading of topical events, as the programme note makes clear:

> The artists responsible for the present production have adopted the same attitude towards Liszt as Liszt did towards Dante. The ballet is therefore a freely symbolical interpretation of the moods and form of the music and, though it represents the warring attitudes of two different groups of equally tortured spirits, it tells no set story.

Liszt's score was not so much a direct reponse to Dante as an interpretation of the Victor Hugo poem 'D'Après une lecture de Dante', from which he took his title and condensed structure. The Dantean content of Ashton's ballet was, therefore, several times removed, filtered not only through the minds of Hugo and Liszt but also through the eyes of illustrators of the *Divine Comedy*: Blake, Doré and particularly John Flaxman, whose drawings were the source of Sophie Fedorovitch's economical designs.

If Ashton did read the *Inferno*, it had little effect on his work. The Children of Light (led by Fonteyn and Somes) and the Children of Darkness (Helpmann and Brae), who represent the opposition of good and evil, do not appear in Dante's vision. Rather, Ashton took his images from drawings he consulted during rehearsals and from Hugo's poem. Blake's protoplasmic groupings and Flaxman's floating figures were echoed in the patterns of bodies which formed and dissolved, 'as if thro' aether borne'. The facial contortions of the Children of Darkness (an irritation to Cyril Beaumont, who would have preferred well-designed masks) were a literalization of Hugo's 'Gnashing of white teeth in the dark night . . . The grimacing mask of suffering Hatred.' But the real key to the ballet is the first line of the poem: 'When the poet paints Hell he paints his own life.' As much a Romantic by nature as Hugo and Liszt, Ashton infused the ballet with his own feelings. Although its vision of conflict and turmoil was symbolic of the times, the work derived much of its power from its outpouring of private suffering. It was composed, as Beryl de Zoete confirmed, 'under the influence of a strong personal emotion'. Ashton's despair about the war and its consequences – 'I felt I hadn't said nearly enough to be ready to die on it' – was intensified by the pain of bereavement: the loss of, first, his mother and, now, Michael Somes. A confession of individual anguish was the astonishingly dramatic solo by Pamela May, which expressed 'some terrible unexplained grief' as she ran in broken steps, flinging down one arm, then another, and whiplashing her torso and head.

There were certain moments when *Dante Sonata* did appear to be re-enacting current events. The tramping and surging of the Children of Darkness over the helpless bodies of victims on the ground was considered emblematic of Nazi oppression, but that was not Ashton's intent. 'People said I was affected by the violation of Poland and all that. I don't think I was at all. It was more about the futility of war and how nobody wins in the end.'

Love, the main impetus behind almost all his ballets, was no longer a consolation. Although Liszt saw in the vision of Dante and Beatrice an idealized reflection of his life with Marie d'Agoult, there was no hint of private affirmation in the ballet. When a ray of golden light appears on stage to the sound of a beatific piano trill, it was extinguished as soon as Somes and Fonteyn ran towards it. As Ashton said, there is no victory for either side. Held high in a climactic tableau, the leaders of the Children of Light and Children of Darkness were both crucified. This 'terrible impartial end' was praised by Joan Robinson, the Cambridge economist, in a letter to Ashton, but she, like many others, missed a final, evanescent note of optimism. Just as the curtain fell, a spotlight picked out Fonteyn, walking between the two groups. Fleetingly sanctified into a Beatrice figure 'bathed in the glorious ray', she seemed to be offering a glimmer of hope, while her gesture pointing towards infinity also recalled the 'Serene Virgil' of Hugo's poem, 'who says to us: Let us go on!'

The ballet's crucifixions were considered by Cyril Beaumont to be a lapse of taste on Ashton's part – particularly an earlier incidence, when Somes was punitively 'nailed' to the stage. It is tempting to speculate whether the heavy-handed Christian imagery was prompted by a subconscious personal urge for revenge; but, more probably, Ashton was remembering an episode of the Descent from the Cross in Massine's *Seventh Symphony*. Massine's influence on *Dante Sonata* was pervasive, seen in the mass groupings and Central European flavour of the movements. The bare-footed idiom, so suggestive of Flaxman's drawings, was a departure for Ashton and also evoked his memories of Isadora Duncan – particularly in the women's chiffon drapes and loose-flowing hair, and in the way the dancers appeared to sink in submission to gravity.

The ballet had a therapeutic effect on audiences, although much of its power evaporated after the war. The press hailed it as a landmark in the history of English dance and in Ashton's own development. Of his quartet of wartime ballets, it was the most descriptive of his horror of contemporary chaos. 'He did several what you might call patriotic pieces,' said Ninette de Valois, 'but they weren't directly *out* of him as *Dante Sonata* was. That was the marvellous one. The one he felt really strongly about.' It even converted Ashton's detractors, who had persistently complained that his range was confined to entertaining and elegant subjects. The ballet was a major achievement – all the more so because, as Joan Robinson remarked, 'it's one of those perilous things that if it weren't first rate it would be awful.'

In March 1940, when the company performed in Sheffield, Ashton, Lambert and Helpmann stayed at Renishaw, which, while still not equipped with electricity, was luxuriously welcoming after the chilly lodging houses they had become used to. So apprehensive was Edith Sitwell about the outcome of the war that the trio made little attempt to recapture the frivolity of previous visits. 'How far away everything that we once enjoyed seems,' she wrote to her sister-in-law, Georgia. 'Constant and Freddie and Bobbie have been here. It is so dreadful seeing all these poor young men on the brink of this ghastly catastrophe.' Even if their lives were to be spared, their vocation remained seriously threatened; what G. B. Shaw predicted could be 'the end of our supremacy in one of the finest of the theatrical and musical arts' appeared grimly inevitable. Despite months of string-pulling and high-powered protests in the press, the male members of the company of military age now faced certain call-up. And, as Shaw warned, 'If the Sadler's Wells leading dancers go, bang goes the whole concern.'

Fearing especially for the safety and future of Michael Somes, Ashton had appealed to Maynard Keynes for help. His response was contemptuous at first: 'You could hardly expect the authorities to let a young man off merely because he alleged in a weak voice that he was a dancer.' But, having discussed the matter with R. A. Butler, Under-Secretary for Foreign Affairs, Keynes became more optimistic. He remembered that, during the Great War, the German and Russian governments exempted ballet dancers from service – 'We ought not to be less civilized than they were then' – and Butler had promised to put forward a sympathetic case to the Minister of Labour. Ashton, Lambert and de Valois followed this up with a plea of their own to the Secretary of State for Home Affairs, reiterating the disastrous consequences conscription would have on the thriving new English art form. All was in vain. The final word from the authorities decreed that exemption for dancers would create 'bewilderment and even resentment among the general public'. The only option was for individuals to appeal on grounds of 'hardship' (which is how Somes, called up for military service in January, was granted postponement for six months). In the meantime, the show went on.

War brought the dancers closer to each other than ever before. Their apprehensions about the future were eclipsed, at least for the moment, by relief at the chance to carry on as usual. It was even 'lovely to be on tour', as Pamela May said. One night, while a group of them chatted in their digs over cold meat, apple pie and tea, Ashton announced he was going to read the Bible from beginning to end, promising that, by the time he had finished, the war would be over. (A miscalculation by four years.) Ignoring the groans of protest, he began right away, reading aloud in a sonorous tone of mock-piety. One of the side effects of war, as John Lehmann noted, was that it occasioned 'a great feast of reading'. As well as being an enthusiastic subscriber to the new literary magazines – *Penguin New Writing* and *Horizon*, which he passed on to his old schoolmaster, Alf Dixon, still living in Dover – Ashton was among those Lehmann describes as 'anxious to immerse in art and philosophy rather than in hate, killing and destruction'. The Bible was the first serious text he tackled in a regime of wartime reading that embraced philosophy, metaphysics and mysticism. It marked the beginning of a spiritual quest – a search for peace within himself – which would be reflected in his next ballet.

The Wise Virgins was Ashton's ivory shelter, in Cyril Connolly's phrase, expressing a new-found serenity, in complete contrast to the frenzied action of *Dante Sonata*. The idea grew out of an evening he and Lambert had spent in Cambridge with Boris Ord. When the conversation turned to the music of Bach, Lambert joined their host at the piano and among the pieces they played was Cantata No. 208, 'Sheep may safely graze', which Ashton found intensely moving. Misled, like many, by the pastoral imagery into thinking this a religious cantata, he decided to use it as the basis of 'a holy ballet'.* As a theme, he chose the parable of the wise and foolish virgins from Matthew XXV, for which Lambert selected a further eight numbers to be orchestrated by William Walton. The Baroque period of the music refracted through Walton's transcriptions – 'neither mock-archaic nor extravagantly modern' – made the choice of designer obvious. Rex Whistler (whose completed classical murals in the dining room of Plas Newydd Ashton had admired on his last visit to the Angleseys) combined a genius for academic pastiche with twentieth-century taste, wit and personal flair. He was at his most fluent in the language of baroque, having absorbed the brilliance of Bernini while living in Rome, and having been inspired by the flamboyantly ornate architecture of South Germany. Ashton also looked to the eighteenth century for ideas, studying not only painting in general, but also sculpture and architecture. 'And I tried to convey with the bodies of the dancers, the swirling, rich, elaborate contortions of the baroque period.' He spanned several genres, returning to the early Renaissance to re-create Primavera poses and curlicue arms; and basing tableaux of dancers on illustrations of rococo buildings, writhing with carved whorls and swarming with putti. He even borrowed from Biblical epic – 'the bride's crown was pure Hollywood' commented the *Dancing Times*, who found the mixture of periods 'confusing'.

In his massing of figures in front of Whistler's huge portal flanked by sculptured angels, Ashton must also have remembered Lima's baroque and rococo façades: the vast pillared doorway of the Torre Tagle palace, for example, and the church of San Francisco, with its interplay of columns, arches and stone statues. The visual counterpointing of dance and design gave an impression of genuine craftsmanship. The ballet was constructed like a magnificent edifice: 'You must have all loved building it up,' a fan remarked in a letter to Ashton. Once again, the architectural groups and the wedding theme evoked *Les Noces* as a choreographic influence (although the ceremonial finale, with the Bridegroom's arm raised

---

*In fact, the Christian reference is meant as a pun, alluding to Duke Christian of Weissenfels, whose birthday Bach was celebrating.

in a gesture of blessing, directly quoted the ceremonial last pose from Fokine's *Firebird*). But Ashton had come a long way from the days of *La Péri* and *Leda and the Swan*, with their slavish plagiarism of Nijinska's constructivist pyramids. This time, his sculptured ensembles were there to enhance his subject, their ascending composition expressing a soaring transcendental impulse. And, while the prototypes of the non-dancing parents of the Bride belonged to *Les Noces*, in *Wise Virgins*, Ashton humanized Nijinska's stylized ciphers. Annabel Farjeon was instructed to play her part like a conventional Jewish mother, bereft at losing her daughter: 'Let your ancestor rise up in you,' he told her. 'And WAIL!'

The abiding impression, however, was one of peace. The ballet was a daring exercise in stasis: dancers knelt, slept, posed and walked in procession (another legacy from his memories of Roman Catholic Peru). And yet the ballet was never soporific because, as Edith Sitwell, its unofficial dedicatee, pointed out, 'every picture told a story'. For the first time, he exploited Margot Fonteyn's gift for stillness – the beatific radiance that was later to illuminate *Symphonic Variations*. The Bride was the pivot of the work, a Madonna figure of chastity and grace, whose saintliness was achieved by confining her movements to fresco-like poses and the simple play of head and hands. A lovely solo, oriental in its delicacy, recalled the symbolic hand gestures of the Indian dancer Ram Gopal who had recently performed in London, while the kneels and twisting soutenu turns were inspired by the configurations and barley-sugar columns of baroque art. As the Bridegroom, Michael Somes was cast again as Christ (his bejewelled tunic alluding to the biblical bridegroom's bright ivory and sapphire-laden belly in the Song of Songs) and had little to do except look 'fantastic'. The only dancers who moved with any speed were the Foolish Virgins, led by Mary Honer, whose innate comicality Ashton allowed full rein for the second time. The vivacity of the Foolish Virgins, heightened by the brassy can-can spirit of their music, provided a well-planned contrast to the stillness, though some felt that their boisterousness unbalanced the rest of the work.

The Wise Virgins was slow to attract audiences and it divided the critics. Countering P. W. Manchester's virtual dismissal of the ballet, Audrey Williamson declared that it was the finest abstract achievement since *Les Sylphides*. Ashton's friends were full of admiration. Kenneth Clark pronounced it 'a masterpiece' and Edith Sitwell was effusive with gratitude and praise. 'It is *most* lovely, and has a singular youthful innocence which is just like that of the Adorations of the Primitives . . . it moved me very deeply. I am more proud than I can say that you should have dedicated it to me.' Edith Sitwell was in the habit of dedicating her work to one of a coterie of friends, which may have prompted Ashton to follow suit, even though he no longer felt under pressure to please her. Their friendship was now easy and sound (the last time they saw each other he brought his sister, Edith, along to meet her), and there was a reciprocal enjoyment of each other's gift for barbed repartee. Ashton noted that Edith Sitwell was well aware of the effect she created, remembering how amused she was by a waitress at the Sesame Club who remarked, 'Oh, Miss Sitwell, you *do* look queer today. Lily, doesn't Miss Sitwell look queer today?' The pair had supper at the club before a performance of *Wise Virgins*. Edith was wearing all her rings – huge aquamarine rocks on her beautiful, etiolated Gothic hands. Seeing Ashton staring at them she said, 'Shall I take them off? Does it look as if I didn't care?' War had changed Edith Sitwell: in contrast to the enfant terrible of the 1920s and 1930s, she had become a far more sympathetic and responsible figure. Of the three Sitwells, who all played important roles in the new literary and artistic world that emerged during the next few years, she, in particular, was deeply affected by the 'unspeakable' waste of human life.

There was one venture which the Foreign Office considered important enough to defer the call-up of Sadler's Wells' male dancers for two months. At the instigation of the British Council, the English ballet was sent to Holland as a propaganda exercise. On Saturday, 4 May, they travelled overnight to Rotterdam sardined into two cabins of a small Dutch boat. The town which, days later, would be pulverized by German bombs, was looking naively celebratory. It was a public holiday and cyclists thronged the sunny streets, their necks and handlebars garlanded with tulips. The company's headquarters was the Hotel du Passage in The Hague, thirty minutes' drive away. At first, it was all such fun. There were no blackouts or rations. The food was plentiful and wonderful – especially breakfast: a banquet of assorted hams, sausages, cheese and butter! The first-night gala was a triumph (*Dante Sonata*, in particular), and the company was given an overwhelming ovation and showered with tulip petals as they took their final call. There seemed to be a special bond between performers and public, intensified by the shadow of impending doom.

The next day, they went by bus to perform in Hengelo, eight kilometres from the German border, where the atmosphere was chillingly different. The journey there had alerted them to the increase in military activity: bridges were heavily guarded and partly blocked by concrete, troops stood with fixed bayonets, and there was barbed-wire fencing everywhere. When they reached the town, they heard that all the railways had been closed. There was hardly much incentive to sightsee – in fact, the dancers were advised not to go out. Some of the girls had already

LEFT: Frederick Ashton's father, George, in his youth

RIGHT: Ashton's mother, Georgiana, in 1916

BELOW: Georgie Ashton with her children and stepson, John,
photographed in England in 1906. *From left to right:* Charlie, John,
Tony, Frederick (in a dress), Georgie, and Alex

Charlie and Frederick Ashton, *center*, with a friend in Ecuador

ABOVE: Edith,
Ashton's sister

RIGHT: Georgie Ashton
in Lima

BELOW: Frederick on
holiday in Devonshire
with his guardian,
Maud Lawson

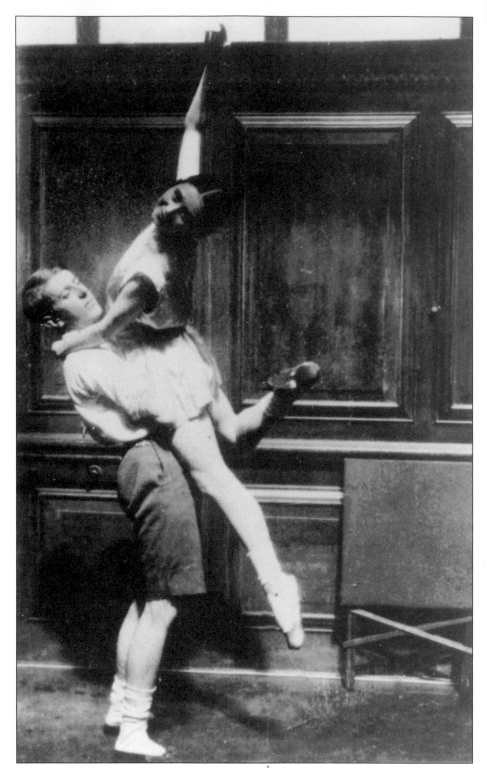

Ashton partnering Frances James in the Ballet Rambert studio,
circa 1925

ABOVE: Billy Chappell
by Edward Burra

TOP RIGHT: Edith's
wedding, 18 June 1932

RIGHT: At Charleston, 1932,
left to right: Ashton, Lydia
Lopokova, Duncan Grant, and
Billy Chappell

Photographs from Barbara Ker-Seymer's album, Les Sablettes,
Toulon, 1931. TOP LEFT AND RIGHT: Bunny Roger. CENTER: Billy
Chappell. BOTTOM LEFT: Jean Cocteau and friend. BOTTOM RIGHT:
Ashton in a pose from *Les Biches*

LEFT: Iris March, Ashton's first fling,
during a weekend together
at Buster Tonge's house

TOP: Ashton's great friend, the
designer Sophie Fedorovitch,
at Brancaster

In France, Bronislava Nijinska (center, front row) with dancers
from the Ida Rubinstein Company: Ashton is on Nijinska's left;
Billy Chappell is behind Ashton; Arthur Mahoney is at far left.

Ashton's Impersonations

LEFT: As Nijinsky in *L'Après-midi d'un faune*

TOP: As Gertrude Stein, with Bobby Helpmann, on the left, as Alice B. Toklas

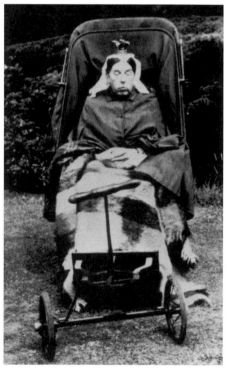

LEFT: As a *Vogue* model: Ashton helps Barbara Ker-Seymer with her first assignment as a fashion photographer

RIGHT: As Queen Victoria

ABOVE: Alice Astor photographed for *Vogue* by Cecil Beaton with Pavel Tchelitchew's series of eight charcoal studies of her

RIGHT: June Brae as The Rich Girl (inspired by Alice) in *Nocturne*, with Ashton in the role of The Spectator

LEFT: Ashton with cabaret singer Jimmy Daniels, who inspired Virgil Thomson to choose an all-black cast for his avant-garde opera *Four Saints in Three Acts,* which Ashton directed

Michael Somes in Cambridge, from a page in an album belonging to Ashton devoted entirely to photographs of Somes

ABOVE: Ashton and Gerald
Berners collaborating on
A Wedding Bouquet at Faringdon,
observed by Cecil Beaton

RIGHT: Pamela May and
Michael Somes as the lovers in
The Wanderer

LEFT: Dick Beard of the American Ballet Theatre in a pose that helped to inspire Ashton's *Valses nobles et sentimentales*, 1947

RIGHT: Alexander Grant, whose feral sensuality influenced the ballets of the fifties

ABOVE: The Royal Ballet on tour, *left to right*, Ninette de Valois, Margot Fonteyn, Moira Shearer, Ashton, Michael Somes, Robert Irving

BELOW: On holiday in France, *left to right*, Gertrude Stein, Alice B. Toklas (in shadow), Ashton with Stein's poodle, Basket, Bobby Helpmann, and chauffeur Gilbert

RIGHT: Tony Lizzul, a young chemistry student who was the secret muse of *The Two Pigeons* and *Persephone*

LEFT: Martyn Thomas, a life force in Ashton's last twenty years

BELOW: Tony Dyson, Ashton's loyal companion in the 1980s

RIGHT: Brian Shaw, a talented technician who was one of the most striking exponents of Ashton's style

TOP: Dressing-up at Chandos Lodge: Princess Margaret, *center*, and *clockwise from top*: Martyn Thomas, Ashton, Jean-Pierre Gasquet, Sarah Armstrong-Jones, David Linley, Fiona Penn, and Alexander Grant

ABOVE: In the pool at Sternfield: Ashton, Princess Margaret, Lord Snowdon, and Jocelyn Stevens

LEFT: Ashton in his beloved Gothic folly at Chandos Lodge

Ashton at Chandos Lodge in his Le Nôtre-inspired garden, which
he designed with Martyn Thomas

been jeered and spat at in the street for wearing make-up and silk stockings, but, that night, they played once again to a packed and enthusiastic house. Their third engagement in Eindhoven was, to everyone's relief, much further from the frontier, and, after another standing ovation, they motored back to The Hague.

Arnhem was their final port of call. At the supper party after the show, the dancers were told to hurry and board the bus waiting to return them to the capital. On the return journey, the long straight roads were crowded with heavily laden Dutch people trudging in the opposite direction towards the coast, and soldiers heading for posts on the border. By 3 a.m., they were back at the hotel and some of the dancers had just got to sleep when they were woken by the noise of fierce aerial fighting. Ashton was sitting on the lavatory looking out of the window as the dawn lit the sky, when he saw parachutists and propaganda pamphlets floating down like a surreal equivalent of the tulip petals at the theatre. Some of the dancers raced on to the roof to watch the action. Lambert and Fonteyn joined them (having been caught in bed together by a dancer who had burst into Lambert's room to break the news of the invasion), until all were chased down by a burst of gunfire. Ashton was a less enthusiastic spectator: 'It was absolutely terrifying,' he said, and his fear was noted by the others throughout the tour. 'There was a kind of terrible anxiety and barely suppressed hysteria with him,' said Annabel Farjeon; although faced with the grim actuality of war, the mood among them all, she admits, was one of 'cowardice, hysteria and humour'. When the sun came out and the cafés started to fill up, the dawn invasion seemed like a bad dream. Ashton sat at a table on the hotel pavement with Lambert and de Valois, until they were driven inside by a stray bullet from a low-flying German plane, which smashed the plate glass window directly behind them.

Then the waiting began.

Ninette, Constant and I had to go back and forwards to the Embassy to see what was going on, what our orders for the day were. We were told 'Be ready at 8 o'clock', which we would be, but nothing would happen. And then, 'Be ready at five' and nothing happened again. This went on for two or three days. Finally, we got on the bus with soldiers who had hand grenades in their *hands*.

At about six o'clock in the evening, they set off for an unknown destination. They had made their own sandwiches in the hotel kitchen, and each carried a small suitcase packed with essentials, which was all they were allowed to take. Scenery and costumes of all the ballets they had brought were left behind, but, although they included four of Ashton's, he seemed more distraught at having to abandon his new dinner-jacket. De Valois came to the rescue, volunteering to wear it for him over her summer coat. For nine hours they travelled through the darkness until they reached a wood where they were told to disembark and stay together. They were at Velsen, their base a large shuttered house filled with sleeping refugees. Here they collapsed on to the floor, wherever they could find a space. Their spirits were revived the next day by the tranquil beauty of the surroundings, with peacocks and deer wandering about the grounds. A few of the Sadler's Wells boys found a football and began an impromptu game against their Dutch guards. 'For all the world as if it were a midsummer's day on the village green,' remarked Fonteyn. With nightfall, the company's fears and misgivings returned – most of them had not eaten properly for forty-eight hours. At around midnight, they were instructed to form a long crocodile and board the bus, together with a convoy of refugees. The journey to the port of Imuiden was slow and nerve-racking: whenever there was an exchange of fire, the bus would stop and everyone would fall flat on to the floor.

A cargo boat awaited them at the dock and, like a herd of cattle, they were driven into the hold. Lit by a few hurricane lamps, the boat held about 400 people huddled together on a layer of straw, de Valois still incongruously dressed in Ashton's dinner jacket. Straw served as the only lavatory for the passengers, with an army blanket strung up on a piece of rope to provide a degree of privacy. On the fifteen-hour voyage across the North Sea, it was 'bombarded the whole way', according to Ashton, as, they found later, the Germans suspected that Queen Wilhelmina, fleeing to England, was aboard. 'We only *just* got out. It was a miracle. *Crazy* to have sent us there at all.' But their ordeal was not over. Having anchored off Harwich at about lunchtime on a Whit Monday, they were told they would not be allowed to disembark until the following morning, when, as Lambert put it, a 'Mr So and So would be back'. So there the old tramp steamer waited, 'without food or sanitation, a target for bombs, maddeningly within a few yards of shore . . . It was like trying to wake up a country stationmaster on Sunday afternoon.' They did eventually get ashore that night and, five hours later, in the early hours of the morning, boarded a train for London.

Some of the dancers slept for twenty-four hours when they got home, but Ashton was impatient to see his friends. The next day, he lunched at Cecil Beaton's house in London and regaled the group (which included Juliet Duff, William Acton and Oggie Lynn) with his adventures. Risk and privation had made him especially appreciative of upper-class life, which, in certain circles, continued regardless. The day France fell, Ashton lunched with the recently widowed Alice Wimborne, last vice-reine of Ireland, whose reaction to the news was, 'But where are we going to get our *hats*?' An elegant, youthful sixty-year-old, Lady Wimborne was immensely grand, although, as Ashton commented, 'quite a gel'. She and her husband, one of the richest men in Britain, had led independent lives, and she had acquired a reputation for preferring artistic men much younger than herself. Since the mid-1930s, she had been in love with William Walton and was now offering to marry him – a situation parallel to, if less complex, than that of Ashton and Alice. The two women had much in common and, in time, became quite close. 'They both had their . . . whatever you would call Willie and me.' Alice Wimborne was also a generous benefactress, a fact of which Ashton was well aware, although he never profited artistically from their friendship. 'The hostesses of that period were *powerful*. They were patrons. If they took you up, they could do something for you.'

His own Alice was as committed to him as before, but she had given up hoping to be his wife. She had recently married Philip Harding, a financial journalist now serving in an anti-aircraft regiment. For Alice, it had been an arrangement made on the rebound. On the morning of the wedding, she telephoned Ashton's sister, Edith, and said, 'I just wanted you to know that I still love Fred, but I must have someone to hang his hat up in the hall.'

Not that Philip Harding was the conventional marrying kind. Although he looked an upright, pinstriped, colonial type, he was, in fact, a Communist, who antagonized Alice's friends by reading Marx on the smooth lawns of Hanover Lodge – the epitome of a Beluga Bolshevist. Moreover, many people, including Ashton, suspected that Harding was a homosexual. 'I was staying with Osbert Sitwell when Harding was courting her,' said Ashton, 'and Osbert told me to warn her against him. I said, "It will come very badly from me." But he insisted, "You've *got* to. You must take Alice for a walk and tell her all about him, what he really is." So I did and Alice dismissed the whole thing. "Oh no, no. He'd changed. That was all over."' In fact, Harding was a courteous, good-looking and intelligent man, whose main faults were extreme shyness and a rather dull personality. Alice's daughter, Romana McEwen, recalls dinners of agonizing stiffness; the most interesting thing about him, she said, was his close friendship with John Betjeman. (The two had been to Marlborough and Oxford together, and spent a memorable holiday in Dorset, Harding's home county, which inspired Betjeman's poem of that name.)

Alice took a house for the duration of the war near Dorchester in

Dorset, where, in December 1942, her fourth child, Emily Sophia Philippa Frederica, was born. 'Everyone thought she was Fred's child,' said Lincoln Kirstein, but Ashton denied this, pointing out there was no physical resemblance between them. He was one of Emily's godparents, as well as namesake, although her father's Marxist beliefs prevented a christening (until twelve years later in New York). For a short time, Harding was to exert as much influence on Alice as Ashton had done previously. Like many women who lack self-confidence, she lived through her men. She became engrossed by Communism, which Ashton found hard to take seriously. 'I remember sitting on a beach when she was going on about it and saying, "Come *on* darling Alice, you're a very rich woman. If this is the way you feel, give the whole lot away, but don't *talk* about the values of Communism." I think that's why she liked me: I was the only one who told her the truth.'

Alice certainly sought Ashton's company at that time, inviting him, in Harding's absence, to grand dinners and luncheons in the garden at Hanover Lodge. But his millionaire era was nearing its end. Alice was soon to move out of Hanover Lodge and into one of the cottages in the grounds, dividing her time between London and Forsten, the Dorset house where Emily, a nanny, and Basil, Alice's chef, were installed. Towards the end of August 1940, she and Ashton spent a final wartime weekend with Juliet Duff at Bulbridge. Even in the heart of Wiltshire, there was no escape from air-raid warnings, one of which interrupted Ashton's Sunday-afternoon swim in the pool. The Blitz began in earnest three weeks later. On 7 September, Ashton left London, travelling to Polzeath in Cornwall with Beryl de Zoete, Margot Fonteyn and Pamela May. 'We all wanted a bit of a holiday away from the bombs,' said May, whose idea it was to stay at Greylands, a private hotel, which she had visited the previous year. They spent a week devouring clotted-cream teas, and luxurious breakfasts of eggs, bacon and exotic yellow tomatoes. It rained continuously, but that did not deter them from going on long cliff-top walks. 'Fred insisted we took towels with us.' The scientist Alan Hodgkin was staying at a nearby cottage and met the group on several occasions. 'Freddie had terrible toothache but dreaded the dentist and went around in an absurd bandage that sprouted rabbits' ears on top of his head.'

When Ashton returned to London, it was not to Wharton Street, but to 1 Wharton Cottages, in a tiny enclosed mews immediately opposite his old front door. With his mother gone, he no longer needed such a large house and he was anxious to break away from its associations. Number 1 had two bedrooms and a cosy, bow-fronted sitting room looking out towards the old stable wall. It was furnished in a half-elegant, half-cottagey style, with large chintz armchairs competing for space with Alice's Regency pieces and Edith's baby grand. At the back was a small lawn and patio, secluded by high ivy-covered walls. It was here that Ashton discovered gardening, a passion which was to last the rest of his life. He began by growing rhubarb as a wartime measure, planted his first roses (which Edith was instructed to look after in his absence), and nurtured a lilac tree from a cutting taken from his grandmother's garden at Yaxley.

With only two other cottages in the mews, it was a neighbourly little enclave. Ashton used to drop in for tea with Mr and Mrs Miller, an elderly couple who lived in Number 3; and Number 2's Ena Norris, a cheerful Cockney, who worked as a nippy at Lyon's Corner House, would 'tidy 'im up', and keep a gossipy eye on the comings and goings, which Ashton appreciated more when he had to go away.

For four weeks in October, the company was sent on an ENSA tour 'to brutalise the troops', as Edward Burra remarked with irony. The repertory included *Les Sylphides*, which was asking for trouble as it guaranteed clanking seats and hoots of derision at the leading man's floppy-sleeved blouse. (At garrison theatres, the danseur noble was allowed to go without the Lily Elsie wig.) To make themselves seem more alluring to the troops, Pamela May and Margot Fonteyn wore strings of pearls and earrings on stage. But the most applause anyone can remember was for Julia Farron, when her shoulder strap snapped during a penché arabesque in *Façade*, and Leslie Edwards had to cover her bare breast with his hat. The company was billeted in various houses in and around the garrison towns, and revived their flagging spirits after performances by playing records on Ashton's wind-up gramophone. There was the occasional party on stage, including the one Billy Chappell gave when the ballet arrived at his army barracks at Larkhill on Salisbury Plain. One of the first dancers to sign up, he was serving as a gunner, but was given preferential treatment as he was 'useful'. He had cast himself in the role of entertainment organizer, staging old-style revues, and was even allowed to liven up the communal rooms with 'very symbolical' Picasso-type murals.

Back in London, the company was homeless, as the Wells had been commandeered as a rest home for air-raid victims. The bombardment of the city continued relentlessly and Ashton escaped whenever he could. Maude Lloyd, living in the country because of enemy damage to her Victoria flat, received a note from him, pleading for a proper night's sleep away from the bombs. When he arrived, he made straight for a heap of foliage Maude and her husband, Nigel Gosling, had swept on to the lawn, and performed an impromptu imitation of Pavlova's 'Autumn

Leaves' solo, running about, flinging up handfuls of floating foliage. It was a very congenial weekend: the Goslings always indulged Ashton, and were about to open a treasured bottle of old claret for him when he spotted neighbours coming down the path. 'That's *far* too good for guests,' he exclaimed, and hid the bottle behind the sofa until they had gone. In November, he spent a few days at Plas Newydd, where an adoring audience of friends once again drew out his frivolous side. Rose Paget remembered a fancy-dress evening in which he appeared as Queen Mary, with Lady Anglesey as Queen Anne. 'Freddie with a handmade toque on his head and Mummy with tiny gold crown on hers. Both of them smoking non-stop!'

He had been much cheered by the prospect of a new refuge for the company, which, while only temporary, at least provided a well-earned break from relentless touring. At the invitation of American philanthropists, Mr and Mrs Leonard Elmhirst, the Sadler's Wells Ballet were to base themselves at Dartington Hall in Devon. Run, like a kibbutz, on a co-operative basis, it had proved a successful experiment in self-sufficient rural living, combining an academy of arts with farming and furniture making: over 800 people were employed on the estate. Since 1934, it had been the headquarters of the Ballets Jooss, but the outbreak of war had stranded the company in America, where they had been on tour, and Jooss, a German citizen, had been interned in a prisoner-of-war camp on the Isle of Man.

The Sadler's Wells company settled in gratefully. Edward Burra pictured Ashton spending Christmas 'in ear stoppers a tin hat weak tea well sugared against shock & an anti panic tablet', but, in fact, Dartington proved to be an excellent solution. In a communal dining room, they ate wholesome meals produced off the land, and the estate had its own theatre and studios, in which Ashton was to complete his next ballet. There was even a church, and a pub where the dancers played darts and shove ha'penny in the evenings. On New Year's Eve, the wife of Hein Heckroth, Jooss's resident designer, threw a party in his studio, and Ashton and Bobby Helpmann drank toasts to the future. Pamela May remembers Ashton being particularly happy at that time, giggling and energetically joining in the games. The dancers shared campus-type rooms, one of which held a nightly ritual of strip poker. The regulars were Lambert, Ashton, Helpmann and Pamela May, and once, for a joke, Julia Farron was sent for. 'They obviously felt it was about time I was initiated.' She sat on the end of someone's bed, simulating loud yawns, until she was allowed to return to her room.

Although her parents were staying in the village for Christmas, Julia had recently dismissed 'Mummy Farron' as chaperone. Her romance with Somes was at its most intense, although she remembers that 'a lot of people tried to stop it'. Joy Newton was one of them.

Everybody was in and out of each other's beds at Dartington and I just had to keep Julia and Michael working – not let them get together too much and become too involved with each other. I tried to guide them without letting them know it. For Michael it was a real tug of war: he was not sure which side he wanted to be on. I tried to help him but there was so little I could do because Fred's personality was *so* strong and from a dance point of view Michael was very important to him at that time.

Julia Farron maintains that, instinctively, she kept her heart in check. 'Even in my innocence I realized it wouldn't have been a good thing to pursue.' Looking back, she believes that Somes was exploiting the situation as an act of defiance against Ashton – 'it was always there, that sadistic thing in him' – although he was still artistically, if not emotionally, dependent on the choreographer. 'You can't be a young, ambitious boy and have someone like Fred fall in love with you without it meaning something to you. It was a very great part of his life.'

Watching the vicissitudes of young lovers once again cast Ashton in the role of outsider. But, this time, he capitalized on the experience in the form of a new ballet. *The Wanderer*, named after Schubert's Wanderer-Fantasie D.760, centres on a Byronic mental and emotional traveller, who is, by turns, observer and victim of the passions, pitfalls and lures of human life. Pamela May recalls how eager Ashton was to begin work on her duet with Michael Somes, knocking on her door on Christmas morning and asking if she would mind rehearsing instead of going to church. Somes told David Vaughan that stormy scenes accompanied its creation, 'often ending with Pamela May reduced to tears', but this account contradicts May's recollection of a serene atmosphere, enhanced by the beautiful adagio which Lambert played for them. There was no reason for tension on May's part: she was now happily married to Paignton Cowen, who even joined her for a few days at Dartington. 'Michael and I *loved* our pas de deux. So did Margot who said she wished it was hers.'

When the dancers arrived in the rehearsal room, there were drawings spread over the floor: Ashton's own sketches of positions he wanted to use, reminiscent of José Clara's simple line drawings of Isadora dancing. They faced, circled and cradled each other, entwined and engrossed in sensual complicity. The dance then developed into a stately game of statues, with one frozen pose replacing another. Although the intimacy of their embraces was frowned on by some critics, the duet was by no means overtly erotic. 'Fred said, "You've got to be terribly pure – all charm and love and softness."' The two were cast as emblems of young love, a union which was both sensual and spiritual, anticipating that of the self-absorbed lovers in *Illuminations*. Dramatizing Ashton's own ideals, *The*

Wanderer duet was a love poem to Somes, allowing the choreographer to recapture memories of idyllic moments they had shared. He perfected the skimming-on-air lift that resurfaced in so many of his ballets, his leitmotif for rhapsodic feeling, which usually signalled his own imaginative appropriation of the ballerina's role. (The pairing of Somes with May, rather than Fonteyn, was, in itself, a reminder of the reality of times past.) But, at the same time, through his protagonist, danced by Robert Helpmann, Ashton was able to maintain a more worldly and detached perspective. In the completed work, after reliving the precious memories of his love, the Wanderer is immediately 'beset by every kind of mental stress'. Only when he has emerged from his own inner conflict can he gaze on the lovers with a measure of intellectual and spiritual detachment. This rather forced resolution was the climax of the ballet, in which, as the curtain fell, Helpmann was triumphantly held aloft as the pinnacle of a Petipa-like tableaux.

It would be a mistake to interpret too literally the extent to which the ballet enacted Ashton's own state of mind. Psychoanalytic ballets were as fashionable then as the theme of exiles wandering in perpetual dissatisfaction had been in Schubert's day. Massine led the way in 1933 with *Les Présages*, in which personified abstractions confronted the hero; while, in the same year, Balanchine, also using the Wanderer Fantasy, choreographed *Errante* – 'a fantastic and highly introspective study of the morbid workings of the mind.' The war also contributed to the shift in focus, in literature and the arts, from documentary realism to a more introverted, reflective sensibility. Billy Chappell illustrated this development in an autobiographical essay confessing his aversion to army life (published in *Penguin New Writing*). 'My life being free, I did not have to think at all. These days I think all the time . . . and I feel in my brain that an endless transformation scene is taking place.' Drawing attention to this new subjective trend, John Lehmann included the war paintings of John Piper and Graham Sutherland – the artist whom Ashton chose to design *The Wanderer*. At this period and throughout the war, the ballet became the primary site of English neo-Romantic art, its preoccupation with spiritual quest closely reflecting Ashton's own priorities. But although he gave Sutherland his first dance commission and owned one of the paintings, the choreographer remained equivocal about his work. Ashton was made uneasy by the menacing anthropomorphism and mutable configurations of the landscapes. 'It has to go,' he remarked to a friend about a Sutherland gouache hanging on his wall (a study of two hills). 'I've seen a gasmask in it.'

The Wanderer invitation came when Graham and Kathleen Sutherland were living as guests of Kenneth Clark at Upton, the Georgian house he had recently rented in Gloucestershire. Margot Fonteyn was staying near by with a painter friend, Theyre Lee-Elliot, and, on her twenty-first birthday, Clark took Sutherland to meet her. This introduction was the starting point for the commission, although Clark, Sutherland's patron, would certainly have encouraged Ashton to follow it through. The first planning meeting took place at Upton House, where Ashton and Lambert joined Sutherland and Edward Sackville-West – another friend of the Clark's in residence – to discuss *The Wanderer* over lunch. The two back-cloths Sutherland produced were superb, in Michael Ayrton's view (although he complained that, from the upper circle, the designs were only half-visible). The first scene was a blown-up version of the gouache of Monk Haven, Pembrokeshire – the disquieting, contoured landscape, where the artist discovered his identity as a painter. The other cloth was a subdued version of his 1940 *Mountain Road with Boulder*. There were moments in the ballet when, as Beryl de Zoete said, the dance groups seemed 'to take mobile form from within the canvas'. The performers, however, were not impressed. To Alan Carter, Sutherland's sets were 'not *smears* exactly, but very very sketchy and indecipherable'. 'We didn't understand them,' admitted Julia Farron. 'They reminded us of some ghastly disease under a microscope.'

Their most vehement contempt was reserved for the costumes. *The Wanderer* had its first run-though without designs at Dartington. When the dancers saw what they had to wear for its London première at the New Theatre, they were so disturbed that they went on strike, refusing to perform in the clothes. 'Not that it did any good,' said Julia Farron. The corps girls were dressed in mud-brown shifts, while the four bare-legged boys in khaki shorts, who flanked the Wanderer, looked, as David Vaughan commented, like Boy Scouts or representatives of Hitler Youth. A be-plumed Margot Fonteyn, representing worldly allure, was described in the *Spectator* as 'something between the Worst Woman in London and an equestrienne'; while Julia Farron, in the allegorical role of Compassion, appeared 'in purple rags looking like King Cophetua's beggar maid'. Ashton made several improvements for subsequent productions (including putting the boys in tights), but, although Sutherland took the changes in good heart – 'I always knew I'd done wrong . . . Tights, tights all the time' – he retaliated with a complaint that the new dress of the adolescent girl personifying Innocence (Margaret Dale) made her look like 'a bridesmaid from Palmer's Green'. Sutherland would never again design for the stage.

More successful was the close integration of dance with the music, prompting Beryl de Zoete's description of the ballet as 'a symphony of movement'. The score, in four sections, is recognized as the model for César Franck's *Symphonic Variations*, but *The Wanderer* did not anticipate Ashton's interpretation of this work, which he was to choreograph six years later. Rather, inspired by the music's variety of mood, pace and bravura style, he returned to the classical technique, carried to new extremes of virtuosity. As a Balanchine-like siren, Fonteyn dances 'with a magnificent and tingling vitality that showed a completely new facet of her art'. Her movements are hard, sharp, fast, sophisticated and dangerous. She is spun through the air in a dizzying display of athletics, at one point plummeting down the length of the Wanderer's body like a dive-bombing Spitfire (one of several topical fighter-plane references). 'Fred was getting a bit wild at that time and Margot didn't like it much,' said Pamela May. 'She was always rather scared of doing it, it was not at all what she was used to.' In the title role, Helpmann never leaves the stage – an impressive, if overwrought, performance, which influenced his own unravelling of a life through the mind of Hamlet, the ballet he was to choreograph a year later. Audiences were mystified by his strange semaphoric gestures; indeed, some found the entire work baffling and incoherent. 'It is, one feels, Mr Ashton's wits that for once have wandered,' quipped the *Spectator*, although Beryl de Zoete declared *The Wanderer* to be 'a triumph for all concerned'.

The Wanderer was Ashton's swan-song before military service. In the summer, he would leave Sadler's Wells, appearing for the last time as a member of the company in *Dante Sonata*. After the performance, Ninette de Valois announced on stage that Michael Somes and Alan Carter would also be leaving. Ashton and Carter were to travel together to sign up, but, even though they 'held hands, so to speak', the companionship brought little consolation. 'I saw Fred,' Billy Chappell reported in a letter to Ashton's sister, Edith. 'He's off to the RAF . . . quite bewildered by it all.'

CHAPTER TEN

ASHTON'S WAR
1941–1944

A shton's induction into the RAF took place in June 1941 at Cardington, a reception centre for recruits. He and the young dancer Alan Carter caught the train to nearby Bedford, and together they spent the day suffering the ignominies of feeling the lowest of the low. They were among hundreds of men quizzed, examined (eyes, ears, nose, teeth), kitted out, marched from place to place, and bawled at by an officious corporal. In a hangar as big as St Paul's, a warrant officer sized up everyone and made a crack about the two ballet dancers who would be joining them. 'The whole place fell about,' said Carter, 'and we felt our faces just drain.' Next, they were told to collect 'irons' and go to the cookhouse, where lunch was served: bangers with a hunk of bread and dollop of marge. Having lost sight of Ashton, Carter spotted him outside, a 'pale, heaving figure', vomiting as he held on to a sign which read 'Airmen's Mess'.

Having begun his service as an Aircraftsman Craft II, the equivalent to a private, the thirty-seven-year-old Ashton was soon promoted to Acting Pilot Officer (amended by Terence Rattigan to 'Over-Acting Pilot Officer'), and received his commission on 4 October. His first posting was to have been as a supernumerary for photographic interpretation at Medmenham in Buckinghamshire, the powerhouse of the Central Interpretation Unit, which identified and dispatched top-secret reconnaissance information. Although its principal employees were highly experienced and capable of making instant decisions, the unit's Second Phase was staffed by a motley group of academics, artists, musicians and writers, among whom Ashton would have immediately felt at ease. Most of them had been commissioned directly, with no service in the ranks, and were regarded with tolerant amusement by their CO. In August, like all new recruits, Ashton underwent an intense training course at Borlase Academy, Marlow, a few miles from the unit itself.

In a Dover College exercise book, he took scrupulous notes from a series of lectures on photographic reconnaissance, illustrating them with wavery freehand angles, circles, grids and maps. But, when it came to working out, by representative fractions, the size of a vessel by measuring it against a map, Ashton found himself completely lost. Although some claimed that it was possible to do the work with little or no mathematical ability, in fact, a rudimentary knowledge of algebra was essential to calculate scale; just as a smattering of physics was needed to determine the speed of vessels from wave patterns. As someone who 'didn't know the rudiments of anything, or even how to learn', Ashton was forced to admit failure. 'Everyone tried to teach me but I just couldn't take it in.' It would, he admitted, have been 'a lovely war', if only he had got to Medmenham, where acquaintances and like-minded colleagues included Sarah Churchill, Charlotte Bonham Carter, composers Robin Orr and Humphrey Searle, and the actor Dirk Bogarde (who described himself and his colleagues as 'clever little fellows planning D Day [who] were all BIGOTS. A splendid name for "top secret"'). But Ashton had to leave: 'I was no use. I just couldn't do it.'

He next became an Intelligence Officer attached to various squadrons in Number 13 Group, beginning with RAF Usworth in County Durham, where, according to Edward Burra, he spent the autumn 'reading a lot . . . and feeling out of it'. Unlike 'Madame de Larkhill' (Billy Chappell), who, as Burra said, was now 'a veritable stone-henge Conti . . . (She'll never be allowed away from the withering planes [sic] and go on producing shows for ever.)' Ashton refused to stage revues for the troops. 'They wanted me to but I said if I'm going to do entertainment, you can send me back where I can do something useful' (meaning not the war effort, but what he did best). His hauteur did not win him friends, and he became intensely lonely. If he received any letters from Michael Somes, he did not save them; although he did keep two love lyrics from a mysterious suitor called Donald. Their 'intermittent' encounter was founded on a shared nostalgia for songs of the 1920s, such as 'Tiptoe through the Tulips', to which one poem specifically alludes. Its title is 'Lyric for 1941 and F.A.':

> More tulips on the gramophone
> More records to the tear
> Than bells upon the telephone
> Or beds within the year.
>
> More kisses in the cornered night
> More strange-felt hearts to learn

Than inward creeping back of sight
Or love affairs to burn.

But still you turn behind the dance
The heartbeat of my day
With eyes whose intermittent glance
Says what I cannot say.

The second poem, a sonnet tinted with Petrarchan oxymorons, and even more sentimental and obscure than the first, opens with a riddle, which could refer to Ashton's unremitting attachment to Michael Somes:

Three loves that turn and tangle in the glass
One loving one, and loving, love loves two . . .

It is preceded by an invitation to drinks ('There are still a lot of the twenties records you haven't heard') and a *Concise Oxford Dictionary* definition of 'love'. But Donald's 'affectionate devotion; warm affection, attachment . . . ' would have made little impression on Ashton, with his predilection for being the pursuer and not the pursued.

Lively letters from Burra, spared conscription through ill-health, continued to arrive, keeping 'l'Aiglon' up to date with his set. Designed to cheer him up, they were spiked with caustic anecdotes about 'Nero Helpmann', whose self-aggrandizing behaviour was making him increasingly unpopular with them all. 'Goodness knows what heights Bobbie has reached by this time.' Burra had heard that Ashton was considering buying one of his paintings. 'I'm very flattered dear and have quite a selection would you rise to 30£?' Never had Ashton's appreciation of his friends been so intense. On a few days' leave, he spent an 'enlivening' evening with Cecil Beaton, to whom he confided how much he hated his present life. Even the discipline which he hoped would act as 'a sort of spiritual cleansing' had failed to take effect. 'I think I shall emerge – if I do – even dirtier than Casati* and with no black velvet or crumpled violets, just trails of bullshit.'

His next posting at Drem, near Edinburgh, was less dispiriting. At the beginning of February, he began work as Intelligence Officer with the City of Liverpool Squadron 611, his new role requiring him to deal directly with the pilots. As soon as they returned from sorties, he would

*Marchesa Casati, the epitome of the 1920s vamp.

rush over to their planes, debrief them, then file a report. He was also supposed to assist with aircraft recognition, but this proved a problem as 'he didn't know the front from the back of an aeroplane – let alone a German one'. However, not only was it easier to bluff his way through this job, but he found a pair of allies who liked him enough to cover for him.

Michael Graham and Emanuel Galitzine were pilots in their early twenties whose comradeship made bearable Ashton's first real experience of life in the forces. The pair met him in the messroom at Drem while playing snooker. Miscueing a shot, Galitzine, the son of White Russian refugees, Prince Vladimir and Princess Catherine, swore in his native tongue, to which 'this funny little man' said something Russian in reply. As they began talking, Galitzine recognized Ashton, having seen him on stage, and was 'most impressed'. Like his more celebrated elder brother, the late Prince George,* who became a grand dragoman, Emanuel was a balletomane, whose London childhood was coloured with memories of Ballets Russes dancers visiting the Galitzine house. Ashton, who remembered Princess Galitzine from Ballet Club days, when she would arrive at rehearsals with boxes of Rumpelmeyer's cakes for all the dancers, was enormously relieved to find someone in the squadron who not only knew who he was, but admired him for sacrificing his career. The two pilots and their commanding officer, Douglas (Dirty) Watkins – 'a great hero of ours' – immediately befriended Ashton and helped him to settle in. When he got into trouble for going on leave with no pass, they all stood by him, and in return, he put himself out to make fun for them – so successfully that he claimed they would not go anywhere without him. In April, when the squadron moved to Kenley, Watkins made sure that their Intelligence Officer was transferred with them.

While he was in Scotland, Ashton was plied with invitations from rich dowagers who, having evacuated themselves from London and bought large houses in Edinburgh, were keen to establish themselves in local society. Discovering the choreographer as a local celebrity, they put Ashton high on their lists. Sometimes he would ask if he could bring his 'boys' along, which raised an occasional eyebrow, but usually resulted in Galitzine, Watkins and Graham accompanying him to 'these *marvellous* parties' with plenty of black-market food and liquor. When one evening proved hard-going, they plotted their escape, climbing through a back window, over the garden wall and ending up in a dilapidated nightclub. They sat drinking rounds of Near Beer, until eventually one of the Burraesque hostesses came over and asked, 'Don't any of you boys dance?' Ashton got up and led her on to the floor, where they performed 'the

*It was George who had carried out the dramatic sea rescue during Ashton's holiday at Airds, Appin.

most amazing jitterbug that any of us had ever seen before or since'. 'When we went out at night to dancing places I was their pimp,' Ashton said. 'I used to get them girls.' Ashton certainly made life in the forces more fun for them. Recognizing that the pilots were still schoolboys at heart, Ashton became their nanny: 'They loved me because I took trouble with them. I even wrote their love letters. I was on their side – fuck the ground staff – I always acknowledged that they were the ones that mattered.' He was pleased when, years later, one of his ex-colleagues thanked him for being 'the most wonderful intelligence officer we ever had'. 'Well, I may not have been intelligent,' he replied, 'but I *was* in amongst you all.'

Ashton entered into everything – '*everything*, whatever they did.' Dining-In Nights was the ordeal he dreaded most. They started off formally, with smoking forbidden and everyone in full uniform, and ended up as a riot. Once there was a competition timed with a stopwatch to see who was the fastest at riding a motor bike through the mess, the kitchens and ante-rooms, out the back door and back again. 'I can't tell you the rough-house those nights turned into. One of the games, called High Cockolorum, involved getting on someone's back and another couple would do the same and we'd have to pull each other off. Then there were all sorts of other things on the floor. *Ghastly!* Can you imagine me entering into all this and *having* to because I would have looked so awful if I hadn't.' Participation was his way of coping, even though his colleagues saw through his act. 'He put on a jokey veneer,' said Graham, 'but that was the only side we knew.'

So eager to endear himself to his charges, Ashton would crib on their behalf as well as his own. 'There were all these little models and you were supposed to know what they were and *they* were supposed to know. I hadn't a clue and had to cheat. I used to fill in all their papers for them and one day the station master congratulated me on the standard of my boys.' Ashton tried to take the work seriously, but, as Graham remarked, 'Let's face it, he just wasn't good enough.' Half-intentionally, he took on the role of squadron buffoon, constantly entangling himself in farcical *Carry On* situations.

There were some awful moments. At the end of the day we had to take the flag down; there would be about six people who had to do it and I had to appear as an officer and give orders. Well, I never knew what the orders were and used to say, 'Carry on, Sergeant,' and one day the sergeant didn't arrived and I didn't know what to say so I told them to '*Scram*'. They looked at me as if I'd gone mad [presumably wondering if he meant 'scramble', the familiar RAF command]. 'SCRAM!' I shouted, and they all rushed away giggling. And then another day, there was a church parade; I had to take my section or whatever it was called into the chapel and I didn't know how to order them there. I couldn't say, 'Left, *turn!*' or whatever it had to be, so I sat up all night and learnt what I had to do. But then I had to tell the senior officer in charge, 'I'll be able to get them *to* the chapel, but I can't get them *in.*' 'Well,' he said, 'I'll take over.'

Commanding neither respect nor disrespect, Ashton was popular with his squadron because he was so entertaining. Protean as always, he went out of his way to fit in – even to the point of adopting the common lingo – 'I have not uttered anything but Cockney,' he complained to a friend. And privately, he was languishing like a parched flower. 'None of us really appreciated how terrible it was for Fred,' said Margot Fonteyn. Fans kept him in touch with his former life to an extent, sending him cigarettes, chocolates and encouraging messages, but his true feelings he kept well hidden from all but his closest friends. In an affectionate, nostalgic letter to Marie Rambert, he evoked memories of 'our good times, quarrels and successes . . . those early exciting days when every step was important and you guided my delicate arches and long nose', and recalled how Ashley Dukes used to roar with laughter at the thought of him and Billy Chappell in uniform. 'Tell him it's not funny and very boring.'

Ashton revived his spirits on leaves to London and sorties to grand houses. He had an open invitation to Faringdon from Lord Berners, who sent him occasional racy accounts of their friends. 'I hope Constant or Bobby told you about how we frightened Willie [Walton] at Oxford where he came to be canonized or whatever it was. He has been getting above himself lately – owing, I presume, to adulation of ecstatic females.'

Often, when Ashton had a day off, he visited Lady Cecilia Fitzroy, whose Scottish mother, the Duchess of Grafton, had a house in Edinburgh. 'She was an incredible old character. Cecilia was getting rather keen on me, and one day she asked me to come into her room and gave me a glass of South African sherry and said, "I want you to realize that Cecilia is a very precious daughter and must make the right marriage."' Having no designs on her whatsoever, Ashton found the situation more amusing than embarrassing. 'I loved the way she did it. I loved her directness. You're a very nice boy, *but . . .*'*

---

*The Duchess did, indeed, make a good match for her daughter, who married George Howard of Castle Howard, though, with a touch of schadenfreude, Ashton pointed out that the Earl 'was a drunk and in the end, she out of sympathy took to the drink with him. He was cured, but she went on.'

*   *   *

The Station Commander at Drem was the war hero Group Captain Peter Townsend, whose romance with Princess Margaret was to make international headlines in the 1950s. Decked with medals, and as dashing as a young Gregory Peck, Townsend instantly captivated Ashton. 'He was *beautiful*. Really, you couldn't have met a better-looking man.' Townsend was sitting in his office when the new Intelligence Officer first arrived to report to him. 'In came this rather slight figure who did a couple of pirouettes, so to speak, before saluting. I took a liking to him straight away. We had lots of good laughs and became very good friends.' Like everyone else, he was amused by Ashton and set him some provocatively challenging tasks.

> One of my fellow officers had been pinching petrol and I had to go round all their cars to see who it was. You can imagine how popular that made me. I discovered the three culprits and went to Townsend and asked him to be lenient. 'I'm *not* going to be bloody lenient,' he said. 'I've got them by the short hairs.'
>
> And once when I was working, or supposedly working, he tapped on the office window and beckoned to me. So I said to the officer, 'The Station Master is beckoning to me.'
>
> '*Most* irregular.'
>
> 'Well, he's still beckoning, what should I do?'
>
> 'I suppose you should go out and see him, but it's *most* irregular.'

Townsend wanted Ashton to go out on a 'flip'. Having recently been grounded and tranquillized, after twenty months of air battles, he had regained his nerve at Drem and was flying again as of old – fast, hard and low. The opportunity to be a fighter-pilot's passenger was the last thing Ashton wanted because he was terrified of flying, but, enslaved by infatuation and rank, he agreed to sit in the open cockpit, pale with fear, as Townsend rolled, looped and plunged the aircraft through his repertoire of aerobatics. 'It was absolute agony. I hate heights so I'd say, "*Please* Sir, don't go any higher – God's sitting on my head" – which he thought was very funny. And I'd beg him to "hedge hop" which was *far* more dangerous – the only people allowed to fly low were the C.O. – but I was near the ground, so I didn't care.'

Ashton's attraction to his Station Master was mutual. 'He was infatuated in his way,' said Townsend, 'and I was in mine. He was warm and friendly, he made me laugh, and he was very sensitive. Maybe some of the others thought less of him for being an ex-ballet dancer, but if anything, this made me *more* determined to be friends.' The two met again after the war when the Townsends were neighbours of Edith Russell-Roberts, but Ashton never forgot or quite forgave Townsend for once failing to acknowledge him when, as equerry to King George VI (an acknowledgement of his fighting record), he accompanied the King and Queen to the ballet. 'He wasn't nice to me at all, for which I gave him very bad marks.'

Life in 611 proved to be the high point of Ashton's war. The routine of military life may have been spiritually stultifying, but at least the camaraderie was cheering, and he was relatively comfortable, with his own room and batman. By the end of the summer, his larky ménage had broken up, with Dirty transferred to the Air Ministry, and the two pilots posted abroad. Michael Graham believes that the authorities deliberately separated them after a couple of their pranks went too far. One rainy day, the trio had set off for an air test and ended up spending three nights in London. 'On the way back, Emanuel got lost and the next thing we saw on our left *above* us was a church steeple.' There was also trouble over what they refer to as 'the Ipswich Incident' ('someone got shot in the balls'), which almost resulted in a court martial for Graham. Ashton was the first to leave, posted to an RAF station at Ouston, near Newcastle-upon-Tyne, where he was miserable and spent his time writing beseeching letters to important friends in the hope they could help get him released.

The only relief throughout the Northumberland posting were visits to Ursula Ridley, Lutyens' favourite daughter, whose lively company was, in a line from her father's limerick about her, 'Receipt against boredom and other ills'. The wife of Viscount Ridley, she lived at Blagdon, the eighteenth-century family seat on the northern outskirts of Newcastle, where Ashton had first stayed with Helpmann and Lambert during company tours to the city. There was a quarry garden and yew walk designed by Gertrude Jekyll, and Lutyens had added a canal and a sunken tennis court. To Ashton, it was an oasis to which he returned whenever he could. Lady Ridley, who would have studied ballet seriously had her father not frowned on the idea, was a dedicated follower of Ashton's work, although she found it hard to tell him. 'Everything sounds so platitudinous,' she wrote. 'Only criticism is vocal, so that your ballets make me feel silent.' The sympathetic atmosphere of Blagdon made the contrast of his new squadron even harder to bear, especially now that Ashton had become the victim of a sadistic CO. A misfit and ineffectual at his job, Ashton was easy prey for the officious, humourless Belgian, who took against him on sight. His ex-schoolmaster Alf Dixon wrote to sympathize, 'Poor Freddie! You say that efforts are being made to get you out of the RAF . . . make sure you don't go from the frying pan into the fire:

life in the ranks for one of your temperament would be unendurable.' Alice was pulling every string she could on his behalf and did, in fact, achieve some success, thanks to her friend, Harold Balfour, then Parliamentary Under Secretary of State for Air. Ashton had asked to be transferred back to 611, even though his chums were no longer there (Peter Townsend had also moved on), and, although he was told this was impossible, at least he was able to escape the Belgian. 'Balfour said he couldn't send me back; but what he did was move us both.'

RAF Acklington, a dismal, windswept aerodrome, polluted with Newcastle's industrial fumes, was hardly an uplifting new environment, but at least it provided an escape. Ashton continued to occupy his free time writing plaintive letters to friends like Beaton, whom he begged to use his connections.

> Do work for me, dear Cecil . . . being a poor old bourgeois I have no pull or aristocratic uncles & aunts & cousins . . . If you can fix [Sir Stafford] Cripps, speak to Balfour – everyone, & inspire K[enneth Clark] to continue his efforts. I'm exhausted by the whole thing & when the war is over will just fall back & laugh & weep alternatively, my hair parted in the middle in thin air force blue with a touch of mauve unable to do anything again. It's time my luck changed, I have been sorely tried . . . I am slowly getting like an old maid expecting nothing of life in my bitterness – 'so good of you to write' – 'oh don't bother about me, I'll be alright' 'very good of you to bother about me I'm sure' & so on in that sad line.

Martyrdom was making him ungratefully play off one friend against another. To Kenneth Clark he accused Maynard Keynes, who had mediated on his behalf with the Air Ministry, of being 'really a philistine', and peevishly complained that Keynes had not made as much effort over his exemption as he had over that of the interned German choreographer, Kurt Jooss. Knowing that Ashton had reached the point of despair, Clark did everything he could to lift his morale, while making strenuous attempts to get him released. As well as approaching Cripps, then Minister of Aircraft Production, he was busy appealing to the Ministry of Labour which, as Ashton was competitively aware, had exempted John Gielgud and Emlyn Williams from service. Vacillating between complete defeatism – 'I am glad that you think there is still hope, though I myself hold none' – and clutching at straws, Ashton interpreted the Air Ministry's negative comment, 'We should be most averse to releasing him', as 'not absolutely final'; and he told Clark of his meeting at the première of the film *The First of the Few* with a fat man from the Ministry of Labour, who asked what he was doing in uniform. '[He] said that they had never meant to call me up and they must have slipped up somewhere. I wish I could remember his name, but I think he sat next to that American boy, Hirams friend, whose name I cannot remember either.' It was hardly much to go on. At this point, though, Ashton was not counting on being released altogether, hoping rather to be placed in a more suitable position, like the Censorship Office, where his fluency in Spanish and French could be put to use, instead of 'trundling round all the aerodromes releaving [sic] officer after officer like a dose of salts . . . oh God how waring [sic] to my poor talent'.

He had gone to war with the highest ideals – 'He felt he ought to be *doing* something,' said Kensington (Ken) Davison (who was to become organizing secretary of the Friends of Covent Garden). Then a fighter pilot, Davison remembers Ashton curled up in a corner of the Mess, avid for ballet gossip and grizzling about his lot. The waste of his gifts, especially now that 'the stirrings of creation were beginning to rumble within me so strongly', exacerbated Ashton's discontent. He was full of ideas for ballets, and particularly anxious to begin a new collaboration with Gerald Berners and Cecil Beaton. He had applied for leave to work on *Les Sirènes*, set on the French Riviera at the turn of the century, and was 'broken' by the rebuff. Although the ballet would not be created until the war was over, he was reluctant to let it go, imploring Beaton to do everything he could to help. But underlying his frustration was fear, specifically the fear that he was literally about to be 'sent to Siberia'.

Since Hitler's invasion the previous summer, bases in northern Russia were being established using RAF personnel. There had been rumours that 611 would be among the detachments posted there, but, according to Ashton, the operation was called off at the last minute 'because of the bombing of the aircraft carriers' (possibly the Luftwaffe's destruction of the ill-fated convoy PQ17 on 4 July 1942). Anyone destined for Murmansk would have had serious qualms when they looked at their maps and realized where they were bound, but the relief Ashton felt at being spared the dire Arctic conditions was short-lived, for now he faced a much greater possibility that 'the Steppes [would] call again'. So agitated was he by the prospect that Maynard Keynes, whom he implored to intercede, had sought de Valois' advice.

Maynard said, 'What am I to do? Fred's in an appalling state because they want to send him to Russia. He's put down on his papers that he speaks Russian and it's making things very difficult for me to get him out of it.' But I said, 'For Fred to spend the war in Moscow or Leningrad would be far the best thing for him to do.'

Ballet went on there the whole time. I know what they're like, as soon as they'd have found out about someone like that, they'd have invited him to join one of the companies as a guest. From the angle of comradeship, we would have loved it. I think he was silly not to go – he might even have got a job in the Embassy – but he was frightened and that was it.

Looking back, Ashton was scathing about de Valois' reaction: 'She doesn't know what she's talking about.' Had he been posted to Russia, he felt sure he would have been attached to a squadron and not free to choreograph 'as if there wasn't a war on'. In the event, Keynes did manage to help him, despite Ashton's bogus claim to speak fluent Russian, which he naively assumed would help secure him a job in the Censorship Office. In October, he moved to RAF Catterick, another northern-based squadron in Number 13 Group, where he continued his intelligence duties. With his fear now superseded by resentment, he became even more misanthropic. Burra describes him disgorging a stream of reproaches and abuse during his leaves to London, and then retiring to Catterick, 'where he writes insulting letters'.

The main target of his venom was Bobby Helpmann, whom he and Billy Chappell had nicknamed 'La Helpmann', shortened to 'La', because he had become so lah-di-dah. The Three Bears bonhomie had given way to strained relations on all sides; even the equable Chappell complained, 'I feel La is a total loss these days . . . She used to be such a marvellous companion but I feel I bore her now.' Helpmann's reputation as an actor was fast catching up with his standing as premier danseur (he was performing simultaneously in *Swinging the Gate*, a revue at the Ambassador's, and with Sadler's Wells at the New Theatre). He was being compared to Sinatra as a new public idol, and off-stage, too, he had become increasingly prominent, appropriating the role of acting director in de Valois' absence. He was, Fonteyn has written, 'The person who more than any other kept the company going during the war.' Morale boosting was all very well, but Helpmann had started to instigate changes which implied criticism of Ashton. The shoe-string tours that kept British ballet alive in the early stages of the war were dismissed by Helpmann as 'shoving ballet at [the soldiers] with a stand-up piano and no orchestra like a pill to be swallowed'. From now on, the ENSA performances would be staged with orchestra, scenery and costumes. 'We were sensational,' boasted Helpmann. 'After that we were sent to camps all over the country.' But the rift had another cause, far more unsettling to Ashton. As Chappell remarked, 'Fred couldn't forgive Bobby for *daring* to choreograph in his absence.'

Partly out of strategy – 'She wanted to keep Bobby' – and partly because, with Ashton away, she needed to divide the burden of providing a new repertoire, de Valois had asked Helpmann to create a ballet for the next London season. It was a risk, as he had virtually no choreographic experience; but he already had a doting public, he knew the dancers and their capabilities, and de Valois trusted what she called his 'severe theatrical discipline'. The result was a staging of Milton's masque, *Comus*, with music by Purcell and designs by Oliver Messel. Helpmann's combination of words, mime and movement was only moderately successful, but five months later he followed it up with *Hamlet*, a work of enough importance to challenge Ashton's omnipotence as company choreographer. Writing about the artistic renaissance taking place, and in particular the revival in stage design by the neo-Romantic artists, John Lehmann glancingly acknowledged Ashton's 1941 *The Wanderer* for anticipating what was to come; but hailed Helpmann's ballet, with its striking designs by Leslie Hurry, as the work which 'most stimulatingly' displayed these new possibilities. 'It was an entirely original creation, not just a clever attempt to put *Hamlet* into terms of dance, and said something to us at that moment about war, and youthful death, and the destiny of nations, that was movingly topical and yet of no time or place.'

At the end of the war, Ashton would counter Helpmann's style of literary ballet with *Symphonic Variations*, intended as 'a kind of testament' to restore the purity of classical dance, but now, isolated and frustrated in his northern squadron, his gall, as Burra observed, was 'all for Veuve Joyeuse Helpmann for having managed to escape everything'. 'I thought he was a traitor,' said Ashton. 'I had done so much for him and the moment I left, he just plunged in.' Margot Fonteyn confirmed an element of opportunism, or at least eager compliance, on Helpmann's part. 'I don't know if Bobby would have thought of doing choreography if Fred hadn't been away.' She noticed too, that Ashton's imitations were conspicuously less frequent when he returned to the company, as if 'maybe he thought something about Bobby'. So intense was their rivalry at this stage that Billy Chappell believed Helpmann took up acting seriously 'through one-upmanship of Fred'. Six years later, Ashton would caricature the tetchy, maiden-aunt hostility between them in the guise of the Ugly Sisters in *Cinderella*. But, although time and humour sugared the bitterness, he remained cynical about Helpmann for the rest of his life. Hearing him describe the presents he had bought for Laurence Olivier and Vivien Leigh one Christmas, Ashton muttered, 'That's not generosity, it's *investment*.'

Ashton also accused de Valois of disloyalty. 'She claimed he was invaluable; she let *me* go and hung on to Bobby.' He was feeling so insecure and misprized at this time, that he facetiously signed one letter to Kenneth Clark from 'the invaluable and irreplaceable Fred'. He could not see that de Valois was acting in the interests of her company: with no virtuoso male dancers left, Helpmann's mime-based, demi-caractère choreography was essential. Despite Ashton's suspicions, no favouritism was intended. If Helpmann had had a British passport, she would not have kept him. 'I didn't see the difference, frankly, between pianists, violinists and dancers. If the other artists had to go, to make an exception of dancers would have been terrible.' Having retracted her initial support to exempt dancers from service, de Valois took no part in the current attempts to secure Ashton's release. 'I'm sorry, but I didn't think one should do that. Fred was right to have what I call a clean war slate; he would never have been a CO or anything stupid like that. And he recovered his choreography very quickly: it was much harder on the dancers who *did* have a tussle to get back. Four years is a long time.'

Ashton was not alone in his misgivings about Bobby Helpmann's caretaking of the company. Dissatisfied with 'its present artistic performance', Constant Lambert had threatened to resign unless Ashton could be brought back in control. In an unofficial letter advocating the guardianship of the Old Vic and Sadler's Wells by CEMA, the forerunner of the Arts Council, Kenneth Clark made an urgent case for Ashton's return. 'Helpmann is an admirable dancer, but he is a virtuoso, who does not command the confidence of the company as a whole in the way that Ashton would do. If Constant Lambert leaves, I am afraid that Margot Fonteyn would leave also, and the whole Ballet would break up.' Clark's warning took effect, if only temporarily, as Ashton was soon to be granted leave of absence from the Air Force to choreograph a new ballet. But before he rejoined the Wells, he faced the prospect of an equally intimidating foreign posting, this time to West Africa. Another friend of Alice's, Patrick Guimareans, a great ballet fan, persuaded an important contact, Air Vice-Marshal Douglas Colges, to intervene. 'I was terrified that you might get yellow fever or some dread disease,' wrote Guimareans, 'just the sort of stupid posting they would do to our finest choreographer.' But, with Colges' help, he 'wangled it', using the excuse that Ashton was about to create *The Quest*.

The idea of a ballet based on Spenser's *The Faerie Queene* had come up five years earlier when Doris Langley Moore, 'an assiduous reader' of the epic poem, sent Ashton her scenario drawn from the self-contained Book One. With its pageant of Seven Deadly Sins, and trio of virtues in the House of Holiness, the poem offered rich visual possibilities and contained stock ballet characters, such as the evil magician, Archimago – a

Rothbart figure, with a touch of Kostchei – who deceives the knight, St George, with a false version of his beloved Una, a heroine of Odette-like purity. Ashton was immediately 'taken with the notion' and thought of Walton as the most suitable composer, although he never, in fact, approached him. In March 1938, Langley Moore wrote to her friend Jack, Viscount Hastings, who had got to know Walton through the Sitwells, asking him to put in a tactful word about it. 'Freddy himself suggested it would be just the thing for music with that humorous quality which Walton writes better than anybody living.' She and Ashton had worked out some basic details of the action, and, in July, she sent a more complete version of her 'St George ballet' to Billy Chappell for him to 'put under Freddy's nose' and explain her intentions. But Ashton was having second thoughts and returned the synopsis, commenting that it was 'too literary'. Although she was disappointed, Langley Moore did not press things and had almost forgotten about the idea when, in 1942, she received a letter from Ashton saying that he felt its subject – the conquest of evil forces by England's patron saint – had become appropriate for the times.

The destruction of the country was having a profound effect upon artists and writers, altering their perceptions and forcing them to find new ways of expressing themselves. Responding to the spiritual loss of their day, the New Romantics took as their emblem 'the quest . . . a search whose object is the shrine, an Eden or Arcadia'. The apt visual style for a world in turmoil was the dark Gothicism adopted by the painter John Piper, and it was he whom Ashton felt to be the most appropriate designer for the new ballet. As an alliance of three of the foremost contemporary minds in choreography, music and painting, *The Quest* should have had real importance, but the outcome was far from satisfactory. For a start, there was no interaction between the collaborators: Piper, working in ballet for the first time, praised Ashton for his indulgence, lack of interference and practical help, but perversely advocated 'no collaboration whatever' on matters of taste, his object being to achieve what he called 'an "accidental" unity'. Doris Langley Moore, who all along had found it hard to deal directly with Ashton – 'Communicating with Fred by post is a business fraught with difficulties' – stayed away from rehearsals because she felt slighted by a remark he had made. 'It got back to me that Fred had said, "I suppose we'll have Mrs Moore around advising us about everything."' Relations between them cooled considerably as the ballet progressed. Feeling burdened with what had turned out to be an unwieldy scenario – the episodic format of romance does not translate well to the stage –Ashton ungenerously made a scapegoat of Langley Moore. Una's lion, a symbol of loyalty, which she did not include in her original scenario 'because I thought it would be like a pantomime cat', was added by Ashton, then eliminated in later drafts. Naturally, she was 'amazed' to find that she was being blamed by Ashton for introducing the lion, which he used as evidence of a difficult and overpopulated libretto.

Uninspired by the subject and unable even to remember his librettist's name, William Walton composed the score piecemeal, 'on backs of envelopes, practically'. Because of Ashton's limited leave from the RAF, the composer had only five weeks in which to write forty-five minutes of music and would 'bribe guards on trains to take a minute or so's music to wherever Freddy happened to be with the ballet – to Wolverhampton, Preston or somewhere'. On days when nothing arrived, Ashton had to ask the rehearsal pianist, Hilda Gaunt, to improvise. Composer and choreographer obviously discussed the work when they both stayed with Alice Wimborne at Ashby St Ledgers, her fourteenth-century manor house near Rugby, and Ashton provided Walton with a minutage inspired by Petipa's instructions to Tchaikovsky. But although some exacting requests were met – such as the delivery of 'compassionate' music for Charity and her Girls, and 'the most movingly lyrical passage you have ever written' for a duet reuniting Una with St George – Walton badly impeded the flow of Ashton's imagination by making it impossible for him to immerse himself in a completed score. The choreography, as David Vaughan wrote at the time, appeared 'distinctly forced'.

Even though the first-night audience welcomed Ashton back with a heart-lifting reception, the ballet's flaws could not be ignored. With the exodus of male dancers into the forces, it was hardly the time to create a work enshrining knightly deeds. Borrowing a powerful image from Book III's Masque of Cupid, Ashton resorted to using a corps of 'Hermaphrodites', girls in fancy dress whom Cyril Beaumont dismissed as 'very insipid fare'. Especially disappointing was Ashton's interpretation of the Seven Deadly Sins, an allegorical set-piece enacted with embarrassing literalness and – in the case of guzzling, belching Gluttony – with uncharacteristic vulgarity. But, although Ashton's divertissement for Pride was equally unimaginative, with her repetitive penché arabesques swooping towards a hand mirror, everyone noticed the lucid line and 'shining beauty' of the seventeen-year-old redhead who created the part. *The Quest* launched the careers of Moira Shearer and Beryl Grey, who, at only fifteen, gave the Odile-like Duessa a slinkiness and flinty attack remarkable for her age. 'She was strong, angular and fast,' says Shearer, 'but the rest of the choreography was very pedestrian.' There were, however, other highlights, such as the staccato pointwork and quivering crossed hands of Archimago's bats; and the lyrical, stage-skimming duet for Margot Fonteyn and Robert Helpmann as Una and St George. Yet no amount of clever choreographic incidentals could redeem the ballet. Ashton was clearly defeated by his narrative and came into his own only when the story was over.

In the final scene, he returned to the ritualistic, religious mood of *The Wise Virgins*. The House of Holiness, depicted in Piper's stained-glass colours, looked like a page from an illuminated manuscript, but its serenity was obliterated by what Walton called the 'ghastly' end, when the girls, like GI brides, pulled out their handkerchiefs and waved off an invisible train. In straining to make his ballet topical, a jingoistic call to action, Ashton exposed his inadequate grasp of his source. *The Faerie Queene* is not the patriotic work it appears to be. Although its various quests are reflections of the great English myth of King Arthur's search for Gloriana or Elizabeth I, the endings become more and more inconclusive: Arthur never gets to Gloriana, none of the other knights complete their missions, and the poem relapses into a strange combination of pacifism and mysticism. By turning it into a celebration of national glory, Ashton misinterpreted Spenser, but he was only being true to the times: fighting the war by drawing upon English literature and history at a time of emergency, as Laurence Olivier was to do in his famously propagandist *Henry V*.

There is no final victory in *The Faerie Queene*. Far from being a paragon of valour, Book One's Red Cross knight is a 'faint harted', 'clownishe younge man', who, despite his spiritual recharge in the House of Holiness, tries to abandon Una and his quest, and retreat into the sanctuary of New Jerusalem. There was a painterly mood of hieratic tranquillity in Ashton's House of Holiness, but the Florentine groupings were decorative and one-dimensional; and even the partisan de Zoete complained that the ballet had 'no spiritual depth'. The libretto's exclusion of the dragon eliminated the central theological reference – the old serpent, Satan – and, whereas Spenser deftly integrates religion with romance, Ashton took the chivalric story at face value. As he later admitted, it was a struggle for him 'to give any idea in the ballet of the richness of Spenser's imagery' and portray allegorical characters in dance terms: 'to convey clearly their humanity and to bring them to life on the stage as Spenser [did] . . . in his great poem.' Dance, expressive of what Arthur Symons called the evasive, winding turn of things, is, by its nature, more suited to symbolism than the black and white certainties of allegory. And as an art which idolizes the body, it cannot be expected to convey the moralistic, medieval doctrines of Spenserian allegory. Living proof of this was the portrayal of St George by Robert Helpmann, whose garish makeup and Afro wig suggested to Beryl de Zoete 'dedication to anything but

Holinesse'; while William Walton thought he looked more like the Dragon than St George. He can have had little guidance from Ashton who, quite apart from his own uncertain concept of the role, was still feeling resentful towards him. He even changed the final tableau in order to screen Helpmann from behind a white gauze. 'It is better than seeing that sinful face sanctified.'

After six weeks' leave of absence, Ashton rejoined the RAF in the office of the Assistant Chief of Air Staff, based, until the end of the year, in London. Alice lent him the gardener's cottage at the gates of Hanover Lodge, a Mrs Tiggy-Winkle dwelling, comprising a damp little sitting room, a bedroom with just enough room to accommodate a divan, a galley kitchen and tiny bathroom. The main house had been requisitioned as nurses' quarters, and Alice was living in the twin gate cottage opposite. 'I don't think she was ever happier,' says her daughter Romana McEwen. 'War removed all the social obligations and she at last got rid of her mother, who took us off to America in the summer of 1940. Except for the fact that friends were being killed, it was wonderful freedom for her and great fun: lovely evenings with Fred on leave making toast in front of the fire.' Although they had spent Easter at Faringdon (a nostalgically convivial gathering, which included Cecil Beaton, Daphne Weymouth, Clarissa Churchill, Peter Watson and Peter Quennell), Ashton in fact saw very little of Alice, who was either in Dorset with her baby, Emily, and the nanny, or else volunteering her services around the country, driving an ambulance and doling out food to the troops. On free weekends, Ashton sought his sister's company, staying at the cottage she and her new husband had bought in Datchet, near Windsor.

At the beginning of 1941, after almost nine years' resistance, Edith had married Douglas Russell-Roberts, then serving as a Lieutenant Commander in the Navy. She was not in love with him, but he was tall, good-looking and brave (recipient of the Legion of Merit award), and timid little Edith, who was terrified of the war and any kind of violence, grew to see him as 'this brick' in her life, and finally agreed to let him take care of her. There were moments of panic when, alarmed by their incompatibility, she would disappear, tormenting Douglas into believing he had lost her. 'Oh poo, don't frighten me . . . ' he begged in one letter. 'Could you not be a little more generous to me in your "escapes"?' As he was well aware, Edith thought of him as 'belonging to another world', but the doggedness of his devotion, which began when he would sit and watch her in her club, eventually took effect, and they were married in a register office near his ship, with only Edith's sister-in-law, Helen, in attendance. Douglas went back to sea, buying her a wireless set as a wedding present because, as he wrote to his mother, she would be 'so much alone'.

Not for long. It was during the war that Edith began a 'most passionate' affair with Kenneth Clark, for whom she had nurtured a girlish crush ever since she had sat next to him at a ballet performance in the early years of her marriage to Trevor Richards. 'I loved him all my life,' she said. Although she was one of several dalliances in Clark's life – the painter Mary Kessell was her main rival – Edith felt, as they all did, that she was the only one. When she became pregnant, she was sure that Clark was the child's father and wrote, asking him to visit her in the nursing home. Later, she told her son, Anthony, how relieved she was to see how closely he resembled Douglas. Constrained by her unsatisfactory marriage, Edith was swept up by the romance of it all, sending Clark postcards illustrated with eighteenth-century paintings of lovers meeting, and treasuring his letters, tied together with red ribbon. Handsome and urbane, Kenneth Clark was the omnipotent cultural authority at that time and wildly impressed Edith, who regarded him as her mentor. 'He taught me everything I know.'

'She was quite unsophisticated when he found her,' said her friend, Lady Margaret Douglas-Home. 'She loved him, my goodness how she loved him, and he was very devoted to her. But that's where he was so naughty. Because she wasn't in the smart set, he would hardly refer to her even.' However, according to Susana Walton, the composer's widow, Clark was more serious about Edith than his friends knew. 'K thought he'd seen the light of day and proposed this wonderful scheme.' The idea was that Walton, who had recently declared his love for Clark's wife, would 'go off with Jane' so that Clark would be free to marry Edith. 'But William just scuttled,' said Lady Walton. 'He knew that Jane was a difficult character, well known for having a tremendous temper, quite apart from the fact that he was still involved with Alice [Wimborne] and would never have hurt her.' Edith and Clark made a plan to elope, but on the chosen day he rang to back out, using the excuse that he had had to rush Jane into hospital with an artichoke thistle stuck in her throat. His wife could be useful protection when it suited him.

The important question is how much Clark's involvement with Edith influenced his championship of Ashton at this period. His daughter, Colette, insists that, given his official role as Chairman of the War Artists Advisory Committee, Clark 'would have helped Fred anyway'. Certainly, he admired Ashton's work. 'I know nothing about ballet and don't understand it at all,' Clark wrote to him, 'but if I know anything about the nature of art as a whole, I am sure you are one of the greatest living artists.' The two men were not particularly close; Ashton, who was in-

timidated by Clark and cynical about his professional charm (his reticence was noted by Clark, who described him in his memoirs as 'a master of evasion'), was much friendlier with Jane Clark, whom he loved for
her warmth, impulsiveness and generosity. He used to recount how,
whenever he arrived at their house, she would come to the door, holding
out a pound note to pay for his taxi. 'Jane used to do it to embarrass him
in front of people,' claimed Susana Walton. On the contrary, Jane Clark
knew Ashton well enough to realize that his motto was always to accept
an offer of money, even though it fuelled jokes about his stinginess. As he
explained to a fellow guest, taken aback by his audacity, 'A pound's a
pound.' Despite his fondness for 'darling Jane', it is quite likely that Ashton, obsessively exploiting his contacts to escape his current situation,
would have encouraged her husband's affair with Edith. Whatever the
underlying motives, Clark's impact on both their lives dominated brother
and sister's conversations during the Datchet weekends.

Church Cottage, with its Elizabethan timbers, lattice windows and
climbing roses, was a charming refuge, overlooking the village green. Peter and Rosemary Townsend were neighbours, living across the river in
Adelaide Cottage, another pretty house, originally built by William IV as
a tea garden for his Queen. Rosemary and Edith had become very close,
as, being interested in the arts, they 'spoke the same language' and they
were both experiencing problems in their marriages. Edith, at this point,
was 'very up and down', given to flinging herself on her bed and sobbing
like a schoolgirl. 'She just longed to be out in life and Douglas didn't like
that,' said her oldest friend, Sophie Pearson. She would have loved to
have been more involved in her brother's world, into which she fitted
very well. Sophie Fedorovitch and Alice were devoted to her, while Kenneth Clark was not Ashton's only friend to appreciate her allure. 'Willie
Walton was always making passes at Edith,' Ashton said. 'She was always very successful with highbrows. Henry Moore was mad about her
too and tried to seduce her, but she wouldn't go with him . . . Edith was
quite a one; she was such fun and had enormous charm. Men adored her
femininity. If something touched her, her huge eyes would fill with tears
and she would clutch your hand to her cheek.' Edith was well aware of
what Billy Chappell called 'her real *way* with gentlemen' and enjoyed seeing it work. At the Townsends' annual Gold Cup Day party at Ascot, to
which the Royal Family were invited, she went up to the King, rested one
of her little soft hands on his sleeve, and whispered, '*Sir*, next time you
drive through Datchet, *please* look up at my window boxes: they look so
lovely at the moment.' Rosemary Townsend's Brigadier-General father
was 'really shocked' by her presumption, but the King was delighted. 'He
loved it,' she said. 'He was awfully shy and liked people to talk to *him*.'

Edith's flirtatiousness tormented Douglas, who retaliated either by being 'bloody to her', or by sinking into one of his moods, when he appeared possessed by what he referred to as his 'devils'. First nights would
always bring on a black mood. He had no interest in ballet and Ashton's
artistic friends made him feel inferior; they, in turn, found him a bore,
nicknaming him the Ancient Mariner. He was 'insanely jealous' of Edith's
rapport with Ashton and homophobically suspicious of her brother's influence on his son. He was so intent upon destroying any aesthetic ten-
dencies the little boy might have, that Anthony would be made to wear
Fair Isle and corduroy at children's parties, rather than the customary
velvet and lace. But, with Douglas away at sea, Datchet weekends with
Edith were cosy and fun for Ashton, as they shared the same sense of humour and used to 'giggle like mad'. They made a running joke of Mrs
Russell-Roberts, an intimidating, eccentrically fastidious character, who
washed her spare change and mattress springs with vinegar. But, for Ashton, good times with Edith and his friends were short-lived. Early in
1944, he was posted north again, this time to Liverpool, where he spent
most of the year as Air Advisor in Intelligence.

In the requisitioned Littlewoods Pools building, he began working as
head of a department, sharing an office with three colleagues, one of
whom, sitting opposite him, was his personal assistant. Pamela Mortimore remembers a pleasant, quiet and unassuming man, who specifically
asked her not to reveal his true identity. 'So F/Lt he was and remained
amongst the many hundreds of people in the building. Being very honest,
he said that he would move heaven and earth to get a posting back to
London.' With the invasion of North Africa and the preparations for the
Second Front in Europe, Britain was on the offensive and the priorities of
Ashton's department were to maintain security and boost the morale of
the overstretched Air Force. As Air Advisor, his main task was to sift intelligence information from correspondence gleaned from all over the
world (although his language skills were still not put to use as the material was already translated for him). He carried out his duties conscien-
tiously, without any show of impatience, but, at every opportunity, he
would dash back to London. Billeted in Liverpool's comfortable Rac-
quets Club, he spent his time off-duty reading Sir Arthur Bryant's history
of England and listening to jazz records – Fats Waller's 'My Very Good
Friend, the Milkman' was a particular favourite. Pamela Mortimore
found herself mothering him out of office hours: pleading poverty, he got
her to carry out running repairs on his uniform and used to borrow her
scissors to cut his toe nails, his excuse being that all his personal belongings had been lost in Holland. In return, Ashton entertained her with imitations: 'Queen Victoria, and also of his sister burping her baby.' After

the war, they corresponded for a while, remembering their days in the forces: 'I was never in more danger than being shot at by the C.O.,' Ashton wrote in one letter. As a parting present, he gave her a new Rosamond Lehmann novel which he inscribed, 'Thank you so much for looking after me so well. Hope the next time you see me will be across the footlights and not across a desk.'

Ashton got his longed-for posting home in October 1944, transferring to the Censorship Office, described by Pamela Mortimore as 'our branch in London'. Before he left, he asked her to accompany him to the Ministry canteen while he had his fortune told by one of the Welsh waitresses, an amateur clairvoyant. As Pamela moved tactfully out of earshot, she could not help overhearing the opening remark, 'that he should beware of a dark man near him'. A look of grim satisfaction crossed Ashton's face. 'It's Bobbie Helpmann, of course!' As, indeed, it was.

CHAPTER ELEVEN

MIDWINTER SPRING
1944–1946

A shton's cri de cœur had finally been answered, and he spent the last phase of the war as a civil servant in London, based at 271 High Holborn, a nondescript modern building near the old Empire cinema. On his first day, he was shown round the open-plan room by Wing Commander Reckitt, who introduced him by saying, half-facetiously, 'This is Flying Officer Ashton: we're saving him for the nation.' His new job as an Air Advisor involved briefing the Censorship Officers, who sat on the other side of a partition, and answering their queries. Because his desk was nearest the door, he was inevitably approached first: 'He hated it,' said a former colleague. 'He never really knew what the answers were.' There was one man he particularly dreaded, who was constantly asking questions, and who also happened to be deaf. The other officers used to stop what they were doing and listen, grinning, as Ashton, who could never bear to raise his voice, was forced to shout out facts that he himself did not understand.

The Censorship Department dealt mostly with Intelligence information, but material was also scrutinized for offensive content by 'old girls' whose prudishness irritated Ashton intensely. 'There they used to sit, opening and sealing letters saying, "Oh, but this *must* be censored." And I'd argue, "Nonsense, it's not giving anything away." Supposing an airman was writing to his wife and said, "Prepare yourself, for the next fortnight you're going to see nothing but the ceiling . . ." They'd say, "Oh, that must be cut out," and I'd say, "*Why?* It has nothing to do with you."'

But Ashton himself could be more than a little irreverent with the correspondence he handled. 'Any letter that had something entertaining it was treated most indiscreetly,' remembers Sylvia Loeb, a deputy from Censorship, who used to 'pick out letters that looked "stagey" and bring them over to his desk for marvellous gossips'. She was a friend of Edward

Burra's and the granddaughter of the conductor Hans Richter (for whom Ashton was to create an off-stage role in his 1968 *Enigma Variations*), so she found much in common with him. As another excuse for a chat, she used to deliver batches of sentimental postcards of loving couples, confiscated from Italian soldiers, which Ashton was collecting to make a screen.

Sitting opposite him was Richard (Dicky) Smart, a good-looking, cultivated Australian, who, Sylvia Loeb says, was 'very much one of the boys and mad about Bobby Helpmann'. A connoisseur of dance, opera and art (he was a friend of Paul Nash and owned a drawing of himself by Augustus John), Smart was a source of urbane conversation much appreciated by Ashton after so long a period of cultural abstinence. Another colleague, Kathleen Evison, sat next to them, and all three became good friends. They all smoked incessantly, too, with Ashton selecting his cigarettes from a jewel-studded Fabergé case, a present from Alice. With Kitty, as he called her (after the comedy *Old Mother Riley and her daughter, Kitty*), he developed a jokey rapport: 'He just took to me for some reason. He was Old Mother Riley, and used to pass me very funny notes instructing me how to live.'

Ashton appeared shy and deferential towards his seniors, but there were one or two he would mimic as soon as their backs were turned. 'The Censorship Office was full of every peculiar, eccentric brand of English person you've seen abroad,' recalls Sylvia Loeb. Reflecting this, his repertoire became zanier, almost Dada-esque during his stint with AI S(8). There was one act where he pretended to be sick into a waste-paper basket, and another involved a woman whose hair gets caught in the ventilator and is scalped. 'Then he found some rope that a parcel had been tied in and he became a sort of Gretchen. And there was a wonderful performance he did of Mozart playing the piano and conducting and getting carried away.'

But at 12.30 sharp, when the squadron leaders went out to lunch, Ashton would push his Censorship duties to one side and settle down to serious work. 'Fat tomes he used to read,' said Kitty Evison. 'He really educated himself during that hour and enjoyed the fact that nobody bothered him.' Some research must have been for *Les Sirènes*, because she recollected one book being full of Edwardian period detail – 'the sort of spoons and forks they used' – but most of Ashton's studies at this time were in preparation for *Symphonic Variations*. He rarely read for pleasure; to him, literature existed to nourish his art: 'I read everything to feed me subconsciously.' But there were personal gains as well. Increasingly immersed in metaphysical texts, he was becoming 'contemplative and almost mystical'. The visionary theology of St Theresa of Avila and

St John of the Cross was a particular source of consolation, reconciling him to the idea of death and making him much more fatalistic. Kitty Evison described how, during an air raid, all the staff would dive under their desks except for Ashton, who simply carried on what he was doing. He remembered walking home during 'the most tremendous Blitz. There was no way of getting back and I had to walk to Hanover Lodge, getting there at dawn when the all-clear was going. I saw St Anne's in Soho burning and just went through it all. I must have been brave in those days: occasionally diving down into a cellar and coming up again.' Ashton's move to the Censorship Office coincided with the arrival of the doodle-bugs, the flame-tailed V-weapons that spluttered over London at all hours of the day and night. Sometimes, when he came home, he would go for a stroll in the grounds of Hanover Lodge with Gilbert and Gracie, Alice's chauffeur and his wife, but one evening he had a 'strange feeling' and rang up Edith in Datchet to ask if he could stay the weekend. While he was there, a V2 hit the top of a huge copper beech, blowing out the rose garden, killing Gilbert and seriously injuring Gracie. Ashton was very shaken by the tragedy; quite apart from his narrow escape, he had been very fond of Gilbert and was grateful for the kindness he had shown his mother at the end of her life.

At work, too, Ashton came close to being killed when a bomb exploded only yards from his office, a direct hit on a street market. Rather pruriently, Kitty Evison took him along during their lunchbreak to witness the devastation. 'He didn't say a word; not a word. He just looked. He *hated* all the killing. And then he said, "Now I'm going to show *you* something."' They walked to St Ethelreda's Church in Ely Place, the only pre-Reformation church in London restored to Roman Catholic worship. Inside, Ashton went straight up to the candles and lit one. 'I asked who it was for: "I'm not going to tell you," he said.'

It may have been for Georgie (in his 1948 ballet, Cinderella lights a candle and places it next to the portrait of her dead mother), but often, before embarking on a new work, Ashton would go into a Catholic church, usually Brompton Oratory, and light a candle, as much a talisman of good luck and love of ritual, as a declaration of belief. His was a very private faith, fusing pantheism and Roman Catholicism with peasant-like superstition. Largely through laziness, he hardly attended a service, yet described himself as 'fairly religious'. Theological orthodoxies did not convince him; but while he was not entirely persuaded by the existence of an afterlife, in his old age he used to envisage a heaven populated with artistic deities such as Mozart and Petipa, before whom, on arrival, he planned to kneel in homage. His religious leanings were predominantly Catholic – 'If I was going to embrace God I'd get myself converted' – but he believed in pagan omens just as devoutly. In 1987, when the tree he had planted at Eye in memory of Sophie Fedorovitch began to die unaccountably, he fell into a deep depression, interpreting this as a portent of his own imminent end. His God was a Diaghilev-like impresario, a master puppeteer, whose sorcery controlled his art. 'I rather put myself in the hands of a superior power. I make some kind of receptive preparation. I am almost like a wireless. I feel that if I turn the right knobs the stream will flow through me.'

This 'wise passiveness', in Wordsworth's phrase, involved steeping himself in the relevant score, playing it (and nothing else) continuously, day and night. If he came home slightly drunk from a party, Ashton would put on the record, 'because you never know how it soaks through you . . . then gradually, from the music everything comes to me.' Pamela May remembers César Franck's *Symphonic Variations* playing 'over and over' on a wind-up gramophone in the dressing room and, again, back at her digs. Ashton wanted the score to inhabit his dancers to the point of possession, because it was they who would be making the music visible. 'Right from the word go he said, "Now you see, the boys are the orchestra and the girls are the piano."' Friends were also expected to listen repeatedly to the record while he outlined his ideas. On one occasion, sitting in front of the fire at Datchet, he demonstrated many of the movements he had in mind to Vera Volkova, the celebrated teacher who had become a close friend, as well as a vital influence on the new work. At rehearsals, she would discuss and rework minute details with Ashton, the purity of her Russian heritage guiding the ballet's radiant delineation of classical line.

Volkova had been pupil of Vaganova and contemporary of Ulanova, and gave inspiring classes, which drew crowds of acolytes from Margot Fonteyn to chorus girls from London musicals. She was particularly good with male dancers (her protégés would include Rudolf Nureyev, Erik Bruhn, Peter Martins, and Stanley Williams, America's greatest teacher), and she was responsible for easing Ashton back into shape. Her studio in West Street was draughty and dingy, with the only light during winter-afternoon power cuts and blackouts coming from two candles on top of the upright piano. Volkova was a hard taskmistress, especially towards her favourites: 'That was what the French call *moche* – rubbish!' she once remarked to Fonteyn after a difficult adagio. She spoke with a thick Russian accent, which she combined with an effective onomatopoeic lexicon of sounds, instructing a pupil, for instance, to 'Svooooosh' the floor with his foot before an assemblé. The similes she used to help a dancer achieve the effect she wanted were eccentric, but invariably spot-on. 'Pull God's beard!' she cried, correcting a limply raised arm. She continually strove to get more out of the dancers than they thought they were capable of giving. 'I always imagine zat ze leg should hug something,' she told a pupil standing poised in attitude. 'You are hugging one of zose red English pillar-boxes. You must hug *ze gasworks!*' She always insisted on clean, academic line and yet choreographed upliftingly lyrical enchaîne-ments. As one Wells member remarked, 'Vera used our technical ability and taught us how to *dance.*' An original character, wearing a silk turban, with a cigarette absent-mindedly unlit between her lips, in some ways, she must have reminded Ashton of Nijinska – most significantly in that both women instilled in him the quest for *more.* (Margot Fonteyn described how he would literally bend, push and pull her into positions she never thought possible.) More épaulement – the torso eloquently angled – was their lifelong decree, something which, more than anything else, remained the signature quality in his own work.*

In November 1944, portly and stiff-limbed, Ashton filled the few weeks' leave he was given with an intense course of Volkova's classes, combined with rehearsals of *Nocturne* (in which, fortunately, his first post-war role as the Spectator, was physically undemanding). To show his gratitude to his Air Ministry colleagues for allowing him the time-off, he – or, rather, 'one of his posh friends' (probably Alice) – threw a luncheon for the whole department and invited everyone to the first night. 'Oh, Freddy did get an ovation,' said Kitty Evison. 'We were all on our feet – I've never seen such a reception.' Silencing the applause, Ashton made one of his rare speeches from the stage. 'I want to thank you for the affection with which you have remembered my ballet and to tell you how pleased I am to discover that, after three and a half years absence, I can still raise my arms.'

The ballet, as P. W. Manchester wrote in a letter of congratulations to Ashton, had retained its allure: 'Such glorious movement and everything really *danced* – it must have come as a revelation to those seeing it for the first time.' Edward Burra, however, divulged juicier revelations, telling Billy Chappell that, while Fonteyn was 'beautiful, wonderfully distracted and romantic . . . behind the scenes, dearie, it was more distracted than romantic'. Going backstage after the performance with Bumble Dawson, he found 'Mrs Siddons [Ashton] and Mrs Bracegirdle [Helpmann] or

---

*After the war, Ninette de Valois took Volkova to lunch at the Ivy, after watching a class in her studio next door, and offered her a permanent position with Sadler's Wells – on condition that Volkova close her West Street school. This she refused to do, and, as a result, the offer was withdrawn and the company were forbidden to attend her classes. It was an ill-judged decision by de Valois, which robbed her company of one of the finest teachers of the century.

should it be the other way round standing washing in a minute dressing room like a couple of land mines waiting to go off. Mrs Brace G said, producing 2 grey rags, "please be more careful of the towels they cost coupons". Mrs S almost in tears said, "she's buggered it up again" referring to poor old Alice who'd gone off in the hired car.'

The corrosive effects of Ashton's embittering wartime experience are most tellingly shown in the deterioration of his friendship with Bobby Helpmann. However 'impossible' Helpmann had become – and his début early that year in Tyrone Guthrie's production of *Hamlet* had made him even more brazenly self-obsessed – the root of the problem lay in Ashton's dog-in-the-manger resentment over Helpmann's escape from the services. 'I know what you mean about people who are not in bondage not being really sympathetic,' he confided to Chappell. 'I feel that with La . . . she gets away with everything.' Chappell understood. He knew how 'bitter-making' and frustrating it was for a creative artist to be prevented from working, 'to have to listen to wonderful plans made by other people for other people'. And he had seen how Ashton's spirits, which fed on the kind of aesthetic sustenance Alice provided, had been sapped by the ugly Nissen huts and concrete wastelands of his air force surroundings. Added to which was Ashton's understandable indignation that a talent he knew to be inferior to his own seemed, in the eyes of the world, to be overtaking him. Helpmann was a more self-seeking person – 'determined to be famous and caring more about the trappings of fame' – who was quick to promote himself at the expense of friendship. A remark in a letter from Cecil Beaton to Boris Kochno bears this out:

> Freddie Ashton is very hurt that Bobbie Helpmann told him you wanted to do a ballet with Helpmann 'as you thought Freddie's work was imitation & weak Balanchine'. I am repeating this silly potin in case you feel like contradicting Helpmann who is a charlatan & not to be compared as an artist to Freddie. If you saw the 'Miracle in the Gorbals' you will know exactly how true this is! Freddie has had 4 years in the R.A.F. is very sensitive about not starting work again. & as he has great respect for your judgement is quite upset.

Ashton, with his X-ray vision regarding character and motive, was right to be wary of Helpmann, but mixed with justifiable suspicion was straightforward jealousy. 'The toast of all the armies' was hogging the limelight, and Ashton did not like it. He and Helpmann were the original Ugly Sisters, whose relationship had always been spiked with petty rivalries – 'If Bobby bought an Aubusson, Fred had to have one too' – and, as in the ballet, instead of holding his own against the bossy exhibitionist Helpmann, Ashton was made to feel timorous and insecure. Or, at least, that is what he claimed to Billy Chappell:

> Believe it or not, I no longer feel interesting and I imagine I bore everybody when I am out dining or with La's theatrical friends. I really see very little of her now & as I always make her pay for my supper & she is so mean, I really only see her about once every three weeks & then she is staring at all the other tables afraid of missing something & all the time pursuing her own egotistical thoughts and horrible though it is I see boredom in my friend's eyes. She is not a sincere friend really & it was somehow those very qualities that were lacking in her performance.

Few who knew them both would deny that Ashton was the more likeable of the pair; as Michael Powell put it, 'Bobby was a wasp and Fred was a bee.' Both had a virulent wit, but, in public, Ashton was never as vicious and insulting. Even Helpmann's critics, however, would consider the accusation of meanness rather steep coming from Ashton, while the antiphone of complaint in his correspondence with Chappell soon begins to grate. And yet, however camp and trivial it may seem, the débâcle is crucial, not only because it fuelled their most famous interpretations – the two Step Sisters squabbling over a shawl could be a rerun of the dressing-room scene between Mrs S and Mrs Brace G – but also because their attempts to outsmart each other (subconsciously or not) helped to generate a masterpiece. 'I saw that everything was becoming too literary, with Robert Helpmann doing ballets about big subjects. I thought they were losing the dancing element and this worried me. And I began thinking in terms of pure dance.' The result was *Symphonic Variations*.

For a brief period, the two rivals appeared to be reversing roles: Helpmann was thinking of choreographing a ballet with a commissioned score by Benjamin Britten, while Ashton was turning his hand to projects outside the company. He, too, planned to work with Britten, not on a ballet, but an opera, *Peter Grimes*, in which, according to Edward Burra, he was to make a silent appearance. Neither scheme materialized: Britten abandoned the ballet to concentrate his efforts on *Peter Grimes*, and the 'princesse du geste or reine de l'atitude' never made his operatic début. Two months earlier, Ashton had collaborated with 'Old Ma Gielgud' on a play, Nevill Coghill's production of *A Midsummer Night's Dream*, which opened at the Haymarket on 25 January 1945. Conceived as a Jacobean masque, it had music not by Mendelssohn but by Leslie Bridgewater, and hardly any choreography (no corps of fairies, for instance). Like the critics, Ashton was unimpressed with Coghill's production.

'What a lack of taste . . .' he told Billy Chappell, '[Gielgud] really must stop using these Dons. How they all need Diaghileffs, dozens of them.'

Ashton's main task was to teach 'a few dancing steps' to John Gielgud and Peggy Ashcroft (Oberon and Titania): 'Not very successfully, I fear,' said Gielgud, 'judging by some of the critics' remarks.' 'One, two, three, twirl, one, two, three, twirl. Just as I hoped they were going to do a rumba,' wrote one reviewer, 'it degenerated into a minuet, and then with a smile and a kingly gesture Mr Gielgud dismissed the lady.' Gielgud admits he was 'very bad indeed' in the play; both he and Peggy Ashcroft were too old for their parts – indeed, the whole company was 'distinctly middle-aged'. Ashton claimed that Gielgud, coated in eerie green make-up, 'like Wotan, rather than the God of [morning?]', was 'very grateful' for his contribution and he enjoyed working for him. However, twenty years later, when the young Derek Jarman told Ashton about his commission to design the sets for John Gielgud's *Don Giovanni* at the Coliseum, 'Freddie's face fell when I said who the director was and he actually warned me, "You've got to do it, but it will be an absolute disaster. He can never make up his mind."' (Ashton was right, as it turned out, and the production was slated.) Gielgud, for his part, maintained a rather guarded acquaintance with Ashton, whose 'malicious repartee' had, on occasion, been directed against him. 'Very Sarah Bernhardt', he called Gielgud's Romeo, which the actor took to be more of a compliment ('*voix d'or* I imagine he meant') than was probably intended. Notwithstanding, he was 'vastly entertained' by Ashton, envying the 'wonderful series of imitations' he performed at parties given by their mutual friend David Webster during the 1940s and 1950s.

Civil-service hours gave Ashton plenty of time for a social life and, as Burra cynically noted, he appeared to move only 'between the censor and the grande monde'. He told Kitty Evison that he had accompanied the Queen to a matinée, 'although he didn't swank about it.' However, this appears to have been wishful thinking on Ashton's part, as The Queen Mother has no memory of the occasion, maintaining that she got to know Ashton only after the war. He still spent weekends at Faringdon, and saw a great deal of the Clarks, whose ubiquity in wartime London society prompted the line (sung to the tune of the hymn, 'Change and Decay') 'Jane and K in all around I see'. Like many of his male friends, Ashton frequented the decadent downstairs bar at the Ritz, which had a special cachet for pick-ups, and was consequently closed down after the war for being 'too queer'. 'That's where I used to meet people like Terry Rattigan. We all used to go because it was right down in the cellar and you couldn't hear bombs or guns' – its nickname was 'l'Abri' (the shelter). Barbara Ker-Seymer spotted Ashton one night in a 'dinge' club, the Caribbean, 'with a posse of pink-faced young officers, barely out of their teens. Madame was in charge', she reported to Billy Chappell. 'She sat there longing to be whirled into a jitterbug sequence by a handsome negro, but nobody asked her to dance. Maybe her WAAF's uniform put them off.' Ashton was on the prowl. As he confessed to Chappell, 'Pussy is out for all she can get.' He described a louche weekend with an old friend, whom he betrayed by being 'naughty with the husband – a thing I disapprove of so much but he was so insistent and Pussy was weak. Quoi faire? Pussy also took up with a ballet boy. Very nice . . .'

Sixteen-year-old Brian Earnshaw, from Golcar, outside Huddersfield, was a student at the Sadler's Wells School when he first caught Ashton's eye. A prize pupil of Volkova, he was such a dedicated exponent of her style – 'To Brian épaulement was everything' – that, eventually, he became one of the company's foremost teachers (known affectionately as 'Shaw-Shaw'). Ashton insisted that de Valois take him into the corps, telling her, during a class they watched together, 'Earnshaw is the boy who can dance.' With his jaunty virtuosic technique, innate musicality and terre-à-terre precision, Brian Shaw, as Ashton persuaded him to call himself, shone at a time when Britain's male dancers, etiolated and unfit, were just starting to return from the services. Harold Turner rejoined the ballet in April 1945, and, in no time, Shaw had appropriated his most famous roles, eclipsing him as the Bluebird in *The Sleeping Beauty* and the Blue Boy in *Les Patineurs*, the ballet Ashton bequeathed to Shaw in his will.

Ashton's evaluation of Brian Shaw was based as much on personal infatuation as on merit. Short and chunky, with a scrubbed schoolboy face, he was not a conventionally pretty 'flop-haired Cecil Beaton golden boy', but he had a sinewy, perfectly proportioned body and a high sexual drive. When he was seduced by Ashton, forty-two years old and unhealthily overweight, Shaw was hardly more than a child. Although not in love, the dancer grew emotionally dependent on Ashton: 'Fred was the first person who was ever really nice to me.' He was a typical Yorkshireman: taciturn, introverted, with salt-of-the-earth intolerance of flamboyance. (He shared a dressing room with Rudolf Nureyev for a number of years without speaking to him, because he deplored his self-aggrandizing ways.) Ashton used to claim that Brian Shaw had more personal integrity than anyone he had ever met. It was a match of opposites: unsuccessful socially ('at parties he'd just sink into a corner'), Shaw was poorly educated and dyslexic, but had a dry wit, and amused Ashton with his naivety and north-country dourness. 'And yet I always felt that Fred found Brian boring.' The new ballet boy, as Ashton told Billy Chappell, was 'not Pussy's type, but Pussy has no type now'.

Not strictly true. Michael Somes was out of sight (at the time, he was recuperating after an operation in an Army convalescent home for light casualties), but by no means out of mind. Ashton was still in thrall to his 'Miski Bu-Bu', which Somes knew and would sometimes play on with near-sadistic calculation. They were in close touch. When the dancer had to undergo a serious spleen operation as a result of a lorry accident, Ashton responded with prayers, letters, telegrams, telephone calls, money and books. In return, Somes wrote him rambling accounts of his family worries – his brother's delinquency and his mother's nervous illness – while also chivvying Ashton to galvanize his spirits. One Friday towards the end of the war, they met at the barrier at Waterloo and caught the 6.15 to Datchet, where they spent most of the weekend playing *Symphonic Variations* and discussing ideas for the ballet.

In the gardener's cottage at Hanover Lodge, Ashton also played the record to Brian Shaw, whose reward for 'Amor [*sic*], S.V. & lots more' was to be given the second of the three men's roles in the ballet, an opportunity considered so unfairly partisan by a group of second principals that they presented de Valois with a petition protesting about the advantages shown to Ashton's latest romantic attachment. 'Ninette was pushed into a corner,' said Alard Tobin. 'She called Brian into her office and told him that if he gave up Fred, she would manage his career.' Shaw refused to be bullied, but found little support from Ashton, who was unwilling to get involved, probably because it was not a relationship upon which he placed great value. Both he and Somes were dispensable when it suited Ashton. Neither accompanied him to Chips Channon's VE Day party, the occasion on which he had cautioned Nicholas Lawford about turning up with a young parachutist, who was clearly his lover. 'Alas & alas, he says I can't possibly take P to smart parties without everyone drawing the strangest conclusions,' wrote Lawford in his diary.

Earlier that evening, there had been a riotous performance of *Coppelia*, the last act of which got completely out of hand, with Bobby Helpmann improvising his own celebrations on stage. Although no one knew it at the time, the festivities heralded not only the resumption of peace, but the début of a national ballet, the significance of which would be commemorated nine months later by the company's move to its grand new home.

When the idea of establishing a resident opera and ballet company at the Royal Opera House, Covent Garden, was first discussed (with a second ballet company based at Sadler's Wells), de Valois, with uncharacteristic lack of vision, was not convinced.

> It was a great theatre haunted by the shades of exotic Russian ballet: it was a theatre that had formed the habit of graciously open-

ing its doors for the summer season . . . We were setting out on the adventure of making this building extend its hospitality to us throughout the year, challenging it, at the beginning, with nothing more than a bedraggled, war-weary Company. It could be likened to a crazy nightmare, wherein I might be given Buckingham Palace, a few dusters, and told to get on with the spring cleaning.

Intimidated by the unimaginable scale of the venture and the exacting standards the post-war public would demand, she considered that the move from Islington would present 'one great danger': a diffusion of the company's creative energies. 'I visualised the possibility of a sudden weakening – a position akin to that of an army, its lines stretched to a point where a break through could be effected almost anywhere.' Even the ballets, she felt, would not necessarily be 'aesthetically any better' on the larger, grander stage.

De Valois, as Ashton realized, was quite wrong. '"If you won't," he told her, "I will."' Bringing about the project was so important to him that he considered forming his own company and taking it to Covent Garden himself. 'He didn't want to supplant Ninette, but he felt that if he did not, the Russians would be back and English ballet would be on the fringe forever.'* Ashton may have been emboldened by the fact that the music publishers Boosey & Hawkes had approached him for advice. They had taken over the lease of the Opera House from Mecca, under whose management it had flourished as a dance hall throughout the war.† Michael Somes maintains that Ashton's ultimatum was simply hearsay: 'He certainly was of an opinion that going there was the right thing to do, but I don't think it's something he would ever have done – he had no means. He would never have deserted Ninette; that's why he stayed in England instead of accepting the offer to work in America.' In their letters, he and Ashton discussed the requirements of the existing company in order to emerge from the shadow of the Ballets Russes: a stronger corps, improved technique, and priority given to new choreography. In the event, de Valois, overruled by her Board of Governors, accepted the challenge. On 20 February 1946, for the first time, 'the traditional two eighteenth-century powdered footmen [parted and closed] those great gold and crimson curtains for an English ballet.'

Appropriately, *The Sleeping Beauty*, which the company had pre-

---

*In a letter written in August 1951 to Moira Shearer, Sacheverell Sitwell remarks, 'I believe Freddy, even, would like to oust [Ninette] de Valois from Covent Garden, which is mad from his point of view.'
†It was now being run by a Covent Garden Trust established by CEMA, whose chairman was Maynard Keynes.

sented on a moderate scale in 1939, was chosen to reawaken the new theatre.* The gala night, with the entire Royal Family and full Cabinet in attendance, was a brilliant occasion, but the ballet itself lacked lustre and, for the first few performances, it looked as if de Valois had been right. 'Large groups of courtiers or fairies were not making their presence felt sufficiently,' wrote Mary Clarke, 'and although the performance was beautifully rehearsed and well executed it did not have any great strength of impact.' Even Margot Fonteyn as Aurora, the role she later made her own, 'had yet to take the measure of the great auditorium.' Ashton decided to put things right. 'I went all over the house and said [to Fonteyn], "You're *still* not registering. I don't know what's the matter. I've been upstairs, I've been downstairs," and then one day she held one pose a fraction longer and I went back and I said, "I've got it. You've been used to a small theatre. This is a huge theatre. You've got to *hold* everything much more, so as to register . . . Show everything clearly." It worked.'

Ashton appeared in subsequent performances as Carabosse, one of his exuberantly malevolent character roles, whose tetchiness, in this case, owed something to his observations of the formidably plain, caustic Margot Oxford. He also contributed new choreography to the production: a wittily phrased and patterned Garland Dance; and a pas de trois for Florestan and his Two Sisters, faithful to the style of the ballet, but full of Ashtonian embellishments. Watching Petipa's *Sleeping Beauty*, Ashton always maintained, was a private lesson in how to handle crowds, devise entrances and exits, build up a climax like a beautiful edifice and then effect a decrescendoing of atmosphere. 'I'm not looking at the dancers at all, I'm looking at the way he achieves the effect that he's after.' His working on the ballet had an even more significant and lasting impact, with both *Scènes de ballet* and *Cinderella* (made two years later) paying direct homage to Petipa. For Ashton, as for Stravinsky who regarded Petipa as 'the greatest artist of all', *Sleeping Beauty* was 'the gateway' to neoclassicism, a fact which would have been underlined by the scheduled première of *Symphonic Variations* two nights later. As it turned out, because Michael Somes had injured his knee, Ashton postponed the ballet until April, using the extra time to continue paring away everything but the essence of the dance itself.

Symphonic *Variations* was born out of five years' bitterness and despair, a lily-flower 'whatever horror nudge her root', and marked a new development in British dance: a radical change in terms of scale and style. Like

*This version was again based on the notation of Nicholas Sergeyev, who had staged the original 1890 production at the Mariinsky.

a film director working with CinemaScope for the first time, Ashton was liberated by the challenge of filling what seemed an infinity of space, even eliminating the corps he had originally planned to use, in favour of six soloists on an empty stage. 'Quite unbelievable,' says the choreographer Richard Alston. 'I've only ever once worked at Covent Garden, and it just filled me with awe . . . you get lost in that space.' Despite the feelings of inadequacy he confessed to Billy Chappell, Ashton's confidence in his artistic capabilities was soaring. He proved his new-found independence by disregarding Constant Lambert's advice against using the César Franck score: 'Constant said, "It's complete in itself," which is what he told me when I wanted to do *La Mer*. In that case I listened – I saw I'd have had my mouth full of seawater and drowned – but with *Symphonic Variations* I didn't care what he thought and went on with it. In the end he came to me and said, "*You* were right."' Triumphantly so. Never before had Ashton shown himself in such command of the music; the dance visually enacted Franck's antiphonal writing and thematic variations, yet sometimes departed from the score with a Cunninghamesque freedom. Soft circuiting leaps juxtaposed with rapid stage-skimming enchaînements correspond to no detectable beat. Yet when Ashton does react literally to the music, he seems to uncover extra subtleties: generating a flicker of wit in the circling wrist movements that accompany a passage of semi-tonal semiquavers; or in the fast backward diagonal for two girls, which is so attuned to the piano that it calls to mind the drolly synchronized dance of the Cygnets, or the Sapphic pair in *Les Biches* (which it deliberately echoes).

It was Sophie Fedorovitch with whom Ashton had a virtually telepathic collaboration throughout the making of the ballet. She was as much involved in the choreography as the dancers, sitting by his side at rehearsals and discussing the work way into the night. It was she who urged the economy of its final form – a result that came about through a process of elimination on both sides. While Ashton simplified and purified the dance, Sophie modified her original idea for the backdrop. Preliminary sketches that were recently discovered in the backing of the framed finished design (which Ashton owned), show the way in which faintly naturalistic imagery – a suggestion of the tree and slanting sunrays – was refined into an abstract pattern of lines.*

When her friend Captain Goodliffe died in a Cambridge nursing home in 1940, Sophie moved from Marsh Farm to an adjoining barn,

---

*See Beth Genné's article, 'My Dearest Friend, My Greatest Collaborator', in *Following Sir Fred's Steps: Ashton's Legacy*, edited by Stephanie Jordan and Andrée Grau.

which she converted with characteristic simplicity, and where Ashton spent many a weekend. For her, too, the English countryside, especially in springtime, had a profound emotional impact, 'refuel[ling] her spirit as it were' and formulating ideas for designs. The view, from the barn's large kitchen window, of foggy marshland merging with lowering Norfolk skies – mile after mile of open space – was the main inspiration for the empty panoramas of *Dante Sonata* and *Symphonic Variations*. 'They were together in my mind,' she told Simon Fleet. 'Reaching for a higher plane, paradise really. In my mind there is a definite connection, using line . . .' (Fleet says she left the sentence unfinished, providing a suggestion and allowing the audience's imagination to fill in the rest.)

Sophie and Ashton were bicycling near Brancaster, towards the end of the war, when the idea for the colour of the design struck them like an epiphany: 'We came up a hill and suddenly there was the most marvellous glade filled with sunshine, and this had the most terrific effect on us.' So mesmeric and suggestive was the result – a backcloth washed 'a sort of greenish yellow' and scored with sweeping, looping parabolas – that to Alastair Macaulay writing in *The New Yorker* its pastoral spirit evoked Marvell's garden, 'Annihilating all that's made/To a green thought in a green shade'.*

When the curtain rises, the 'sextet of perfect instrumentalists', on which Ashton always insisted (he never let this ballet, his signature work, out of his sight), stand like classical Greek statues in elegant repose: arms relaxed, head tilted and lowered, one foot crossed over and resting on its point. It is a continuing motif and the position to which the dancers return as the curtain falls – 'In my beginning is my end' (it was one of three possible conclusions which Ashton finally chose at the dress rehearsal). The first cast has never been surpassed; in fact, they remain so intrinsic to the ballet that, even today, as Macaulay points out, the music seems to call out their names: ' "Margot *Fon*-teyn . . . Moira *Shear*-er . . . "; then "Michael *Somes*; Brian *Shaw*; Henry *Dan-ton*." Though Franck quickly embroiders variations on the theme ("and *Pam*-ela May") he keeps returning to devout announcements of it.' Once set in motion, the dancers

---

*There are several intepretations of these curving black lines: Fedorovitch told the dancer, Gilbert Vernon, that they were suggested by a weather chart with its high and low pressures; Ashton and Marie Rambert claimed that they reflected the outline of telephone wires patterned against the Norfolk moors; Pamela May remembered Sophie muttering something about the illustrations of patterns made by electrical currents she'd seen in a book. The critic Beth Genné believes that the original inspiration of a sun-filled country glade is reflected in the enclosing shape of the 'protectively' bending lines.

never leave the stage; and, although the steps themselves are not taxing, the twenty-minute ballet is such a marathon that performers rehearsing it for the first time have sometimes been physically sick. During the initial run-throughs, the dancers would lie on the floor, panting and in tears, but Ashton was ruthless: ' "Get up and do it again," he'd say', until they were able to create the effect of effortless lyricism he wanted.

To begin with, there is a sense of dormancy on stage, as the trio of women – striking in the original cast, with their matching heights, and contrasting black, red and blonde hair – are screened, purdah-like, by their outstretched arms. They are, Ashton has said, 'like women waiting to be fructified, so to speak'. He intended the ballet to progress from chastity to fertility, darkness to light, following the pattern of Shakespeare's last plays: death to rebirth was the obvious metaphor for the times. 'It has that breath-taking quality of serenity, a sense of the morning of the world,' a friend told Ashton, to which he replied, 'Quite right.'

The dominant theme of the seasons in the ballet held a perpetual fascination and mystery for Ashton. He endorses it in the ballet's four-part, cyclical structure and in the recurring circular patterns created when the dancers take hands and run in a chain, their 'ringlets' evoking English May Day dances, while also alluding to the new international amity (traditionally, in court and country dances, held hands signified harmony). At the time of making *Symphonic Variations*, however, there were many other things on Ashton's mind. The original concept was far more complex, as these jottings from his notebook reveal:

a) *Poco allegro* – Part 1. The women, Winter, the period of waiting, the Moon period, the Underworld, the Darkness. The Earth, Venus mourning. The Virgin's faith.
b) *Allegretto* – Part 2. The arrival of the Men. The Sun's rays, the Summer, the World, the Heavens, the Light, Adonis returns to the Earth, Life, Love, the Lover excites the love of his Spouse.

a) *Molto piu lento* – Part 3. The Search, The Wound of Love and Rapture caused by the spark of love. The Dance of Union, Fertility.
b) *Allegro non troppo* – Part 4. The Call of the Bridegroom. The Festival. The Summer. The Marriage. The Heart's joy in union. 'Art and Faith united in one unseverable bond.'

The ballet is steeped in subliminal religious references. Ashton considered the notion of introducing a nun taking the veil, an idea he abandoned only to suggest it fleetingly when the ballerina kneels, as if in supplication, as the Bridegroom approaches. The medium, he felt, had become 'anti-God, if you like', by which he meant that the symbolic power of dance 'to whisper private and sacred things' was diminishing, while the literary, theatrical ballets of Helpmann and de Valois were taking precedence. 'I am frankly bored with too much characterisation in ballet . . . I would personally prefer to see somebody moving beautifully and expressing nothing but "line", than all the characterisation in the world.' *Symphonic Variations* was Ashton's manifesto, in which dance d'école is paramount. Yet, while it appears to be 'simply steps, pure dancing', its emotional impact on audiences reveals another dimension: an atmospheric potency Ashton described as a 'personal fount of emotion from which the choreography springs'. 'It's not abstract. It's not steps,' Antoinette Sibley has said. 'It's intoxication of everything that's beautiful on another, not human, plane . . . it's what heaven must be like.'

Ashton was not only under the influence of the Carmelite mystics when he made the ballet; he was also responding to César Franck's 'very religious' score. Franck's devout music, which, with its mystical ascent 'towards pure gladness and life-giving light', is the progression to which the ballet itself aspires, an exultant expression of Ashton's renewed faith. Dazzlingly lit, *Symphonic Variations* possesses the clarity of a vision. Margot Fonteyn, as he said, gave 'the clue to it': hypnotically still, she represents a soul in a state of grace, in that state of suspension during which, St Theresa claimed, 'visions so sublime' can appear. The ballet's main motif of stasis – anomalous in a medium which glorifies movement – is a direct reference to St John of the Cross's teachings on Quiet: 'The soul waits in inward peace and quietness and rest.' Repose, of course, is crucial to the ballet, for mundane as much as mystical reasons: the dancers need to recover their breath. When Fonteyn stood as the other dancers swirled around her, a symbol of ever-fixed eternity contrasting with worldly flux, she was, in fact, saving her strength for a scherzo solo which immediately preceded her smooth, floating pas de deux with Michael Somes. And while the doctrine of St John of the Cross is a major source for *Symphonic Variations*, Ashton keeps it submerged, in the same way T. S. Eliot does in *Four Quartets*, a work with its own 'secret history' of mysticism. 'Little Gidding' is particularly close in spirit to the ballet. Written under the shadow of the war, it, too, is lyrical and visionary, a poem 'of greatest comfort and illumination'. But, whereas Eliot embraced the via negativa, Ashton encompassed the sensuousness of the Spanish mystics, their baroque 'indulgence of emotion' being fundamental to his background and sensibility.

A covert eroticism is also embedded in the ballet. When Franco Zeffirelli, 'still bruised by the war', first saw *Symphonic Variations* at the Florence Festival in 1948, he was struck by its impact.

At the times they touched one another you felt the *love* they had for each other. They had suffered, they studied hard then suddenly came into the world. They managed to make us feel all of that. At my age it was very important. It taught me that you can't achieve anything in the performing arts unless there is reciprocal love. It has to be an act of love.

Even the spatially cool pas de deux, where 'male and female have become almost as impersonal as electrons', contains allusions to the sexual act: Ashton wanted the ballerina to 'really stretch herself open on those high ecarté lifts, making an arc with delayed climax and arrival'. And in a confessional subtext, Ashton dramatizes his life story to date. While remaining the cynosure among the three danseurs, Michael Somes is momentarily eclipsed by Brian Shaw, whose solo culminates in what Beryl de Zoete aptly described as a 'breath-taking ecstatic renversé, winging a pirouette' – a feat which contemporaries say no other dancer has equalled. The ballet, as a friend told Ashton, is 'almost Greek in feeling', emphasized by the women's white tunics (a variant of practice dress), and by its evocation of Grecian statuary. And like the Platonists, Ashton sees carnal love as a shadow of a higher, more spiritual devotion. Here, Michael Somes is once again the Ideal; deified in the original scenario as the Bridegroom of the Song of Songs – just as he was in *The Wise Virgins*. In the final version, he remains a magnetic force, drawing the three women around him in a tribute to Balanchine's Apollo, whose three muses curl round his body like tendrils. He is the life-giver, inciting the trio, 'moving alone coldly, unfertilized' into dance, like dull roots stirred by spring rain. Later, he also reactivates the two sentinel men, leading them by his example.

Ashton would have discouraged an over-elaborate interpretation of *Symphonic Variations*. It is, after all, a simple ballet, devoid of story and character. And yet, for him, as for Schiller, whose work he was then reading and transcribing, the human element was always inseparable from the abstract. None of the dancers – not even Somes or Fonteyn – knew of the existence of a libretto. He was reluctant to put his ideas into words, even to himself. 'Perhaps I was afraid . . . I might deflect myself from creating the work in terms of dancing, and that it might become literary, and that the fluid nature of my inspiration might crystallize into something I did not really intend.' Like Mallarmé, purging poetry of didactic content, Ashton made it his priority to reinstate the dance equivalent of poésie pure – steps and not ideas. But, at the same time, he recognized that choreography needed to be more than just an exercise in abstract dancing; that, without a basic idea behind it, a personal fount of expression, 'a cold complexity emerges which ceases to move an audience'. Similarly, in an early draft of 'Little Gidding', Eliot acknowledged the lack 'of some acute personal reminiscence (never to be explicated, of course, but to give power from well below the surface)'.

Symphonic Variations is 'a revelation of the power of classical dancing to evoke romantic reactions' – a fact proclaimed by the ballet's euphoric reception in April 1946. 'Hardly have I read such unanimous praise in the press. There seemed not one dissatisfied critic to be found,' wrote Adeline Genée, the famous, turn-of-the-century Swanilda, who remembered when Ashton and Georgie called on her in Hanover Terrace just as he was beginning to choreograph. 'How she protested at [your] upsetting her drawing room with all your papers and drawings. Today she would be very proud of you.' The ballet, as everyone agreed, was a landmark for Ashton and for English ballet. Arnold Haskell, recognizing *Symphonic Variations* as a masterpiece, also reminisced about the early days, commenting, 'It has been a wonderful journey and a rapid one.' Among other fan letters was one from Sacheverell Sitwell, who, likewise, declared the ballet to be Ashton's 'best work . . . quite lovely and without one jarring or discordant note, a real classical creation and a wonderful test of your creative powers . . .'

Symphonic Variations is a paradigm of native classicism: lyrical, idiosyncratic, yet true to its academic origins. Its personalized neoclassicism – a brilliant reminting of the language of Petipa – was not only a breakthrough in the development of English dance, but, at the time, spoke metaphorically of a brave new world. The ballet holds its own among the great war-generated works, including 'Little Gidding', Evelyn Waugh's *Sword of Honour* trilogy, Henry Moore's Shelter drawings, and the paintings of Graham Sutherland and John Piper. In its celebration of the sanctity and eternity of the English countryside, it belongs in the neo-Romantic tradition, although it rejects the heightened realism that characterizes the genre. Charged with feeling, *Symphonic Variations* is a modern evolution of ballet blanc (in *Studies in Ballet*, Billy Chappell includes it in his chapter on Romantic Ballet). 'Its emotional appeal expresses in some inexplicable abstract way, as much, or even more, of the human heart as any ballet with a definite plot or obvious theme.' It is as subjective, in its way, as *Dante Sonata*, but 'the emotional stream [which came] rushing out with all its rocks and stones and trees', as Beryl de Zoete wrote, has been distilled into 'heavenly serenity'.

Appearing on the same bill as *Symphonic Variations* was Robert Helpmann's *Adam Zero*, the first new English ballet to be produced at Covent Garden in 1946 and as different from Ashton's conception as it was possible to be. 'Entirely and completely of the theatre', it was an ill-conceived cocktail of elaborately staged, allegorical dance-drama, deriving from German Expressionism, Thornton Wilder's *The Skin of Our Teeth*, Japanese Noh plays and ancient Chinese Theatre. 'I don't mean to go for I know I should not enjoy it,' Juliet Duff wrote to Cecil Beaton, having received a report of the ballet from her friends Sophie Fedorovitch and Simon Fleet. 'It's such a pity that the Ballet have given up dancing and taken to walking.'

With Terpsichore restored to her true element, Ashton's influence upon British dance became as dominant as Balanchine's was to become in America. Now that de Valois had ceased creating new work and gave no further commissions to Bobby Helpmann, Ashton's position as the company's resident choreographer seemed invincible. But this was not to last. Ashton's next work, a resounding flop, countered everything he had set out to achieve. Furthermore, it would not be long before he would feel, once again, the stab of competition.

CHAPTER TWELVE

INTERPRETERS OF LOVE*

1946–1947

Jean Gilbert was an elegant young Canadian musician of outstanding talent who joined the company as a rehearsal pianist after the war. When she started alternating with Angus Morrison as the accompanist of *Symphonic Variations*, Michael Somes began to fall seriously in love with her, and Ashton stood by in his familiar role of distraught witness. Jean had been recently widowed, her pilot husband having died in action, but for Somes it was precisely her vulnerability and inaccessibility which made her so appealing. His pursuit had begun during the company's travels through the war-damaged cities of Hanover, Berlin and Dusseldorf in the winter of 1945 (a tour Ashton withdrew from in order to begin work on a new collaboration with Lord Berners). Still in mourning, Jean rebuffed Somes's advances, but, on her return to London, she faced more intense pressure, this time from Ashton himself.

> Typical Michael; after the war when he knew that I loved him, he came to me and said he was *mad* about Jean . . . she was in a terrible state and he was longing to get her and have her. And he said, 'Please will you speak to her?' Charming. And I said, 'Yes, I will,' and I did. I took her out to supper and spoke to her and she said, 'No, I can't possibly,' and I said, 'That's all over. This is your future, don't be ridiculous.' And as a result of my speaking to her, she then gave way to him. I was noble beyond words.

It was a repetition of the Pamela May situation and just as humiliating for Ashton, who may have yearned for reciprocal desire and affection, but could not help tenaciously clinging to a relationship defined by

---

*'And oft the pangs of absence to remove/By letters, soft interpreters of love' – Matthew Prior, *Henry and Emma*.

an imbalance of power. 'Fred was just like Terry Rattigan,' said a mutual friend, 'his emotional life ate him up but it all went into his work.'

What was now 'a very serious get together' between Somes and Jean Gilbert soon became deeply troubled. There were terrible arguments, and Violetta Elvin* (the company's new Russian ballerina) remembered many occasions when Jean was in tears. 'We felt Michael was still playing a game with Freddie and Freddie also considered he could make a game of it because Michael was really closer to him and had avoided marrying Jean. That's how it came out, the story that Freddie almost enjoyed suffering.' Professional success, it seemed, could be won only at the expense of personal unhappiness: Ashton's emotional life had reached its nadir. 'It was the end of Michael,' said Violetta Elvin, 'and very much a moment of [Fred] trying to remake his life – his personal life.' 'I think he was terribly lonely,' Lincoln Kirstein concurred, 'particularly after the war when it all blew up with Michael.'

Brian Shaw was no longer around to provide physical consolation, having been called up soon after the première of *Symphonic Variations*. Innumerate and dyslexic, he was drafted into the pay corps in rain-sodden Co. Antrim, where, afflicted by psychosomatic pains, he became 'a mental reck [*sic*]'. (Shaw believed that it was his traumatic experience in the Army that accounted for the loss of his hair at only twenty.) The dancer's letters describe his 'boring, dragging' days, while continuing to supply the reassurance and encouragement he knew Ashton needed. 'I shall never change as regards my thoughts for you, you can rely on that. Nothing could ever make me leave you . . . Well, Darling, you must do a wonderful Ballet and think of me as a seagull.'

Ever since the war, when Ashton confided to Cecil Beaton his dream of wafting 'on gulls wings into forgetfulness', he had endowed seagulls with Chekhovian significance as symbols of freedom and escape. Watching their 'wheeling, strange and remote' flight, while he was walking by the sea one day, gave him the idea for a ballet to be set on a Riviera beach at the turn of the century. *Seagulls* was his original title, changed to *Seagulls and Sirens*, before becoming *Les Sirènes* (possibly because of the superstition that seagulls are unlucky). Ashton pressed ahead with plans for a November première, and, in May 1946, he wired Beaton in New York, asking him to return immediately to begin the designs. Privately, however, he was having misgivings about his Edwardian ballet, triggered by the London season of Les Ballets des Champs-Elysées. With innovative works by Roland Petit, décors by Christian Bérard, Jean Hugo, Marie Laurencin, and thrilling performances by Renée Jeanmaire and the virtuoso Jean Babilée – 'the sensation of a sensational month' – the troupe had

*Violetta Prokhorova, as she was first known.

proved a revelation, dancing 'with a youthful zest which seemed the greatest possible contrast to the habitual cold correctness of Sadler's Wells'. Ninette de Valois 'wore an air of chilly disapproval' and was not seen again at the Adelphi Theatre season; while Ashton was left worrying that his romantic, lyrical style was out of date. But not for long. The other visiting company that summer, although equally stimulating, had a much more positive impact upon him.

The arrival of New York's Ballet Theatre at the Royal Opera House in June 1946 jolted audiences out of their patriotic complacency by its vitality and contemporary repertoire. The virile physiques and technical accomplishment of the men were particularly impressive, emphasizing the enfeebled state of English male dancing. As one of ABT's members remarked, 'The English boys had been through a war, and it showed.' The most interesting production, *Pillar of Fire*, was the first of the new works by Antony Tudor to be seen in Britain. Dramatizing the warring urges of sexual release and social conformity, it had revealed the outstanding dramatic gifts of Nora Kaye, who was soon to play an instrumental role in Ashton's life. For him, the key moment in the ballet was when Kaye, as the yearning Hagar, pressed herself up against a transparent scrim, through which one of the Lovers-in-Experience was silhouetted. This was Richard Beard, a twenty-year-old dancer, with the brooding charisma of a young Brando. 'I remember you so vividly,' Ashton would later write to him, 'that vibrant intensity, the plastic beauty of your poses and the shining sensuality that drew all light toward you.' Beard had made a similar impact on Antony Tudor, who invited him to join ABT after seeing him simply walk across the stage in a de Cuevas production of *Sebastian*. Tudor then cast him as the Bridegroom in *Undertow*, a role which exploited the dancer's physical magnetism, but his career had yet to fulfil its potential. 'Dick should have been a star,' said Philip Dyer, a fan who became a friend. 'He had so much going for him – Nora Kaye used to say that he had the best pair of legs since Serge Lifar – but he was lazy. He rested on his glamour.' A serious, idealistic young man, Beard had been 'completely mesmerised' by Pavel Tchelitchew, who enshrined the dancer's erotic hold on him in a series of ink-wash nudes. It was Tchelitchew who had first told him about Frederick Ashton. 'Pavlik regarded him as possibly second to Balanchine but somewhat superficial, "as most English artists are".' At that point, however, except for *Les Patineurs*, which Beard found well made and attractive but of no great artistic interest, the dancer knew nothing about Ashton's work. 'After Tchelitchew, Fred wouldn't have been serious enough for Dick,' says Dyer.

Determined to ensnare him, Ashton enlisted Nora Kaye as his go-between. They had met at one of many parties given for the visiting company and, although Ashton did not especially admire her as a classical performer ('She's a one-ballet ballerina,' he used to say, meaning *Pillar of Fire*), they instantly became friends. Nora was 'a marvellous dame', sexy, smart (her father had been a student of Stanislavsky at the Moscow Art Theatre), and full of vitality. She loved anyone who made her laugh and was exceptionally generous in return, plying her English friends with food coupons and clothes (she once gave Margot Fonteyn, with whom she was particularly close, a silver-fox stole). Ashton enchanted her: 'Nora considered Fred to be an absolute genius,' said Herbert Ross, her second husband. 'She adored his choreography and thought him a more important artist than Balanchine.' Returning to New York, Nora Kaye became ecstatically evangelical on Ashton's behalf. 'I've been talking of "Symphonic Variations" to everyone. I sound as hysterical as if it were almost a new religion with me – and in a sense it is. It has changed a great many of my theories . . .'

It was Ashton's refinement and romantic sensibility that Nora, with her Brooklynese drawl, found particularly beguiling. In her eyes, he epitomized everything she loved about England, all the glamour of performing at Covent Garden and living at the Savoy; her 'great longing and nostalgia' for the country were now focused on him, producing 'stirringly sweet emotions', which developed into what was, for her, a love affair of sorts. 'Everyone thinks I'm madly in love with you and I am,' she wrote, confessing that his letters left her 'wandering about for days in a sort of glow . . . If we do not go to Europe this Spring, I will surely die of a broken heart.' It was neither the first nor the last time that she would be physically attracted to a homosexual man. In 1948, she came to London theoretically to marry the American choreographer and ballet master John Taras. She knew perfectly well where Ashton's interests lay, but nevertheless, whether through a vicarious desire for amorous intrigue, or masochistic devotion (a situation with which Ashton himself was all too familiar), she volunteered to play the role of pander. Famous for her iron will, Nora set out to make the seduction of Dick Beard a trophy she would win for Ashton at whatever the cost.

> August 21 1946, [Beard records in his diary,] 'Nora Kaye has been exceptionally nice to me lately. She tells me that Fred Ashton, the English choreographer, had seen me in performance and says that he can make a great dancer of me, adores my body and wants to meet me.'
>
> August 22: 'Tonight I met Fred Ashton in Nora Kaye's dressing room on her request.' [A meeting Beard remembers as 'brief and silent, almost "how do you do" and I left. Fred seemed rather shy and self conscious. I wasn't good with trivial conversation . . . His appearance was not impressive (to me) but not inelegant.']

August 23: 'Nora Kaye asked me to supper with her and Ashton – I declined.'

During the London season, Ballet Theatre commissioned a new production of *Les Patineurs*, and even though he was not called to learn a role, Beard heard through the dancer Hugh Laing that the choreographer wanted him to perform the romantic 'white' pas de deux. The company returned to the States towards the end of September, and, on 7 October, while working on *Les Sirènes* with Gerald Berners at Faringdon, Ashton wrote his first letter to Beard, 'using the American première of "Patineurs" as an excuse'.

> Dear Dick
> Please write and tell me about 'Patineurs', what you thought? As you were not (regrettably) dancing in it perhaps you saw my ten-year-old ballet, so please, if you can spare the time, write me particulars, how it was received, what people say, you can imagine the things that I'd like to hear. I somehow worry as to whether you liked it or not. I want you so much to do the pas de deux. You would look so elegant and utterly charming and I *so* regret that I saw and yet hardly know you, but it was somehow difficult and you would never turn up at the places I was at! Perhaps you won't answer this scrawl but I am a fan and like fans I like answers and I like photos! . . . I had cables from Cecil Beaton and Lucia Chase very nice and enthusiastic. But I would like to hear from you –
> Yours sincerely
> Frederick Ashton

Predictably, Ashton had also received 'particulars' on the ballet's reception from Nora Kaye, who had been thinking of him 'incessantly with great joy'.

> Oct 6th [1946]
> Freddie my darling,
> Enclosed are the reviews as promised. 'Patineur' [*sic*] went off like a dream – the first, and I'm sure only, successful ballet to be seen in New York this season. The stupid 'war' between the two companies is of avid interest to the theatre-going public with all the sympathy on the side of Ballet Theatre. Hurok is so hated and his De Basil company is really the dregs. Seeing all the old chestnuts performed again – and badly – makes one realize how few great works there are in Ballet . . . *So* – in the midst of all the moth-eaten corn, 'Patineur' came like a cool, clean gust of air –

Balanchine said, 'At last one can breathe'. He loves it – adores the charm, the movement. I keep telling him of 'Symphonic Variations' he's most curious and anxious to see it. We are friends and more in sympathy with each other . . . With the fiasco of the De Basil repertoire, there has been a strengthening of forces. There is much hope for the standards of Ballet in America now . . . Dearest . . . I adore you – do nothing but speak of you in raptures to all . . . You're a genius and now New York by my ravings is intrigued and perishing to see your works – I hope it's very soon . . . So happy about riding on this ecstatic crest of the wave . . .
    My love always
    Nora

A second letter from Nora followed a fortnight later. While reassuring about the ballet's reception and gently chiding in tone ('It is wholly unnecessary to have, as you put it, a message or social significance, in fact nothing is as abhorred'), it contained a conspiratorial snippet of ballet gossip which, while fuelling Ashton's insecurity, also brought news he would have considered more than adequate compensation:

Also, my dear boy, your reviews for 'Patineur' were excellent – obviously you don't know what a really bad review in New York can be like . . . It's true John Martin was bitchy, but only because Agnes de Mille, a close friend of his, pumped him full of misinformation . . . It seems the fair Aggie has to all of her 4000 nearest and dearest and to anyone else willing to lend her an ear, spread the word that Antony chose 'Patineur' for our company merely because it was harmless enough not to give him serious competition. And when asked if you would do one of your more meaty works instead you blithely answered you didn't think our company capable of handling it . . . Aggie is a vicious girl with a most venomous tongue but it's exactly the sort of thing Martin would believe and disapprove of . . .

    I've come to the conclusion, after, mind you, much thought, that I am really madly in love with you, that it will very likely be the great tragedy of my life. And as I am resigned at last to the inevitability of unrequited frustration, I am campaigning to at least make your life a full one. I am very chummy with Dick at this point and have talked him into the 'wonder' of you – a sacrifice, for I fully realise the outcome. As he doesn't know you at all and is usually of a reticent nature this was no mean feat – and only the clarity and enthusiasm I have when I am on a subject I relish, brought it off. So if you receive a rather shy and hesitant letter from him in answer to your own, I want you to immediately put pen to paper and start one of histories [*sic*] most fervent correspondences. I have no doubt that one day this will be one of the great loves of all time.

Throughout the London season and a subsequent six-month tour of the States, Nora had spent a considerable amount of time with Dick Beard, talking mostly about Ashton and his ballets. 'She took me up. For a reason.' Back in New York, she brought up the possibility of Beard's joining Sadler's Wells Company in order to be with Ashton. 'I was only mildly interested as I was not convinced about him as a choreographic force and talent. Nora then made a different approach. How did I believe I could make further progress with Ballet Theatre and Tudor as Hugh Laing would never allow it – Hugh, she said, was already bordering on jealousy of me even then.' Nora's proselytizing worked. 'It's in the bag . . .' she told Ashton. 'He is sweet, Freddie – with a charming rather whimsical wit.' On receiving Dick Beard's reply to his letter, Ashton immediately wrote back.

9 November 1946, Faringdon House, Berks

My very dear Dick,

I can well imagine that my letter was a surprise to you and it was insolent really of me to have written on so slender an acquaintance – but it just happened and before I knew it was in the post and me full of misgivings at what I had done. Thank you for taking it so well and giving so kind a welcome to my faltering words. You see when I met you I was tongue-tied, gauche and embarrassed. I am not usually that way, generally quite at ease most places, but this was different. I was before golden Apollo and I a poor dithering mortal floundered and the vision vanished. Like a mystic, every time I tried to recreate you, you never appeared again. I would catch disturbing glimpses during my rehearsals, and later would watch you from the red and gold theatre which I love more than any other in the world and you were dancing on my favourite stage. I used to think how wonderful if it were a ballet of mine with him in it and that after we might leave the theatre together. I wonder will we ever. I didn't dare whilst you were here embarrass you as I longed to do by talking to you, as I am diffident, stunted, middle aged and unattractive and you are all beauty – radiant, upstanding and aloof. Now that you cannot see me – measure me – I feel more confident and dread the day when we must meet, which may never be, who knows. Nora was appalled when she first saw me. Only later did she learn to like the Cyrano-like figure and the mellow melancholy of my nature. For I talked so much in the later summer evenings – of you, of ballet, of love, life – endlessly we talked and I grew to like her so much, her warm humanity, her clear-sighted and just summary of people and things, her humour and the straight way she looked into my eyes. Keep her as a friend and she will guide you wisely and I like to think of you two, perhaps even remembering me sometimes. But how can I hope to capture your imagination as you have mine? I who passed unnoticed before you. But write to me please from time to time, about anything, how you are, your work, even your loves and I will keep your confidence as in a casket. I loved your letter. It was as I imagined you, generous and reacting charmingly to my held out hand. I was made very happy indeed and re-read it constantly. I am being over-worked like an old donkey but my ballet is finished (Les Sirènes) thank God for the release and this ballet like Patineurs must be a success immediately or fail. What will be the verdict? I just wait. It is crazy, nostalgic, I am told witty (whatever that means in ballet) but understated and not vulgar, and the pas de deux I think is good, in the Petipa tradition, exciting and full of drama of movement (the only drama I like in ballet). Pray for me on the 12th. It is going to be a brilliant audience, Duchesses, Marchionesses, Countesses [illegible] in their tiaras to get in. So I leave you dear Dick trembling on the brink.

> Yours ever
> Freddie
> Fans like photographs

Obtaining photographs of Beard now became a priority. One November night, the critic Phyllis (Bill) Manchester invited Pip Dyer to supper. Arriving at her flat in Chelsea, he was flattered and intrigued to discover that Ashton was there too. After a pleasant evening, the two men left together, and the moment they got into a taxi, Ashton came straight to the point. 'It began like this: "Bobby told me that all summer you had an affair with an American dancer, Dick Beard." "Not at all," I said, "but we're great friends."' Dyer then explained that he lived with the *Life* magazine photographer Hans Wild, who just happened to have taken a series of pictures of the dancer. 'Bring them to me next week,' said Ashton. 'I'll give you supper.' From then on, although he never admitted it to Dick Beard, every time Ashton met Wild and Dyer, he 'prised' another photograph out of them. 'Hans was very wily,' says Beard. 'He rationed them in order to socialize with Fred.' The sequence shows the dancer dreamily posed in black tights and a white shirt with sleeves rolled above his biceps – the embodiment of male sexual power. Ashton craved the photographs not only as homoerotic icons, but as inspiration for his work. He had already experimented with still poses in *Symphonic Variations*, and Wild's studies of Beard (which may themselves have been influenced by the ballet) provided him with the impetus to sublimate male glamour even further. Firstly, however, although his heart was not in it, Ashton was obliged to concentrate on a more immediate project.

Les Sirènes, like *Le Train bleu*, which Lord Berners had seen the Ballets Russes rehearse in Paris in 1924, was an opérette dansée, in Diaghilev's term, in which the smart set parade their flirtations and foibles on a smart Riviera beach, the main difference being that Jean Cocteau's ballet, with costumes by Chanel, was set in its present, rather than the past. Like its predecessor, *Les Sirènes* featured characters modelled on real people: Ashton's appearance as King Hihat of Agpar was based on King Farouk of Egypt (much in the news at the time, owing to the Arab–Israeli partition scheme); and Fonteyn danced La Bolero, a caricature of La Belle Otéro, the turn-of-the-century Spanish dancer and grande horizontale. But, while the new ballet echoed *Le Train bleu*'s mood of 'coloured picture postcards' – Beryl Grey's portrayal of the Countess Kitty reminded Arnold Haskell of 'a postcard of Lily Elsie' – its main source was the Trouville opening of *Moths* by Ouida. Her writing had influenced the society comedies of Wilde and early Shaw, and her witty, flamboyantly romantic works had been first brought to Ashton's attention by Doris Langley Moore, aware that the novelist's gift for period detail would appeal to him. Ouida's flippant Lady Dolly was the original for Lady Kitty; her sentimental hero, the tenor, Raphael Corrèze, was travestied beyond recognition by Robert Helpmann as 'Adelino Canberra (of the Adelaide Opera)'.

On a scrap of paper, the back of which bears an inventory for a wooden filing cabinet signed for by P/O Ashton, and a Taunton address for Michael Somes, Ashton had faintly pencilled an outline of the plot, written while he was stationed at Tangmere during the war.

Open 2 Seagulls
Enter children? Enter grown ups/Poteniere [?]
Enter La Belle Otero & Tenor & Guardee
Enter King of Egypt
Pas de Trois & Wooing of Otero. King wins by giving her diamonds
Exit Otero & King, she throwing a kiss to Guardee & a flower to tenor
General dance of Bathers

Re-enter Otero & Tenor to undress & bathe – singing
from either bathing machine Pas de deux, re-enter all
King to find them, demands his diamonds, scandal: no diamonds.
Degringolade
Otero & Tenor left & exit weeping. When all exited gulls come
out & put jewels on female.

With a few variations, this was the basis of the synopsis which featured in the programme the following year. Like the earlier Ashton–
Berners collaborations, *Les Sirènes* was an exuberant burlesque, spiced
with in-jokes and double entendres, such as the allusion in Adelino Canberra's name to Berners' own nom de plume, Adela Quebec.* The appearance of an Oriental carpet-man, who rushes on and lays down his
wares, may even have been a joke made at Fonteyn's expense: one of her
suitors at that time was a man whom Ashton used to call 'the Armenian
rug-seller'. The composer's invention of the 'Faruka' dance punningly
linked the name of the Andalusian Farucca (famously performed by Massine in *Le Tricorne*) with that of Egypt's playboy king. It was, in fact, a
pseudo-oriental number, accompanying a grave, exquisitely funny Egypt-
ian sand dance, which Ashton performed as a send-up of the well-known
music-hall act by the etiolated, deadpan trio, Wilson, Keppel and Betty.
The score was the usual cocktail of pastiche and self-parody. It mixed a
Spanish dance in the style of Berners' own 'Fantaisie Espagnole' with
what the *Dancing Times* mystifyingly called 'balloon music of 1904 or
thereabouts'. It also included mock-Italian opera, themes from Wald-
teufel — even a snatch of the *Les Patineurs* waltz. Once again, creating
the ballet turned out to be a pleasurably social experience. Cecil Beaton
elaborates:

> While Gerald Berners worked at his piano in the drawing-room . . .
> I laboured, with more detailed love and care than usual, upon the
> designs in an upstairs bedroom. Lunch was not only a pleasant in-
> terlude but a gastronomic treat. At the end of the day I would
> show Gerald my progress, he would play his score, while Freddie's
> imagination was fired to further frivolities. After dinner, upstairs
> again to paint another filigree row of struts in the Trouville pier or
> more ducks'-eggs pearls on Otero's costume.

---

*As Clement Crisp points out, D'Ardath, the name of the tenor in Ashton's orig-
inal scenario, was a jokey reference to the singers Jean and Edouard de Reszke.
Ardath and De Reszke were brands of cigarettes.

As in the case of *Cupid and Psyche*, however, the indulgent working conditions took precedence over artistic objectivity. The result seemed more like a charade at a weekend house-party than a considered work of art. Extravagantly overdressed, with costumes that were fetchingly authentic but inadequately adapted for dancing, *Les Sirènes* ended up as a version of *My Royal Past* sur la plage. And like Beaton's 'realistic confections', Ashton's choreography was lamentably over-literal. This lack of stylization can be seen in the coy, pedestrian dance of the seagulls. Far from capturing the strange, wheeling, flight which had inspired the choreographer in the first place, the pair of gulls (Margaret Dale and Alexis Rassine), in banal costumes, were grounded and 'as vulgar as humans', with wings attached to their arms. As Richard Buckle commented at the time, 'In ballet it is the bird-like movements, not the feathers, that denote the species. After all, no one needed to wear skates in *Les Patineurs*.'

The most embarrassingly literal instance was when Robert Helpmann launched into audible song, yodelling 'O Cara mia dolce amor' with mock-operatic affectation.* Although Helpmann's performance delighted his fans, who on the first night demanded an encore, it left the majority of critics cringing. Undeterred, Helpmann seized an even more exhibitionistic stunt. On the first night, Ashton, as King Hihat of Agpar, made his entrance by landing on stage in a hot-air balloon, but he was so traumatized by vertigo that, on disembarking, he forgot his steps and had to be prompted by his two henchmen, who performed the sand dance in front of him. 'Fred refused ever to do it again,' said Alexander Grant, who was one of them. 'Bobby, of course, thought this far too great an opportunity to miss.' Beryl de Zoete thought otherwise. 'When, as the Eastern potentate, [Ashton] entered from the wings on the second night, instead of making a solemn descent in the balloon, one hoped he had traded this pleasure against Helpmann's song, which was really past a joke. But no; Helpmann descended blowing kisses and sang as well.'

For all its silliness and superficiality, *Les Sirènes* had its good points. The most notable was a tight, clever structure, built round the symbol of a necklace found by the Seagulls, which strings together the disparate elements of the plot. (*Moths* is named after a necklace, 'the moth and the star'; La Belle Otéro was as famous for her necklaces as King Farouk was for his collections of expensive trinkets.) Beaton claimed that all three of them took the ballet very seriously, even if their initial intention, 'to create an atmosphere that was mysterious and vaguely sinister', was lost in the finished

---

*This was an idea similar to one Berners had tried before in *The Triumph of Neptune*, when a baritone in the orchestra pit intoned 'Tis the Last Rose of Summer' like a bad drawing-room ballad singer.

work. Only Berners' nostalgic, aqueous prelude hinted at 'the sense of desolation behind all the mondaine [*sic*] high-jinks' inherent in the original conception. 'Perhaps,' said Beaton, glibly exculpating himself, 'Lord Berners' "pop-goes-the-weasel-tin-trumpety" music infected Ashton with its gaiety.'

It was true that the score did not fulfil the promise of its overture. Berners was beginning to suffer from the illness from which he died four years later, and his 'perverse and comic music' was no longer sufficiently substantial to carry an evening. The ballet soon disappeared, even though, at the time, many people, including a couple of the critics, found it very funny.

Les Sirènes was finally sunk by the unnecessary lavishness of the venture. As Richard Buckle wrote at the time, 'The more elaborate a joke the more embarrassing is its failure.' Having distilled his last ballet to its essence, Ashton felt obliged to make use of all the resources at his disposal. However, Cochran-style gimmicks such as a vintage car, hot-air balloon and mechanical waves looked misplaced in the Royal Opera House, and the production was roundly criticized for its extravagance. In terms of Ashton's own career, it was a puzzling reversal of the artistic credo he had so triumphantly established in *Symphonic Variations*, but he maintained that the inconsistency was deliberate. 'I think the way to keep oneself alive is never to follow that line up with saying, "This kind of ballet has been successful. I will now do a series of this sort." I do the contrary thing . . . I immediately take something that is completely different and in that way you develop yourself, I think, and increase your horizon.'

The timing of the ballet was obviously ill-judged. The aftermath of a war was hardly the opportunity for Ashton, Beaton and Berners to parade their love affair with the Coty-perfumed atmosphere and swishing skirts of the Edwardian era. Time had moved on. Within days of the première of *Les Sirènes*, Balanchine showed his austerely modern *Four Temperaments* in New York. Ashton's judgement of his own venture was surprisingly defective; the ballet was neither 'witty' nor 'understated', as he had reported to Dick Beard. But, if making an impression had been his main concern, why should he admit the truth?

Ashton sent Beard the two favourable reviews of *Les Sirènes*. It was followed by a Christmas present of four sapphires set as cufflinks, delivered by Ashton's former teacher, Margaret Craske, who was joining ABT as ballet mistress. The accompanying card was inscribed

Dearest Dick:
    Sapphires are my favourite stones. Wear these with my love or sell them if you would rather have something else. All my love for Christmas.
    Freddie xxxxxx

The lead-up to Christmas was spent hard at work on Purcell's masque *The Fairy Queen*, a compilation of dancing, singing and spoken verse, based on Shakespeare's *A Midsummer Night's Dream*. The occasion was intended to inaugurate the newly formed English opera company at Covent Garden, and Ashton's role as choreographer and producer was paramount. To him fell the task of inventing set dances for the three masques, as well as giving unity to the whole spectacle by incorporating actors, singers and dancers into the overall choreographic design. He had met a similar challenge before in *Four Saints in Three Acts*, and, once again, the corps de ballet in undulating groupings provided a decorative and unobtrusive background to the semi-static singers. He was helped on this occasion by Helpmann, whose beautifully spoken portrayal of Oberon was an uncharacteristic performance of quiet dignity. Ashton's own contribution was impressively confident. Working for Cochran had taught him how to instil grace in non-dancers, and Margaret Rawlings' Titania was praised for her gestures and movements in perfect accord with those of the dancers. Against a background of Michael Ayrton's masterly designs, inspired by Inigo Jones, Ashton produced several exceptional sequences. Having decided against a slavish reproduction of traditional baroque, with 'everyone strutting about in high-heels and periwigs, weighed down by cumbersome costumes', he chose neoclassical ballet as his idiom. The pas de deux for Margot Fonteyn and Michael Somes as Spirits of the Air recalled the low, drifting moments in their *Symphonic Variations* duet. To George Harewood, it was 'one of the loveliest things' he had ever seen. Also memorable was the Echo Dance, in which Beryl Grey's sweeping movements were echoed by a second, then by a third dancer, becoming less pronounced each time – a clever parallel to the triple-echo effect in the music. The Third Act's Masque of the Seasons provided Ashton with something of a practise run for his outstanding Spring, Summer, Autumn, Winter solos in *Cinderella*, which he was to create in 1948.

The spectacle was considered only 'a fifty per cent success', largely owing to the poor quality of solo singing. E. M. Forster, an admirer of the choreographer's work, claimed to enjoy much of it, although admitted he would rather have seen *Symphonic Variations*.

Ashton and Forster had met each other through Maynard Keynes, and, to the novelist's evident bemusement, Ashton had recently taken to sending him food parcels. 'One present is pleasing enough,' Forster wrote in his letter of thanks, 'but you keep on sending presents and such welcome and rare ones. This year I shall have a butter party I think.' Such uncharacteristic largesse is hard to explain, unless, with opera rather than ballet on his immediate agenda, Ashton had Forster in mind as a future librettist.* At that time, Ashton was deliberately taking on opera commissions as a form of security, concerned that he might, one day, run out of choreographic ideas.† As a director, his all-seeing eye served him well. 'He worried about the whole thing from beginning to end,' said Michael Rennison, a young producer who learnt a great deal from watching Ashton. 'He went into such detail and although singers are notoriously difficult about taking detailed correction, they had enormous respect for Fred. He would get to know them and talk lucidly to them, dropping in a point here and there that would change their interpretation. You never saw the same fault again.'‡ Ashton's approach was predictably choreographic – Geraint Evans and Ileana Cotrubas have both acknowledged his help with their movements on stage – and, although he could not read a score, his intuitive approach served him well. 'Only in *Manon* produced by Frederick Ashton and *Der Rosenkavalier* produced by Joan Cross were musical considerations allowed to take precedence over dramatic and visual ones,' commented Harold Rosenthal, writing about the first decade of opera at Covent Garden. Massenet's *Manon*, the second in a series of three operas that Ashton tackled in quick succession, proved more taxing than he had anticipated. With the première almost upon him, he wrote again to Dick Beard.

January 20 1947

Dearest Dick,

Your last letter made me so happy because you were so sweet about the links, after I sent them I worried because Americans don't wear links very often. Nora tells me that they are the colour of your eyes, how lucky she is to be able to gaze into them ... How I wish I could look into them but my fears would keep me back for your beauty frightens me. Your youth alarms me and I tremble at the thought of you, for what match can I be to you in my dowdy middle age? The gaze of your pale eyes will shrivel me and I shan't dare to look again, for you are golden and I am grey, you firm and I am shrivelled, you are straight and exquisite and I

---

*The novelist's radio talk on George Crabbe was the germ of Britten's *Peter Grimes*, and, in 1949, he adapted *Billy Budd* for the stage.

†Until the end of 1947, when he was replaced by the brilliant twenty-five-year-old Peter Brook, Ashton was credited in the daily opera programmes as 'Production Consultant'.

‡Ashton found his work in opera as valuable in helping to perfect his own craft as his experience in the theatre with Cochran had been. Balanchine used to claim that it was from Verdi's operas that he learnt how to handle ensembles and to make soloists stand out against the corps de ballet.

am slumped and melancholy, and beauties only like beasts in fairy stories and transform them into Princes and your beauty does have a magic glow. My beloved I am so tired today. I have been alone and I have contemplated on you as I do often – it is Sunday and last week I had a hellish time with Manon. The chorus is like moving 70 grand pianos by oneself and their immobility tires and exasperates me and I am worn out by the end of the day. I have 9 horror days ahead and then the première and then I will rest, perhaps to Paris for a week to change my outlook, if only you were coming with me that would be joy itself . . . The next best thing will be to take your letters – I always have your last with me and when I am depressed or dissatisfied with my work I read and feel better and when I see one on the rack I sing for days. So promise to write often and don't apologize for your letters, they are all I like. They give me an aroma of you, your sweetness, your simplicity, the beauty of your nature comes through and I love simplicity in all things and people and if you write to me we will learn to know each other without knowing so to speak and each will preserve his mystery. This situation is entrancing to me, strange, unexpected, nicer almost for knowing you so little and I often wonder how we shall feel when we see one another again. We have become so familiar at a distance. How did we get the idea of thinking of one another and how did the first illusion concerning our destinies come into being? Perhaps if we stay at opposite ends of the world our story will be the ideal of happiness. I certainly fear to face you for physically I am a poor thing and your pale eyes that steal their colour from sky will – will leave me gasping and transfixed. I long for that day nevertheless or do I sound like someone in a Cocteau play? – when I await to be awakened, or killed. Write often, a scrap, send me your laundry list, anything just to see your writing continually.

My love always, Freddie

I want a present very badly, *a picture* of you *please*

Letter writing, Ashton always maintained, was 'a terrible hardship' for him. Lord Berners spoke for them both when, explaining a long silence, he said, 'I'm no Sévigné. Once, in my presence, a lady said that a French letter was agony to her. An English letter is the same to me.' Only a lover could unleash anything more than a few bread-and-butter lines from Ashton. For him, love letters were not only conduits for the romantic declarations he needed to give and craved in return, they were also an aphrodisiac. 'Physically the tide of emotion rose in me and I was stiff with anticipation,' he confessed to Dick Beard, describing the effect of seeing his handwriting on an envelope. Ashton's marginalia in his letter of 20 January promised copies of Shakespeare's *Sonnets* and Plato's *Symposium*, as well as Gertrude Stein's *Everybody's Autobiography of Alice B. Toklas*. Although resorting to clichés of homosexual courtship, he now realized that the only way to seduce Beard was to solicit his admiration. Stein's avowal of Ashton's genius would provide interim evidence until the time came when he could prove it himself.

Despite the difficult rehearsals, Ashton's production of *Manon*, the new opera company's second venture at Covent Garden, was acclaimed as both musical and professional, although, as in *The Fairy Queen*, the singing was considered deficient. 'All the minors sang louder than the principals,' wrote Philip Hope-Wallace, adding that Virginia McWatters, the 'pretty and vivacious little soprano from America, was just not big enough to get the pathos across'. But praise for Ashton's achievement was inadequate recompense. 'Fred resented the fact that suddenly he wasn't asked to do ballets,' said Alexander Grant. And, although he did not confess the cause in his next letter to Dick Beard, Ashton was in a severe depression over the success Massine was currently enjoying at Covent Garden. Massine had been touring England with a doomed production of *A Bullet in the Ballet* when David Webster asked him to stage two of his early successes for the company, *Le Tricorne* and *La Boutique Fantasque*. Having had designs on the Royal Opera House after the war, Massine needed little persuasion. The acquisition of his two ballets, combined with his guest appearance in both, was considered a landmark in the history of British ballet. 'Massine brought something to the Opera House which a few years later Maria Callas was also to bring – if he was a dancer he was also a Presence, a reminder and an embodiment of the possibilities and the highest aspirations of his art.' His influence upon the English dancers was strikingly evident: the corps de ballet were infused with life and rhythm, in contrast to their all too frequent apathy. It was hardly surprising that Ashton felt overshadowed. His spirits were further cast down by the sudden death from a brain tumour of Pearl Argyle, compounded by one of the worst winters on record.

17 February 1947
Faringdon House, Berks

Dearest Dick

You have been constantly – as always – in my thoughts, but it has been so terribly cold in London that it has congealed my thoughts and my mind, almost my feelings and the only warmth seems to radiate from you, but is that strictly true? No, better the thought of you, for your letters are cold and reserved, but please realize that *I expect nothing* and encourage me. It is the only way to set me writing and at this distance letters must be warmly written for they are apt to chill on the way as they speed across frozen seas from you to me – or is the cold in my mind? and is it because I am now lying in a four poster bed in a warm well run and comfortable house with heating – imagine?! and wonderful food and drink, for my host is rich and I assure you that there is nothing nicer in the world than the well run country houses of the aristocracy in England – even now crippled though they are in all ways, the atmosphere is charming, the conversation brilliant (depending on the house) but always a tradition of good living and civilization and a true understanding of the arts of life. I pine if this the best of English life will vanish like everything else in this poor benighted Isle. I am wallowing in creature comforts, for London has been cruel, spartan and relentless. I complain of nothing usually (but bad artistry) but cold is my most unfavourite element so I need your warmth my beloved, send it to me enclosed in an envelope – soon – or my heart will get frosty and cold. 'Manon' I don't know if I told you was a success – because of me, many people said, which pleased me. Would you have felt proud for me? But I think I tackled my problem well and my gambling scene gets much applause. Miss McWatters whom I like because she is American like you, is delighted with me, but why do I tell you all this? Do I need to impress you? I must think I do for I am not boastful. I am only relieved that I conquered my problem and must tell you of it. Tricorne is a great success for the company and Massine, the corps are inspired by him and never danced better, the decor is still wonderful – most wonderful and the music too. The ballet I find tedious after repeated seeing except for the corps numbers and his great dance . . . I am resting now, they have been plugging me too hard at the Garden and I feel the need for new impressions and to restore my mind afresh . . . Dick please realize that I work daily on Webster to get you over and if you come shall we meet? Or shall we write only? I fear you would not like my appearance, I cannot be looked into too closely. Nora was shocked by my appearance, how much more so will you be? I cannot wait for the picture that you are sending me. I will carry it everywhere and look at it continually, speak to you, look at it in lovely places, because you will make them more beautiful and in ugly places because your image being there will mitigate the horror – so you see what a necessity it is for me. Please hasten it to me – don't forget my need. How pleased I am that you work hard. She [Margaret Craske] will give you a sense of line which is the most important thing in a dancer, for it is line that gives the lyrical note that drugs the spectator. I am getting sleepy . . .

Ashton's professional insecurity was seeping into his private life. His letters to Brian Shaw, who continued to see him on weekend leaves, beg for devotion and promises of fidelity, despite his own double-standards. Although hardly monogamous himself, Shaw wrote to quell his fears. 'How dare you get any ideas about someone else, I don't want anyone else and there is no likely hood [*sic*] of even seeing anyone down in this dead hole. So you may set your troubled mind at rest, *for good*.' Artistic success had always helped to sustain Ashton's emotional self-esteem, 'For the choreographer in me has absorbed the person and without my work I am as nothing.' So, when his supremacy in the field was threatened, as it was by Helpmann and now Massine, Ashton felt bruised and affronted. Once more, de Valois bore the brunt of his hostility. Towards the end of the war, they had begun to argue over the idea of using guest choreographers at Covent Garden, and one of their confrontations led to an acrimonious exchange.

[undated]

My dear Fred

Your letter is rather what I expected after the interview I had on Saturday. I think that you must see the wisdom of dividing the possibility of guest choreographers into two divisions:

a) Those who are not established – but show abilities that are as much our business to develop, as others made it their business to develop our work in the beginning. These artists should be trusted with one production only – and no further surety of work guaranteed.

b) Those who are already famous, and must eventually visit us *for a period of time* in which they should be given free scope – and 2 or 3 consecutive productions at least offered to them.

In the first category I place for the moment Tudor &, in a smaller degree, Howard. In the second such artists as Nijinska, Massine & possibly Jooss. The war makes the second type of producer, at present, rather out of the question. When the time comes to approach them – surely you realise that it will mean the standing down for some time of one of the two resident choreographers. Needless to say, as the director of the ballet, but 2nd choreographer, it would be my wish & right to step out temporarily.

There is very little done – except in the completely internal policy of the theatre – without everything you say [supported?] by me. But I feel that it is inevitable that I should have the last word over a young choreographer – as it has something to do with the fundamental policy of the theatre. If a mistake is made, the blame will naturally fall on me.

I do not understand your present fears. You are completely established. Your argument that you protest because of 'standard' hardly coincides with your request, or rather suggestion that you and this young choreographer [identity unknown] should change over companies for a year. Indeed I can't take such a remark seriously – if you mean it, it would appear that you have very little concern for the welfare of the ballet. This I cannot & will not believe of you.

As I explained to you on Saturday, the opera was submitted in all good faith, and *not in place* of a ballet production, but as a extra scope for your choreographic abilities . . . I did not press the point as you persisted in misunderstanding the situation . . . Will you, after reading this letter, please come & see me? There is so much that one cannot say in a letter. This is only a reply to yours . . .
Yrs
Ninny

Ashton's hostility towards de Valois' invitation to Massine was entirely self-obsessed: once again, he chose to ignore the fact that she was acting only in the company's best interest.

It was necessary. I did it for the men who were madly weak after the war. It wasn't as if I'd brought in some little Englishman; I brought in a distinguished choreographer from the last generation. Fred wasn't interested in the men, he never was. He was principally a woman's choreographer. I knew the girls were alright with Fred; I was worried about the boys. Massine did the men a lot of good, and if anyone benefited it was Alexander Grant: I did it for him as much as anything. Massine was on to him at once and when Grant tackled Fred's ballets afterwards, he was a different person. That's what I was working on. I knew Fred would like him as a character dancer.

Alexander Grant's success in Massine's work only exacerbated Ashton's grievance. He had picked out the sixteen-year-old dancer himself, twinning him with Donald Britton in the Popular Song duo in *Façade* after spotting them leaning together against the barre during class. In *Les Sirènes*, apart from using Grant as one of his two henchmen, Ashton cast him as a child who jumps through a hoop. It was the sort of eye-catching moment that he had given Michael Somes in *Les Patineurs*, and was just as prescient: what was to become one of the most important relationships in Ashton's life was now in its nascent stage.

There was more to Massine's involvement with the company than his galvanizing influence on the men. Sensing (correctly) that Ashton's immediate interest lay in abstract ballet, which she considered 'a bore', de Valois was anxious to extend the range of her company's repertory. Although she paid tribute to its 'completely satisfying' neoclassicism, she did not consider *Symphonic Variations* to be a masterpiece. 'People scream at me, but it has never been my idea of an Ashton work. It doesn't stress his individuality.' She was not likely, therefore, to appreciate Balanchine's influence on this and on Ashton's two subsequent plotless ballets, *Valses nobles et sentimentales* and *Scènes de ballet*. Although de Valois was always absurdly prejudiced against America's achievements in dance – 'They're not demi-caractère dancers as we are; the English school has a wonderful sense of *variety*' – she was astute in realizing that Massine would resuscitate the character element of dancing, which she valued so highly, and on which she no longer had time to concentrate herself. While Ashton still retained strong feelings of admiration and obligation towards Massine, a sense of personal grievance got the better of his finer feelings. Purely out of pique, he began casting his net beyond the confines of the company. 'I did many things,' he said. 'I went to America . . . I went anywhere that asked me.'

Glyndebourne asked first. When the resident producer, Carl Ebert, refused to stage Benjamin Britten's new opera, *Albert Herring*, because he did not like Eric Crozier's libretto, Ashton agreed to step in. He had taken an instant liking to Britten when William Walton invited them both to dinner in the spring of 1938. 'Is this *really* your adorable self?' Ashton wrote soon afterwards on a Bronzino postcard, referring to the resemblance Britten bore to curly-haired Don Garcia de Medici, a painting of whom he had seen at the Ashmolean Museum in Oxford. Shortly before the war, they had discussed the idea of a ballet using the 'Frank Bridge Variations'; after his release, from the RAF, Ashton wrote to 'Beloved Ben', promising 'definitely' to schedule *Les Illuminations* for forthcoming production. 'You know my dream is to work with you and more than ever now.' *Albert Herring* came at a particularly opportune moment; not only occupying Ashton artistically, but also allowing him to leave London for a month while renovations were carried out on his new house. Life was starting to improve: summer had arrived, which, to Ashton, meant the imminent arrival in London of Dick Beard.

4 May 1947

Dearest Dick

Yes I am a pig dog, but somehow I felt discouraged – but surely you are right, it was the cold. Today was hot and I have just come in from a walk round the square which is a mass of lilacs white and mauve and I can never smell lilac now without thinking of the most beautiful boy I know, or don't know.* But you were there in spirit and I thought how lovely it would have been if we could have been silently walking together in perfect communion of spirit. I have been very unsettled lately. I had to leave my other house which was so lovely, situated on the edge of a lovely property in Regents Park and the only place I could find was a derelict 18th century house in Knightsbridge. So I set myself the superhuman task in this day and age in England to get it put right. What a task! I would rather do ten ballets and how exhausting. There was no water, light or gas or anything. I hope it will be tolerable by the time you get here, but it has been very unsettling getting out of that place and into this junk-hole surrounded by workmen in every room all day, who do no work . . . The ballet have started on rep again having done almost non-stop 'Sleeping Beauty' Margot dancing like an inspired beauty. We started with 'Symphonic Variations' which again had the most fantastic success and the best press I have ever had for a ballet, wonderful. I was happy – you would have been too I'm sure for your old boy. I do wish you could see it, but of course there is the possibility that you would not like it. For if you don't like my work there is nothing to like in me . . . unlike you who walk God-like in the Lilac Garden while all heads turn to admire how lovely you are.

Please write to me. I shall be so busy and longing for letters from you. You don't know what a state the sight of your writing puts me in . . . That promised picture never arrived. I have waited long for it, impatiently. Work well and think of me sometimes a little tenderly. Think of Mr. Ashton who is obsessed with Mr. Beard.

Love from Freddie

The pastoral surroundings of Glyndebourne should have provided a welcome escape from intractable builders, dust and rubble, but this turned out to be a very fraught few weeks for Ashton. John Christie, the eccentric connoisseur, who, in 1934, had added a theatre to his country house in Sussex on the South Downs, had not liked *The Rape of Lucretia*. It had been Britten's first project for the Glyndebourne English Opera Company, staged the previous year, and Christie was greatly out of pocket from its tour. He liked Britten's simple country fable even less. 'He hated Ben's music and said so out loud,' said John Piper, *Albert Herring*'s

---

*Dick Beard performed the second male role in Tudor's *Lilac Garden*: 'Fred's fantasy of our walking together through a lilac garden actually happened when he later took me to the location that had inspired Tudor.'

designer. 'He couldn't bear the work and claimed they'd only got it because they couldn't get back to their German connections. He was *beastly* to Ben; they were absolutely at loggerheads.'*

'When Britten fell out with Glyndebourne, I was in on it,' said Ashton. 'Ben wouldn't speak to Christie or allow him inside his own theatre. We weren't allowed to stay at Glyndebourne or go into the bar. The moment the rehearsal was over, we got into a bus and went to a house on the cliff somewhere. We weren't allowed to have any contact with anybody except Kathleen Ferrier [performing there in *Orfeo*]. Christie used to come up to me and say, "What's happening?" And I'd say, "I'll smuggle you in." If Ben had known he was in there he'd have stopped the whole thing. Frightfully small-minded. I don't know what it was all about.' Donald Mitchell believes that Ashton was exaggerating. Britten, he said, was 'preternaturally polite' by nature and John Christie was not the type of man to be kept out of his own theatre. But Joan Cross, who was there at the time performing a superb Lady Billows, insists that it was 'all true', although she believes they did not stay at Glyndebourne because 'the *Orfeo* crowd' were occupying the house. Compounding the tension was criticism of Ashton's interpretation of the libretto by Britten and Crozier. 'We did the prologue,' said Joan Cross, 'and obviously got it all wrong as Ben and Eric sat there getting lower and lower in their seats and looking very miserable about it.'

Albert Herring is a comedy set in a Suffolk village – a prim English rite of spring – in which the timorous hero, a grocer's son, is elected by the local dowager, Lady Billows, as May King of the Loxford pageant. During the celebrations, Albert's friends lace his lemonade with rum and he spends the night carousing in the countryside, released at last from maternal constraints and, probably, from his virginity too. Instinctively drawn to the opera's homely Suffolk setting and especially to its mother-dominated hero, Ashton seemed ideally suited to direct *Albert Herring*. ('I love him,' he later told Britten, '& I was pleased with my production.') Not only did he enjoy the story, but he was unable to resist performing himself, making the initial rehearsals very amusing for the cast, most of whom took his side and almost mutinied when, in response to Britten and Crozier's opposition, he offered to resign. The collaborators wanted the comedy to be played 'straight', but Ashton's approach verged on caricature, with jokey preparations of the work resulting in near-farce on stage – as in the case of the later Berners ballets. Their disapproval was a shock to him and severely shook his confidence, even though he suspected jealousy on the part of Crozier, who had wanted to direct *Albert*

---

*It was outrage at Christie's bullishness, coupled with appreciation of the working conditions he provided, that led Britten, Peter Pears and Eric Crozier to form their own opera group at Aldeburgh.

Herring himself. 'Eric was very hurt and upset and so Fred had a lot of problems with that. He used to talk about "Eric's disappointment",' said Colin Graham, who later produced the opera. Joan Cross remembers how downcast Ashton was at the time. 'It must have offended Fred very much indeed. We were all staying at a farm house on the coast and one night I was just going to bed when Fred came into the room and said, "I *am* a good producer, aren't I?" He spotted a box of my chocolates and sat down and went through the lot. Luckily I was able to be a comfort to him.'

Extravagantly affectionate towards each other and sharing a similar sense of humour, Ashton and Cross became friends for life. 'They admired and fed off each other. It was a perfect marriage of director and star.' Ashton loved Cross's portrayal of Lady Billows ('Darling, you're exactly like my Aunt Millie,' he told her), which she made a composite of Lady Bracknell, Lilian Baylis and her own Suffolk-based mother, 'always caught up in village bazaars, committees and flower shows'. Ashton found later interpretations to be over-grand, including Patricia Johnson's in Peter Hall's 1985 Glyndebourne production – 'Lady Billows behaved like the Duchesse de Gramont' – although he considered Hall's Albert Herring (John Graham Hall) to be much better than Peter Pears, whom he never liked in the role. Colin Graham agrees that Pears gave 'a mawkish performance', but says that Ashton could have done little to improve it. 'It would have been difficult for Fred to criticize Peter in rehearsal, it was always a case of Ben and Peter against the rest of the world.' Ashton disliked Pears, believing him to be an amateur and an opportunist, but kept it to himself. Nancy Evans – on whom Crozier, her future husband, based the character of Nancy – recalled an entertaining evening at their digs, when Britten played snatches from *Swan Lake* on the piano, and Pears and Ashton trotted through the Little Cygnets' dance. Britten was also 'a great giggler'; but, although Ashton liked and revered the composer, he tried to avoid seeing too much of him and Pears during the staging of *Albert Herring*. 'He found their little empire very difficult to take,' says Myfanwy Piper. 'Walking through Glyndebourne garden, Peter could be heard to say things like, "Have you seen Mozart?" Fred didn't want to get into the Ben/Peter self-supportive situation.'

Despite the hostilities at Glyndebourne that summer, once Ashton had capitulated and toned down the burlesque, he produced what Britten considered to be the definitive *Albert Herring*. 'Those of us who subsequently did it were expected to reproduce Fred's version,' remarked Graham. Other friends and colleagues of Britten's agree that Ashton's was a classic production. 'Never to have been surpassed.' '*Wonderfully* funny with a precise sense of period I've missed with other stagings.' There were a few dissenting voices among the critics, *The Times* judging the piece to be 'a charade', whose music failed to engage the heart. For Ashton, it had far more significance than he was aware of at the time, sowing the seed of his masterwork, *La Fille mal gardée* (1960). Like the ballet, *Albert Herring* is a pastoral French tale* translated into a Suffolk setting, and with the same charm, sexual innocence, gentle humour and commitment to everyday life. Just as Britten distilled music out of children playing ball, street-corner whistling and an attack of the hiccups, so Ashton went on to choreograph the ordinary – from hens scratching in the yard to farm labourers returning from a day in the fields. *Albert Herring* showed Ashton how to make a virtue of simple subject matter, giving him the confidence to develop his own demotic style. As Ninette de Valois shrewdly noted, 'It did Fred good to do things elsewhere.'

There was, in addition, a more immediate, tangible gain for Ashton. With his fee for *Albert Herring*, he bought an Aubusson rug – 'large enough for Versailles' – which covered his new drawing-room floor from wall to wall. Number 25 Yeoman's Row was, like Wharton Street, a congenial, villagey neighbourhood: Edith Russell-Roberts was minutes away in Lennox Gardens Mews; Bunny Roger, with whom Ashton had stayed for two months while the house was being completed, was in Walton Street; Cecil Beaton in Pelham Place; and living among the residents in the terrace itself was Oliver Messel. Ashton had taken the cottage for a negligible rent, on condition that he would move out at short notice. He devised the décor – described by one friend as 'very John Fowler in the best sense' – and chose burgundy-striped wallpaper for the hall and stairs because it reminded him of Covent Garden. Above the formal drawing room, furnished with Alice's Regency antiques, was Ashton's small, red-papered study, crammed with his books and records, prints, and statuettes of Pavlova and Taglioni. There were two bedrooms, one of which was reserved for Brian Shaw and, in his absence that summer, for Dick Beard. Through Bunny Roger's 'permanent called Cora', Ashton found his first housekeeper, Mrs Lloyd, a white-haired, plumpish woman, who always wore blue. Single-minded and 'very superior-looking', according to Roger, 'she could have been the wife of a rich iron-monger'. At Ashton's invitation, Mrs Lloyd and Cora frequently watched his ballets at Covent Garden. 'You'd see these two charladies sitting frightfully grandly in his box while we all squashed into the stalls.' Ashton never called her anything but Mrs Lloyd and kissed her on the cheek every night before he went to bed. He grew to dote on her, to the extent that his friends thought he might marry her. 'At every meal Fred had her sitting opposite him at the head of the table, which was very tedious and inhibiting for us,' said Billy Chappell. But Ashton maintained that it never occurred to Mrs Lloyd to worry about 'any goings on'. Which was just as well.

*Maupassant's 'Le Rosier de Madame Husson'.

On 9 July 1947, Ashton met Dick Beard and Nora Kaye at Southampton docks. Even though Beard had been led to expect he would be staying in a hotel, 'this was all swept aside and I found myself moved directly into Fred's house without any say in the matter'. It was not a propitious start. On their first day in London, Ashton took the American dancers to lunch with Terence Rattigan at his sparsely elegant Albany rooms. The four sat formally in the dining room, waited on by a white-gloved manservant, and Beard remembers 'cringing with embarrassment' as he realized he should have put his salad in the crescent-shaped side-dish rather than on his plate. Pygmalion-like, Ashton soon began to instruct him in social graces, including how to eat an artichoke, elaborately 'making an orgasm of it' by slowly peeling off each leaf until he reached the climax of the heart. Keen to parade his friends before Beard, and vice versa, he laid on a hectic social round, which did not have quite the effect he intended.

> Don't misunderstand me, I was very impressed. It's just that there was never a minute as we were rushed into the circle: Rattigan, Helpmann–Benthall, Chappell, Beaton, Britten–Pears, Gielgud. Looking back, it was simply Fred trying to entertain us, and Nora absolutely adored it, but there was no chance to establish a rapport with Fred – only to see him performing all the time. 'He seems self-centred, vain, conceited', I wrote in my diary. None of the things I had expected from his letters.

It was hard for Beard to share Ashton's enthusiasm for his work, as the company was not performing and he was unable to see any of the ballets; on top of which, he was given no independence or opportunity to see the friends he had made in London the previous year. 'Instead I felt manipulated and constantly hauled around on show. I didn't like it and I began to fight back.' Beard and Ashton were also prevented from getting to know each other by the ever-present company of Nora Kaye. Having claimed she was reasonably content with the situation – 'but must it be Tchaikowsky and Von Meck? Can't it have perhaps a bit of the flavor of Shaw and Mrs Pat Campbell – far more amusing' – her reserve broke down one night when all three were sharing a taxi and she confronted Ashton with a wild declaration of her feelings. 'Fred was very good with her; kind, gentle and chiding, although he knew I was sitting there listening to this whole thing. She'd been drinking a bit and became absolutely hysterical, shouting, "I love you, I love you." It was rather embarrassing as Nora was always in such control of herself. Funnily enough, Fred and

I never referred to it. I've since wondered how sincere he was towards her; whether he simply *used* her obsessive crush to advance his own.'

On 14 July, a date Ashton commemorated as 'France's day of freedom and mine of enslavement to beauty', he and Beard made love for the first time. Although the physical side of the relationship was less appealing to Beard than it was to Ashton ('I was used to people with glorious bodies'), his good manners, respect and affection made it natural for him to acquiesce. Two days later, Ashton took Dick Beard to Paris, with Nora, naturally, in tow. Hans Wild, on an assignment for *Life* magazine, met them at the station and drove them to the Hotel de la Trémouille, where Margot Fonteyn was staying. Devastated by the recent collapse of her relationship with Constant Lambert, and feeling she had reached a stalemate in her career, Fonteyn had persuaded de Valois to give her a few weeks' sabbatical leave. Classes with Boris Kniaseff, 'exactly the teacher I needed at that time', were helping to restore her confidence, but the recklessly passionate affair she had begun with Roland Petit provided the emotional and physical replenishment she sought. When Constant Lambert fell in love with the painter Isabel Delmer, whom he married in October of that year, Fonteyn, according to Ashton, 'just cut out the whole episode. Sewed herself up and became virginal again.' She never again acknowledged the affair, whereas she admitted to a deep but harmless crush on Petit, describing his attempts to persuade her to leave the restricting conditions of Sadler's Wells to dance 'new, exciting ballets'.

Fonteyn's defection greatly exacerbated Ashton's sense of betrayal. 'Fred wanted Margot on tap,' said Alexander Grant, 'to create when he wanted to.' He understood her wish to increase her range, but was very concerned, when she went on to perform in Petit's ballets, that the cabaret-like veneer of his work might in some way tarnish her restrained classicism. 'I was more afraid of that than of his smartening her up in a boulevard way.' Petit introduced Fonteyn to the bell-shaped dresses of Dior's New Look and encouraged her to have her slightly bulbous nose resculpted. 'She came back with a *disaster*,' said Ashton, 'and had to have it done again by the surgeon [Sir Archibald McIndoe] who did all the pilots.' Finding himself supplanted as 'the person whom [she] loved most and depended on most' was more hurtful for Ashton than Fonteyn realized at the time. (Later, in barely disguised revenge, he was to make her feel equally jealous and slighted.) But, for the time being, in love in Paris and reunited with Fonteyn, who 'managed to simplify everything into "dancers on a summer holiday,"' Ashton soon forgot his grievances. The friends laughed 'from morning to night through idiotic adventures', despite the fact that within a couple of days of their arrival Ashton had faced a minor setback with Dick Beard. Determined to escape – 'to be free at last from all those extravagant declarations which I hadn't yet learnt to digest' – Beard had bolted to Vichy for the weekend where Roy Tobias, a lover 'before, during and after Fred', was dancing with the Grands Ballets de Monte Carlo.

When I returned, Nora became openly difficult and demanding. She had brought me as a gift for Fred, and I wasn't behaving according to plan. It was quite the contrary with Fred, who was delighted to have me back and was charming. Things began to ease. Margot helped enormously; she was so sweet and attractive and seemed to grasp the situation immediately. She didn't mind who Fred was with, she just wanted him to be happy.

Ashton and Beard began to talk at last, 'about things beyond social trivia. He took me to the Luxembourg Gardens which he loved; showed me the hotel nearby where he stayed when he worked with Ida Rubinstein; and the church of Sainte-Clotilde where César Franck had been organist.' Ashton took charge of the four of them, designating 'Rich Days' spent on the Right Bank, with meals at the Relais Plaza, and 'Poor Days' at Left Bank bistros and street fairs in Pigalle. They went to a Bal Musette – 'very Toulouse Lautrec with a band on a balcony high above the room' – where Ashton danced with Beard, swooning with delight like a nineteenth-century mistress. Others joined their group: an American diplomat, who danced with them all, but finished up with Nora; and a hard-drinking dancer, Dick Reed, who saw the situation between Ashton and Beard, and tried to break it up, sitting outside their hotel room all night. 'Fred loved this sort of thing: it made our relationship more romantic for him and therefore more real.' Balanchine was, at the time, in charge of the Paris Opera Ballet, and took Ashton and Beard out for dinner one night to the Cloche d'Or. Although relations between the two choreographers were never easy, on this occasion they were relaxed and jokey with each other. Things would have been different, however, had Balanchine foreseen Ashton's irreverent behaviour a few days later during a performance of *Apollo*. It was the sight of Michel Renault's brown body make-up spreading itself over the white tunic of Maria Tallchief as Terpsichore that made Ashton lean across and loudly hiss a scatological quip, which left them doubled over in paroxysms of stifled giggles. (As if in retaliation, Balanchine would repeat a similar discourtesy two years later, during an evening of the English ballet in New York.)

On 23 July, the quartet of friends went to the seaside, staying in Villers-sur-Mer on the Normandy coast. They rented bicycles and cycled around Trouville in homage to Ouida and Proust, whose *A la Recherche du temps perdu* Beard and Kaye were then reading in preparation for a Tudor ballet (never completed). 'As we arrived in Cabourg, Fred said,

"*This* was Balbec," but he was nasty about Tudor, telling us *he* was the one who should be doing the ballet, as only he understands the manners of the period.' While they were by the coast, Beard and Ashton went for long walks. 'We talked a great deal and I remember him speaking of *Symphonic Variations* as if it were a new beginning for him.' From Villers, Ashton sent a letter to David Webster about the possibility of Beard joining the company and enclosed the dancer's application. They returned to London at the end of the month and, shortly afterwards, Nora went back to New York, leaving Beard with Ashton in Yeoman's Row.

Days passed pleasantly enough – particularly a summery Sunday spent in Datchet with Edith, walking through the fields to Eton – but Beard noted in his diary, 'I am not right with Fred.' The main problem was the dancer's concern about his career. 'Fred wouldn't get round to *doing* anything and that made me very impatient and mean.' Dilatoriness on Ashton's part was compounded by the company's policy in hiring only Commonwealth subjects. De Valois had been formally introduced to Beard; but, although she invited him to take class with the company, she had not asked to see him dance. She was implacably against any form of sexual favouritism. 'Madam was so hot against homosexuals that Fred said she was unbearable,' remarked Myfanwy Piper. 'She never understood male love.' Ashton frequently commented that 'Ninette had absolutely no grasp of male glamour' – a criticism disproved years later by her ardent championship of Nureyev. To Beard, it all seemed much too casual. 'Nora had given me the impression that getting into the company wouldn't be a problem. But there I was with a very limited time before the new ABT season began, and nothing seemed to happen. It was frustrating for me and I took it out on Fred, often unfairly I'm sure.'

Among all the friends who observed the tensions, Sophie showed the most concern. Suspecting opportunism on Beard's part, and anxious to prevent Ashton from being hurt, she was rudely abrupt to the dancer whenever she saw him. 'She wanted Fred to herself and didn't want me in the room: "I don't want to talk in front of *him*," she said.' Naturally, Brian Shaw was even more jealous. Having enjoyed playing a devoted, if unfaithful, wife – scolding Ashton for ironing an unlaundered shirt, and taking Ashton's dirty clothes home for his own mother to wash – he now found himself in the position of scores of English soldiers cuckolded in their absence by handsome, healthy American GIs.

It's my turn to be hurt. God knows I seem to have done the same to you often enough. What is there between you and this American . . . If you really do love him, I'd rather you told me. I couldn't bear going on with it if you were . . .

But Ashton was remorseless about prolonging his affair with Beard, regardless of the hurt he was causing. On one of his weekend leaves, Shaw, accompanied by his mother, turned up at Yeoman's Row to find Dick Beard installed there. He was pleasant and friendly enough to Beard, but on subsequent occasions when the two dancers met, Shaw was so surly that Ashton, obviously relishing the situation, urged him to speak to Beard. From his digs in Leeds, Shaw wrote a heart-rending letter to his 'Most Treasured Poscection'.

> I can't even spell your title correctly . . . I aint no good for nothing, am I? . . . Fred, I think maybe I love you more & more, & when I think of Dick Beard I almost lose my grip. Tell me Fred, do you love him, or have you, maybe lost something of what you had for me? Tell me, & please be truthful. I know that being apart can make a difference, but if you want to have some-one else, tell me. This is a great worry to me, & also I know theres nothing wonderful or attractive about me, & so many of your friends have everything to help them gain these objectives. Beard was able to mix amongst people who you knew & go where I could never be taken, lest I embarres you or everyone. He's gay & has everything that goes to make one attractive. Enough. I'm getting no where, only depressing myself more & more . . .

As his next ballet would obliquely suggest, Ashton intended two-timing for as long as he could get away with it. When he left for a provincial tour, Beard went back to France to visit Roy Tobias, feeling that, despite the constant 'telephoning, wiring and writing' about his joining the company, he had no option but to return to Ballet Theatre. Ashton wrote to him in despair. Without mentioning Somes's name, he relates a story, as rhetorical as a fairy tale, of how his own heart had once been 'turned to stone'.

> 26 August 1947
> North British Hotel, Edinburgh
>
> Dearest Beloved Dickie
>
> When driving yesterday from Manchester to Edinburgh we stopped by a mountain stream. As I stooped to bathe my face I saw at my feet a heart – of stone. I picked it out of the clear water and thought, is this a portent of good or bad. Is it a heart of stone at my feet, an unfeeling heart cooled by many waters? Or is it a reflection of myself. Your letter moved me *deeply*, to tears and plunged me into an absorbed mood from which I cannot stir myself. I have spent 2 days in my room seeing no one and going only to the theatre at

night and very unhappy. I will not, no never, try to justify myself in your eyes. But I can only say that you did not look deeply enough into my heart or you would have found more than you did. I will tell you dearest Dick that I had a most sensitive heart, that has suffered such anguish as I hope you will never know. I laid that heart at somebody's feet with all the ardour, the faith, the fullness of passion, in fact my being was my heart and was inhabited only by one person. It was trampled, mutilated, distorted and crushed, with each wound and each thrust my heart shrank, but I grew as a person and as an artist . . . I fell exhausted, the war came and I went, years after I returned, my heart had turned to stone. That is why I told you that story at the beginning of this letter, and that is the story of my heart. I tell you this because I have longed for someone to bring my heart to life in a happy way. Only you could have done it.

In a valedictory final paragraph, Ashton asks Beard to send him the photographs they took at Villers, offers him the use of Yeoman's Row while he is away on tour, and begs him to say if he needs money. 'If you pass through London I won't come to you, but let me speak to you on the phone.' The one thing Beard did want – a place in the company – Ashton was either unable or unwilling to provide. The dancer had been asked to join the 'second company' based at Sadler's Wells, but had refused. As things turned out, Beard's future was decided for him by a cable that arrived in Vichy. 'Ballet Theatre started rehearsals accepted your absence to replace you good luck with Decuevas and Devalois – Antony Tudor.' Apart from Ashton, the only other person who knew his whereabouts was Nora Kaye. 'It was her last big play to force me to stay with Fred whether I got into Sadler's Wells or not.' Beard never spoke to either Tudor or Kaye again.

A week later, on 17 September, Beard returned to Yeoman's Row to find Mrs Lloyd waiting for him. She told him to take a taxi immediately to Sadler's Wells, where Ashton was working on his new ballet. 'And remember,' she said, 'it's his birthday.' When Beard walked into the studio, Ashton stopped the rehearsal. 'A dead silent room of dancers stood waiting to see what would happen next. We went towards each other and Fred said, "I have made a ballet for you. About us. And I want you to see it." "Happy Birthday," I replied and then we sat with our backs to the mirror and watched "my ballet". From then on we were perfect together. I had seen the work and it was good. Everything else fell into place. When Fred talked about his work, his art, the art of dancing, there was no pose or affectation. There seemed no end of things to say. These were the great days of our relationship.'

CHAPTER THIRTEEN

MR A OBSESSED WITH MR B

1947–1950

Ashton admitted that *Valses nobles et sentimentales* was 'suggested by actual people and events', but he never revealed anything more, and very few knew about his secret muse. 'It is . . . supposedly about nothing, but you and I know differently,' he wrote to Dick Beard. 'I love your ballet, because it is yours and because I owe so much to it and because I think it has some of the essence of your beauty in it . . . I love to watch it because I share it with you.' Behind each dreamy, photogenic attitude of the five boys lies the image of Beard. Whether sitting with a profile fetchingly tilted, or standing contemplatively, with one leg resting across the other, they faithfully replicate Hans Wild's studies of the dancer and yet remain resonant of Ashton's own style. Stillness, as in *Symphonic Variations*, is the recurring motif; but here it is mainly the prerogative of the male dancers, whose narcissistic poses have the studied elegance and veiled erotic charge of fashion plates. The ballet is a reworking of *Valentine's Eve*, which Ashton made in 1935 to the same set of waltzes by Ravel. Although this early piece is just as autobiographical, circumstances had changed in Ashton's favour; rather than appearing in what amounted to a self-parody of a romantic suitor thwarted by unrequited love, Ashton altered the gender of the leading dancer, casting a young girl (Anne Heaton) in a role which alluded to his own life at the time.

> Two (boys) were both attracted by the same girl, at least she was always present in their thoughts, even when they were dancing with other girls. At the end she returned to them after an absence, and I was left in doubt as to which of them, if either, she would eventually choose.

The action, such as it is, is far more elusive than Richard Buckle's summary suggests. Relationships and rivalries are implied, never defined;

feelings, no more than innuendoes. Although Ashton can only have read about the ballet for which Ravel orchestrated his waltzes, *Adelaide, ou le Langage des fleurs*, its perfumed plot and over-stated symbolism filtered into *Valentine's Eve*; whereas *Valses nobles et sentimentales* is an abstract work, with the 'sensualité un peu sèche' of the score itself. The ballets were visually very similar, with Sophie Fedorovitch again using rose and burgundy colours, gauze screens, and shadows of potted plants stylishly evoking a ballroom or conservatory. The girls, who could be débutantes, wear white gloves and beribboned tulle gowns, deliberately recalling Bérard's designs for *Cotillon*. The three principals of Balanchine's ballet were baby ballerinas aged between twelve and sixteen, and Ashton, who wanted to recapture a similarly youthful, evanescent quality, created his work on dancers in their teens – members of the newly formed Sadler's Wells Theatre Ballet, one of whom was the eighteen-year-old Kenneth MacMillan. *Valses nobles* is a ballet which, like Balanchine's, exudes atmosphere, style and period (Ashton 'adored' *Cotillon*, rating it higher than the later, pristine masterpieces). Other influences, Nijinska and Pavlova, are behind the girls' lush épaulement, drifting arms and pliant torsos. The abandoned, frilly flourish with which a port de bras suddenly unfurls is one of Pavlova's insignia encoded in the ballet as part of a private dialogue with Beard. (He was equally smitten by the ballerina – 'To begin with, Pavlova was all Fred and I had in common' – and collected her films, pictures and books.)

Valses nobles et sentimentales, as Ashton told his dancers, is 'just a party'. The mood shifts, in tune with the waltzes, between joy and wistfulness, but never, as in *Cotillon*, is the gaiety undercut by a sense of impending doom. Balanchine 'evokes a pretty world and undermines it at the same time', but Ashton, although he leaves the conclusion open-ended, with the ballerina passed in arching leaps from one suitor to the other, did not feel that his nostalgic re-creation of youthful chic was naive or anachronistic. Asked to define the potency of *Valses nobles*, he said, 'Just poetry, my dear. Everyone spits on it now, but all the great ballets have poetry in them: it's the one thing ballet can express really well.'

Like *Cotillon*, which Balanchine rehearsed for the last time in 1940, *Valses nobles* disappeared for several decades until the late 1980s, when, within a year of each other, both works were recovered and restaged. Neither has stood up well to time, their nuances concealed by over-emphatic performances. '*Valses nobles* was such a gentle ballet,' said Anne Heaton, 'flirty and elegant and underdanced. But [in the 1987 restaging] they just bashed away at it, missing everything that one thought it was about.' Arlene Croce has pointed out how Balanchine, believing that the poetic 1930s had perished in the war, resurrected *Cotillon* as *La Sonnambula* (1946), before refurbishing it once more as *La Valse* (1951). Having himself recycled *Valentine's Eve* in 1947, Ashton went on to incorporate elements from *Valses nobles* (the circular 'reaping' step, for instance) into his own *La Valse* (1958). Whether or not he was consciously retreading the same ground, Ashton was profoundly influenced by Balanchine in these post-war years.* Lincoln Kirstein maintained that there was 'a mutual contempt' between the two choreographers, but this may be too inflammatory. Ashton's feelings towards Balanchine were much more equivocal (reminding Moira Shearer of Mark Antony's famous speech of denigration, then eulogy, in *Julius Caesar*, 'but in reverse'). He admired Balanchine more than any other choreographer after Nijinska, but resented his condescension: 'He was always *holding forth.*' There is certainly no evidence of any Ashton influence on Balanchine's work, although it has been noted that he tended to avoid any ballets for which Ashton had already used the score. It could have been a performance of *Valses nobles*, playing at Sadler's Wells in April 1950 when Balanchine was in London mounting *Ballet Imperial*, that prompted the choreographer to use the score himself as a prelude to *La Valse*, created a year later.

Valses nobles was popular with audiences (it was given 101 performances in its first two years), but it was not a critical success. It takes more than one viewing to detect the subtleties behind its sugar-plum surface: what may seem, at first, to be merely 'neat pink scenery and dresses, some pretty movements, some beautiful lifts', in fact contains choreography as innovative as its score. The harmonic daring, displaced accents and dissonance, with which Ravel contrasts his plush melodies, is reflected in the ballet's combination of lyrical but forward-looking classicism. (Reviewing the revival, Alastair Macaulay noted how the pas de trois sets a compositional precedent for *Monotones*, made eighteen years later.) The lack of a story or discernible theme, combined with the 'discord' of the music, proved too much for several reviewers, but Ashton was unconcerned, already planning a work that would present a far greater challenge. He was pleased with *Valses nobles et sentimentales* – 'It is poetic and charged with rich undercurrents of feeling' – as was, gratifyingly, Dick Beard. 'When I saw Fred had done something beautiful, my whole attitude changed. Just like that – in one afternoon. I was just about to leave, so we made this great regeneration, as it were.'

---

*He, too, made a point of naming ballets after their scores: *Symphonic Variations*, *Valses nobles et sentimentales* and *Scènes de ballet* (Stravinsky, 1948).

They parted that October, with Ashton promising to telephone if he had anything positive to report about a position in the company. If nothing changed, they agreed to spend a part of each year together. Beard had heard that Balanchine and Lincoln Kirstein wanted him to join their recently formed Ballet Society. 'Fred understood, but begged me to stay. I wanted to – and looking back, probably should have – but at the time, I didn't like the idea of being "kept".' Although Ashton always avoided and mocked domestic ménages among homosexuals – 'I don't like queer marriages – having to live with someone's ingrown toenails. Queerness can't be permanent: queers are tarts and mistresses, not wives' – what he craved at that time was a companion with whom to share his artistic life and to be by his side: 'Inactive, an inspirer.' 'Fred often said, "I don't want to revive my ballets, I want to do new ones for you." He would have been perfectly happy if I'd stayed there in the house and met him after rehearsals and performances. But I didn't want to do that: I was young, ambitious and I wanted a career of my own.'

Beard's return to New York generated a vital outpouring of letters from Ashton who, despite being denied the dancer's physical presence, depended on the creative complicity they had established.

> I have all the time thought of what you said and carried your orders to me in my head and tried to carry them out . . . I think that you should not have been capricious with me and written to me continually to keep me up to scratch and to infuse inspiration into me, you do it so easily. You have so apt a means of expression that I understand immediately what you want me to do. I think that it is so wonderful that you who are so beautiful want to use your beauty to make more beauty to inspire beauty and spread beauty from out of your being. It is remarkable and you are never cheap or use your gifts in a menial and bestial way. Beloved keep them for me. I have so few years to cherish them and you who have disenchanted me from being a beast will one day lift your magic and leave a husk.
>
> I have thought of you all the time as I arranged my ballet, on the way to rehearsal, during it and after. I have said I wonder if my Dick would be pleased with the old boy today. Is it good enough for him. Would you kiss me tenderly and say, 'you did well today'. I am getting to the end of it and today I went through it . . . All of it, my darling, for what it is worth, I dedicate to you with my love.

The idea for *Scènes de ballet* came to Ashton when he was in the bath one Saturday morning, listening to the weekly broadcast of gramophone records on the wireless. Hearing what seemed to him 'the most fascinating and perfect music for dancing', but having missed the announcement of the score's title and composer, Ashton telephoned the BBC, who arranged for the music to be played privately for him as there was no available English recording. *The Seven Lively Arts* had been commissioned in 1944 for a Broadway revue, with choreography by Anton Dolin; the eighteen-minute piece of music had been composed by Stravinsky in Hollywood, a fact which accounts for its sophisticated veneer. Ashton intended to comply with the composer's original conception of a plotless work, even to the point of approximately following his choreographic plan. But the dance needed a context, and he turned to his friend and neighbour Richard Buckle for ideas. Buckle came up with a scenario centred on a hero whose inner thoughts and 'associates in the journey of life' were somehow to be realized in plotless dance. The focal point of the design was to be a fantastic, proscenium-like pavilion which, 'for those who troubled to look for symbolism, was the inner theatre of the hero's mind, in sleep, solitude or death'. Aware that all this was over-elaborate and obscure, and wanting a pivotal role for Margot Fonteyn, Ashton rejected the outline, but agreed that the designer should be André Beaurepaire, whose work for Les Ballets des Champs-Elysées he had seen and admired. He was persuaded that Beaurepaire's style of 'intricate, nightmare baroque' was what was needed for *Scènes de ballet*, and Buckle, as a friend of the young painter, volunteered to act as go-between.

Although barely twenty and unschooled in technique, Beaurepaire was already a sought-after figure in artistic Paris, encouraged by Cocteau and commissioned by Boris Kochno. At the time, he was living at the top of his parents' house in Passy; his latest work was heavily influenced by Picasso, whose equal he considered himself to be. Beaurepaire's sense of fantasy and outrageously inflated ego provided Buckle with enough material for an enjoyably comic chapter of a book (*Adventures of a Ballet Critic*), but, to Ashton, faced with the task of bending the designer to his will, Beaurepaire very soon became 'tiresome and superficial'. Buckle describes his dilemma:

> Ashton was in turn confident, determined, diplomatic, despairing, plaintive and resigned to the worst . . . Doubts would suddenly assail him: was he perhaps suppressing the original conceptions of the greatest genius of the age? Should he not modify his plans to embrace some of the French designer's excesses? After all, our English ballet was in need of a little Parisian fantasy. But no, it was really too monstrous: he had *said* what he wanted and he was *not* getting it. It was Dicky's fault. He should have employed James

Bailey all along. Anyway he would refuse to see or speak to Beaurepaire ever again, either before or after the first night . . . Oh! Why couldn't he be left alone to work on his choreography undisturbed! Must he do everyone else's job besides his own? And as long as his ballet was good, who cared how awful the designs were?

Beaurepaire's décor – a perspective of arches, executed in pinky-mauve pastel on a black background – suggested 'a railway bridge or aqueduct in the Hittite or Babylonian style, but seen through the eyes of a northern pupil of the early Chirico'. Ashton liked the grandeur of the set, even though he felt it more suitable to a Greek play than to his ballet. For the apotheosis, Beaurepaire produced an additional edifice – a spiky screen of arches, 'rich in sadistic detail' – presumably a version of the pavilion Buckle had initially envisaged. It was a striking, if incongruous, conception, intended to be 'a sort of fantastic pavilion of love', Ashton said. His idea was to create a climactic transformation scene for the ballerina and her partner (Fonteyn and Somes) by positioning them in the pavilion, which rose up slowly, while an aqueduct descended in front of them, making their ascent appear even higher. 'It is quite effective,' Ashton wrote to Dick Beard, 'and curious you should say in your lovely letter that it should "all sink into oblivion before their eyes".'

Ashton virtually designed the costumes himself, as Beaurepaire refused to defer to his ideas. 'I have had much trouble with him . . . in fact we almost quarrelled. But by dint of simplification I have I hope arrived at something.' With his letter to Beard, along with a photograph of himself captioned 'La Bête Ashton', he enclosed two pages from *Ballet* magazine showing Beaurepaire's designs, and two ink drawings on which he had written, 'It's not like this at all.' His own rough sketches illustrate his alternatives:

> The girls *may* wear hats like this [drawing] they look well on – of
> black velvet encrusted at the side with pearls and diamonds sewn
> tightly together, pearl earrings and pearl chokers. They look a
> cross between a Greek column [drawing] and a toreadors hat –
> tutu of pale blue and white and a bodice like this [drawing] black
> gloves. The boys sort of Sylphide jackets, rather Chinese and
> rather Joseph's coat of many colours [drawing] Margot in yellow
> and her hair perfectly plain and diamond choker and earrings.

Beaurepaire at first refused to reproduce the style of tutus with embellishments that Ashton had liked in Petit's *Concert de danses* – '*Surtout, pas de diamants!*' he hissed, wanting to make the new ballet as different as possible from his last. But Ashton evidently got his way, his insistence on diamonds unwittingly echoing Stravinsky's 'only scenic idea' for the ballet: 'a black tutu with diamond sequins for the ballerina and a classical gilet for her partner.' Ashton was unsympathetic towards Beaurepaire's bid for versatility, considering it modish and shallow. 'The French desire to astonish, [is] tiresome to me who prefer things to be right rather than outré – and elegant rather than chic.'

Elegance is integral to Stravinsky's score: the *Spectator* critic compared it to 'a copy of *Vogue*'. Outdoing Roland Petit, Ashton dressed Fonteyn in a couture combination of yellow and black, offset by a diamond tiara, earrings and double string of pearls – an effect to which she rather over-responded, adopting 'a mocking Parisian glitter' that she later toned down. During her sinuous andantino solo, Somes and a quartet of male dancers – once again used throughout the ballet in decorative, mannequin poses – sit watching her, one arm outstretched and resting on a knee, like Michelangelo's Adam. As the curtain opens, the four are paired on each side of the stage, one shadowing and half-clasping the other in what Buckle calls the 'David and Jonathan position' (the erotic daring of their embrace having been all but eradicated by Ashton's austerely angular stylization of the position). The four boys – one of whom was Alexander Grant, twinned again with Donald Britton – are given more prominence in the ballet than the danseur noble, Michael Somes, which indicates a waning of interest on Ashton's part. Rather than the pas de deux, which Stravinsky planned to accompany a soaring, Tchaikovskian trumpet solo associated with the male lead, Ashton choreographed a pas d'action, in which Margot Fonteyn is partnered by all five men. 'I set out to display her with all the full richness of the classical ballet at my disposal.' His model was the Rose Adagio from *Sleeping Beauty*, a homage to Petipa, whose compositional devices provide the basis of *Scènes de ballet*. But, while the hierarchical structure of female corps, male cavaliers, premier danseur and ballerina derives from Petipa (as well as direct quotations such as the Lilac Fairy attendants' line of travelling coupés), the divisions of the ensemble into twelve women and four male soloists are based on the twelve months and four seasons of the year. This time, however, a seasonal theme is not even implicit in the ballet. Ashton was determined to confine himself to purely abstract dance in order to stretch his choreographic imagination to the limit. Like Stravinsky's score, in which 'nothing goes on too long, everything is always changing, thus giving great variety and mood to the spectacle', he set out to derive interest through the work's structure and constantly shifting dynamics, boasting of how he had orchestrated three or four rhythms at the same time.

For the visual counterpoint to the music, Ashton's model was the patterns produced by Euclid's theorems, in the same way as de Valois had used chess strategies to frame the choreographic action of *Checkmate*. At school, he had been 'clueless' about any form of mathematics, but he surprised himself by developing a late interest in the subject, possibly whetted by his training for Photographic Intelligence, as well as by da Vinci's notebooks, which he had read with fascination during the war. He bought a second-hand volume on advanced geometry in Charing Cross Road and began to invent original patterns. 'I used to place the dancers in theorems and then make them move along geometric lines and then at the end I used to say, "Well, QED" when it worked out.'

Ashton choreographed *Scènes de ballet* to be seen from any angle – 'anywhere could be front, so to speak' – but, in order to appreciate the Euclidean diameters, triangles and squares within a circle formed by his dancers, the ballet is best viewed from above. In this way, one sees more clearly how he softens a static, geometric male grouping with a swirl of running corps girls; or moves a block of dancers diagonally upstage, like wavelets chasing after each other. Ashton was extremely pleased with the ballet and claimed it was his favourite: 'If God said, "You have one left" – that would be it.' His pride shines through his account to Dick Beard. 'The choreography is very classical, naturally my own particular extension of the classic vocabulary, with moments I think of poetry and real beauty and very much on a grand scale and a certain mystery and elegance and an aristocratic aura.' It is all he describes and more. Inspired by Stravinsky's 'featherweight and sugared' music, the ballet is packed with playful, Ashtonian embellishments: wrists flick, heads nod, 'shoulders and feet exchange jokes'. (Its lightheartedness is infectious. The Royal Ballet dancer Michael Coleman began a tradition of standing in the wings as a quartet of girls travelled towards him. At a given moment, he would proposition them and, grinning, wait for four heads to nod in unison.)

Yet while the choreography of *Scènes de ballet* is intensely personal, it is one of Ashton's least subjective works. As he told Dick Beard, there is no implication of himself in it 'as there is in your ballet [*Valses nobles*], only that in the apotheosis the man and woman are united in bliss and rise on the lift . . . away from all the slander of the world, and live for each other only'. Stravinsky also admitted to an emotional element in the apotheosis, which he composed on the day of the liberation of Paris. But the jubilation of his rising chords is not matched in the ballet. On the first night, it was clear that the elaborate apotheosis was a mistake: machinery failed to work, the lighting was crude, and the original idea of a rising platform for Fonteyn and Somes was scrapped. *Scènes de ballet* ends conventionally with the danseur supporting the ballerina's Petipa-style pirouette into a deep penché finished with a flourish on the final chord.

Ashton's subdued climax only partly explains the mixed response the ballet has received since its première. Lacking the emotional immediacy of *Symphonic Variations*, it has what he described as 'a hidden beauty . . . a cold, distant, uncompromising beauty which says I am here, beautiful, but I will make no effort to charm you'. In terms of Ashton's own development, the ballet was a major advance, his mastery of Stravinsky's diverse time-signatures and epigrammatic dance incidents attesting not only to his musical accomplishment, but also to his continuing independence from Constant Lambert, whose hostility towards the composer is well known. Critics today recognize the work as 'a marvel', but at the time of its première, opinion was clamorously divided between those, like Beryl de Zoete, who foresaw that the ballet would 'come to be regarded as one of Ashton's finest compositions', and those who contributed towards the general crying-down. Illustrating the way that *Scènes de ballet* polarized the dance world, Buckle published a spread of extracts from the daily papers with headlines ranging from 'AN AUSTERE NEW BALLET GHOSTLY SCORE'; 'SMILE, PLEASE'; 'THE NO-STORY BALLET' to 'STRAVINSKY BALLET HAS GREAT BEAUTY'; 'PLEASANT DESIGN TO STRAVINSKY'. Even the *Dancing Times* contradicted itself, with Dyneley Hussey's recognition of Stravinsky's delicately scored, 'elusive' melodies in the same issue as the Sitter Out's emphatic dismissal of the 'skeleton-like' music, 'devoid of warmth and melody'. What André Beaurepaire described as 'certaines opinions à réflexes négatifs . . . critique prête matière à discussions: "sans queue ni tête"'* provoked a battery of indignant letters from friends and fans; while critics who had praised the ballet found themselves being personally thanked by the choreographer. Ashton reported the confusion to Dick Beard.

The ballet had its 1st performance – it went moderately well. I don't know how to begin to tell. I wish somebody else would write to you about it, it is painful for me, for it is your ballet and I love every moment of it and it is beautiful, but many people rave about it and say it is the best I've done, which I think, and Stravinsky's son adores it. One paper says wonderful and another rubbish and they all contradict themselves. People who never liked me before praise me, the public bewildered. It's wonderfully danced, full of invention and never strained. R. Petit, and Karsavina and K. Clark etc were in raptures. Only I was sad as I wanted your ballet to be acclaimed. I will send you notices good and bad and you'll see how confused everybody was.

*'Opinions of knee-jerk negativity . . . the endless chit-chat of the critics.'

A modernist masterpiece which alienates the general public is often, as the composer Hans Werner Henze told Ashton, 'the best proof of its worth'. The twenty-two-year-old Henze saw *Scènes de ballet* when it toured in the autumn of 1948 and considered it to be a ground-breaking creation, comparable to the work of Schoenberg, Satie and Picasso. 'Getting away from direct human feelings, concentrating on the abstract . . . It was modern, cool and its beauty was so high-class that it could not and must not be accepted by everybody.' News of the ballet reached Balanchine, who invited Ashton to choreograph a piece for Ballet Society, a commission that had to be postponed because of Sadler's Wells Ballet's visit to Holland in March. 'I was pleased at his hand of friendship,' Ashton told Beard, 'for I admire him beyond all other choreographers.' Lincoln Kirstein wanted *Scènes de ballet* for Ballet Society, but, with plans afoot for Sadler's Wells first tour of New York, Ashton was unwilling to let it go. David Webster, who had flown to America to begin negotiations with the impresario Sol Hurok, volunteered to contact Beard while he was there, but Ashton would have none of it. 'The brute wants to make you and had the audacity to say so to me. I said, "*Try*," dryly.' Had Beard met Webster in New York and complied, he might have had more success than Ashton in sealing an agreement with Sadler's Wells. The choreographer claimed to have remained working on the case, sending him yet another telegram.

> Believe me have tried without success. One hope left. Can you fix it? Of course I will be responsible in my way. Must see you somehow. Do write. No summer without you.

The reference to fixing something was (and remains) confusing to Beard, but the obfuscation could have been deliberate. Although Ashton maintained he was delighted by the change in the dancer's feelings – 'Dearest one, I praise your fidelity and above all I am so moved by your impatience to hear from me, as though it really mattered to you! I even like to think, as though it were necessary for you. Oh! would that were so' – it is quite possible that Ashton was being purposely ineffectual; he knew that if Beard came to England to live with him, the relationship would not last. Quite apart from the disparity in their ages, Ashton, like many artists, needed to guard his gift by maintaining his independence to the point of reclusiveness. 'You would find if you were with me a lot that I live a great deal within myself – must be alone – & that would be no life for you . . . I like so much an inward life now, a life of the imagination.' Like the dancer muse of the Symbolist poets – impersonal, abstract, an embodiment of the incomprehensible image of art – Beard was now more inspiring to Ashton as a distant vision of an ideal, rather than a flesh-and-blood presence.

> You live now in my imagination, absorbing it and though you are miles away you are always with me. As I create my new ballet you are at my side, encouraging, dissuading what is wrong, approving what is good (I hope) and when we return to my little room you are tender to me and loving, for I am tired and preoccupied and I feel that flow of your affection and you refresh me . . . Often at rehearsals to make you more vivid to me I bring out my handkerchief which I have previously soaked in Jicky, for that is the perfume that brings you readily before me and Margot knowing this, gave me a bottle for Xmas!

Sensing a change in the nature of Ashton's feelings towards him, the dancer grew more dependent on their correspondence, his own writing style becoming so floridly romantic in imitation that Tchelitchew reprimanded him for sounding like a Victorian chorus girl:

> I realize a wonderful, but delicate spell holds us together, and not even a visible force is needed to break it. When your letters stop, I think the spell is broken forever . . . Please (M. Prevost) try to recreate me in your visions so that a letter will come from you to keep me from wilting forever.

Beard admitted to being jealous of John Taras, who was then staying with Ashton in Yeoman's Row, even though he was no rival. 'I imagine you are going out a great deal perhaps because of Taras. I like to blame him and I like to believe I am not a part of you because you are going out with others.' Ashton had met John Taras the previous year when, on a tour with Metropolitan Ballet, he came to London, bearing letters of introduction from Lincoln Kirstein, Virgil Thomson, Tchelitchew and Alice. They found they had much in common and, after dinner, zigzagging between Taras's rented house in Belgravia and Hanover Lodge cottage, would have the sort of all-night, mobile conversations that Ashton had once shared with Billy Chappell and Doris Langley Moore. 'Fred wanted to hear *everything* about New York.' When Taras returned to London in the summer of 1948, this time delivering a suit and some shirts from Alice, Ashton insisted that he stay with him. They went for a weekend in Paris, where they spent most evenings at the Relais Plaza, drinking Specials and 'just giggling all the time'. Ashton took Taras along to talk to the French designer Jean-Denis Malclès, whom he wanted to design *Cin-*

derella, his first full-length ballet. Ashton considered Malclès, who had done impressive work for Roland Petit, to be an artist 'not of genius but of talent and elegance who loves the stage'. After his experience with Beaurepaire, he had to be careful.

While they were in Paris, he and Taras saw a performance of *Les Demoiselles de la nuit*, the ballet Petit had made for Margot Fonteyn, in which she danced the part of a cat called Agathe. The costumes and rooftop setting were by Léonor Fini, a fashionable surrealist just beginning to make her mark in the theatre,* whose autobiographical libretto and décor Ashton was to use in *Le Rêve de Léonor*, choreographed the following spring. 'Superfeminine' is the word Max Ernst chose to describe Fini's work: a bizarre fusion of boudoir sugariness and necrophilia, with its decomposing corpses and baneful nudes shrouded with cobwebby dustsheets; a nightmarish world, populated with 'swollen images of desire'. Fini could also be classified as an erotic artist (her coyly sadomasochistic illustrations for Pauline Réage's *L'Histoire d'O* are kept under lock and key at the Duke Humfrey Library in Oxford), and there are provocatively Sapphic undertones in her portrait *Margot Fonteyn et son Amie*,† painted in 1948, the year of *Les Demoiselles de la nuit*.

The ballet caused quite a stir at the time, and Fonteyn found herself the conquest of Paris, lionized, much to her surprise, as a sexual icon: 'Ah! la derrière de Margot!' was one compliment she overheard. The sight of Fonteyn in a short cut-away skirt, performing what can only have seemed a parabolic tale of a young man (Roland Petit) whose intense infatuation succeeds in making a woman of a pure white cat, confirmed Ashton's fears. 'Fred was very upset and felt that Margot had deserted him,' said John Taras. In fact, it was not Fonteyn but Ashton himself on whom Fini and Petit would have a disastrously adverse influence.‡

---

*Balanchine's 1945 *Le Palais de Cristal* (now known as *Symphony in C*) was designed by Fini.
†Sold at Christies in 1987 for £40,000.
‡Ashton claimed to have been 'bullied' into making *Le Rêve de Léonor* for Les Ballets de Paris in April 1949, after Petit, who planned to choreograph it himself using music from *Tristan*, had fallen out with Fini. Her libretto, described by Richard Buckle as 'halfway between Dali and the third act of *Casse Noisette*', was (fortunately) cut in half by Ashton's decision finally to use Britten's 'Variations on a Theme of Frank Bridge'. But while the episodic character of the music was not really suited to the slow, dream-like unfolding of the dance, the choreography, being Ashton's, inevitably contained movingly lyrical passages. 'As a final confession of failure, speech was introduced: a Sphinx, one of Fini's pet symbols, sat in a bath and let out a cackling laugh, and the dancers cried out "Léonor! Léonor!" as the curtain fell.' The whole enterprise was, as Clement Crisp said, 'deeply silly'.

Resigned to a summer without Beard, who, through work commitments, was tied to New York, Ashton cancelled plans to go abroad and spent a fortnight at the English seaside with Sophie, followed by another fortnight at a health farm. He hoped to lose two stone on a strict fast, becoming 'physically cleansed, mentally cleansed, alert and spiritually uplifted' as a result, but self-denial was having a contradictory effect, provoking dreams of dissipation. His letter to Beard from Bedfordshire contained 'nothing but erotica – erections etc'. He also wrote to Richard Buckle while he was there, thanking him for sending a pin-up of the young Mexican dancer Luisillo: 'What an enchanting face it is – but God he was difficult to get at.' Like Babilée the year before, Luisillo, a member of Carmen Amaya's troupe of gypsy dancers, had been the revelation of the summer season. He was small, soft-eyed and timid – until he started to move. 'He does not dance,' wrote Buckle. 'He is a galvanized homunculus – the instrument of some god's will.' Coveting the vibrantly sexual Luisillo – he and his partner Teresa were like two 'fierce and beautiful birds love-making' – was not so much an infatuation as a form of Method Research: sex as subject matter for a ballet was now occupying Ashton's mind.

He had begun to think about using the Don Juan legend while in the Air Force. Then, having heard Strauss's tone poem at a concert, he wrote to Edwin Evans, who contributed the programme note, asking him to send further details, including the quotations from Nicholas Lenau's poem with which the composer headed his score. If Ashton received the information (Evans died three years before the ballet was made), he disregarded it, except for the fact that he follows Lenau's depiction of a group of Don Juan's mistresses by appending a silent prologue to the music, in which the betrayed women glide into view and vanish like haunting visions. To begin with, Ashton had considered the idea of basing the ballet on Zorrilla's play *Don Juan Tenorio*, even though he had found it a struggle to read. Eager to help, Edward Burra, whom Ashton wanted to design the ballet, sent him a ludicrously long-winded, characteristically misspelt and virtually unpunctuated précis:

> It starts off during carnival with mascaras etc Don J & Don Luis
> have a bet & meet in the Tavern to count how many people they've
> poked. Don J wins by a cool 50 & is overheard by various Fathers.
> Dona Ines Father at once shuts up Inez in a convent & Don J says
> hes going to get Don Luis girl. He does & then breaks into the
> cloister carries off Inez, kills Father & Don Luis & escapes to
> Naples from which he returns & finds the Palace of the Tenorios

has been turned into a pantheon with the tombs of his victims all round he meets 'The sculptor' who has just put the finishing touch to Dona Ines having flung a bolsa de oro at the sculptors head. He apostrophises Inez who suddenly appears in an apotheose in a mysterious light & says she has exchanged her soul for his then some bright sparks arrive & carry Don J off to dine he invites El comendador. at dinner theres an extra place. & in the middle a loud bang at the door, which they take no notice off, followed by a further bang in the house, & a furthur bang Don J accuses the sparks of playing a joke on him. There then a fearful bang & Don locks the door but El Comendador El convidado de piedra materializes through the wall the 2 guests fall down in a fit & El C says the D dies that night & has 6 hrs to make his peace with eternity & then vanishes . . . The guests & Don J then all accuse each other of putting drugs in the wine & challenge each other to duels. The next scene is the pantheon & Don J arrives the statues come to life an entire dinner table laden with deaths heads hourglasses vipers twined tumblers of boiling blood abortions in aspic etc whirls out of a tomb . . .

And so on, for another two and a half pages. Insisting that all this would make 'a very nice little peice of romance', Burra also enclosed an idea and sketches for a divertissement, 'a Rat D'hotel dressed in skin tight black tites who terrorizes the guests of a hotel, & is followed about by a brand of hysterical chamber maids. Rather like carnival only "nastier". Quite a simple thing.' An alternative synopsis, this time by Burra himself, also arrived, focusing on Don Juan, Dona Ines and her father, El Comendador, who is stabbed by the Don. At a 'little dinner with a few sparks & courtisans', the ghost of El C presents the Don with a small card '(RSVP au cimetiere)', where the final scene takes place. Here, a tug of war ensues between Dona Ines pulling one of Don Juan's arms and a crowd of demons pulling the other. 'Quite plausable . . . though not quite Zorrilla.'

Hardly surprisingly, Ashton decided to use only the essence of the Don Juan story; Burra, despite his wasted efforts, was unfazed. 'It's what I hoped he would do instead of cooking up some crazy plot,' he told his designer friend Beatrice (Bumble) Dawson. His accommodating manner, a welcome change after the battles with Beaurepaire, was much appreciated by Ashton. 'If I showed the least hesitation in approving a design he would immediately produce a flood of alternative ideas.' He liked Burra's darkly romantic perspective of crumbling arcades, but the critics were bored by 'chi-chi ruins', and complained that the décor lacked a sense of location. Rather than indulging his relish for Spain – with its brothels, boîtes, Holy processions, fiestas and bullfights – Burra abandoned even his initial evocative ideas (including a large baroque portal and a cardboard Jerez barrel for a tavern scene), presumably because Ashton did not want a décor too specifically suggestive of time or place.

In keeping with the libretto and the design, the choreography was also pared to its essence, and was considered as severely classical as *Scènes de ballet*. 'The ballet hardly touches the emotions,' wrote Audrey Williamson, 'but its geometric and architectural line is of amazing beauty.' *Don Juan*, which has not survived, was a choreographic experiment that did not come off. Associations with the legend were so vivid that Ashton's attempt to create an abstraction of the story appeared bloodless and inadequate. The electrifying force of Strauss's music, composed to express the effect of a passionate new love affair, found no counterpart in the ballet, which was as cool and polite as the applause. The main problem was Robert Helpmann's ineffectual portrayal of the Don. According to Moira Shearer, who played the unfaithful Young Wife, he was 'bored to tears and spent all his time sending everyone up, including Fred'. Unresponsive in return, Ashton gave Helpmann, who had now returned to the company as a permanent member, so little to do that he was forced to attempt to project the drama through facial expressions. 'This Don Juan . . . is a glum static figure, who even when the swelling music demands some virtuoso dancing, can do no more than run futilely across the stage.' Helpmann's role, as Cyril Beaumont remarked, was mainly that of porteur, 'an onerous task . . . which clearly weighs upon him more than the burden of Don Juan's sins'. With a complete absence of Luisillo-like sparks between Helpmann and Fonteyn, or any of his other amours, 'what was intended to be a picture of blissful polygamy, looked more like a daisy chain'.

As La Morte Amoureuse, Fonteyn was literally a femme fatale, conspicuously similar to the character in Roland Petit's *Le Jeune homme et la mort*. She even moved in the style of a Petit dancer, splitting her legs like compasses, stabbing her pointes, and performing violent acrobatic contortions. As Cyril Beaumont complained, Ashton the romantic, the lyric poet, had closed his ears to his Muse, allowing himself to be carried off 'by two importunate Sirens: Fashion and Novelty'. As if subconsciously sabotaging this giddy new direction in Ashton's career, Fonteyn tore a ligament on the first night of *Don Juan*, and relinquished her part to Violetta Elvin. But for Ashton, the 'really bitter blow' was the fact that her injury prevented her from creating the role of Cinderella, scheduled for the Christmas season.

Since 1939, when *The Sleeping Princess* was revived at Sadler's Wells,

Ashton had wanted to choreograph a full-length work, but the war had ruled this out. Soon after the company's move to Covent Garden, he considered Delibes' *Sylvia* as a possibility, again consulting Buckle over the libretto and designs, but he postponed the project in favour of Prokofiev's *Cinderella*, which had recently been presented in Russia. England's first evening-length ballet was a momentous event for Sadler's Wells and Ashton's greatest challenge to date. It *had* to succeed – a three-act failure could never be hidden in the repertory – and, consequently, as he told Dick Beard, the responsibility weighed heavily upon him.

> I finished it last week in a really remarkably short time as some of the music is not easy. It is really quite extraordinary to sit there and see 3 acts unroll themselves before me and I feel that gratified at my achievement whether it has any worth or not, it is still an achievement to have done it all in 4 weeks. We open with it on the 23rd and all your love & concentration must be directed towards me that day, for it is a big moment in my life & a terribly anxious one.

The title role in a full-length Ashton ballet belonged to Fonteyn by right and prestige (she had been waiting for this for years), but hers had been a double blow. When she discovered, from an announcement in *The Times*, that Ashton meant her to alternate in the role, she felt angry and humiliated. 'In the past, any part created for me by Fred belonged to me; or so I felt, with a possessiveness equal to jealous love . . . The idea that Moira [Shearer] or anyone else should share *Cinderella* from the start, hit me like a slap in the face.' Allowing Fonteyn to learn the news from the press, rather than telling her himself, was Ashton's retaliation for the hurt her defection had caused him. Nevertheless, his motive for making her share the role was sound enough: a full-length ballet was far too taxing for one ballerina to dance on consecutive nights. Also, as she was forced to acknowledge, there were younger stars coming up behind her who deserved the sort of opportunities she had always been given. Anne Heaton was chosen for the initial rehearsals. She had been the lead in *Valses nobles et sentimentales* and was tipped at the time to be Margot Fonteyn's successor. But, without any explanation given to Heaton, Moira Shearer was cast as Cinderella. In box-office terms, she was a far greater draw – the new sensation, then at the height of her *Red Shoes* fame. Tall, spirited and glamorous, with her film-star figure and spectacular red hair, Shearer was already proving a threat to Fonteyn's position – a situation widely resented in the company. On the first night, not a single person wished 'Gingerella' good luck.

As things turned out, however, this was not to be Cinderella's evening, but the 'Ballet of the Ugly Sisters', as *Picture Post* titled their cover story. Its real stars were Robert Helpmann and Ashton, whose timid, flustery charm was definitively described at the time by the American poet and critic, Edwin Denby.

> She is the shyest, the happiest, most innocent of Monsters . . . To do a little dance step transports her, though she keeps forgetting what comes next. At the Prince's she is terrified to be making an entrance; a few moments later, poor Monster, in the intoxication of being at a party she loses her heart and imagines she can dance fascinatingly – in the way Chaplin at a fashionable tango-tea used to imagine he could slink like a glamorous Argentine. But after the Slipper-test she accepts the truth as it is, she makes a shy state curtsey to the Princely couple, to the power of Romance and Beauty, and paddles sadly off. No wonder such a Monster wins everybody's heart. Ashton does it reticently, with the perfect timing, the apparently tentative gesture, the absorption and the sweetness of nature of a great clown. He acts as if he never meant to be the star of the show and very likely he didn't. He cast Helpmann, England's greatest mime, as the First Stepsister and gave that part the initiative in their scenes; he himself was only to trail along vaguely, with one little solo in the second act . . . Ashton's unexpected triumph on stage is the sort of accident that happens to geniuses.

In the 1944 Soviet version of Prokofiev's *Cinderella* (which Ashton had heard about but not seen), the roles of the Ugly Sisters were played by women, which had been Ashton's original intention. However, because of the unavailability of one of the dancers he had selected, he decided they should be performed by men, probably remembering Fokine's version, brought to London in 1939, in which two character dancers based their comic mime on pantomime dames. Helpmann's bossy Sister corresponded to this English tradition more than Ashton's, but each invented a character so real to the audience that the joke of the pantomime dame – the comic tension created by burly men wearing female clothes – did not apply. Both performers borrowed traits from female eccentrics they knew: Helpmann claimed to have modelled his Sister on the forthright Jane Clark; while Ashton incorporated 'a bit of Edith Sitwell' – most noticeably, the famous profile. But the genius of the two portrayals lies in their revelation of self-caricature. It is all there: Ashton's love of dressing up in Edwardian finery, his early dreams of dancing like Pavlova, his self-deprecation and constant insecurity; against which Helpmann's thrusting, preening egotism – equally true to life – provides the perfect foil. The blur between fact and fantasy is summed up in the scene where Ashton's Sister forgets her solo enchaînement: a literal re-creation of the choreographer's own memory lapse in rehearsal. 'I had the whole production in my head and sometimes forgot steps and said to Bobby, "If I don't remember, then you must correct me."'

The homey familiarity of *Cinderella*'s pantomime is, as Denby says, a ritual the audience has known all its life, awakening childhood echoes and largely accounting for its success. 'At last, you have come to your triumph,' wrote Lydia Lopokova. 'My mind beams and my heart beats for you. You must have suffered before you achieved it . . . Come to Tilton and give me a kiss.' The ballet's charm lies in what Denby calls its 'English sweetness of temper', a mild, gentle tone, which was reflected by Malclès in his felicitous designs. Yet, despite the understatement of the mime scenes, which Ashton deftly modulates into the dance, the comical Ugly Sisters come close to overbalancing the ballet: like Dickensian grotesques, their dramatic vitality reduces the protagonists to ciphers. 'Aren't they in love?' Denby wrote of Cinderella and her Prince. 'Watching them, the eye doesn't catch any luminous movement-image of a dazzling encounter, a magic contact, the release of romance . . . What a cold fish she is! . . . Her shy Ugly Sister has more heart than that.' When Fonteyn appeared in *Cinderella* the following year, she was able to bring more pathos and innocence to the role than the technically ravishing but porcelain-brittle Shearer. The Act I solo with the broom, metaphorically preparing for the glass slipper, is a choreographic poem to Shearer's famously eloquent feet, but it took Fonteyn to instil poignancy into the dance. 'It was her eyes,' said Clement Crisp, 'she *acted* it all.' And only Fonteyn conveyed a real sense of sustained ecstasy as she descended trance-like down the ballroom steps, enouncing each step on pointe in a slow transport of wonder, without once looking at the ground.

Although there are dance highlights for Cinderella and the Prince – her manège of pirouettes, for instance, whipping up a sense of mounting exhilaration – their final grand pas de deux is disappointingly anticlimactic. Ashton's most inspired choreography occurs in Act I. The twelve Stars look like sisters of the twelve corps girls in *Scènes de ballet*, their ray-like limbs and floor patterns marking out in contrapuntal, driving waltz rhythm the accelerating passage of time. The variations of the four Seasons are also brilliantly conceived, each a conceit fusing attributes of weather with personality. Twenty-one-year-old Nerina, fresh from South Africa, a plump, bouncy soubrette – 'Nadia couldn't walk through Covent Garden market without being whistled at and given apples' – created the role of Spring. 'We were in a basement studio one rainy day,' said Nerina, 'and Fred asked me what I associated with spring. "Buds bursting," I told him. "Well *do* it," he said, and so I proceeded to *burst* and the solo came out of that.' Summer was the sensuously lovely Violetta Elvin, whom Ashton used to tease about her amours and her laziness. 'She was always complaining in her languorous way that she couldn't do things and I would laugh and say, "What do you want to do then? *Walk*?"' Summer, with her sinuously rippling shoulders and swooning fondus, has the languid sensuality of an odalisque. The speedy Pauline Clayden was Autumn, flinging herself into a whirlwind of chaînés and giddying off-kilter turns. 'It absolutely suited her: daft and dithery, with feet going mad as if she was kicking autumn leaves aside.' For the final solo, Ashton used Beryl Grey's strength and physical control to enact the gripping power of winter; in a series of icicle-sharp fouettés, her leg seemed to freeze mid-air, before melting into fluid renversé turns.

A major figure in Act II is the Jester. Part Harlequin, part Buttons, with the plaintive, white-painted face of a classical French clown, he dominates the Ballroom scene to such an extent that Cyril Beaumont felt the role to be 'something of an anomaly'. Among sketches of the original cast featured in *Ballet*, Brian Shaw is pictured as the Jester, but, although Shaw helped to create the role, Ashton 'suddenly' gave the first night to Alexander Grant, now reckoned to be the company's most interesting male dancer. 'Everybody was mad about Alexander at that time,' said Richard Buckle, 'Denby in particular.'

> Like a jet of force he darts forward . . . bent sideways, bent double, leaping down a flight of stairs, springing into the meagre dances of the guests with a smiling threat.

The Jester is attendant to the Prince and, in Grant's interpretation, had a story of his own. 'When my Prince fell in love, I was happy for him but also terribly sad that I was going to lose him and could never have someone like Cinderella myself,' a regret which told on Grant's face as he wistfully held Fonteyn's train. This ability to convey the contradictions in a role – sweet sorrow; a 'smiling threat' – gave Grant a unique quality as a character dancer. Paradox was inherent in his own make-up, too. His dark, delinquent looks, and the hint of danger in his dancing, was matched by a jaunty, winning personality. Small and chunky, 'very well-hung and uninhibitedly sexual', he also had a satyric appeal similar to that of Brian Shaw. From now on, there would be great rivalry between the two dancers, which Ashton, igniting creative sparks, may have exploited, as he did by making Grant provocatively upstage Michael Somes. (While the Jester leads the courtroom dances, the Prince stands redundantly at the back until, eventually, he shoos him into the wings.)

Brian Shaw was still living with Ashton in Yeoman's Row, but they were no longer romantically involved. 'Brian wasn't out of the picture, he was just out of the bed,' said a colleague. 'They were both playing the field.' Shaw was soon to fall in love with Gilbert Vernon, a handsome young South African dancer, with whom he shared a house for twenty years. Although Vernon also maintains that 'Fred and Brian kept together long after "it" had stopped', Ashton's transferral of interest to Grant was now manifesting itself on stage. 'We felt very sorry for Shaw-Shaw,' said Nadia Nerina. 'Suddenly Alexander was getting all the first nights.' Ashton's reasons were, as usual, not entirely subjective. Although Grant was not as accomplished technically as Brian Shaw, he was the greater artist, transmitting a warmth and charm that Shaw lacked. Off-stage, too, he was more outgoing – 'much more human than Brian.' 'Everyone loves Alexander,' Ashton once told a friend, 'men, women, dogs, children. He's been through the ballet both ways.'

During the company's tour of The Hague the previous spring, Grant had begun a relationship with Nadia Nerina. 'Alexander and I learnt about life in Holland. We were most amazed by the whole thing, because neither of us knew anything about it. We were very young and very happy.' Although Ashton had singled out Grant as 'the next one', his importuning had not yet begun in earnest. There had always been an element of favouritism in his casting, and he was now playing flagrant sexual power games. 'All the boys are suffering from "Ashtonitis",' one of the male soloists complained to Richard Buckle over dinner, explaining that a good part now carried with it certain conditions. 'I once said "no" to Fred and didn't get another role,' said the dancer Ray Powell. Despite the romance and femininity in his nature, Ashton could be aggressively predatory: 'He *wanted* it,' as Dick Beard put it. The greater the obstacle in Ashton's way, the more relentless and ruthlessly unswerving was his appetite for the chase. Countering his physical demands, however, was a continual yearning for ideal love; the sacred versus the profane. It was the subject of his next ballet, and the dichotomy that would recur throughout his work during the following decade.

While Dick Beard remained an icon of youth and beauty for Ashton, the choreographer's most recent letters, with their sonneteer's stream of poetic figures, rhetorically inflate a feeling that no longer exists.

17 January 1949

My Most Dearest,

In spite of the complexity of one's life my thoughts turn constantly to you – the most beautiful, the most ideal, the most terrifying, the most forbidden, the most destructive. You who holds the prize, the gift of happiness, the realization of bliss, of misery, of fruitfulness . . . What do you not hold in those blond caresses, that passionate yield, that surging passivity. I fear you and long for you. Perhaps we should never meet again. I can give you nothing but decay, you most living of creatures. I am the crisp frost of winter – the bleakness, the latent period, you are the summer, the warmth, the flower-laden breezes, the promise. I am the sad fulfilment, the melancholy, the summer's toll[?], the varigated autumn, the amber the russet the faded green the fallen leaf – you the fragrant blossom-laden youth, my dried leaves of passion falling about you. I fear your glance as at dawn I fear the sun & I curtain myself against its rays & I fear you, dissipate my doubts. Only your great love can lift the mists of doubt.

Love to my only love, F.

Always the down-to-earth partner, Beard was more realistic about the outcome of the relationship, more honest about acknowledging inevitable 'runnings about' on both sides. To Ashton, however, the romance was all, however illusory it had become. 'Remember,' he wrote, 'Yours is the thread of Ariadne & we should be tied however far we wander so that the slightest tug brings one racing back to beloved arms.' What did he care about rival lovers? He was above them. Even if they held Beard's heart and body, he had hold of his imagination. A far more serious threat to the tenuous link between them was the dancer's increasingly long silences. 'Don't leave me so long without news . . . I will get used to living without you in my thoughts & force myself to efface you.' Beard's reply was bitterly reproachful.

Dear Fred,

You could never have said you could and would forget if you had not already begun to care very little . . . When I left you that morning on the bridge . . . I carried a certain fragment of it all . . . the essence of you and that time – how can such a thing change. I came back and what had always taken place here took place, quite naturally: I could not have hoped part of that time with you would spill over into this other world. So all that has happened has been only a continuation of my usual life, of which you were never a part – I was part of *your* life . . . You are going to come here to New York, I have wondered, and will probably never know, whether you have given a single thought to me . . . We will meet – it is inevitable . . . and our meeting is what I fear most terribly. It has been so long – and so long since I have believed you have thought of me . . . If you do not answer this I will know I cannot speak to you when we meet. But if you will give me some sign, any sign . . . I will write again so that we may meet in secret and in that way discover how much has been forgetfulness or how much lost love . . .

Goodbye my dear Freddie.

Ashton responded almost immediately, but a new tone of cynicism and disillusion had infiltrated his usual florid style. It was *his* right to be hurt when, as he had heard, Beard had been in Paris and Rome without getting in touch. 'I knew you would come back to Europe without my sadnesses, disappointments, my tears, my happinesses.' In fact, Beard's appearance in Italy would have been less welcome than Ashton suggests, intruding on an encounter he had begun with a twenty-two-year-old dancer whom he had met during the company's season in Florence. But Ashton continued to insist on the perpetuity of their spiritual ties, which transcended everyday dalliances and incompatibilities. '*I* do not fear meeting *you* – loving arms will be held out, fingers will entwine, & it is all above others sorrow, others pain, for it is inevitable. I will meet you in secret in silence and alone in love.'

They met on the first day of the company's visit to New York, in October 1949. When Beard arrived at the Gladstone Hotel, Ashton was still in bed, shuddering over the ordeal of his journey (his BOAC plane, grounded in Iceland because of appalling weather, had landed at La Guardia fourteen hours late). Although they were to spend a good deal of time in each other's company, seeing several plays and reuniting later on the tour, according to Beard 'it all seemed to have burned out'. Within a year, each had fallen in love with someone else. They remained friends well into the 1960s, however, with Ashton taking an avuncular interest in Beard's emotional happiness. His memory of their affair remained with him as 'a particularly agreeable' period of his life. And for Beard? Despite having been denied the professional reward he craved, the dancer bears Ashton no ill will, and (together with Tudor and Tchelitchew) considers him one to be of the three most enduring influences on his life. His dismissal was couched by Ashton in the most lyrical, flattering and self-denigrating terms: 'I'm not worth it. Go & find your equal. Look amongst the Gods.' Yet Beard is well aware that his affections had been manipulated in much the same way as Nora Kaye's: 'We fitted into a plan to get Fred what he wanted.' Beard's role was ultimately to nourish Ashton's art – whatever the cost to his own career. In an uncharacteristically altruistic letter, written shortly after the dancer's return to America, Ashton confesses how self-serving his motives had been.

My conscience has to be put at rest that I have done nothing for you but muddle your life – made you lose the trust of one who could help you [Tudor] & took from you only & gave you nothing in return. I praise the nobility & dignity of your nature that you never flung it at me . . .

And yet, however 'painfully' he mishandled the situation, Ashton considered that he had bestowed on Beard a much greater gift. The dancer, as Ashton commented, was never one to commit himself: 'I like to take sides & affirm it, declare it & pledge. Not so you.' Their liaison, despite its difficulties and disappointments, had kindled in them both 'the essence of all that is poetic'. The day Dick Beard left England, on an unscheduled, black-market flight, Ashton accompanied him, by taxi then bus, to a foggy airfield outside London. Dawn was rising as they embraced and Ashton said, 'Well, it may not have been what you expected, but at least I have *moved* you. The most important thing in life is to be moved. Nothing – nothing else matters.'

During Ashton and Beard's first morning together in New York, Alice was also in the room. She was showing Ashton the different American coins. 'It *would* take one of the world's richest women to care about the value of a dime,' he hissed to Beard. The Gladstone was now Alice's home in New York, she having taken a floor for her children, their Scottish governess and a full-time seamstress. And it was Alice who, according to her son, Ivan Obolensky, was 'single-handedly' responsible for the company's first visit to New York. 'My mother went to Sol Hurok, and said "Why don't you bring over Sadler's Wells Ballet?"' Hurok was unenthusiastic; ballet, as he had learnt to his cost, was not an exploitable commodity. But Alice persevered and eventually won him round by agreeing to help sponsor the trip and throw a welcoming party for the company at the Sherry-Netherland Hotel. The House of Worth was among the couturiers to have dressed the girls, as ambassadors of British fashion, but the boys had received nothing, so Alice made an arrangement with a Fifth Avenue men's outfitter for them each to choose two free shirts.

Sadler's Wells Ballet's inaugural season in New York is a legend in the history of British ballet. The company caused a sensation, breaking box-office records at the Metropolitan Opera House, which was sold out weeks in advance. Outside the theatre, in an Indian-summer heatwave, scalpers were asking $80 a ticket and standees queued for places at the back of the auditorium where they would be sardined four deep. Hurok chose *The Sleeping Beauty* for the gala première, attended by almost every important name in American dance and society. The grandeur and scale of the production – never before seen in its entirety in the United

States – combined with the sweet restraint of the English dancers, 'filling the house with lilac fragrance', made an overwhelming impression. When the curtain came down after the Prologue, Mayor O'Dwyer, host of the first-night party at Gracie Mansion, leaned across his flag-draped box and bawled to Ninette de Valois above the applause, 'You're in, lady!'

The sight of Margot Fonteyn, the personification of youth and spring, appearing under the arches of Act I almost brought the performance to a standstill. New York had never seen anyone like her. With her natural charm, lack of ostentation, sensitive phrasing and unhurried attention to simple details, Fonteyn was the supreme exponent of native English style. As de Valois said, 'It was only Margot then,' eclipsing even the nation-wide fame of Moira Shearer. 'They didn't really see beyond her or *The Sleeping Beauty*. Then later they started to accept the choreography of the country.' The mixed bills, with ballets by Ashton, de Valois and Helpmann, were much less successful: *Façade* and *Wedding Bouquet* were regarded as enjoyable juvenilia; *Apparitions*, 'a big pseudo-romantic bore'; *Symphonic Variations* as 'inferior Balanchine'. It was the large-scale ballets the Americans wanted to see – 'production miracles', with their lavish designs and consistency of classical style. Praise for Sadler's Wells' schooling and meticulous preparation inevitably implied criticism of native achievements. The British had given 'a terrific wallop' to American national pride, and, not surprisingly, a certain sourness prevailed. Lincoln Kirstein, founder of New York City Ballet, criticized Ashton's performance as Carabosse to Richard Buckle, remarking that he had only 'a limited number of denunciatory gestures – six in all'.* Trivialities apart, this was a time of crucial allegiance between the two ballet worlds. Kirstein, a great patron of literature and the arts and a man of immense erudition and organizational energy, passionately loved England. It was his dream to instigate a transatlantic exchange of companies, dancers and choreographers. By the end of the American season, it was arranged that Balanchine would stage *Ballet Imperial* for Sadler's Wells, and Ashton was invited to create a new work for New York City Ballet the following

---

*Balanchine caused offence at a performance of *Sleeping Beauty* when, a guest in Ashton's box, he turned round during a heavy rallentando at the end of the Bluebird sequence and raised a sardonic eyebrow at the conductor, Robert Irving, who was sitting behind him. 'Balanchine and I had looked at each other with rather a sad expression – that was all,' said Irving. 'The story was distorted. By dear Fred. He went out and called several people including Lincoln and Balanchine and I got faced with this by Lincoln. Fred had put it about that Balanchine had been very rude.'

year. The shouts of 'Come back! Come back!' that resounded during the first night's forty-nine curtain calls gratifyingly took effect: Sadler's Wells did return to America (and has continued to do so throughout the following half-century), while New York City Ballet made their first visit to London in the summer of 1950. This was the beginning of what Buckle called 'Lincoln's Exchange & Mart', largely made possible by a real-life Lilac Fairy behind the scenes.

Alice, in the view of her close friend George Dix, was still obsessed by Ashton. 'It wasn't the ballet that interested her, it was Fred. She talked about him constantly and could only think of what Fred wanted and Fred didn't want. I think she still wanted to marry him.' At the time, she was growing apart from her fourth husband, David Pleydell-Bouverie,* whom she had met at the Gladstone Hotel. He claims that they 'weren't really introduced', implying that Alice had picked him up, which, in a way, she did. Spotting the effetely attractive young man across the restaurant, she asked Billy McCann, her dinner companion and a mutual acquaintance, to invite him over to their table for coffee. Alice was delighted to discover that Bouverie was English and (superficially, at least) had the manners of a gentleman; otherwise, they had little in common. Within no time she had fallen in love, optimistically anticipating 'the most lovely new start'. They married in 1946 – Bouverie, a promising architect, willingly forsaking his career to be kept by Alice. (Her wedding present to him was a cheque for £1 million.) She saw this marriage pulling her life together and created a dream home in California, a 500-acre ranch in the Sonoma valley,† planning an idyllic outdoor life for her children. Sanya Lubitsch‡ was Alice's confidante at the time. 'From what she told me she was deeply in love and it didn't work out because . . . well I don't think David should ever be married. He was one of the ones who *did* take advantage of Alice and yet he neglected her quite thoroughly. If he went walking with her he'd just abandon her and vanish. She was very unhappy, but couldn't make up her mind at that time to leave him. It turned into a very nasty relationship; there was no affection between them.'§

When Ashton came to America in 1949, Alice, because of the problems with her marriage, had begun to make a life of her own, centred at

---

*Grandson of the 5th Earl of Radnor.
†Now a nature reserve managed by Bouverie.
‡Widow of the film director Ernst Lubitsch.
§After Alice eventually divorced Bouverie in 1956 (having hired private detectives to follow him), he immediately began an affair with the heiress Barbara Hutton, this time declining an offer of marriage.

Rhinebeck in the Hudson Valley. She had kept the grey-stone Queen Anne manor that she and Serge Obolensky had built on a high slope of Vincent Astor's land, and at weekends the house was full of writers: Tennessee Williams, Evelyn Waugh, Truman Capote, and the twenty-four-year-old Gore Vidal, a new protégé, whom she was soon to encourage to buy a magnificent, neighboring Greek revival house. She and Vidal were intimate friends, but there was no question of romance – at least on his part. 'I was going through my older-woman phase with Anaïs Nin and not about to take on Number Two.' Ashton, on the other hand, was immediately captivated by Vidal's wit and sensuous, exotic looks, and urged Alice to invite them both for a weekend. 'Fred decided that he had a thing about me and was giving me a big rush, but I wasn't remotely interested. He amused me, that was all.'

'Not much sex . . . and what chances I have Alice kills,' Ashton reported on a postcard to Richard Buckle, which was one of many grouches about Alice. 'She was constantly giving him presents which he was constantly complaining weren't really good enough,' said Vidal. ' "Too many langues de chat," I remember him sighing. Fred could be terribly rude to her and often reduced her to tears, but he was an intuitive man: he saw that was what she wanted and so behaved accordingly. Alice played roles with people and with Fred she was the put-upon but loyal helpmeet of a great man.'

Like a true benefactress, Alice introduced Ashton to an ambience in which he could flourish. In the palatial mansions along the banks of the Hudson, homes of the railroad kings and patrician landowners, including the Roosevelts, Ogden Millses, Livingstons and Stuyvesants, there still survived the life Edith Wharton portrays of Edwardian affluence and social exclusiveness. But Alice had created a world apart. Her country house was manageable in size and subtly English in atmosphere, fostering weekend party games of charades and cross-dressing – an atmosphere in which Ashton and 'visiting Brits' like Cecil Beaton and the Sitwells felt immediately at home. When Ashton returned to America in February the following year to collaborate with Beaton on a new work, the piece was planned in the congenial surroundings of Rhinebeck.

When Ashton first read the poetry of Rimbaud, while stationed at Drem in 1941, he wanted to make him the subject of a ballet. The transcendental content of many of the *Illuminations* formed part of Ashton's wartime reading programme of visionary texts; and he found Rimbaud, with his St Theresa-like religious fervour and passionate search for la vraie vie, a deeply sympathetic though unbearably tragic figure. 'I used to weep when I read about him.' Ashton first heard Britten's *Les Illuminations*, sung by Peter Pears and conducted by the composer at a Promenade concert at the Albert Hall, in September 1945, and he promised Britten that a ballet to the score would soon follow. But even though he kept returning to the idea, it was not until the New York City Ballet commission that he began to think seriously about the subject which he had abandoned as too risqué for the English. Many of the prose poems, of which Britten used only nine fragments, were written during Rimbaud's 'shameful' sojourn in London with Verlaine, a wild debauch of drugs, drunkenness, vagrancy and forbidden passion, terminated finally by their famous roulette with death. The two poets had roamed the city streets and docklands like spectators watching the passing show – the reason, perhaps, that Ashton approached Christian Bérard, the designer of *Les Forains*, Petit's ballet about a troupe of strolling players. Bérard, working in London for Massine in 1948, made some preliminary drawings on the brown-paper sleeve of Ashton's record of the music, but died before the project could be realized. Ashton and Lincoln Kirstein both agreed that Cecil Beaton, in New York at the time, should take over.

While Ashton was suffering another traumatic transatlantic journey to New York – 'Terrible voyage, a day late, mountainous waves. Terror & boredom & sick,' he reported to Britten – Beaton and Kirstein were planning *Illuminations*.

> Kirstein and I agreed on certain essentials for the ballet. It must have a child-like quality, it must be provocative and as daring as Rimbaud's poetry itself . . . We agreed everything should be tawdry tattered, splashed with mud; everything should be extremely poor, patched, darned, mended and torn again . . . We looked at the paintings of Klee . . . [who] seemed to be in the same spirit as that of Rimbaud . . . We investigated many aspects of circus life, and of under-the-sea life, and then Ashton arrived from England.

Alice met him at the docks and invited the three collaborators to 'the Schloss up the Hudson' for the weekend. Presented with what seemed a fait accompli, Ashton 'peremptorily' dismissed their ideas – or, rather, Kirstein's, whose enthusiasms Beaton was soaking up 'like an expensive sponge'. Ashton, who had come equipped with his own Rimbaud library and visual sources, showed them postcards of Picasso clowns and produced a Van Gogh night-scene; but, finally, it was a book that Alice gave Kirstein, showing children dressed as pierrots, that provided the key to the ballet. 'A troupe of pierrots are disguising themselves as Rimbaud, as his townspeople, as his muse, and as kings and queens.' A pierrot painting by Tchelitchew also had a profound influence on the ballet. Ashton had bought the portrait of Iya Abdy's son, Valentine, in 1948 because it reminded him of Dick Beard.* 'It is so very like you and I will leave it to you when I die.† His eyes follow me round the room.' Beard was his original inspiration for the role of Rimbaud, and, in December 1948, he sent the dancer an inscribed copy of Enid Starkie's biography of the poet. 'We had talked a lot about the ballet; I think at the time he saw a great deal of Rimbaud and Verlaine in the two of us – or concerned himself poetically with the idea. Later he told me Lincoln had insisted that he use Nick Magallanes because of his seniority with the company and loyalty to them. They "owed" him. My guess is that at this point Lincoln tried to interest Fred romantically in Nick, and succeeded.'

Born in Mexico, Nicholas Magallanes had trained at the School of American Ballet, and had danced with Kirstein's Ballet Caravan and with New York City Ballet since its inception. With his glamorous Hispanic appearance and masculine magnetism on stage, he was exactly Ashton's type. The choreographer needed little persuasion to use Magallanes, but was also, as Beard pointed out, 'whipped up' by Kirstein, who referred to him as Mr Nick 'Basket' Magallanes and sent Ashton a full-frontal nude drawing of the dancer by Tchelitchew. In rehearsal, Ashton made no secret of his attraction. 'You'd be blind not to have noticed but it didn't get in the way of anything,' said the ballerina Tanaquil LeClercq, who danced the part of Sacred Love. 'Freddie just came in and flirted a little.' Which was all Ashton was able to achieve. Magallanes, as John Taras remarked, 'liked his boys very young'. 'He was absolutely fixed about it,' said Dick Beard, who had himself been a lover. 'There was no give and take for the sake of career. He did exactly what he wanted to sexually and it didn't have anything to do with gain or loss.' The part of Rimbaud was a great success for Magallanes, enhancing what came naturally to him: sensual plasticity of movement and a compelling romantic intensity. In terms of the ballet as a whole, his role was vital, providing a unifying link between the fragmented sections. He was also a surrogate for Ashton himself.

Dance, the most symbolic of the arts, is well suited to convey the intuitive, suggestive nature of *Les Illuminations* which, in words of no rational order or meaning, powerfully externalize the poet's emotions. Right from the beginning, when the hero sets the ballet in motion by an-

---

*Bought for £300 from Richard Buckle; sold in the Ashton auction in 1993 for £5,500.
†Ashton did not carry out his promise to leave the painting to Beard.

imating the frozen clownish figures grouped round the stage, Ashton establishes the analogy of the Poet as Choreographer. Counterpointing episodes from Rimbaud's life and work, he also incorporates dreams and conflicts of his own. The Being Beauteous section pays tribute to the 'glorious, golden, beauteous youth' of Dick Beard, transforming him into Tchelitchew's pierrot by offsetting his features with a large white ruff. The dancer appeared with three other cavaliers, who, in a grand, Petipa-style adagio, partner the ballerina, Sacred Love. (One of them, Arthur Bell, was black, lending an exotic, Venetian touch and alluding to the Ethiopian servant who accompanied Rimbaud on his North African travels.) With her Taglioni-length skirt, whimsically pom-pommed by Beaton, Sacred Love is a modern descendant of ballet blanc's vision of an ideal, a Sylphide or an Odette, whose ports de bras she in fact mimics at one point. Using Tanaquil LeClercq's sweeping extensions, Ashton created an innovative yet lyrical pas de cinq, which ends with her being carried off the stage in splits. 'Tanny's legs are used like a callipers to divide the world,' Kirstein reported to Buckle. 'And the whole number is done by her off the floor, when she is not burrowing like a mad memory of Pavlova.'

Her counterpart, a hungrily wanton bacchante, wearing a Grecian tunic and only one pointe shoe, was danced to great acclaim by Melissa Hayden. Her duet with the Poet was a tour de force of explicit abandon, in which the pair appeared joined at the groin, until, in a convulsion of self-contempt, he casts her violently to the floor. As the *New York Times* critic, John Martin, remarked at the time, Ashton could not have made *Illuminations* for his own company, despite the fact that other controversial elements – the pissoir and *Faune*-like masturbatory episode with a scarf – are so glancingly done that it is hard to imagine why the ballet caused such offence in London later that year. In contrast to the 'sordid' imagery, such as the shooting of the Poet which involved a loud bang and mock-blood, are enigmatic episodes, such as the solo to Rimbaud's 'Phrases': 'I have stretched ropes from steeple to steeple; garlands from window to window; golden chains from star to star, and I dance.' After some very literal mime, in which the Poet stretches out and knots imaginary ropes, he reaches into his pocket and flings up a handful of confetti: an image of falling stars and, also, in an earthy, Rimbaud-type paradox, an emblem of ejaculation, enacting a line from one of Ashton's love letters to Beard: 'How can I forget where you showered me with stars.'

Ashton brilliantly establishes the half-angel, half-vagabond antithesis in Rimbaud's nature. If the ballet comes across as slightly frivolous, it is mainly the fault of Beaton's winsome designs. Although faithful to Rimbaud's vision of childhood – his deliberate attempt to capture vivid, intuitive impressions unalloyed by experience – the sets and costumes are, as John Martin wrote, 'too pretty, too chic, too fancy, for so grimy and brutal a life'. They are also too fussy. 'Pom-poms and things kept falling off and littering the stage,' said Tanaquil LeClercq. 'The costumes really annoyed me; I felt more like a model in a Cecil Beaton creation.' But, apart from its designs, the ballet was outstandingly successful in New York, 'The most impressive choreography by Mr Ashton that we in America have seen.' The dissolving, semi-hallucinatory sections were a vast improvement on Ashton's previous attempt at surrealism in *Rêve de Léonor*; and the acrobatic idiom – 'the clutching eroticism', popularized by Petit – did not appear derivative and gratuitous, as before, but was smoothly assimilated into a style that was Ashton's own. The American dancers' dynamism, rhythm and lack of inhibition seemed to liberate Ashton into new realms of expression, just as they had done in *Devil's Holiday*. But although his cast, particularly Magallanes, responded to the challenge of performing in a much more theatrical way, there were, Dick Beard said, difficulties that Ashton had a battle to overcome.

> Fred wasn't very respected during the time of *Illuminations*, because Balanchine had everyone mesmerized. He was God. You didn't fiddle around with lesser mortals, and it was hard for Fred to put up with that in his own mind. He admired Balanchine so much and probably thought Balanchine *was* a greater genius, but he didn't want to have those feelings of inferiority. Also, one had the feeling that Balanchine was messing with Fred's rehearsal hours.

Ashton himself believed that Balanchine deliberately sabotaged his rehearsals, complaining to confidants like John Taras how the choreographer would come into the studio and take away his dancers. 'George didn't like *Illuminations*; I suppose because Fred used Tanny whom he was very fond of at that time and who came out of it very well.' Probably as a result of Balanchine's attitude, LeClercq, who became his fourth wife two years later, was extremely cavalier about the ballet. One day, after the dancer had arrived late again for a rehearsal, Ashton, in mock-fury, pointed a Carabosse-like finger at her and said, '*A genoux!*' She obligingly sank to her knees, although, Beard said, 'She just didn't care. Fred couldn't fire her.' Ashton was so unhappy about the situation that he threatened to leave. 'He went to Mr B and told him, "I'm a guest in your country and I haven't been treated well."' Rehearsal conditions improved after that, but Balanchine continued to take no interest in the progress of the ballet: 'I asked him to come and see what I was doing, but he never came near it, which was rather wounding.' The final snub was Balanchine's departure for Italy on the day of Ashton's première.

Although the critical reaction to *Illuminations* could not have been more positive, it was Balanchine's approbation that Ashton sought. 'Fred is very sweet and frightened,' Kirstein told Buckle. 'He is so much in awe of Balanchine that he is flying in the other direction and wants to produce something never seen before.' Ashton felt so bruised and defensive as a result of his treatment that, overhearing someone disparaging the ballet at a party, he turned on him and snapped, 'I may not have talent, but I have craft and I have taste.' There was harsher criticism in store.

Ashton returned to London immediately after the first night, and Balanchine followed soon afterwards, to mount *Ballet Imperial* at Covent Garden. The discipline and musicality of the English dancers were appreciated by Balanchine, whose presence inspired them to attempt new risk-taking levels of technique. In Margot Fonteyn, however, he met a measure of resistance not dissimilar to that experienced by Ashton in Tanaquil LeClercq. Fonteyn, as she later admitted, danced her first and only Balanchine ballet very badly, making no attempt to achieve the off-tilt, diagonal angling of the body that the work required. Only Moira Shearer made a genuine effort to grasp American neoclassical style, and Balanchine rewarded her by coaching her himself for a matinée performance.

Balanchine never discussed rehearsals of *Ballet Imperial* with Ashton, even though he was staying in the spare room at Yeoman's Row. His only indication of preparations on the ballet were the passages from Tchaikovsky's second concerto, which he played on Edith's piano before leaving for the theatre. As the house was unheated and Balanchine was always cold, Ashton made constant journeys to his guest's room with rugs and electric fires. Conversation, monopolized by Balanchine, centred on gastronomy, wine and his own aesthetics – none of which interested or impressed Ashton: 'Balanchine could talk a lot of cock, m'dear.' Although they enjoyed some good times together, the two choreographers never became friends.* Ashton resented the fact that Balanchine did not return his hospitality (a charge famously levelled against himself); while Balanchine, according to Lincoln Kirstein, considered Ashton to be

---

*More than anything else, Ashton envied Balanchine's heritage. In a review of Bernard Taper's biography written for the *Sunday Telegraph* in 1964, he wrote: 'George Balanchine, a contemporary and colleague of mine, is the choreographer that I most admire in the world. Balanchine has had all the necessary environment and background for the making of the great choreographer he is. Unlike myself, who had to make all my opportunities from the beginning, and fight my way against every kind of prejudice, in order to be allowed to dance. He started as a child in the Maryinsky School where he received the best available tuition. He came from a musical family and all the Russian fairies must have gathered at his christening to bestow on him all his great gifts.'

'one of the least generous men he'd ever met in his life'. As personalities and as creative artists, they were total opposites. Ballet deities adored by Ashton, such as Pavlova and Isadora Duncan, were ridiculed by Balanchine. Balanchine was passionately industrious, founding a school to nurture his personal classicism and teaching company class every day; Ashton was passionately lazy (the 'Old Turkish Lady', Kirstein called him), he never taught class and took no interest in the school. Ashton's admiration for Balanchine's work dwindled after the 1950s, when, echoing obtuse English opinion, he found it 'much too dry'. Balanchine, according to Kirstein, never did take Ashton seriously, mistrusting his musicality and judging him to be inadequately professional. 'Fred followed the music but he never analysed it and he couldn't play an instrument. George could work with Stravinsky as a partner. He could have forgiven Fred if he'd been committed, but he deplored that kind of lightness and feigned silliness.' Balanchine's disregard is summed up by an anecdote told by Tanaquil LeClercq which, however innocently recounted, contains a barely implicit put-down, which would certainly not have been lost on Ashton.

> Talking over those good old days together, my husband turned to Sir Fred and said, 'You know you really taught me something.' Eavesdropping on this conversation, I half expected he was about to make public a useful pointer on choreography, or perhaps the management of difficult ballerinas . . . 'Yes,' continued my husband, 'you taught me always to pile up the dinner dishes in the sink and run water over them before your charwoman arrived.'

Ballet Imperial was well received by London audiences, but Cyril Beaumont's complaint that it lacked warmth provided a foretaste of the criticism of New York City Ballet's Covent Garden season three months later, when the Balanchine repertory was pronounced barren, soulless and lacking in range. Although it was this London engagement which established its international reputation, the company was not the triumph that Sadler's Wells had been in New York. And yet one of the two most pilloried works (along with Balanchine's *Firebird*) was Ashton's *Illuminations*. Beaton reported the savage reception of the ballet to Greta Garbo.

> There are a few artists who like it, but the highbrow critics say it is decadent, nasty, chi-chi and chic. We really had brickbats thrown at our heads. It is most surprising and baffling as I think it a lovely work and very near to Rimbaud . . .

One of its few admirers was E. M. Forster, who found it 'really lovely and most moving', but the Duchess of Kent, whom Ashton had invited to the first night, was so shocked by the 'pornographic dance' that she was unable to compliment him on the ballet when they dined afterwards at Lady Rothermere's fancy-dress ball. (Later, Ashton told Richard Buckle that it was not the ballet itself that had shocked Princess Marina but the 'Royauté' episode, 'where Rimbaud rushed at a Royal Procession and dismantled it'.) Ashton, to whom 'anything that was not a bouquet was a bomb', particularly where royalty was concerned, was visibly shaken that night. Critical vitriol and tragic personal losses were to darken the next decade. But first came a welcome respite: a five-month tour of America, the country he loved more than any other, and which he felt loved him as much in return.

CHAPTER FOURTEEN

ANTIPODEAN MOONSHINE
1950–1956

'The Ballet Special', Sadler's Wells' home for 21,000 miles through American and Canada, comprised four scenery wagons, a diner, club car, and six Pullman sleeping coaches. The corps de ballet were relegated to the upper, less well-ventilated bunks (compensated by a dollar per week extra), soloists and principals took the lower ones; while the stars and the three artistic directors – Ashton, de Valois and Lambert – had their own compartments. Although Ashton liked to surround himself on tour with a small entourage of friends from the company, he remained very much part of the team. 'Don't leave me out,' he used to say, and would sit watching the dancers' swallow-diving displays, join in their Canasta games and entertain them with imitations of his idols: an evocation of Isadora's abandoned run, down the train corridor; a performance of Pavlova's Dying Swan, in a swimming-pool. At the traditional Half-Way Party, he appeared in a low-fitting felt hat and a raincoat with up-turned collar, in an impersonation of Garbo, with whom he had become even more infatuated after an evening they had spent together in London with Cecil Beaton.* In New Orleans, he led a crawl of jazz clubs, where he and a lively group drank absinthe cocktails and danced to a jukebox until morning. 'But as soon as we got back to England,' said one of the dancers, 'Fred became very grand again.'

Although Alexander Grant and Nadia Nerina appeared almost inseparable throughout the nineteen weeks, it was during this tour, which took place during the autumn and winter of 1950, that she began to realize 'things weren't quite right': Ashton's overtures towards Grant had be-

---

*His adoration was not unqualified. When Beaton first introduced them in New York, Ashton had arrived with an armful of yellow roses and fallen to his knees as Garbo lay reclined on a chaise-longue, telling her, 'You must come back' – later remarking to a friend, 'I didn't say through ten gauzes.'

come much more pressing. 'Alexander asked me what he should do,' said Gilbert Vernon, 'and I said he said he should follow his heart. But it was clear that Fred was being very manipulative.' Ashton felt he was getting nowhere and was in very low spirits.

One night in Tulsa, Oklahoma, Jane Edgeworth, the company's 'den mother',* found him in tears. 'It was Alexander. We drunk a bottle of Old Grandad whiskey and passed out on a bed together – *plastered*.' The other dancers cynically observed what was happening, but Grant was far too popular for anyone to begrudge the favouritism. With one exception. After Sadler's Wells' début in Los Angeles – a dazzling success, attended by an array of movie stars – Grant, dressed up for the occasion, went into the hotel bar. As he paused by a table, Michael Somes stood up and, without saying a word, poured a jug of water over him. 'Extraordinary,' said Grant. 'Professional jealousy, I suppose.'

Somes was especially volatile at that time. His behaviour towards his girlfriend, the rehearsal pianist, Jean Gilbert, had been so 'autocratic and appalling' that, when Jane Edgeworth remonstrated with him, he vindictively ripped her dress 'from top to bottom'. But things would soon improve for Somes. Not only did his roles in new Ashton ballets become more substantial than they had been of late, but he was about to fall in love with Deirdre Dixon, a young dancer, who would become his first wife. Lincoln Kirstein maintains that Ashton was 'broken' by Somes's marriage, which is something of an overstatement. Ashton was fond of Dixon, 'a *beautiful* girl', and, in a sense, remained symbolically wedded to Somes for the rest of his life. Ashton's wedding-ring finger, said to have been fractured by the dancer in an attempt to wrench off a ring (reports vary as to whether this was a ring given to Ashton by Somes or by Alice), was never reset 'out of romantic nostalgia'. In contemplative moods, he used to sit with the bent finger hovering against his lips. A perpetual tie existed between them. 'Life is so strange,' said Ashton in his final years. '*Now*, Michael would die for me. Michael, who has abused me and attacked me in front of everyone, would really die for me.' Ashton had a particular gift for keeping a retinue of ex-loved ones close at hand: 'However awful anybody was to me, I was never bitter. I never closed doors.' All the same, Somes must have known that he was being overshadowed; his drenching of Grant, however farcical and retaliatory, was a form of baptism, subconsciously endorsing the young dancer's succession as one of the most important and enduring relationships in Ashton's life.

The son of New Zealand hoteliers, Alexander Grant had been brought up in Wellington, where he started to dance at the age of six. He was in-

*PA to the general administrator.

spired to make ballet a career by the Russians who toured the country in the late 1930s, particularly by Leon Woizikovsky. In Nijinsky's role as the favourite Slave in the original *Schéhérazade*, Woizikovsky left such an impression that a trace remained in the faintly menacing, panther-like quality of Grant's own dancing – what Edwin Denby described as 'the beautiful suspense of an animal pounce'. He also followed the Russian in becoming one of the great character dancers of his time. Grant was an original. Audiences adored him: he had a potent allure; a merry, erotic susceptibility, which manifested itself off-stage as well as on. 'Alexander was like a puppy dog sniffing round a lot of trees,' remarked an American friend. 'His sexual persuasion was not very certain then,' said the dancer, Ray Powell. 'I should know.' Nerina was aware that 'Alexander was learning', but she was made so unhappy by his cavalier behaviour towards her on the tour that one of his colleagues, Michael Boulton, who was infatuated with Nerina, confronted Grant. 'I knew exactly what Nadia felt about Alex; she was besotted with him and almost demented because he was treating her very badly.' There was a violent argument – 'it was the only time I saw Alex absolutely furious' – but, by the final lap of the tour, the couple were still together, up till 3 a.m., drinking hot chocolate in an all-night café in New York. Ashton was already in London, having left after Chicago, to begin work on *Daphnis and Chloe*, missing as a result a satirical preview of the ballet in the Christmas cabaret, 'Poor Chloe', performed by Anne Negus and Kenneth MacMillan, 'with apologies to Frederick Ashton'.

Immediately after his return, Ashton took Tamara Karsavina, the original Chloe from Fokine's 1912 production, out to lunch. 'I said to her I'm thinking of doing *Daphnis and Chloe*, because I think it's a great piece of music, and I'd like to rescue it from the concert hall and bring it back into the theatre where it belongs. And she said, quite right.' Although drawing on the Longus legend, Ashton did not want to portray the Greece of classical antiquity. Rather, he wanted to create a contemporary love story, to give the impression that the gods were alive and alert to the destinies of the youthful shepherds and shepherdesses depicted on stage. Oliver Messel and Mary Kessell (Kenneth Clark's idea) were among the designers he considered; a more serious contender was Tchelitchew, who had received word of the ballet through Lincoln Kirstein, and had written to Ashton the previous spring, inviting him to Paris to see his paintings and to exchange ideas on the new work. He was in need of inspiration, he said. 'Because M Petit's influence of oriental fucking rhythms à la Massine – is a great danger of putting Mme la Danse in a whorehouse . . . I like the theater that creates a life strange peculiar life – where enigma and sphinx sing duettos.' Tchelitchew's rhetorical concepts may have changed Ashton's mind: he did not want a repetition of the Beaurepaire débâcle, and he had a more down-to-earth collaborator in mind, someone who could convey Greek mythology in a modern Mediterranean spirit.

For this reason, Ashton approached the young neo-Romantic painter John Craxton, whom he had met during the war and who now lived on the Greek island of Poros. When Craxton flew to London to discuss the ballet, Ashton was recovering from flu. Craxton did a demonstration of Greek dancing in his bedroom, and they talked about the idea of dressing the cast in everyday clothes: soft, swirling skirts for the girls; trousers and open shirts with rolled-up sleeves for the boys. Later, they went to the British Museum to look at ancient Hellenic costumes, but Ashton decided he did not like what he called 'those shit-on [chiton]', and said he was bored by 'Greek ballets with people running around in tunics and veils and scarves'.

The ballet that emerged is essentially a classical work, into which Ashton has introduced folk-dance figures adapted from illustrations published in Maurice Emmanuel's *Antique Greek Dance*, a second-hand book he had bought from Cyril Beaumont in the 1930s. His other main source was a painting by John Craxton of male taverna-dancing. The result is an ingenious choreographic fusion with a modern, Mediterranean flavour, established right from the beginning, when peasant youths and girls, grasping each other's shoulders, form kalamatianos lines and circles, their frieze-like positions also incorporating a signature of Ashton's: the contemplative opening pose from *Symphonic Variations*. In a natural transition, their ancient chain walk is transformed into a Petipa line of corps de ballet, leading the eye to the entrance of the hero (Michael Somes).

Richard Buckle denounced the passive Daphnis as a 'sissy', but, true to the source, he is simply a conventional pastoral lover, whose dreamy nature is offset by the darker machismo of Dorkon, who vies with him for Chloe's affection. Dorkon's preening, pseudo-pyrrhic dance immediately precedes a romantic solo in which Daphnis dances with his arms stretched along a shepherd's crook, echoing the rod-straight arms of the kalamatianos. Following Longus – rather than Fokine, who prudishly omitted it – Ashton submits Daphnis to a sexual rite of passage with a married townswoman (arrestingly danced by the glamorous Violetta Elvin). In an extraordinary stylized enactment of female sexual ecstasy, Lykanion hooks her leg round Daphnis in a classical attitude, whips it behind, in front, again and again, getting faster and faster as her arms and head flail uncontrollably, until her climax subsides with an imperceptible quiver of her foot.

Daphnis and Chloe is yet another work that reflects Ashton's abiding interest in the tug between innocence and experience, pure and profane love. As the embodiment of purity, Fonteyn's Chloe was unsurpassable. No other ballerina conveyed the same sense of wonderment and pathos, or performed the simple academic steps with such radiance and lack of mannerism. Watching a revival of the ballet with John Craxton, Ashton admitted that 'without Margot, it doesn't take off the ground'. 'Fred really found her personality in that role,' said Nadia Nerina. 'The elegance, the correctness – that really *was* Margot.' Chloe's extreme vulnerability was highlighted by a violent scene in which she is abducted by the Pirate Chief, Alexander Grant. He, too, was unforgettable in the role, which proved to be the most exhausting of his career. Grant picked up Fonteyn with one hand, ran round the stage with her, slung her across his shoulders, twisted her round, threw her to the ground and immediately started jumping. They were the wild, unclassical jumps that Grant had patented as his own, combined with Russian-style athletics and sheer physical panache. It was a superb performance, in which Grant seemed alarmingly invincible. When he left the stage door one night, he was pleased to hear one fan whisper to another, 'That's Alexander Grant – but he's so *small.*'

As a complete contrast to the percussive frenzy of the pirate scene, Ashton made the lovers' reunion an event remarkable for its tranquillity. 'I find that often the better the music is, the stronger it is, and the more emotional, the more you can stand still and do nothing.' Responding to the Wagnerian echoes in the music, he wanted to capture 'that same quality of standing still – when Tristan turns and sees Isolde and for what seems like half an hour they just stare at each other'. To one of Ravel's most luscious surges of music, Chloe, gazing into Daphnis's eyes, slowly bourrées towards him through a frieze of corps. She hangs on his neck and he swings her around in slow motion, almost like a father with his child, until she is flying around him horizontally.

The pas de deux, like Fonteyn's plaintive solo with tied hands in the pirates' lair, was a masterstroke of understatement, its semi-static, photographic poses recalling their tender duet in *Horoscope*. Rather than trying to compete with the music, Ashton, through the economy of movement, provided 'a kind of visual overtone'. However, several reviewers decided that dance could add little to the flawless score and the ballet was grudgingly received. Although Ashton liked Craxton's sunbaked set and youthful costumes, the critics, as he rightly predicted, did not. 'I fear we will be debagged,' he cabled the artist. A small coterie of critics continued to champion *Daphnis and Chloe*, but not until the New York showing was it given the acclaim that it deserved.

After one of the first Covent Garden performances, the American choreographer Ruth Page came backstage with her husband, Tom Fisher, to congratulate Ashton and Fonteyn. They had met during the last tour when the Fishers entertained the company in Chicago. When they met again in London, sitting in Fonteyn's dressing room, where John Craxton had joined them, the five were enjoying themselves so much that Fisher suddenly proposed they should spend the summer holiday together. Craxton suggested a cruise around the Greek Islands, which was immediately taken up, and they agreed to rendezvous in Athens the following month. In Piraeus harbour, Fisher rented a boat, the *Eliki* – not 'what you would call a swank yacht . . . just a small fishing boat', but he ensured a certain amount of luxury by hiring a chef from the Grand Bretagne Hotel, a steward from the British Embassy, and bringing aboard several cases of fine champagne.

They decided that it would be a good idea to have a guest on board who spoke fluent Greek and who knew the islands, so they arranged 'by accident on purpose', as Craxton put it, to bump into the Graecophile Patrick Leigh Fermor at a café in Athens. He and his wife-to-be, Joan Rayner, whom Ashton had known in the 1930s when she was Joan Eyres-Monsell, came along 'as stowaways, really'. Leigh Fermor was able to direct the captain to islands where no tourist had ever set foot; to bays where a pleasure cruiser was such a novelty that a Navy speedboat came racing up to investigate. The seven friends spent the days walking, climbing, swimming and sightseeing. They went by motor boat to Bourtzi, a Venetian fort built on the tip of a rock off Nastriou, which had been converted into a hotel. After lunch, they stripped down to their bathing suits and sunbathed on the taverna wall that overhung the bay. There was a rather surreal element to the holiday. The chef, who was an old man and had never been to sea, was bitten by a fish on the first morning and refused to get up for several days, 'saying that he was reading about Geisha girls'. So at night they ate in waterside tavernas, watching sailors dance and perform astonishing feats, such as balancing cluttered wooden tables with their teeth. 'Margot and Freddie joined in once,' said Craxton. 'They danced amazingly well, picking up the steps so easily.' The cruise ended prematurely with a terrifying storm, during which Ashton and Ruth Page clung to each other, convinced they were going to drown (an experience that Ashton would later brilliantly re-create on stage, with the queasy pitching and tossing of the ship in *Ondine*).

The next day was calm and beautiful. The group were on deck drinking champagne and watching the sunset, when a school of dolphins appeared, a sight so moving that Ashton and Fonteyn fell into each other's arms. Their affection for each other was especially apparent on holiday, when Fonteyn was irrepressibly vivacious and completely at ease. 'She was marvellous,' said Ashton. 'If anything went wrong, she always made light of it. She was wonderful in the sea because she was so svelte; she swam like an ondine with her hair hanging down. And she'd drink red wine and really be relaxed. But she'd still do her exercises every day. Even on a yacht, she'd be hanging on to the railings.'

In melancholy mood, Ashton confided a fear that had been preoccupying him at the time, that he was going to be usurped by the fast-rising choreographer, John Cranko, whose *Pineapple Poll* – a spirited ballet-bouffe – had been a great success that spring. Cranko was an ambitious young South African, emerging from the influence of Massine, who was then being hailed as the first major choreographic discovery since the war. 'Fred was terribly worried by this and we were always having to console him,' said Craxton. But a shadow of premonition may also have darkened his holiday spirits.

The moment he returned from holiday, Ashton, as he told Edith Sitwell, began 'working like a dog' on *Tiresias*, the ballet which was to have a dramatically damaging effect on the company's stature. Its score and libretto were by Constant Lambert, its décor by Lambert's wife, Isabel. Since the Camargo days, Lambert had wanted to make the legend the subject of a ballet. The story concerns a Theban youth who is blinded by the vengeful goddess, Hera, for agreeing with her husband, Zeus, that sex is more satisfying for women than for men. Although Ashton felt somewhat fazed by his libretto – 'How do you explain in a ballet who enjoys sex more?' – as an allegory of bisexuality, it was an issue much closer to his heart than Lambert's. It has been suggested that the composer was drawn to the subject out of suppressed guilt about his own homosexual predilections, but his close friends refute this. 'Constant was as normal as can be,' said Ashton, an opinion seconded by Billy Chappell. 'He loved being with queer people, but there was not a sniff of it in him.' Ashton, on the other hand, had been, until recently, genuinely bisexual, unable to comprehend the distaste felt by friends like Chappell and Helpmann at the idea of making love to a woman. 'I knew what I was but I couldn't deny a whole section of society: one's got to go ahead and *see*.' Like Tiresias, he believed that a woman derives more pleasure from sex: 'Of *course* she does. She gets penetrated.'* And having experienced the act of

---

*A former lover argues that Ashton's attitude towards penetration was 'entirely homosexual: he was the female partner'.

love from both points of view, it was the frissons of the woman in love, in particular, that he portrayed so poetically and convincingly in his ballets, with what, indeed, seemed a first-hand knowledge.

Michael Somes (understudied by Alexander Grant) appeared as the male Tiresias, asserting his virility in a non-stop dance of athletic prowess. However, his technique had declined considerably of late, and he failed to make the impact Ashton intended. '[It] would hardly have won third prize at a Prep school sports.' Symbolizing his dual sexuality, a pair of 'copulating snakes' appeared: Brian Shaw held Pauline Clayden upside down by one leg and she coiled round, down and over him, until, breaking up their coupling, Tiresias killed the female snake and, in a trick of light, disappeared. Immediately, Margot Fonteyn, the female Tiresias, wearing the same combination of white and gold, emerged high above a massive Minoan bull. Endorsing the conclusions of the legend, the most lyrical music and choreography were created for her. A solo with a white scarf, performed to a soft Siciliana, was followed by an ecstatic, sexually ambivalent pas de deux (with John Field), which 'fizzed up into a kind of orgasm', after which the pair lay on the floor in stylized, post-coital stillness.

This passage of music was Lambert's last love poem to Fonteyn. Although he was now married to Isabel Delmer, the dancers noticed that there was 'still something lingering between Margot and Constant – we all felt it'. Fonteyn does not even mention Tiresias in her autobiography, although it is the ballet which, according to Mary Clarke, she danced with a passionate intensity not equalled in any other role. When Tito Arias came back into her life, determined to marry her, he was made so jealous by the rapturous duet and by her seemingly transparent, Cretan-style bodice, that she relinquished the role to Violetta Elvin, telling a friend, 'Tito has made such a carry-on, I just can't do it.'

The third scene, which Richard Buckle described as 'pointless and vulgar . . . [an] absurd wrangle of pedestalled deities', was similar, in its gesticulating pantomime style, to the quarrel between Jupiter and Juno in Cupid and Psyche, only this time it was portentous rather than flippant. Ashton was bored by the idea of treating the gods' dispute in dance terms and so he handed over the choreography to Alfred Rodriguez, who played Zeus. 'Just get on with it,' Fred said, 'but don't be too filthy.' The result was unintentionally comic, 'like an opera without singing'. The ballet ended with Tiresias as a blind old man, groping miserably off stage, the sound of his tapping stick providing the final notes of the score. This last section was the ballet's nadir. It was too long (Tiresias ran for an hour) and too solemn for the occasion it was intended to celebrate: the 1951 Festival of Britain. The first-night reception by a gala audience in

the presence of The Queen was polite but unenthusiastic. It was rumoured that there had been three deputations from the palace to ensure
the work's suitability for royal viewing, but the principals who visited the
royal box after the performance felt a distinct froideur: when Fonteyn
entered, having covered her provocative top with a cardigan, Princess
Elizabeth turned her back and looked away. Lambert's euphemistic
programme note had disguised the fact that the ballet dealt with sex; but,
from the slash of two whips with which his stridently percussive score began, there was a tangible erotic charge on stage. 'We thought it was a
tremendously exciting ballet,' said Anya Linden,* who appeared as one
of the Priestesses. 'The stunning pas de deux which wasn't at all Fred's
usual romantic style; the sexy snakes and bare-bosomed designs by Constant's wild-looking wife . . . all seemed extraordinary to us.'

The critics thought otherwise. Every review was negative, and those
by Richard Buckle and Richard Johnson† were almost libellously hostile.
Lambert, in fact, instructed his solicitor to demand an apology from
Buckle, whose review in the *Observer*, entitled 'Three Blind Mice', implied that Sadler's Wells' three artistic directors were incompetent. De
Valois, he said, was too busy to supervise every detail of production; and
Ashton (who, with Lambert, completed the triumvirate) was 'too easily
reconciled to compromise'. Buckle followed up his review with further
articles questioning the directorial policies of Sadler's Wells, a campaign
de Valois interpreted as a take-over bid by the critic himself (although, in
print, he had proposed the appointment of Boris Kochno as a Diaghilev-
type figure to guide artistic decisions). At 'Madam's' summons, the dancers
convened in the corps girls' dressing room as she explained the position
and asked them not to make independent statements to the press. The
company closed ranks – they felt that Lambert, in particular, had been
unfairly treated – and when the composer suddenly died six weeks later,
they held the ballet's detractors responsible. In his obituary of Lambert in
the *New Statesman and Nation*, Osbert Sitwell, who had written a
protesting letter to the journal after it had published Richard Johnson's
attack, reiterated the opinion that Lambert would still be alive had it not
been for the savage onslaught on *Tiresias*.

Lambert, however, had been a sick man for some time. He was an un-
diagnosed diabetic, whose symptoms were exacerbated by heavy drinking. Despite his genius as a collaborator – an enriching influence on most
of Ashton's early ballets – his importance in the history of English ballet
has always been undervalued. To Balanchine and Kirstein, he alone was

*Now Anya Sainsbury.
†The pen name of John Richardson, Picasso's biographer.

the hero of the Wells' triumphant début in New York. 'A divine conductor,' Kirstein reported to Buckle, 'the greatest ballet man in the business.' Although Ashton was now less dependent on Lambert's musical counsel, he continued to respect his judgement and to appreciate his scholarship and knowledge of the arts. 'Constant knew about everything; Maynard Keynes told me that he was potentially the most brilliant man he'd ever met.' Ashton denied that Lambert had moulded his musical taste: 'No one did that. But I would listen to his opinion.' And Lambert would listen to Ashton's, particularly on matters of the heart. They had in common a fatal weakness for the unattainable; in Lambert's case, 'the remote, the inaccessible, the exotic, the unsuitable'. 'I suppose I was his closest friend – or at least his confidant,' said Ashton. 'Every misery he went through I had to share. I saw him through it all with Margot.' Ashton still took no part in Lambert's Fitzrovian life – indeed, he had not even heard of the term: 'They were such drunks I couldn't keep up with them.' But the composer's death, so closely following that of Lord Berners the previous year, caused him great sorrow. Ashton had lost two close friends and collaborators in quick succession, which was to be only the beginning of a macabre rollcall of the death of friends.

It was time to take stock. Sadler's Wells had had a particularly uninspiring season, marred by poor performances and the absence of injured dancers. After a terminal show-down with de Valois, Robert Helpmann had left the company in the middle of the tour. He had not been a success in America, particularly as a choreographer. 'Take the Ham out of *Hamlet!*' one critic had quipped; while Kirstein, in private, compared the ballet to a *Reader's Digest* abstraction, and was damning but perceptive about Helpmann's own performances: 'a sort of dwarfish vengeful narcissism explodes with little nodules of unlove.' Many prominent people began to proclaim that ballet was 'finished' and, determined to prove them wrong, de Valois put aside everything to get the repertory back into shape. Despite its unpopularity, *Tiresias*, cut by twenty minutes, continued to be performed. It was not a complete disaster; the score, as Alan Rawsthorne has written, is 'evocative, pictorial and . . . charged with the spirit of the theatre', and Ashton's fusion of neoclassicism with the silhouetted, angular style of Greek dance was first rate. One of the few critics to acknowledge this was James Monahan, whom Ashton wrote to thank for his sympathetic review, 'like a sponge of water after being buffeted in the ring'. Only Monahan, he felt, had understood his aim: to extend the boundaries of classical dance, uncovering latent drama and giving it a contemporary slant without resorting to the grotesque. Ashton received further support for the ballet from indignant friends and fans, but de Valois' decision to commission new works from Massine (*Donald of the Burthens*) and John Cranko (*Bonne Bouche*) was a scouring of salt in his wounds. He must have experienced a touch of satisfaction from the fact that neither piece was a success, but nevertheless, nursing a familiar sense of rejection, he made a point of accepting assignments elsewhere.

In January and February 1952, Ashton went to Hollywood to arrange the dance for *The Story of Three Loves*, a film directed by Gottfried Reinhardt and Vincente Minnelli. Ashton was involved only with the first story, 'The Jealous Lover', starring James Mason and Moira Shearer, a banal, derivative tale of a beautiful red-haired ballerina dancing herself to death under the influence of an autocratic impresario. This was Ashton's first handling of Rachmaninov's 'Variations on a theme of Paganini', the score he was to use for his 1980 ballet, *Rhapsody*. His choreography is elegantly lyrical: tailored, first, to Shearer's stiletto shoes and evening dress; then, when she performs in costume in the impresario's house, growing increasingly flamboyant. Pavlova's imprint is everywhere; one sweepingly circular port de bras borrows a well-known sequence from her performance in *La Nuit*. Dance critics praised the beautiful flow of the choreography but failed to point out that Ashton was either recycling his own material or else being deliberately self-referential. From a choice of three costumes, 'Air, Earth, Fire', the ballerina chooses the first, twinning her with Fonteyn (in *The Fairy Queen*) as a spirit of the Air; while the snippet of a production we see at the opera house, with its red and orange costumes, and set of flaming streamers, bears more than a passing resemblance to the Fire section in *Homage to the Queen*.

Ashton had worked with Moira Shearer the previous year, in Michael Powell's *The Tales of Hoffmann*, also a story of three loves told in a fantastical synthesis of three genres: opera, dance and cinema. It was a daringly uncommercial venture, made possible only by the huge success of Powell and Pressburger's *The Red Shoes*. *The Tales of Hoffmann* reassembled the main players from the earlier film, and Ashton, who was brought in as both choreographer and a performer, felt something of an interloper, 'edged out' by Massine and Helpmann.

> They *loathed* each other and were always fighting for the best position. I'd ask Bobby where I was going to be and he'd say, 'There' (with my back to the camera). I'd agreed to do the choreography on condition I didn't have to do Massine's dances. He was supposedly one of the greatest choreographers and I felt I couldn't possibly. I'd been his pupil. So I did all the other parts, which of course

he resented, but Michael Powell didn't want him to. He wanted him as an artist.

Powell was aware of the rivalry between Massine and Helpmann, but, as a fan of both, was happy to indulge them. 'Massine took charge of the whole production. I was his camera man', while Helpmann, 'knowing which parts Massine would grab for himself . . . made a clean sweep of all the villains'. Ashton, on the other hand, 'had better manners'. Unlike his two colleagues, he appears only in the first third of the film, in two character roles, each spiked with self-parody. As Kleinzack, he is the hunchback jester, with a potbelly and Cyrano nose, who is enamoured of a disdainful medieval beauty (Moira Shearer). Her obsession with her reflection recalled Pearl Argyle's *The Lady of Shalott*; and another echo from an Ashton ballet is evident when Kleinzack, holding the woman's train against his cheek, mimics the Jester in *Cinderella*. But the main interest of the role is its caricature of 'La Bête Ashton', the persona he had mocked in letters to Dick Beard: 'I am diffident, stunted, middle aged and unattractive and you are all the beauty radiant, upstanding and aloof.'

The puppetmaster, Cochenille, impersonates Ashton the choreographer, responsible for setting the dancers in motion. With his painted, pouting lips and tripping hobble walk, it is a performance of 'inspired stupidity', a foil to the effete exhibitionism of Spalanzani, played by Massine. Ashton would mock Massine's 'proud, peacocky' behaviour off camera, but, having endured his mentor's constant upstaging, he gets his revenge through Cochenille, who pokes out his tongue at his overbearing master. Like the puppeteer, whose role it is to wind-up the clockwork doll, Ashton was responsible for her dance, a solo in which Moira Shearer performs ballet's equivalent of coloratura: scintillating footwork and virtuosic fouetté turns. A more unusual contribution is the Dragonfly Ballet which opens the film: a flitting, fluttery dance, made in homage to Pavlova's famous solo, which also borrows speeded-up images from *Swan Lake*, conflating them with modern contortions. In a bizarre ending, the dragonfly suddenly transforms into a Petit-like sexual predator, aggressively miming the murder of her mate, who is left undulating, like a reed in the water, as she dances off into the night, silhouetted against the moon.

As choreography for the camera, neither piece is particularly impressive. Movements are not adapted for high angles, and the dance is mostly shot full length, tracked by a camera that is frequently taken by surprise. Powell claimed that Ashton showed a keen, but limited, sense of cinema. He did not sit in on the editing and had little enthusiasm for trying new resources available to him.

I'd say to Freddie, 'Would you like a guide track?'
'Well, Michael, I don't think I do, if you don't mind.'

At the time of its release, *The Tales of Hoffmann* was not a critical or box-office success, although it has since acquired a certain cult status, mostly owing to the fact that Martin Scorsese claims the film influenced him more than any other.

Ashton flew straight from Los Angeles to New York to begin work on his second assignment for New York City Ballet, *Picnic at Tintagel*. Reunited with Lincoln Kirstein and Cecil Beaton, he spent the weekend with Alice at Rhinebeck. As always, she was an attentive hostess, although this time she did not involve herself in the collaboration. Alice was in love again. Through Gore Vidal she had met John Latouche, a puckish, thirty-three-year-old lyricist, best known for the Ethel Waters movie *Cabin in the Sky*. It was he, and no longer Ashton, who now benefited from her patronage. 'Touche was brilliant,' said Vidal, his closest friend. 'Winning, charming and feckless. Women loved him; he came on so. There are people who make the weather and Touche – a writer, actor, singer, dancer – made the weather for everyone round him.' Latouche was fascinated by psychic research and, chameleon-like as ever, Alice steeped herself in his obsession. 'They used to be in a room muttering about this and would shut up when I came in with my bright sneer,' said Vidal. From now on, Alice became involved in a way of life that was alarmingly alien to her family and friends. 'Alice is just mad,' Kirstein reported to Beaton. 'I am distressed, but there is nothing to be done. She has quite lost any contact with exterior reality . . . I don't THINK she will marry Touche, but she spends all her time with him and she is so strange and daft . . . she won't put up a nickel for me or Fred or anything.'

The show went on regardless. Ashton had already worked out the libretto of *Picnic at Tintagel* with Robert Irving, who had replaced Constant Lambert as Musical Director. Set among the ruins of Tintagel in 1916 (the year Arnold Bax composed 'The Garden of Fand', which Ashton used as his score),* the ballet tells the Arthurian tale of Tristram and Iseult in flashback, in parallel to a narrative of adulterous love among a group of Edwardian tourists. Its theme of forbidden, repressed yearning, a perennial concern in Ashton's work, was one with which he acutely identified at the time. Lucian Freud, whom he had met through Ann Fleming, was his first choice of designer, but Lincoln Kirstein told him that the artist would want too much money and proposed Beaton as a more suitable choice. Once again, Kirstein was deeply involved with the project, assailing the collaborators with 'divine ideas'.

*He considered it more suitable to dance than Bax's score *Tintagel*.

Iseult at Tintagel must be mist-bound and vague glowing and golden, fierce and dark etc. Fred has tomes of letters from me about how the roses are drained of fire and ruby-blood etc . . .

Ashton's source for the journey back in time was a famous account by Miss Moberly and Miss Jourdain of a dream-like walk, *An Adventure*, written in 1901. Sightseeing in Paris, the two friends decide to visit Versailles and, while making their way to the Petit Trianon, come upon figure after figure in late-eighteenth-century dress, placed in a landscape which had become as flat, still and lifeless as a tapestry. The sinister kiosk-keeper, wearing a heavy black cloak and slouch hat, was the originator of Ashton's Caretaker of the castle, 'a strange half-hobo', who, in Scene Two, assumes the character of Merlin the Magician (played by Robert Barnett, a character dancer, 'very like Alexander Grant', who could spin and move at super speed). The eerie, oppressive atmosphere the women describe permeated the ballet: Beaton's ruined Tintagel was 'shadowy, mysterious, fascinating'; and Arnold Bax, whose music was linked inextricably to the Celtic twilight, was a master at conveying wild seascapes and a mystical, magical sense of place.

All that remains of *Picnic at Tintagel* are a few minutes of fuzzy, jittery, black and white film.* Without an evocation of atmosphere, the choreography looks dated and over-charged, although the dancers' histrionic gestures were, at the time, not seen as flawed. To eliminate 'the Wagnerian [illegible] overtones', the title was changed from *Iseult at Tintagel*, but Ashton did not want to erase the ballet's operatic origins entirely. Having portrayed a euphoric, Tristan-like sense of frozen anticipation between the lovers in *Daphnis and Chloe*, he tried a more daringly operatic medium for *Picnic at Tintagel*. Keeping dance to a minimum, he concentrated on the mime. But rather than using a static semaphore, he rhythmicized the gestures, setting them in motion and extending them into the action. As in *Tiresias*, the most interesting choreography was the ballerina's solo and the pas de deux for the lovers. Iseult was danced by Diana Adams, the company's rising star – 'She has a chance to be the American Margot,' Kirstein told Buckle – and Tristram, the seventeen-year-old Jacques d'Amboise – 'Fresh and touching . . . big and strong, he is going to forge ahead.' The two dancers found Ashton's method of working rather alien at first, not realizing that he expected them to perform for him. 'Balanchine gave us a count and a step for every note,' said d'Amboise. 'Fred didn't give steps, he gave ideas – he would say to me, "*Swirl!*" and Balanchine would say "*Chaîné.*"' At the time, d'Amboise considered Ashton to be lazy and somewhat inferior to Bal-

*Held in New York Public Library's Dance Collection at Lincoln Center.

anchine, in that he frequently made the dancers invent their own choreography.

> '*Throw* yourself at her feet,' Freddie would say. 'Make up something, dear boy, don't wait for the steps.' It was only much later that I realized what he was trying to achieve: he wanted me to do what came out of my head and nature, and then he'd edit it. He was allowing me freedom. He'd say, 'You put in what you want and I'll put in what I want, and then we may have something.'

Diana Adams's Iseult was the prototype Ashton woman, who, like Natalia Petrovna in *A Month in the Country*, falls desperately in love against her own volition. The ballet's rendition of Isolde's long wait for Tristan was dazzling in its simplicity: throughout a long passage of music, she performed trembling, Pavlova-like bourrées on pointe, her weight falling forward as she made small supplicating gestures with her hands. 'Years later I stole that idea and used it,' said d'Amboise. Their duet was the centrepiece of the ballet, passionately sensual – 'it was fornication on stage' – and yet transfigured by Ashton's sublimation of the movements. Apart from Edwin Denby, who found the whole enterprise rather risible ('Ashton's Isolde behaved like a Potiphar's Wife with a willing young Joe'), all the critics praised the work. It was not, as Beaton reported to a friend, 'a great event in the ballet world, but . . . our Tintagel ballet . . . has great charm and a strange atmosphere . . . & will be useful'.

Picnic at Tintagel provided New York City Ballet with the sort of theatre piece that was lacking in a repertory of mostly plotless works. It was one of which the company could be justly proud, even though its origins – what Kirstein described as Ashton's 'traditional gift of narrative pantomime and domesticity' – were English and antipathetic to Balanchine's aesthetics. 'It is primarily a theatre style, not a musical one – his big influence is not Balanchine but Sarah Bernhardt.' Understandably, Balanchine did not like the work, but, according to d'Amboise, was 'a little envious of its success'. *Picnic at Tintagel* continued to be performed for a few seasons and then disappeared. The costumes and sets were said to have been destroyed by a warehouse fire, which, Ashton sourly told friends, 'was probably lit by Balanchine'.

Ashton completed *Tintagel* by the end of February 1952 and returned home in time to enjoy spring in the English countryside. In a nostalgic excavation of his roots, he had bought the Old Schoolhouse in Yaxley, his mother's village, situated diagonally opposite the graveyard where

Georgie and her Fulcher antecedents are buried. He acquired Church Cottage, as he renamed it, in 1948, a pretty, thatched and gabled cottage washed Suffolk pink, which he bought along with five freehold cottages (sold to their sitting tenants in the late 1950s). Ashton spent over two years extending and renovating the property, using a local firm to build on two bedrooms, overhaul the plumbing and rethatch the roof. With Sophie and Edith's help, he created a cottage garden, planting old-fashioned roses, pink jasmine and wild flowers. After months of feeling 'dull, dispirited, frustrated, and eclipsed by antipodean moonshine', Ashton's long courtship of Alexander Grant had finally taken effect. Nadia Nerina had given the dancer an ultimatum: 'When Fred fell for Alexander,' said Nerina, 'he [Ashton] became very jealous of me. Terribly jealous. And I had to find my own way because I didn't know about these things either – hadn't a clue. But I understood, and I said to Alexander, "You've got to choose."' In fact, the circumstances surrounding Grant's decision had little to do with either Ashton or Nerina. Since 1946, he had been sharing the top floor of St Alban's Clergy House in Holborn with David Gill, a young dancer in Sadler's Wells Theatre Ballet, whom he had befriended when they had been briefly in the school together. Older than the other students, they were both alone in London for the first time and became very close. 'David was someone to talk to and come home to.' Gill was dating a good friend of Nerina's, the dancer Pauline Wadsworth, and they were 'a very happy foursome'; the girls would come for tea at the Clergy House, they all went away on occasional weekends, and would joke about having a double wedding some day. But although Gill maintains he was unaware of it, Grant was becoming increasingly infatuated with him. 'David was the love of Alex's life.' Gill announced his engagement to Pauline Wadsworth in April 1952, at the end of Sadler's Wells Theatre Ballet's* long American tour, a time Grant dates as the beginning of his relationship with Ashton. He felt heartbroken by the news, but Ashton was there to console him. 'Fred saw me almost in tears in a passageway at Covent Garden and asked me what was wrong.' Grant told him, and when Ashton invited him to Yaxley, he accepted.

Weekends at Church Cottage soon became a regular routine. Domestic by nature and an enthusiastic cook, Grant settled easily into Ashton's Suffolk life. They would take the train to Mellis and be met by a local taxi driver; go for bicycle rides, and walk to Mr Ley's junkshop in Eye to look for Wemyss ware and Staffordshire corn-on-the-cob jugs to add to Ashton's growing collection. He taught Grant how to mix a vinaigrette in a wooden spoon and to time perfectly the boiling of quails' eggs. 'And

---

*A second company was formed by de Valois after the Second World War.

then all the cooking was left to me.' 'That was a wonderful relationship. Alex really took care of Fred.' Affectionate, outgoing and practical, Grant would help Ashton with the garden, mend things, move furniture around. 'Freddie was wonderful at directing – "*Move* this," he'd say and the next day want it back where it was.' He would also chivvy him out of his fits of melancholy. There was the inevitable agonizing, on Ashton's part, over Grant's fidelity. He remained very jealous of Nerina – 'Fred had a way of looking at her round the corner of his eyes' – and, despite Grant's reassurances, remained wary of David Gill for at least three years after his marriage.

Although Grant was ambitious and aware of his exceptional dramatic gifts, tensions over the dancer's career, as there had been with Dick Beard, did not surface. On the contrary, when Brian Shaw was away in the army and Grant replaced him in *Symphonic Variations*, he was embarrassed that, as a character dancer, he was not up to such a technically demanding role, even though he had danced it many times before in the late 1940s. Also, he was a great deal more adept than Shaw at winning round de Valois to his relationship with Ashton. 'Ninette adored Alexander and he could deal with her. He'd flirt with her and charm and manipulate her.' Grant may have enjoyed the privilege of his position – and, according to colleagues, he guarded it jealously – but he understood Ashton well enough to know that pressuring him professionally would have a countereffect. His sensitive, ungrasping nature was greatly appreciated by Ashton, who, the previous year, had terminated a liaison with an Italian dancer after receiving a long begging letter:

> Why don't you take me in London with you Freddie, why don't you find a work for me in the Sadler's after all I've been studying classic dance for some time, I really could do something, at least the littlest part . . . I want to work Freddie, I want to work with all my strengths for the theatre, but I am no one and someone must help me . . .

It was an experience that Ashton was unwilling to repeat. Grant, however, never once asked the choreographer for a role: 'I wouldn't know if I was in one of Freddie's ballets until I saw my name up on the board.' To begin with, as he had done with Dick Beard, Ashton introduced the dancer into his social round, taking him for weekends with Terence Rattigan and to dinners with grand friends, 'But it didn't last long: I wasn't a big success.' (Grant got rather drunk at a party given by Lady Diana Cooper and complimented his hostess on her beauty, a remark considered out of place by Lady Diana, who cut him for the rest of the evening.) Ashton was very good at compartmentalizing his friends, and Grant was someone whom, in the end, he preferred to keep to himself. A tender complicity existed between them which superseded any words. 'We could talk quite easily, but sometimes we didn't need to.' In these moods, without saying anything, Grant would go and fetch the Chinese Chequers game that Ashton loved to play because it reminded him of his art. 'He enjoyed the way everything got in a muddle and then resolved itself. He used to say: "That's choreography."' Their rapport also had professional undertones, corresponding to the mysterious symbiosis between a choreographer and his muse. But it was less the sort of spiritual kinship that had developed between Ashton and Beard than an affectionate, domestic companionship – possibly the most rewarding relationship of Ashton's life – which ultimately transcended rival affairs and lasted until the day he died. He manifested his love and gratitude towards Grant, long after the physical side of things was at an end, in some of the most singular, personalized character roles ever created.

Ashton did not invite the dancer on his second summer holiday with the *Eliki* group: Fonteyn, John Craxton, Ruth Page and Tom Fisher, who had rented the famous Villa Cimbrone in Ravello, where Greta Garbo had spent a romantic holiday with the conductor, Leopold Stokowski, and where, a year later, in 1937, William Walton wrote his Violin Concerto. Jutting a thousand feet above one of the most stunning stretches of coastline in the world, it is an intoxicating place – 'A cross between being on a yacht and in an aeroplane,' as Kenneth Clark told Craxton – as well as relaxingly sylvan, with its shady, grape-festooned terraces and Moorish cloisters. The friends went on several excursions by boat to explore nearby islands. One trip – which Grant would certainly have relished – was to Gallo Lugo, the largest of three rocky islands, Li Galli, about a mile from Positano, which Diaghilev had persuaded Massine to buy. 'There was nobody about when we landed,' said Craxton. 'We walked up to the house where we found Massine asleep. We decided not to wake him, but Fred wrote a visiting card and stuck it between his toes.' Massine then arrived unannounced at the villa a couple of days later.

With Ashton in a mythopoeic frame of mind, contemplating *Sylvia*, his next ballet, Cimbrone's formal gardens and classical statuary provided an inspirational setting. The 'columns through which a magnificent view of the coast and sea can be glimpsed' could be a description of the backdrop for Act III; while the Temple of Bacchus, with its lovely marble youth, must have influenced his decision to cast Alexander Grant as Eros, posed, statue-still, in a shrine throughout most of Act I. When the curtain rose, Grant, hardly breathing and wearing nothing but a silver-silk body suit and a fig leaf, looked so convincingly marmoreal that the audience assumed he was a piece of scenery.

Sylvia was Ashton's second full-length work and the company's most ambitious venture to date. Intended to rival the famous productions of the past, it had been preoccupying him since 1947, when he had accepted, then rejected, a libretto by Richard Buckle. Delibes' melodious score continued to attract him, and, in 1952, propelled by an upsurge of interest in the three-act form (several critics were then urging a return to a genre that Diaghilev had renounced as degraded and shallow), Ashton decided that the moment had come to do *Sylvia*. Rather than reinventing a classical myth for modern times, he created a charming pastiche of Paris Opera conventions. The Arcadian rococo designs (by Robin and Christopher Ironside) were Claude-inspired; the choreography, unashamedly old-fashioned.

At its most basic, *Sylvia* is a pastoral love story very similar to that of *Daphnis and Chloe*: 'Boy loves Girl – Girl captured by Bad Man – Girl restored to Boy by God.' Ashton's one mistake was not to follow Sacheverell Sitwell's advice to make the plot 'as simple as possible, so that all the accent can be on the music and the dancing'. His libretto, which stayed close to the original production of 1876, is complex and unengaging, narrating not only Tasso's tale of a shepherd's love for Sylvia, the huntress nymph, her abduction by the villain, Orion, and indifference to the machinations of Eros, but also alluding to Diana's passion for the sleeping Endymion – a final twist which no one without a knowledge of classical mythology or a programme note would understand.

Ashton's raison d'être for *Sylvia* was to provide a showcase for Margot Fonteyn, who, since her recognition in America, had reached the summit of her career, eliciting heady superlatives for her 'miraculous', 'astonishing' performances. The audience had never seen an Amazonian Fonteyn before. Shadowed by her troupe, she leads the hunt with martial swagger, one recurring leap wittily mimicking the firing of an arrow. But the role is full of contrasts. The section ends with Sylvia joining hands with her huntresses and leading them out of their regimental lines into a softly flowing Grecian chain. And when Sylvia thinks Aminta is dead, she instantly turns into one of Ashton's helplessly romantic women in love, her foot stuttering forward in a movement that conflates past and future: paying homage to Pavlova's Dying Swan and looking forward to the expiring heroine of *Marguerite and Armand*. In Act II, Fonteyn plays the seductress, feigning interest in Orion's advances; in the final scene, she appears in her element as the classic assoluta.

> The part has everything for Fonteyn. It exploits her imperiousness, her tenderness, her pathos, her womanliness, her bravura. It gives us Fonteyn triumphant, Fonteyn bewildered, Fonteyn exotic, Fonteyn pathetic, Fonteyn in excelsis. The range of her dancing is

unequalled, the heart-splitting significance she can give to a simple movement unsurpassed. The whole ballet is like a garland presented to the ballerina by her choreographer.

As part of Ashton's homage, the choreography enshrines highlights from her career: an inspired enchaînement with tiny cymbals (crotali) recalls her delicate oriental dance in *Wise Virgins*; a luminously simple pizzicato solo salutes her Aurora. But he also challenged Fonteyn's technique in a way he had never done before. '*Sylvia* was the best thing Margot ever danced, she was glorious in it,' said her colleague Annette Page. 'Her technique in the mid-fifties was phenomenal – her Black Swan left us breathless.' The part of Sylvia's lover, Aminta, was danced by Michael Somes, whose own technique showed a marked improvement after an intense course of classes with Alexander Volinin in Paris. In recognition of this, Ashton gave him what Cyril Beaumont described as 'a Volinin-like solo', drawing attention to his newly polished academic precision. His Act III pas de deux with Fonteyn was the climax of the evening; until that moment, several critics felt, the ballet had failed to pack the sort of virtuosic punch traditionally associated with a full-length work. Sylvia was carried on stage in a magnificent arc high above Aminta's head to a violin solo interpolated, along with much of the music for this act, from Delibes' *La Source*. This duet had all the excitement and authority of a grand pas de deux in the Petipa manner, but Ashton also humanized it into an avowal of their love. There is a wonderful moment when Aminta, supporting the ballerina with a touch of his fingers on her temples, lowers her head and then raises it against his cheek, as she seems to melt into his body, his arms spreading along hers.

Much of *Sylvia*'s choreography for the corps de ballet relies on formulaic enchainements, reflecting the fact that, for Ashton, creating dance for large ensembles was often something of a chore. 'The first thing Freddie did when he came into the studio was go up to the piano and see how many more pages he had to fill.' In this case, however, the conventional, even texture of the choreography is in keeping with his pastiche of the period, and gives the ballet a 'peculiarly French' quality of delicacy. 'Hearing this 19th-century music, it's impossible for me . . . to depart from the spirit of the music . . . I try to be inventive, but I think I have a very adjusted sense of what the music is trying to say to me.' Not that the ballet lacks originality. When Eros enters disguised as an impish sorcerer, his droll hobbling run, picked up by the watching ensemble, is a touch of the sort of pure nonsense that only Ashton could bring off. The ballet, as Richard Buckle wrote, was 'a confusion of excellence and weakness', the lowest point being a winsome duet for a pair of goats (Brian Shaw and

Pauline Clayden), but the general view at the time was that, as a full-length work, *Sylvia* had failed. '[Its] dance composition for Acts I and II do not rise to the heights one expects of a master.' In response to the criticism, Ashton, in 1967, distilled the ballet into one act, eliminating not only the silly goats but also the sorcerer and several other highlights. Those who had loved *Sylvia* 'felt cheated' by the cut version, while its critics continued to complain that the subject was too anachronistic for the times.

In January 1953, Ashton returned to classical myth as both choreographer and director of a new production of Gluck's *Orpheus*. The title role was sung by Kathleen Ferrier, who was dying of cancer at the time. 'Dear Freddie', as Ferrier called him, was sweetly solicitous towards her, doing everything he could to save her from undue exertion. 'She found it unusual to work with someone who, without a word being openly said, instinctively knew just how to help her save her failing energy, inspiring her to put forth all her strength at exactly the right time and place . . .'

Whereas in many operas dance exists only as a form of divertissement, the ballet in *Orpheus* was as integral as the singing. Ashton conceived a highly stylized production in close collaboration with Sophie Fedorovitch, whose near-abstract designs were in perfect accord with the beautiful simplicity of Gluck's score.

The first night was scheduled for Tuesday, 3 February 1953. A choral run-through took place on the Sunday before, at which Sophie failed to appear. This slightly surprised Ashton, as she never missed a rehearsal if she could help it, but, like everyone else, he assumed that she had gone to Paris for the weekend to work on a new Birger Bartholin ballet for the de Cuevas company. On Monday morning, he was nearly late for the rehearsal because he had not been woken by Sophie's usual alarm call. When by midday she had still not arrived at the Opera House, he sent her assistant, Alan Tagg, to her studio in Bury Walk. There was no answer when Tagg rang the bell, and, concerned by the smell of gas in the street, he let himself in with the key Sophie had given him. She was lying on the floor beside her bed, with one arm stretched out towards the telephone. She had been dead for two days. Tagg summoned the emergency services and broke the news to Ashton, who came immediately.

> He was stunned. It was awful, *awful* for him but he took it silently, with a set face. There were stretchers, police, gasmen, reporters crowding the room but he and I just sat there until the evening. At one point I told him I had to go and give someone a lift and he panicked and said, 'I mustn't be left alone.' Billy Chappell came round

and at about ten o'clock we went to Yeoman's Row and stayed up until the early hours. Fred was very very upset. He didn't know how he was going to go on with *Orpheus*.

The tragedy was, as the *Daily Express* termed it, a 'riddle', in that Sophie was not 'the sort to commit suicide in the least', as Ashton said. Her work was going well and she had been in tremendous good spirits. An inquest recorded a verdict of accidental death: she was poisoned by escaping gas caused by a defective thermostat in an ancient central-heating boiler, which her builder had begged her for years to replace. Ironically, the economy for which Sophie was so highly regarded in her work – 'There is genius in such Spartan austerity' – had inadvertently led to her death. Ashton told Richard Buckle that it was one of the hardest blows of fate he had had to bear.

Sophie Fedorovitch had designed eleven of Ashton ballets, from his first, *A Tragedy of Fashion*, to his most flawless, *Symphonic Variations*, in which her method of scrupulous elimination profoundly influenced his own purging of the dance to its essence. He never found a collaborator as in tune with his ideas or a friend who could take her place. Her forceful influence affected not only his art but his way of life. His favourite pastimes, such as cycling in the countryside and foraging in junkshops, derived from Sophie, whose fondness for pastel colours, old roses and wild flowers inspired his own. 'She was very before her time: planting cowslips and buttercups in the grass long before it became the popular thing to do.' The love they shared of simple things filtered into their work. Sophie's design for *Symphonic Variations*, her masterpiece, was so fresh and delicate that Bérard called it a lily-of-the-valley. Simplicity has always been a hallmark of Ashton's ballets – as Edwin Denby famously remarked, 'The more trivial the subject, the deeper and more beautiful is Ashton's poetic view of it.'

It was to be five years before he could bring himself to go back to Sophie's 'Gothic Box', even though he was a friend of Simon Fleet, who inherited it. Fleet himself died in the house (he was found at the bottom of the stairs), convincing Ashton that it was jinxed. He was equally superstitious about *Orpheus*, especially after learning of another death: Covent Garden's stage manager, Louis Yudkin, who was killed in a plane crash. For Ashton, the opening scene of mourners surrounding Eurydice's tomb was unbearably moving: it was almost as if Sophie had deliberately created her own memorial. The chilling sense of déjà vu, described by Fleet, gives some indication of what Ashton was forced to endure:

> As the first performance went on, the atmosphere grew more and more tense; it was appalling when in the scenes in hell, smoke filled

the stage as S. had intended; for we couldn't help being reminded of the escaping gas at 22 Bury Walk.

Towards the end of the second night, Kathleen Ferrier almost collapsed on stage. She managed, with amazing fortitude, to get through the final aria, but it proved to be her swansong: the two remaining performances of the opera were cancelled and she would never again appear on stage.

Of the production itself, there was the usual divergence of opinion between the music and dance press: The 'stately dancing' and 'unadulterated sublimity', which the critic of *Opera* magazine found so soporific, was championed by Mary Clarke, particularly the solo Ashton choreographed for Svetlana Beriosova, the leader of the Blessed Spirits. Over the last two years, this beautiful, Lithuanian-born twenty-one-year-old had begun to show unmistakable stature. As well as a joie de vivre and distinct flair for comedy, she had a rare quality of tender graciousness, purity and calm, which Ashton drew on for the first time in *Orpheus*. To the famous cor anglais passage, a barefooted Beriosova danced an Isadora-like series of running steps, and poised on her outstretched hand was a white dove. Visually, Ashton's staging was superb, particularly the first scene when the singers and dancers appeared united in a single pattern, a slow-moving tableau in which the contrasting colours and swathes of twisted chiffon in Fedorovitch's costumes were incorporated into the choreographic line. His inspiration for the grouping of mourners were the funeral dances represented in *Antique Greek Dance*, the book which had been such a vital influence on his last three ballets. Here, imitating the silhouettes on Greek vases, the lamentations were symbolized by gracefully cadenced gestures, based on hands decoratively resting on the head. The choreography was at its weakest in the underworld. Ashton 'failed lamentably' with the climax of the opening of hell's gate – 'Orpheus strolled down the Stygian ranks as if at a review' – and the Dance of Furies, despite being led by Alexander Grant, was 'cute rather than fearsome'.

A nasty bout of flu had dampened Grant's performance, otherwise his dancing was on thrilling form. In a speedy Neapolitan tarantella specially created for him and Julia Farron (for a revised production of *Swan Lake*), Ashton used his frenetic energy and scampish charm to show-stopping effect. Just as Britten exploited the strange, distinctive register of Peter Pears's voice, Ashton's dance was defined by Grant's idiosyncratic style: his quirky inflection of the steps (so minted to his own body that other dancers found it almost impossible to take over his roles), the reckless jumps, darting changes of direction and sudden slips to the floor, not to

be found in any classical lexicon. And it was not only the dancer's ath-
leticism and sense of risk that Ashton utilized; in roles such as the leader
of the Furies and the Spirit of Fire, a solo from *Homage to The Queen*,
he caught the very essence of Grant's personality – an impetuosity that
had once led him to join the Spanish youths running with the bulls
through the steeets of Pamplona.

> He was always bubbling, talking arguing – he *loved* arguing. He
> and Fred would row so badly . . . they'd even argue about who
> liked sweetcorn the most. And he had to be absolutely on edge to
> perform, very much like Nureyev used to be. Alex never even
> warmed up. He would just *burst* on the stage. And he would make
> himself late in the theatre, so late that everyone else was panicking
> that he wouldn't make it.

The early summer of 1953 brought the Coronation and, having orga-
nized two tickets for the grandstand in front of the Duke of Wellington's
house at Hyde Park Corner, Ashton and Grant sat in the rain from 7 a.m.
to watch the procession. Through a courtier acquaintance, he had obtained The Queen's permission to create a new ballet as part of the festivities: *Homage to The Queen*. Its composer was the young Malcolm
Arnold, who, in his first ballet commission, provided a danceable, appropriately descriptive score. 'Fred loved the way the music came so
quickly and easily out of Malcolm,' said Anya Linden. 'He was a heavy,
lovely, jovial man and would stand by the piano to watch us, twinkling
and laughing. If Fred didn't like a particular passage, he'd happily write
something else.' Created to display the achievements of the whole company, the ballet opened with a grand defilé by a quartet of ballerinas, the
Queens of the Four Elements, with their cavaliers and attendants. Then
there followed four miniature ballets, each enacting the chosen element,
in much the same way as Ashton had dramatized the four Seasons in *Cinderella*. This time, however, presumably because he was deliberately extending their range, the ballerinas were not as typecast. The buoyant
Nadia Nerina was grounded as Queen of the Earth, given terre-à-terre
footwork and heavy steps en fondu, which emphasized the pull of gravity. The Queen of Water, with her rippling arms, perfectly suited Violetta
Elvin and anticipated the watery conceits in *Ondine*, choreographed five
years later. For the corps, Ashton created striking baroque tableaux, architecturally amassed like Bernini fountains; and, in a change of music,
gave the effect of pattering rain with clipped, tapping pointework on
spot. The noisily percussive Fire section, led by Beryl Grey, was more un-
even. Serene Svetlana Beriosova, cast in the pas de quatre, was conspicu-

ously out of her element; and even Grant, with fiery hair and arms licked by writhing flames of red ribbon, made only a tepid impact. But the scene which followed, for Fonteyn and Somes as Queen of the Air and her Consort, effaced any flaws. It was a development of their Spirits of the Air duet from *The Fairy Queen*, their ethereal lifts offset by the corps wafting in flurries from side to side, considered by Clive Barnes to rank 'among the finest pieces of classical choreography ballet has yet produced'.

Homage to The Queen ended with an apotheosis, in which the company saluted the lavishly costumed figures of the two Elizabeths, one handing on to the other a sceptre and orb. As the curtain came down, the dancers were grouped in the shape of a crown, with Fonteyn poised as the priceless jewel on top. But, in spite of its rather sycophantic conclusion (which everyone agreed should be cut), Ashton's Coronation ode was heaped with praise. Barnes went so far as to call it a masterpiece: 'Mr Ashton has done his job too well to get full credit for it. It was wayward of him to produce possibly his best classic ballet for an occasion like this.' As a laureate, Ashton had succeeded where Benjamin Britten had failed. *Gloriana*, the composer's own contribution to the Coronation festivities, was 'kicked around' by the critics and pronounced 'one of the great disasters of operatic history'. Ashton, on the other hand, keenly sensitive to the limitations of court entertainment, produced exactly the kind of patriotic paean that was expected, choosing as his designer Oliver Messel, expert in the Inigo Jones tradition of courtly splendour and fantasy. Britten, by contrast, had contrived a waywardly unflattering portrait of the monarch and an opera that almost sent its gala audience to sleep. But of the two works only *Gloriana*, now recognized as a passionate tender drama, has survived; *Homage to The Queen*, for all its enjoyable originality, proved to be as ephemeral as the occasion for which it was created.

A month after the première, Ashton went to Spain on his first and only holiday abroad with Alexander Grant. It was unbearably hot in Madrid, but the dancer remembers being wearily 'dragged' round museums and churches in a relentless quest to see 'all the Goyas in Spain'. They went to Tangiers where they stayed with friends, swam a lot, and tried, without success, to get visas to visit Fez and Marrakesh. Ashton spent most of August in Suffolk, and in September he set off on a company tour of the United States. Although, as far as their colleagues were concerned, they were now considered a couple, Ashton frequently chose to stay in a grander hotel than Grant and see friends independently, including Terence Rattigan ('They used to go to Schrafft's together with all the mauve-rinsed old ladies') and Irene Worth. The actress had hoped to persuade

Ashton to direct her in *Agamemnon*: 'I thought Freddie would do it so simply in a very stylized, pure way. He used to talk about the power of gesture, the significance of a movement of the head, and I felt he would have added the movement and imagery of the pre-classical.' Having met through the Clarks during the war, they had been reintroduced by Alice, whom Ashton saw several times on this trip, but usually with Grant there, too. 'Freddie didn't want to go out alone with her.' They would rendezvous in the nightclub of the Sherry-Netherland, where Alice, evidently disappointed not to have Ashton to herself, 'sat in melancholy silence'. The dancer noted how very fond she was of Ashton, making sure his hotel room was filled with flowers. Grant always accepted that Ashton had a world outside the dance and, unlike Brian Shaw, was not affronted by his exclusion from it. At the time, though, Ashton was keen to cultivate him, and, when the company performed in Boston, he took Grant to an Isaiah Berlin lecture at Harvard. 'He spoke faster and faster and afterwards, when we went to say hello, Freddie told him that we could hardly catch a word of what he'd said. "I'm like an aeroplane," he told us. "If I don't get revved up and go at full speed, I'll crash."' Despite their twenty-year age difference, Grant loved being in Ashton's company and was touchingly in awe of his social aplomb:

> Ever ready Freddie,
> Always, entre nous,
> In every situation
> Knew exactly what to do

To Ashton, Grant was 'Someone to Watch Over Me', his favourite song,* who never minded being there when he was needed. 'Freddie expected it of me. He didn't like to be abandoned. He'd say, "Where are you going? Don't leave me alone." There had to be a certain amount of attention, but it wasn't an imposition for me – Freddie has always been part of my life.'

The 1953 American tour was a time of personal triumph for Ashton, whose recent ballets, particularly *Sylvia* and *Daphnis and Chloe*, were given a far more enthusiastic reception than they had received in England. Night after night, Ashton, having been mobbed by adoring 'standees' at the stage door, walked with Grant across the street to Bill's restaurant, the company's second home. The proprietress, Sis Conovitch,

*From *Oh, Kay!*, 1926.

another ardent fan, would cup his chin in her cool hand, tell him how wonderful he was, and lead him to the bar, where half a dozen dry Martinis would be lined up waiting for him. Soon after the New York run, Ashton developed violent stomach pains. A surfeit of alcohol was an emergency doctor's diagnosis, which Ashton preferred to call 'Martini poisoning', adding defensively, 'Some people drink when they're failures. I drink when I'm a success. And I've been a very, very big success.' The high living continued, intensified by the fact that Tito Arias, in pursuit of Margot Fonteyn, was flamboyantly entertaining her friends as part of his seduction strategy. At one of his parties, Ashton went one better, performing what Fonteyn describes as the most sensational series of impersonations she had ever seen at one sitting.

Pavlova, Isadora Duncan, Lopokova, Carmen Amaya, Pastor Imperia . . . His dancing between the restaurant tables was more pliant and supple than ever before, his body completely flexible and his soul ablaze. This firework display was climaxed by a flying leap into the arms of the headwaiter.

Ashton, she noticed, had been 'horrified' by the extravagance of the party invitations, in the form of thirty-word telegrams to each guest; but, having claimed 'never to be able to marry anyone who didn't have his approval', Fonteyn would have been distraught had she known how scathing Ashton could be about Arias behind her back. Not that he was against the ballerina marrying money. 'I was very practical. I'm so tired of seeing wretched dancers having to peel their own potatoes when they retire.' It was Arias's vulgarity he scorned: the gold bracelets, pomaded hair and glib Latin charm. But for all that, Ashton made no attempt to prevent Arias from paying every restaurant bill and willingly came along for the free rides. In Los Angeles, Arias chartered John Wayne's boat and took a group of Fonteyn's friends on a trip to Catalina Island. It was the day on which she decided, after much procrastination, to become his wife. Ashton gave the couple his blessing, 'I suppose only because she wanted me to,' and, from then on, adopted the role of officious mother-in-law, instructing Arias how to take care of his beloved charge. The three ended the tour with a cruise off the coast of Nassau on Arias's own yacht. 'We were an odd lot': a small party, including the dancer Leslie Edwards, Jean Gilbert and Danny Kaye's wife, Sylvia. 'Fred adored every moment. He didn't get up till late and he loved being hot and swimming all day. We were lavishly treated by Tito; Mrs Kaye was charming and witty with a great knowledge of the theatre; and there was a piano on board on which Jean played all Fred's favourite tunes.'

Ashton and Fonteyn went abroad again in the early summer of 1954, when he took a small troupe of dancers to the Granada Festival and created a new solo for her with a costume by Christian Dior. Inspired by his boyhood memories of seeing Vera Trefilova in a Japanese dance, *Entrada de Madame Butterfly* was, in fact, no more than a jotting for a larger project, *Madame Chrysanthème*, which Ashton had in mind for the following year. Performances in Granada took place under the stars, on a stage built among the fountains and cypress trees of the Generalife Gardens. But although Ashton enjoyed the entrancing setting, particularly an evening they spent watching gypsies dance flamenco at a little house once owned by Manuel de Falla, his colleagues noticed that 'things were a little fraught between Fred and Alex'. The problem was that Grant, a conspicuous presence on the mixed programme chosen by the choreographer, was as much in demand off-stage. 'When you're young, attractive and everybody wants you,' said Ashton, 'you're not going to be restricted, you're going to enjoy it. Can you *imagine* Alexander being faithful?'

Sexual activity, for many dancers, is an extension of their occupation; their virility, simply another form of athletic prowess. Not surprisingly, Grant, one of the most physically charismatic performers of his time, 'adored sex' and was very good at it. 'He was extremely animal and prodigiously endowed which was a large part of his charm.' 'He was a loveable animal. So warm and gentle with marvellous hands.' 'He had a fabulous body – better than most dancers: chunky and savage and very physical. Like a wild animal in a way.' With Grant in the forefront of Ashton's mind, it was no coincidence that, throughout the early 1950s, he used sexuality as a subject in his ballets and treated it more graphically than ever before. Yet however inspiring Grant's sexual dynamism was to his work, it was not easy to come to terms with in private.

> I'd be in love with him and he'd go off and that was how the queer world worked. I wasn't promiscuous but they were. If I loved somebody I loved somebody. That was all I wanted, I didn't *want* anyone else. But anybody I loved wanted everyone else. They liked me but I wasn't enough for them and if someone said, 'Let's go to bed,' off they'd go. If I didn't put up with it they'd just go off, that's all. Michael wasn't queer, he liked girls, so he went off with the girls. And all the others who liked boys went off and had them. Every bloody one of them. Nobody was prepared to be devoted to me. They wanted that and they also wanted to fuck around. Well I perfectly understand. I probably didn't satisfy them physically, so

they were all onto something else. In the queer world, you can't expect fidelity, dear.*

By now, Ashton knew the stakes and, in Grant's case, 'tolerated it all because he really loved Alexander'. The bond between them was impregnable, proof of which were the roles that kept on coming. In a programme of two new works, both minor pieces, designed as showcases for the company's rising stars, Ashton gave the dancer a pivotal part in *Variations on a Theme by Purcell*, which used the Britten score better known as 'Young Person's Guide to the Orchestra'. The three soloists (Elaine Fifield, Rowena Jackson and Nadia Nerina) were each given variations identified with a particular instrument; Grant, as part master-of-ceremonies, part *Cinderella*-like Jester, was there to conduct their performance. Wearing dusky make-up and one black, one white glove, he was an enigmatic figure, whose dramatic hand gestures were derived from his Massine roles. Ashton's choreography for him also contained a parody of Dolin's *Bolero* and a loose-wristed soft-shoe shuffle to the rhythmic percussion section. The combination, however, was considered 'exceedingly feeble' and the rest of the work, despite strong classical performances from the three young ballerinas, failed to make much of an impact.

Rinaldo and Armida, to a Malcolm Arnold score, was also 'a very honourable near-miss'. It was, in effect, a long pas de deux created to display the lofty, lunar beauty of Svetlana Beriosova, who, as a sphinx-like enchantress, loses her heart to her mortal victim (Michael Somes). Aware that his collaboration with Fonteyn, having reached its zenith, would inevitably begin to wane, Ashton had begun focusing his attention on other ballerinas. Violetta Elvin held his eye for a time – 'Maybe it was a little bit of a case of a stale marriage. Margot was more reserved, and maybe I put something different . . . maybe more of a woman into it.' But although Vera Volkova had alerted Elvin to the choreographer's interest, 'being a little bit rebellious', she was unwilling to entrust herself to him, to be 'obedient', as she put it. Beriosova was more malleable, and in her Ashton divined a touch of the quality shared by Pavlova, Karsavina and Spessivtseva. 'There is something in her arms, in her back, in the way she holds her head and uses her eyes, that cannot be taught, and for which technique is only a frame.' He planned to cast her as Lady Macbeth in a 'tremendously elaborate' version of Shakespeare's play but eventually

*Ashton, a former lover argued, 'took it when he could get it. I heard him preach this sermon once to a friend and thought at the time it expressed some kind of romantic ideal but it had nothing to do with nature's order of things.'

abandoned the ballet 'because I like to have a thing of love and there is no real love in it'.

Rinaldo and Armida relied upon Beriosova completely to give expression to the story's gradations of mood and passion. (As Rinaldo, Somes was no more than a supportive cipher.) Although unremarkable for their originality, the movements were designed to enhance chaste, sweeping line, eloquent port de bras and the tilt of her aristocratic profile. The ballet, with its chic black and white designs by Peter Rice, was charged with atmosphere, and yet somehow unsatisfying. While to some, *Rinaldo and Armida* provided evidence of a new creative partnership which roused hopes for the future, others felt that the choreographer and ballerina 'didn't really spark one another off'. Ashton, it is true, was never sufficiently challenged by Beriosova, who was 'so purely set in her own image'. Nevertheless, he remained fascinated by her mystique and continued to enshrine it in his work.

Three months later, Alexander Grant was again given the male lead in a new Ashton ballet, playing a French sailor in *Madame Chrysanthème*, based on Pierre Loti's autobiographical novel about his temporary marriage to a geisha (the story that inspired *Madame Butterfly*). Ashton conceived some nautical, predictably lusty dances for the dancer – 'great bounds, and jumps with his legs raised horizontally to hip level' – but, although Grant was pleased to be given his first Ashtonian love pas de deux, this was not a role that he was able to dramatize convincingly.

> I saw Buckle the other evening [who] . . . thought I was miscast . . . he thought that the sailor should be more wistful and romantic and I was always too positive. So I asked him how wistful and romantic you could be and then break into a gay hornpipe, he hadn't thought of that.

The ballet belonged, essentially, to Elaine Fifield, an Australian ballerina to whom Ashton had developed a strong attachment. As pertly pretty as a young Elizabeth Taylor, Fifield had first come to his notice in *Valses nobles*, where she showed natural sophistication and poise. 'Fred was *intrigued* by Elaine and she was almost in love with him,' said Anya Linden. 'I heard that she wanted to marry him. I think she was seeking some sort of father figure at the time.' Fifield, however, insists that her rapport with Ashton was based on a mutual understanding that was professional rather than private. 'It was absolutely our work. A sort of spiritual thing. When you love your work like Sir Fred did and I did, there's an affinity; a belief that you were put here for a reason. Words aren't necessary.' Yet there is no doubt that, when Ashton created *Madame Chrysanthème* for her, Fifield was badly in need of support. Her marriage to the conductor John Lanchbery was in pieces, she had become anorexic and seemed to her colleagues to be on the verge of a breakdown. 'Fred helped her through the dancing,' said Annette Page. 'He never wanted to get involved with people's emotional problems, but by giving Elaine the ballet, he probably saved her life.' Fifield's thin, wistful fragility was exactly the quality Ashton wanted for Madame Chrysanthème, the quaint 'little mousmé' with a mercenary heart, whom Pierre discovers testing his silver dollars with a 'dzinn! dzinn!' tapping of her mallet. Exploiting the fact that Fifield could and would do anything for Ashton, he pushed her technique to the limit, at one point instructing her to fold from a position on pointe straight down on to her knees. He also used her doll-like expression and kittenish qualities to great effect: 'She folds up into a cosy bundle: she pats and wriggles and turns up her toes, then points them to reveal her noble instep.'

Japan was in the air in the spring of 1955. Kurosawa's films were finding an English audience (*Seven Samurai* won an Academy Award that year); Miho Hanayagui's troupe of dancers had aroused much interest when they appeared in London the previous autumn; and the Azuma Kabuki company was scheduled to appear at the Edinburgh Festival in August. Transferring his attention from Ancient Greece to the Far East, Ashton tried experimenting with Japanese techniques, including kyogen – visible scene-changing by shadowy stagehands. He called in Japanese advisers to teach the women how to perform small shuffle steps and to incline their heads in order to achieve 'that sort of humble feeling'. His dance idiom was a conflation of faux-Japanese mannerisms and classical ballet, an effective motif being Madame Chrysanthème's quirky pointing and flexing of her foot, which also contained a private tribute to Fifield's strikingly arched feet. Buckle considered *Madame Chrysanthème* to be Ashton's best ballet in years, and Mary Clarke pronounced it 'a lovely and delicate work of art . . . free of all sentiment . . . a very nearly perfect collaboration'. But, despite Isabel Lambert's subtly evocative designs and an aptly satirical, if somewhat tinkly, score by her future husband, Alan Rawsthorne, the ballet was treated by the majority of the critics as no more than an amusing novelty. It soon disappeared from the repertory.

Immediately after the première, keeping up the astonishingly productive pace he had maintained throughout the last five years, Ashton left for Copenhagen to start work on his first assignment for the Danish Ballet, a full-length version of *Romeo and Juliet*. De Valois had prevented him from doing the work for his own company, as, at the time, she did not want more than one Prokofiev ballet in the repertory. She was, Ashton said, 'a little Tory in these matters', but he was more embittered by her decision than he admitted. Creating the ballet elsewhere was a gesture of retaliation which, he believed, delivered its point quite clearly. 'She was worried when I went to Copenhagen. She came over to see what I was at.'

As his lead, Ashton 'stuck to Shakespeare', as he had not seen any other production. The Bolshoi's groundbreaking *Romeo and Juliet*, which was to define the epic versions by Cranko and MacMillan, did not come to London until the following year (although, a month after his première, Ashton was to attend a private viewing of the 1954 film of Lavrovsky's ballet at the Soviet Embassy). It was almost as if he had seen the Russians 'pantomiming their way through the music' and had decided to do the exact opposite: a chamber piece, which concentrated on the dancing and the two lovers. Prokofiev had supplied a ready-made scenario – 'Anybody could get up and do *Romeo and Juliet*, it's all there structured for you' – and Ashton cut any music he did not like. There was to be nothing extraneous in the ballet, which achieves much of its effect through its symmetry. Important characters are clearly introduced, their entrances framed in an arch of Peter Rice's skeletal, colonnaded set: first Tybalt, King of Cats, caricatured as an Old Vice figure, with a scratchy, feline leitmotif; then Benvolio; then Mercutio. The arches focus key moments, such as when Juliet, centrally framed with Paris, first sets eyes on Romeo. The Montague–Capulet feud is established emblematically by token representatives from each house – one red, two green – who clash during the confrontation between Benvolio and Tybalt.

Beside the large-scale versions, with their seething crowds and aggressively naturalistic swordfights, Ashton's *Romeo and Juliet* seems as unambitious as a school play – the reason he was reluctant later to revive it. 'If I'd done it for us I would have had to open up the seams, so to speak – enlarge it.' But the concentration and formality of his approach is just as valid, and also true to Shakespeare, whose dramatis personae are symmetrically aligned and express themselves through rhetorical devices and stylized attitudes – the lovers address each other like sonneteers. And just as artificiality exists side by side with realism in the play, the formal rhetoric giving way to a sudden clearing of the verse, so Ashton contrasts old-fashioned mime with some wonderfully natural touches. When the Nurse comes in to wake Juliet, bawdily itching and adjusting her corset, her little morning shudder to a trilling arpeggio in the score not only establishes the early hour, it presages her terrible discovery a minute later.

Ashton had always been interested in love, not darkness; which is why he abandoned his ballet version of *Macbeth*. Minimizing the threat of death, his *Romeo and Juliet* is fundamentally a love story that turns out tragically. He does link love with death – the wedding bed becomes Juliet's tomb – but as unobtrusively as a Shakespearean pun. Seeing a revival of Ashton's work, MacMillan's Juliet, Lynn Seymour, felt that the choreographer was 'frightened' by the rhapsodic intensity of Prokofiev's score. Yet rather than responding literally to the music, like MacMillan's Juliet with her 'Anna Magnani-size passions', Ashton lets the music communicate the lovers' thoughts, while maintaining an element of aristocratic reserve between them. The emotional weight is contained in their knotted hands and arched backs; in tremulous floor-skimming lifts, rather than dizzying aerobatics. Because the choreography is understated, it falls on the lovers to convey internally their passion and impetuosity. In the original version, Juliet was danced by Mona Vangsaa, a ballerina whose lyricism more than compensated for her rather weak technique. Romeo was twenty-one-year-old Henning Kronstam, one of the most romantic-looking male dancers in the world, whom Ashton picked from the corps. Only after a battle with the management, however, was he able to instate his two leads.

Unknowingly, the choreographer had walked into a situation almost as discordant as his story. Ever since the 1952 'Lander Scandal' (the dismissal for misconduct of director Harald Lander, who defected to Paris, taking all his ballets with him), the Royal Danish Ballet had been riven in two by opposing factions. On her arrival in Denmark, Vera Volkova, the company's artistic advisor responsible for Ashton's commission, had found a company set in amber by their traditions, and decided to make some changes. She brought on a new generation of young dancers – 'Henning Kronstam was totally a Volkova product' – but, when it came to casting, the old guard stood firm. Mona Vangsaa's husband, Frank Schaufuss, who was tall and very handsome, demanded to know why he was cast as Mercutio instead of Romeo. Ashton made a pact with him, 'I said . . . when I've finished, you don't have to dance Mercutio unless you're satisfied that it's a good meaty role: we'll get someone else. Well, he did it.' The casting of Juliet caused all-out war. Ashton, supported by Volkova, wanted Vangsaa, but this was considered an insult to Margrethe Schanne, adored by the press and the only dancer of her time to be featured on a postage stamp. As light on her feet as a ballerina in a nineteenth-century lithograph, she personified the Bournonville school and appealed to 'something deep in the Danish soul'. But Ashton, who felt that Schanne had neither the passion nor the poetry for Juliet, stood by his decision, despite the fact that Schanne did everything she could to revoke it. 'She was a sharp operator and led a great cabal against me.'

The rancour caused Ashton such distress that, every morning, when he walked across the street from the Hotel d'Angleterre to the theatre, he would have to stop to be sick in a doorway. Hearing of his predicament, his friends tried hard to raise his spirits. 'You tell me you got a black eye through nervous tension but one can't help thinking?' wrote Grant in one of several letters, full of cajoling support.

> Don't pine away buck up its not forever . . . don't let yourself get to the stage where you don't know what is right anymore. I have faith in you even if you have no knowledge of it . . . Be strong and take no notice . . .

Marie Rambert also wrote to console him.

> With that immense vocabulary of yours and all the gorgeous words to inspire you, plus the music, you are bound to produce great beauty, specially having intelligent, gay and sensitive Vera at your side all the time . . . So be of good cheer and not miserable.

For all its problems, *Romeo and Juliet* was an enormous hit with the Danes (performed so many times that the scenery and costumes eventually fell apart and it dropped out of the repertory), but Ashton was unplaced. One night, Stravinsky appeared at the theatre, causing great excitement among the journalists who were there. 'We met in the foyer and embraced and I said "What are you doing tonight?" and he said, "I'm having dinner with you." So the press who'd ignored me completely because I hadn't chosen Schanne, came to me afterwards and asked me what we'd talked about. And I said, "If it's taken Mr Stravinsky's friendship with me to bring me to your notice, I have nothing to say to you."'*

Although Ashton would always crave approval and be quick to take umbrage, there is no doubt that he over-reacted to his treatment by the Danes. His trials with New York City Ballet had proved him quite capa-

---

*Although Stravinsky never suggested collaborating on a ballet with Ashton, they enjoyed each other's company and would speak French together. 'He could be tremendously dogmatic. I remember once being at a party when Stravinsky went into a whole tirade against Berlioz. He went on and on and on about the horror of Berlioz, until finally I said, "Mais Maître, je ne suis *pas* Berlioz."'

ble of handling a disagreeable situation; there had to be something else compounding his misery.

> You say it is my fault . . . [but] I think of you a great deal as you know I must, for the past year especially you have made me so much part of your life that I could hardly help it . . . I think much much more of you on top [sic] physical and intimate as well . . . Don't let yourself get the melancholy blues Freddie, with your knowledge, experience, and talent, with that story, fall in love with that for a little while. With no other distractions you can do a great ballet.

Although Grant's letters pledged his devotion and made jokey reassurances of his fidelity, Ashton, fifty years old, with 'quite a little belly on him', knew that it was unrealistic to expect the romantic side of their relationship to last. 'Fred was not his type sexually – Alex liked young people.' The dancer had planned to come to Copenhagen for the first night, but was called in to see de Valois at the last minute, who read him the rule book about dancers not being permitted to travel beyond a certain radius. He believes to this day that Ashton put her up to it. He was hurt at the time, suspecting 'a romantic interest in Freddie's life'. But although, like most of the ballet world, Ashton was half in love with Henning Kronstam and took every opportunity to dance with him when rehearsing, this was more a fascination with him as a performer than a real infatuation. It was more likely de Valois' impending arrival that influenced his decision to keep Grant away from Copenhagen. Possibly, though, Ashton was deliberately bringing things to an end. While he was in Denmark, he suggested that Grant should invite Michael Boulton and his girlfriend, Anya Linden, to Yaxley for the Easter weekend. 'Alex had always had a slight thing for Michael, so it was either Fred giving dancers a good time or else playing some kind of game.'

B y the summer of the following year, Ashton had detached himself enough to encourage Grant in a new liaison. It was his idea that Frank Raiter, an amiable young American actor, should move into the Battersea house the dancer had just bought with the help of an £800 loan from Ashton. 'Freddie thought I'd be lonely and that Frank could help with expenses.' Raiter maintains that the transition in the relationship between Grant and Ashton was smooth. 'It was still going on, but as a very deep friendship.' Ashton was fond of the actor, whom he nicknamed 'Mother' because he gave teas for the company between his shows, but he never questioned him about Grant. 'And I never brought it up because I didn't want to hurt Fred.' They all spent several weekends together in Yaxley, joined by Brian Shaw and his current lover, the dancer Derek Rencher. It was a ménage that rather overwhelmed Raiter, a 'naive twenty-year-old, just becoming aware sexually', although, as a keen ballet fan, he relished the company. Ashton got Raiter to read aloud passages from de la Motte Fouqué's *Undine*, his next major project, and gossiped about the ballerinas he had begun rehearsing in *Birthday Offering*.

> Fred described how he'd be sitting in the Covent Garden canteen and would summon Violetta Elvin over and want to know about all her lovers. He used to call her a tramp. Fred could say the worst words and make them sound elegant and inoffensive.

Created to celebrate Sadler's Wells' Silver Jubilee, *Birthday Offering* was the second of two short pieces that Ashton choreographed over the next two years, both of which reinstated Fonteyn as their cynosure. The first was *La Péri*, a new version of a poème dansée to a Dukas score, which he had first devised for himself and Markova in 1931. His main reason for reviving it was to provide a new showcase for Fonteyn, whose fantastic and exotic simplicity as the keeper of the Flower of Immortality recaptured her arresting unwordliness as the Firebird, a recent début. But its tale of a man feeling the approach of old age and searching for eternal life was one with which Ashton could now identify. Echoing the choreography's grafting of Eastern mannerisms on Western dance, the new designs attempted to marry the oriental chic of the costumes (by André Levasseur) with a neo-Romantic pastoral setting by the British painter Ivon Hitchens. It was not a successful match, unlike that of its two stars. With Michael Somes as Iskender, the ballet paid tribute to a partnership now considered to be the most distinguished in Western ballet. Strong, handsome, dependable and self-effacing, Somes was the perfect foil to Fonteyn. 'He was completely there for her and sort of melted behind her so that you were not aware of her being supported.' But circumstances had turned Somes into a parody of himself. A last-minute decision by Dukas's music publishers insisted on obedience to the composer's original instructions – that the male role be limited to mime and partnering. 'The little ballet thus became virtually a supported solo for Fonteyn with a be-turbaned Somes in walking attendance.' Like its hero, the ballet was destined for a short life.

Birthday Offering, a series of classical variations in the Petipa manner imprinted with Ashtonian embellishments – 'half a tribute to *Beauty* and half a commemoration of temps perdu' – was intended to promote the individual qualities of seven ballerinas, who were given much more prominence than their seven cavaliers (the reason for its nickname, 'Seven Brides for Seven Brothers'). Although, as usual, Ashton expected each dancer to improvise for him, the ballet is also a remarkable testament to his genius for impersonation. Elaine Fifield performed the first variation, her rather vacant prettiness and mechanical precision satirized in a solo very like the Doll Dance in *The Tales of Hoffmann*. Rowena Jackson came next, lunging and darting to and fro and showing off her championship turns; then Svetlana Beriosova, beautifully poised and expansive; Nadia Nerina was fourth, leaping 'spring-like in lemon, revealing once again those qualities of spontaneity and enjoyment in dance that first endeared her'. Violetta Elvin followed, with languorous waltzes sweeping the floor; then Beryl Grey, showing off her strength and superb control; finally, Margot Fonteyn in a staccato solo, consisting of tricky terre-à-terre steps. 'They're all going to have to look at Margot's feet,' Ashton had said at the time. The ballet was full of in-jokes. Beryl Grey was allotted her piece of music because Ashton claimed he could hear her arpeggio laugh in it. He gave Fonteyn an unusual step – pas de bourrée à cinq pas, from the syllabus of the Royal Academy of Dancing – because she had just been made RAD president. And, in response to the gymnastic flamboyance of the Bolshoi, and as a personal jibe at John Cranko, whose *Lady and the Fool* was full of lifts, Ashton announced that he was going to choreograph the pas de deux without a single one. By highlighting the accomplishments of Sadler's Wells' ballerinas – six of whom had recently performed Aurora – *Birthday Offering* reflected Ashton's own strength as a choreographer. As de Valois said, 'Fred was always much better with the women.' It was an unqualified success, proving how richly the company deserved their new title, 'The Royal Ballet', conferred later that year. But, once again, the perfection of Ashton's work was achieved at the expense of his personal life.

As the decade drew to a close, with no new love interest to sustain him, and still bereft by the loss of Sophie, Ashton's moonshine moods grew more pervasive. To avoid Sunday melancholia, he regularly spent the day at Rosenau Road with Alexander Grant, who produced a large roast lunch for him as he sat in his usual chair, 'the Ashton chair', under a portrait of Pavlova. Ashton lost two more friends within the next two years: Tchelitchew, who died at the age of fifty-nine, and Alice, whose sudden death remains a mystery. 'None of us knew if she was murdered or killed herself,' said Lincoln Kirstein.

The last time Ashton had seen Alice, he had thought it slightly strange that, when she said goodbye to him, she remarked, 'Don't worry, I'll always see you're all right.' It was as if Alice knew that she was going to die. Through a medium friend of John Latouche, she had recently met and fallen in love with the parapsychologist Andriji Puharich, who was considered by her family to be the catalyst in her tragedy. A charming character – 'pure Cat-Nip to women' – Puharich had persuaded Alice to fund his research foundation and take part in its 'odd adventurous work', in Aldous Huxley's description, testing the effect of magic mushrooms on extrasensory perception. Unnerved by her performance under hypnosis, Alice began to fear that she might be coming under the spell of outside agencies. 'She was very glum that summer,' said Gore Vidal. 'It was a hot July and she hated the heat. And she had stopped eating.' On the morning of 19 July 1956, Alice was found lying dead on the floor of the bathroom of her East Side New York house by her maid. An autopsy ordered by her brother, Vincent Astor, certified death by natural causes, but the rumours persisted. According to the photographer Horst, there was 'a story going round of someone Alice knew who'd suddenly had to disappear', and Ashton remained convinced that Alice had been murdered. The alternative suicide theory was fuelled by the fact that, the day before she died, Alice had summoned her solicitor Max Perl to make changes to her will. 'She felt something was going to happen,' he said.

Alice's new will, a handwritten draft of which was left on a train by a partner in the legal firm, has caused almost as much controversy as her death. It was either, as Huxley maintained, a case of 'lawyers double-crossing', or simply a farcical episode. 'I was the one who suffered from that lawyer,' Ashton complained. In her previous will, Alice had bequeathed him an annuity of $400. This was changed to an outright bequest of $2,500. Edith was a beneficiary in both wills: first, inheriting $1,000, which was amended to a lifetime annuity of $500. Through Arnold Goodman, Ashton contested the 'lost' will and, as a result, received an additional $2,000 over and above his second legacy. But he continued to feel disgruntled about the paucity of his inheritance, remarking ungratefully that Alice had named him 'amongst the servants'.

As things turned out, Sophie had seen both him and his sister 'all right'. Edith inherited the barn overlooking the moors at Brancaster, and the remainder of Sophie's estate went to Ashton. With a fraction (£6,000) of his £35,000 inheritance he bought Chandos Lodge, a pretty Victorian hunting lodge in Eye, three miles from Yaxley, which he Gothicized in her memory, and where he himself was to die. He would go to Chandos Lodge to replenish his spirit and, as he put it, 'question my talent', and it was where his great works of the 1960s and 1970s were first conceived.

Ashton used to insist that his country routine was entirely inert: 'I do nothing. I sit and stare.' But, as he sat for hours on the terrace, listening to music, sipping Martinis and chain-smoking, his mind was all-seeing, projecting visions of filigree arms and Garbo-esque profiles, lyrical youths and love-smitten heroines, on to the backdrop of his darkening lake and garden.

CHAPTER FIFTEEN

SPRING CHICKEN
1956–1963

On a warm August night in 1956, W. H. Auden and Chester Kallman were having dinner in the piazza of Forio, Ischia. Ashton sat at a table near by, in earnest conference with the thirty-year-old composer Hans Werner Henze. It was at Maria's Café, the focal point of the village, that the first discussions about their ballet, *Ondine*, took place. Henze had recently left Germany to live in Italy – a rejection of his country and its restricting cultural values – and was renting a house on the island. Although he and Ashton would sometimes join Auden's table that summer, they did not ask him for advice about the libretto. 'We didn't even tell them what we were doing,' said Henze. 'Fred didn't want to be influenced by Auden who might have dissuaded us from doing this as a ballet. He was probably terrified of his authority.' Their conversations continued on the beach, Ashton's copy of de la Motte Fouqué's *Undine* (a 1909 edition, with illustrations by Arthur Rackham) becoming sandier and more sun-curled by the day. '"What is *Ondine*? Who is Ondine?" we asked ourselves. "Is she the soulless mermaid, obsessed by the desire to gain a soul? . . . What drives her to go among mortals? Is it curiosity, playfulness, or is it the wish of the human being who summons her?" We kept coming back to these questions.'

William Walton is generally assumed to have been Ashton's first choice of composer for *Ondine*. 'William was busy with something else, but always one to do a favour to a pal, he suggested Hans Henze,' said his widow, Susana Walton. 'The establishment at Covent Garden were not inclined to engage a fairly unknown composer, and so it was a question of William forcing David Webster to accept this.' Henze, however, insists that this was not the case: the Waltons were his neighbours on Ischia and they saw each other almost every day. 'They would have told me.'* Ashton may well have sought Walton's reassurance that the young composer was capable of sustaining a three-act work, but he did not need an introduction. Henze was hardly an unfamiliar name to him; not only were they close friends, but they had been discussing the idea of working together for the past eight years.

It was through the cultural office of the British Army that Hans Werner Henze was invited to Hamburg in 1948 to see the Sadler's Wells Ballet for the first time. The programme began with Ashton's *Scènes de ballet* and, that night, Henze has said, 'a new world of aesthetics' opened up to him. As he had never before heard Stravinsky's score, or seen a classical ballet in the hands of a modern choreographer, the combination was a revelation, showing him the possibility of presenting traditional material in a new and transformed context. 'In my world,' he once wrote, 'the old forms strive to regain significance, even when the modern timbre of the music seldom or never allows them to appear on the surface.' Henze's romantic sensibility and belief in music as a means of communication had distanced him from the cold atonality of the Darmstadt school, but he was, nevertheless, exploring radical new forms of expression which *Scènes de ballet* seemed to him to encapsulate. In his then imperfect English, he wrote Ashton a fan letter,† the first of many to come.

> Dear Sir,
>   . . . I'm a composer of 22 years of age, who (by fate and by Schott Editors) became known quickly through different concertos, orchestra pieces and an opera . . . Here in Germany has raised a movement through all parts of art, whichs main interest is abstraction, going away from painting, writing, composing themes of direct human feelings. 'We' use (in a more or less individual way) art as a medium to overwhelm personal mourn, disappointment, catastrophes and death. We intend to concentrate the demonstrations of human situations to glass, to ice – only the individual intellect is at work during the conception of a piece of art . . .
>   When the curtain raised at 'Scènes de ballet': this music: like steel, the dancers: like fanatic, apassionate appearances, the prezision of the movements, and this absolute beauty . . . it made our time in Hamburg here like a dream . . . It was completely ade-

---

*In her memoirs, Susana Walton mistakenly maintains that it was in 1958 that Walton had suggested Henze to Ashton (the score was completed in 1957). When, shortly before Ashton died, Henze mentioned Lady Walton's claim that he was second choice, the choreographer dismissed it as 'Absolute nonsense'.
†16 October 1948.

quate to our ideas. We were absolutely enchanted and deeply touched . . . Let me thank you in the name of my friends for your coming to Germany . . .

Ashton's reply no longer exists, but he later told Henze that he had liked his letter and his attitude: 'I have always loved the idea of you . . . & I have kept you in my thoughts.' After finding out more about him from Bill Fedrick, a mutual friend in the Army cultural department, Ashton wrote the composer 'a very kind and interesting letter'. By this time, under the influence of *Scènes de ballet*, Henze had written a twenty-minute piece, *Ballett-Variations*, which he hoped might be of interest.

This ballet will never be produced if not by you . . . It was been composed for you, and for your dancers . . . not in order to show the dancers' technik but to produce a suite of symbols, cool and abstract, standing instead of heart-rendering pantomime . . . I've even tried to find out what sort of music you like most, and though being very strong in my modernism I seem to have succeeded in mixing memories of 'Les Patineurs' 'Symphonic Variations' and to the Tchaikovsky ballet style . . .

By the spring of 1950, Ashton had heard a piano score of the ballet (which was dedicated to him), but did not commit himself to using it. Henze was unconcerned. He had heard, through Bill Fedrick, that Ashton wanted to create a ballet with him in direct collaboration. 'I assure you that this would be the fulfilling of a wish which I did not dare to express.' In the autumn of 1952, when the company performed in West Berlin, Henze was able to play his music to Ashton. They spent only a few days in each other's company, going to parties and to the theatre, a period during which they developed an intense and lasting affection for each other. 'How strange the way our love & sympathy grew,' Ashton later recalled. He was immediately drawn to Henze, investing him with the kind of 1930s Sonnekind attributes extolled by Isherwood and Spender. 'To me you are Berlin & the whole charm of Germany – your blondness, your sentiment, your forthcoming warmth.' But, although he made no attempt to take his physical attraction any further ('Fred was much too tactful'), the letter he wrote on his return to London is full of bitter-sweet regret about an affair that was 'not to be'.

I loved you & had it not been that I knew & respected your other ties & against which I could not compete – I would have asked you to accept my love, all of which is as well for now I would be suffering to be parted from you . . . When I got back I played your records & thought of you. I wished that we had known each other, but seduction is not a role I like. I like the overwhelming surge of mutual attraction . . . Had you been free & I younger (sadly I say this) all might have been different. But I am your friend, certainly for as long as you wish, fervent & true.

Henze's reply reciprocates Ashton's tenderness, but redirects his romantic declarations towards a more platonic bond.

A good deal of the things you told me, I have very well felt . . . and I am as sad as you are about the facts. The one important thing I have to implore you, is, not to be sad about being older than I am . . . You should not have had to ask me to accept your love, I have accepted it, and I must ask you to accept mine . . . the situation between us is really a beautiful one, and friendships like ours can become important and eternal and marvellous, especially if they are not melange with what one calls 'an affair'. And, my dear Fred, so it will be creative and productive . . . For so long a time I have wanted a friend like you. I was always very lonesome in spite of the boys. It is quite a new mood for me, and I feel security and a strange sort of being-at-home.

As he was to do with Visconti five years later, Henze assumed the role of a pupil in the hands of a master, 'someone I should try to please'. Unwittingly using an image famously associated with Ashton and Pavlova, he told the choreographer that he felt he had been 'injected with poison'. Failing to make the connection, Ashton wrote a defensive reply.

I could make you drunk & I could derange your senses, but I could not poison you. I am not an angel of death I am a life giver. I might disturb you & rearrange your thoughts for greater stimulus but not for sterility – not for oblivion. I want you to be great & deep not superficial & earnest & heavy & pompous, but clear & true . . . You & I must be big, open . . . we must fly. All has been said in European music – but you must say your music, your own true music, personally felt & new.

The concept of Ashton as a 'life giver' is one to which Henze often returns. 'He was for me like a rope to climb out from the sea.' To the provincial German boy, 'full of sentiments and full of desire to be nearer to the abstract, to the other side', Ashton was a figure of great authority, someone he strived to emulate. ('He tried to teach me manners.') Henze was 'astonished to say the least' by the ease with which Ashton accepted his homosexuality, and was inspired by his integrity and morality. 'Not Victorian morality, a very personal ethos. A sense of elegance in human relationships.' In an extensive, highly articulate correspondence, Henze, 'like a schoolboy making first confessions of his nightly secrets', confided his thoughts and anxieties about art and love, and encouraged his mentor to do the same.

When Ashton was on holiday in Spain with Alexander Grant in the summer of 1953, the composer tried in vain to persuade them to travel on to see him in Ischia. They lost touch that year, but saw each other in November 1954, when Sadler's Wells performed in Naples, and again, a month later, when Henze came to London for the première of Walton's *Troilus and Cressida*. Next autumn, he heard through Susana Walton that Ashton wanted to commission a ballet score from him (*Ondine* was not mentioned, but this proposal may be the source of the confusion). In his reply, Henze included a brief outline for a twenty-minute work, an elegy for three or four couples awaiting the departure of the boat to Cythera, island of eternal love. The tone of this letter is uncharacteristically testy: time and again, he had begged Ashton to let him know his intentions so that he could plan his working schedule, but not having heard, he had taken on other projects. 'Now I really wonder if I can do something or not.' At this point, Ashton must have brought up the subject of *Ondine*. They arranged to spend a few weeks together in Ischia the following summer to work on the libretto. A month after his return from Italy, Ashton surprised Henze by arriving in Berlin unannounced to see his second opera, the richly evocative *König Hirsch* – 'He came to see what effect my music made in the theatre.' Soon after that, the commission was made official.

De la Motte Fouqué's tale of a mortal's love for a water sprite had been the source of several operas, ballets and plays, of which Louis Jouvet's magical production of Giraudoux's *Ondine* in Paris in 1939 made a profound impression on Ashton. At the time, he and Pavel Tchelitchew, its designer, discussed a one-act ballet on the subject, and, although this came to nothing, Ashton kept returning to the idea. He studied the libretti of two Romantic ballets produced in London in the 1840s,* and decided to go back to the novel, simplifying the plot and the Germanic names. He and Henze wanted to evoke, rather than reconstruct, a Romantic work, avoiding nineteenth-century clichés and types. His original

*Jules Perrot's *Ondine; ou, la Naiade* and Paul Taglioni's *Coralia; or the Inconstant Knight*.

conception was a 'dissolving' of the story into abstract dance, but it soon became apparent that this was not possible to prolong throughout the three acts; a coherent narrative depended on a certain amount of mime: 'brief fleeting communications with the audience, which then make it possible to enter into the pure fantasy world of absolute dance with all the more freedom.'

Ondine would arise from an intimate collaboration, similar to that between Petipa and Tchaikovsky. Ashton provided a detailed minutage for Henze, and they both worked closely with the designer, Lila de Nobili, to whom he had also given careful instructions, even sketching his requirements for the first scene. De Nobili had been the creator of the exquisite Proustian sets and costumes for Visconti's 1955 production of *La Traviata* with Maria Callas, and was then one of the most revered designers in Europe. She was both an aesthete and an artisan (painting backcloths herself, to preserve the delicacy of the brushwork), whose meticulous sense of detail and period was filtered through her own singular vision. 'Lila loves musty old décors which look as if they had been brought out of the store of the Théâtre Sarah Bernhardt and dusted and hung,' Ashton told Kenneth Clark. They established an immediate rapport. Even though she was eccentrically shabby, with her shawl and laddered black stockings, Ashton described 'Lila the beloved' as one of the most aristocratic women he had ever met. 'She consoles me a little for the loss of Sophie.' Her meetings with Ashton and Henze took place not on a beach but in the drawing room of Yeoman's Row; yet, as an Italian, she was immediately sympathetic to the Mediterranean spirit of the score, the shimmering colours reflecting what Henze called 'the strange Scirocco atmosphere of last summer'.

Ondine promised to be an ideal match among three romantic temperaments: Ashton's recent collaborations with John Craxton and Michael Powell had re-explored English neo-Romanticism; Henze, whose music at this time was tuneful and full of fantasy, has been called 'the last of the Romantics'; while de Nobili belonged to the Paris-based school of neo-Romantics, led by Christian Bérard. Of the same generation, and sharing similar tastes, Ashton and de Nobili's concepts of the production were more in harmony, compared to that of Henze, whose main concern was to make the Ondine myth contemporary. Like Michael Powell, who, in 1953, planned to make a film of Giraudoux's play (starring Audrey Hepburn and set on the French Riviera – 'a modern aqualung film rather than a medieval romance'), he envisaged a twentieth-century *Ondine*, but soon discovered that his collaborators had a great mistrust of modernity for its own sake. 'Fred was full of traditional ideas and Lila worked within certain well-marked, self-established rules and limitations. She lived in a very retrospective world and was influenced considerably by her collaboration with Visconti. Her technique of stage design was definitely and outspokenly 19th century.' Henze realized that he was going to have to adapt his 'own sound world' and his ideas in order to conform to the visual style that was being developed by the choreographer and designer. 'Fred wanted me to follow him . . . he wanted to be served.'

Conceived in the Mediterranean warmth, the score of *Ondine* was created during an English winter. Henze spent the first few months of 1957 in London, where he stayed with Alexander Grant in Battersea. Ashton had installed a piano for him in the small front room and he spent the days composing, then he would take his material to Yeoman's Row. 'Fred was quite pitiless. When I played new stuff I'd written, he'd stab at me with his finger and say, "Give me a *tune*."' One day, an excited Grant reported to Ashton that his cleaning lady, Mrs Griggs, had heard the most beautiful music coming from the living room. 'Well, let's hear it,' Ashton said impatiently to Henze that evening. He played what he had written and watched their faces cloud with disappointment: he had spent the afternoon playing Schubert sonatas 'for my personal edification'. Although Henze knew that he was not able to provide the nineteenth-century melodies with which Ashton would have been happier, he tried hard to please. He went to the ballet almost every night 'to see how the steps go with the music, what is danceable music and what isn't', he had long consultations with Alexander Grant, the company's spokesman 'against the music', and attempted to 'build in their feelings and wishes into my researches and experiments in the score'. Ashton often accompanied Henze to Covent Garden to instruct him on what he did and did not like – 'He would say "Don't you dare to write anything like *that*."' He even forbade the composer to initiate a reconciliation with a lover whom he had left behind. 'You must pour all your feelings into the music.' He later admitted to being hard on Henze, but it was out of love, Ashton insisted: it was his way of trying to stir the composer to his greatest efforts. 'I think that all our talks and doubts were of immense importance for we delved deep into this subject & though at times we were submerged in the darkest watery depths of it, I hope that it will also be blue & radiant & sad & suspended like your beloved Mediterranean.'

The score of *Ondine* was completed in the spring of 1957, after Henze had returned to Naples, leaving behind a tape-recording of the whole work, now orchestrated, which Ashton heard for the first time.

Dearest Hans,

Your music is wonderful & I am thrilled with it . . . *but* it is very difficult & on the tape it is very different from the piano. It is all so much more sustained & intense. The result of all this is that I have had to revise all the work I had done before in the light of the orchestration & bring it all much more 'au point' . . . The 2nd Act is magnificent, better than Tristan, but it requires a new approach choreographically to anything I have ever done before. My only complaint is that it is fiendishly difficult but that must be overcome somehow . . .

Work progressed very slowly. Neither Ashton nor the dancers felt they could get to grips with the orchestration. Henze's score, Fonteyn said, 'just didn't seem to say the same thing as the scenario'. Rumours filtered back to the composer that Fonteyn and Ashton hated the first act, and that he had either to rewrite it or to give the whole thing up. When Ashton's minutage for Act III failed to arrive, he felt even more hurt and upset, and, hearing that the production was being further delayed because there was not enough space at Covent Garden for Lila de Nobili to paint her décor, Henze was in despair. 'Try to have some phantasy and to imagine that I would like to know how things are going . . . that is only human . . . If you want music to come out of me for you, it is dependent on your attitude.'

Ashton wrote to placate him.

Well I think you are very silly to listen to absurd & malicious gossip . . . I love your music otherwise if I did not believe in you, is it likely that I would have risked my reputation on a 3 act work with you . . . Perhaps I should have been more encouraging to you, but it is strange to me that you did not feel my loyalty for I am that above all things.

There were further delays. While he was at Chandos Lodge in June, Ashton ruptured his Achilles' tendon and, with his foot in plaster to his knee, was out of action for six weeks. Then came the company's five-month American tour which Ashton 'abandoned' midway to carry out two commissions at La Scala, Milan. He had been introduced to the general administrator, Antonio Ghiringhelli, 'whom I like & who likes me', at a party of the Waltons in Ischia. Although, at the time, he showed a lack of interest in 'the Sovrintendente's' invitation to work in Milan, Ashton soon had second thoughts. La Scala was then the place to be: Maria Callas was at the height of her career; Victor de Sabata, Carlo Maria

Frederick Ashton as Monsieur Duchic and Marie Rambert
as Orchidée in the first performance of *A Tragedy of Fashion*
at The Lyric Theatre, Hammersmith, 15 June 1926

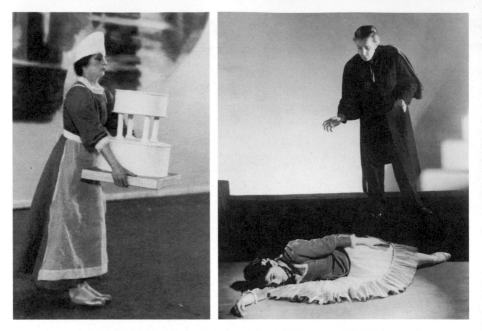

ABOVE LEFT: Ninette de Valois as the officious maid, Webster, in
A Wedding Bouquet. ABOVE RIGHT: Frederick Ashton as the
Spectator with Margot Fonteyn, a poor flower girl, in the 1936
Vic-Wells production of *Nocturne*

BELOW LEFT AND RIGHT: Beatrice Appleyard and Walter Gore as
the Queen of the Port and her Sailor in the 1935 Vic-Wells production
of *Rio Grande*, in which Margot Fonteyn and William Chappell
appeared as the Creole Girl and Boy.

ABOVE: The 1947 Sadler's
Wells Ballet production of
Valses nobles et sentimentales

RIGHT: Margot Fonteyn and
Frederick Ashton perform the
tango in a revival of *Façade*

LEFT: Grouping from *Symphonic Variations* with Michael Somes, center

BELOW: Margot Fonteyn, Michael Somes, and the four cavaliers from *Scènes de ballet*

ABOVE: Nicholas
Magallanes in New York
City Ballet's 1950
production of *Illuminations*,
based on the poems of
Arthur Rimbaud

RIGHT: Margot Fonteyn and
Michael Somes in *Sylvia*,
with Alexander Grant as the
statue of Eros

LEFT: Lynn Seymour and Christopher Gable as the reunited lovers in *The Two Pigeons*

BELOW: Nadia Nerina and David Blair perform a ribbon dance from *La Fille mal gardée*

ABOVE: Antoinette Sibley and Anthony Dowell as Titania and Oberon with Alexander Grant as Bottom in *The Dream*

RIGHT: Derek Rencher as Elgar and Deanne Bergsma as the muse figure, Lady Mary Lygon, in *Enigma Variations*

RIGHT: Margot Fonteyn and Rudolf Nureyev in 1963 in *Marguerite and Armand*

BELOW: Frederick Ashton, *left*, and Robert Helpmann as the Ugly Sisters in *Cinderella*—roles that caricatured their offstage rivalry

Giulini and the young Leonard Bernstein were conducting there; designers included de Nobili and the brilliant Piero Tosi; and a new generation
of directors had begun gaining international recognition, one of whom
was 'Visconti's boy', Franco Zeffirelli. By the time Ashton arrived, Zeffirelli, having fallen out with the theatre's old guard, was working at La
Piccola Scala. Along with Lila de Nobili, they spent a lot of time together,
and charmed by Zeffirelli's lively company and audacious good looks,
Ashton 'fell frantically in love. Nothing happened, of course,' he told
Henze. 'Freddie was a bit wild, yes,' said Zeffirelli. 'But of course I had
too much respect for him. He was an adorable man. So jovial, humane,
yet bitchy beyond the power of the word. But so funny. He loved the
work I was doing. I had La Scala in my hands and I was practically a kid.
He was fascinated by that.'*

Ashton's first task was to choreograph a new production of Ravel's *La
Valse*, a score which, as he told Marie Rambert (in a letter written in pid-
gin Italian, spiced with a touch of Spanish), he interpreted with a tenaciously retrospective romanticism.

> Il vecchio maestro . . . fada La Valsi di Ravello cui, dicie tutto la
> gente qui e molto bello e riempito la grande scena con un movi-
> mento di danza feroce e poesia . . . io no po dire ci bueno o no . . .
> Il vecchio maestro no po fare il balleto moderno e brutto e dedi-
> cato a la bellezza e il lirism, que cosa fare? . . . Sa veccio elevo Fred-
> erico, dolce com un fico.†

La Valse has been staged by many choreographers, including Nijinska, in whose first version for Ida Rubinstein's company Ashton himself
had danced. 'I loved the music but was never very happy with the way it
was first presented,' he said. 'Nijinska made it a completely abstract
work.' While his interpretation pays glancing homage to his mentor in
the ballerinas' extravagant épaulement and the bouncing classroom beats
of the men, Ashton's main lead, initially at least, was Ravel. He follows
the composer's description of the opening of his score as precisely as a libretto, the curtain rising on a mysteriously misty scene in which 'through

---

*Their fondness for each other continued. Ashton remarked how sweet Zeffirelli
was to him: 'He always bows and calls me "Maestro".'
†"The old maestro Ashton has done the Ravello waltz which, as everyone here
says, is very beautiful and fills the great stage with fierce, poetic dance movement . . . I can't say if it's good or not . . . The old maestro can't do ugly, modern
ballet. He's dedicated to beauty and lyricism, and what can be done about
that? . . . Your old pupil Frederick, sweet as a fig."

whirling clouds couples of waltzers are faintly distinguished'. The clouds then lift, the lights go up, and André Levasseur's huge chandeliered ballroom is seen peopled with twenty-one dancing couples.

It is significant that Ashton's programme note omitted the rest of Ravel's outline – his vision of 'a kind of apotheosis of the Viennese waltz, which I have mixed in my mind with the impression of a terrifying and awe-inspiring vortex' – in that the ballet all but ignores the latent drama in the music, the edgy, obsessive, 'féroce' quality, graphically summed up by Arlene Croce as 'real hellfire under red cellophane'. Ashton's *La Valse* is pretty, poetic and chic – an encapsulation of period style, feminine allure and nuances of courtship, reminiscent of his own *Valses nobles et sentimentales* – but it is uncharacteristically thin on invention. Enchaînements are perfunctorily repeated rather than contrapuntally varied; and Ashton has recycled his own work, once again relying on the hectic *Daphnis and Chloe*'s 'reaping' motif to whip up a climax. In other sections, the manic swirl of the music is subdued by the elegantly classical idiom of the dance. It may be that, as Diaghilev believed, Ravel's score is inimical to ballet – 'it lacked scenic action, and so paralysed every possibility of choreographic development.' Yet, when Ashton's version was premièred at Covent Garden the following year, it was generally considered a disappointment. At La Scala, however, *La Valse* had an enormous success, the sophistication, musicality and enthusiasm of the Italian dancers generating an exhilarating performance. Francis Poulenc, who was among the first-night audience, told Ashton that it was the only successful realization of the score he had seen.

His second assignment for La Scala was to choreograph the dance in a new production of *Orfeo ed Euridice*, with the Italian ballerina Carla Fracci cast as the leader of the Blessed Spirits. It was directed by Gustaf Grundgens, the brilliantly versatile German actor, who inspired Klaus Mann's *Mephisto*. Mann described Grundgens as 'all talent', a character driven by vanity and a persecution mania: 'He glittered and suffered and seduced.' Ashton, on the contrary, found him 'quite sympathetic but with no taste'. He amused Zeffirelli by his imitations of Grundgens, a 'most outrageous queen, tall as a lamppost and completely bald', who wore pastel-coloured shirts and flamingo-pink panstick on his face. Ashton was not only intrigued by his pinkness but would mimic the Gestapo-like harshness with which Grundgens was always saying, '*Vas?*' While he was in Milan, Ashton had discussed *Ondine* with Ghiringhelli, who expressed an interest in bringing it to La Scala. There was also talk of the Royal Ballet including the ballet in their repertory on a proposed tour of Italy, but a firm date had not yet been set for its première. On Ashton's return, a letter arrived from Henze, begging for a September staging.

It was not to be. On the last night of the season, Ashton and Grant threw a party at the dancer's house in Battersea. 'Freddie said, "You provide the food and I'll do the drink."' As usual, Ashton was the last to leave, and, at 5 a.m., Grant drove him back to Yeoman's Row only to be told to fetch him the next morning at 9 a.m. (they were going to Chandos Lodge for the start of the summer holidays). 'He said, "We've got to leave early, because I've told Mrs Lloyd she can't go to church."' When Grant returned, he had to clear up after the party; by the time he had finished, he was due at Yeoman's Row.

It was a beautiful day and Freddie said, 'Let's go on the side roads, it's much prettier.' He fell asleep and I must have dozed off too, because the next thing I remember is him shouting, '*Look out* Alex!' just before we went off the road and into a lamppost. Mrs Lloyd, who was sitting in the back with piles of luggage pushed him forward through the windscreen, he put out his hand to save himself and broke his nose and wrist.

There was a farmhouse near by from which they called an ambulance. Mrs Lloyd was concussed, but, as a Christian Scientist, refused to see a doctor. Ashton was given an injection of morphine and, before he was driven to hospital, whispered to Grant, 'If they ask you if I've had any morphine, tell them "no". I want some more.'

More shaken than hurt, Ashton rather enjoyed the attention his accident caused. He was photographed for the *Tatler*, made front-page news in *The Times*, and was the talk of his friends. 'Freddy Ashton and Lucian Freud have suffered broken and lacerated noses,' Ann Fleming reported in a letter to Evelyn Waugh, who was unlikely to have been sympathetic. As dismissive of 'Assheton' as of her other homosexual friends, Waugh had always made his hostility towards the 'unarmigerous dancer' quite plain – on one occasion, objecting to Ashton's dandyish cravat, he arrogantly upbraided him for not owning a tie. Ann Fleming, on the other hand, whom Ashton first got to know after the war when she was married to the newspaper proprietor Lord Rothermere, was full of commiseration and affection. One of London's last great hostesses, she was now his substitute for Alice, so extravagant towards him that her second husband, the novelist Ian Fleming, claimed he had to 'work twice as hard to keep Lucian Freud, Peter Quennell, Freddie Ashton et al. in champagne'. There were 'jolly dinners' with Stephen Spender and the Devonshires – 'Freddy was a great success with Debo . . . If she is going to frat. with Teddy boys she might as well meet the nicest of them' – and caviar luncheons at Wiltons, with her favourite coterie of 'Teds': Freud, Bacon and 'little Cecil Beatnik'.

Hating 'the pale and the placid', Ann was intrigued by the netherworld of friends like Bacon, and she was amused when, having left one of their gatherings for Leicester Square after much talk of bicycle chains and razors, he returned to Wiltons 'with an undergrown youth'. Of the two artists, Ashton was more impressed by Bacon. 'He was the master. It was wonderful when he held forth, he had so much to say. Mostly though, our conversation was quite general, quite frivolous. We weren't on deep subjects by any means.' Ian Fleming did not attempt to participate in his wife's social circle, but with Ashton he made an exception. 'Ian could be difficult but he liked Freddie and found him frightfully funny,' said Loelia Lindsay,* who first introduced them. Preferring men to women, and dismissing anyone whom she designated a 'bore', Ann was even trickier – 'as pointu as her nose', as one friend remarked. 'She was very intelligent, very very arriviste but with a good understanding of things and people. She was really a collector of people.' Ann was a tremendous gossip, at the same time greatly disliked and adored, depending on her allegiance. She loved Ashton for his wit and social aplomb, and grew dependent on his company. 'Beaton and Ashton are in America,' she wrote to Waugh, 'so who can we invite?' Violent in her partisanship, she once 'screamed abuse' at Richard Buckle in the Crush Bar of Covent Garden because of his unfavourable review of one of Ashton's ballets. As in several of his close relationships with women, there was an element of flirtatiousness on both sides. 'Bags I be the first Lady Ashton and to hell with Madge Garland,'† she wrote, congratulating him on his knighthood in 1961.

Throughout the late 1950s and early 1960s, Ashton and the Flemings were frequently together: at several weekends with Loelia Lindsay at Send Grove; at Goldenhurst with Noël Coward; at Drumlanrig Castle, Dumfriesshire, with the Duchess of Buccleuch, who took her guests for long country walks. 'Freddie in little light shoes skipped along admiring the scenery whereas *tough* Ian Fleming gave up and had to rest his legs.' But despite Ashton's social distractions, *Ondine* remained in the forefront of his mind. While visiting the Angleseys in North Wales, he gave an amusing interpretation of the nymph emerging from her fountain; choosing the largest fern in Bodnant's conservatory, Rose McClaren‡ filmed him parting the fronds and peering through with an expression of mock-wonder. Staying with Clarissa Eden* in Wiltshire, they walked along the Vale of Pewsey and she pointed out a 'charming little stream with willows either side', which he went back to study three or four times.

---

*Ashton's friend from the 1930s, Loelia Westminster.
†Madge Garland became Lady Ashton when she married Sir Leigh Ashton.
‡Rose Paget.

The première of *Ondine*, with Henze conducting, finally took place in October 1958 – more than a decade after he had written his first letter to Ashton. In the overture, seeping through the percussion, were the strange sea sounds he had promised would be there – 'all the whispers, the allusions to water, to woods, to the Mediterranean air' – but as soon as the curtain rose, it seemed, as Henze now admits, 'as though the dancers listened to another music that is not in the pit'. Like the 'chance procedures' of Merce Cunningham and John Cage, there is a disjunction between the ear and eye, as if Ashton has created the dance independently of the score. The first moment of true harmony is when Margot Fonteyn appears through the fountain. The lambent, other-worldly texture of the music is perfectly echoed in Lila de Nobili's iridescent wisp of a costume, and in Fonteyn's tremblingly delicate movements. Ashton's choreography for her pays homage to other roles and other dancers: her Gothic intertwined arms is a recurring motif, imitating Pearl Argyle's fishy poses in Andrée Howard's ballet *Mermaid*; the playful shadow dance re-creates Fanny Cerrito's famous solo in Perrot's *Ondine*; her timidity with the hero, Palemon, alludes both to the Firebird and Odette. Nevertheless, the ballet is, as one critic commented, a Fonteyn-concerto. With her long, loose black hair, she is the 'ondine' Ashton described swimming off the Fishers' boat in the Mediterranean; her own qualities of simplicity, girlish directness and lack of flamboyance, are all invested in the role.

A ballerina, Arlene Croce has written, is as inseparable from music as a water nymph is from her fountain; in *Ondine*, Fonteyn, one of the most musical dancers of all, is in her natural element. Images of flowing water, as in Seamus Heaney's poem 'Undine', frequently suggest parallels with the act of creation, a freeing of inspiration, and Ashton's ballet seems to enact the mysterious spiritual kinship between the choreographer and his ballerina. Deliquescent and elusive, Ondine is more than just a water nymph fleeing from her human pursuer; she is a vision of the unattainable, her myth an allegory of the artist and his muse. During rehearsals Fonteyn told him, 'Things you've been trying to get me to do all my life, I'm at last beginning to understand.' Ashton's tutelage is imprinted everywhere: in the low, Pavlova-inspired arabesques, and in the animation of her fingers, wrists, shoulders and, especially, her eyes. 'Dancers today don't understand what eyes are for,' he would complain. 'With your eyes properly used, you can distract everybody from your technique. You

---

*Wife of the Rt Hon Anthony Eden, who was succeeded as prime minister in 1957 by Harold Macmillan.

draw the public to you through your eyes' (as Fonteyn demonstrates, when she steps tentatively through the fountain, her eyes speaking of Ondine's wonder at the brave new world).

Shakespeare's Miranda was the role Ashton originally had in mind for Fonteyn, but, because she felt it 'rather a dull character for me', he abandoned *The Tempest* – though not entirely. When Ondine first hears Palemon's heartbeat, her naive amazement echoes Miranda's marvelling appreciation of Ferdinand's brave form; the play's storm at sea provided a model for the ballet's realistic tempest in Act II; while Tirrenio, abruptly ending Bertha and Palemon's nuptial revels in Act III, has inherited Prospero's implacability, fused with the elemental wrath of Oberon (his commanding stance, high above the enchanted forest, anticipates that of Oberon in *The Dream*, choreographed six years later). Lord of the Mediterranean, Tirrenio, was danced by Alexander Grant with his usual zeal, flinging himself into abandoned leaps and turns, his silky, scalloped cloak swirling round him like a wave. Apart from Ondine, it is the ballet's only successful role; the other characters, barely sketched at all. Created by Michael Somes, Palemon is as pallid as his name, another 'handsome dummy', there to provide noble support. His earthly beloved, Bertha, was danced by Julia Farron, who did all she could to make sense of an alluringly mannish, but conspicuously undeveloped character.

Ashton was always less interested in story ballets than in 'poetic potency'; in *Ondine*, he attempts (not entirely successfully) to absorb the emotional stylization of an abstract ballet into a nineteenth-century framework. The result, in spite of its narrative flaws, is 'full of the true poetic spirit', a daring, evasive work, haunted by the presence of water. It is Ashton's ode to the sea, his childhood love, and he reproduces its changing moods and surging flow with masterly accuracy. 'I wanted the movement to be fluid like the rhythm of the sea rather than set ballet steps.' Ashton makes great play with watery conceits: the 'swimming' lifts, where Ondine floats above Palemon's shoulder; or the human fountain of watersprites, a citation of Busby Berkeley's tiers in 'By a Waterfall' from *Footlight Parade*. But it is in the choreography for Fonteyn – the capricious changes of direction, rippling bourrées, drifting arms and seamless continuity of movement – that Ashton has most ingeniously caught the multiple characteristics of water. Classical ballet's clearly defined lines and crisp variations have liquefied into a new, free choreographic style. *Ondine*'s idiom (influenced, to a certain extent, by the Bolshoi's method of allowing the dance to emerge naturally from the story) takes the ballet emphatically into the twentieth century, and yet somehow it seems old-fashioned. Ashton's mistake was to try to extend a slight, enigmatic story over three acts: a decision that Lincoln Kirstein, in a lengthy diatribe to Cecil Beaton, blamed on outside pressures.

My private opinion is that he works under conditions that cannot produce really great work. He should refuse to do three acts ballets; they are not in our tempo. He is not Petipa. Margot is a marvelous dancer, but she should be shown as herself, not as some echo of a 19th-century star. Ninette is not Nicholas II. Today is 1958. The Maryinsky Theater is not Covent Garden and Henze is not Tchaikovsky. No one can write music for a THREEEEEE ACCC-CTTTT ballet, not Stravinsky, nor God . . . I am so bored with the kind of thinking that makes Henry Moore THE SCULPTOR, Benjamin Britten THE COMPOSER and Fred THE CHOREOGRAPHER. The weight imposed is incommensurate with long-term prestige earnestly desired by Imperial Agencies; no one can deliver in these terms; England is NOT in decline in sculpture, the novel, the theater; it is not neccessary to have to force these things. Fred is not in contact with much vitality and de Nobilis is a gifted designer but its all in the international chic-set which died in 1940. Why has nobody done a horror number of the Angry Young non-U's with Francis Bacon? Because Ninette doesn't like queers; so, – we have Fred as a non-queer doing something gloriously done by Pavlik [Tchelitchew] 20 years ago . . . The Royal Ballet has no intellectual direction, no contact with neccessity, that is WHAT IS ACTUALLY NEEDED for its public . . . it has a great theater, a subsidy, and it is a national object of veneration, and Ninette is a combination of Montgomery of Alamein and Mrs Bowdler. If I had anything to do with it, I would blast the place open . . .

Kirstein was right; Ashton was straining to fulfil expectations. De Valois regarded *Ondine* as 'a noble and perfectly conceived work on the grand scale which is the only scale for you to concern yourself with from now on'. After the première, in spite of her aspirations for him, Ashton took a vow to do no more three-act ballets. Although everyone agreed that *Ondine* was an admirable showcase for Fonteyn, the general opinion was that it did not 'quite come off'. Only one or two critics saw the ballet for what it is: a work of intense poetic imagination with a strange, brooding sense of enchantment that becomes more potent at each viewing. It is vital to the Ashton canon in that, as his last major ballet for Fonteyn, it marks the end of an era. And yet, being a supreme statement of neo-Romanticism, *Ondine* is very much of its time. When it was restaged at Covent Garden in 1988, it looked as dated as a Piper Gothic ruin, its set dustier than de Nobili could ever have intended. (Living as a recluse in Paris with her cats, she had declined to participate in the new production.) The ballet is no longer popular with audiences, although, with one or two exceptions, the revival was politely received by the critics. What the revival made clear was *Ondine*'s dependence on its original star. Although pretty, fey and technically more accomplished, the new interpreters had little of Fonteyn's ability to convey wonder and to express a kind of spiritual grace, tapping intuitive symbolic meanings that lie beneath the drama. The subtext of *Ondine* explores the evanescent nature of inspiration and, without 'his violin', as Henze called Fonteyn, Ashton's concerto appears only half-scored.

In the original production – and even thirty years later – it was Henze who bore the brunt of the criticism; Noel Goodwin's complaint of the lack of a personal signature seeming particularly unfair in retrospect. Yet, despite Ashton's manipulation of his score, the composer showed him nothing but gratitude and admiration.

> It was such a very beautiful ballet, a great wonderful Nocturne about Love and Beauty and you have done a masterwork . . . My very adorable Friend you gave me the greatest artistic help by letting me work for you . . . people will discover more and more all the details of wonderful accordance between you Lila and myself. Don't you ever forget me, and call me for anything you need, and consider me your spiritual lover, your interpreter, your poet.

They remained great friends; and, although they spoke of further ventures – 'I could even produce your operas. We will learn from this collaboration and improve on any mistakes we make, for it is rare to find a really understanding partner' – Ashton did not work to a commissioned score for almost a decade.

Soon after the première, Ashton moved out of Yeoman's Row (due to be demolished and reconstructed), into a compact three-storey Georgian house in Marlborough Street, South Kensington, which Edith had persuaded him to buy. Surrounded by small local shops, it had the village atmosphere he liked and was a few minutes' walk from the King's Road. Substantial renovations were carried out and Ashton made a pretty, camellia-covered patio, with steps leading to the french windows of his drawing room. Most of his energy, however, went into creating his garden at Chandos Lodge. Again, it was Edith who had urged Ashton to take on the property, as the amount of land, about ten acres, had 'horrified' him at the time. 'How on earth was I going to cope with all that, I thought, having come from a tiny cottage with only a patch of ground.' His first step was to plant box hedges and old-fashioned roses round the house, Edwardian beauties whose titles – Mme Alfred Carrière, Mme

Louis Leveque, Mme Abel Chatenay – he would recite with the same pleasure he took from naming well-born acquaintances. Later came a grand, Le Nôtre-inspired topiary, its clipped box triangles, swirls, pompoms and crinolines as aesthetically placed as an Ashton corps de ballet. Although he tried to emulate the architecture of French gardens at Chandos, its combination of rigid formality with a profusion of roses and cottage-garden flowers – classical line, with romantic embellishment – is more of a Sissinghurst-style alliance. It is also the hallmark of his art.

Like Church Cottage, Chandos Lodge was painted Suffolk pink with white shutters. The furniture was a mixture of Alice's Regency hand-me-downs and bargains bought from Mr Ley. 'Junk,' wrote Cecil Beaton, but 'extremely pretty and individual. The house of an old aunt or of the girl in Spectre de la Rose.' There were ribbons and roses everywhere – in paintings, on china and chintz – displayed with whimsical collections of pottery chickens, cabbages and corn-on-the-cob jugs. Chandos Lodge was 'drenched with Fred' said his nephew, Anthony Russell-Roberts, who was to inherit it. Its fusion of femininity, elegance and rustic simplicity mirrored the 'Ashtonian' qualities in his work – and never more resonantly than in his next ballet.

With no touring throughout the year and no emotional distractions, Ashton spent the summer of 1959 and every possible weekend in Suffolk. He had fallen in love with the English countryside, which gave him a sense of peace and fulfilment that his relationships were not able to provide. First came the joy of arrival, when he would walk round his garden picking nosegays of flowers, which, like Vita Sackville-West, he liked to arrange in tiny vases grouped round the house. Then followed 'days of contemplation and endless staring and dreaming'. Ritualistically, he always played Beethoven's 'Pastoral' Symphony, its first movement – an expression of the composer's own elation on arriving in the country – providing 'a sort of confirmation that I am there'. Feeling not only spiritually in tune with Beethoven, for whom nature was the most enduring and significant love, Ashton was also reading Dorothy Wordsworth's *Journals*, 'swept away by a longing for the country of the late eighteenth and early nineteenth century'. The homeliness and simplicity of her account of day-to-day living was close to Ashton's heart, but not its reality: the rural destitution she describes. More romantic than the Romantics, his vision was of an idealized ordinariness, a sanctified rural England. 'There exists in my imagination a life in the country of eternally late spring, a leafy pastorale of perpetual sunshine and the humming of bees – the suspended stillness of a Constable landscape of my beloved Suffolk, luminous and calm.' This was his 'period of preparation', during which he was evolving his own tribute to nature, a 'poor man's *Pastoral Sym-*

phony', his description of *La Fille mal gardée*. A work of genius and the most popular of his career, it drew on the two sources which had absorbed him that summer, imposing the serenity and noble simplicity he found in Beethoven upon everyday country life.

Staged in Bordeaux in 1789, the original ballet had marked realism's first major entry into the genre, substituting authentic country inhabitants for conventional nymphs and fairies. It was Karsavina, one of the great interpreters of the role of Lise, who 'really sold' the idea of *La Fille mal gardée* to Ashton; but, reluctant to take on another long work, he kept procrastinating about it, until de Valois finally forced his hand by advertising its upcoming première. 'I said you've got to get on with it now and he started at once, without any trouble.' After copying in longhand Jean Dauberval's libretto in the British Museum, Ashton, sitting in his little Gothic folly at Chandos one fine afternoon, wrote out his own version. It is a simple story of a widow's daughter in love with Colas, a young farmer, who thwarts her mother's plans to marry her off to the doltish Alain, son of a wealthy landowner. Having taken as his source an old French tale, Ashton, like Britten with *Albert Herring*, naturalized it by drawing on his own Suffolk surroundings as the setting. The ballet's atmospheric inspiration also derived from a series of nineteenth-century English rural prints which he lent to his designer, Osbert Lancaster, and later hung in maple frames on his bedroom wall. The scenes of harvesting and country dancing provided the general flavour, with their details of farming implements, vegetables and stacked sheaves of corn. And there are three prints – 'The Cottager's Daughter', 'The Farmer's Son' and 'Madame Auriole as Columbine' –on which the costumes are so closely modelled that they could be illustrations from the ballet itself. There is also 'The Happy Morning', a group portrait of mop-capped mother, pretty daughter and eager suitor, which could not only be a scene from *Fille*, but exactly encapsulates the bucolic sentiment which, with exaggerated archness, Lancaster's designs attempted to caricature.

The music required more extensive preparation. In the Municipal Library at Bordeaux, the score for Dauberval's ballet, by an unknown composer, was discovered by the dance historian Ivor Guest, who also found in the Paris Opera archives the derivative 1828 version attributed to Hérold. There was another score, by P. L. Hertel, used for the Petipa–Ivanov production in which Karsavina danced, but Ashton did not like it and decided he wanted what amounted to 'an old house with new bricks'. He commissioned John Lanchbery, principal conductor of the Royal Ballet, to carry out the work, giving him 'absolute carte blanche' to compose the new links. He also made suggestions of his own. One day, he told Lanchbery, his neighbour in Marlborough Street, that he had heard an 'absolutely awful' piece by Weber on the wireless, but he liked the fact that it kept stopping and starting. 'So we put those stops in Lise's solo.' He also took Lanchbery to see Lancastrian clog dancing in a folk-dance festival at the Albert Hall, resulting in one of the ballet's highlights, a jaunty clog dance for Widow Simone, the accompaniment of which was a tune by Hertel, combined with a passage of Lanchbery's own. Despite its hybrid composition and caramelized melodies, the score of *Fille mal gardée* is a delight. Ashton told Kenneth Clark that it was 'a holiday after *Ondine*'s music', its easy tunes spurring him to a continuous flow of invention. There is no padding whatsoever, and the choreography for the corps is exceptionally felicitous, its energy and impulse illustrating 'the accumulative waves of movement' that Ashton attributed to Beethoven and 'imposed on poor Hérold'. (Although Hérold had based his storm scene on Rossini's *La Cenerentola*, Ashton's little scene when Lise and Colas kneel in prayer is a tribute to the 'Pastoral' Symphony's fifth movement, the shepherd's hymn of gratitude and thanksgiving after the storm.)

The 'musique concrete of farmyard noises', which he described listening to at Chandos as a real-life accompaniment to Beethoven, colours the opening bars of *Fille*. It is dawn as the curtain rises, the farm-hands enter yawning and stretching, a cockerel crows and performs his own feathery stretch, mimicked by a quartet of hens. Their opening number of strutting, hoofing chickens is a droll send-up of a Cochran-style revue, and sets the tone of whimsical good-humour that continues throughout the ballet. The setting is one Ashton based on a hazy first memory of a visit to his grandmother at Valley Farm. He was barely two, but claimed to remember standing with his nose pressed against a lead-framed windowpane, looking down on the farmyard at the side of the house. The first scene is devoted mostly to Colas's courtship of Lise. Their delicately flirtatious encounter at the butter churn was one of several episodes described to Ashton by Winifred Edwards, a Royal Ballet teacher, who appeared in the 1912 version in which Pavlova danced.* But Karsavina's memories formed the basis for Ashton's *Fille*, her 'enchanting and marvellous' demonstration of a mime reverie, in which the heroine anticipates her married life, convincing him to revive the ballet. Alone in the cottage, Lise sits on a bale of straw, which the labourers have brought in to dry out after the storm. Unknown to her (and the audience) it is 'a trojan horse' hiding Colas.

Then she starts to think about when she is married. I will wear a lovely dress, carry a bouquet and walk like a great lady. Then per-

---

*Among Ashton's papers is an undated programme of divertissements by Pavlova and her troupe at Covent Garden. It includes *La Fille mal gardée*, arranged by Petipa, with Hilda Butsova in the role of Lise.

haps have children 1, 2 and 3 (counts them out in sizes.) 'Have you learned your lessons?' she asks an imaginary child. 'No' then slaps it. A baby falls down. Picks him up and rocks him in her arms and sings to herself. Colas appears and she is ashamed to be caught in such day dreaming. Colas takes her by the hand and both sit on the straw and look different ways and then at each other. He takes a kerchief and rolls it, then each puts a kerchief on the other's neck and they kiss.

Ashton follows Karsavina's directions to the letter, and not only in this instance. A four-page transcript of a 'conversation with Madame Karsavina', recorded in October 1959, virtually serves as a libretto, outlining exact details – from Alain playing hobby-horse with his umbrella, to Colas finding the ribbon left for him by Lise, kissing it, tying it on a stick and parading with it on his shoulder. Karsavina even provided Ashton with one of *Fille*'s jokes: Lise pretending to trap a fly as her mother wakes and catches her trying to steal her keys. But Ashton never acknowledged the extent of Karsavina's contribution, maintaining that apart from the mime passage, 'choreographically it's all entirely mine'. He was always hypersensitive when questioned about influences on his work, misinterpreting this as a charge of plagiarism, an attempt 'to undermine me'. But, just as Shakespeare's pastoral romance *As You Like It* steals the plot of Thomas Lodge's *Rosalynde* and unrecognizably transforms it, it is Ashton's enhancement of his source material that elevates the ballet to a new plane of sophistication and emotional depth – the way, for instance, that Colas not only consoles Lise with a kiss for embarrassing her, but tenderly spaces three separate kisses along her arm to an echo of the '1, 2 and 3' children music: it is a heart-rending gesture of gently allusive, sweet-humoured understanding. The most personal of Ashton's ballets, *La Fille mal gardée* is also the most eclectic – a masterly potpourri of borrowings from beginning to end. The chickens were suggested by the famous Felsentein production of Janáček's *Cunning Little Vixen*, which he saw in East Berlin; while the coda, where Alain steals back into the cottage to fetch his umbrella, imitates the ending of *Der Rosenkavalier*, where the little page returns for the Marschallin's handkerchief. He based two key moments – the maypole dance and Lise trying to steal her mother's keys – on illustrations from a 1937 book on *La Fille mal gardée*, published in Leningrad. Yet perhaps Ashton's most audacious plundering (which he tried to keep secret from all but his dancers) is to be found in the ribbon patterns, which identically reproduce the hand-tinted designs in a set of nineteenth-century German prints.

The pas de ruban was first introduced in the Mariinsky version of *Fille*, in which Karsavina danced. She insisted that the big roll of ribbon must stretch across the whole stage and described its use in the pas de deux. The idea was captivating to Ashton – pink ribbons, like pink roses, were appealing enough in themselves – and in *Fille* he developed the motif into 'one of the most resonant metaphors in the whole of ballet'. The ribbon-dances in Act I are full of charm, with a blithe solo for Lise, and a duet where she and Colas reel and unreel the ribbon by chaîné-ing along it, in a similar way to the ballerina entwining herself along a length of chiffon in *La Bayadère*. Following Karsavina's instructions, they play horse and cart and then take ingenuity a step further by twisting and ducking until they have conjured a cat's cradle (which always wins a round of applause). The use of ribbons reaches the virtuosic during the harvest festivities. Here, Lise's friends, imitating the nineteenth-century patterns, spell out a row of kisses, using four girls who hold the criss-crosses with their chins and, recalling the lovers at play, transform the ribbons into the spokes of a cartwheel. Softening the geometry are the lyrical exchanges between Lise and Colas, who yearningly weave towards each other, humanizing the picturesque posturing. The climax of this section is breathtaking. Balancing Lise in an attitude at the epicentre of the corps' wheel of ribbons, Colas leaves her slowly to promenade in a full circle, supported only by a handful of satin, as her eight friends run round her. 'The first time we did this Fred couldn't believe it and was shouting, "Keep running, girls, keep running!"'

Superb balance was but one of Nadia Nerina's outstanding gifts. The ballerina was not Ashton's original choice for Lise – Karsavina wanted him to use Fonteyn – but, as Ashton said, 'If you have a company you have to keep the elements in the company happy. You've got to do ballets for people who necessarily you wouldn't choose as perfect instruments for you.' Until her break in *La Fille mal gardée*, Nerina was regarded as 'a problem ballerina': technically she had no equal, but she was not particularly musical and her performances lacked depth. She did, however, have something rare: a virtuosic exuberance straining to be released. Ashton had already exploited her spiritedness in the Spring solo in *Cinderella* and in *Birthday Offering* – both jottings for the role of Lise – and, although he may have been reluctant to cast her at first, it was Nerina and her partner, David Blair, also a formidable virtuoso dancer, who, in effect, set Ashton free. For the first time, he was able to choreograph without giving a thought to technical limitations.

For years he has used Fonteyn and Somes as his subjects, and developed a whole style of ballet around them, serene, passionate and lyrical . . . Yet suddenly Ashton has started afresh with Nerina and Blair in a new vein of *bravura* choreography . . . Blair aggressively confident and defiantly elegant . . . holds Nerina right above his head in ecstatic Bolshoi lifts . . . she jumps and curvets round the stage with the athletic power of a man, yet with a completely feminine flounce, madcap and girlish.

Both performers were continually striving to extend the limits of their technique. Blair had started a club among the male dancers to which the 'entrance fee' was the ability to execute eight pirouettes, later increased to twelve. And when Fonteyn was on stage performing the Rose Adagio in *Sleeping Beauty*, Nerina would enlist the nearest available partner to help her practise behind the backcloth, her balancing invariably outstripping Fonteyn's. She thrived on a challenge. Ashton had seen a company of Georgian dancers in London and dared Nerina to attempt their show-stopping feat and run on her toes. She was able to do so dazzlingly, her flying feet goose-stepping into a blur of speed. Having no fear, she also volunteered to perform the dizzying lifts she had learnt from the Bolshoi's Nicolai Fadeyechev during a spell in Russia and which no English ballerina had ever attempted before. The grand pas de deux for Nerina and Blair culminated in what dancers call 'a bum lift': a Soviet tour de force, where the ballerina sits high above her partner's head and balances on the palm of one hand.

David Blair, a handsome young principal with Sadler's Wells Theatre Ballet, had first made his name in John Cranko's ballets and was now being groomed to take over from Michael Somes as a new partner for Fonteyn. Technically flamboyant and academically polished, he was able to achieve with ease Ashton's desired combination of classroom precision and Bolshoi bravura. Blair's neat beats, terre-à-terre footwork and fast crab-like pas de bourrée runs also paid homage to the Bournonville school, which Ashton was able to observe during his period in Copenhagen. (*Fille*'s storm scene is reminiscent of that in Bournonville's *Napoli*.) Stimulated by his two new stars, he worked in a state of great excitement. '*Fille* went like the wind' and was completed in only four weeks. His euphoria was infectious. 'The whole cast always enjoyed it so much because, whatever you felt like, after a few minutes with *Fille*, you forgot everything.' More accomplished performers, such as Nureyev and Baryshnikov, have since danced Colas with far greater aplomb than Blair, but Nerina has remained unsurpassed. One solo in particular (preserved by amateur film-maker, Edmée Wood) attests to her thrilling attack.

Competing with Blair's manly virtuosity during the harvest dances, she reverses a grand fouetté sauté sequence, jumping in different directions, her leg saucily flinging up her skirt in swinging battements en cloche. It is a passage lasting only thirty seconds, which leaves Lises of today looking daintily restrained. After seeing Ashton's new interpreter in *Fille*, Fonteyn began to consider retiring. For twenty-five years she had been the most eloquent practitioner of English classicism, helping to define not only Ashton's personal style but also that of Royal Ballet itself. Many ballerinas, even today, have moulded themselves in her image, although none has ever matched her astounding musicality – her way of bringing out the nuances of a phrase and of dancing '*in* the music', as Ashton put it. Radiantly composed and perfectly proportioned, she could make even a line distorted by contemporary choreography look classical and harmonious. Ashton loved these qualities and had enshrined them in almost every Fonteyn role, and yet clearly the time had now come for him to look to other dancers to extend his range. The virtuosity of Nerina and Blair was exactly the intoxicant he needed, their inspiration just the beginning of a sublime new phase in his career.

When the company presented *La Fille mal gardée* on its first tour of Russia the following year, the Soviet-style athletics were greeted with rowdy approval; but in Copenhagen, Ashton's Bournonville borrowings were misinterpreted by some as burlesque. In fact, Ashton has superbly integrated the different idioms, merging cosmopolitan classical styles with pantomime, English music-hall routines and native country dances – Morris, Maypole, Lancastrian clog-walloping. In *Fille*, unlike *Cinderella*, everything dovetails perfectly; nothing goes on for too long and the comedy is never allowed to unbalance the ballet. This might not have been the case had Robert Helpmann decided to remain in the travesti role of Widow Simone. After only a few rehearsals, he asked to be released, with the excuse, 'It's not really me. All I do is scold my daughter.' Ashton was privately relieved, knowing how solipsistic his performances could be. 'I'm glad you're doing it,' he told Stanley Holden, Helpmann's replacement, 'you never camp it up.' During the lovers' final pas de deux, described by Edwin Denby as 'quite miraculous', Helpmann would probably have been 'knitting or something', said Ashton. Holden was more suited to the role in every respect. Widow Simone was intended to pay homage to the legendary pantomime dame Dan Leno, who, while playing the music halls of Lancashire, became 'Champion Clog Dancer of the World'. Holden had similarly begun his career as a hoofer in the North of England, and had become All England Champion at the age of nineteen. He was familiar with the rolls, kicks, taps, twizzles and shuffles of Lancastrian clog dancing and demonstrated a break step that Ashton then used as a motif in the dance. Holden played the part with subtlety and imagination, never pushing a joke too far. He devised one of the best comic moments when, having admired her reflection as she ties on her bonnet, Widow Simone goes back to the mirror for a second look. A happy mistake, Holden claims, 'I got to the door too early and had to fill in time.' But it is Ashton's wit and observation of human behaviour that takes the character far beyond that of any pantomime dame. He drew upon a favourite impersonation of an elderly dowager nodding off during a concert in the scene in which Lise plays the tambourine for her dozing mother; and memories of his own mother infused the Widow's domineering nature and grudging, undemonstrative affection.

Alain is an even greater comic creation, a gift of love to Alexander Grant. The rejected simpleton is never the maudlin figure he could have easily become, but combines the radiant stupidity that characterized Ashton's Cochenille in *The Tales of Hoffmann* with an endearing eccentricity encapsulated in his affection for his red umbrella. 'Fred didn't want him to be an idiot. He's not trying to be silly, it's just his nature.' His weak knees and turned-in toes recalled Grant's acclaimed portrayal of Petrushka, another role which he took great care not to make self-pitying. Alain is a performance of perfect pitch; even his oafish dances are underplayed, with Ashton incorporating a private tribute to Grant's own idiosyncratically abandoned jumps. The dancer's main model came not from ballet but the theatre. Grant took his character's happy-go-lucky independence from Oliver Goldsmith's spurned suitor, Tony Lumpkin, whose catchphrase is 'Ecod! I'll not be made a fool of no longer': the heroine could marry whom she pleases, and Alain, like Tony Lumpkin, would be 'his own man again'.

Possibly through nostalgia (or even settling old scores), Ashton gave Alexander Grant, rather than Nerina, the end of each act – a perfect balance, whatever the motive may have been. Clutching his umbrella, he takes flight in the storm as the curtain falls at half-time; in the final scene, he creeps back into the cottage to retrieve it. The epilogue may be derivative, but Ashton makes it seem not only original but also predestined: a good-natured, good-humoured indulgence of Alain's umbrella obsession, which sends the audience home chuckling. 'Neither an American nor a Russian company could have sustained for so long so airy, childlike and unemphatic a good time,' remarked Edwin Denby. Countering the ballet's gentle whimsy is the earthy authenticity of the characters. Both Colas and Lise are full of lusty vigour, leaving the audience in no doubt as to what they are up to when they are locked in a bedroom together. Sexuality in *Fille* is frankly enjoyable. It emphasizes the elemental, biological nature of love, with none of the guilt and equivocation that defines the ballets of the 1950s. Unlike the effete mannequins of *Valses nobles et sentimentales*, Colas is exuberantly heterosexual, while Lise's peasant-like fecundity is summed up by the candid pleasure with which she indicates her pregnant bulge. For once, Ashton was happy to celebrate requited young love, with no intimation of wishful thinking or personal exclusion.

Although a charming period piece, as Karsavina wrote in her programme note, the ballet is 'singularly compatible with the artistic trends of today . . . an artistic reaction to contemporary life'. This remark contains an implicit challenge to Ashton's critics. Under the influence of the angry young generation of writers like John Osborne, dance in Britain had begun to show a new awareness and involvement in the problems of twentieth-century life. Disconcerted by this direction, Ashton had begun to 'sense an attitude of "He's finished." And I am,' he confided to Kenneth Clark, 'if it means today's problems. I am no blue genius.' His anxiety over Cranko's rise had been exacerbated by MacMillan's growing authority. Yet in the same way that the insecurity he felt about Helpmann after the war goaded Ashton into asserting his choreographic superiority with *Symphonic Variations*, so *La Fille mal gardée* emerged, to some extent, from a sense of one-upmanship. Working in the same demi-caractère genre as *Pineapple Poll* and using Cranko's designer and lead dancer (Blair made his name in the ballet), Ashton went one better and created a masterpiece. 'I suppose it is the biggest success I have ever had,' he wrote to Kenneth Clark. 'Which surprises me as there are others that I prefer . . . Success always alarms me it makes the next so difficult.'

In January 1960, 'carrying the applause of *Fille* in [his] ears', Ashton travelled to Milan to stage *La Péri* at La Scala, with Fonteyn and Somes as guest artists. Balanchine and Massine were also there, mounting ballets of their own and 'fighting for the stage', Ashton told Kenneth Clark. 'Only the Scala could have achieved having us all three there & also all to not much purpose.' He found the lack of applause, except for a claque, 'sobering' after his recent success. But he was able to relive his triumph with *Fille* later that year when the company went for their biannual tour of the States. The New York première of *Ondine* proved to be less rewarding. Although pronounced 'a knock-out' by *The New Yorker*, the ballet was dismissed by Edwin Denby as 'foolish and everyone noticed it'.

To steady his nerves during one of the intermissions, Ashton went across to Bill's Bar for a Martini. There, talking to John Cranko, he spotted an alluring youth, with full lips and a quiff of hair flopping over one eye. Cranko introduced them, but Tony Lizzul, a keen ballet fan, knew exactly who Ashton was. 'Hearing I was still in college, Fred asked what I was majoring in. When I told him it was chemistry, he seemed relieved that I was not someone in the theatre looking for his help.' They arranged to meet after the performance at a party given by John Taras, and after a 'wonderful night' together at the St Regis Hotel, they were almost inseparable for the rest of the New York season. Although they were not seen together in Ashton's box at the ballet –neither de Valois nor Webster approved of open indiscretions and 'Fred was always very conscious of what people thought' – they met for dinner after most performances. If Ashton was committed to another engagement, Lizzul would go to his room. 'Oh the delight of opening the door to you & to know that you would be with me for some hours, hours of bliss & happiness.' He continued to take comfort from the fact that, although flattered by the attention, Lizzul had nothing to gain from him professionally. 'I could give Fred companionship without an ulterior motive. He expected devotion and I think I gave it to him. I got the impression that he needed to be alone and quiet and one of the things that helped our relationship was that we could have long silences without feeling uncomfortable.'

Lizzul was a thoughtful, earnest young man, and had a 'sweet sympathy' in his nature which Ashton appreciated: 'You seemed to understand me.' He was not only attractive, but an easy companion, 'a nice boy and cosy', and was considering a career in perfumery. He also had a romantic streak, which, naturally, appealed to Ashton, who was delighted to be given a personalized cologne, an infusion of lemon verbena in gin, and touched when, on his return journey to England, he found his cabin filled with his favourite flowers.

> I was overcome with emotion & tenderness towards you when
> I . . . found the exquisite tuberoses. I grasped them with delight &
> I 'blubbed'. . . they were so special not just a bunch of roses but so
> selected & personal. You are a dear boy . . . I am pining for you
> with real suffering no matter how stupid I tell myself I am. My
> time in N.Y. with you was an idyll, but it is not of my success that
> I think . . . but of you. Of your sweetness to me of your attentive-
> ness & the devotion & time you gave to me . . . Oh that it were
> true when you said I had 'done it' I am beset with doubts . . .

They had been sitting in the King Cole Bar of the St Regis, Ashton drinking his usual dry Martini, when Lizzul told him he had 'done it', meaning that the choreographer had made a profound impression on him. 'You did something to me and created something in me which I can never forget.' The phrase became a refrain in their letters and telegrams, with Ashton demanding constant reiteration – 'I feel I have "done" nothing *please* re-assure me' – and Lizzul obliging, 'Yes you did it, and *it* will probably die with me, please believe me.' Lacking emotional inspiration,

Ashton was searching, perhaps even consciously,
him up creatively', in Billy Chappell's phrase, to
once again the romantic's craving for the unattaina
counter with Lizzul provided him with an after-in
Beard's, causing him hours of unfulfilled yearning:
that hurts for those nights at the St R when I cou
slept & drank in those wonderful looks.' But, lil
grit into pearl, it would poetically transmute itself

After brooding obsessively about Lizzul throughout the voyage – 'As
I stare at the waves you rise like my Ondine out of them everywhere' –
Ashton was dismayed to find no letter awaiting his return at Marlborough Street. A few days later, a formal little typewritten note arrived
from Lizzul, blaming his silence on an attack of flu and avowing that he
had been behaving himself. 'I have missed your companionship for the
past week, and the calls about 11 AM.' Ashton was not convinced.

> By now I suppose you are back into your own complicated life &
> my image must be receding. Please cling to it a little for you won
> my love & devotion whether you wanted to or not. Maybe for you
> it was only a joy ride, but I alas as an artist am impressionable &
> sensitive & you made a great impact . . . I managed to keep some
> of your dear flowers for almost a week after I got back. For ever
> now they will symbolise you.

Lizzul's first letter had been written before he had received Ashton's.
His next is infinitely more responsive.

> When I said 'you've done it' in the King Cole Bar I meant it and
> again I say to you, 'you've done it' . . . Your image is far from re-
> ceding, as a matter of fact, the association that I make disturbs
> me . . . OH how you are mistaken if you feel that I don't miss you.

Yet, even though Ashton was elated to find his ardour reciprocated,
subsequent letters were more cautious, and Lizzul's reticence – his 'Arctic
breezes' – spread doubt and insecurity. 'I was more important to Fred
than he was to me. At the time I was too young to appreciate the intensity of his love.' Lizzul led what they euphemistically referred to as a
'complicated' life, the focal point of which was Fire Island, then, as it is
today, a sanctuary for homosexual men, 'flamboyant, promiscuous and
free'. Lizzul's attempts to spare Ashton's feelings rarely took effect. 'You
say don't worry, how can I help it? With those big blondes forever making demands on you, of course I worry. Where do I stand?'

uestion and the answer Ashton wanted to hear are written into
t work, *Les Deux pigeons*, a fantasy about infidelity and reconcil-
on, based loosely on a la Fontaine fable about an errant pigeon. The
allet, as the programme note revealed, is an allegory, but only the choreographer knew of its additional, hidden dimension. Ashton's plea to Lizzul to 'Leave the wild inhabitants alone' could serve as its epigraph, the
temptations of Fire Island transferred to a gypsy encampment, where a
young man is lured into a sexual rite of passage, before returning con-
tritely to his true love.

Reflecting the new social realism in dance, Kenneth MacMillan's *The
Invitation*, premièred two months earlier, had graphically depicted the
rape of an adolescent girl, an astonishing performance by his twenty-one-
year-old protégée Lynn Seymour, from whom Ashton was to draw contrasting qualities of whimsy and melting tenderness. But despite the fact
that Clive Barnes felt compelled to compare the new Ashton ballet with
John Osborne's *Look Back in Anger* – 'Think of that passage of the
lovers' conversation about "bears and squirrels"' – *Les Deux pigeons*
was an unashamed idealization of old-fashioned romance. Still indulging
himself after *Ondine*, Ashton was digging in his heels. Like *La Fille mal
gardée*, it has two acts, a nineteenth-century source (the first version
choreographed by Louis Mérante) and a sweetly tuneful score (by André
Messager). Ashton quoted extracts from the la Fontaine poem in the programme, but, in effect, created a new tale of his own, setting it in a studio in Bohemian Paris. When the ballet opens, a young artist (Christopher
Gable) is painting his fidgety mistress, Lynn Seymour: plump, gauche and
as substantial as a Degas model. She tries her best to be alluring – flirting,
nuzzling, teasing and tickling him – but he grows increasingly irritated.
He expresses his exasperated defeat in a memorable image: legs slung
over the back of a chair, torso arched, head and arms resting on the floor –
casually contemporary and gracefully sensual. The pair are distracted by
friends and soon a white pigeon flies across Jacques Dupont's backdrop
of Parisian rooftops, signalling the lovers to adopt their allegorical roles.
Chests puffed out, hands on hips, elbows fanning, heads pecking back
and forth, they perform their comical pigeon strut. As his ballets and letters reveal, Ashton loved metaphor; he would take an idea and run with
it, as he did with the ingenious use of ribbons in *Fille*. Arms akimbo, the
corps mimics the couple's avian motif, prefiguring the Young Man's later
flight by forming the shape of an arrow: an image of migrating birds and
a quotation from *Swan Lake*, a pervasive influence throughout.

Half-way through Act I, a group of travelling performers appear, and
the Young Girl realizes she has a rival in the Gypsy Girl (Elizabeth Anderton), whose mock-challenging, hands-on-hip shimmy wittily eroti-

cizes the pigeon motif. Anderton gave an exhilarating performance – 'Here was something of the elevation and physical bite of Nerina', and one that has never been equalled. 'She could *jump*,' said Ashton. 'The girls who do those split jetés now are always pulling their groins and splitting their fannies.' There follows a dance duel between the two women, similar to that in *Daphnis and Chloe* but more combative. It is all rather obtrusive – a crudely caricatured portrait of jealousy, which Ashton would later refine with Shakespearean insight and control in *A Month in the Country* – and redeemed only by Lynn Seymour's solo. In rehearsals, Ashton had reprimanded the ballerina for being 'too stiff and English'.* What he drew from her, as a result, is extraordinary: frantically intricate footwork; arms flying, as her torso lurches tipsily back and forth in antic, hiccupy, devil-may-care movements that plumb the Dionysiac qualities of Seymour's dancing and exploit her unconventional persona. A member of the Royal Ballet touring section (the company for which Ashton created *The Two Pigeons*),† she was proving to be a performer of rare dramatic intelligence and natural expressiveness. If MacMillan used Seymour to convey the dark life of the psyche, Ashton brought out her adorable appeal. But, anxious that she was being made too 'cute-sy', the ballerina smuggled MacMillan into the balcony one day to watch a stage-call. 'I removed the girl's pouts and moues, substituting some impish mischief and wilful sexuality . . . Fred, who misses nothing, caught the minuscule changes and expressed his hesitation, but everything fell into place at the première.'

Aware of allaying the sentiment, Ashton originally cast as Seymour's partner Donald Britton, a dancer in his mid-thirties. He was injured at the dress rehearsal and replaced by his twenty-one-year-old understudy, Christopher Gable, who gave the part a very different inflection. Instead of being Ashton's *Age of Innocence*, in which the hero grows sated with his winsome ingénue and seeks a dark-haired, sultry alternative, *The Two Pigeons* evolved into a portrait of an inexperienced young man keen to stretch his wings (an idea obviously more conducive to the central metaphor). Gable was less remarkable for his dancing than for his natural charm: 'The way he grins and lets his arms swing loose at the end of a solo, his boyish "Anyone for tennis?" manner is something quite new in ballet.' Ashton thought so, too, and even though Britton reclaimed his role (and Alexander Grant danced it in New York), the piece became intrinsically identified with Seymour and Gable.

Fittingly, with Tony Lizzul as its muse, its leading role is the Young

---

*Although she is, in fact, Canadian.
†As it became known from October 1962.

Man rather than the ballerina, who is off-stage for most of Act II. Humiliated by the gypsies who have trussed him up and flung him out of their camp, he heads for home. As he stretches out his arms, the ropes attached to his wrists take the form of wings, alerting the audience to the resumption of the bird imagery and anticipating the appearance of a white pigeon that flies onto his hand – the token he carries to his love, symbolizing peace and his return to her. Their reconciliation, delicately conveying the gradations of the Young Girl's feelings from numbed grief to growing rapture, is one of the most poignant romantic encounters in dance. When the painter enters, she has sunk, like the Dying Swan, to the floor. Standing behind her, he slides his arms through hers and draws her back towards him. Instinctively, she arches responsively, only to collapse forwards, too hurt to surrender. He repeats the gesture and then eases her into a duet that affectingly recasts key moments from the lovers' adagio in *Swan Lake*: like Odette, she hides her head under one wing; like Siegfried, he folds her wings in his arms and tenderly rocks her from side to side. Seymour's easy extensions, yielding upper back and Pavlova-like feet, displayed so exuberantly in Act I, are, here, given poignant emotional weight: in the high développés that 'yearn upward', then yield in fluttery tiny battements.

Ashton is a poet of rejection, who spoke from the heart; like many of his works, *The Two Pigeons* is charged with his own feelings. 'There are tender pas de deux,' he confessed to Tony Lizzul, 'in which I have injected my love.' As the ballet comes to an end, the lovers recline on either side of a wicker chair, its lacy oval back framing their faces like a Victorian Valentine card. Completing the picture, a second white pigeon flies on stage to join its mate perched on the chair. Invariably eliciting a gasp of appreciation from the audience, this wittily romantic coup de théâtre not only celebrates the fact that the ballet was premièred on 14 February, but is also an encoded Valentine's Day message to Lizzul.

> It is your ballet & I have put all that I feel for you in it & the moral is that after much wandering & disappointment the Pigeon returns to roost. Would that could [be] the case with me but I feel there would have to be many other species of birds to be pecked out of the way, some of them quite big! What chance has a poor English pigeon got & a rather molting one, also, against American Eagles? . . . Remember Pigeons can fly & high too.

The ballet was too cloying for some – 'a sentimental piece of pseudo-Victorianism,' remarked Annabel Farjeon, '. . . it is tiresome that Frederick Ashton should fritter his talent on such mush.' Yet even though most reviews were favourable, Ashton insisted that he had been turned into 'a pot au feu of pigeons' by the critics. 'Everything is done to make me appear frivolous and nonsensical,' he complained to Clement Crisp. 'Since when are "subjects" the all-important matter of works of art. [You] may as well say Chardin was a bad artist because he painted cabbages & what about the adored Britten and his subjects. However, I begin to think some critics can neither see nor hear and have acquired what I call a Traditional modern outlook. Why can't I be left to my livestock?'

In sounding off to Crisp, Ashton effectively delivered his own artistic manifesto. With pigeons, chickens, field creatures, cauliflowers and potatoes as inspiration, he was, indeed, the Chardin of dance, ennobling humble material by the poetry of his art. But, with the current emphasis on weighty contemporary subjects – 'We are ripe in ballet for a *Hiroshima Mon Amour*,' wrote Peter Brook that year – Ashton continued to feel out of sync with the times. He need not have worried. *The Two Pigeons*, despite not being successful in America – 'I can't sell it,' said Hurok. 'You know what pigeons do to our park benches?' – has lasted far longer than its detractors predicted, as popular with audiences today as it was on its first night.

Although Ashton enjoyed the success of the Valentine's Day royal gala, boasting to Lizzul that The Queen Mother had invited him to supper in her box – 'Alas, I couldn't go as I was involved with the cast' – he was depressed and feeling his age. He had developed a hernia (which he blamed on lifting Karsavina as a young man) and had put on weight, his distended belly and chest turning him into a comical parody of his latest protagonists: 'He looked like a little puff-pigeon,' as one friend put it. Cecil Beaton was also taken aback by the change in Ashton's appearance. 'Freddie's face has become very exaggerated – the lips more pursed, the nose beakier, the eyes waterier – the colour is almost purple.' Ashton's physical deterioration compounded his insecurity, and no amount of morale-boosting from Lizzul that he was home 'almost every night' could assuage the doubts. 'How can I not have them. There is the disparity in our ages . . . & the shadow of the tall . . . [Lizzul had a predilection for tall young men] I am only human . . . we must re-assure one another continually.' A long silence from Lizzul, studying hard for his degree, provoked a panicky telegram and two letters. 'I am haunted by your image & it is awful, spring is here & my heart is leaden . . . I can't work or think of anything else.' Lizzul reaffirmed his love by cable, prompting a euphoric reply from Ashton, who was left in no doubt that he had 'done it': 'But alas, one wants to hear it all the time & over & over again.'

Ashton was soon to have his wish. Lizzul was coming to see him that summer before setting off on a tour of Europe, a graduation present from his parents. Before that, however, Ashton was to embark on a landmark trip of his own, accompanying the Royal Ballet on its first visit to Russia.

Originally scheduled for November 1957, the tour had been cancelled following the Soviet invasion of Hungary. This time, there was to be a reciprocal arrangement between the two countries: on 15 June 1961, the Royal Ballet gave its first performance in Leningrad; four days later, the Kirov opened in London (the European season during which Rudolf Nureyev had defected in Paris). The first ballet was *Ondine*, which was well received, although critics found Henze's music 'difficult & unsympathetic & anti-Soviet in ideas'. *La Fille mal gardée* proved the hit of the tour. It was 'a triumph', Ashton told Lizzul. 'They just wouldn't stop clapping & rushed to the front of the stage & threw flowers . . . & applauded me as I left the stage door. All very gratifying. They would be more friendly still if they dared.'

Ashton had been 'full of dread' about the Soviet trip – 'I hate policed states & resent forfeiting my freedom even for 4 weeks' – and the reality did little to change his mind. After performances, he would walk out into the white nights, but there would always be footsteps behind him and someone steering him back to the hotel. He had asked to see Guy Burgess, whom he knew from his Trocadero days. 'I liked him very much, we used to meet at the Café Royal. He was fun and lively. We never talked about politics (if you'd asked me who the Prime Minister was in those days I would not have been able to tell you). He sent a message to me somehow to come and see him. I went to Embassy officials and said Guy Burgess is a friend of mine, I'd like to see him, but they said no.' In Moscow, the Bolshoi's director, Leonid Lavrovsky, wanted to meet Ashton, but refused to come to his hotel. 'I said we won't be talking politics, so what's it matter if we're bugged?' Lavrovsky suggested that they meet in the public gardens, but Ashton did not relish the aspect of subterfuge and declined. Finally, a meeting took place in the small anteroom off the Bolshoi stage, where grand dukes once dallied with ballerinas and where the two choreographers talked about their art.

Ashton found Moscow 'hideous except in odd corners', but he was enchanted by Leningrad – 'dusty but beautiful & on a grandiose scale', he wrote to Ann Fleming. 'It all made a tremendous impression on me & I never thought I should be ready to lay down my life for freedom especially of the arts.' Nevertheless, it was a relief to get home, 'bent double with hunger' because the food had been so grim, 'apart from the odd slice of bread spread with a millimetre of caviar scrounged from the British Ambassadress'. A week later, he met Tony Lizzul off the boat-train at Waterloo.

Although Ashton preferred to keep Lizzul a secret (Alexander Grant knew nothing about him), a few close friends were allowed to meet him.

Billy Chappell was asked to paint his portrait, which he did, thinking it was a commission. 'But Fred took it and gave it to Tony and there was no mention of any money.' Chappell found Lizzul 'a sweet boy, but frightfully boring'. To Ashton, however, he was a quiet, sympathetic presence, someone willing to be with him night after night, listening, engrossed, to his stories, or sitting in comfortable silence, allowing Ashton his thoughts. Domestic by nature, Lizzul never seemed to mind the 'dull time' and Ashton adored it, 'just being with you alone'. They went to Chandos for an idyllic summer weekend, where they walked and gardened and made love in the Gothic folly. (From then on, the folly became a keynote in their correspondence, a code word symbolizing physical longing, almost exclusively on Ashton's side.)

Leaving him to spend the rest of August in the country, Lizzul set off for Italy and Germany, where there was always a letter, telegram or message awaiting his arrival in each city, such as, 'Don't make it too much of a roman holiday only you count.' Ashton had agreed to direct the Royal Ballet touring company's Middle Eastern trip, possibly because it took him to Athens, where he and Lizzul arranged to meet at the Hotel des Ambassadeurs for a few days. Although Ashton encouraged the young man to expand his horizons – 'I can only hope that the more you see & the more variety you have the more you will cherish me . . . & that I will be a haven in your life where you can come & go at your will.' – he nevertheless kept a vigilant eye on his movements. While Ashton rehearsed, Lizzul admitted to 'doing [his] own thing', but he was always tactful and discreet, and was capable of making Ashton ecstatically happy. For Ashton, Athens was a 'glorious time', which he recalled with a poet's sense of wonder and rapture. 'I never knew that a tiny room could contain the whole of happiness in that way,' he told Lizzul, unconsciously paraphrasing Donne's celebration of love's power to make 'one little roome, an every where'.

> To have you sharing life with me in intimacy was bliss itself & how well & easily we got on. To come back & find you in the room was real fulfilment but to find you loving, tender, affectionate & forever trying to look after me was paradise . . . To sleep with you there & to wake up & gaze first thing at your beautiful & tender face & you always extended a loving hand towards me. I was all such happiness I returned glowing & people continually say to me 'I have never seen you look so well' & only I know the answer . . . You did it up to the hilt & touched my heart.

As soon as he returned to England, Ashton went straight to work on his new ballet to Stravinsky's *Persephone*, a musical realization of André

Gide's poem based on the Homeric Hymn to Demeter. 'I think only of two things, you & Persephone & more of you,' he told Lizzul. He was briefly diverted by having to choreograph a solo to launch Rudolf Nureyev in London. After a sensational season with the Marquis de Cuevas company in Paris, the young Russian defector had been invited by Margot Fonteyn to perform at her annual matinée in aid of the Royal Academy of Dancing. The dancer asked if a new piece could be specially created for him by Ashton, who 'agreed nervously', Fonteyn said. He need not have worried, as Nureyev knew exactly what he wanted. He chose the music, Scriabin's 'Poème Tragique'; the choreography, 'mostly written by Rudolf', evolved behind closed doors. Although struck by his great beauty and presence, Ashton found Nureyev 'rather reticent, rather suspicious' and was surprisingly over-awed by him, aware that the Kirov star had had the benefit of a great dance heritage which he himself lacked. 'I felt that he already knew everything about it and had nothing to learn from me.' He never questioned Nureyev's 'vast feeling for movement' and made a point of listening to him. The dancer's London début, sandwiched between the usual gala fare, took place at the Theatre Royal, Drury Lane, on 2 November. The audience was divided between society figures in the stalls and 'hyena-baying' fans in the gallery, who screamed for Nureyev as if he were a reincarnation of Valentino. Cecil Beaton described his performance:

> The huge stage was empty except for the scarlet-shrouded object standing centre . . . Suddenly the cloak moved more swiftly than the eye could follow, and was violently whisked away to reveal a savage young creature, half naked, with wild eyes on an ecstatic, gaunt face, and a long mop of flying, silk hair, rushing towards the footlights. The force and dynamic power of this unexpected figure was shocking and compelling.
>
> The dance upon which he had embarked was so strong in its impact that the theatre became an arena of electrified silence. The wild, faunlike creature, with the parted pout, was darting round the stage, dipping and weaving . . . then turning in screws like a whiplash . . . I noticed the marvellous precision with which his feet were returned from space to the boards of the stage . . . These legs were strong, but not over-muscular . . . they moved with molten glass fluidity . . . The torso was broad-shouldered, and rather narrow at the waist; the arms were strong and long and swayed with an ineffable grace and strength . . . Here was something almost perfect in the taste of today. Diana Cooper, next to me, whispered: 'He's better than Nijinsky!'

Nureyev's wild, Slavic poem came to an end. The audience was for a moment stunned. Then, recovering, it produced its storm of lightning and thunder applause. The boy responded with charm, dignity and superb Russian pride. He was obviously pleased and touched by such friendliness. His obeisances were lengthy, leisured, and completely relaxed. This twenty-three-year-old creature from the woods was now, beatnik hair and all, a Russian emperor imperiously accepting the acclaim of his people.

Nureyev's curtain calls, rather than Ashton's choreography, convinced Ninette de Valois of his genius as a performer. 'This marvellous presence; the *port de bras* as he swept the ground . . . all I could think of was seeing him in *Giselle*. The solo had been done very quickly for him and didn't show to great advantage the man that I saw standing in front of the cloth.' Ashton admitted that he had put in 'too many ingredients' – 'in fact, it was so charged with things that we really had to eliminate quite a lot because it was too exhausting to get through it.' Fiendishly difficult, the solo exposed a few technical flaws that did not pass unnoticed, although everyone agreed that Nureyev's rapturous stage personality transcended all else. 'A hymn to freedom . . . a great outpouring of passion and sadness', *Poème tragique* may have been symbolically over-literal with its casting aside of a constricting red cloak, but, theatrically, it had great impact. 'Tragic clutching arms, falls on the knees, hair all over the face – thrilling!' wrote Richard Buckle. Nureyev, however, like de Valois, felt that the choreography did not do him justice, telling Cecil Beaton, 'Everyone says it was a bad dance – the wrong thing to do. Someone showed me a very bad critique . . . they say it was a mistake.' He was not only wrong, Beaton indignantly noted in his diary, but ungrateful.

Little did he realize that Freddie had been responsible for presenting him for the first time to the British public in the most dramatic & spectacular manner possible . . . Freddie's idiom of yearning wanderers, of D'Annunzio romanticism & 1910 mysticism combined with this Soviet's ruthlessness to bring about a revolutionary masterstroke . . . He would have made little impact if just seen in a classical pas de deux.

Ashton returned to doing 'nothing, *absolutely nothing* but work on Persephone', which was due to be premièred in a month's time. His synopsis, in three scenes, followed Gide's text closely: Pluto's abduction of Persephone; her exile in the underworld; and her resurrection, when she brings springtime to the earth. Once again, the ballet's secret muse was Tony Lizzul, Ashton's private personification of spring – 'Le printemps est toi' – with whom he would ritualistically share a pomegranate, a symbol of Persephone, each time they were reunited. 'It was a way of celebrating the rebirth of our friendship.' Chilled by Lizzul's last letter, 'a cold breeze off the Alps', Ashton increasingly identified with his subject, feeling he was 'still in the underworld awaiting "le retour du Printemps". That will be when you return to me warm, golden & loving.' The Persephone myth, however, contained deeper reverberations that went beyond the immediately personal. Its theme of regeneration born out of death – what Northrop Frye called 'the drama of the green world . . . the triumph of life and love over the waste land' – has inspired English poets from Shakespeare to T. S. Eliot; for Ashton, too, it was a potent influence in both his life and work. The rhythm of the seasons frequently infiltrated his ballets: either overtly, as in *Cinderella*, or covertly, as in *Scènes de ballet* and *Symphonic Variations*, where the three women frozen in their wintry purdah are akin to Persephone's people waiting for the arrival of spring. Ashton was continually preoccupied with the changing seasons. His conversations and letters chart his despair that winter would never end. Easter was more important to him than any other Christian celebration. Surrounding himself at Chandos with his closest friends, he would insist on their participation in a private rite of spring. Alexander Grant, Billy Chappell, and whoever else was there, would each be made to collect a hat from the hall – a motley assortment of flowered straw sun-hats, trilbies and cloth caps – then form a ring round a statue of Bacchus. This was a beautiful seventeenth-century tall marble youth, which Ashton had bought at great expense and rechristened 'Daphnis' (with his modern, open shirt, he looked very like the hero of his ballet). After performing pastiche Greek dancing in a circle, the revellers concluded by 'doing what we thought were pagan things': throwing their drinks over the statue as a libation and whipping him with twigs. In winter, the statue was swaddled with polythene, and every spring ceremonially unwrapped once more for the annual ritual. 'Fred loved this coming to life of Daphnis,' said Grant.

'A veritable Russian Easter', Stravinsky's *Persephone* had been originally commissioned in 1933 by Ida Rubinstein, who, nearing fifty, had seen Persephone as a stately dance-mime role for herself. At five feet ten inches, with a striking tawny mane, she had the stature and the voice – 'grande diseuse . . . with a tint of plums about the tone'. With choreography by Kurt Jooss, *Persephone* had only three performances and was not revived again until Ashton produced his version, with Svetlana Beriosova in the title role. Fluent in French, she, too, had a beautifully

resonant voice, but was capable of dancing far more demanding choreography than her predecessor. Three months before the opening, Ashton
took the ballerina to hear Stravinsky conduct a concert performance
of *Persephone* at the Festival Hall. They later went backstage to pay
their respects and Beriosova read a passage from the libretto. Stravinsky
nodded his approval which, she said, 'really made us feel that we're on
our way'.

The ballet begins with a spring setting, Greek painter Nico Ghika's
grassy bank and scattered flowers evoking a romantic atmosphere, 'almost like a Botticelli painting'. Curled in a foetal position in the lap of
her mother, Demeter (Gerd Larsen), Persephone accompanies her vocal
celebration of the first morning of the world with 'a wonderful stretching
out after a long winter under the earth'. The integration of music, speech
and movement showed Ashton in complete control. 'For this Stravinsky
should be grateful,' wrote Clive Barnes, 'for to a surprisingly large extent
Ashton seems to have unflawed a flawed masterpiece.' Enhancing the silences in the score which coincide with the natural pauses of the words,
he again made skillful use of stasis and ritual – what Barnes referred to as
the 'art of "no-choreography"'. A chorus of Persephone's friends grouped
themselves in visually arresting tableaux vivants, echoing and amplifying
Beriosova's movements. 'There was great gentleness in the poses. If she
sighed we all sighed with her.' And, once more, Ashton drew on illustrations from Maurice Emmanuel for the Greek lines of the choreography,
which he fused with a modern, angular idiom, mimicking Stravinsky's
syncopated rhythms. Some considered the corps' jazzy cakewalk strut in-
appropriate to the action, Ashton's approach reminding Barnes of
Stravinsky's syllabic treatment of Gide's libretto: 'He has apparently used
the score as if it were abstract music innocent of specific stage action.'
Others, however, like Andrew Porter, found the deliberately bizarre element exciting, because it showed Ashton developing the free, unclassical
movements that he had begun to explore in *Ondine*.

In choosing to remount *Persephone*, Ashton may have wanted to participate in experiments in 'Total theatre', a fashionable genre that year
(with three examples, including Balanchine's *The Seven Deadly Sins*,
shown at the Edinburgh Festival). But the result was considered to be a
set of compromises between all the elements involved. 'Nothing predominates, no key is set, no single theatrical quality is aimed for or achieved.'
The work aroused a wide variety of reactions – from stifled giggles in the
audience at its portentousness, to unreserved admiration. There were a
few serious flaws. Alexander Grant as Mercury was disappointingly typecast, 'a cross-breed between his Eros and his Tirrenio'; Demeter (Gerd
Larson), embarrassingly melodramatic. 'What should be stylized sobs of

frozen grief have been made into a patter harangue sadly reminiscent of Hera in *Tiresias*.' But it was unanimously agreed that Beriosova carried the evening. Despite practical problems – a short-circuiting microphone, cumbersome wigs which had to be accommodated in her duet with Pluto (Keith Rosson) – she was brilliant, her radiance and poise a perfect complement to the music. Persephone's last recitation, which, in its transcendental tranquillity, rivals Gluck's 'Elysian Fields' music in *Orfeo et Euridice*, also recalled Beriosova's luminous performance in the Dance of the Blessed Spirits. Suffused with Ashton's own emotions, there was, in *Persephone*, an almost religious sense of exultation, a joyful tribute to youth and beauty as embodied by Tony Lizzul. 'It is for you my only love. To celebrate the glory of my love for you . . . I can only say that without you & the way you sustain me I could not have done it.'

Tony Lizzul returned from his travels to London just in time for the first night. Ashton had warned him that Webster was 'going to pry' – as, indeed, he did. But whereas, in the past, Ashton had always maintained 'a cool distance' between them in public, for once he dropped his guard and even presented Lizzul to The Queen Mother. He was too happy to be circumspect. What had began as a creatively stimulating emotional spree had developed into something much more lasting. Although they spent only a short time in London together, Ashton had grown to love Lizzul 'very deeply & profoundly'. The young man's kindness towards him and understanding of his artistic temperament – '& the way you put up with it' – were qualities he valued more and more. For Lizzul, the relationship was 'almost like one you read about in Socrates' – Ashton was someone to admire, who educated him on art and on life. Dance was a mutual passion, and Lizzul had even spent time earning money as a 'scalper', selling black-market tickets in order to see as many performances as possible. He also loved going to the opera and art exhibitions, which they often did together. As his parents had given him a generous allowance, Lizzul was not interested in material gains – not that, with Ashton, there was ever much on offer, beyond the odd scarf or cufflinks at Christmas – although he was well aware of the privilege of being the inspiration for such a remarkable man. Lizzul may have succumbed to the lures of 'whorish Fire Island', but he was genuinely committed to his 'loving old boy', and took selfless pleasure in making him happy. Basking in warmth and affection, Ashton, who, until now, had resisted a domestic liaison, became increasingly dependent on Lizzul's company. He was so touched by Lizzul's attentiveness that he even kept among his papers a pencilled scribble, reminding him to put the cooker on to heat the supper awaiting his return. They cooked breakfast together, ate 'funny lunches at very odd hours', and, night after night, sat alone together at Marlborough

Street. 'Everything was so easy & natural & pleasurable that I grew to love you . . . My desire [was] to have you only to myself even at the risk of boring you . . . We were together & so close, so easy & so loving.' Lizzul's departure after Christmas shook him badly.

> . . . I find my life empty of affection & my house a void I think it is easier for you for you have gone to a place where I have never been, but here you have emptied my house of your presence, the sun has gone down & I live in the shades – returning is painful. You are not here, you are not upstairs taking hours to prepare my meals . . . you are not opposite me in the chair typing those endless letters & lists. All this I learnt to love & expect as part of my daily life. To go to the theatre with you to sit through Persephone together . . . & so so many other delights which you can guess. I feel that life for me is too short & that you should be with me till *you* can stand it no more. I have been wrenched apart . . .

Distance renewed the doubts – 'always doubting you see, please tell me again & again that you love me for I cannot live without it' – producing a rush of despairing telegrams and letters questioning Lizzul's silence.

> I was imagining all sorts of things; orgies with the marquis de Sade after a dose of damaroids & every other kind of vice with sad regrets & fears for the pollution of my very dear one . . .

'Fred knew I carried on my life, but liked to think I was a monk,' said Lizzul, who dutifully continued to pacify Ashton, his letters proving almost as arousing as his presence: 'I wouldn't open it, like delaying an orgasm to prolong the pleasure.'

Ashton spent his summer holiday at Eye, longing to recapture the peace and contentment of the previous year. 'I hanker round an empty folly and re-live happiness not only there but everywhere.' The two pigeons he had nostalgically installed in a dovecote had increased to ten 'and would have fluttered round you as I would have'. Feeling lonely and sorry for himself, he planted a memento to Lizzul near the folly of Bleeding Heart.

> What is life without all this? Without you to look after me & care for me. I feel sometimes that I work for the enjoyment of others & get so little for myself & that on the one occasion that somebody comes who seems to reciprocate my feelings we are torn apart

most cruelly & what was wonderful for me is that though I am hundreds of years older than you you never made me feel that it made any difference & with me you never looked to right or left you were always warm, affectionate & loving & tender & always looked after me & my needs . . .

One consolation that summer was Ashton's knighthood, an honour to which he had aspired for some time, although he claimed never to have 'scrabbled for orders'. Hearing of John Gielgud's arrest on charges of homosexuality in 1953, he muttered with exasperation, 'He's ruined it for all of us.' Among the congratulations to 'Frederick (the great)', as Lydia Lopokova saluted him, were Vivien Leigh, Mary and Douglas Fairbanks, Edith Sitwell, and fellow knights John Gielgud, Michael Redgrave, Isaiah Berlin and Malcolm Sargent. The following month, Ashton (together with W. H. Auden) was awarded an Honorary Degree by the University of Durham, the first of several, which confirmed his new status of grand seigneur. Increasingly portly and patrician, as Beaton noted, Ashton had acquired, over the years, great weight of character and the 'most miraculous' self-confidence. But his portrait of 'a most fulfilled & contented person swimming so serenely into old age, without racks & torments' is evidence that Beaton, like most of Ashton's friends, had no real understanding of the man behind the persona.

> He speaks with enormous authority & seriousness – as well as a frivolous cynicism . . . He now has the assurance of a Czar – & I must say that when walking slowly with fur cap & stick in the garden this is just what he reminded me of. I suppose that a ballet master always has great authority – that by degrees he becomes accustomed to ruling with unswerving power over the little rats at the Barre. But Fred is now a grand old man. He has acquired the authority of being able to talk & move slowly – to give a big knowing look – to know the value of a pause. Seeing him sit, like Buddha, & listen to the younger generation or to make his summations was like watching someone with twenty years added to his own 60 . . . I don't think I know of anyone who has become before my eyes – in my lifetime, a grand old man. It is achieved by knowing himself through & through & by never pretending to be anything he is not.

When Beaton gave a luncheon for The Queen Mother, in November at Pelham Place, Ashton was among his five guests, 'friends who are creative and interesting', comprising Edith Sitwell, Truman Capote and June Osborn, the pretty widow of the pianist Franz Osborn, whom Beaton had recently contemplated marrying. 'I explained that my guests were all rather eccentric but I hoped that this would be amusing.' The Queen Mother relished Capote's shout of joy when the summer pudding appeared, and later told her host that she had loved Freddy Ashton. Although Ashton claimed that he used to 'tango her up and down 145 Piccadilly' (the house in which the Duchess of York had lived before she became Queen), Queen Elizabeth has no memory of this. It was not until the early 1970s, when Ashton began to spend weekends at Sandringham and to lunch regularly at Clarence House, that he and The Queen Mother became close friends.

Around the time of his luncheon, Beaton was working with Ashton on a new collaboration: a ballet based on the Alexandre Dumas play, *La Dame aux camélias*. 'Another love poem,' he told Lizzul. 'And there is another theme for us.' By the autumn of 1962, however, the situation between them appeared to have reversed, and Ashton was writing to reassure Lizzul that his feelings had not changed. For his birthday, Ashton sent him £20 to buy tuberoses and a Martini: 'Drink to our love, drain the glass & think only of me whilst you do & wish for your reunion & deeper love.' Although separation had, inevitably, cooled his ardour, Ashton's silence, as he told Lizzul, reflected nothing more ominous than the 'hellish tensions' he was undergoing at work. He had had to postpone the new ballet scheduled for December because Nureyev had injured his foot. He spent Christmas at Chandos, 'atrophied' by a relentless cold spell and imagining that every plant had been killed by frost. The folly was 'like a fridge' and he eagerly anticipated the spring, when he was to see Lizzul once again on the company's tour of America. 'Then you can really thaw me out . . . though my heart is packed in ice there is an ember which is you burning in it.'

The heat soon intensified: *Marguerite and Armand* was near completion and sparks were flying. At the dress rehearsal, in front of a battery of fifty cameras, Nureyev was characteristically explosive, and even Fonteyn turned diva-ish, coyly refusing, 'for reasons of modesty', to wear red camellias because of their symbolic association. 'I could have kicked her,' remarked Beaton in his diary. Having cut off the tails on his jacket, Nureyev tore up two shirts and was about to attack a third when de Valois stepped in. 'It was really dreadful. I said to him, "This can't go on, if you tear that shirt, you'll have to wear it. What's worrying you?"' 'I am *not* a waiter,' stormed Nureyev, who got his way with the shortened tails, though still looking, according to Edward Sackville-West, like a handsome footman. Early rehearsals had also had their difficulties, the 'anguished choreographer, impatiently chain-smoking, frequently having to wait for his stars to run through *Giselle* or *Swan Lake*. After only four rehearsals, they flew off together to Australia and Panama. When he did have the dancers to himself, Ashton complained that Nureyev 'would sit down every two minutes'. He could handle the Tartar tantrums – 'I gave as good as I got, my dear' – but he could not tolerate Nureyev's 'biting remarks' to Fonteyn. Understanding Nureyev better than anyone, she was unperturbed by his outbursts – a defensive reaction, she believed, triggered by nerves: 'Rudolf is Rudolf, a law unto himself.' Ashton, however, was 'brought up to believe that a ballerina is a sacred being. Margot never minded in the least, it was only me with that exaggerated sense of courtesy, I suppose you could call it.' But the tensions helped to detonate the ballet. Rather than starting at the beginning, as was his custom, Ashton, feeling very nervous, began with Marguerite and Armand's first meeting. It is a highly theatrical moment, combining the heightened suspense of the climax of *Tristan and Isolde* with the freeze-frame, statuesque artificiality of *Last Year in Marienbad*, Alain Resnais' controversial film released earlier that year, which Ashton acknowledged as a major influence. Standing at opposite ends of the stage, transfixed by each other, they freeze for two phrases of music, until, slowly, like a crouching predator, Nureyev begins to edge towards her. In permitting himself what Peter Brook called 'the audacity of stillness', Ashton subordinates choreography to an expression of personality, to his dancers' delivery of themselves. The wild charisma of Nureyev is a foil to Fonteyn's eloquent poise. 'There's an enormous sexual impulse behind it all,' said Ashton, 'a kind of animalism, a violence, a sort of tremendous physical intensity.'

The following day, still working unchronologically, he choreographed the scene with Armand's father, played by Michael Somes.

> Michael was standing with Margot, very stern and stiff, and I saw the door open a crack and Rudi looking in very cautiously, in his scarf and everything. I could see him tiptoe round behind me as we went on working and when we began to come to the end of the scene he started stripping off his coat and things and just at the right moment he flew out from behind me into Margot's arms; it was wonderful.

Fonteyn also marvelled at Nureyev's feral eruption – 'one of those fantastic moments when a rehearsal becomes a burning performance.' It became a motif in the ballet, repeated several times, recalling not only the 'electrical storm of emotion' in the studio that day, but also the way 'Rudolf [had] burst headlong into our world.'

It was seeing a rehearsal of the play *Lady of the Camellias* in 1961, with Vivien Leigh, that gave Ashton the idea of adapting Marguerite Gautier's story for Fonteyn. 'This was before Rudi Nureyev had been invented, of course.' A score already existed (by the French composer, Henri Sauguet), but it did not inspire him. 'Sauguet wanted me to do it and sent it to me but it was too elaborate. And then quite by chance when I heard this Liszt Sonata, I saw the whole thing . . . pared down to nothing.' The cyclic structure of the Piano Sonata in B Minor, beginning and ending 'in a vein of gloom' and characterized by the Gothic romanticism Ashton loved, helped him to visualize how he could compress the Dumas narrative into what he described as 'a kind of tabloid, a pillule . . . strong enough to kill'. Then he discovered how extraordinarily apt his choice of composer had been. *La Dame aux camélias* is based on the author's love affair with a consumptive young courtesan, Marie Duplessis (the source of *La Traviata*). Fascinated by her graceful beauty and simple tastes, Ashton read everything he could find about her and discovered that, two years before she died, she had fallen in love with Franz Liszt. 'This seemed a marvellous thing . . . that somehow this music had fallen into place . . . one doesn't know how much of the piece was Liszt's memory of her. It may not have been so, possibly not in the least. But you see, it *could* have been.'

Marie Duplessis was not Ashton's only inspiration; the ballet draws most of its power from the characters of the two dancers. For Armand's first entrance, Ashton uses a pose from Nureyev's signature role, *Le Corsaire*, and the solos blatantly incorporate his steps and style: extra high retirés, tucked-in fifth positions, very deliberate placing. Some critics felt that the conventionalized role did not do Nureyev justice; but on the contrary he was destined to dance Ashton's Armand, sharing not only the character's passionate ardour but also being almost a reincarnation of Liszt himself. Similarities abound, from their flared nostrils and expressions of seraphic ecstasy aroused by their art, to the mass hysteria they induced in their fans. Marguerite is also a composite. With her jet-black hair and perfectly proportioned oval face, Ashton considered Fonteyn to be the epitome of Marguerite Gautier; and yet, more prevalent than in any other role is the imprint of Pavlova. The ecstatic whorls of arms above the head, the animation of her eyes, are highlights of the kind he borrowed from her performances. 'Pavlova was radiant from *here*,' said Ashton, indicating the upper body. 'It was all up here.' The early scene in which Fonteyn sits on a chaise-longue surrounded by a group of attentive young men is based upon two images of Pavlova in the same situation.

The first is from a fragment of her film *Christmas*, in which, with an alluring undulation of her shoulders, she removes her shawl. The second
re-enacts an occasion in Lima at which Pavlova was guest of honour. It
was described to Ashton by his brother Tony, who was among her coterie
of admirers. Her pose, with her front leg angled from the knee (as if in a
seated balletic fourth position), is one that Ashton adopted for himself
and instilled in others. 'Turn your *foot* out,' he would instruct a pigeon-
toed guest.

Inevitably, the film *Camille* was another influence on the ballet. Ashton was 'Garbo-mad from the word go', loving the way she pronounced
her lovers' names, the way she dressed and did her hair. Once, in a Soho
restaurant with Cecil Beaton, she and Ashton had enacted a silent love
scene together, and it is this quality of extravagant romance – head flung
back, hands half in prayer – that Ashton absorbed into the dance idiom
of *Marguerite and Armand*. The ballet exploits what he called 'the impact of personality', the stage presence of his stars. 'People now think it's
camp. How stupid they are. Everyone wants to be stirred – personality is
so utterly important.' The choreography itself is less memorable than the
performance Fonteyn and Nureyev played as actors. 'Extraordinary actors,' wrote Peter Brook, 'who bring to each moment and each movement
that quality of depth which makes the most artificial of forms suddenly
seem human and simple.'

When Ashton and his designer, Cecil Beaton, first began discussing
Marguerite and Armand, they both agreed that, ostensibly, 'the ballet
must be completely unrealistic'. One evening at Beaton's house in Pelham
Place, Ashton was introduced to Nancy Mitford's great friend Anna-
Maria Cicogna. The Contessa Cicogna was from an aristocratic Venetian
family, a witty woman with outstanding taste, and so Ashton was somewhat taken aback when, hearing of their plans, she groaned with mock-
dismay. She had seen Sauget's 'realistic ballet of intolerable length' and,
as they outlined their conception – a death-bed fantasy in which, in a series of hallucinatory flashbacks, Marguerite relives her romance with Armand – the Contessa relentlessly continued to send up the whole thing.
Ashton knew he had chosen an 'old hack story', but Beaton considered
that the 'little comedy scene' had been useful 'because it prevented Fred
from falling into any of the usual booby traps'. Their ballet would be an
evocation poétique; the set simple and contemporary, with Brechtian projected photographs and a Noguchi-like metal construction half-circling
the stage (Marguerite's 'gilded cage'). Assuming the audience's familiarity
with the plot, the programme note barely outlined the action: Prologue –
The Meeting – The Country – The Insult – The Death of the Lady of the
Camellias; and, having experimented with half-sketched subsidiary fig-

ures in *Ondine*, Ashton took this to a more daring extreme, making the Duke and the Father shadowy, static figures, modelled on the marble, watchful but indifferent, anti-naturalist performances in *Last Year in Marienbad*. The stylized symbolism of Kabuki acting was also in his mind. 'The way they just stand while the emotion builds up inside them and then suddenly alter the fold of a sleeve or something and that tells you everything.'

Like Resnais' film, itself a representation of memory merging truth and fantasy, *Marguerite and Armand* is not a conventional narrative. Rather, it is a series of dramatic pas de deux, the gradations of which clearly reveal the development of the lovers' relationship: driftingly dream-like at first, with rippling arms and arched backs swaying to and fro; ecstatically playful in the 'Country' scene, Fonteyn's frothy white dress and thrillingly fast bourrées heightening the music's frilly rapture. As the ballet builds to a climax, Marguerite's growing passion for Armand, and her dependence on him, is enacted in the high melodrama of the choreography – reckless lifts, where Fonteyn is flung, swung and double flipped by Nureyev. 'It was so exciting and they got so carried away that Rudolf had to stop and pull the thing together, saying, "Let's get down to basics, what steps are we actually doing?"' But Ashton was aiming for something above and beyond pure classicism, as Clive Barnes wrote in his review:

> This hectic choreography, with all its plunges and its grapplings, still bears traces of classical elegance; but is far wilder than anything Ashton has created before. Nureyev seems to have prompted the same revolution in Ashton that he earlier prompted in Fonteyn . . . He has challenged both of them to discard their inhibitions . . . Fonteyn acts with every nerve naked with every emotion exposed . . . the last shred of artificiality has been cast aside.

Nowhere is this better illustrated than when Marguerite stands in a state of dazed anguish after she realizes that she must give up Armand. Flat-footed, arms and body lifeless, it is a display of crude, unballetic, 'embarrassing' emotion, of the kind associated more with MacMillan than Ashton. This was the realism, the truth, the lack of artifice, to which Peter Brook referred, something so alien to Fonteyn's image that Clive Barnes interpreted the scenes with the Father as an allegory of British ballet, depicting Somes's silent disapproval at the new excesses of its ballerina assoluta and her choreographer. Intentionally or not, *Marguerite and Armand* appeared to be full of real-life allegories. David Vaughan saw the story as 'a fable of [Fonteyn's] attainments and inevitable decline'; while the receding image of Somes and the other male dancers spoke of Nureyev's eclipsing effect on the rest of the company (he was once compared to the Great War 'because he destroyed a generation of young men').* When Armand, misunderstanding Marguerite's motives, publicly insults her, there were those who could not help recalling Nureyev's 'awful' treatment of Fonteyn during rehearsals. But what generated the most excitement about *Marguerite and Armand* was speculation that it confessed their off-stage love affair.

Anxious to spare her husband, Fonteyn was always extremely reticent about her passion for Nureyev. 'In fact,' said their mutual friend Maude Lloyd, 'I always felt that she was less generous in her praise of Rudolf than she would like to have been because she didn't want to upset Tito.' Yet she teasingly fuelled the rumours by not denying them. 'Hardly anyone knew where truth ended and fantasy began.' Understandably, Ashton 'was a little bit upset' by Nureyev's hold on his muse. It was not so much that Fonteyn was visibly in love – 'Rudolf's romanticism and the sort of ecstasy he had at that time lit her up' – but because, as Maude Lloyd said, 'Margot gave herself so utterly to Rudolf. Fred felt in a way that she was deserting him.' Only twenty-five years old, the Russian had released her final reserve as an artist, and was able to impart the sort of technical expertise that Ashton was unable to give her. 'She was in a state where she was willing to be refructified,' he admitted. 'She accepted from him.' There would be other reasons why he never choreographed another major ballet for the two stars, but his jealousy of Nureyev was paramount and continued to rankle for many years to come. 'Il m'embête,' he told a friend while on holiday in the South of France in the late 1960s. The dancer tried several times to contact him there, but Ashton did not return his calls.

Marguerite and Armand has never been performed by another cast. At the time, it was criticized for being a star vehicle – 'a specimen of the personality cult which is out of fashion nowadays' – but, as Ashton commented, 'even a vehicle has to stand on its own wheels to run'. All the same, he knew very well that two lesser performers might tip the balance into empty rhetoric. Peter Brook believed that, even with Fonteyn and Nureyev, the romance of *Marguerite and Armand* no longer 'held water'; others were even more censorious, Nadia Nerina dismissing it as 'that dreadful ballet – it couldn't have been more kitsch'. Her remark is partly true of the version with which most people are familiar, the film of *Marguerite and Armand* incorporated into the Nureyev documentary, *I Am a Dancer*. Misty-edged and sentimental, it strips the ballet of its emotional

*A remark attributed to Michael Wood.

truth, fastidiously looking away from Fonteyn's visceral anguish and prettifying things all round. Its only advantage is that, unlike the stage version, it uses the Liszt Sonata in its original form. 'I felt *very cross* with Humphrey Searle for his barbarous scoring,' Edward Sackville-West wrote to Ashton about the orchestration. 'Constant, I believe, would have used far more piano, as he did in *Dante Sonata*. If it had been better scored, the music would have "carried" the ballet more effectively.'

Roused by the phenomenal advance publicity and the erotic chemistry between the two stars, the first-night audience (including The Queen Mother and Princess Margaret, who had observed several rehearsals) gave *Marguerite and Armand* a tumultuous reception. 'TRIUMPH', Ashton reported in a telegram to Tony Lizzul. 'ROYALS AND SUBJECTS DE-LIGHTED 21 CURTAIN CALLS THANKS FOR YOUR CABLE YOU NEVER FAIL LOOK FORWARD TO NY AND YOU'.

He did not have long to savour his success. Three days after the première, an official announcement broke almost unimaginable news: de Valois was to retire as director of the Royal Ballet at the end of the season, two years earlier than expected. Ashton, to his dismay, was now in charge.

CHAPTER SIXTEEN

THE PUPPY

1963–1970

'It won't be my season this time in N.Y.,' Ashton told Tony Lizzul. 'I have only two new things – The 2 Pigeons and Marguerite and Armand – whilst Kenneth McMillan [*sic*] has 3 much more sensational ones . . . [*The Invitation*, *Symphony* and *Rite of Spring*] So it will be his season.' It was neither. The Royal Ballet's spring tour of 1963 belonged to Rudolf Nureyev. *Time* and *Newsweek* ran simultaneous cover stories on the dancer, and 'Rudimania' was at its most extreme. Mounted police were called out to protect him from screaming admirers; fans stood in ticket queues for up to four days and nights, sleeping in the subway tunnel near the theatre; and one devotee was able to live in Europe for most of the year on the money he earned selling photographs of Fonteyn and Nureyev at the stage door. When the two stars danced the *Corsaire* pas de deux together, the applause lasted twice as long as the ballet, carrying on through the intermission and stopping only when the curtain rose on the next item. Audiences were enraptured by the 'double sorcery of Fonteyn/Nureyev', and programmes which did not include them were lightly attended. Realizing what an inspiration Nureyev was to the English dancers – 'I thought that he would be a marvellous example to everybody,' said Ashton. 'His example would lift the whole technical standard of the company. And of course it did' – neither de Valois nor Ashton hesitated to exploit Nureyev's box-office potential. But there were vociferous complaints in the dance press that the image of the Royal Ballet was being dangerously distorted, the company becoming no more than a beautiful backdrop against which the two dancers could shine. Newspapers allotted most of their space to Nureyev; new ballets and new names received only scant attention. 'It left one with the impression that a meteor had obliterated moon and planets and rising stars.' It would be Ashton's first challenge as director to readjust the balance.

With Nureyev in the company, life off-stage brought new excitements every day. Jacqueline Kennedy sent a private plane to New York to fetch him, Fonteyn and Ashton for tea in Washington. She showed them round the White House, then introduced them to the President. In Toronto, Nureyev was arrested for walking along the middle of the road at three in the morning pretending to be a tram, but the international brouhaha this caused went virtually unnoticed by the company's director. Tony Lizzul was with him, having offered to fly up to see him for twenty-four hours. Although each had wondered if they could recapture the closeness of the previous summer – hearing no word since March, Lizzul worried that the 'European cold' had chilled Ashton's feelings – they discovered in New York that nothing had changed. Lizzul had wanted to meet him at the airport, but Ashton discouraged him, knowing there would be 'a clutter of Huroks etc', so they met at the St Regis, where they spent their 'long overdue' first evening together. Ashton had begged Lizzul to 'clear the decks of others' and concentrate on him for the short time he was in New York, but there had been no need to ask: Lizzul was as devoted as ever. 'I don't expect ever to find anybody who can replace you in my affections,' Ashton wrote gratefully. 'You are so good to me, so understanding & think only of me & you enrich my life so by having somebody I can trust & believe in, it is rare you know. I think always about your unselfish attitude, so rare in someone attractive as you are.'

After the summer holidays, Ashton officially took up his duties as director of the Royal Ballet. He had been dreading the prospect of succeeding de Valois months before her retirement was announced. 'I feel rather like James the First succeeding Queen Elizabeth,' he had remarked, and Cecil Beaton noted in his diary, 'Fred said how awful his future was. As he was by nature an Indian – extremely lazy & hated any power, loathed making decisions & wanted only to do – if any work at all – only creative things.' This, of course, was Ashton's main anxiety: an administrative job might blunt or completely stifle his choreographic imagination. He was also concerned that he lacked the temperament for ballet politics. 'I *dread* all those girls coming in my office to weep,' he told John Craxton; and many years later, when he was sitting in his garden, a background whine of a strimmer still brought back memories of the endless complaints of disgruntled dancers. On the other hand, Ashton's inert self-image was deceptive; he may not have had de Valois' autocratic qualities of leadership – her nickname was 'the Games Mistress' – but he could be as uncompromising, in his way, and just as hurtful. He once went into a ballerina's dressing room straight after a performance, gathered up her bouquets of flowers and flung them on the floor, saying, 'You've no right to these until you learn to point your feet.' 'He could see at once what was wrong and would always tell you what he thought,' said Peter Wright, a Royal Ballet dancer, who went on to direct the touring company. 'Sometimes the truth was very hard to take.' An ungifted dancer who asked for a particular role would be told, bluntly, 'No dear, you'll be no good in it.' And anyone with a physical imperfection that required correction would have no choice but to carry out Ashton's wishes. Ann Jenner received the following note from the director: 'I believe that it would be worthwhile, from the point of view of your career, if you could manage to deal with the gap in your teeth. Therefore I suggest that you find out what can be done to make it less noticeable.'

De Valois maintains that, when Ashton took over, she handed him 'everything on a plate', including three assistant directors, who would help to relieve him of administrative duties. John Field took charge of the touring company; John Hart oversaw rehearsal schedules and day-to-day organization; and Michael Somes worked as répétiteur, teaching roles and maintaining levels of performance. Noel Annan, who became a member of the board, considers Somes to have been 'an evil influence' on the company. 'He killed talent. He wanted to keep things petrified in what they had been in his time.' And Lord Drogheda, chairman at Covent Garden, also saw him as 'a problem' to the administration. There was an extraordinary contrast between Somes, the gracious, self-effacing partner, and his fierce off-stage persona, 'the castigator of the inadequate'. Almost impossible to satisfy, he could be sadistically exacting in the rehearsal room and notoriously antagonistic towards his colleagues. 'He was a very tied-up-in-knots fellow,' said Lord Drogheda, 'terribly difficult to other people around him'. But Somes's 'ferocious irascibility' (his own description) was, more often than not, a result of his impassioned guardianship of standards (of Ashton's ballets, in particular). 'He felt that somehow the soul of the company was entrusted to him.' When he overstepped the mark – as de Valois said, 'Somes had a terrible temper and had this habit of hitting people, you see' – Ashton would always defend him. Their dependence was mutual. Each time Ashton created a new ballet, he needed Somes as a sounding-board for his ideas. The dancer was useful to Ashton because of his unusually retentive memory and his gift for breaking down music into counts and phrases. Several observers, however, considered that his influence was too intrusive. 'Michael really browbeat Fred,' said Derek Rencher, 'but he seemed to thrive on it. He needed that in some funny way. It was like a relationship going on all the time.'

Although Ashton preferred to give his colleagues the impression that he 'had no organisational skills whatsoever', this, again, was not entirely true. He had been at the helm of the company before when, in de Valois' absence at the beginning of the war, he had kept everything going, leading a nucleus group of dancers around the country. And, as he often boasted, 'If it hadn't been for me, the Royal Ballet would never have moved to Covent Garden.' One of his first surprises as director was a blatant reversal of his lack of interest in second casts. This had always been a point of contention between him and de Valois. 'He saw the first couple he chose and that was that. But I'm afraid I had to ignore that otherwise we wouldn't have got the curtain up sometimes.' In retaliation, Ashton frequently chose 'the most terrible second cast that Ninette couldn't possibly put on. It was my way of getting back at her.' But when he choreographed his first ballet as director, pinned to the noticeboard was a list of both first and second casts. 'This is most unusual,' Alexander Grant said to him. 'Yes, it's different now,' he replied.

But the friction continued, with Ashton complaining that de Valois was always breathing down his neck. Unlike Balanchine, whose single vision defined the identity of New York City Ballet, Ashton was never able to make the artistic direction of the company entirely his. Ever since the war, de Valois had ensured that the classics formed the backbone of the repertory and, against Ashton's will, brought in outside choreographers such as Massine to enrich its style. And whereas Balanchine had Lincoln Kirstein working from behind the scenes towards the same end, between Ashton and de Valois there existed more of a power struggle than a collaboration. 'We fought like cat and dog', he admitted, confiding to the author a mysteriously intense degree of animosity towards de Valios that lasted almost to the day he died. 'There are things I have to say about Ninette which nobody knows, but I'm not going to tell you while she's still alive.'

Even as director, Ashton was never fully in control. 'Fred had a helluva time with her,' said Kirstein, 'she was so strong-minded and disapproving of so many things he did.' De Valois had always considered Ashton to be something of an amateur, because he had not had a thorough classical training. She also saw 'laziness, nothing but laziness' in his assimilative choreographic method – what one short-sighted dancer described as 'doing that man's ballet for him'. 'Real old pros wouldn't attempt anything like that,' said de Valois. 'Balanchine didn't and Nijinska didn't – I worked with them both. You did what you were told.' But what disappointed de Valois most was what she felt was Ashton's lack of interest in the Royal Ballet School. 'Fred did not have a pedagogue's mind at all. Balanchine was the one extraordinary case where pedagogy and creativity went hand in hand, but it's a very exceptional thing to find. The school dropped very badly when Fred was Director. I tried hard but I was only able to cope with the top class.' De Valois maintained that teaching the graduates herself, in order to provide Ashton with a good selection of well-groomed young dancers, was her only involvement with the Royal Ballet. She insists that she did not interfere. 'He did it all himself . . . I had nothing to do with what was going on in the theatre.' Events were to suggest this was not entirely true.

Of the two directors, Ashton was more popular with the dancers. He seemed more human, more approachable, and he took an interest in their lives outside the theatre and noticed small but significant things, such as the way a girl styled her hair. 'I used to teach them manners. When we were on tour and we went to embassy parties I used to say, "Go and talk to so-and-so and *dress* properly. Don't leave without thanking your host and hostess." Nowadays they steal the silver.' To most of the dancers, Ashton was a figure of formidable authority. 'He always brought with him a great sense of occasion when he came into a room,' observed Anthony Dowell. 'There was a sort of buzz about it.' 'Fred was like E. M. Forster,' said Lord Annan. 'The most diffident of people but he jolly well expected respect.' And Ashton won it, because everyone felt they could trust his taste and knowledge, and learn from him. The mix and balance of the programmes was an immediate reflection of his good judgement (opening a triple bill with *Scènes de ballet*, for instance, 'because it's like a dry Martini before the main course'.) He wasted no time in enriching the repertory, bringing back Balanchine's *Ballet Imperial* and importing a signature work, *Serenade*. Against some resistance, he fought to commission Nureyev to stage the Kingdom of the Shades scene from *La Bayadère*. 'I simply insisted. I was adamant that time should be found to put it in.' The ballet starred Nureyev and Fonteyn, but also called attention to three fast-rising new soloists – Monica Mason, Merle Park and Lynn Seymour – while its hypnotic opening défilé became a showcase for the corps de ballet, which, under Ashton's direction, was considered the best in the world.

Less successful was a new production of *Swan Lake*, which Ashton misguidedly delegated to Robert Helpmann. Its most controversial departure was the addition of a Prologue to clarify the story, but Ashton was disparaged for 'tinkering around' with the choreography 'until the whole ballet had come to pieces in his hand'. The changes were a concern only to the purists, as the new dances and Ashton's final act – an elegy steeped in romantic melancholy – are outstanding in their own right. Even the production's most rigorous critic, Clive Barnes, had to admit that the new pas de quatre was a 'dazzler' – as, indeed, it is. In the solo variations for Merle Park and Antoinette Sibley, Ashton has incorporated jaunty keynotes from the charleston, cha-cha-cha and the twist, almost unrecognizably transmuted into a classical idiom; and Brian Shaw and Graham Usher are twinned in a dance that wittily and exhilaratingly exploits their mirror image of each other. 'It's bliss. I love it, it's very exciting,' said Peter Wright. 'You can't say that it's Petipa, it's pure Ashton and it's not even Ashton copying Petipa.'

The substantial amount of new choreography for *Swan Lake* had left Ashton feeling 'rather depleated [sic]', his fatigue exacerbated by the fact that he had not heard from Tony Lizzul for some time. Since his return from America, their correspondence had dwindled, but mostly on Lizzul's side. Ashton continued to fret. 'Why this silence? Have your feelings changed? Is there somebody else?' When he, in turn, failed to write and was rebuked by Lizzul, Ashton responded with a long letter blaming the pressures of his new job.

> My life is quite hideous . . . no longer my own . . . Do try to understand the strain I am under & help me by being sweet & forthcoming & not withdrawn & distant . . . Do be behind me & support me write to me, re-assure me, don't forget our memories together . . . I do wish you could come over to enliven me, & enfold me & strengthen me . . . How is dear N.Y. I love it because of you – whimper, whimper whimper. Do you remember? No, you put me out of your mind, forget me & recriminate. Don't. I love you & remember it & cherish me.

Lizzul did not reply and, by Christmas, as Ashton complained in a reproachful telegram to him, there was 'still no news'. The reason was that Lizzul's mother had died. Although she had been ailing for some time, he had been a dotingly solicitous son and the loss affected him badly. In his letter of condolence, Ashton tells Lizzul that he loves him and often thinks of him, but months went by before they were in touch again. The tone of the letter Lizzul wrote in May 1964 is cold and hurt. He realizes that Ashton's new position absorbs most of his time, 'but I thought our friendship meant something to you'. Ashton's last letter, written from Eye in June, is affectionately apologetic. Lizzul had mentioned that he might return to England, news Ashton greets as 'too good to be true'. There is nobody else, '& I would most certainly tell you if there were . . . The Folly awaits you.' But there was someone for Lizzul. In the spring of that year, he had fallen in love with a young stock trader on Wall Street, William Newton Funck, who was to become his partner for life. 'The shadow of the tall', an ominous refrain in Ashton's letters, had been prophetic: Bill Funck is six foot two. When the Royal Ballet were in New York the following year, Lizzul went backstage, but, by this time Ashton was involved with another young man, a relationship that was to prove equally enduring.

Ashton spent the beginning of 1964 preparing a one-act adaptation of *A Midsummer Night's Dream* for a programme commemorating Shakespeare's quatercentenary. Nureyev would seem to have been the obvious choice for Oberon, possessing in abundance the hauteur and plasticity of movement that the role requires. But not only was he already starring in two ballets on the triple bill (Helpmann's *Hamlet* and MacMillan's *Im-*

ages of Love); Ashton also wanted to work with a more malleable dancer. 'I once told Rudi, "You don't put yourself in my hands. You don't let me mould you." ' In the early days of Nureyev's defection, their regard for each other was extremely equivocal. 'They wanted to get along,' said Billy Chappell, 'but something in them bristled every time they were together.' Quite apart from his feelings of hurt and jealousy regarding Nureyev's hold over Fonteyn, Ashton resented his resistance to him as a choreographer, a lack of trust which the dancer grew to regret.

> First of all, big handicap was that I was protecting my school . . . and trying, let's say, to keep my style undiluted . . . Ashton wanted very much to work with me . . . and I thought he doesn't understand classical dance. 'Not this year, next year,' I said, and again, 'Not this year, next year.' I was not willing. I was willing in my head but my heart just wouldn't do it. And that took a long time and finally he lost interest and got cool hands.

De Valois, however, had the impression that it was Ashton who was reluctant to work with Nureyev. 'Most of Fred's ballets were inspired by English dancers and he wasn't sure they'd suit Rudi.' A case in point was *Symphonic Variations*, which Ashton allowed him to dance only once. Although one critic described this as 'a performance to remember', the choreographer was displeased.

> That ballet is a sextet. Like a sextet in music, it all has to be dovetailed and nobody can shine out. They can, of course, if they have a radiance. Apart from that, you've got to be together with the other two boys.

In the early 1960s, Nureyev was less willing to submit to an ensemble. 'He thought only of himself in a role, not the ballet itself.' When Ashton offered him Colas in *La Fille mal gardée*, the dancer replied, 'What happens to me in the second act?' 'I said: "If you feel like that, that's all right, but I'm not going to change it." So we dropped the matter.' Twelve years later, Nureyev telephoned Ashton and asked if he could appear in *Fille*. 'I said, "But what happens to you in the second act?" He laughed, because by then he had changed his mind.' When Nureyev first came to the West, his only god was Balanchine; Ashton, he felt, had 'no formal knowledge', an opinion he was later to revise.

> In the end [Ashton and Balanchine] knew as much as each other but they came at it differently. Somehow Fred was completely

open: he made himself see how elements could influence him . . .
He understood theatre very well. He was a theatre animal.

Ashton explained that he did not do more for Nureyev – who was, after all, at the peak of his career – because he had to look after the rest of his company. 'I couldn't concentrate only on Fonteyn and Nureyev. You can't run a national company for the benefit of two people.' As if to prove this, in *The Dream*, the first work he created as director, he cast two home-bred dancers as Oberon and Titania: twenty-one-year-old Anthony Dowell,* who was still in the corps de ballet, and Antoinette Sibley, a fast-rising young ballerina, whom he had, until recently, conspicuously ignored – 'Perhaps because she was Ninette's golden girl.' (Tellingly, 1964, the year of *The Dream*, also saw her marriage to Michael Somes.)

Somes and conductor John Lanchbery were both working on the libretto. Ashton gave them copies of Charles Lamb's *Tales* and asked them to come up with a draft to compare with his own. His idea – retained in the ballet – was to omit the play's outer acts and to 'not get bogged down' with the story of Theseus and Hippolyta. He concentrates, instead, on the discord between Oberon and Titania; the two pairs of lovers (stylized as Feydeauesque types); and the rustics, singling out Alexander Grant as Bottom, another rewarding and original comic role in which he performs on full pointe, his black shoes mimicking the neat trotters of a donkey. Ashton said he chose this particular Shakespeare play because it is 'the most balletic' and because, 'I could do something of my own with it.' Far from being what Clive Barnes described as 'a digest version [which] scampers through the reduced plot with a numbing conscientiousness', the ballet is ingeniously distilled and immensely personal. Barnes complained that the ballet failed to add a new dimension to Shakespeare's play. On the contrary, there are times when the ballet transcends its source, such as the sublime reconciliation duet for Oberon and Titania, next to which Shakespeare's eight lines of tetrameter seem only serviceable. 'I had the play always by my side and then found out that I'd done something quite different . . . gone off the track.'

Ashton's *Dream* is a conventional interpretation only in its appearance. Seen through a misty gauze, the set and costumes are early Victorian and re-create Lila de Nobili's insect-wing textures and woodland colours (the designers, David Walker and Henry Bardon, had been her pupils). Atmospherically, it fuses an Old Vic-style production – Ashton had Tyrone Guthrie's 1937 version in mind – with traditional Romantic ballet. Mendelssohn was an admirer of Taglioni, the icon of this era, a

*Currently director of the Royal Ballet.

fact Ashton acknowledges in the fairies' mimicry of the ballerina's famously foreshortened poses. Choreographically, the work is ground-
breaking. Titania's band of fairies flitting intricately round about the
stage to Mendelssohn's buzzing violins may look like a pastiche corps of
nineteenth-century sylphs, but Ashton has characterized them and set
them free. Like the chorus in *Persephone*, they serve to amplify the heroine's moods, but this time their contribution is slightly satirical. Titania's
shirty walk as she leaves the stage with the changeling boy is picked up
by the whole ensemble. When she voluptuously fawns over Bottom – a
charming episode, highlighted by a balletic version of 'footsie-footsie',
which, as Sibley says, is 'pure Fred' – one or two fairies freeze in mock-
amazement. Even a speeded-up Fred Step (performed back to front) becomes a brief comic turn, as Peaseblossom realizes that she is the only
one left on stage.

Ashton's casting of Antoinette Sibley as Titania was an inspired departure from standard Vivien Leigh-type interpretations. Sibley's attractiveness is shot through with what he called 'a farouche quality': a willful,
subversive streak, not dissimilar to Titania's, which brought out the sensuality of the role and made it far more interesting than it has since become. As a student she was a maverick, reluctant to step into the Margot
Fonteyn mould; her models were Ulanova and Pamela May, her teacher,
whose habitual cigarette and stiletto heels pronounced a 'real flesh and
blood woman'. Resisting the original conception of Titania as 'very *La
Sylphide*', fey and lithograph-like, Sibley began waywardly to extend the
line of her arms, and to make the role more naturalistic and modern.
'Fred didn't mind because he saw that it worked.' Ashton had already exploited Sibley's instinct for 'doing something a bit differently', giving her
a solo characterized by a series of unusual, straight leg pirouettes – 'because I could do them faster that way' – which are contrasted by 'Fred's
whooshes', a sensuous yielding of the arms, head and upper torso. With
her swan neck, long thin limbs and pliable back, she was an ideal instrument for Ashton, for whom expression derived 'from the *top* of the
body'. But, despite the touch of zany abandon in her dancing, Sibley's impact was not the reckless passion of Seymour but a very English sensuality and classical correctness. Like Anthony Dowell, she was a perfect
practitioner of the Ashton style.

The two dancers had already discovered each other: 'I saw this young
boy sitting on the ground and I asked if he would mind just holding me
up. He was very shy and did his Princess Diana look . . . but it just
worked. We hit the right balances, heard the music the same way, which
had never happened with anyone else.' *The Dream* forged their partnership, second only to that of Fonteyn and Nureyev in English dance. 'It
was purely a look' that Ashton liked, their complementary proportions,

timing and line. They also had a natural sophistication on stage and a slight arrogance, particularly crucial to the role of Oberon, who is a commanding but static presence for a major part of the ballet. Although it took some time for Dowell's performance to grow in authority, Ashton foresaw that this 'fetching boy god', in Arlene Croce's description, was capable of 'throwing out glints of darkness and devilry'. With the exception of Helpmann in the Guthrie production, no dancer has ever made more theatrical use of his or her eyes. But to begin with it was Dowell's musicality and technical flawlessness that the critics applauded; his legato control off-set by the bounding allegretto agility of Puck (Keith Martin). Dowell was a protégé of Nureyev, and the Russian's influence is engraved on the elastic poise of his dancing – the way, for instance, he could run a sequence of multiple pirouettes into a penché without interrupting the musical phrase. He seemed, as Croce wrote, to have reserves of pliancy available to him. 'The extra stretch he can always produce . . . and in that little bit more there is never a suggestion of thinning power; the line does not attenuate.' Nureyev also influenced Ashton's decision to give, for the first time, an equal share of the pas de deux to the male dancer.

The Nocturne – the most skillfully crafted and dramatically resonant duet in the Ashton canon – became a signature piece for Sibley and Dowell. It is a brazen statement of male supremacy, of a woman's surrender to her husband and lord; but it also allows Titania, as Sibley said, to give herself 'her way'.

> She's as great as he is in her own right, and she's not going to let him win anything off her until she finds that he *is* winning, and then she has to completely wilt for him and mesmerize him again.

Ashton wanted Titania to appear to Oberon suddenly, like an apparition, and when he turns with one arm raised and one stretched towards her, he fleetingly impersonates Nureyev in the Shades scene of *La Bayadère*. As he leads her bourréeing forward, she instinctively strains away, but then is folded in two by him in an extraordinary promenade in which she jack-knifes under her leg and re-emerges the other side. The movement had come to Ashton in a dream and was, Sibley said, 'totally impossible unless I cut off arms and legs because the body was in the way. We tried and we tried and Fred started getting really grumpy and told us he was going off for a coffee leaving us to work it out and eventually, of course, we did.' After his imperious manipulation of Titania, Oberon appears to have reclaimed and tamed her. But there follows what can only be described as a danced conversation. Oberon's series of looping, pike-like leaps is interrupted by Titania's idiosyncratic solo – all shimmying shoulders and quirky little dives. Their dialogue continues until, as if signifying a new accord, they dance in unison, their soaring manège round the stage giving air to the debate and drawing attention to the physical twinning of Sibley and Dowell. A stately adage reinforces their mirror image, until flashes of Titania's recalcitrance appear in her quick, darting tugs away, and, as the momentum gathers, Oberon only just catches her as she flings herself through the air with mounting *Marguerite and Armand*-style abandon. At last, Titania 'wilts for him'; her arrow-sharp arabesques melt into Ashtonian swoons. Cradling Oberon's head, she submits to him completely, sinking down into the splits again and again, until, in a postcoital diminuendo, she falls asleep in his arms, rocked from side to side.

The Dream was not immediately recognized by the critics. 'A disappointment but not in any sense a failure,' wrote Barnes. 'One of his second best ballets.' But, as Roy Strong later pointed out, it summed up the essential Englishness of Ashton, drawing on layers of allusion from Shakespeare and Victorian romanticism to the native feeling for natural phenomena and liking for rich Hogarthian humour. As in his other great works, there is a quality of improvisation in the choreography, a sense of dance discovering itself. And although, as he predicted, today's performances are 'getting mingier and mingier', with few ballerinas able to emulate Sibley's expressiveness in the upper body, almost every step is stamped with his signature. The fairies are Ashton prototypes – 'Watch how those bodies bend, how the feet trip through small steps, how the arms wave, swish and flutter' – and *The Dream* still stands as one of the best examples of his artistic credo: a personal reinterpretation of classical ballet.

Nijinska, a pioneer of personal classicism, had taught Ashton the importance of an individual choreographic style; as a tribute to his mentor, he asked her to mount *Les Biches* at Covent Garden and, two years later, to stage *Les Noces*, 'one of the most significant revivals of the decade'. It was the fulfilment of a long-standing ambition. 'The moment I have anything to do with running the company I will bring Nijinska over,' he told John Lanchbery. Lanchbery had enquired why *Les Biches*, a twentieth-century classic, was not already in the repertoire. 'Because de Valois is jealous of her,' Ashton replied. At first, the company was a little wary of the old woman with her crackling hearing-aid, who could communicate only in French; but *Les Biches* became 'a love-match between Nijinska and Sir Frederick's dancers', who, thanks to the guidance of both choreographers, gave a superbly subtle evocation of louche Diaghilevian style. An invitation to Antony Tudor to choreograph a new ballet for the company, after a cold-shouldering of nearly thirty years, was made at de Valois' behest, confirming her vigilance over Ashton's regime. In a letter, he promises to get round to the 'problem of Tudor', and in January 1967 *Shadowplay* was premièred to considerable acclaim. No one could accuse the new director of being unwelcoming to rival choreographers. He had planned to revive his *Romeo and Juliet* for the Royal Ballet, but deferred, knowing that MacMillan wanted to do a version of his own. 'As the director I *had* to say go ahead.' The Board would have preferred the Bolshoi's version, but Ashton championed MacMillan and won. 'Kenneth was quite touched that Fred did that for him,' says Deborah MacMillan, his widow. 'Before he became established, Fred was enormously encouraging. That's why he was so confused by what happened over *Romeo and Juliet*.'

MacMillan's first full-length ballet was the sensation of the 1965 season, but its success was tainted by a dramatic rejection of his original cast. MacMillan had created the ballet on his muse, Lynn Seymour, and her partner, Christopher Gable; but Ashton, reaching a compromise with the Board and under pressure from Sol Hurok, advised him to give the première to Fonteyn and Nureyev. 'I told him that if he wants a local success he should use Seymour and Gable, but for an international success he must have Margot and Rudolf.' MacMillan was, at the time, neither strong enough nor old enough to oppose him, although, from a commercial point of view, Ashton was right: the appearance of the two stars was exhilarating for the fans, who gave them forty-three curtain calls. To the cognoscenti, however, the forty-six-year-old Fonteyn's 'moonlit' romantic interpretation negated the ballet's new realism, just as her uncontemporary physique diminished much of the choreography – the oblique scissor shapes, for instance, which MacMillan had moulded on the beautiful sway-back line of Lynn Seymour's legs and feet. For Seymour, the discovery that she had been relegated to fifth cast was 'the ultimate betrayal'. Unaware that Ashton was behind the decision, she had always assumed it had been made by Webster and de Valois. 'Fred knew that it hurt and was very sweet to me about it. He said, "It's a part made in heaven whichever night you do it." ' Despite the fact that Seymour, with Gable, danced the second performance, replacing an injured ballerina, she was devastated by the rebuff, while MacMillan, disillusioned with the unsupportive management – 'Kenneth always had an inadequate kind of paranoid fear of the administration' – suffered a lengthy depression. When he was approached to direct the Ballet of the Deutsche Oper, Berlin, he consulted Ashton, hoping that he would encourage him to stay, but Ashton advised him to accept the post, telling him it would be good experience. Taking Seymour with him, MacMillan left for Berlin the following year. It was a blow for the Royal Ballet, but for Ashton it meant that the choreographic field was left liberatingly clear.

In complete contrast to the seething Cecil B. de Mille canvas of MacMillan's *Romeo and Juliet*, Ashton's next ballet, created for a gala a month later in March 1965, presented only three dancers spotlit on an empty stage. *Monotones*, to Satie's *Three Gymnopédies*, recalls the pared down neoclassicism of *Symphonic Variations* carried to minimalist extremes – what Clive Barnes called movement without moving. As usual, Ashton was motivated by the music, but not since *Symphonic Variations* had he shown such an uncanny affinity with his score, or such a grasp of its compositional procedures. The clear lines and calm flow of the dance are so attuned to the music that they appear to have emerged from one and the same inspiration. The painter Puvis de Chavannes' slender tracings, which so greatly influenced Satie's melodic lines, seem to be the source for Ashton's harmonious groupings – 'the continuity of his line is like that of a master draftsman whose pen never leaves the paper', wrote Arlene Croce – while *Monotones*'s 'athletae Dei', the androgynous figures in their glistening white bodystockings, could be abstract reincarnations of the naked youths performing dances and gymnastics at the Gymnopaedia festivals of Apollo which provided Satie with his title.

The curtain rises on the sculptural trio: Anthony Dowell, Robert Mead and the streamlined Vyvyan Lorrayne, who is slowly raised from the ground in the splits, her head resting on her outstretched knee, and rotated by each partner in turn, 'playing' her like a harp. This movement, followed by a plunging promenade, in which her legs form a straight line like a fully extended compass, is an acrobatic version of Titania's 'chicken on a spit' contortion which Ashton had seen in a dream. The effect, however, is not rhetorical but chaste and serene. Like the music, there is a bare, abstract quality to *Monotones*. As they stand side by side, the three dancers are a visualization of a Satie chord, an illusion heightened by their enactment of the musical ideas. The cubist quality of the *Gymnopédies*, with its repetitions and juxtaposition of familiar phrases with slight variations, also defines the ballet, a choreographic collage which, as Constant Lambert remarked of the music, can be viewed from any angle like a piece of sculpture while remaining a plastic whole. With colour and contrast deliberately suppressed, the smallest deviation has a momentous impact. A simple changement performed in unison, and given the lofty ceremony of a grand adage, coincides with an important key change in the music – an effect, as Croce remarked, like a shock to the senses out of all proportion to the humility of its means.

Satie's technique of mesmeric repetition anticipated by nearly a century the trance music of Steve Reich and Philip Glass; and, with its title giving the clue to his intention, Ashton's new work indulges his own avant-garde explorations, constricting the natural development of the dance and negating any sense of progression. Occasionally, he breaks free of his score, allowing a dancer to travel across the musical beat and cracking open the nutshell constraint with a running passage round the stage. Nevertheless, *Monotones* is, as Croce has written, 'a luminous, peculiar, and disturbing ballet', and – for the average ballet audience – 'an uncompromising experiment in concentration'. By this time, Ashton had reached a stage in his career when his own interests came first.

> When I was younger . . . I wanted very much to please my audience and I thought it of great importance that I should entertain, amuse and charm them. Now I don't think that way. Up to a point I don't care what the audience thinks, I work purely and selfishly for myself and only do ballets which please me and which I feel will both develop me as an artist and extend the idiom of the dance.

A certain model for *Monotones*, a contemporary offshoot of the ballet blanc genre, was Act IV of *La Bayadère*, which had been recently mounted by Nureyev. Its opium vision of thirty-two shades, hypnotically repeating the same step, is a nineteenth-century forerunner of minimalist art. A more obvious modern influence is Merce Cunningham, whose first London season, in the summer of 1964, included two Satie works (*Nocturne* and *Septet*), and who alerted Ashton to new ways of relating shapes against space. And yet the ballet enshrines the very essence of the Ashton style. 'Good old British Cecchetti technique – all chaste and flowing arabesques, limpid contrapposto harmonies, impervious balances, and (especially ravishing to the deprived American eye) strict épaulement.' Although there are typical embellishments – a swishing business with the arms and a curious wing-shaped curve (which Ashton called 'Goldie', referring to the eagle that had made the news by escaping from London Zoo), *Monotones* is as abstract and non-pictorial as its score.

In 1966, he doubled the length of the ballet, preceding the *Gymnopédies* with Satie's *Three Gnossiennes*. He told its cast of three (Brian Shaw, Antoinette Sibley and Georgina Parkinson) that the white figures in *Monotones II*, as it became known, were heavenly bodies, whereas they, the Gnossiennes, were terrestrial. Their costumes were greenish yellow, and, as the ballet opens, they seem to be shielding their eyes from the heat of the sun. There is an eastern flavour to some movements, alluding to the quasi-orientalism in the *Gnossiennes*. Peter Williams detected a glimmer of narrative, 'a physical attraction which doesn't work out because emotions are too much involved', but he is mistaken: the later piece is as impersonal as the first. There are strong reminders of *Symphonic Variations* in key formations, such as the dancers' running chains, and especially in the presence of Brian Shaw, the creator of one of the six roles, who, exactly twenty years later, brought the same incisive line and shading of épaulement to his new role. This time, however, there is no romantic impulse behind the work, only dance expressing nothing but itself. Balanchine's *Apollo*, which Ashton had recently incorporated in the repertory of the Royal Ballet, influenced the work, most noticeably in a version of the famous 'troika' grouping and a reference to the muses' cupping of each other's chins. But, once again, the inspired moments in *Monotones* are achieved through simple means. Three abreast, the dancers hop continuously forward in arabesque, the famous corps de ballet step from *Giselle*; then, as the two women progress, Shaw travels backwards, introducing a note of surprise which Ashton elaborates with variations that seem, in this low-key context, as startlingly original as Stravinsky's opening syncopations in *Le Sacre du printemps*. The effect of Number Two, as James Monahan wrote, 'is to make Number One look even better than it looked on its own.' It is the *Gymnopédies* section with which *Monotones* is associated (revived alone, for example, in 1992); recognized today, as it was at its première thirty years ago, to be a small masterpiece of classicism.

The first-night reviews were unanimously favourable. Soon after the gala, Ashton left London to join the company for the New York run of their spring 1965 tour of the United States. Watching the plane's take-off from the observation deck at Heathrow was twenty-three-year-old Martyn Thomas, a trainee interior decorator, whom Ashton had recently met at a Chelsea cocktail party. The young man was not especially good-looking but had a charismatic masculine allure, or, as an admirer put it, an 'enormous and outrageous sex appeal', which he emphasized by wearing flamboyantly tight trousers and half-unbuttoned shirts. 'Martyn was very aware of his looks and the impact they had on people.' To Ashton's friends, however, Thomas did not seem 'the sort of person that Fred would have been interested in'. They believed Thomas to be 'a high-class cocotte', 'a butch type with pretensions', who 'ran Fred ragged' for the next two decades. And yet they admit that his early death in 1986 marked the beginning of Ashton's end. 'He just disintegrated after that.' While there was unquestionably something of the cad about the boy, for Ashton, Martyn Thomas was a lifeforce whose influence in the final phase of his career proved as intoxicating and rejuvenating as Nureyev's had been for Fonteyn.

Born in Cleethorpes, Humberside, Thomas was the son of a formidable ex-headmaster, a violently explosive character who had been an invalid for many years. He and his sister were brought up by their grandmother as his mother, Peggy, earned the family living selling her fashion designs to Grimsby trawler owners' wives. After her husband died, she later remarried a local interior decorator, Edward Tuplin, a gentle man by contrast, whose interests would draw his stepson into the same field. Thomas was a talented child. He drew and painted well, and shared the family flair for needlework. Although he had no formal musical training, he had taught himself to play the piano by ear, and, years later, would spend hours with Ashton working on 'the scaffolding' of a ballet by fitting the action to the music, making suggestions, replaying and splicing up tapes. He was a prefect at his school in Brigg, having been sent there to board when he was eleven, in fear of his father. 'Martyn's real father was a very difficult man. His rages were monumental and then he would spoil you to death. That was hard for a small child to understand.' Thomas, who inherited similarly dramatic mood swings (so violent at times that some feared he was mentally unbalanced), never talked about his father. But when he met Ashton, nearly forty years his senior, he was clearly seeking some sort of father substitute: 'We rather hoped that Fred would do a parental job for Martyn,' said Peggy Tuplin.

Rather than going to university, as his parents had hoped he would – he won a place at Cambridge to read Fine Arts – Thomas went to London, taking with him a portfolio of drawings and designs for school productions. Gregory's, an antique shop in Bruton Street, gave him a job; two years later, he went to work for Mann and Fleming, the antique dealers and decorators. With Princess Alexandra, Evangeline Bruce, Mrs Gilbert Miller and Lady Jellicoe among its clients, the Mount Street firm gave Thomas a glimpse of a world of which he longed to be part. Meeting Ashton was his passport, but, sooner or later, even without him, Thomas would have arrived. 'People were drawn to Martyn like moths to a flame. He had this electric effect on them.'

Because he was appealingly youthful, fun, cheeky and eager to please, Ashton nicknamed Thomas 'the Puppy', an image to which, initially at any rate, he responded with jokey enthusiasm. 'The subject is fully house-trained, *reasonably* well behaved and quiet, but is inclined to do strange things if left alone too long,' Thomas wrote to Ashton during his first week in New York, sending a flurry of letters every few days. Aware of Ashton's greatness as an artist, and also appreciating 'Fred as Fred', Thomas was elated by their romance, even though he was, and always would be, in great demand elsewhere. Apart from an endless series of John, Dick, Brad and Harrys, there were two more serious contenders. The concert pianist Moura Lympany had met Thomas a couple of years earlier through Mann and Fleming, and was devoted to him, relishing his youth, energy and ideas. 'Martyn was Moura's Apollo,' said his sister,

Jennifer Mellors. 'She *adored* him. He flattered her and took an interest in her clothes and her performances. They had quite a steamy relationship for a short time and when it calmed down they were still very close.' The astrologer Patric Walker posed more of a threat, or so Ashton believed. He and Thomas shared a flat in Upper Wimpole Street and, although Walker claimed they never had an affair, friends describe it as a 'strange relationship'.

> Fred didn't trust Patric and he didn't like their friendship at all. Patric wasn't a rival and I think he knew that but he just didn't like him. He felt that he led Martyn astray.

Walker, 'a kind of Svengali to Martyn', may have brought out the rogue in him, but he was, in his way, as bewitched as Ashton. 'He was one of those most special people who come into one's life. I've never known anyone with such creative talent.' They had the same sense of humour and Walker 'polished Martyn's edges', according to a friend, 'honing his wit and attitude to life'. 'They bounced off each other,' said Gabrielle Crawford, who, with her husband, the actor Michael Crawford, spent many a lively evening with them as a foursome, dancing till the early hours at Angelo's, a piano bar in Albemarle Street. 'Fred resented the joy Martyn and I had together,' said Walker, who was involved at the time with a well-known American film actor, and, to Ashton's disapproval, was 'always whirling Martyn off' to glamorous locations. But, although Thomas found this lifestyle most seductive, he allowed himself to be increasingly at Ashton's beck and call. They spent the summer holidays, Christmas and Easter at Chandos Lodge, with which Thomas was enchanted. He virtually took over the garden, creating a parterre of new boxed beds, planting an avenue of hawthorns to blossom in spring, and delighting Ashton by clipping the box hedges into the shape of birds, squirrels and teddy bears. Gardening became a major bond between them, and they discovered mutual enjoyment in slow twilight walks, discussing plants in flower and future plans. Thomas obligingly carried out manual work to choreographic specifications – 'A little to the left; no, that's *far* too much' – and every time they passed a weed, he would be instructed, 'Puppy, pull that groundsel up!' If Ashton went away on tour, Thomas would go to Chandos to keep things under control, taking photographs of the roses to show Fred on his return. He also took charge of the London patio: replanting, weeding, watering, dead-heading, hosing down the terrace. When Ashton went to Greece and Italy with the company in June 1966, he left Thomas with the keys to Marlborough Street – his main motive being to part him from Patric Walker. Thomas slept in

Ashton's bed, and took his sister and brother-in-law to the ballet, sitting in the director's box. 'Madam [de Valois] was there and poked her nose into the box and scowled. I think she has caught on to who I am, but respects my position as she should!! . . . I look down at my ring and see how real a marriage it is . . . Aren't we lucky my love?'

What Thomas had envisaged was an old-fashioned homosexual affair, where a young man is kept in a certain style by a wealthy older lover. 'He'd read the biographies and heard the stories.' Consequently, he made the most of the prerequisites he felt were due to him. At Ashton's request, he was given tickets for every performance, and he became more and more interested in dance and involved with the company. If Ashton was away, Thomas included reports in his letters about dancers he had seen: praising Merle Park's *Two Pigeons*, for instance; vilifying Paul Clarke's Oberon.

> Lady Ashton was treated with the respect which is due to a lady of her standing – being married to a genius. She was involved in the interval with a whole crowd asking after her husband and begging that I do everything in my power to persuade you to do Symphonic Variations again *quickly* . . . I was rather apprehensive about your messing around with 'Sylvia' . . . I wish you would leave it alone.

Some colleagues were alarmed by Thomas's increasing power over Ashton, and it was not only pillow talk about castings that caused concern. This confident, free-spirited young man, in shocking-pink trousers and Mr Fish shirts – a living emblem of the Swinging Sixties – was now influencing the ballets themselves. *Sinfonietta*, premièred by the touring company in February 1967, was clearly an attempt by the master to swing with the times. According to its composer, Malcolm Williamson, it was Thomas's idea to make a feature of psychedelic lights in the ballet. Changing optical projections by Hornsey College Light/Sound Workshop competed 'murderously' with lurid horizontal stripes on the dancers' cat-suits designed by Peter Rice, who describes them, in retrospect, as 'very King's Road'.

The music for *Sinfonietta*, 'a cheerful and extrovert work', was a 1965 BBC commission; nevertheless, Williamson claims that the ballet was 'very much a collaboration'. Williamson was recommended to Ashton by Billy Chappell, who had directed one of his operas and who provided the choreographer with a selection of gramophone records of various symphonies. A deciding factor appears to have been Williamson's score for *The Display*, a ballet written for Robert Helpmann and the Australian Ballet, which Ashton liked very much. At a dinner after the first night, he toasted the composer in champagne and later summoned him to Marlborough Street to discuss the prospect of a ballet. 'Freddie said, "I'm not musical like Mrs Chappell. I have to sit up night after night with a wet towel on my head to absorb the music."' But Williamson soon discovered that Ashton's lack of confidence was unfounded. 'He was meticulous about minutage down to a quarter of a minute and the ballet followed the structure so brilliantly that you couldn't tell which had came first.' Ashton later proved positively dictatorial about the music and when Williamson pointed out that the orchestra was playing one of the fast movements too slowly, he 'snarled' at him, saying, 'Well we'll do it at your tempo if you want to *ruin* the ballet.' (He later conceded that the composer had been right.)

The score was originally in three movements, but Ashton commissioned an additional 'dreamy moonlight introduction' to accompany the lightshow. Described as 'an explosion of ice-cream sundaes', mutating in the middle section to 'giant mauve and grey frogspawn', its shifting patterns were echoed by four dancers in the opening Toccata, with their fluid changes and interchanges of direction. The adagio middle section was in the style of *Monotones*; the dancers, a sparkling white stellar group comprising an airborne ballerina (Doreen Wells) manipulated by five cavaliers, an idea MacMillan later borrowed in *Manon*. The final Tarantella launched the young David Wall in a virtuoso solo, and 'What could be seen of the master's choreography looked pretty good' (although, apart from a Royal Ballet School revival in 1979 and another by Sadler's Wells two years later, the ballet has not lasted).

Perhaps identifying himself with the central ballerina role, the cynosure of many admirers, Martyn Thomas believed that *Sinfonietta* had 'a special meaning' for him. He was delighted when Lord Snowdon, accompanying Princess Margaret to a performance, acknowledged 'Lady Ashton's presence' and waved and smiled. 'I was very elated my status was royally acknowledged.' Being accepted into Ashton's world was becoming increasingly important to him. A dinner invitation to them both from *The Dream*'s designer, David Walker, prompted him to suggest, 'Don't you think he would be fun to have in the country for a weekend? I love it when people are sweet about you and me. It really makes marital status seem extra real which I like.'

Thomas had sent packing two current suitors, with every intention of changing his ways. 'I don't want any further complications,' he wrote to Ashton, 'I know what lines my life should follow now – and hope you do too.' During the Royal Ballet's European tour, he wrote dutifully every few days. 'I am the obedient wife whose husband has gone away on a business trip.' Although Ashton's friends were extremely suspicious of this Chester Kallman figure in his life – 'Quite honestly, we all knew what Martyn was' – his devotion to Ashton was genuine, as was the 'vast, deep pride' he took in the choreographer's work. Thomas was sincere when he wrote, 'All sorts of things may happen, Fred, but at this stage in my life, July 5th '67, I can truly say that I have never loved, admired, and worshipped you more.' And yet, as Patric Walker admitted, 'it would be a mistake to canonize Martyn'. Free love was almost an imperative in 1960s London and he was, as a friend said, 'quite irrepressible in that way'. This was tormenting for the romantic, emotionally possessive Ashton; but, however much he longed for more constancy from Thomas, he must have appreciated that it would have been unrealistic to expect him to sacrifice his youthful libido on someone twice his age. Thomas knew this, too – even though, at the time, he half-wanted to oblige.

I wish I could dig the house and garden up and transplant it miles from anywhere or anyone so that I could live with you without the complications of anyone else.

In their first years together, however, the problems were caused less by Thomas's infidelity than by misunderstandings over the definition of his role. 'Martyn had an image of himself,' said Gabrielle Crawford. 'He was quite a strong person and unwilling to be thought of as an accessory.' Whereas, in the past, Ashton's lovers had always allowed him to continue his life apart from them, Thomas, seeing himself as a Robert Heber-Percy figure to Ashton's Lord Berners, expected to be included in his social world. He was companionable, he had the repartee, and resented the fact that he was being treated like a puppy, only allowed out on certain occasions. Holidays were a particular cause of contention. In 1964, Ashton began regularly to join the Baroness de Courcel and her family in the South of France – an exceptional and very private milieu, into which he had no intention of introducing Thomas.

Martine de Courcel, the wife of Baron Geoffroy de Courcel, the then French Ambassador in London, first met Ashton at a dinner she gave for Princess Marina, who had asked specifically if he could be invited. The Baroness was a brilliant hostess, 'Worth a hundred Ann Flemings', and Ashton was immediately attracted by her elegance, taste and intelligence. When they sat together on a sofa after dinner, they discovered 'a mutual confiance' and many shared interests. Ashton was fascinated by Baroness de Courcel's Proustian world (one of her friends was the daughter of the Duc de Gramont, model for St Loup) and she found him genuinely Francophile: knowledgeable about French art and literature 'and what he called "Le raffinement"'. Although they had only just met, the Baroness invited Ashton to the South of France for a family holiday – 'père, mère, enfants, grand-mère (plutôt plus jeune et plus folle que les autres)'. The plan was for Ashton to come to Ramatuelle for a long weekend and stay in their house in the village, but he said that he could not possibly come for less than a week and would much rather be with them in their ca-banon near the beach. So in August 1964, and every summer for the next ten years, he stayed with the de Courcels, sleeping in Martine's study, 'a monk-like little cell', with just a bed, small cupboard and desk, but with a glorious view across the vineyards to the sea. It is known to this day as 'la chambre de Freddie'.

A certain amount of international entertaining went on – Sam Spiegel, Edward Heath, Garret Drogheda, and Jeremy Thorpe were among their guests – but holidays there remained very informal. When Raine Dart-mouth, expecting an ambassade d'été, arrived in a large Bentley for lunch one day, wearing a suit, stockings, white gloves and white shoes, she was met by her hosts dressed 'like vignerons', in slacks and shirts with rolled-up sleeves, although she soon adapted herself to the surroundings. The atmosphere was genuinely familial and they all enjoyed playing at the simple life, with barbecues on the terrace and lashings of local wine. Ar-riving with a carrier bag full of Carnaby Street outfits, Ashton made him-self instantly popular with the de Courcel boys, who soon discovered what good value he could be. 'Faîtes une imitation de la Queen Mum,' they would beg, and, 'rather reluctantly', he performed his routine, bor-rowing Martine's bathing cap, a 1960s version with fake hair, and enact-ing the following conversation:

'What would you like to drink, Ma'am?'

'What do you have?'

'Sherry . . . champagne . . . Dubonnet? [No reaction.] Martini?'

'That would be lovely,' he would smile sweetly, touching an imaginary lace décolletage. (When, at a dinner in honour of President Pompidou, the Baron met The Queen Mother, he was amused to watch her perform 'word for word the whole scene of Freddie's imitation'.)

Geoffroy de Courcel, who had been Secretaire-General de la Prési-dence de la République when de Gaulle returned to power in 1958, in-timidated Ashton, who never called him anything other than 'Monsieur l'Ambassadeur'. 'Geoffroy is a charming man,' said Poppet Pol,* a Ra-matuelle neighbour, 'but they didn't hit it off and Freddie always hoped he wouldn't be there.' Knowing nothing about politics, let alone French politics, Ashton could never think of anything to say to the Baron, but conversation with his wife was unlimited. They would sit together on the

*Augustus John's daughter.

terrace, Ashton drinking pastis and chain-smoking, until two or three in the morning. 'We were very sincere and intimate in things we said,' Martine recalled. 'And yet he was always very vague and so was I. What mattered was relating the experience.' A trained psychologist, Martine had learnt to be objective. 'Freddie liked that. He felt there was no judgement.' Once or twice, to her surprise, he became rather passionate about her – 'what we call in French "entreprenant", but it was sans lendemain.' They were extremely close – 'in the way you remain close to people you have been in love with' – and it was, for Ashton, as it was for her, an amitié amoureuse, a deep understanding and a mature affection, that he was soon to recapture on stage.

While Ashton was in Ramatuelle, a letter arrived from Martyn Thomas reporting on the first week of 'Pups Antiques Ltd', their private name for a shop in Elystan Street, on which Ashton had taken a lease. Thomas, who had unquestionable visual talent – 'He was a genius with colour,' said Moura Lympany – was just beginning to establish himself as an interior designer: the actor, Michael Caine, whom he had met at a party, was among his first clients. By helping to start him off professionally, Ashton was, as Thomas realized, making the most beneficent gesture of his life.

> Thank you my love a million times for making it all possible. I haven't exactly enthused with thanks for all your financial aid but you must know deep down how grateful I am for giving me this chance to start. I shall work very hard now to begin to make some money.

Round the corner from Marlborough Street, the shop was on two levels, its circular staircase to the basement having been installed by eight Opera House stagehands. On sale were inlaid satinwood antiques and well-chosen pieces of porcelain and glass. Thomas loved going out to buy stock, but the business itself bored him: he was not prepared to sit in a shop from nine to five. A sunny afternoon usually found him sunbathing in the park, although it was Patric Walker whom Ashton blamed for enticing him away. Ashton's friends looked on uneasily, Thomas's cavalier attitude confirming their anxiety that he was 'exploiting Fred'. They might have felt even more disquiet had they known that Thomas had become one of the main beneficiaries of Ashton's will. In 1963, Ashton had written a makeshift will on a sheet of blue writing-paper leaving all his 'worldly goods and monies' to Edith. The following year, he drew up a formal document in which he bequeathed Chandos Lodge with all its furniture and personal effects to Edith; and Marlborough Street and its contents to her son, Anthony Russell-Roberts. In this version, Billy Chappell was to inherit £1,000; Michael Somes, £500; Brian Shaw, £1,000 and Alexander Grant, £5,000. But, in 1967, he made an important change. He still left Chandos and Marlborough Street to Edith and her son, but gave Martyn Thomas the largest share of the legacy, £7,000; and dropped Alexander Grant's bequest to £3,000. Ashton considered that he had received more than enough from Thomas, who, initially, had brought him 'nothing but joy'. 'Martyn came into Fred's life at exactly the right moment,' said Patric Walker. 'His input was tremendous; helping to stir his creativity and forcing him to break a pattern and think in new ways.' Ashton's next ballet would confirm this – a showcase of fun, frivolity and modernity, but which also reveals him as straining to keep up with the pace.

Jazz Calendar was, according to its designer, Derek Jarman, 'a crash job'. With the postponement of a production of *Aida* at the Opera House, Ashton was asked, at very short notice, to come up with a light-hearted divertissement to help fill a gap in the new programme. On the advice of the critic Nigel Gosling,* he approached Jarman, giving him a tape recording of Richard Rodney Bennett's jazz score, based on the children's rhyme 'Monday's child is fair of face', and asking him to produce, in the space of a weekend, a portfolio of ideas. Although the twenty-six-year-old artist had recently had a successful exhibition in Edinburgh and had been tutored at the Slade by *Romeo and Juliet*'s designer, Nico Georgiadis, Ashton, as Jarman knew, was taking a risk. 'It was a master/student relationship except that he never made it seem that way. As far as I was concerned, he took me on as a genuine collaborator. One of the things he said was, "If you have problems with dancers, I'll sort it out, but Nureyev you'll have to deal with yourself."' Ashton liked Jarman and continued to see him socially, spending one Christmas at his converted Bankside warehouse where, after dinner, guests smoked joints rolled in papers patterned with the American flag, and watched Ashton and Jarman start the charades. 'Fred was Wallis Simpson and I was Edward VIII.'

The artist had recently worked on a project at the Lisson Gallery, using installations and dancers as 'objects in space', and he developed this idea for *Jazz Calendar*, making bright abstract cut-outs form part of the performance. Miró had done something similar for Massine's *Jeux d'enfants* in 1932, using brightly coloured costumes and a large free-standing circle and triangle (a décor with which, interestingly, Martyn Thomas was familiar, as Michael Caine, whose Grosvenor Square flat he was currently decorating, owned one of the designs). Ashton's ballet followed the

---

*The *Observer*'s dance critic, Alexander Bland – the pen name of Gosling and his wife Maude Lloyd.

seven-part structure of Bennett's score but was, as Jarman admitted, 'too tied to the Sixties'. Revivals have since been attempted, but, like any calendar, it has not outlasted its year. Ashton, however, never intended it to be anything more than a topical revue. When a dispute erupted over the lighting, he reprimanded William Bundy, the lighting designer, 'Stop behaving like Maria Callas. This is a *little* ballet.' It is closest in its approach to *Façade* and *A Wedding Bouquet* and, like these, is full of in-jokes and parodies of contemporary choreography, including his own.

Monday's Child is a hymn to narcissism which flaunts the astonishingly sleek physique of the dancer Vergie Derman. Framed in one of Jarman's circles, her face tilted up to an imaginary mirror, she is a contemporary Lady of Shalott, while her cool, stylish androgyny, and palms poised flatly on her thighs, also pay tribute to Nijinska's Garçonne in *Les Biches*. Tuesday is a *Monotones* pastiche, once again pairing Anthony Dowell and Robert Mead, dressed in identical white catsuits and skullcaps, with Merle Park completing the trio. Like a newly washed poodle in her frivolously fringed costume, she enlivens their sculptural groups – '*Monotones* gone a-Charlestoning' – with whizzing chainés and supported cartwheels (a jazzed-up quotation from the *Gymnopédies*). Like Vergie Derman, she is a 1960s reincarnation of an early Ashton ballerina – the girl from *Valses nobles et sentimentales*, here seen through a triangle of perspex bubbles rather than a gauzy screen, her two cavaliers posed dreamily on the floor in a nod to the 1947 male mannequins.

With her long black wig, and arms knotted round her head, Wednesday's Full of Woe (Vyvyan Lorrayne) parodies Nadia Nerina's interpretation of Elektra in Robert Helpmann's ballet – all splayed hands and grande tragédienne grimaces. Surrounded by four reptilian attendants, she also recalls *Sleeping Beauty*'s Carabosse and even faintly impersonates Aurora when, partnered by each one in turn, she performs a malevolent, crotch-baring distortion of the Rose Adage. Thursday's variation begins and ends with a Chaplinesque imitation by Alexander Grant, who is joined by six bubble-wigged girls enacting different interpretations of 'far to go': strap-hanging on the Tube, and forming a human rowing boat and propeller plane. While it has its amusing moments, this is the silliest section and, without Grant, Mary Clarke wrote, would be 'totally unbearable'. Fortunately, it is erased by Friday's blues duet, the high point of the ballet, which starred Sibley and Nureyev in a raunchy dramatization of 'loving and giving'. It was, as Sibley said, 'raw sex through classicism', which brazenly plagiarizes the classical-erotic-acrobatic idiom of Roland Petit's *Paradise Lost*, recently choreographed for Fonteyn and Nureyev. But there is further self-parody. With Jarman's cut-outs of intertwined serpents providing the clue, the dancers, in their unisex costumes, are a modern-day embodiment of *Tiresias*'s copulating snakes.

The most in-joke of all is Saturday's send-up of a male ballet class. Sauntering over to the barre, the dancers drape dressing gowns and towels over Jarman's installations and begin their hard day's work, driven to dropping point by a sadistic ballet master (Desmond Doyle) – a caricature of Michael Somes. Teacher's pet was the nineteen-year-old Wayne Sleep, who performed a tour de force of spins – a reference to his triumph as the Blue Boy in the 1966 school performance of *Les Patineurs*. Michael Coleman also excels, nonchalantly knocking off twelve pirouettes, and *Jazz Calendar* ends with a jaunty Sunday's child (Marilyn Trounson) leading the finale through their paces and into a rotating cluster of waving dancers – a tableau borrowed from the closing ritual of the television show *Sunday Night at the London Palladium*.

Dancers and audience hugely enjoyed *Jazz Calendar* – it was as amusing to see stars of the stature of Nureyev and Sibley bumping and grinding as it was to see Ashton at play: 'Like the Queen Mother lifting her Hartnell crinoline to reveal a pair of kinky black boots.' The ballet achieved its effect by what Martine de Courcel called 'the balance, the measure, the irony, the absence of vulgarity or more exactly the purification of a theme which could have led to facileness'. The critics disagreed. David Vaughan considered it to be not only slight but inconsiderable. 'There is a fatal lack of conviction in what seems to be an attempt to show that he could be "trendy".' The *Dancing Times* was equally as scathing. 'Ashton Out of Date' was the headline of Mary Clarke's review, a verdict that was about to have an unintentionally cruel resonance.

In April 1968, Ashton was summoned to the general administrator's office and told by David Webster that in two years time, when he himself retired, Ashton would also be required to leave. 'But aren't you going to consult me about a successor?' he asked, completely stunned by the news. It had already been decided, said Webster. Kenneth MacMillan's contract in Berlin was soon to expire and he would be taking over as director of the Royal Ballet, reigning jointly with John Field. The matter had been brought to a head because Field was thinking of accepting the directorship of the Festival Ballet and Webster did not want to lose him. 'When I went into the room,' said his assistant, John Tooley, 'there was a very crestfallen Fred who looked at me in his inimitable glum manner and said, "That's it." I asked him what he meant and he said, "I've been sacked." And David said, "No, it's not a question of being sacked, Fred is just going with me."'

Ashton had always talked about retiring in 1970, when he was sixty-six, but, when the time came, he fully expected to be persuaded to stay on for a couple more years. 'I wanted everyone to *beg* me to do it,' he admitted. By now, he was enjoying the job and knew that his term had been an enormous success. There had been some criticisms. In a controversial interview, Nadia Nerina spoke out against his regime – 'As a company we seem to be in a muddle. Freddie finds it hard to make decisions' – but most people knew the personal grievance behind her complaint: not promoted to be Fonteyn's successor as Prima Ballerina Assoluta, she left the company in 1966, the year of MacMillan and Seymour's departure. As Lord Drogheda acknowledged in his memoirs: without de Valois, the Royal Ballet would not have existed; without Ashton, it would not have achieved its fame and distinction.

His enforced retirement has always been an issue 'wrapped in terrible mystery', which de Valois attributes to Ashton's initial negativity.

Fred knew he was going to be Director, but he did nothing but say he didn't want to be. He was always boasting that he was off as soon as his time was up. To such an extent that we all believed him. He'd pretend he didn't want to stay on; and he rather overplayed it and misled a lot of people. Very childish. It was an extraordinary act he was putting on.

Several well-placed sources, however, believe that de Valois herself 'was behind the whole thing'. Although she was teaching in Turkey at the time – 'It was all settled when I came back' – John Tooley maintains, 'Ninette had been rooting for Kenneth for a long time.' 'I've always heard that Madam was to blame,' concurred Lord Hastings, a governor of the Royal Ballet. 'She was looking ahead and probably saw in MacMillan a new style of choreography that the company wouldn't get from Fred. You couldn't have Fred as director and Kenneth as principal choreographer. Fred was a jealous character and couldn't have tolerated another choreographer making marvellous ballets.' In fact, the story begins a year earlier when, unbeknown to Ashton and quite possibly encouraged by de Valois, Webster flew to Berlin to offer MacMillan the directorship of the Royal Ballet when his contract expired.

The first challenge to Ashton's regime, of which he had been aware, had taken place in a meeting with Webster and Tooley in March 1967, the gist of which was a discussion about the unpopularity of his two lieutenants, Jack Hart and Michael Somes. The dancers, Webster claimed, were demoralized by Hart's cold, unavuncular approach, and even more so by Somes's Draconian rehearsal methods, amounting to what he called 'a form of cruelty'. Ashton's lack of interest in the touring company was also questioned, and, in a follow-up letter, Webster suggests that John Field, who had run it as a happy ship and could offer the very things they lacked, should be embraced into the management to take an overall in-

terest in both companies. Webster was not proposing that Field supplant
Ashton, but he was criticizing his loyalty to his two assistants, neither of
whom would have agreed to serve under Field. As far as Ashton was concerned, losing Somes and Hart was out of the question. 'Fred was devoted to them, particularly to Michael, and although he regarded Jack as
a bit of an operator, he relied heavily on them both.' Things continued as
before, but Ashton made his resentment known. In the June issue of
Dance and Dancers, the following notice appeared: 'Intention to retire
was announced by Royal Ballet director Frederick Ashton. He expects to
remain until about 1970 but is determined not to stay indefinitely.' 'I
can't remember any official announcement,' said John Tooley. 'That was
Fred saying something and somebody picked it up.' A year later, 'the fatal interview' occurred.

Ashton's main concern, when he came out of Webster's office,
was how he was going to break the news to Hart and Somes. If they
resigned immediately, he threatened to go with them. Visibly upset, he
broke down in Nureyev's dressing room one night, confiding what had
happened. Iris Law, Ashton's secretary, recorded subsequent events in her
diary.

> Rudi promptly phoned John Tooley and told him if they want the
> Royal Ballet to remain a great classical company they must keep
> Somes . . . In the meantime the Company, now getting wind of the
> story are very much behind Somes and Hart, especially Somes.
> Kenneth Mason said that 75% of them would sign a letter to
> Drogheda backing Somes and Hart.

Yet, although word had quickly spread, it was not until the Royal Ballet's season in New York that an official announcement of Ashton's
impending departure was made. 'We were absolutely in shock,' said
Antoinette Sibley. 'Everyone was in tears, crying their hearts out, and Anthony [Dowell] and I had to hold the company together during a performance. We had to keep it all going. Fred was very much our mentor. Our
love for him was boundless.' Rumours were multiplying to such a degree
that Webster called a meeting. 'You may have heard that a lot of dancers
are going to be sacked, but it's not true,' he said, referring to the proposed amalgamation of the two companies, which took place in 1970.
He was cut short by Jack Hart predicting 'dangerous times ahead' and
warning that the Royal Ballet would now be run along the lines of the
Paris Opera, full of political intrigue. 'Fred's departure caused David
Webster a great deal of trouble,' said John Tooley. 'I'm afraid it was a serious error of judgement on his part and at the beginning of the New

York season he had a very rough time. The atmosphere round the place was dreadful and he was constantly on the phone, "What will I do, what will I do?" He wasn't well and I think this was one of the reasons why it was so badly handled.'*

David Webster emerges as the villain of this tempestuous affair, selfishly determined to take Ashton with him when he retired at whatever the cost. 'I think Webster was rather naughty,' said de Valois. 'He should have changed his mind.' But was he entirely to blame? Having been 'part of the Ashton fanclub' since the 1930s, he was a great admirer and belonged to the same homosexual cultural network that included John Gielgud and Terence Rattigan. They often saw each other socially, Ashton taking advantage of the good food and Dom Perignon at Webster's famous Weymouth Street parties, while privately decrying his lower-middle-class origins. 'That Liverpool department store manager' was how he once described him to a colleague. According to Isaiah Berlin, Ashton 'loathed' David Webster, considering him 'a vulgarian, coarse and inartistic – all of which was true'. In turn, Webster, a shrewd businessman accustomed to what de Valois called her 'tough, professional get-down-to-earth-in-the-office approach' was unimpressed by Ashton's disdain for the administrative side of his job. Webster was also, she claims, 'very angry' about his grudging attitude. 'And that's why, you see, in the end he wouldn't push Fred into staying. But dear old Fred had done it himself and nobody knows why.' De Valois also admits that she was disheartened by Ashton's approach. 'When I was leaving, I wrote a letter saying it was my dearest wish that he should follow me. He never answered it and when I met him he said, "Oh I've no intention of going on a minute after my time." I remember thinking, "Oh God, really," and being rather upset about this. You can't go on saying something without eventually people taking you seriously.'

It was de Valois who more than once told Tooley, 'Fred's been around a long time, he's getting to an age when he ought to retire and I would love to think that Kenneth succeeded him.' And, even though she insists that, being abroad at the time, she had nothing to do with the negotiations, her colleague Richard Glasstone, who was then director of the Turkish Ballet Company, overheard her almost daily telephone calls to David Webster. 'Madam was certainly behind it all. I'm quite convinced of that.' Ashton, who, as Lord Annan once remarked, 'took umbrage and then enjoyed a jolly good hate', blamed not only de Valois but also MacMillan – 'He felt sure Kenneth had a hand in engineering it' – and John Tooley – 'Fred used to say, "Never trust anyone with fair eye-

*David Webster died in May 1971, at the age of sixty-seven.

lashes." ' The abrupt termination of his contract was a key episode in his relationship with the Royal Ballet, influencing his thinking for the future. 'From that moment Fred was embittered.'

Feeling unprized and insecure, Ashton sank into a severe and long-lasting depression. Although he was made a Companion of Honour in recognition of his achievement as director, and was awarded two more Honorary Degrees,* no amount of official recognition could dispel his private despair. Not even Martyn Thomas was able to reach him; he was too young and too flighty to understand. 'If you won't tell me what is bothering you – I can't help you,' he wrote impatiently to Ashton. 'You are suddenly entirely different – and it is not only me who has noticed it. I can appreciate and understand that I can never expect enthusiasm from you, but a life that entails no fun from you is not for me . . You have played the old man, end of an era, finished professionally game for too long.'

Forty years earlier, another great figurehead of British culture had experienced the same sense of professional neglect and secret unhappiness. In the early 1920s, with the emergence of modernists like Stravinsky, the work of Edward Elgar, the acknowledged leader of his field, began to be ignored. Hurt and almost Timon-like in his resentment, he fell silent and withdrew to Worcestershire, becoming increasingly aloof from his friends. The affinity between Elgar and Ashton is profound: both regarded the English countryside as a vital creative stimulant; both were Edwardians by temperament, out of sympathy with the new age; and both were emotionally divided men, subject to dark moods and self-doubts, which 'not all the adulation of an era could wash away'. And yet, until now, Ashton had never liked Elgar's music. In 1968, when he told his surprised friends that he was planning to make a ballet to *Enigma Variations*, he explained that 'Elgar is in the air', referring, perhaps, to Michael Kennedy's biography published that year. Sure enough, the new work, a danced interpretation of the masterpiece that had brought Elgar long-awaited fame, heralded a resurgence of interest in the composer and his period. The 1970s, as Roy Strong has pointed out, was a decade marked by the rediscovery of Edwardian life: the film *The Go-Between*, Edwardian costume serials on television, *The Country Diary of an Edwardian Lady*, photographic books depicting Edwardian England – all were part of a trend inaugurated by Ashton's ballet.

The idea had been brought to his notice early in the 1950s, when Sir Hugh Casson left a series of designs by a gifted Royal College of Art pupil at the opera house, marked for de Valois' attention. After waiting

---

*University of East Anglia, 11 November 1967; Doctor of Music, Hull, 3 July 1970.

months, Julia Trevelyan Oman collected her portfolio from the stage door, assuming they had not been seen. In 1966 she received a telephone call from Ashton, who had not forgotten her sketches, telling her that the time was now right to do *Enigma Variations*. They decided to set the ballet in Elgar's Worcestershire – 'as derived from plump Victorian photographic albums, plush covered and copper clasped' – setting its action in 1898, when the forty-one-year-old composer, tormented by lack of recognition, learns that Hans Richter will conduct his score. At first, Ashton had 'enormous qualms' about how to tackle the music. 'Then I hit upon the idea of using the actual people who were written about musically and this began to fascinate me. I did a lot of study of them . . . to try and get under the skin of it.'

Capturing the essence of a person or a mood had always been Ashton's forte – his own impersonations were as much fieldwork for his ballets as his novelistic asides about strangers who caught his eye – and *Enigma Variations* would depict the personalities of Elgar's friends with 'an accuracy which is almost psychic'. When the composer's daughter, then an old lady, came to see a performance, she congratulated him afterwards, saying, 'I don't understand how you did it because they were exactly like that.' But even more interesting than his brilliant delineation of character are the departures Ashton makes from his source; the undramatized Chekhovian nuances, which sublimate a nostalgic re-creation of Elgar's world of friendly chamber music, local gentry and genial eccentricity into an English masterpiece in its own right.

When the curtain rises, the composer (Derek Rencher) is studying his score, surrounded by his wife and friends posed so tranquilly that, apart from a few falling leaves, the opening scene could be a sepia-tinted photograph. Dorabella (Antoinette Sibley) enters and playfully steals between Elgar and his manuscript. She is the 'Variationee' Dora Penney, frequently invited to Malvern because the melancholic Elgar was cheered by her enthusiasm and merry chatter. Reading between the lines of her memoirs,* Ashton obliquely suggests that their feelings for each other ran deeper than they appeared. As Elgar sways her to and fro, Dorabella's back is sensuously arched; but, when he attempts to kiss her, she turns away, a little disconcerted, and, immediately and unguiltily, turns to greet Lady Elgar. To recount the incident in words is to load it with an importance that Ashton did not intend; the romantic undercurrent is so fleetingly and delicately conveyed as to be hardly detectable. *The Invitation*, MacMillan's ballet about an older man's infatuation for a young girl, was currently in the repertory and Ashton was wary of appearing derivative. 'We must be careful', he told Sibley. 'We mustn't poach.' But

---

Edward Elgar: Memoirs of a Variation, Mrs Richard Powell.

more to the point, ambiguity, rather than a conventional narrative, was Ashton's prime concern.

Once again, an important model was Alain Resnais' *Last Year in Marienbad* – 'An enigma, the most monstrously elaborate enigma' – which tantalizingly evades any definite interpretation of plot. The statuesque positioning of the actors in the film also influenced the ballet. Lady Elgar's vigilant stance at the top of the stairs during the opening scene with Elgar and Dorabella creates a faintly sinister air of equivocation: is she aware of her husband's attraction for their young friend? Ashton exploits the poise and personality of both his leading dancers, their ability to inflect the simplest gesture with meaning. With his stagey moustache and sad hooded eyes, Derek Rencher looked physically identical to Elgar, and Ashton uses his solidly eloquent presence to focus the whole piece. Cutting out more and more of his dancing ('It seemed wrong . . . even when he does a few steps it kind of jars on me'), he makes Rencher a static, watchful figure for much of the ballet – the artist viewing his creations.

The role of Lady Elgar was the greatest of Svetlana Beriosova's career. As soon as she begins to dance, an enchaînement that distils classical technique into little more than graceful swaying, she embodies to perfection the serene and lovely Lady Elgar, who would listen to her husband's music in 'a state of seventh-heaven beatitude'. Their duet is an encapsulation of Edwardian married love, seemly and restrained, with moments of freedom, such as the diving lifts that fan the skirt of Beriosova's padded costume into a shape as sculptural as her scissoring calves. In a beautifully cadenced ending, she kneels at Elgar's feet, her head against him, his hand touching her hair.

An abrupt change of tone is introduced by three comic variations, which take their cue from the composer's manuscript and from the memoirs of his friends. Hew David Steuart-Powell (Stanley Holden), an amateur pianist, appears on a bicycle, an authentic prop borrowed from the Victoria and Albert museum. His characteristic diatonic run over the keys before beginning to play, travestied by Elgar's semiquaver passages, is given a dance equivalent in a short, flustery sketch of antic runs and skidding on the heels. The author Richard Baxter Townshend (Brian Shaw) rides round, ringing his bell on a tricycle, his amiable eccentricity mocked by the children who dance round him and encircle him with their hoop. Alexander Grant enacts Elgar's description of William Meath Baker's forcible personality, the 'inadvertent bang of the door' as he leaves the room expressed by Grant's jump on to the staircase while raising his hat.

Avoiding further episodic treatment of the music, the next vignette runs together two individual variations, linking a couple who were not romantically involved in life. Matthew Arnold's son, Richard (Robert

Mead), a contemplative young scholar who has been picturesquely swaying a Malvern lady, Isabel Fitton (Vyvyan Lorrayne), in a hammock,
dance a typical Ashtonian love-duet, its dreamy pace disrupted when Anthony Dowell explodes on stage as 'Troyte', a Malvern architect. His
brusque, boisterous manner and bungling attempts to learn the piano are
captured in an astonishingly accomplished 'bat-out-of-hell' scherzo, ending with a mimed 'final despairing slam' of the piano lid. A stately solo
follows, danced by Georgina Parkinson as Winifred Norbury, a neighbour whose characteristic laugh heard in the music is choreographically
interpreted as a slightly folksy twitching of her skirt from side to side.
This variation, like those of the 'galaxy of grotesques', and Wayne Sleep's
lively impersonation of George Robertson Sinclair's bulldog Dan later in
the ballet, amount to little more than witty literalizations of biographical
notes – costumes in motion, as in *Lord of Burleigh* or *The First Shoot*.
But the famous 'Nimrod' variation, which follows, elevates the mood to
an entirely different plane.

Ashton admitted that he was alarmed by the grandeur and solemnity
of this piece, Elgar's record of a long summer-evening talk when he and
his great friend and publisher, A. J. Jaeger, discussed the slow movements
of Beethoven. 'I did several versions and in the end I eliminated more and
more and more and just let the music speak for itself and created a
mood.' He confines the men's dancing to a semi-walking, slightly querulous 'question and answer' sequence; and, when they are joined by Lady
Elgar, she seems to smooth their dissent and draw them all together. Their
pas de trois, although appearing to be staidly Edwardian, takes *Monotones*' experiments with restricted movement to an even more daring extreme. Aligning himself with the post-modern pioneers of the 1960s,
Ashton adopts their strategy of non-dance; but, in his hands, natural
walking movements are weighted, made rhythmical and modulated into
low lifts and long classical lines. Towards the end, the friends, who are
facing the back of the stage, slowly raise up their arms, turn, surge forward, and begin to raise them once more. They instinctively freeze, their
hands falling to their sides, their feet sinking from half-pointe to flat foot
– 'as if we're back to earth again' – and then slowly walk away, arm in
arm. The episode, so prosaic on the page, has an almost epiphanic power
on stage, established, exactly as Ashton intended, from music and mood
alone. In a note of congratulations to Ashton, John Sparrow described
Nimrod as 'almost unbearably moving: something swelled and swelled
inside me and seemed on the point of breaking, and was then appeased
by the noble resolution – all passion spent upon the stage. You are a wonderful imaginative poet.'

Ashton had originally wanted Dorabella to be part of this sequence,
but Sibley felt unable to go straight into the taxing solo which immedi-

ately follows (fortunately, as her youthful presence would have dissipated Nimrod's expression of mature accord). Her own variation is a delight. Its fractured pace, the way Dorabella keeps breaking free from Elgar to dance alone, may have evolved from Dora Penney's description of his exasperation when she dashes off on a shopping trip almost as soon as she has arrived. Her edgy purposefulness ('I really can't stop now . . . I simply must go'), competing with her romantic nature, is wonderfully caught in the sharp arabesques which subsequently liquefy into Titania-like abandon. Ashton loved Bournonville's *Napoli* and instructed Sibley to capture the Danish trait of holding a step and melting out of it. 'He wanted that accent. He thought it described Dorabella's way of saying something and then shyly covering it up.' Elgar's staccato semiquaver chords and the pizzicato bass, which parody her stammer, are translated into chirrupy hops on pointe and an irregular series of steps, where he 'sneaks in' an extra pas de chat to mimic the broken rhythm of her speech. Sibley was known for her strong pointework – as a young girl, she would run along the shingles of Brighton beach without shoes to strengthen her metatarsal arches – and she was told by Antony Tudor, after a performance of *The Dream*, 'Your feet are just like Spessivtzeva's. They talk.' Sibley insists that Ashton's highlighting of her footwork – 'in every ballet he created for me, he's got jumps on pointe' – contained an element of mock-revenge. As a young sprite in *Ondine*, she had once been severely reprimanded by him for dancing a step on half-pointe; she believes he never forgot. 'Fred always treated me like a naughty child. He was gruff, he'd prod me, he'd cajole me . . . and of course it was lovely and endearing once I knew that he really liked me.' Theirs was a relationship similar, in ways, to that between Elgar and Dora Penney. Always chattering and laughing, Sibley worshipped Ashton (who referred to her as his 'Beloved Dorabella'). 'He knew that I just adored him and would try *anything* for him. I had absolute trust and such a warm love for him. I truly truly would like to have embraced him all the time.' Although there was, of course, no parallel in her own life, Sibley danced the role convinced that Dorabella was infatuated with the composer 'and vice versa'. It is this intimation of hidden yearning – for Elgar, the lure of youth and beauty, which Ashton understood so well – that cuts through the girlish winsomeness of the variation. Dorabella is a key to the private side of Elgar's divided nature, a dichotomy central to *Enigma Variations* and made literal in Julia Trevelyan Oman's interior/exterior set.

'The Composer as First Dancer' is the title of Lincoln Kirstein's essay in *Movement and Metaphor*, in which *Enigma Variations* is the only Ashton piece included in a discussion of fifty seminal works. The musician, Kirstein says, is portrayed in 'a domestic rather than tragic or romantic ambience'; but, on the contrary, Ashton's portrait of Elgar is a combination of all three. An atmosphere of almost Lisztian romantic despair pervades the ballet, enhanced by Rencher's sympathetic interpretation – 'I was expressing my feelings in my life . . . a sense of failure in a way, a sense of need and of solitude' – and made almost tangible by Ashton's identification with his subject. 'We all knew what Fred was choreographing about,' said Beriosova. 'But when he was thinking about Elgar he forgot himself.' The final scene between the composer and his wife is one in which the anguish and loneliness of the creative artist is most keenly felt. Their closeness, symbolized in a hand gesture which has been a motif throughout the ballet, is made even more potent by the subjective weight that lies behind it.* 'L'amour c'est ça,' Ashton used to tell Martine de Courcel, putting one hand gently on her knee and removing it with his other, in a gesture of exasperated rejection. 'He had a very desperate conception of love.' And, in a sense, the Baroness was Ashton's surrogate Lady Elgar: her tender sympathy – 'He knew I understood him, not the personnage, the person' – compensated for the lack of constancy from Martyn Thomas. 'I do not have the temperament to be a Prince Consort,' Thomas admitted, 'merely to be in attendance to support you.' But, although Ashton may have envied the unselfish nurturing of Elgar, he depicts the composer as withdrawn, at times, even from the comfort of his wife, who can only move solicitously in his shadow as he kneels in a world of his own.

Elgar is alone on stage when the final character appears, the enigmatic Lady Mary Lygon (Deanne Bergsma), whose billowing veils and gently rocking movements allude to Elgar's account of her absence on a sea voyage. It has been suggested that this delicate tone-poem was a confession of 'lost love still longed for', an interpretation hinted at in the ballet by the poignant intensity of Elgar's mood before her entrance. Her name was denoted in the score by asterisks, which Dorabella said stood for 'My sweet Mary'; and, although Ashton retains an element of mystification about her identity, she is, in essence, a traditional balletic vision of the unattainable, a Muse-like apparition, far removed from the earthy vitality of the other characters. Her participation in the celebratory final scene is the ballet's only real flaw. After a telegram has arrived announcing that Richter will conduct the *Variations*, the whole cast position themselves for a photograph, a denouement Ashton had employed once before in *A Wedding Bouquet*. This finale, which uses Elgar's original

---

*This passage of music, in fact, belongs to Basil G. Nevison, performed by Leslie Edwards. Nevison was an amateur musician and devoted friend, who is playing his cello at the beginning of their duet.

composition rather than the extended version which he wrote at Jaeger's suggestion, was criticized for being too abrupt – 'How dare he tamper with the music!' Lord Harewood exploded to Buckle. But Ashton, uninspired by the militaristic fervour of the conclusion, said that he found it 'impossible to reach up to the full sonority of that ending'.

Although *Enigma Variations* was hailed as one of the most beautiful ballets Ashton had ever made, there were those who found it old-fashioned and sentimental, while Alexander Bland regarded 'two stiff-collared gentlemen arabesquing together with their watch-chains flying . . . uncomfortably near to the comical'. Fittingly, it was Ashton's friends who were most appreciative. 'It reduces me to tears,' Kenneth Clark told him. 'What an incomparable maestro you are – no one else has had such a range and brought so many different things to perfection.' And writing to Nicholas Henderson, Ann Fleming remarked, 'Freddy has most perfectly evoked the tranquillity of late summer, a touch of Chekhov, a touch of mystery, a little magic. I was entranced, and think the critics carping who infer one cannot dance in a bustle, for somehow this did not detract from a small work of art.'

Ashton's close circle, particularly Martine de Courcel, Alexander Grant and Billy Chappell, would always be there when he needed them; but, increasingly, he longed for a more stable domestic life, which Martyn Thomas, as he himself acknowledged, was unable to provide. 'I am beginning to feel that you would really be happier with someone of a calmer nature – a male combination of Iris [Law, Ashton's devoted secretary] and Alexander.' The shock of the Royal Ballet's mishandling of Ashton's retirement had coincided with one of the most volatile and precarious phases in his relationship with Thomas. 'Fred wanted a peaceful life and Martyn would scream and rant,' said a friend. Money and long-term security were the two recurring issues. Ashton provided an allowance, but it was not large enough or regular enough to satisfy Thomas – 'more a form of hand-out when things got desperate.' As companion, cook, housekeeper, gardener, 'quite apart from lover', Thomas expected more for his efforts than 'a bunch of flowers or some dollars in an envelope'. He resented not being included in Ashton's future plans, often being invited to an event only the day before, or told at the last minute that he could watch a performance from the wings. 'Your lack of commitment is what hurts me,' he told Ashton, 'and I retaliate in my own way and try to hurt back.' He was 'sickened' by his role of mistress 'as opposed to wife', but would have been the first to admit that he did not have a Lady Elgar-like virtue of steadfastness in adversity. He could not comprehend Ashton's desolation: 'It is so alien to my nature and I do not understand how to cope with it.' Bursting with life and enthusiasm, Thomas was full of ideas to improve Marlborough Street and Chandos Lodge, but found his plans repeatedly quashed by Ashton, who was, by nature, over-cautious – or, as many would say, simply mean: 'If Fred sent you out with £10 to buy groceries which cost £9.99, he expected the penny change.' Thomas was the complete opposite, not grasping, his family and friends insist, but generous-spirited and impulsive. Suddenly, his life seemed to lack all spontaneity and to revolve round Ashton and his 'sad Fred act – "everything is over, finished, shan't travel, no money coming in etc" . . . I have heard it ad infinitum, & it does bore me . . . It would do you a lot of good to sit down and realize how marvellous your life has been *and*, more important, how marvellous it could be. If you persist in clinging to the black side of everything then it would be wrong of me to stay . . . You will wallow in self-pity until you drown.'

Lament of the Waves, Ashton's new ballet about two drowning lovers, could almost be a direct response to Thomas's remark, reflecting the sense of doom they both felt about the future of their relationship, as well as dramatizing the dark mood that was engulfing him. He admitted to David Vaughan that the work was autobiographical, confessing only to an abstract emotion, his own 'morbid feeling of being submerged by time'. But, however personal its motivation may have been, *Lament of the Waves* is barely recognizable as an Ashton work. In a defiant challenge to the charge that his ballets were out of date, he chose a young composer, Gérard Masson, whose avant-garde score, the grimly atmospheric 'Dans le Deuil des Vagues II', makes Henze seem as melodic as Meyerbeer. The designer, Bill Culbert, was also young – a Lisson Gallery artist, whose light projection sphere emerged from the darkness of the background 'like a monstrous sea-anemone'. The cast of two were little-known corps de ballet dancers, Carl Myers and Marilyn Trounson, their long hair and natural good looks enhancing the ultra-contemporary idiom of the dance. Most of the movements are startlingly untypical: scrabbling arms and unballetically flexed feet, as if Trounson is fighting to get to the surface; grotesquely distorted and upended bodies transmuting into strange lurking molluscs, and seaplants buffeted by underwater currents; or, more chillingly, simply a boy and a girl undulating under water, not waving but drowning. There is a great deal of Petit-style floorwork, particularly effective in the moments where the couple replay their sexual intimacy. Peter Williams saw in the ballet's re-enactment of their love a parallel to Ashton's creative life with the Royal Ballet, 'the end of his love affair with it', citing references to his previous works: air walks from *Symphonic Variations*, a tremulous foot from *Two Pigeons*, swimming lifts from *Ondine*. But these movements are given such bizarre inflections that they appear completely new. It is his next ballet that Ashton offers as an allegory of his own achievement.

The uncompromising starkness of *Lament of the Waves*, which seemed longer than its seventeen minutes, drew a tepid response from the first-night gala audience, and Ashton was further demoralized that evening by another confrontation with Martyn Thomas. This time, their dispute was over friends, specifically Patric Walker, whom Thomas was about to join in Torremolinos. 'All I wanted to establish,' he wrote from Spain, 'was that we each have a life and couldn't possibly approve of everything that the other one does or believes in. I do love you very very much and you must stop doubting it or you will wither my feelings.' Time apart provided a respite from their differences and brought home to Thomas 'how much I need and depend on you (despite all my hideousness and difficulty to live with)'. With Ashton spending his annual fortnight in Ramatuelle, they were accustomed to separate summers. The previous year, Thomas had also been to Spain, helping to decorate Moura Lympany's house. He loved nothing more than holiday living – sunbathing, swimming, night-clubbing until five in the morning – and was elated to be part of the Mar-bella Club set: 'Baron Thyssen etc etc; every opportunity to dress up and have fun . . . I'm sure I have been typecast as the gigolo – sure that will put you at ease rather than have me create the gay decorator image!!! I am being a very good dog.'

Despite his bid for independence, Thomas continued to reassure Ashton about his commitment. 'Please don't let me return to any problems with you. The last weekend was something special and it *must* continue like that. It is difficult for you to believe but I do love you above all else.' But, however much he reiterated that his 'kennel is spotless', Ashton, quite understandably, remained unconvinced. Rather than sitting at home, imagining the worst, he began seeking the company of even the most casual acquaintances, frequently telephoning John Stuart, a Chelsea neighbour, and inviting himself for a drink. 'He hated being alone. I think he felt he was getting older and his choreography was being pushed aside.' There were other anxieties. Edith had recently left her husband, bolting to Ischia to stay with the Waltons, and her husband was refusing to give her a divorce. Money also was preoccupying Ashton, his main worry being that his pension and the income from royalties on his ballets would not provide enough for him to keep both his properties. But with his finances in the capable hands of Mark Kerr, a Lloyds banker friend whom he had appointed his trustee, there was no cause for alarm. A com-bination of his Cazenove shares and savings certificates meant that he was then 'worth over £110,000'. As Kerr wryly pointed out, 'The way you live you will not really ever have to worry about money!'

Ashton had recently lost much of his investment in the Elystan Street shop. Thomas, who, as he said, had 'many capacities but lacked application', had shown so little interest in the business that it went into liquidation after three years. The shop was bought by Gabrielle Crawford and, in his will, Ashton released Thomas from debt, bequeathing a third of the shares to his family, who had also put money into the business. 'Martyn was mortified that he'd let us down,' said his sister, Jennifer Mellors. 'He was never secure about his future and needed our love very much and thought he might have jeopardized it. His relationship with Fred had taught him that love is conditional.' Early one Sunday morning, when Ashton was still asleep at Chandos Lodge, Patric Walker rang to tell him that Thomas was in hospital after having taken an overdose. Ashton returned to London immediately. Although Thomas was now feeling contrite, his insecurity remained just as acute, frequently manifesting itself as aggression. At a party after a New York gala for Ashton in May, there was 'a terrific clash' between him and Nureyev. 'Martyn got into a terrible rage and was challenging Rudi who must have been so provoked but had to control himself. You can't have a fight in public with Sir Fred's friend.' It had been Ashton's evening, a farewell tribute which comprised (at his request) the Shades scene from *La Bayadère* as an honour to the corps de ballet, *Daphnis and Chloe*'s finale, *The Dream* pas de deux, *Symphonic Variations* and *Façade*. The response from the audience was rhapsodic. As Ashton often remarked, his following in New York was far more demonstrative than in Britain. 'It was extraordinary. When I arrived at the stage door there'd be a crowd outside and as I stepped out of the car, they'd all *burst* into applause. Well, that was heartening.' But, to Thomas, unwilling to be in Ashton's shadow, it only brought home his own inadequacies and increased his demands. 'I feel in my deepest heart,' he wrote, 'that you do not regard me firstly as a permanency and secondly on an equal basis with you.'

Trying to oblige, Ashton agreed to pay Thomas a fee for helping him with his next project, *Creatures of Prometheus*, made for the touring company and premièred in Bonn in June 1970, as part of the Beethoven bicentenary celebrations. Although his sister claims that 'Martyn did a bit of the choreography', none of the leading dancers can remember him in the studio, suggesting that he was involved only in the early planning stages. The original scenario, an heroic-allegorical spectacle, created for Beethoven by Salvatore Vigano in 1801, has been lost, although contemporary accounts helped Ashton to reconstruct a plot. Consisting of a prologue and one act, it dramatizes Prometheus's animation and his educating of two figures he himself has made – an obvious analogy with the task of the choreographer, which Ashton underscored by quoting in the programme the conclusion of Goethe's ode, 'Prometheus'.

> Here I sit, forming them
> In my image,
> A race that will resemble me;
> To suffer, to weep,
> To enjoy and be glad,
> And not to heed you –
> Like me

As in Goethe's lyric poems, many of which concentrate on the artist and the process of creation, Ashton's recent work had become reflectively self-conscious. He, too, saw in Prometheus, 'the very type of the solitary creator', a symbolic representation of himself. Surrounded by figures he has made in his own image, Goethe's hero spoke for Ashton when he says

> Here my world, my all!
> Here I feel myself;
> Here all my desires
> In bodily shapes

Moulded by his personal style and sensibilities, every dancer in the Royal Ballet was a living emblem of his legacy.

Set in 1801, the date of the score, *Prometheus* was Ashton's foray into German Romanticism.* Prometheus (Hendrik Davel), with his white shirt, breeches and boots, is presented as a revolutionary artist who escapes to the sanctuary of his studio with a brand of flame stolen from Heaven. Like Dr Coppélius with his dolls, he brings his two stiff-limbed creatures (Doreen Wells and Kerrison Cooke) to life, and, to endow them with a spirit and emotions, leads them to Apollo and Eros before invoking the various muses to complete their enlightenment. A sprightly solo by Alfreda Thorogood as Thalia (Muse of Comedy), together with Brenda Last's amusing portrayal of Terpsichore as a cane-wielding ballet mistress ('I was supposed to be Madam'),† were two highlights in what was generally an unimpressive enterprise. The main problem was the dancers' uncertainty as to whether or not the ballet was meant to be hu-

---

*Ashton had considered using *Prometheus* in the 1920s: among his papers there is a copy of the score annotated 'For Harold [Turner] and Billie [Chappell]'.
†Ninette de Valois.

morous. Adrian Grater, who led his bloodstained army as a caricature of Napoleon and imagined his role to be tongue-in-cheek, claimed that Ashton was 'very disturbed' when he heard laughter from dancers watching the rehearsal. John Percival, however, praising the new work in *Dance and Dancers*, described it as 'a ballet that makes you chuckle'. According to David Vaughan, *Prometheus* 'did not look like an Ashton ballet at all'; but how much this can be attributed to Martyn Thomas's contribution will never be known. Jennifer Mellors sensed some ill-feeling over it. 'Martyn was very uncommunicative at that time. He seemed very nervous as if he didn't want us to ask any questions about it. There were times when he and Fred did a lot of work together, and times when Fred said, "No. Mind your own business. Don't push me."' Despite the recent blow to his self-esteem, it is unlikely that Ashton, never having allowed his private life to affect his professional integrity, would suddenly be deflected from making the ballet he had in mind. Its subtext, a portrait of the artist, was one that had been preoccupying him for some time. And, as if nostalgically replaying his own career, there are several reminders of past works, including a chain-like entrance of peasant girls and boys in wide-brimmed hats and smocks, 'who might have nipped over from Widow Simone's farm for a fête champêtre on Parnassus'. But, if driven to anthologize himself through a sense of being undervalued, Ashton was soon to be recompensed. A month later, on 24 July, like his drowning couple in *Lament of the Waves*, he saw his whole life pass before him.

Preparations for the special farewell tribute to Ashton, devised by Michael Somes, Jack Hart and Leslie Edwards, had been conducted in secret. 'I didn't know anything about it. They never allowed me to have a rehearsal that was going on at the same time as the gala rehearsals.' Several meetings took place at Barbara Ker-Seymer's house in Islington, where Billy Chappell, who wrote the linking commentary, was then living. Kept in the dark until the last moment, Ashton became increasingly perturbed when, on several occasions, he telephoned Charlton Place to ask 'Mrs Chappell' if he could come to supper and, each time, was firmly rebuffed. Not even the audience, who were only given programmes as they were leaving the theatre, had any idea of the performance they were about to see. Tickets were priced no higher than usual. 'That meant that everybody who ought to have been there got in,' said the writer Patrick O'Connor. 'It was a real balletomane, not a socialite, audience. The contrast with David Webster's rather pompous gala a few weeks before could not be unnoticed.'

When the curtain rose, Robert Helpmann was seated at a table on the side of the stage, sipping a glass of champagne *Wedding Bouquet*-style and delivering his lines with arch aplomb. Projected photographs, recovered by Edith when her brother was out of the house, accompanied his account of Ashton's childhood and early days, then the dance began. The frivolous mattachins quartet from *Capriol Suite* (1930) was the first and oldest of thirty-seven items covering a period of forty years. Several lost treasures had been recovered through what Helpmann called the 'choreographic archaeology' of dancers' memories. Among them was Walter Gore's eccentrically jazzy solo from *Rio Grande* (Alexander Grant), an elegant dance with a fan from *The Lord of Burleigh* (Deanne Bergsma), and the lovers' duet from *The Wanderer*. Rudolf Nureyev's exhilarating interpretation of the Idzikowsky role in *Les Rendezvous* drew delighted applause, as did the appearance of Fonteyn in five of her original roles. But the end of the evening is remembered as the most moving part. When the entire company were waltzing on stage in their assorted costumes, Helpmann quoted a line from Gertrude Stein: 'They incline to oblige only one.' 'Only one,' he repeated, and the curtain rose at the back of the stage to show Ashton descending on a lift. The applause thundered out and flowers began raining on stage. He tried to speak, but broke down. For him, as for the performers and audience, it had been an overwhelmingly emotional occasion, one of the most remarkable in the history of English ballet. 'Even my old horny eyes were moist,' Robert Heber-Percy wrote afterwards, and among the many other messages of congratulations was a telegram from Nijinska: 'My admiration for your magnificent artistic achievements in the Royal Ballet who under your outstanding direction reached greatest heights in ballet world.' Michael Somes wrote to thank his 'Darling Fred' for their glorious years together. 'You know (in spite of my rough exterior) how devoted I am to you in every way . . . I only hope you will consider this performance as my humble and inadequate tribute to my dear friend & master.' Jack Hart was leaving to work abroad, but Somes was to remain in the Royal Ballet under the new regime, performing as a guest artist and taking charge of all Ashton's ballets. Their gala had been, in the words of Peter Williams, 'as demonstrative an expression of love as I have ever seen in the theatre'. But was Ashton reassured? When Barbara Ker-Seymer saw him later that evening and remarked how wonderful it had been to see him receiving such adulation, he looked at her dolefully and said, 'I'd have given all this up for one kind word from Martyn.'

CHAPTER SEVENTEEN

EYE SOCIETY

1970–1977

The beginning of Ashton's retirement promised to be a welcome restorative after the wretchedness of recent years. Financially secure and (apart from a grumbling hiatus hernia) blessed with good health, he spent much more time at Chandos Lodge. Here, he planned to perfect his French by having someone come in to read to him. 'We'd read Racine. But of course I never did it.'

His everyday needs were well catered for. At Edith's instigation, he had dismissed Edward, his manservant, who had been running Chandos as if he were the lord of the manor, inviting Eye lady friends to tea and becoming increasingly involved with Salvation Army activities. Often, when Ashton rang to announce that he was coming down for the weekend, Edward would dissuade him by saying that he was going out. 'He was a terror,' said Billy Chappell. 'He always talked too much and joined in the conversation at lunch' – an intrusion Ashton appeared to resent more than Edward's 'frightfully bad cooking'. 'Fred was perfectly awful to him,' said Elizabeth Cavendish. 'I used to say, "You *can't* speak to him like that."' Edward was replaced by Mrs Dade, a russet-cheeked treasure, who brought Ashton tea and toast in bed, baked his favourite lemon-curd tarts and sat opposite him in the morning, perched on the edge of her chair, helping him with the *Telegraph* crossword. With her, he was as teasingly affectionate as he had been with Mrs Lloyd; whenever she asked, as she habitually did, if there was anything else she could do for him, he would chuck her under the chin and instruct her, with mock-imperiousness, to 'Clean the silver. And then scrub the kitchen floor.'

Ashton now had several good friends in the area. Benjamin Britten and Peter Pears had bought a retreat in Horham, a few miles away, to escape the noise of aeroplanes above Aldeburgh's Red House. The photographer Angus McBean lived nearby with his young lover and assistant, David Ball, in Flemings Hall, an imposing early-Tudor manor. There were frequent lunches, dinners and parties, to which Ashton was invariably invited. Ball would also drive over to visit him at Chandos Lodge, where they sat on the terrace on summer evenings, drinking their way through a pitcher of Martinis. Ashton liked to leave the jug inside the house, explaining that when he could no longer get up to refill his glass, he knew he had had enough. He amused Ball by telling him long stories about a fictitious lover, a character he had invented called Reggie, a North-country businessman he 'couldn't take anywhere'. 'Fred would say things like, "Do you know the actress Judi Dench? Well, Reggie's just left me for her."' Forty minutes away at Sternfield, a Queen Anne house set in 300 acres, lived Prudence Penn, the tall, attractive wife of Sir Eric Penn, Comptroller of the Lord Chamberlain's Office. Prue was fun and flirtatious – 'a composer's moll', beloved by both Britten and Walton – and one of several well-born women who were happy to act as chauffeur-companion to Ashton. He would be driven over to Sternfield for luncheon and stay for supper, settling down after everyone had gone and launching into a 'frightfully rude' post-mortem on the other guests. One hot Sunday, he choreographed water ballets in the Penns' pool, with Prue and Princess Margaret, a close friend, alternating in the ballerina role, balancing with hoots of laughter on Lord Snowdon's shoulder. Ashton caused further delight by teaching The Princess's daughter, eight-year-old Sarah Armstrong-Jones, Mrs Tiggy-Winkle's dance in the garden. Although he claimed to avoid local society – 'I don't go anywhere. I don't want that when I come here' – Suffolk neighbours contest that, on the contrary, he loved being invited out and would be inclined to telephone even a slight acquaintance to announce that he had arrived. Sunday was always a melancholy day for Ashton and he went out of his way not to be alone. He spent many a Sunday with Anne Renshaw, an elegant widow who also lived in Eye and who enjoyed looking after him, cooking him tomato jelly rings filled with scrambled eggs when he began having trouble with his teeth. 'Fred allowed himself to be nannied by Anne,' said Janie Henniker-Major, a young friend whom Ashton used as a foil for the county types. It pleased him that Janie, whose father was Lord Henniker, a descendant of the Fulchers' landlords, owned Valley Farm, his mother's family home in Yaxley. 'He made me promise I would never sell it.' She saw her role as a prompter, to drink and smoke with him until four or five in the morning, asking him questions about his past life – 'well-honed stories and social gossip from the Thirties.' He would occasionally complain that he was being pestered by well-meaning, possessive neighbours. But if Suffolk society became too intrusive, Ashton could always escape into the tree-house built to avoid the vicar, who took to calling round when Ashton had first moved to Chandos Lodge. It was equipped with children's seats and even a bar of sorts, so that when Ash-ton spotted the clergyman coming up the drive, he could sit in the trees, glass in hand, and watch the poor man ring the doorbell. 'I have now been vicar here for three months and regretfully have not been able to catch you at home,' the Revd John Larter wrote in vain.

The garden at Chandos Lodge continued to give great pleasure. The topiary was now established and, to its left, Ashton had recently had dug a lake surrounding a small island – 'I must have water to look at' – on which he had planted a tree in the centre, in memory of Sophie. Later in the year, with his fee for choreographing the film *The Tales of Beatrix Potter*, he would have a swimming-pool installed in the old laundry room, a source of as much irritation as pleasure, in that it cost £6,000, the price he had paid for the house, and it continually needed servicing. Martyn Thomas's contribution towards the improvement of Chandos Lodge was as prodigious as ever. It was his idea to ask Angus McBean, gifted as an amateur carpenter, to fretsaw Gothic wooden curves for the bay windows; Thomas reduced the 'airfield' of gravel in front of the house, making it part of an extensive lawn; and he persuaded Ashton to convert an adjoining outhouse into a light morning room in which to dis-play his collection of Wemyss ware. But, although Thomas, in turn, had benefited greatly from being with Ashton – 'All my standards and appre-ciations stem from you' – their visual taste was incompatible. Ashton loved the faded elegance of tea-stained chintz and worn Aubusson car-pets that he had seen at grand houses, whereas Thomas favoured vivid Mediterranean colours and 'everything decorated to the nines', according to his friend David Scott-Bradbury. 'Fred tried to teach Martyn to create a little disorder.' Thomas's bedroom at Chandos Lodge was so showily done that Ashton called it the Elizabeth Taylor Suite. The Wemyss exten-sion, too, with its orangey walls and leather sofa, was not really in char-acter with the rest of the house, and yet, because of its associations, it became Ashton's favourite room. If it was too cold on the terrace, he would sit there most of the day and evening, propped up by Thomas's embroidered 'Fred' cushions, chain-smoking, his hand posed gracefully away from his face like the Hostess's in *Les Biches*.

His country routine grew increasingly sedentary. 'People don't believe me when they ask me what I've done all day and I say, "Nothing. I do nothing. I sit and stare."' Yet whereas in the past he had always needed time to himself, to lead what he called 'an inward life', lately, insecurity about his future, both emotional and professional, had instilled in him a dread of being on his own. Despite assuring Martyn Thomas that he would never ask him to waste his 'beautiful young life' by sharing his pastoral seclusion, Ashton craved his continual presence. Not only was

Thomas a lively companion, but he was also an exceptionally good listener. 'There would be fights, but then they'd have a whale of a time,' said Patric Walker. 'Sitting there having an all-day lunch and giggling. Just the two of them.' Thomas, however, was growing restless; after their five years together, he had heard most of the stories before and he began to resent Ashton's dependence on him. 'I am *not* a prop to be rested on or an injection to give you life – not all the time anyway.' Ashton's plea, 'I must have *some*one sitting opposite me,' only increased his irritation. 'You make me feel like a utilitarian piece of furniture. An apt simile but frightening since you are always changing round your rooms.'

According to Patric Walker, the first year of Ashton's retirement was the turning point in his affair with Thomas. 'That was when Fred no longer had power and importance. He stopped going to the Opera House every day and started to have time to worry about where Martyn was. And the moment you started to put the clamp on Martyn, he was sure to misbehave.' In an attempt to fetter him, Ashton had installed Thomas on the floor above Billy Chappell's flat in Battersea, a house owned by Alexander Grant who lived next door. 'Fred wants to get me away from Patric and he's stuck me out here,' Thomas complained to David Scott-Bradbury, who said that Grant and Chappell would observe the 'goings on' in Rosenau Road and report back to Ashton. The growing realization that Thomas was leading a double life tormented Ashton, but his remonstrations went unheeded. 'It would be foolish to disregard the fact that my age demands that I pursue my own goals and friendships professionally and otherwise,' Thomas replied, and his friends were equally implacable. 'What did Fred expect?' said Patric Walker. 'Surely by sixty you have sufficient experience in life to realize that it's the friendship that counts.' In theory, Ashton did, in fact, have a realistic attitude to occasional infidelity. 'What does the odd fuck matter,' he would say, relating a story Diana Cooper had told him about how she had sent out a search party for her husband when he failed to come home one night. 'Wasn't it idiotic of me?' she had remarked to Ashton. 'He was only in bed with Daisy [Fellowes].' Confronted with the reality, however, Ashton, the poet of romantic love, found it impossible to sustain a stance of worldly detachment. Relentlessly and flamboyantly libertine, Thomas made him suffer as he had never suffered before.

Ashton's confidant at the time was Alard Tobin, a young dancer with the opera ballet, who was the partner of Brian Shaw. At Shaw's request, Ashton had found a job for Tobin as his lighting stand-in on the film *The Tales of Beatrix Potter*, in which he danced the role of Mrs Tiggy-Winkle. 'We were vaguely the same size and Fred said, I can't run across fields, I'm too old. You can do that.' Every day, Ashton offered Tobin a lift to the studios in the chauffeur-driven car the film company had provided, and, on the journey to and from Elstree, he would unburden himself. Tobin listened attentively, but, because he had not taken to Martyn Thomas, whom he found 'rather pretentious' and over-cocky about his position, he was not particularly sympathetic. 'After all, Martyn was a very young man and Fred by this time was getting on.' Tobin observed the way in which the film 'grew out of the depths of Fred's despair', but said that on the set Ashton did not appear to be cast down by his problems. 'It was only in the mornings and in the evenings that he really thought about Martyn and got it all out of his system.'

Ashton's first reaction to the prospect of choreographing a ballet based on *The Tales of Beatrix Potter* was one of apprehension. He was uncertain that the time was right 'for such an explosion of sheer charm' and imagined other people commenting, 'The old man's gaga.' But swayed by the enthusiasm of the couple whose idea this had been (producer Richard Goodwin and his wife, the designer Christine Edzard), Ashton eventually agreed. The calibre of the collaborators was impressive. Goodwin had been assistant producer on Zeffirelli's film *Romeo and Juliet,* on which Edzard, a protégé of Ashton's beloved Lila de Nobili, had also worked. The director was Reginald Mills, who had edited *The Red Shoes* and *The Tales of Hoffmann.* More significantly, it was the union of Ashton and Beatrix Potter that seemed predestined. Quite apart from their old-fashioned sensibilities and fondness for simple things – cabbages and roses, sprigged calico, flagged kitchen floors, pink and white pottery – each was able to catch the smallest nuances of character. (Potter once named a family of snails and claimed she could tell them apart.) Christine Edzard's costumes and Rostislav Doboujinsky's masks re-created each character with painstaking authenticity, while Ashton's English restraint and skill as a miniaturist guaranteed fidelity to her spirit.

Mrs Tiggy-Winkle opens the film, tripping along a Lakeland path. Her quirky movements, with swaying hips and feet sashaying from side to side, are so idiosyncratic that Alard Tobin, on whom Ashton tried out the choreography, had trouble executing it. 'Fred saw Mrs Tiggy-Winkle as a great, fat, jolly black mammy with enormous hips waddling down with the laundry basket. I couldn't really do that sort of hip walk but he knew that he could do it himself.' Ashton rejected the original piece of music that John Lanchbery had chosen for him from the selection of Victorian and Edwardian theatre music which forms the basis of the score. 'It's too rhythmical for me,' he said. 'I want something nearer to a blues.' As this was not in period with the other numbers, Lanchbery found 'a kind of cake walk' played chiefly on the guitar. Mrs Tiggy-Winkle's solo is nonchalantly low-key, its bluesy looseness merging naturally with Ashtonian motifs, such as busy circling wrists, a soft-shoe shuffle of a Fred Step, and the flexing and pointing of a black-buttoned boot drawing attention to the choreographer's celebrated insteps.

There are droll self-references throughout the film. The Mouse Waltz, which follows, converts *La Fille mal gardée*'s ribbon-play into an intricate use of tails, two-and-a-half-yards long. The mice make patterns, skip rope, interlace like maypole dancers on a village green – a reminder of Ashton's Garland Dance from *The Sleeping Beauty*. Peter Rabbit's frenetic tarantella reinvents Ashton's Neapolitan Dance, a lettuce and bunch of carrots in each hand replacing the beribboned, waving tambourine; while the courtship of Pigling Bland and Black Berkshire Pig parodies an Ashtonian love duet. Several moments derive from *The Dream*: like Bottom, Pigling Bland dances hobblingly on point and the couple repeat the footsie-footsie motif – the joke being that both he and Peter Rabbit are danced by Alexander Grant, sending-up two of his most popular roles. Grant, more than anyone else in the cast apart from Ashton himself, is able to project his own character through the huge, inhibiting mask; his interpretation is imbued with his kindness and good nature. In other performances, the personalities of the dancers are transmitted through their movements: Michael Coleman's high jump and famously neat beats define his portrayal of Jeremy Fisher; the dainty footwork of Hunca Munca announces a sparkling new young talent, Lesley Collier; while Wayne Sleep is instantly identifiable through the blurring spins and technical élan of Squirrel Nutkin.

Unfortunately, Sleep's impact is diminished by Nutkin's appearance towards the end of the film: after an hour, and with another thirty minutes to go, the viewer has, by this time, seen enough. The humour Ashton elicits from the conjunction of balletic grace with cumbersome costumes has long since palled. The finale, in particular, seems endless, which Ashton realized, but he could do nothing to rectify it. 'Fred was very unhappy with it,' says Alard Tobin, 'and probably would have done it differently, had he been given an opportunity.' Although Ashton had sufficient experience of filming, he was not at ease working unchronologically or against the clock. He did not attempt to choreograph especially for the camera, composing 'just as I would for the stage' and leaving it to Reginald Mills to work out the angles. What he enjoyed were the perks of film-making: the chauffeur at his disposal; the personalized director's chair; tea served to him in a silver pot; an inlaid table placed at his side. 'Fred was treated like a star,' said Alexander Grant. With Lord Brabourne, Lord Mountbatten's son-in-law, as the film's executive producer, there was an almost daily rota of grand visitors to the set, includ-

ing Prince Charles and Princess Anne, whom Ashton conspicuously monopolized. 'As soon as any member of the Royal Family arrived, we
would have to disappear, even though we might have been chatting to
Fred at the time,' said Tobin. And, although the cast were not invited to
the Royal Command Performance, for which *Tales of Beatrix Potter* was
chosen, Tobin derived some satisfaction from hearing that, when Ashton
was presented to The Queen, she told him her favourite part of the film
had been when Mrs Tiggy-Winkle runs across the meadows. 'And did
you tell Her Majesty that it wasn't you?' asked Tobin. 'No, of course
not,' Ashton replied indignantly.

It is Mrs Tiggy-Winkle who remains the film's abiding image – one
which became increasingly representative of Ashton himself. Congratulating him on his OM award seven years later, Mountbatten addressed
the choreographer as 'Mrs Tiggy-Winkle', and Britten and Myfanwy
Piper would refer to him as 'Fred Tiggy-Winkle'. In his old age, when his
teeth were causing him pain, Ashton frequently supped on hedgehog fare
of bread soaked in a bowl of milk, sitting in his kitchen at Chandos
Lodge, a replica of Mrs Tiggy-Winkle's parlour, with its scrubbed pine
table and painted plates displayed on the dresser. The resemblance was
not lost on Ashton: when Martyn Thomas begged to be allowed to mod-
ernize the room, he was firmly rebuffed. Mrs Tiggy-Winkle is undoubtedly one of the choreographer's greatest creations, an acknowledgement
of which is the tiny carved hedgehog on his gravestone. Yet he must have
known that, despite its popularity, the film, as a whole, was unsatisfactory. 'It *was* a success, wasn't it?' he urged Alicia Markova, when they
met one day for tea. 'Fred was in a terrible state,' she said. 'He hadn't received any money for the film yet and desperately needed reassurance.'
Although Ashton's version of Beatrix Potter's *Tales* achieves much of
what it set out to do, his gentle satire keeping any mawkishness at bay (a
balance aptly described by Lincoln Kirstein as 'avant-garde innocence'),
with no real outlet into which he can funnel his emotions the result is
somehow unfocused and diffuse. The fact that, by the end, the film could
be described as 'wearisome' is proof enough that he was not on form at
that time: boring an audience was one thing Ashton vowed never to do.

At a private preview of the film, Richard Goodwin introduced him to
a young colleague, Michael Rennison, a twenty-three-year-old assistant
stage manager at the National Theatre, who experienced 'an immediate
spark of recognition' on meeting Ashton. 'Before I knew what was happening, I was being invited to have dinner with Fred at Daphne's.' Notic-
ing how lonely Ashton appeared to be, Rennison was quick to assess the
situation. 'Fred was having a rough time with Martyn Thomas and I
seemed to fill some sort of gap in his life. Every now and then he and

Martyn would have a break from each other and Fred would find friends, usually young friends, to fill in.' Now that Thomas was tiring of his company, it was a relief for Ashton to discover that he could still captivate someone with his conversation. Passionate about the theatre, Rennison loved listening to him reminisce about his past, 'There was something so poetic and emotional about sitting in an ever-darkening room with Fred telling these wonderful stories. It made a tremendous impression on me.' Ashton was also grateful to find that Rennison did not intend to use their friendship to advance himself professionally. He may have had ambitions to work at the Royal Opera House, but he was determined to do so without Ashton's help.*

For the next couple of years they met once or twice a week, sometimes at Marlborough Street and sometimes for the ritual Sunday lunch at Alexander Grant's house in Battersea. Because there were very few buses on a Sunday and Ashton was reluctant to pay for a taxi, he would insist that they should walk there, one of several economy measures which took Rennison by surprise. 'We cooked spaghetti one night and I remember Fred saying, "Don't forget to count out the strands": a portion had to be exactly twelve strands each.' Unlike Thomas, however, he was amused rather than exasperated by Ashton's frugality, and, if anything, took his side. 'Martyn struck me as being a sort of a leech; and because I never wanted to be like that myself, I rather abhorred him for it.' Ashton, he found, was generous in other ways. 'He was an educator, a social educator who showed me areas of my life that needed to be improved.' Yorkshire bred, and rather unworldly at the time, Rennison admitted to having had 'a lot of rough edges which Fred gently and subtly sanded down. There were things he corrected that have never left me, infinitesimal things like the way I held my knife and fork, which probably wouldn't have any significance for anybody else but for me was mind-shattering. He was very much the instructor and I was the instructed.'

Rennison had always been drawn to older men; yet, while there was 'definitely a romance' between him and Ashton, their relationship was never consummated – the closest they came to physical intimacy was a naked swim in the new pool at Chandos. 'We talked about sex a lot, but it was something that didn't develop between us. There were kisses on the cheek but never a trip to the bedroom. But Fred seemed to quite like hearing about me going to bed with other people.' A mutual friend was a well-known opera singer, whose social life was 'much more notorious' than Rennison's, and who would sometimes accompany him to Marl-

*When, in 1975, they worked together on a farewell gala for Lord Drogheda, Rennison had already become a staff assistant producer in his own right.

borough Street. 'We'd go and see Fred and tell him what we'd been up to, which gave him rather a vicarious thrill.' It occurred to Rennison that, in addition to relishing his company, Ashton might have been using him as bait to recapture Martyn Thomas's interest. When the two young men were invited together to a Royal Ballet School performance of one of Ashton's ballets, Rennison detected 'definite jealousy' on Thomas's part. 'Fred may have been playing me off against him; I sensed an element of "I can find someone younger than you".' As far as Ashton was concerned, his relationship with Thomas was now reduced to a half-abstract, intense yearning. As he sat in the twilight with Rennison, Massenet's achingly sweet 'Meditation' playing in the background, it was Thomas alone who pervaded Ashton's thoughts.

The Massenet music was to be the score of a new pas de deux, *Thaïs*, a vision of unattainable love, named after the opera from which the six-minute symphonic intermezzo is extracted. Thaïs is a courtesan who later repents and enters a convent, and, although the ballet has no narrative as such, it hints at the Eastern, pseudo-religious eroticism of its source, the exotic colours of some movements imparting a flavour of the opera's luxurious Alexandrian setting. On her entrance, the ballerina (Antoinette Sibley) is mysteriously veiled. 'Anticipate with your *eyes*, something strange is arriving,' Ashton told her partner, Anthony Dowell, cast as a traditional poet-dreamer. Conceived as a vision scene, like the Shades act of *La Bayadère*, the ballet pays homage to nineteenth-century classical convention. Sibley appears on stage like an apparition and, when Dowell lifts her as if in a dream, she slips elusively from his fingers. Ashton wanted the ballerina to convey a sense of disembodied weightlessness. 'Push her on on on on, so it *flows* on,' he instructed, and Sibley bourrées past Dowell so smoothly that it is as if she is being pulled on a string. 'Fred wanted the float . . . The whole thing was a mystery and it all had to be done with silence and arms and wafting so you hardly were really there yourself.' *Thaïs* enacts Matisse's comment about the fluidity of Ashton's choreography, in that every step dissolves into the next. The smoothness enhances the illusion, and the sense of mystery is heightened further by the chimerical nature of Thaïs' identity. Who is this exquisite vision? Is she simply a dream? Like the music with its shimmering texture, *Thaïs* is a work of evanescent layers and allows no single interpretation. If Dowell represents the solitary figure of the artist, Sibley is an image of his muse, specifically Pavlova, whose spirit she recaptures in art-nouveau arms framing her face and moments of swooning abandon. Yet she also projects an earthy allure, seeming to be, at times, an embodiment of the opera's courtesan heroine and, in the recklessly romantic impetus of the choreography, also invoking Ashton's Marguerite Gautier. Towards the end of the duet, Thaïs plants a passionate kiss on her partner's lips, but then drifts away, returning to her original incarnation as an incorporeal ideal. The carnal–spiritual dichotomy not only recalls the Massenet source, it recapitulates the perennial Ashtonian division between sacred and profane love – 'reality and illusion, spirit and flesh, innocence and sexuality all tantalisingly blurred.'

Thaïs shows Ashton in complete control of his art. Its latent drama, gymnastic virtuosity and the grafting of Eastern motifs, such as a minaret-shaped port de bras, are never allowed to distort the classical line. He cast Sibley and Dowell because they were 'true to the text', as he put it, innately sensitive to the purity of the idiom. 'Fred created it for us as a very personal thing,' said Sibley. And, although the ballet's motivating force is autobiographical, its real subject the ephemeral nature of romantic love, there is no flicker of self-indulgence or self-pity. As Judith Mackrell has written, 'Ashton never strained after emotion, fantasy or sex. Yet these qualities are implicit in every step.' Despite its fragile length, the ballet – a masterly alchemy turning erotic feeling into art – was considered by Marie Rambert to be one of Ashton's three masterpieces (along with *Symphonic Variations* and *La Fille mal gardée*). When Nureyev first saw the *Thaïs* pas de deux, he turned to Fonteyn, sitting with him in the auditorium, and said, 'The bastard – he's done it again!' The ovation, unusually forthcoming for a gala audience, went on for so long that Ashton announced that the dancers would perform the whole piece again as an encore. There were one or two dissenting voices among critics who found the work hackneyed, but even Ashton admitted to being surprised by the enthusiastic response. All the same, its success did not spur him into producing anything more substantial. Still bitter towards the Royal Ballet, he would choreograph little more than pièces d'occasion for the next five years.

In August, Ashton went to Ramatuelle for his annual fortnight with Martine de Courcel. He travelled there, on this occasion, with Piers de László, the thirteen-year-old grandson of the society painter Philip de László.* After checking-in their luggage, although it was only 10 a.m., Ashton insisted on going straight to the bar where he 'more or less polished off a bottle of brandy'. Despite frequent cross-Atlantic journeys, he

---

*Piers's mother was Edith's great friend Rosemary, whose first husband was Peter Townsend.

had never lost a terror of flying, and, once having boarded the plane, grasped the boy's hand tightly until they landed in Nice. 'I remember being very upset that everybody would think I was off for a naughty weekend in the South of France with him,' said de László. 'I tried to look as macho as possible and winked at all the air hostesses.'

It was always a pleasure for Ashton to be reunited with Martine, who lavished affection on him. 'La tendre amitié que je vous porte et que chacun de vos séjours à Ramatuelle fait entrer plus profond dans mon cœur,' she told him in one of her letters. Late one night, they made a rash vow to each other to rise at dawn for an early-morning bathe. Woken by their alarm clocks, they dutifully staggered the 700 metres down to the sea, almost speechless with exhaustion. 'It's exactly like catching an early plane,' Ashton groaned. The beach was deserted until, suddenly, a beautiful girl emerged from the bushes and made her way towards an upturned boat, placing a piece of paper underneath it. The minute she had gone, they guiltily went over to the boat to examine the note, but found only two words written on it: 'Moderato cantabile', a musical term meaning 'at a gentle pace', as well as being the title of a novel by Marguerite Duras. 'Of course Freddie and I were thrilled by this,' said Martine. 'It was so enigmatic. We went again and again and looked under the boat but never found anything else there.'

Ashton was in noticeably good humour that week, performing Mrs Tiggy-Winkle's dance on the beach wearing fake-patchwork shorts and a large matching floppy hat. One night, he went out late with Martine and her husband to a restaurant, where a roistering group arrived still later and began spraying each other with soda syphons. 'We were getting slightly alarmed and thinking of leaving, when a chap came over and bowed in front of Freddie, saying, "Voulez-vous danser avec moi, monsieur?"' Without hesitation, Ashton got up and led the young man round the room in a spirited tango. 'It was the real thing, and the poor chap could hardly follow. He had no idea who he was dancing with and was amazed and absolutely exhausted by the end. Although he thought he was being funny, Freddie had made such a fool of him. But they sent us over a bottle of champagne after that.'

Although he and Thomas had parted on bad terms, an apologetic and affectionate letter arrived while Ashton was in France. 'I hope you weren't unhappy about me before you left,' Thomas wrote. 'It is just one of my silly mental blocks.' They were about to have a rare holiday together, staying in Ischia with the Waltons, visiting the ex-ballerina Violetta Elvin, in the small hotel she owned on the Naples coast, and ending up in Venice, where Ashton was treating Thomas to a few days in the Danieli. 'Long, long for Venice more and more, in the same way that I love you more and more,' Thomas told him. 'It's funny that you have to go away and be missed before I can say it.' Their time at the Danieli was to have been the high point of the trip, but, for Ashton, it turned into a nightmare. One evening, standing alone on the bedroom balcony, overwhelmed by the romantic beauty of the city, he looked down and saw Thomas disappearing along a calle with a young stranger. Ashton returned to London on his own. A colleague remembers coming across 'this pathetic little figure' at Venice airport, who admitted that he had 'been ditched'. 'I gave him six or seven double brandies and shoved him on the plane.' From that moment, according to a mutual friend, Ashton's relationship with Thomas was 'always on and off'.

It was on when Ashton took Thomas on a trip to Australia in February of the following year, off when they returned a month later. Ashton had been invited by Peggy van Praagh and Robert Helpmann, joint directors of the Australian Ballet, to stage *La Fille mal gardée* and *Cinderella*, in which he and Helpmann performed the Ugly Sisters. The dancers were struck by his kindness and calmness – 'certainly a contrast to the tense and often ruthless atmosphere we were used to' – but Ashton's equability was achieved against considerable odds. In Sydney he found himself having to appear in twenty-one consecutive performances of *Cinderella*, his exhaustion compounded by yet another setback with Martyn Thomas. Thomas had met a young Australian with whom he quickly became so infatuated that he invited him back to London, where the two of them were to live together in Rosenau Road for nearly a year. Although Ashton could not have foreseen the audacity of Thomas's duplicity, the rebuff he received in Australia was humiliating enough to prompt him to retaliate. In the past, while quite capable of running more than one affair simultaneously, he had always preferred attachments to passing encounters. He rarely sought out casual sex – in his position, he did not dare – although he admitted allowing himself to be importuned on one occasion by a guardsman who demanded his watch as payment for his services. 'I told him – wasn't this quick of me – that I knew his Commanding Officer and would get him to arrange an identity parade.' Unfazed, the soldier asked for some shirts (which Ashton gave him) remarking pleasantly as he left, 'I'd like to see you again some time.'

Two years short of his seventieth birthday, Ashton decided to prove to himself, as much as to Thomas, that it was not too late to seize the day. His quarry was Mark Brinkley, a good-looking first-year corps de ballet dancer whom he had spotted sitting in the wings during a rehearsal in Melbourne. Only eighteen years old and greatly revering Ashton, Brinkley was flattered by the attention, but embarrassed that he might be thought opportunistic by his colleagues. An ebullient and articulate per-

sonality, he was amusing company and quite prepared for the relationship to be physical. He and Ashton would go to the cinema and to restaurants, and talk for hours. Ashton knew that there was no question of
such a liaison being anything other than transitory; nevertheless, he could
not help investing it with all the trappings of a proper love affair, requesting billets-doux and photographs on his return to England, 'so I can
gloat over them'. However inconsequential it was in terms of his life, the
experience undoubtedly influenced his work. *Siesta*, a duet choreographed as a seventieth 'birthday card' for William Walton, was an indi-
rect reflection of Ashton's Australian encounter. With sunlight filtering
through a slatted screen, its setting is a sultry afternoon, during which
a bare-chested youth (Barry McGrath) and a young girl in a filmy skirt
and bra (Vyvyan Lorrayne) prepare to make love. Taking place on and
around a large mattress, the dance was 'by turns playfully acrobatic
and sensually entwining', its emphasis being on tenderness as well as
passion. It was Ashton's second attempt at this Walton piece, a wistfully
romantic miniature suffused with Italian warmth; the first, in 1936, had
been performed by Pearl Argyle and Robert Helpmann. The new version,
in David Vaughan's view, 'would have seemed rather shocking then', although he concedes that its eroticism is mild enough. The ballet was premièred in July at the Aldeburgh Festival, during an evening of Walton
works which included *Façade*. Ashton had also helped celebrate the composer's birthday on 29 March, when the Prime Minister, Edward Heath,
gave a dinner at Downing Street at which The Queen Mother was present, together with many of Walton's friends, including Henry Moore,
Kenneth Clark, Benjamin Britten and Laurence Olivier.

In August, while Ashton was having what was to be his last holiday with
the de Courcels in Ramatuelle, Martyn Thomas went to Mykanos in
Greece with Jimmy Hardwick, a pianist friend who, at the time, was renting a room in Rosenau Road. The island was fast becoming a mecca for
homosexual men and Thomas, according to Hardwick, 'had a ball there'.
By now, he was adept at compartmentalizing his private life, explaining
to friends, 'Fred is something else. He'll always be there.' But so were the
perennial problems between them. Ashton complained that Thomas was
'bleeding him'; at the annual Chelsea Flower Show, for instance, he
would order profligately, charging everything in Ashton's name. 'Sir
Frederick was very careful with his money and didn't want to see it
squandered,' Ashton's housekeeper, Mrs Dade, said defensively. From
Thomas's point of view, Ashton was irrevocably miserly and unapprecia-
tive of his efforts, fobbing him off with a £10-per-week allowance which

was doubled only after he had made a scene. Thomas's rages were becoming more frequent and more violent. 'When I first knew him you couldn't have wished for anyone nicer,' said Mrs Dade. 'The nasty side didn't come out until much later. There would be terrible rows if Mr Thomas couldn't get his own way. Sometimes I'd take his tray up to his room and couldn't get an answer, and Sir Frederick would tell me, "Mr Thomas got into a paddy last night and flew off to London."' 'Martyn could have *real* outbursts of anger,' confirmed a friend. 'And if he got into one of his moods he would shut himself into his room and not come out for two or three days. No one could talk him out of it.'

Ashton attempted to reconcile their differences. 'I do not think that happiness is based on material things,' he told Thomas. 'I will not fail you in these issues but I have to do them at my own time.' Cynically refusing to believe that the situation would ever change, Thomas started to take, 'by means fair or foul', what he felt was his due. He was by nature what his friend, David Cope, calls 'morally colour blind'. Early on, when he was working for Michael Caine, one of the actor's paintings went missing, kept by Thomas, Cope maintains, in lieu of payment. Caine still speaks highly of Thomas, although he remembers 'some kind of blot on the page'. 'Whenever Martyn was up to some evil,' said Cope, 'he was so funny about it that you couldn't hold it against him. He'd look for dollars he knew Fred had stashed away in a sock somewhere, saying, "He won't notice." "Oh yes he will," I told him.' Ashton was, indeed, aware that Thomas was 'always filching things,' as he put it, and told friends that Thomas was behind the disappearance of his Graham Sutherland and John Piper paintings as well as a set of Lila de Nobili's costume designs for *Ondine*.* But he was prepared to look the other way, perhaps realizing, as Moura Lympany said, that 'he could never repay what Martyn had done for him – he'd been the most wonderful wife to a man'.

As the 1970s wore on, Thomas's behaviour changed from youthful high spirits into something far more reckless. 'Martyn was over the edge,' said a friend. 'He was worried about his temper and became a much more haunted person.' When Ashton went to South Africa with Robert Helpmann in the summer of 1972, Thomas had filled Chandos Lodge with his friends. 'Hot sunny days & balmy knights', one of them reported on a postcard. He would dismiss Mrs Dade on a Friday evening, telling

---

*Although Ashton's legatee, Anthony Russell-Roberts, was dismayed to discover after his uncle's death that the famous silverpoint portraits of Ashton by Tchelitchew had been replaced with photographs (the whereabouts of the originals is unknown), according to Clement Crisp the choreographer was aware that the frames contained only reproductions.

her he did not want to see her again until the following Monday morning. '*How* many has he got in there?' her son asked, incredulously, one weekend. Neighbours heard rumours of a break-in; some of Ashton's Wemyss ware was broken, but nothing appeared to be missing. 'My opinion was that Martyn had a lot of people there and a fight must have broken out,' said David Ball. Thomas was also becoming increasingly aggressive towards Ashton, 'scaring the living daylights' out of Mrs Dade, who was concerned for her employer's safety. Always remorseful once the mood had passed, Thomas would send his usual letter, apologizing for his behaviour.

I am sorry that I shouted at you to the degree I did – I know how much it upsets you. Whatever I think about you it is stupid of you to suggest that I hate you. I wouldn't become so upset about the state of affairs if I didn't love you as much as I do . . . Small things bottle up inside me and I despair of ever doing anything at all that *really* pleases you. Whatever I do it is never enough . . . Please remember that the gossip that gets flung in my face has its origins with you. My behaviour has been far from blameless over the years but I have never said anything detrimental about you to anyone and I am sick of being cast as the villain of the piece. No villain would spend as much of his time doing things that are intended to make your lot a happier one . . . This does not excuse my abuse. I apologise for it. It solves no problems.

For all the unhappiness, however, a strong bond remained between them. 'I think Fred would have liked the relationship to work more than anything else.' When a young rival threatened to sever it, Ashton responded with melodramatic vengefulness. At Angus McBean's house, Flemings Hall, Thomas met a young farmer with whom he immediately began an affair. Ashton must have known about it because at a lunch given by a Norfolk acquaintance some weeks later, he was walking through to the dining room with the young man when he silently turned and slapped his face. Not a word was spoken by either. 'The next day I rang Martyn to say that I was sorry Fred had done this and sorry that I'd caused him to do it. But after that we went out of our way to avoid each other. I think we both realized there was some affection there and that it was all too dangerous.' Ashton had reacted with extraordinary prescience, somehow intuiting that this was the person to whom, eight years later, he would finally lose Thomas. He even blamed David Ball for introducing the two men. 'From then on there was quite a cooling off from Fred,' said Ball.

* * *

In the autumn of 1973, during the Australian Ballet's London season, Ashton was reunited with Mark Brinkley. He still felt a keen attachment to the young dancer. 'It is so curious how this sympathy exists between us on such a light acquaintance,' he told him. But, at the end of the evening, when Ashton took him upstairs to bed, he had to admit defeat: diminishing virility was but one of several oncoming symptoms of old age. His teeth were another problem – 'I'm fighting to keep what few I have but it is a losing battle,' he confided to Britten – and he found, during a tour of Brazil in the spring of 1973, that he could no longer take the late South American hours. Despite the stimulant of ecstatic curtain calls, sea bathes and doting rich Brazilian ladies, he returned to London 'more dead than alive'. Ashton had been invited by the Royal Ballet to join the company on their first tour of South America, a gesture of goodwill on their part, as he had made it quite clear recently that he was feeling 'put out to grass'. To a certain extent, this was self-induced, a martyred performance of what Martyn Thomas called his 'sad Fred act'. He had ignored many overtures made to him, one of which, overheard in the company canteen, was by Kenneth MacMillan, who failed not only in persuading Ashton to create a new ballet, but also in getting him to authorize a revival of *Symphonic Variations*. 'Fred told Kenneth that no-one in the company then was up to it,' said Deborah MacMillan. The remark, intended as a deliberate slight, had some foundation. Under MacMillan's regime, English classicism had already begun its evolution into the present-day Royal Ballet dance style, its purity replaced by what Arlene Croce calls MacMillan's expressionistic body language. Understandably, as a paradigm of English classicism *Symphonic Variations* was the one ballet that Ashton was reluctant to let go. 'It's too delicate. It doesn't work unless it's properly done.' On the other hand, still suspecting MacMillan of having colluded in his overthrow, Ashton went out of his way to make his successor's life difficult, 'whipping people up' against him. Some needed little incentive. When the new director took his company to New York for the first time in the spring of 1972, he was appalled by the hostility of an anti-MacMillan claque, who booed him and chanted, 'ASHTON! ASHTON! ASHTON!' at the stage door. One woman even followed the choreographer and his wife back to the hotel, making vomiting noises. MacMillan-versus-Ashton factions were in force throughout the 1970s and 1980s: to admire one choreographer seemed to presuppose hostility towards the other. And, having been enormously encouraging to MacMillan before he made his name, Ashton's attitude towards his younger colleague grew more petty and malicious with old age. 'Fred could be very naughty,' said Deborah MacMillan. 'Making sure that Kenneth was looking, he once curtsied to David Bintley [the upcoming young choreographer] and said, "You're the *only* one."'

Despite the frisson of satisfaction that Ashton must have experienced when reports reached him of his fanatical New York following, his spirits during the summer of 1972 were at a particularly low ebb. He grumbled that Martyn Thomas was treating him 'like something the cat brought in – I never get a word of thanks from him', and he was feeling lonely, old and neglected. Consequently, when Benjamin Britten arrived at Chandos Lodge to ask him to collaborate on *Death in Venice*, his new opera, Ashton agreed without hesitation. Aware that Ashton had not forgotten the initial difficulties he had experienced on *Albert Herring*, and that he had felt 'somewhat upset' at not being asked to choreograph Britten's full-length ballet, *The Prince of the Pagodas*, ten years later, the composer was 'frightfully excited' when he consented so readily.* 'You can't believe how thrilled I am at the prospect of working with you,' Britten wrote soon after their meeting, reiterating in another letter, 'Your collaboration has been for me one of the most treasured parts of the whole enterprise. I do need and want you so badly.' To be extravagantly courted again was exactly what Ashton needed, and, in October, Britten promised to fetch him from Eye and play him 'either the best or the worst music I've ever written'. In the event, owing to Britten's failing health, the opera originally planned for September 1972 was postponed until the Aldeburgh Festival season the following summer.

Completing *Death in Venice*, Britten's last large-scale work, proved to be a race against time for the composer, its fusing of creativity and mortality an ironic precursor of his own death three years after the première. Today's interpretation of the opera as a confessional treatise of Britten's 'Tadzio-orientated homosexuality' has intensified its autobiographical status, conferring upon it an importance which overshadows the work itself. For Ashton, too, Thomas Mann's novella contained intense personal resonances. Equating Venice with a debilitating infatuation, it not only brought back memories of his recent experience there, but he strongly identified with the character of Aschenbach, sharing his creative impasse, his idealization of male beauty as a spur to the imagination, and responding, most acutely of all, to the notion of passion as confusion and as a stripping of dignity, the essence of Mann's tale. The absurdity and

---

*Britten told Colin Graham that he had wanted to collaborate on a new ballet with Ashton but at the time, the choreographer had not been available. This was the reason he had approached John Cranko, the librettist and choreographer of *The Prince of the Pagodas*.

abjection to which Aschenbach feels himself reduced – caricatured by Visconti into a portrayal of a 'neurasthenic queen with a ready eye for a pretty face' – would have touched a nerve in Ashton, increasingly alert to the indignities of old age. 'Do I look absurd?' he used to ask, eyeing his blue jeans and sneakers, and referring to his appearance in later years as that of 'a desiccated old lesbian'. He understood only too well the anguish attached to an older man's obsession for a young boy, the surrender to a sexual love which destroys reason. It was a theme which his own final masterpiece would explore with even greater personal commitment.

Another reason Ashton was drawn to the project was that it reunited him with the artist, John Piper, the designer of *Death in Venice*'s romantic-realistic sets, with whom he had collaborated on *The Quest* exactly thirty years ago. Piper's wife, Myfanwy, also a friend, was Britten's librettist. It was her idea to present Aschenbach as a German Romantic caught up with the rediscovery of Greece. Tadzio was to be a reincarnation of Apollo, a stylized vision of Platonic beauty, the beach games with his friends transfigured into an Olympic Pentathlon. Although Britten found Myfanwy Piper's conception convincing, he was worried by a possible confusion in the audience's mind and initially wanted the role to be a singing one. 'Why not a counter-tenor – colder, not manly or womanly, & a sound that hasn't been used before?' But, as Tadzio never speaks in Mann's story – his impact is located purely in his appearance – it was decided to confine him to dance, a device that enabled the boy, his family and friends to exist on an entirely different plane of communication. Thus, as Desmond Shawe-Taylor has written, 'Aschenbach's failure to speak to Tadzio, in the natural way of friendliness, and subsequently to the boy's mother, to warn her of the spreading cholera, [is] due in part to his sense of guilt, but also to the fact that they inhabit different worlds.' Extending the Greek theme, Myfanwy Piper suggested that the boys should dance naked as they had in the original festivals of Apollo, an idea Britten thought excellent at first.

> [It] could be wonderfully beautiful, Hellenically evocative . . . your discovery of the bit in Hessian Tapestry makes it clear that in the 1910s no one worried about children bathing naked . . . There may be some objections – Fred Ashton might raise some – and I am worried lest the work might cause a certain interest that none of us really wants! Thank God the permissive society exists already.

Myfanwy Piper admits that, 1970s values notwithstanding, her proposition was 'pie in the sky'. 'Terrified of the opera being taken in the wrong way', Britten was nervous enough already, insisting on 'a towel for

Tadzio' during Aschenbach's Hymn and asking her to use the word 'built' rather than 'bent', which he had been told 'in the current jargon . . . is used for queer'.* 'We settled for bare feet, but it was an awful job to get them.' Like Colin Graham, Myfanwy Piper had hoped for a more avant-garde approach to the dance, but found that not only was the Royal Ballet School reluctant to allow its students on stage without their ballet shoes, but Ashton himself was playing safe. Their initial suggestion of a contemporary choreographer had been overridden by Britten, who liked to surround himself with a cocoon of friends when he worked. 'The thought of someone new horrified him,' said Graham. 'Ben was absolutely devoted to Fred and admired him enormously.' Attentive, as always, to Ashton's advice, Britten knew that his contribution would extend beyond the dance, helping to evoke a sense of period and atmosphere crucial to the success of the opera. The entrance of Tadzio, danced by Robert Huguenin, a recent graduate of the school, was 'wonderful', according to Deanne Bergsma who played his mother. 'The simplicity of it and the way it absolutely matched the music.' With his blond hair and sculptural physique, Huguenin made a striking impact, although Ashton was not as taken with him as his collaborators. 'Ben, Colin and Peter were all in love with this boy, but Fred thought he was inadequate,' said Michael Rennison, who was seeing a lot of Ashton at the time. 'He thought he was too old for Tadzio and too *knowing*.' Tadzio's solo was compelling, none the less, the eastern tinge to his port de bras enhancing Britten's Balinese vibraphonic overtones, his exotic soundworld for the boy. Otherwise, Tadzio's choreography was conventionally classical, which, despite his colleagues' reservations, was the most fitting idiom for a character embodying the purest perfection of form. Ashton devised a tender, restrained duet for the boy and his mother, but after the first season this was eliminated – apparently at his own suggestion. The Games of Apollo – running, the long jump, discus throwing, the high jump and wrestling – have always been the most criticized passage in the opera, one that begs to be shortened; but this, despite Ashton's pleas, Britten refused to do. The only concession he was willing to make was to 'snip out a bar here and there'. 'We were all aware that Fred wasn't at ease,' said Bergsma. 'He was uncomfortable working with the children and didn't go in for anything remotely creative or exciting. It was all very stilted.' Colin Graham believes that the composer would have reconsidered this section had he been more involved at the time. But Britten was too ill to attend rehearsals and effect the necessary revisions, and his colleagues were over-protective about the music in his absence. Myfanwy Piper now

*As in 'upon that all my art is built'.

admits that the Pentathlon was a mistake. 'I was wrong. It didn't work.' But if Tadzio's impact was diluted during the gymnastic dances – 'which can look embarrassingly like a prep-school sports' – Ashton's choreography for the postlude restored the boy's luminous, emblematic status. In the final scene on the beach, Tadzio is revealed as the messenger of Death, the Summoner god, Hermes, moving away from the dying Aschenbach with his back to the audience by sinking into a series of deep arabesques co-ordinated with ritualized slow swimming arms. The effect was hypnotic – 'absolutely magical', said Bergsma – and subtly reinforced Aschenbach's surrender to obliterating Dionysian forces symbolically associated with the sea.

Although Ashton was unhappy about the longueurs, Donald Mitchell considers his choreography to have been 'quite marvellous. I don't think any production has ever matched it.' Britten was also generous with his praise from the beginning, telling Ashton that his involvement had been 'the greatest encouragement and spur I could have had'. Although the composer was too weak to attend the first night, at a performance of the opera at the Edinburgh Festival two months later Ashton, Britten and Pears enjoyed a celebratory dinner. 'It was a jolly evening,' said Prue Penn, who was also there. 'Everyone was pleased with the way it went and in good form.'

That summer, for the first time in nine years, Ashton decided not to go to Ramatuelle – 'I'm too old. I can't travel,' he explained to Martine – and spent most of August at Chandos Lodge. Martyn Thomas, who had been to Mykanos once again with Jimmy Hardwick, came to Suffolk 'if and when it suited him', said Ashton. The weekend Princess Margaret dropped in with Prue Penn, bringing gifts of Staffordshire corn-on-the-cob jugs for Ashton's collection, Thomas happened to be there, working in the garden and sunbathing in nothing more than a thong. Like many of the choreographer's friends, the two women had never warmed to him. 'I think Freddie sensed it and wouldn't bring him over,' said Prue Penn. Cynical about Thomas's vaunting of his Lady Ashton status, Princess Margaret once joshed him at a Covent Garden opening, 'Good heavens – you're wearing more jewellery than I am!'

Ashton had become acquainted with The Princess in the early 1960s when he became director. Passionate about ballet, she loved watching behind the scenes, particularly when Nureyev was dancing, and 'Freddie was the one who always got me into rehearsals.' Both 'late bedders', they loved to stay up until the early hours. 'I took him home one night after a dinner party and he said, "Would you like to come in? It's very untidy."

It was only one o'clock and we sat there just drinking him dry till about 3.30. It was a darling little place, stuffed with treasures, but he was quite right. It was very untidy.' As Ashton rarely, if ever, reciprocated an invitation – 'I suppose one went to the ballet' – Princess Margaret, assuming that he 'liked people inviting themselves', asked him more than once if she could come for a weekend at Chandos Lodge. Ashton always prevaricated – 'I couldn't cope, you see'. The Princess was known for her exacting standards, and he did not have a cook or enough room in the house for her retinue – or so he claimed. One hot Sunday, Princess Margaret came to Chandos with her two children. Ashton had begged Alexander Grant to come up to Suffolk to help, and, obliging as ever and after combing London for fresh lobsters, Grant and his partner, Jean-Pierre Gasquet, prepared the lunch, while Madame Gasquet, Jean-Pierre's mother, made the mayonnaise. The afternoon was spent swimming in the pool and dressing up for group photographs, the Princess wearing a sundress and flowery hat, Ashton in Tyrolean garb, Grant in *Enigma Variations* tweeds, Gasquet in a Gatsbyish white suit, Thomas, with an impressive new beard, in the guise of a Lawrentian labourer, and the children sitting cross-legged in front.

The less Ashton saw of Thomas, the more dependent he became on the company of old chums. Billy Chappell would 'come and cook and complain', producing deliciously simple nursery dishes, such as boiled tongue and bread-and-butter pudding, which he protested had been ruined by Ashton's habitual refrain, 'Fuck the food. Let's have another drink.' Alexander Grant, increasingly becoming, next to Edith, the most important person in Ashton's life, drove to Eye for weekends whenever he was not performing, prepared the meals and clipped the topiary. Jean-Pierre Gasquet, who usually accompanied him, was understanding about Grant's devotion to Ashton. 'Freddie had a terrific affection for Alexander. He loved his integrity and the fact he always made himself available.' Ashton, of course, would have preferred to have Grant there to himself, but was always courteous to Gasquet, although he could not resist the occasional jibe behind his back. 'What has he been fingering this morning?' Ashton would ask Mrs Dade, referring to Gasquet's interest in his antiques.

In the early 1970s, Grant contemplated buying a place of his own in the country, a riverside property with mooring rights which had come up for sale in Taplow. 'Everybody had their country cottage by then: Brian Shaw, Michael Somes, Leslie Edwards . . . It was nine thousand pounds and I could have managed a mortgage, but instinctively I never mentioned it to Freddie.' He and Ashton were with a group of friends at a restaurant one night when the ballerina Georgina Parkinson leant across to Grant and said, 'Well, are you going to buy that house?' '*What* house?' Ashton asked sharply. Grant explained and Ashton said, in his frostiest tone, 'If you buy that house I'll never speak to you again.' When Grant was offered the directorship of the National Ballet of Canada in 1976, Ashton was bereft. 'Freddie said, "You know what I feel about it." But he wasn't going to stand in my way.'

It was purely through affection for Grant, who had recently taken charge of Ballet for All, the Royal Ballet's satellite group, that Ashton allowed himself to overcome his resentment towards the company and even join forces with Ninette de Valois on a programme entitled *World of Harlequin*, which Grant produced. 'Freddie gave me a letter that de Valois had written to him saying, "We must help Alexander." He did it for me.' Drawing attention to the influence of commedia dell'arte on ballet, the plan was for de Valois to 'do the character bits' and Ashton, the 'usual charming Freddie dances' for Harlequin and Columbine. It was not a collaboration as such – in fact, the two choreographers conspicuously kept away from each other. 'De Valois would *not* go near the rehearsal room when Freddie was choreographing.'

The harlequinade, like his other choreography over the next two years which included dances for a fashion show and a grand finale for the Friends of Covent Garden's Christmas Party, was not in any way significant. *Brahms-Waltz*, which followed in June 1975, promised to be yet another 'little something' for a gala, but, like *Thaïs*, it turned out to be a miniature of genius, exceeding all expectations, including Ashton's. The occasion this time was a homage to Nijinsky, staged by the Hamburg ballet, whose artistic director, John Neumeier, in league with Lynn Seymour, had 'winkled out' of Ashton a dance choreographed in the manner of Isadora Duncan, a major influence on Nijinsky's choreography. 'We were at a party together and both ganged up on Fred,' said Seymour, who performed the dance in Hamburg. It would be the first time Ashton had created a ballet on Seymour since *The Two Pigeons* in 1961. Anticipating that she did not stand 'the ghost of a chance' when Ashton succeeded de Valois as director, she had followed Kenneth MacMillan to Berlin, returning in 1970. Not only was Seymour MacMillan's 'property', but the two of them had been inseparable throughout the 1960s, working and playing together, sharing private jokes and a private language. Associating themselves with the upsurge of nouvelle vague cinema and the naturalistic, kitchen-sink style of Royal Court drama, they found Ashton's work old-fashioned. 'We were like college students – just kids.' He, in turn, was sceptical of MacMillan's uncompromising realism and disapproved of the ballerina's unconventional attitudes which culminated when Seymour, overweight and aggressively disillusioned with the dance establishment, turned her backside to the audience during a curtain call of MacMillan's slated production of *The Seven Deadly Sins*. By 1975, things had changed. MacMillan and his muse were now estranged – 'as Fred was well aware' – and, despite having recently given birth to her third child, Seymour had emerged from pregnancy, and a severe depression, slim and on top form, the dramatic resurgence in her career heralded that spring by an unforgettable performance in Jerome Robbins' *The Concert*. Not only was there no breach between them, but Seymour found working with Ashton after a ten-year gap 'very private, very cosy and unstressful'.

Wearing a Titian-coloured wig and a transparent wisp of pink chiffon, Seymour was to impersonate the heavy, middle-aged Isadora, whom Ashton had seen perform at the Prince of Wales Theatre in the 1920s. 'Keep your fingers crossed,' he told her, 'you know it might look terribly silly today, that sort of leaping around.' He did not intend to re-create Duncan's choreography – as several dance revivalists have done – but wanted, instead, to give a personal impression of her impact, merging his own memories with images from Isadora iconography. He brought Arnold Genthe's photographs of the dancer to the studio, line drawings by de Segonzac and Walkowitz, and a 'charming programme he had kept since he was a boy in Peru with petals he had watercoloured in'. It was Duncan's famous petal dance to a Brahms waltz, the inspiration behind 'the rose-petal hands, the loosely drooping fingers' of *Le Spectre de la rose*, that Ashton wanted to recapture. Seymour enacts the beginning of her solo exactly as he remembered it. 'She had her hands full of petals and as she ran forward the petals streamed after her. It sounds terribly corny but it was wonderful.' With her robust upper arms shaping a wide-open generous gesture, its solidity countered by a sudden frisky little jump, the dancer conveyed to perfection the paradox of Isadora's style: the plain, natural movements contrasting with surprising lightness and grace. The solo captured the very essence of Duncan's art: defiantly simple, using only a limited number of steps, it shows the way in which the dancer's magnetism derived not so much from movements themselves, but from her variety of accents, shifts of emphasis, and from her sheer conviction – the way she would suddenly hold a pose and fill the stillness with dramatic nuance. Through Seymour's intuitive understanding of Duncan's style, Ashton proves that this remarkable American pioneer, 'even when she was galumphing around . . . was still very impressive'. The solo was tumultuously received – a great surprise to Ashton, expecting, as usual, to be criticized for being retrospective. Writing to Marie Rambert, in reply to her 'warm & heartfelt' message of congratulations, he confesses his concern, but also hints that there could be more choreography to

come. 'The Brahms are so well known it might shock people by my ba-
nality in interpretation it's so out of touch with the trends of today &
your company would probably laugh at me in my old fashionedness! but
I do like them still & when God moves me & there is time, I might
plunge.'

Ashton extended the piece for a gala performance to celebrate the
fiftieth anniversary of Ballet Rambert in June 1976, making a suite of
dances entitled *Five Brahms Waltzes in the Manner of Isadora Duncan*.
Only eight minutes in length, it is a set of variations on Isadora's movements and moods: pensive, histrionic, revolutionary, whimsical. When
the curtain rises, Seymour is lying on stage in a pool of light, and, as she
begins to move, from her trailing hand you see that she is on a beach sitting in the shallows, tracing a line in the sand with her finger and playing
at knuckle-bones. The action of catching an imaginary pebble on the
back of her hand is turned into a balletic gesture of extraordinary beauty,
an example of the way Ashton has fused Duncan's style with an imprint
of his own. It is a symbiotic union. In the exultant pliancy of Seymour's
forward and backward movements, in the exaggerated yield of her upper
back and in the plastique of her port de bras you see that Ashton's debt
to Duncan is as momentous as that of Fokine and Nijinsky.

Before the gala, Ashton staged a private performance for Marie Rambert who had idolized the dancer. She was in tears by the end, exclaiming,
'That's exactly what I remember, Fred, it's quite amazing.' But Seymour's
contribution was vital. As Arlene Croce has written, 'Lynn Seymour
the actress, the performer of epic daring, but most of all Seymour the
dancer . . . has always possessed the roundness and fullness of contour,
the plastic vigour, and the coherent rhythm to express the sculptural
depth that Isadora's dancing must have had.' Five years later, when Kenneth MacMillan choreographed *Isadora*, his full-length ballet based on
the dancer's life, he overlooked Seymour and cast the quail-boned Merle
Park in the role. It was, Ashton said, 'the biggest mistake of his career.'

The acclaim Ashton received for the original *Brahms-Waltz* was a
much-needed boost, which provided him with the confidence and incentive to tackle *A Month in the Country*, his first important work for eight
years. He spent much of his summer holiday in Brazil, where he arranged
a pas de deux, 'called no less than "The Forest of the Amazon"', for the
fifty-seven-year-old Margot Fonteyn – 'Not too easy for me as I have to
adapt my choreography to suit her present capabilities and avoid all look
of strain.' He found himself the focus of attention at every grand gathering – 'one seems to be kissing all day' – and was somewhat overwhelmed
by the ostentatious warmth and wealth of his hostesses, describing them
to Martine de Courcel as 'rich ladies loaded with jewels in bad settings.

On the whole they are just rich, very kind but not interesting with few exceptions.' He was disappointed with Rio itself, which, apart from its wonderful surroundings, looked much the same as any other international city – 'Everywhere is the same now, noisy & hideous. I wanted to see parrots, monkeys & giant butterflies and orchids hanging from every tree . . . Dali once said to me it was useless to travel, one could always imagine it much better oneself!' By the end of the trip, several weeks of South American social hours had taken their toll: he was exhausted, although sustained by the thought of someone eagerly awaiting his return.

Tony Dyson, a young architect passionate about every form of dance, had declared his admiration for Ashton when they had met at a party shortly before the trip. 'Tony was an idolater,' said Jean-Pierre Gasquet. 'He was very eager to see more of Fred.' Presumably at Ashton's urging, Dyson gave him a set of photographs of himself to take away on tour. With long wavy hair, and a sensual mouth eccentrically framed by a thin circular moustache and beard, he was a striking-looking young man, louchely dressed in a half-open shirt and skin-tight hipster trousers. To begin with, according to Ashton, the relationship was highly charged. Nicknaming Dyson 'the Machine Gun', the choreographer was both flattered and slightly taken aback by such unprecedented attention, which happened to coincide with Thomas's admission that he could no longer continue their physical relationship. It was Dyson's nature to be generous and altruistic, at all times considerate to Ashton's needs. 'Tony was utterly unselfinterested and did everything through affection for Fred,' said Anne Renshaw, while their mutual friend Anne Reid agrees, 'He's incredibly nice and thoughtful and helpful, while not exactly at Fred's beck and call. Tony never lost his identity and went on with his own work.' Endearing himself to Ashton's immediate circle, Dyson soon became a frequent guest at Chandos Lodge. 'He just arrived one weekend with the others, and then started coming down regularly,' said Mrs Dade. 'He was so likeable. He didn't want to be a bother.' Ashton did not attempt to conceal Dyson from Thomas; on the contrary, friends were surprised by the ease with which he 'negotiated these two people in his life', taking them both to the ballet, on one occasion, when 'they all seemed to be smiling'. Aware of Dyson's growing importance in Ashton's life, Martyn Thomas felt at the same time threatened and relieved. He was reluctant to see his position being usurped, but was grateful to share the responsibility of looking after Ashton.

It was around this time, whether or not through fear of losing Ashton altogether, that Thomas made another attempt at suicide. One day, Jimmy Hardwick came home to Rosenau Road earlier than usual and, finding Thomas's bedroom door suspiciously locked, burst in and was able to get him to a hospital just in time. Thomas had staged an overdose of Valium into a mise en scène 'aimed at Freddie', with Ashton's letters strategically placed around the room. It was the usual plea for attention; but if, in Thomas's case, it had been prompted by a sense of rivalry, then this proved to be misjudged.

Although Dyson did, eventually, assume the role of Lady Ashton – at the choreographer's side on foreign tours and on first nights – after the passionate beginning of the relationship, Ashton never came to regard him as anything more than an agreeable and devoted companion. 'Fred wasn't in love with him,' said Edith, an observation confirmed by Ashton himself. 'Tony has certainly been the nicest to me – no question about that. Really marvellous to me. But by that time, I wasn't . . . mad.' Thomas never relinquished his hold on Ashton, who, even in his eighties, while waiting for him to arrive at Chandos Lodge, would get up from his chair repeatedly, in order to gaze expectantly out of the window. His friends continued to shake their heads over 'why Freddie put up with the Puppy when he knew all about his seedy side'. Why should someone famously intuitive about character fall victim to such an 'unscrupulous' partner? Thomas, it is true, was good for Ashton in many ways. 'It bolstered his confidence to be seen in the company of this handsome young man,' said John Tooley. And, apart from his practical help – 'without Martyn, Chandos would have fallen to pieces' – he could be relied upon to admonish Ashton about his work. 'He was always anxious that Fred's reputation shouldn't slip and Martyn made him sit down and get on with it. He would *bully* him into it.' But of most importance is the effect Thomas had upon Ashton's art. Just as T. S. Eliot's widow, Valerie, once said of Vivienne, his first wife, 'She made him suffer and we got *The Waste Land*', we owe *A Month in the Country* to Martyn Thomas. It is Ashton's depiction of an erotic passion that annihilates reason, his admission of the intoxicating elixir of youth.

Turgenev's play, about a young tutor who disrupts the emotional stability of a provincial Russian household, had long appealed to Ashton. Its subject of old and new love, all unrequited, was one with which he could always identify; now, it had come to relate to his own life with extraordinary symmetry. The production he first saw in the 1930s was third-rate and melodramatic, and he must have realized then that dance could offer a unique means of conveying the novelistic aspect of the play: the way it discloses by subtly changing nuances the psychological secrets of the characters. During rehearsals of *Enigma Variations*, he discussed the project with Julia Trevelyan Oman and commissioned her to design it, but, at this point, he had not yet found the right music. A conversation with Isaiah Berlin, translator of *A Month in the Country*, helped Ashton to decide.

Although not close friends, these two great characters were always pleased to see each other.

> Whenever we met, it worked beautifully. Freddie always made a beeline for me and embraced me – La Russe-fashion: three kisses right, left and right again. This was really very melting and I was frightfully pleased that he was always so nice to me. He said, 'The thing about you is you're authentic. You're *echt.*' Well, that is one of the nicest things anyone has ever said to me. On this particular occasion he said he was thinking of doing a ballet of *A Month in the Country* and I asked what the music was to be. 'Oh Tchaikovsky, I suppose,' and I said 'No, no, Chopin is much more suitable for Turgenev who is non-Tchaikovsky in every way. The quality of feeling is very similar, the lyricism, the wistfulness is true of them both.' Freddie didn't need to be persuaded; he took the idea up at once.*

In fact, Ashton had reservations about using Chopin, concerned that Jerome Robbins had 'already picked him over'. But a recording of the early works for piano and orchestra, played by Claudio Arrau in chronological order, at once gave him the idea of how the ballet might work. 'It could have been written for me: he even gave me music for opening the door. And for shutting it.' The integration of action and music was carried out in the Wemyss room at Chandos Lodge with Martyn Thomas. 'I always felt that the time around *A Month in the Country* were some of the best days of their relationship,' said his sister, Jennifer Mellors. After years of feeling undervalued, Thomas was to be rewarded with a formal acknowledgement of his assistance. Although the ballet's dedicatees are Sophie and Nijinska, Ashton thanks Thomas in the programme for helping him 'to construct the ballet to accord with the music'. 'That was the least Fred could do. Martyn really put a lot of work into *Month.*' The arrangement of the score has always been attributed to John (Jack) Lanchbery, who, at Ashton's request, came over from Australia, where he was musical director of the Australian Ballet. 'Lanchbery sort of takes the

---

*Arlene Croce has pointed out that the clue to the music is provided in the stage directions, which describe Vera, Natalia Petrovna's young ward, playing a Chopin Mazurka on the piano, but this appears only in the version by Emlyn Williams.

credit,' said Ashton. 'But I actually worked it out sitting here with Martyn Thomas. We spent *hours* doing it and handed it to him. The only thing Jack did was that he brought back a tune at the end where [the tutor] comes back.'* Although his contribution was more fundamental than Ashton's remark suggests, Lanchbery admits that 'to a considerable extent *Month* was handed to me on a plate. I had the job of making the seams not show.' If this is the case, the collaboration between Ashton and Thomas was a profound achievement – particularly as both men were instinctive, rather than trained, musicians. In her scholarly essay 'A Month in the Country: the Organisation of a Score', Stephanie Jordan describes the use of music as 'remarkable . . . for the score that Lanchbery [*sic*] has fashioned not only clarifies structure but preserves intact the flavour of Chopin's music'.

Friends of Tony Dyson, however, attest to the fact that he also helped with the music. Evidently, Ashton was constructively two-timing, requisitioning them both to feed his ballet, much as he had done with Brian Shaw and Michael Somes during the making of *Symphonic Variations*. Lanchbery describes 'Tony being around and me thinking secretly, I'll put my money on him,' while the dancers remember 'Martyn in the studio for some of the mime scenes. Fred would get him in to see if it made sense.' It was Dyson who prepared a supper of scrambled eggs and smoked salmon on the evening that Ashton invited Lynn Seymour to Marlborough Street to discuss the ballet. 'I had heard rumours about *A Month in the Country*. Was it possible . . . ? I dressed with extreme care. I hoped to look a little grand with a hint of Russian.' The role of Natalia Petrovna, the beautiful, bored wife who becomes enraptured by her son's young tutor, required a mature ballerina: Beriosova had been Ashton's first choice, but she had recently retired, and Antoinette Sibley, whom he also considered, was pregnant at the time – fortunately, as it turned out, as Seymour was the perfect choice. No other interpreter has ever captured so convincingly the gradations of the heroine's mercurial nature: winningly girlish at one moment; unlikeable and devious, the next. Natalia is a manipulator, a belle dame sans merci, who ruins the life of her ward, Vera, because they are in love with the same person. Capable of orchestrating several dramatic layers at once, Seymour could convey Natalia's public persona, her brittle charm and guile, while her yearning port de bras and the rapt arches of her back exposed her emotional submission.

*Lanchbery cut short the Polonaise and returns to material from the Variations and Fantasy, reusing the theme from Mozart's *Don Giovanni*, 'La ci darem la mano', which opens the ballet.

Ashton took Seymour and the rest of the cast to see a production of the play which was running in London, with Dorothy Tutin in the lead, and he encouraged her to research the subject as he had. Rereading *Anna Karenina*, whose story of ruthless adulterous passion coincides with that of the play in several ways, helped to define the portrait of Natalia, but it was the chamber works of Turgenev, not the epic sweep of Tolstoy, that profoundly affected the ballet. The depth of his affinity with Turgenev came as a revelation to Ashton. Both were artists saturated with femininity, whose creativity was inspired by their own experience of what Turgenev called 'l'épanouissement de l'être brought about by love'. Both were considered old-fashioned by their contemporaries, because their art was not weighted with world issues; love was its motivating force and their philosophy on the subject was the same. 'Turgenev believed that love is never equal,' said Isaiah Berlin. 'There is always one who loves and one who is loved.' Turgenev's depiction of the agonies of unreciprocated passion was like a palliative to Ashton, a vindication of his own enslavement to Martyn Thomas. Even the indignity of physical abuse, which he had tolerated during their altercations, is condoned by Turgenev. 'How could one bear to be struck by any hand however dear,' ponders the young hero of *First Love*. 'And yet, it seems, one can, if one is in love.' *A Month in the Country* was also a confessional work for Turgenev. His portrait of Rakitin half caricatures his own romantic servitude to the opera singer Pauline Viardot, trapped like Natalia Petrovna in a secure but loveless marriage. In Ashton's version, it is the heroine, rather than Rakitin, with whom he identifies. 'I am fairly well, fairly happy, fairly unbalanced and mostly bored,' he wrote to Hans Werner Henze during one of his long summer months in the country, his 'taedium vitae', in Turgenev's term, corresponding to his heroine's lethargy at the beginning of the ballet.

The curtain rises on a family scene in the drawing room, designed by Julia Trevelyan Oman as an airy, elegant milieu, with a classic Russian vista of silver birch trees outside. Turgenev's card-players have been eliminated – as Balanchine famously decreed, there can be no mother-in-laws in ballet – allowing Ashton to concentrate on the interplay of emotions among the four central characters. 'I avoided all the characters who were simply talkative and brought nothing to the plot. I swept them all aside.' Arlene Croce, the ballet's most dismissive and yet most eloquent critic, considered the elision of Turgenev's subplot to be a reduction rather than a distillation of the play – a criticism with which many would disagree. Peggy Ashcroft told Ashton after a performance that she thought his version was better than the original; and Brian Friel, who himself composed a very free adaptation of *A Month in the Country*, loved Ashton's ballet.

'That he could reach into the heart of the plot and retell it so eloquently without even one syllable of language erodes even further my wilting confidence in words.' Few would argue that certain omissions, such as the attempted courtship of the maid, Katia, by Herr Schaaf, the German tutor, are a great loss. However, Ashton admitted that, in attempting to compress his ballet from five acts to under forty minutes, he had nervously cut too much. While rehearsals were in progress, he was to restore several passages.

A mood of oppressive summer lethargy is established from the beginning, when the only member of the cast moving across the stage is a footman carrying a tray of drinks. Vera (Denise Nunn) is playing the piano in an adjoining room; Yslaev, a wealthy landowner, reads a newspaper; and reclining on a Recamier sofa, his wife, Natalia, lazily fans herself, with Rakitin (Derek Rencher), her admirer, sitting at her feet reading to her. Rakitin is a non-dancing role, a composite of Rencher's Elgar and the Father in *Marguerite and Armand*: a shadowy, inert figure, denied the ironic vitality he is given in the play. He serves mainly to focus attention on Natalia, whose first solo is intended as a throw-away diversion for him, and which briefly elevates her ennui. It is, as Seymour says, 'a foxy little number', constructed from speedy changes of direction and impossibly intricate footwork, the 'knit one, purl one' patterns visually referring to the lace-makers whom Natalia identifies with Rakitin, isolated in gloomy, airless rooms.

Vera's variation immediately follows, youthfully staccato and Dorabella-like, her legs and arms working in tricky counterpoint, as in a playful backward gallop with circling port de bras. Glimpses of growing maturity are expressed by Vera's mimicry of Natalia's pronounced épaulement, but the audacious expansiveness is not there: pliancy is supplanted by perkiness; drifting, conversational port de bras, by well-drilled classroom precision. The role was an exciting début for Denise Nunn, a young dancer whom Ashton, at Seymour's suggestion, had picked from the corps. 'Fred loved her the minute he saw her. Those feet and the way she just looked the period. She surprised everyone by her wonderful acting and her sincerity.' Ashton consciously duplicated the situation in his source by appointing Seymour as a guardian to Nunn. 'He put me in charge of her; she had big spongy insteps like mine and I was able to help with her shoes and look after her.' He also attempted to re-create the hermetic intimacy of the play by keeping the cast, several of whom were old friends, 'locked up together' in the studio, and refusing to allow understudies to attend initial rehearsals.

The allegro pace of the first two solos is interrupted by a pas d'action, a domestic drama which may be based on a passing reference to lost keys in *First Love*. (The novel had provided Ashton with several other behavioural details, such as a young man bowing with a click of heels, and the token of a rose placed in the buttonhole of his jacket by his love.) The key episode is absurdly farcical, with characters bumping into and leapfrogging over each other, crawling on the floor and being lifted out of the way, but the tedium is deliberate, intended to show the stifling pettiness to which Natalia is subjected. Like George Eliot admitting, in *Mill on the Floss*, that she has deliberately inflicted the dreariness of Maggie Tulliver's life upon her reader, Ashton takes the calculated risk of allowing his audience to experience the family's irksome routine for themselves. A spirited dance with a ball by Natalia's son, Kolya, soon gets things moving once more, created by the impish Wayne Sleep, whose natural ballon and showpiece beats are wittily exploited. Minutes later, Kolya plays Cupid, shooting an imaginary arrow at the hapless lovers on stage. A dramatic ritornello brings an abrupt change of mood; the stage darkens and a sudden breeze stirs the curtains.

The heightening of expectation by a billowing curtain is an old theatrical trick used by Ashton for his elaborate curtain calls, when he would pitter-pat his hands along the velvet to create a flurry of anticipation before he emerged. Beliaev's first appearance is a coup de théâtre which 'could have been insinuated with greater subtlety', in Peter Williams's view. Yet, even though there is no precedent for such a build-up in the play, Ashton is only being true to Turgenev, for whom love, as V. S. Pritchett, has written, 'is like some brief summer whirlwind or storm that sweeps through his people and transforms them'. As the tutor stands on stage with the kite he has brought for Kolya, a muffled rumble of thunder is heard, just as it is in *First Love*, when the boy realizes that he is in love. For a few seconds, all the cast freeze on the spot, like the hero of *Spring Torrents*, 'too amazed to move' when he first sees the beautiful Italian girl. *The Sleeping Beauty* had taught Ashton how to stage a climax: the roll of drums that stirs the blood during Aurora's Rose Adage is Tchaikovsky's version of Turgenevian thunder. More crucially, the tutor's entrance along the back of the stage, from left to right, deliberately invokes Aurora's: in *A Month in the Country*, the sort of fanfare accorded to the ballerina, by right, is transposed to the young hero – 'the sole triumph of the ballet', in Arlene Croce's opinion. (Ashton even considered naming his ballet *The Student*, after Turgenev's original title.) In homage to his muse, whose identity is brazenly signposted by Anthony Dowell's oddly unbecoming strawberry-blond wig – 'Martyn had recently had his hair dyed bottle-blond' – Ashton's portrait of Beliaev is a glorification of 'attractive, vital, vigorous, wild, reckless youth'. By drawing on Thomas' own attributes, but transposing them into heterosexual terms, the choreographer amplifies Beliaev's allure and relish of his own attractiveness, and he becomes, as Croce says, 'almost criminally responsive to women – all women'.

> In the play, he is not a lover but the object of love. Ashton has interpreted him as an unconscious Don Juan – the Don Juan of whom Kierkegaard wrote, 'To see him is to love him' . . . Dowell partners three women in turn – Natalia, Vera, and (in a scene that builds very effectively on a passage in the play) the maid Katia (Marguerite Porter). He is different with each of them – he is *her* Beliaev – but Ashton has made us feel that he is really committed only to Natalia, and Turgenev's ambiguity in this regard is swept aside.

Although Ashton was establishing a private point, it was not wishful thinking on his part. For all Thomas's philandering over the years, he always maintained that Ashton was the most important person in his life. Realizing the extent to which the drama played out on stage corresponded to his own life, Ashton was prepared to manipulate his source in order to achieve even closer similarity. To him, the four main players were all aliases. If Beliaev represented Martyn Thomas, then Rakitin, 'the most gentle and the most considerate and the most understanding. And . . . so permanent', was Tony Dyson, someone on whom Ashton, although not in love with him, depended. Ashton signals the identification of Vera with his own young rival, Thomas's Norfolk friend, by inventing a key incident. After discovering her in the arms of the tutor, Natalia Petrovna slaps Vera's face, a shocking moment in the ballet which exactly re-enacts Ashton's retaliatory slapping of the young farmer. Although he did not confide these aspects of the psychodrama to his cast, Ashton made no secret of the self-portraiture in Natalia. 'He kept relating to her,' said Lynn Seymour. 'Saying things like, well, I'm over the hill now too.' He particularly loved to demonstrate a moment in the ballet when, alone on stage, Natalia feels someone grasp her shoulders from behind. Believing it to be Beliaev, she visibly lights up, only to slump with disappointment seconds later, realizing that it is only Rakitin.

In the duet that follows, Natalia goes through the motion of dancing with Rakitin, but her reaching arm, which he then tightly folds against her, says more about their love triangle in a few seconds than several pages of Turgenev's play. Dance, which takes us beyond language and into the soul of a character, is the ideal medium for *A Month in the Country*, where, as Brian Friel has written, 'the action resides in internal emotion and secret turmoil not in external events'. Vera's quivering instep as she is held aloft by Beliaev betrays her infatuation without the need for words. In the eloquence and variety of each of the ballet's pas de deux,

Ashton has surpassed himself. These are the artefacts of a master craftsman. And rarely in ballet has there been such a swift, seamless transition
from romantic dance passages to interludes of mimed narrative – 'from
poetry to prose, as it were.' Although he did not plan it that way, Ashton
found himself borrowing a Mozartian structure of arias and recitatives,
and this operatic framework, combined with the declamatory style of
some of the Chopin pieces, led him to alternate his delicate, Stanislavskian
approach with episodes of high melodrama (a prime example of which is
Natalia's histrionic exit through double french doors).

The mime sequences are not the only ones to be played fortissimo.
The final duet between Natalia and the tutor is danced with such all-out
abandon that it verges on the parodic. *A Month in the Country* is yet another tribute to Pavlova, whose presence is manifest in Seymour's semi-
camp, silent-movie-star swoons, deep plunges, rhetorical flourishes of
arms, and exposed swan neck. There is also a direct quotation from
Ashton's own *Romeo and Juliet*, when Natalia interlaces arms with
her lover's, first one way and then the other. Their dance climaxes with her
being tossed through the air; Ashton then tempers the passion with a dying fall – a low, rotating, hardly breathing lift, in which the sculptural
curve of Seymour's Pavlovian insteps are lingeringly displayed. By now,
the duet appears to be over; realizing the extent of her folly, Natalia has
torn herself away from Beliaev, only to be irresistibly drawn back. In a
coda of extraordinary beauty, she allows herself to be propelled forward
by him, meandering from side to side as she bourrées, her arms softly undulating like ribbons of water weed. It is one more example, in Ashton's
work, where a moment of utmost simplicity is invested with ineffable
power. The bourrée is a step that makes no claim to virtuosity – its effect,
as Lynn Garafola has written, is psychological. 'In its weightless driftings
the body seems both shorn of its volition and afloat in timelessness.' Ashton uses it here as a symbol of spiritual freedom, articulating Natalia's
trance-like state of altered reality, her dreams of leaving.

The theatricality of Seymour's interpretation owes its inspiration to
Turgenev's opera-singer model, Pauline Viardot. Natalia behaves like a
spoilt diva, self-dramatizing and affected, her true feelings divulged sub-
liminally in isolated, give-away gestures, or in impalpable half-tones of
expression. Seymour's face as she sat stroking Vera's head after the girl's
confession of her love for Beliaev, exposed Natalia's real thoughts. For
Arlene Croce, however, the subtlety of Seymour's performance was
swamped by the insincerity. She saw Seymour's 'new false image of a
grand tragedienne' as a travesty of everything that had made the ballerina
great. 'She's becoming a flamboyant actress, but neatened up, as if she
couldn't bear to bloody herself as she used to in her wonderful mad
scenes.' Her final scene, Croce felt, 'dashes pathos on the rocks of senti-

mentality'. This is an epilogue in which, unseen by Natalia, the departing Beliaev returns at the last moment to kiss the long blue ribbons that trail from the back of her peignoir. He leaves behind the rose she had given him; finding it seconds later, she realizes too late that he has been there. The rose falls to the ground and, raising a hand pensively to her face, she walks towards the audience as the curtain falls.

The source for this interpolation has provoked almost as much conjecture among critics as Elgar's cryptic tune in *Enigma Variations*. Mary Clarke attributes it to the ending of *Le Spectre de la rose*, which, at Ashton's request, Karsavina had twice mimed for him. Ashton himself maintained that his source had been a book of theatrical memoirs by Graham Robertson.* Hamish Hamilton had sent it to him in the hope of persuading him to write his own autobiography.

> There was a lot about Ellen Terry, Sarah Bernhardt and all the people of that period and in it he described the end of a play where this happens. I liked the idea of it and I put it into *Month in the Country*. I never told anybody and dear old David Vaughan was determined to find out. He'd read . . . God knows what and he wrote to me about that and I said, 'Well, what a strange coincidence.'

Vaughan had suggested, at Alastair Macaulay's prompting, a passage from Edith Wharton's *The Age of Innocence* as a model. In her novel, Wharton describes the parting of the lovers at the end of a performance of Boucicault's play *The Shaughraun*, an account which fits Ashton's closing scene almost exactly.

> She rested her arms against the mantel-shelf and bowed her face in her hands. On the threshold he paused to look at her; then he stole back, lifted one of the ends of velvet ribbon, kissed it, and left the room without her hearing him or changing her attitude. And on this silent parting the curtain fell.

When Vaughan later quoted the extract in person to Ashton, the choreographer maintained that he had never got round to reading *The Age of Innocence*, although he had always meant to. However, as no such episode is recounted in the memoirs of Graham Robertson, the mystery of its source must remain.

To Arlene Croce, those two blue ribbons symbolized the failure of the ballet: 'its decline into fussiness and artificiality.' But it could be argued that there is a real point to the frou-frou. As Seymour comes on stage for

Time Was: The Reminiscences of W. Graham Robertson.

this scene, the peignoir ties are draped over her arms in the shape of wings. In a plaintive solo, Ashton's last ribbon-dance, she invokes the boy in *The Two Pigeons*, whose trussings of rope were similarly transformed into images of flight. Earlier in *A Month in the Country*, the kite flown by Kolya in breath-catching circuits of the stage had acted as an imaginative release from the emotional claustrophobia; so, too, the ribbons are used here as an emblem of escape. Far from being confectionery, they are weighted with dramatic resonance. When Natalia, desultorily confronting her fate, allows the two ribbons to fall off her shoulders, the action has the same sense of valediction and tristesse as when Beliaev releases them at the end of the ballet, metaphorically letting her go.

The London première of *A Month in the Country* was ecstatically received and the ballet was considered, as Mary Clarke wrote, to be 'the work of a genius'. The ovations were as much a personal tribute to Ashton as an appreciation of his achievement: a welcome back after so long an absence. The ballet's existence signified a rapprochement between the choreographer and his company, and acknowledging this, a grateful telegram from MacMillan spoke for them all: 'Your ballet is exquisite. Thank you for doing it.' For Ashton, the responsibility of making the work had been a tremendous ordeal; more superstitious than ever, he had insisted on wearing the same pair of trousers for every rehearsal and a bunch of Brazilian charms round his neck 'to ward off ill luck'. He need not have worried. As his good friend Alastair Forbes wrote in a note of congratulations, 'You may lose erections but not yet inspiration.' There were more 'lovely ovations' in New York, where Clive Barnes's review was headlined with the eulogy, 'Ashton Could Be Our Greatest Choreographer'. And there were other rewards to come. A new obsession was beginning to take hold of Ashton which, for once, had nothing to do with unattainable love.

On 8 February 1976, a few days before the first night, Ashton had been invited for a musical evening at Royal Lodge, The Queen Mother's weekend retreat in Windsor Great Park. He and Queen Elizabeth were no strangers to each other, having met many times over the years through mutual friends, and at suppers in the ante-room of Covent Garden's Royal Box.* Nevertheless, Ashton was apprehensive about the occasion, although cheered by the fact that Elizabeth Cavendish, whom he liked very much, had offered to give him a lift. They had been friends for over

---

*Although Ashton made a point of insisting that he had never sought the friendship of The Queen Mother, he did in fact make the first move. In November 1935 Lydia Lopokova reported to Maynard Keynes, 'Fred wrote a personal note to the Duchess of York to come to his first night [*Valentine's Eve*], what an aplomb! and she answered very nicely that unfortunately she had a public dinner.'

thirty years, after being introduced during the war at a ball given by the Duke and Duchess of Marlborough. Elizabeth, a débutante stuck with dreary people at the Dorchester and despairing that she would ever find anyone she wanted to get to know, had been enchanted by Ashton. 'Suddenly meeting Freddie was just wonderful for me.' They danced together, 'charlestoning like anything', Ashton wearing his Air Force uniform, and they had kept in close touch ever since. When Elizabeth took him home to Chatsworth, Ashton had been immediately smitten by her mother, the Duchess of Devonshire – 'He loved people who belonged to the Edwardian past and she adored him. He always said he would chuck anything to go there.' But Ashton valued Elizabeth's integrity and lack of affectation more than her grand origins. He found her an endearing and original character, down-to-earth and dog-loving, her clothes and her car seats habitually covered in Jack Russell hairs. And later, when Ashton was far more assured in royal circles, he would still seek her out. 'If we were somewhere like Buckingham Palace he'd come and find one and stay with one and hold one's hand. He'd feel safe then and we'd go round together. He loved it all but he was always frightened of going. Always very tense before he got there.'

The Queen Mother is also, according to Isaiah Berlin, 'a famous putter-at-ease'. 'She's so easy to talk to and full of life and spirit and she enjoyed all Freddie's stories,' said the Dowager Viscountess Hambleden, one of her ladies-in-waiting. Ashton was evidently such a success with The Queen Mother that evening at Royal Lodge that it was not long before he was invited there again, this time as a houseguest. The weekend of 25 June 1977 proved to be the first of many, when he would arrive at about six on a Friday evening and stay until after breakfast on Monday. He loved the 'very cosy and very comfortable' ambience of Royal Lodge, while its Gothicized 'pink birthday cake' appearance was exactly to his taste. 'It was all wonderfully easy,' said Ashton. 'She knows I won't come down for breakfast, so breakfast was brought up. The food is very very good and the Martinis are *wonderful*.' Weekends at Royal Lodge were informal and bohemian. Apart from musical entertainment, there might be readings by an actor, such as John Gielgud, or a poet, often John Betjeman, who, along with Ashton and David Cecil, were considered the founding fathers of the Royal Lodge set. Not surprisingly, Betjeman and Ashton, both national treasures, much appreciated each other's company: 'John thought Freddie was wonderful and he loved John,' said Elizabeth Cavendish, who was Betjeman's close companion in his latter years. If she were unable to drive him to Windsor, Ashton would often be ferried there and back by Martin Gilliat, The Queen Mother's private secretary, a former Colditz prisoner with a stoop 'like a half-closed penknife', or by her woman of the bedchamber, Ruth, Lady Fermoy, a beautiful woman, with a cloud of white hair and heavy-lidded Dietrich eyes which her granddaughter, Princess Diana, has inherited. Ruth Fermoy was Queen Elizabeth's closest friend, beloved for her matter-of-fact Scottish manner, her warmth and exceptional musicianship. 'The Queen Mother loved Ruth for the same reason that she loved Freddie so much,' said Margaret Douglas-Home. 'They have a lot more to them than the social façade.'

As the organizer of the King's Lynn Festival in Norfolk and animatrice of The Queen Mother's late-July house party at Sandringham, it was natural that Ruth Fermoy, who had grown as fond of Ashton as her 'boss', should include him among the guests. Regulars were the Duke and Duchess of Grafton, Sir Hugh and Lady Casson, Prince Jean-Louis de Faucigny-Lucinge and a handful of devoted retainers. Built by Edward VII when he was Prince of Wales, Sandringham stands in 20,000 acres of windswept parkland, a labyrinthine construction comprising 365 rooms. And yet, as The Queen's private property, not a state-owned house, in which the Royal Family and their friends gather to celebrate Christmas holidays, it still manages to retain a homely atmosphere. Ashton found Sandringham 'grand but cosy – like staying in a comfortable country house'. With carpets worn in places and nothing conspicuously new, its design typifies the understated elegance that he loved.

His routine at Sandringham hardly varied from year to year. He always enjoyed the Flower Show in the grounds, where he would head straight for the stall selling jars of lemon curd. There were visits to Norfolk churches and National Trust houses, and concerts at the Festival in the evening. 'You never feel uneasy. You can go to church if you want to and not if you don't.' A picnic in a log cabin in the woods behind Holkham Sands was the highlight of his stay. Given to the Royal Family by Lord Leicester, on whose estate it stands, the cabin is little more than a hut with a large balcony situated about twenty minutes' drive from Sandringham and a stone's throw from the beach. Queen Elizabeth and her guests would set off in several cars, and a large picnic basket would follow, delivered by her footmen. All her staff and security men then withdrew, leaving her to potter about, playing house. Rather than Glyndebourne-style crystal glasses, silver cutlery and cruets, out of the hamper would come stripy picnic cups, plastic plates and Tupperware containers of 'absolutely delicious food', such as egg and lobster salad, which The Queen Mother laid out on a simple Formica table. She is in charge, like a theatre director orchestrating her group, and guests must maintain a balance between not obviously wanting to be served by her, and not rushing forward and helping too much. 'It's very informal and everyone grabs things from the table for themselves,' said Neiti Gowrie, another sympathetic woman friend in whom Ashton liked to confide. In the afternoon, the party could bathe or, as it was usually raining, don waterproof hats, coats and sturdy shoes, and join their indomitable hostess for a walk. As the path through the pines leads directly to a nudist colony, there were always 'tremendous jokes going on', even though detectives had usually set off ahead to instruct stray naturists to cover up.

More often than not, Ashton was among those who chose to stay behind in the hut after lunch, drinking, smoking, talking and snoozing. Indulged at Sandringham just as he was at Royal Lodge, he would get up 'frightfully late – the only gentleman to have breakfast in his room' – and was always the last to go to bed at night. Out of good hostmanship, a courtier was elected to keep him company. 'One sat up and chatted,' said Ralph Anstruther, who admits he was not remotely interested in ballet, but would listen with interest to Ashton's stories about life in Peru. Although the group were 'pretty geriatric', evenings at Sandringham could be lively enough. With the energy and fun of a woman in her twenties, The Queen Mother – 'a great enjoyer of things' – would champion after-dinner games and entertainment. On Sunday evenings, Hugh McKenna, one of the guests, might sing Victorian songs, Ruth Fermoy was usually asked to play the piano, and it became a ritual for Ashton and Queen Elizabeth to lead the dancing. Guiding her round the room in a sedate and graceful tango, Ashton found his partner 'wonderfully malleable and lyrical', while she, in turn, loved the way he cast her as a romantic heroine, an image their mutual friend Cecil Beaton had perpetuated in his early portraits of the young Queen Consort radiantly backlit, with tiara and tiers of diamonds. Ashton always encouraged Queen Elizabeth to wear her jewels and was known suddenly to kneel at her feet like a cavaliere servente, exclaiming, '*Magistée!*' – a gesture which, although tongue-in-cheek, was underscored with real veneration and awe. His South American upbringing had instilled in him a deep regard for ceremony and tradition. 'He loved the idea that they went back in history,' said Elizabeth Cavendish. 'He found that thrilling. It was more than snobbery.'* Old friends were more cynical; Billy Chappell, for example, began referring to himself as Last-Resort-Chappell, claiming that Ashton saw him only when he had nothing better to do. It was true that

---

*Knowing that Ashton longed to ride in a carriage, Prue Penn's husband, Sir Eric, arranged for the Crown Equerry to take him on a dawn rehearsal for a state visit. Despite his aversion to getting up early, he eagerly rose at 4 a.m. and made his way to Buckingham Palace, from where he rode through the empty London streets.

the choreographer was becoming increasingly drawn into the company of his grand friends. Meeting him at a dinner in the 1980s, Selina Hastings was taken aback by the intensity of Ashton's class obsession. 'Darling, *you're* all right,' he told her. 'You're an earl's daughter.' He had even begun affecting aristocratic vowel sounds, saying 'awf' instead of 'off'. 'I've caught it,' he admitted. 'But I don't say "cawf" [cough], "frawst" [frost], "lawst" [lost].' The aesthetic appeal and comfort of upper-class life was more irresistible to him than ever; but even so, as Isaiah Berlin points out, this did not brand him as a snob.

> Freddie was liked and taken up by a large number of socially prominent people. He didn't resist it, but I'll tell you why I don't think he was a snob. There are various definitions of snobbery. In Proust snobs are people who see people in terms of presentability: could I introduce X to Y. To David Cecil snobs are people who think of others not in terms of what they are but what they stand for. If you find yourself sitting next to a rather boring Duke and very interesting writer, you would still prefer to talk to the boring duke. Well, in neither of these senses was Freddie a snob. He liked being made much of like everyone does . . . He was gay – in every sense – he was charming and had a delicate and extremely sharp wit. He liked society, he had an acute sense of the ridiculous and he told stories with great charm and point, and that pleases society. People like people who amuse them. He was taken up not because he was a wonderful choreographer or a great dancer, but because he was delightful. He sang for his supper and I think he knew this. But he enjoyed the supper very much too.

Unwittingly echoing Berlin, Ruth Fermoy remarked how critical Ashton could be about certain people in society. 'I've seen him be frightfully bored with a duchess who didn't interest him. He was really quite choosy. But in my lifetime, I've never known anyone with his capacity to live in different groups of people and enjoy and feel at home in them all.' 'Freddie wasn't snobbish but he liked the company of grand people,' said Martine de Courcel. 'I think we decided together that when you've seen everybody in all milieux, les gens du monde are the more pleasant.' Ashton seemed most comfortable with what the Countess of Gowrie calls 'the Top of the Pops upper class – people like the Devonshires and the Cecils. If someone whom he thought boring came and sat next to him his face would fall like a child's.' Ashton was always alarmed by the idea of having to talk to the Duke of Edinburgh and claimed to be absolutely terrified of The Queen. With a manner far more formal than her mother's, and lacking the gift for putting people at their ease, The Queen's arrival at Sandringham filled him with dread. As one guest said, the temperature would drop at least twenty degrees. 'I never knew if Freddie was as frightened of The Queen as he pretended to be, he was a tremendous actor,' said Hugh Casson. 'His line was that he was overawed by her presence. But it was an *assured* tenseness.'

With Queen Elizabeth, however, Ashton was in his element; they were, as a mutual friend put it, 'absolutely each other's cup of tea'. Contrary to her sugar-plum-fairy image, she has what Casson describes as 'this streak of strong granite and a sharp edge. Fred was caustic and she liked that.' Both were gifted with the common touch and shared an indomitability of spirit, a legacy from the war years. The Queen Mother's famous remark when Buckingham Palace was bombed – 'Now I can look the East End people in the face' – comes to mind in her page William Tallon's description of an evening at Covent Garden, during which there was a bomb scare and everyone in the building was evacuated – all except Ashton, who sat alone in the Crush Bar, later remarking to The Queen Mother, 'I've lived all my life amongst these bricks and mortar. I'm going down with it.' 'Quite right,' she replied. They were old troupers recharged by public acclaim, who had developed more than a touch of self-parody in their personalities over the years. The Queen Mother's favourite stance, with her winsome tilt of the head and hand posed in a static 'royal wave', was gently caricatured by Ashton in his curtain calls, a parodic composite of HM, Pavlova and himself. She, in turn, has perfected an imitation of him, mimicking the way he would put his head in the air, purse his lips and peer down his Sitwellian nose. They frequently entertained each other with all manner of impersonations. 'We giggle and occasionally we talk French – "Oh non, mais c'est impossible!"' And as much of a bond as their sense of humour was their fondness for 'zonking Martinis', which The Queen Mother relished. 'Her control – by God. She never has too much. Her discipline is so terrific.' Ashton loved to enact The Queen Mother's little shudder of pleasure as she took the first sip of her gin Martini, one plump hand placed upon her chest.*

Although Queen Elizabeth and her circle found Ashton to be completely relaxed, he confided to close friends that he could never be spontaneously funny: there was always a barrier of propriety to be observed. Yet, even though courtiers like Martin Gilliat were constantly refilling his Martini glass, he managed to remain comme il faut, while still being wonderfully entertaining. It was a deft balance: to seem himself and yet keep his bawdy side – particularly his sailor's tongue – well in check. 'It's difficult to be amusing and not go too far,' said Clarissa Avon. 'He told me there had been a terrific frisson once after he said something to The Queen Mother like, "Did you love him?" and he realized he'd gone over the mark.' 'By and large he was perfectly behaved,' said Princess Margaret, 'although he could take great exception to people. He was always hissing to me in a corner, "I can't *bear* so-and-so."' When Ashton asked Ruth Fermoy why he kept being invited back to Royal Lodge, her reply delighted him: 'Because you fit in.' Ashton not only had great charm, he had an unassuming quality which was most appealing. 'In conversation and behaviour Freddie was the least pretentious man,' said Neiti Gowrie. 'If you live in a world like she does, there is a lot of artificiality and so she really appreciates people like Freddie who are very direct.' His humility, as always, was part genuine and part cultivated. He was careful never to take his privilege for granted – 'I never *presume*' – and he continued to be nervous about correct behaviour, frequently consulting Queen Elizabeth's page on matters of etiquette. But he liked to draw attention to the fact that he, 'little Freddie Ashton from Lima, Peru', could have arrived in such elevated surroundings on his own merit. It was an act of mock-submissiveness that he played in front of several people, including The Queen.

Ashton also fitted in because he could be trusted. 'To my certain

---

*The combined joys of Martinis and Ashton's company were celebrated by The Queen Mother in two jocular verses which she and Ruth Fermoy composed in the helicopter after a particularly enjoyable visit to Prue Penn's house, Sternfield, 'c. 1978', when Raymond Leppard and Benjamin Britten were also among the company.

Lament
As we rose to the skies
With tears in our eyes
We gazed at those left below,
At Prue and Ray
And Ben and Fredday,
Our hearts full of woe.

Scherzo
But there the welcome basket stood
To put us in a merry mood,
Martinis for us all to share
In glasses made of Aldeburgh ware,
With loving care each item packed
So not a single thing thing was cracked.

Our sorrow thus was gently healed,
Into the clouds our heli wheeled
And on to Windsor fast we sped . . .
A really spiffing day, 'twas said.

knowledge he saw all sorts of things that were quite all right but wouldn't bear repeating,' said Elizabeth Cavendish. 'They knew he would never betray their friendship.' However close Ashton became to The Queen Mother, he remained suitably in awe, addressing her as 'Ma'am', as all her friends do, 'and dropping in the occasional "Your Majesty"'. He never appeared to push himself, although it amused the Royal Family that if ever he were invited by Queen Elizabeth to stay on at Sandringham for a few more days, unlike other guests who would politely decline, anxious not to outstay their welcome, Ashton would always agree without a moment's hesitation.

He was soon included among the innermost circle, a small group of friends who met every year on 4 August to celebrate The Queen Mother's birthday. Martin Gilliat, 'a great theatre buff', chose the entertainment, often a drawing-room comedy or a musical – provided there was nothing risqué about it. 'It's not that she minds,' said Ashton, 'but if anyone on stage says "fuck" or anything, the entire audience looks up at her to see her reaction.' Ashton could be hard to please on these occasions. 'He was quite critical,' said Ruth Fermoy. 'He'd put on a certain face and you'd know he wasn't enjoying it.' They would meet at Clarence House for smoked salmon and scrambled eggs before they left for the theatre; afterwards, they would go back to Ruth Fermoy's flat in Eaton Square for a lobster supper. At a round marble table, The Queen Mother would sit with her back to an eighteenth-century Brussels tapestry, Ashton always on her left.

In 1977, the choreographer received a letter from The Queen's private secretary, Lord Charteris, asking him to accept the Order of Merit, the most distinguished honour in British public life. When William Walton opened his notification of the award, he burst into tears.* For Ashton, it was the ultimate recognition of fifty years' achievement and he was inundated with celebratory messages. 'You will be the brightest star in the galaxy of OMs,' Ann Fleming wrote to him. 'The dancing and the dancers you inspired were the greatest because of your profound understanding of love and sorrow and the human predicament, youth, old age, fun and laughter. To confine it to the laws of ballet is indeed genius.' Peter Pears also sent his congratulations on Ashton's new initials. 'I like to think that you have inherited Ben's & how happy he would be!' But most

---

*A gift from the Sovereign, the OM, of which there are only twenty-four living recipients at any one time, is a reward for outstanding service in the fields of art, learning, literature and science.

gratifying of all was the note that arrived from The Queen Mother, jauntily illustrated in her own hand.

My dear Sir Frederick,

I do want to send you a line of my very warmest congratulations and hoorays on your receiving the OM.

Everyone is delighted, and when one thinks of your glorious ballets and when you have put our English ballet on a pinnacle [little sketch of ballerina poised on mountain peak] one is full of gratitude and so thrilled that your genius has been acknowledged in this way.

I am, ever yours,

Elizabeth R

The OM service took place in the Chapel Royal, St James's Palace, in November. Prue Penn, then living in Stable Yard, collected Ashton from Marlborough Street, made him lunch and, after the ceremony, 'like his nanny', dropped him back home. Nerves and his hiatus hernia meant that he had not felt like eating anything all day; uncharacteristically, he had not drunk anything either. His OM status – like his role of unofficial courtier – was something that Ashton took very seriously indeed. He was now a grand old man, laureate to the Royal Family, as the next decade would affirm, and he was proud of the fact that he had always maintained what he called 'a clean slate'. He had every intention of keeping it as such. 'If young Apollo came to see me now,' he said, 'I'd give him a drink and send him away.'

CHAPTER EIGHTEEN

BUGGER OLD AGE
1976–1988

With expectations raised by *A Month in the Country*, Ashton devotees waited for more inspired late pressings from the master. He may have been in his seventies, but, as David Vaughan pointed out, at his age Petipa was yet to create *Swan Lake*. Instead, Ashton sunk back into 'Old Turkish Lady' lethargy. He was persuaded by Nora Kaye to choreograph a solo piece for Herbert Ross's film, *The Turning Point*, but he seemed more attracted by the perks involved than by the prospect of working with the dazzling young American ballerina Gelsey Kirkland (who was to appear with Mikhail Baryshnikov in a thinly disguised subplot about their love affair). 'He just wanted to be put up in a hotel of his choice and have lunch and dinner paid for every day,' said Ross. 'Pounds of caviar for lunch and endless Martinis and champagne.' Ashton's encounter with Kirkland was precarious from the beginning. One of the most gifted performers of her generation, tormented by destructive love affairs, and battling against drugs, anorexia and bulimia, she weighed a mere 80 lbs. when she worked with Ashton. She tried to blame her lack of energy in rehearsals on a potassium deficiency, but, with barely disguised derision, Ashton told her that he thought potassium was something that you put on the garden. Kirkland soon withdrew from the film (to be replaced by Lesley Browne) and Ashton's simple, fluent dance to a Chopin étude was seen only behind the credit titles.

Ten years later, when Kirkland performed Aurora with the Royal Ballet, the choreographer was struck by her delicately nuanced interpretation – 'She's a star, there's no doubt about that' – but he remained sceptical about her self-indulgences and he debunked the searchingly analytical approach to dance that she had developed. Hearing how she had asked about 'the motivation' for a particular lift, he said that he would have told her, 'Because *Petipa* put you there.' They met backstage afterwards and, although Ashton was immediately complimentary – 'No one has done what you did with this ballet in years' – Kirkland felt awkward with him, knowing that he remembered their *Turning Point* experience. She intended this performance of *The Sleeping Beauty* to have been her last appearance as a dancer, but a meeting with Ashton a few days later was to change her mind. She and her husband visited him in Marlborough Street, where he launched into his familiar repertory of reminiscences, beginning with his early impressions of Pavlova and ending with an impromptu lecture demonstration in which, with extraordinary conviction, he portrayed glimpses of Natalia Petrovna, Aurora and Carabosse. Kirkland was suitably impressed. By the end of the evening, she had not only promised to return to Covent Garden to dance in a planned revival of *Ondine*, but had also volunteered herself as Ashton's apprentice, with her husband offering to be his chauffeur to and from the rehearsal studio. (When the time came, to the Royal Ballet's disappointment but no great surprise, Kirkland abandoned the role of Ondine as she had developed tendonitis.)

From 1976 to 1979, Ashton produced nothing more than divertissements for various galas, including the engaging trio *Tweedledum and Tweedledee* (for Wayne Sleep and Graham Fletcher, with Lesley Collier as Alice), a typical Ashtonian piece of nonsense to two of Percy Grainger's 'Morris Dances'. To celebrate Margot Fonteyn's sixtieth birthday in May 1979, he choreographed a tactfully sedate, ingeniously evocative solo, *Salut d'amour*, to music by Elgar. In a pensive mood, as if reliving her past, Fonteyn rises from her chair and fleetingly recalls keynotes from her roles in some dozen of Ashton's ballets – evanescent, immediately identifiable images. Although she is almost marking the steps in her mind, like a dancer in the rehearsal studio, Fonteyn's projection of small, understated effects is arresting. The impact comes from the expressiveness of her eyes and port de bras, from her identification with the music and from her radiance – a distillation, in fact, of the qualities that made her great. At the end of the piece, Ashton joins Fonteyn on stage, linking her arm through his and leading her into a gentle 'Fred Step', as he escorts her into the wings. 'Sentimental, yes,' wrote Alastair Macaulay, 'but also history of a remarkable kind.' The picture of a great artist leading his muse off the stage was a perfect ending to their extraordinary collaboration, although Ashton would have been among those attuned to a more cynical analogy. At this point in her career, mostly owing to financial considerations, Fonteyn had shown little sign of retiring, although she had ceased to perform in full-length ballets – in a week or two, she was to dance with Nureyev at the Coliseum. Many years earlier she had made a pact with Ashton that he would tell her when he thought she should stop dancing. 'But of course when the time came, she made it impossible for me to say anything.'

Ashton also celebrated a landmark birthday that year, his seventy-fifth, which was honoured by a tribute on BBC television, and a Royal Opera House gala a few weeks later, with a party in the Crush Bar. 'All tedious to me. I don't like all this glorification of old age.' He appeared to be in good spirits, cutting his three-tier cake with a joke about the inch of his cigarette ash quivering over the icing; in fact, ever since the summer Ashton had been in a state of great distress. His sister, Edith, victim of a sudden stroke, had recently emerged from a coma, but remained bedridden and unable to speak. 'I can think of nothing else,' he wrote to Martine de Courcel, explaining why he had felt unable to visit her in August. 'I am very upset and would be an uneasy guest . . . As you get older the unexpected shocks one.' Edith, then living in Ireland with her third husband, had been working in her garden when, with no warning, she collapsed to the ground. This had proved to be a mild stroke, slightly impairing her speech, but a second near-fatal attack occurred during her hospital stay in Dublin. Her son, Anthony, was with her when she sat up with staring eyes, rigidly grasped his hand and fell back on to the pillows, sinking into a coma which was to last over two months. Ashton came to Dublin almost immediately, making a tremendous effort to try to communicate with her, but it was no good. Desperately morose, he spent much of the two days drinking in a smoky bar near the hospital. Soon after his return, he rang a faith-healer friend, Anna LeGallois, whom he and Edith had both been seeing regularly for over ten years. Like her brother, Edith had great faith in healing; but, whereas she could be sceptical about certain aspects, his own belief was unquestioning. 'Fred had an amazing faith in God. It was like a child's: innocent and pure.' Although Edith was still unconscious at the time, Anna LeGallois went to see her in Ireland, at Ashton's request. 'Rather than her being left paralysed, I think Fred would have preferred her to have gone. He was very very distressed.'

Edith had got to know Harold Grenfell in Norfolk. He was an ex-Naval commander, who had made a fortune dealing in Rhodesian copper and lived near by in Burnham Thorpe. When Grenfell's wife died of leukaemia, he and Edith became extremely close, and (with Martyn Thomas's assistance) she helped him to decorate a Georgian house he had bought in Wexford – 'There's no doubt that she was feathering her nest,' remarked Anthony Russell-Roberts. The discovery that her husband had been having an affair threw Edith into the arms of Grenfell almost immediately. 'It was quite a romance,' said Lady Sylvia Combe, a neighbour. Like all Edith's friends, however, she felt very sorry for Douglas

Russell-Roberts who, despite events, was desperate to win back his wife. In addition to their marital difficulties, he had lost his job, but Edith was too committed to Harold Grenfell to stand by him. After much resistance, including threats of suicide, Douglas finally agreed to a divorce. Soon afterwards, however, his sad life came to a abrupt end when he was fatally injured in a car crash while motoring in France. Filled with remorse, Edith had wanted to say goodbye to Douglas as he lay blinded in an English hospital, but Harold had dissuaded her. A fortnight later, Douglas was dead and Edith attended the funeral alone.

For Ashton, his sister's latest marriage had been as unsatisfactory as her previous two. Grenfell was a 'madly conventional, anti-art type', who was not sufficiently appreciative of Edith; not only that, but he was infuriatingly mean with the drink. Clobemon Hall, his estate near Enniscorthy in Co. Wexford, was an idyllic milieu, with its salmon river, green hills and lovely walled gardens, but Ashton dreaded visiting her there. 'Even before Edith's stroke, he'd have a miserable time,' remarked Billy Chappell. Occasionally, Ashton would persuade Kenneth Clark's daughter, Colette, a great friend of Edith's, to accompany him. Partners in adversity, they would smuggle whiskey into their rooms and after many conspiratorial winks during dinner, meet later, '*Pent up* with Harold's philistinism.' Edith, however, had seemed happy at last; and loved her days doing little else but tending the garden – 'Busy pricking out 500 antirrinums etc', she wrote to Ashton that spring. 'Have 5 plants of the zygocactus you gave me . . . Did you put the kingcup in?' They had grown closer over the years – physically closer, too, with the same large hooded eyes and piercingly wry expression. Like her brother, Edith chain-smoked but did not inhale, and she was also a great flirt with strangers, with a tendency towards exaggerated self-deprecation – 'I'm just a boring old woman,' she would sigh in later life. Above all, they shared each other's sense of the ridiculous and when together became grown-up schoolchildren, collapsing in giggles and delighting in rude private nicknames – 'Miss Fuck-Hole' for a local lady taxi-driver with a prissily pursed mouth, Chuncha (a Peruvian peasant) for Edith and Chancho (a pig) for Ashton. On a bus, for example, sitting behind a woman in an elaborate hat, they spent the journey spluttering as they tried to pull out a feather or hat-pin unnoticed. 'When the lake at Chandos was finished,' said Anthony Russell-Roberts, 'they got into the boat to row out to the middle and something started to amuse them. They became absolutely hysterical and ended up falling into the water and swimming to the island. Covered in mud they just sat there, carrying on and on giggling.'

To see 'darling Chuncha', his lucky charm, robbed of her vitality and sense of fun was devastating to Ashton, who knew that things could never again be the same. After being transferred to St Thomas's Hospital in London, Edith made a dramatic recovery – 'They woke her up. It was amazing' – but she remained paralysed and dependent on round-the-clock nursing at Clobeman Hall. Although her speech was impeded, her mind was alert and she suffered dreadfully from boredom, eagerly awaiting Ashton's visits. For him, however, it was an ordeal he found increasingly hard to bear.

A welcome distraction that year was a reunion with the *Beatrix Potter* team to make another film, *Stories from a Flying Trunk*, freely adapted from Hans Christian Andersen's tales. Ashton was involved only with 'Little Ida', the story of a small girl rebuked in her dancing class for having as much grace as a vegetable, who then dreams about a vegetable ballet. The choreography is wittily graphic – chaîné turns, for example, that plump out the crinoline of Choux Rouge, or a curly flourish of arms in Fifth Position that mimics the heads of Céleris – although less successful is the mock-heroic episode in which a potato realizes his dream to dance with a beautiful princess. At its best, the ballet shows the Chardinesque Ashton at work, making something out of nothing, and it also takes advantage of his genius for impersonation. Although the film itself is slow-paced and banal, the dancing is amusing enough to stand on its own. *Pas de légumes*, as it was entitled (a double entendre, referring to the recent closure of Covent Garden market), was later extracted and performed by the Sadler's Wells Royal Ballet with moderate success.

Ashton now found himself under pressure to produce something more substantial. 'Princess Margaret came to me and said, "You must do something for Mummy's 80th birthday" which also happened to coincide with Baryshnikov insisting that he would only dance with the company on condition that I did a ballet for him. So with a gun held at my head and the Queen Mother's birthday, I pulled out the plugs.' The result was *Rhapsody*, named after Rachmaninov's 'Rhapsody on a Theme of Paganini' and made as a showpiece for Baryshnikov. Although this was the first time the dancer and choreographer had created a ballet together, Ashton was not as intimidated as he had been with Nureyev some twenty years before. They had got to know each other when Baryshnikov had danced as a guest artist with the Royal Ballet in the autumn of 1975, occasionally meeting after a performance at the Carlos Place flat of Terence Benton and his Russian wife, Packly Bicat – ardent ballet fans and friends to many dancers, including the famous Kirov defectors.

After a matinée of *Fille* at four or five o'clock Fred and I used to go back to Packly's apartment. He loved the way she cooked clear consommé for him with caviar and vodka. He always said I don't need anything else. A bottle of vodka and he was fine, his memory was excellent. I learn a lot of things first hand – all these stories he told about Nijinska, sitting on the edge of the divan. Always very composed. Twelve hours later we'd put him in a taxi.

Although Baryshnikov, in Ashton's view, had been '*marvellous*' in his 1977 *Fille* début, the dancer's experience of being pushed by the choreographer into increasingly complicated steps was a foretaste of frustrations to come. As a performer driven to explore new aspects of his art – or, as he put it, 'extend the spectrum of my presence' – Baryshnikov had hoped that the new work would reveal an undiscovered side of himself, and that, by dancing with the Royal Ballet, he would have the chance to learn the language of a new school. Instead, Ashton recast him in the role for which he is most identified: his Soviet bravura role. 'I was a bit disappointed; I wanted English ballet and he wanted Russian ballet. I was trying to escape from all those steps.' But, for Ashton's purposes, they were vital. *Rhapsody* shows Baryshnikov, one of the greatest virtuoso dancers of his time, embodying a balletic equivalent of the amazing feats performed by Paganini, the devil's fiddler. The violinist's medley of tricks – the dramatic leaps, brilliant runs, violent eruptions and double-stops – are personified by Baryshnikov, who hurtles through his technical catalogue, with 'not one skid, lunge, kick, or convoluted air turn' left out. His opening series of bows to the audience, turned into an enchaînement of increasing variety and virtuosity, is both a pun on 'Paganini bowing' and a reminder of the gala occasion (every member of the Royal Family was in the auditorium that night).

A shining golden bullet of energy, with gilded hair and a bejewelled choker, Baryshnikov takes centre stage for much of the ballet and stays there. The Royal Ballet ensemble, silhouetted at the back when the curtain rises, exists mostly as a chorus to enhance his impact, like a pop singer's backing group. He is the visiting superstar, glorified, in Arlene Croce's view, almost to the point of parody.

> He does too much and does it alone, without blending into an overall conception. Although the expansive material suits the melodramatic Rachmaninoff score, it effectively separates Baryshnikov from the rest of the cast and from the Royal Ballet style. Ashton hasn't set down a theme with variations; he's made a Baryshnikov concerto.

Croce is quite right, of course; but, far from being a flaw, the discrepancy between the two schools is a striking dialectic on Ashton's part: English versus Russian classicism is the subject of *Rhapsody* (a contrast that has been eroded by subsequent casting of Royal Ballet-trained dancers in the male role). Although the corps of six men seem infected by Baryshnikov's dynamism, launching into syncopated, bouncing jumps 'like corks bobbing in his wake', they are confined to classroom steps which flaunt the precision of their placing and footwork. The six women, one of whom was the upcoming new star Bryony Brind, have more opportunity to display the hallmarks of their native style, their luxuriant épaulement and neat, petit allegro steps an example of a technique fast disappearing from today's Royal Ballet performances. It is a correct but lyrical idiom, almost courtly at times, as in the slow-motion Fred Step given the stateliness of a pavane; whereas Baryshnikov combines classical technique with dazzling fireworks and demi-caractère panache. Among several pert mannerisms is a moment when he mimics the famous cartoonist image of Paganini, standing in a violinist's posture, imaginary Guarnerius tucked under his chin, his right wrist held in a high arch. Here, Ashton is quoting from Rachmaninov's suggestions to Fokine (who used the score for a ballet in 1939) to show Paganini with 'some devised, fantastic violin'. He also follows Rachmaninov and Fokine by bringing on the ballerina unusually late.

Twelve minutes into the twenty-five-minute ballet, Lesley Collier enters, Aurora-style, from left to right along the back of the stage. After demonstrating her own catalogue of Ashtonisms, she is lifted by one cavalier then another, down a *Scènes de ballet* line towards Baryshnikov. But rather than stepping in to partner her, he watches as she is displayed to best advantage by the company's men, and Ashton sets up a playful tension as to whether or not he will choose her. Like a prince from a classical ballet, he appears to search for her as she stands in a pose lifted from *The Sleeping Beauty*'s Vision Scene, and, still conforming to the traditional role of danseur noble, he finally shadows and supports her in a pas de deux. But too solipsistic to play the prince for long, he soon twins himself with Collier as they perform a romantic waltz that derives its smooth flow and informality from the dancing of Fred and Ginger. Collier, however, never loses her Royal Ballet identity; when Baryshnikov holds her high above his head in a Soviet lift, she embellishes the triumphant port de bras with Ashtonian flourishes of her arms, emphatically marking out the beat. Towards the end of the pas de deux, in a moment that, as Sibley would say, is 'pure Fred', its unballetic simplicity a perfectly judged contrast to the virtuosity that has preceded it, they stroll forward like young lovers out on a Saturday night, his arm around her, her head on his shoulder, until she ducks under his arm to re-emerge on the other side and back again. The finale sees the two performers outdoing each other in their own style of showmanship. From Baryshnikov, we see explosive entrances, streaming Ulanova runs, dizzying skater's spins, every-which-way changes of direction; from Collier, tearing bourrées, lightning footwork, flicking wrists, an audaciously supple upper body. As the momentum gathers, they compete more blatantly for front of stage, until Baryshnikov emerges as the cynosure once more, rotated and flung into the air by the rest of the cast, with Collier running along the outer circle. As she returns to the platform at the back, Baryshnikov, after a final showy entrechat and turn, ends the ballet with a bow that he converts into a Puckish shrug. 'It's been a cinch,' he seems to say, as the curtain falls.

Not so for Ashton. In rehearsals, he clearly felt the strain of keeping his ideas flowing, frequently going up to the piano and paging through the score to see how much more he had to do. Another indication of the pressure he felt was the fact that Baryshnikov's role is over-choreographed: 'Fred would say, "Here we have a few more bars, you can do a few more steps."' Although the dancer gave an exhilarating performance, his disappointment in the ballet was detected by Ashton. 'I always felt he didn't really like it. He didn't want to see that side of him exploited. And to me he never brought it off. He didn't take fire. I wanted to *goose* him at times.' Arlene Croce also sensed the lack of commitment on Baryshnikov's part: 'He performs soothingly, condescendingly, and about as joyously as Liberace ... Baryshnikov doesn't look fresh in *Rhapsody*, Ashton has indulged an image of him which he has outgrown.'

Although he had arrived at the opera house on the first night 'absolutely pea green' with anxiety, Ashton was consoled by the warmth of the response – particularly when he learnt that Queen Elizabeth, the ballet's dedicatee, had been genuinely delighted by his birthday gift to her. 'The Queen Mother and The Queen felt it to be one of the greatest and happiest evenings they could remember,' Claus Moser told him, and many more tributes arrived in the post a few days later. 'It was brave, beautiful and you are a witty old wizard,' wrote Colin Graham. At some cost, in that *Rhapsody* had taken its toll on two close friendships. It had been the first work, in many years, to be created without the collaboration in the studio of Michael Somes, who deeply resented Ashton's choice of Christopher Newton as répétiteur. Billy Chappell also felt slighted. Although Ashton had devised the architectural set based on an eighteenth-century design of classical arches, Chappell was responsible for the costumes which, almost everyone agreed, were over-ornate. Always sensitive to criticism – and criticism from his oldest friend, in particular – Chappell was hurt by Ashton's attempts to effect any changes. 'We were practically passing notes to each other by the end.' Aware of overshadowing him as their careers progressed, Ashton begrudged the fact that he never felt free to speak his mind with Chappell, but was expected to tolerate criticism in return. 'With Billy, it was always, "The trouble with you, Fred . . ." but I could *never* have told him what I thought of him.' Instead, Ashton would frequently voice his exasperation to others – 'I *wish* Billy wouldn't wear that awful cap. He puts it on at such a curious angle, it makes him a mugger's dream.' Yet, for all the minor irritations, they remained devoted to each other and, for the rest of Ashton's life, continued to speak on the telephone every evening.

A more dramatic breach during this period occurred with Martyn Thomas. The issue, which provoked a fight so violent that Ashton feared Thomas was going to kill him, had nothing to do with *Rhapsody* (although, as usual, Thomas had assisted Ashton in the early stages);* it was over the future of Chandos Lodge. Thomas had always assumed that he would inherit the house after Ashton's death. According to David Scott-Bradbury, the plan had been that Marlborough Street and everything in it would be sold to pay death duties, leaving Chandos for Thomas to inherit outright. He, Scott-Bradbury and their friend David Cope would then live together in Eye 'come the time'. Those who dislike Thomas suspect that self-interest had motivated his efforts in the house and garden from the outset – he was building himself a home, or, as Mrs Dade put it, 'Getting it all done with someone else to pay for it.' However, Moura Lympany maintains that Thomas had known for some time that he was unlikely to be sole beneficiary of Ashton's property. 'Martyn said to me, "Well, I don't think I'm having Chandos now that there's Tony and the nephew [Anthony Russell-Roberts, to whom Ashton eventually bequeathed Chandos Lodge]."' Nevertheless, when faced with the reality of Ashton's decision, Thomas became so distraught that he not only announced he was leaving him for good but also began to make plans to emigrate to Australia. His friends urged him not to panic. 'Surely,' wrote one, 'if you continue to pay attention to Fred you will be much better off when he does go even without Chandos.' Even though Thomas was dissuaded from the Australia venture, he continued to have nothing to do with Ashton, moving out of Rosenau Road and into a friend's flat in the Barbican. In the summer, he went to Lindos to carry out a decorating assignment 'and just stayed and stayed'.

The loss of Thomas cut less deeply now than it would have done a few years previously. All the same, this was proving to be a grim time. Shortly before Christmas, Ashton was hospitalized for a prostate operation, his

---

*A rough minutage, linking the action of the ballet to the music, is among the choreographer's papers, written in Thomas's hand.

low spirits lifted a little by the telegrams and messages of sympathy arriving at St Thomas's, among them a note Martin Gilliat had written on behalf of The Queen Mother and all Ashton's 'devoted friends at Clarence House'. The New Year brought another invitation to Royal Lodge, 'the usual weekend with words and music on Sunday', and to Clarence House, where Ashton was among The Queen Mother's regular group, who, on fine days, would lunch under the plane trees at a table laden with crystal, silver and Minton china. In June 1981 Ashton took Tony Dyson with him on the Royal Ballet's trip to New York, travelling on to Toronto, where he was reunited with Alexander Grant. While there, he befriended a thirty-year-old assistant stage manager, Michael Zande, with whom he began the kind of platonic romantic friendship he had once enjoyed with Michael Rennison.

> Fred needed someone to look after him and pay him attention. During those four days I had a wonderful time with him and he felt the same. I think he was genuinely surprised and pleased that someone of my age was interested and seemed to care about him. He never made any advance, which I found very refreshing. I started writing to him and to my amazement he wrote back.

Ashton had hoped to return to New York at the end of the year for a Stravinsky triple bill at the Met, designed by David Hockney – 'the chief delight would be to see you', he told Zande. He had choreographed a duct, *Le Rossignol*, based on Hans Christian Andersen's fairy tale, with Natalia Makarova and Anthony Dowell as the Nightingale and the Fisherman. Dowell's long solo again exploited his line and adagio control, while the pseudo-orientalism of the tale was reflected by the subtle touches of Japonaiserie in his movements – a ceremonial bow, little swaying motions, flexed hands and feet. The lissom Makarova, streamlined in a blue unitard – 'a miracle of nature whose dancing is as symbolic of perfection as the Nightingale's song' – allowed Ashton to make exquisite use of tremulous, soaring, bird-like conceits. By general consent, *Le Rossignol* was considered the triumph of the evening – but, detained in London by the Royal Ballet's first production of *Illuminations*, Ashton was not able to enjoy the acclaim.

During that summer, Martyn Thomas had returned to England to escape various complications that had arisen in Lindos. He had received a blackmailing letter from an ex-lover, now incarcerated in Kos jail, who had learnt 'something very detrimental' about him. He had also fallen out with Patric Walker, a temporary rift exacerbated by the attentions of a young woman who had developed a crush on Thomas. 'According to

P. W.,' she wrote to him, 'I'm in England, being lavishly entertained by my lover in a large country house while the owner is in America. You've got a lot to live up to Martyn now.' Thomas was indeed at Chandos, but he was there on his own. He had returned to collect some clothes and, appalled by the neglect of the 'not-so-enchanted garden', had decided to stay for ten days to put things right. 'I just can't bear to see it like this,' he reprimanded Ashton, claiming to have been equally disturbed by the state of Marlborough Street.

> You practically drove me to despair when I last saw you in London. One thing I had promised myself was that you would not be allowed to sink into squalor and there you were up to your armpits in it. Marlborough Street looked dreadful – not only shabby and cluttered (which is excusable) but dirty and squalid (which isn't). When you return from N.Y. then a plan of action must be formed. I will quite happily get the paintbrush out and clean No 8 up but you must cooperate and clear the piles of rubbish and allow the curtains etc to be cleaned. The garden also needs a blitz . . . I know you will find it difficult to swallow help & support which I had vowed I would no longer give you. Your lack of concern for me made me very angry and later I felt a great hurt. No matter. The fact that Chandos and you have constituted the major part of my life and influenced me more than anything else . . . count for everything. In return for my commitment I think you owe me help and cooperation and not your usual laissez-faire policy of negation . . . You must have things organised correctly or there will be no peace for you at all, only a series of happenings to distract you until the end . . .
>
> It is nearly a year since you announced your 'Chandos not possible' plan to me and I have seen nobody else step forward to help you as I have done in the past. For that reason, this letter . . . I love you very much
> Pup

There was undoubtedly a degree of self-interest behind this display of largesse – Ashton had told Thomas that, on his return from America, he intended to consult his lawyer and Mark Kerr, his financier, about some sort of settlement for him – but Thomas was also feeling guilty. While he was in Lindos, his friend David Cope had berated him about having abandoned Ashton. 'I told him he had to get back and take care of Fred who was getting older and really needed someone to sort him out. Martyn did then knuckle down and start doing things for him again.' Thomas now came in and out of Ashton's life much as he had done before, some-times arriving at Chandos with packets of Marks & Spencer smoked salmon, or leaving with a cuckoo clock that needed repairing. He would even attend to what his sister calls the 'nitty gritty'. For all Ashton's love of beauty and regard for propriety, he was surprisingly oblivious to the state of his immediate surroundings. As he grew older, the public image of the quintessential English gentleman was sullied by a paradoxical streak of squalor. Left alone, he lapsed quickly into slovenliness, wearing three-day-old soup-stained shirts, dropping cigarette ash in his lap, and disregarding the row of false teeth that lay among a clutter of embossed invitations. After a few drinks in the Wemyss room, he would grudgingly apologize for urinating off his terrace, explaining that he could not be bothered to make the journey to the lavatory. For Thomas, the consequences of coping with 'the physical unpleasantnesses' meant that Ashton had toppled from his pedestal a long time ago. He would never have deserted Ashton completely, but he urgently sought to make a future apart for himself. The cavalcade of young lovers, who continued to pass through his life, posed little threat to their bond, but early in 1982 Thomas was reunited with his Norfolk friend. He began spending more and more time at the friend's farm, and Ashton, feeling he was getting next to nothing out of the relationship with Thomas, made his resentment quite plain. The atmosphere when they were together grew intolerable. One night, after an explosive argument, Thomas, having telephoned his lover to come and fetch him, left Chandos Lodge for good. Although he was reluctant to move in with the young man under these circumstances, he had no choice: Ashton told Mrs Dade the next morning that Mr Thomas had gone and would not be coming back. 'He wanted a clean sweep,' said Thomas's lover. 'He was wiping Martyn Thomas's name off the slate.'

It did not take long for it to reappear. 'Most dear Pup,' Ashton wrote to Thomas at the end of the year. 'Not a day passes without thoughts for you & for your well-being.' He was hoping to persuade Thomas to accept as a gift the cottage at the rear of Chandos Lodge. Overlooking the new housing developments in Castleton Way, Chandos Cottage was a mod-ern, boxy construction. Although aesthetically unappealing – 'it could do as a business base for you to dump your purchases' – it was the home of Mrs Dade, and Ashton had led her to believe that it would be hers after his death. He had always stressed, 'I'll see you right' – exactly the words Alice had spoken to him before she died; but, to Mrs Dade's surprise and dismay, he asked her if she would mind moving into one of the converted outhouses, as he intended to give the cottage to Mr Thomas. Despite be-ing extremely fond of his housekeeper, who had now looked after him for over twenty years – he was to leave her £20,000 in his will – Martyn Thomas's needs took priority. If anything, the two men became closer after they had separated, and, seeming to accept that he was indebted to Thomas, Ashton made more of an effort to find ways to reward him financially.

In the spring of 1983, again under duress (Jane Hermann of the Metropolitan Opera had said there could be no Royal Ballet season that year without a new work by Sir Fred), Ashton choreographed *Varii capricci* as part of the Britain Salutes New York Festival. For some time, he had been considering William Walton's five bagatelles; the composer wanted him to use them for a ballet, but Ashton was hesitant. 'They're all right, but not really what I want,' he told Prue Penn, dispatched by Walton to Eye in 1975 'to see if Fred was getting on with it'. Finally, he claimed that he tackled the work 'out of friendship for Willie'. The Waltons' tropical garden in Ischia was the model for David Hockney's set, its vibrant colours, primitivist trees and the abstract outlines of a sunlit swimming-pool intended as a jeu d'esprit to amuse the composer. 'But then he went and died on me': Walton's death took place a few hours after he had completed a razzmatazz finale, written at Ashton's request.

Varii capricci, which reunited Antoinette Sibley and Anthony Dowell, is, as its title suggests, a caprice. Wearing dark shades and a spiv's satin suit designed by Ossie Clark, his hair slicked into a dyed-black quiff, Dowell is Lo Straniero, a strutting young gigolo who dallies with La Capricciosa (Sibley), the elegant mistress of an Italian villa, at a twilit poolside party. As her guests – 'Varii Amici' – Ashton recruited from the Royal Ballet's crop of bright young things four couples whose movements deliberately evoke *Les Biches*, the model for the ballet's mood of indolence and sexual ambivalence. Like birds, the boys are decked more flamboyantly than the girls, their shoulders bared and festooned with chiffon flounces in confectionery colours. 'Who are they interested in – their female partners? Capricciosa? Each other?' Although Ashton disapproved of the new distortions appearing in the company style, *Varii capricci* shows English classicism debauching itself, and he allowed dancers like Philip Broomhead and Mark Freeman to flaunt their hyper-extensions, out-vying each other with 180-degree penchés. Working against the clock, Ashton choreographed the eighteen-minute piece in three weeks, but considered it nowhere near complete by the time the company arrived in New York. Tony Dyson, who had worked on the scoring of the ballet and appeared at most of the rehearsals, was there to lend support, but found himself bearing the brunt of Ashton's agitation.

When Michael Zande went to visit Ashton in his room at the Mayflower Hotel, he was surprised to see him tetchily rebuking Dyson for not having packed his clothes correctly. At the first rehearsal at the Met, the choreographer was beside himself with nerves, snapping at anyone who got in his way – 'Bloody photographers. You can't move . . . Do I *have* to walk through the whole theatre to get to my seat?' This stage call was, as Sibley said, a total disaster, made far worse by hearing that there would not be another. 'Well, I just sat down and burst out crying on stage. Fred was fuming out front; apparently he went mad and he's not someone who loses his temper in public. Anthony had a brainstorm as well. So we got our way and we did do it again.' This time they made it work.

By the first night, Ashton was still sick with nerves, but the delighted laughter that greeted the sight of Dowell, the prince of English classicism, slumming was all the encouragement he needed. The Americans had got the point. *Varii capricci* provocatively subverts every Anglophile's idea of the Royal Ballet: the refinement, eccentricity, reticence and style epitomized by *Enigma Variations* which had opened the programme. Even the romantic pas de deux contains so many Ashton hallmarks that it seems self-parodic. Responding to the applause, Dowell outrageously overplayed his John Travolta transformation, embellishing his sashaying walk, self-preening and employing a pose borrowed from Nijinsky's Faun in which he freezes sideways-on with fingers clenched and thumbs raised. Lo Straniero is a caricature that almost unbalances the ballet, but Ashton wanted it that way, retracting his initial idea of making Sibley an Edith Sitwell eccentric, with 'a very ornate and peculiar' elaborately plaited wig. 'Fred didn't allow me to age. He always saw me as blooming Dorabella.' The ending of *Varii capricci* faintly travesties *A Month in the Country*'s coda. Returning to her sunbed, La Capricciosa, like Natalia Petrovna finding Beliaev's rose, picks up the stranger's dark glasses and puts them on, only to have him return to retrieve them. 'She is left to laugh; it was just one of those flings.'

For Ashton, too, the ballet was a trifle – 'it wasn't meant to stagger' – and once again the Americans enjoyed the joke more than the English. He was soon back for further acclaim, returning to New York the following spring for a centennial gala at the Metropolitan Opera House with *Acte de présence*, another brief evocation of times past for Margot Fonteyn. To a fragment of the Vision Scene music from *The Sleeping Beauty*, Ashton once again appeared on stage as cavalier to his muse.

Because Margot had had such a great success there as Aurora, I thought why not do something to do with that. She was lying on a chaise-longue in St Laurent red taffeta wearing a hundred thousand pounds worth of diamonds from Harry Winston . . . And there she lay looking *wonderful*. I stood away with four roses in my hand and went over like the Prince and kissed her awake. Then she got up and I gave her a rose and she did a turn and I gave her another and so on . . . Then we did a little bit of nonsense. Then what everyone calls my step, but it's not mine at all – it was Pavlova's step and I always put it in as a kind of signature. So then we went off. To *roars* of applause, I must say. They had told us we were only allowed one call and I said, 'Yes, we'll see.' So when we finished we took our one curtain call, and I said, 'Come on, let's go through,' so we went through twice . . . Then I said to Margot, 'Let go of me, I'm going to carry on.' They adore it you see – the ludicrous aspect – they think it's outrageous. No one would *dare* do it there, and I play up to it like mad.

A large part of Ashton's summer was taken up with moving house in London. Finding the stairs increasingly hazardous, he had put Marlborough Street on the market and rented a small flat above a dental surgery in Walton Place, owned by an Australian husband and wife partnership, the Bazants. Jack Bazant, a bloodhoundish, Walter Matthau look-alike, and Flora, known to her friends as Fluoride, ran what amounted to a showbiz practice, counting among their patients numerous dancers, actors and pop singers (Ashton would often wander downstairs into the waiting room and chat flirtatiously with the likes of David Essex). He had met the Bazants through Martyn Thomas, whom they had virtually adopted as a surrogate son. 'They seemed to give Martyn the kind of security and motivation that he didn't get from Fred. They encouraged him and stood up for him whenever Fred's friends put him down.' And having treated Thomas to expensive dinners and holidays in the South of France, the Bazants began extravagantly to court Ashton, too. They became his dentists, and, when they moved their practice to Walton Place, Ashton agreed to take on the flat above.

Number 1a, which Ashton had commissioned Martyn Thomas to decorate, consisted of a drawing room with french windows overlooking the street, a small bedroom with a half-tester bed, and steps leading to an even smaller bathroom and kitchen, its bright-yellow walls offset by Sophie Fedorovitch's *Symphonic Variations* design hanging by the door. Compared with the cosy clutter of Marlborough Street, its effect was clean and airy, the colours light gold as opposed to nicotine brown. Exhausted by the move and irritated rather than cheered by his modern conveniences – the white push-button telephone with a birdie ring replacing his 1940s version, the complicated grill of his brand-new cooker – Ashton was feeling sorry for himself. He complained that he could not find anything he wanted and lamented the fact there were no small shops in the area. 'Oh my darling Chelsea Green – how I miss you.' Even though the food department of Harrods was minutes away, he avoided going there, resenting having to join one queue for a pork pie, then another for a loaf of bread. In the first few weeks, Thomas was often around, facetiously chiding about the ring stains from sherry glasses already appearing on an antique cabinet: 'I don't know why I bother.' One reason was because Ashton had paid him £500 to carry out the move, and was allowing him to make a profit on the sale of Marlborough Street. He had sold the house to Thomas for £100,000, knowing that, redecorated and with central heating installed, it would fetch nearly twice that amount. 'I don't care what he makes on it.'

As usual, on the evening of 4 August Ashton joined The Queen Mother to celebrate her birthday. This year's outing was to *La Fille mal gardée*, which he thought she had enjoyed, 'But then you never know, she's a wonderful actress.' Her letter of thanks more than reassured him.

> My dear Sir Frederick,
>   My mind is still full of the joys of that heavenly birthday evening at Covent Garden . . . I truly sat entranced. It was a very special evening in my life, and as it was all due to you I did want to tell you of my happiness and gratitude.

It was Ashton's eightieth birthday in September, but he refused to feel festive. 'I think a fuss should be made when you're twenty-one and the future is before you; I don't see the point of celebrating the fact you're past it.' On the evening of the 17th, he invited a few old friends to drink pink champagne at Walton Place; a few weeks later, Princess Margaret gave a dinner for him at Kensington Palace. The guests – who Ashton had insisted should be her selection rather than his: 'I'd only offend the people I'd left off' – included the Penns, the Russell-Robertses and Alexander Grant, his only close friend to be invited. After dinner, Ashton uncharacteristically rose to his feet and insisted on making 'the most delicious lowly speech', playing his Little Freddie Ashton role. 'To *think*,' he said, 'I was born in Peru a hundred years ago and I end up by being given a birthday party by a Royal princess.' A fortnight later, the Royal Ballet saluted him in a gala, which, although it did not approach the ambitious range of the 1970 tribute, was, nevertheless, as Ashton himself acknowledged, a moving 'manifestation of love'.

Dividing his time between London and Suffolk, he returned to a life of non-activity and moderate activity, and highlighted by various royal invitations. At Walton Place, he spent long solitary afternoons chain-smoking and chain-drinking thimble glasses of sweet sherry, cursing every time he had to get up to answer the telephone. Callers could be Iris Law, now artistic administrator, consulting him about a cast change; or a botherer (he was listed in the directory), or friends inviting him out. He had no secretary and dreaded the arrival of the post, which brought the inevitable letters from biographers requesting anecdotes, charities entreating his patronage, and bills. 'I'm very middle class and always pay bills immediately.' Any other correspondence was added to the batch he kept in a plastic carrier bag, which he would take to Suffolk, planning to tackle it there – his 'homework', Mrs Dade called it – then bring back to London unanswered. Ashton's Chandos routine remained unchanged. The moment he arrived, he would potter round the garden to see what was in flower, and grimace at the growing invasion of bindweed. The herbaceous border planted by Martyn Thomas was a constant worry to him: it forever needed weeding and he disliked perennials. 'I'm not mad about *colour*. What I really like are buttercups and daisies and cowslips.' Characteristically, though, his preferences for flowers tended to be a combination of simple and grand. Loving the royal rollcall of their names – 'Balmoral', 'Sandringham', 'Windsor' – he would pick armfuls of phlox for the house. He also retained a special interest for plants with high pedigrees, such as the honeysuckle which had begun its life as a buttonhole given to him by the Marchioness of Salisbury, or mignonette grown from seeds he had brought back from Sandringham. By this time, Ashton had lost his sense of smell, a great sadness because, 'like Mme de Pompadour', he had chosen many plants for their scent. But old age had not prevented him from adding new touches to the garden. Despite doubting that he would live another year to see it, he had created a woodland section by getting Mrs Dade's son to scythe a path through shoulder-high grass and nettles, and installing a wrought-iron bench and arch among the trees. 'I love to sit there listening to the birds.' Even on a cold spring day, wearing a seedy old coat and Cossack hat, a 'permanent governess's drip' on the end of his purple nose, he would totter down there and sit, facing his stage of yews. The topiary was, by then, looking very overcrowded – 'More like an Elizabethan garden than Le Nôtre's.' The plants had been only a foot high when he had put them in and he had misjudged the scale. 'It's very much après Le Nôtre, just as my ballets are après Petipa.'

Ashton's morning routine always featured two crosswords after breakfast with Mrs Dade, from the *Telegraph* and the *Daily Mail*. 'He was like a dog with a bone until he finished.' Any guest who wandered into the Wemyss room would have questions fired at them: 'What are those *counting* machines called?' 'Calculators?' '*No.* The things they used to have in nurseries.' 'An abacus?' 'Yes. At *last.*' Around midday, Ashton would have his daily swim in the pool which, even in summer, he kept as tropically steamy as Kew Conservatory. After walking gingerly along the edge – a skinny white figure, with a surprisingly large flat bottom – he would lower himself into the shallows and begin his 'ritual': six pliés, six rises on half point, neck and shoulder circles, followed by six circuits of the pool swimming a stately side-stroke. By now, it would be Bloody Mary time which lasted until about 5 p.m., or, if Billy Chappell were cooking, it would be three when he would finally agree to eat, always starting immediately: 'It's bourgeois to wait.' If he was on his own, Ashton would heat up a dish Mrs Dade had left for him, or make do with something he had found in the fridge: a boil-in-the-bag kipper, wrinkled corn on the cob, or a tin of dubious-looking paté which he had brought half-eaten from London, reluctant to throw it away. He would end the day sitting, smoking and staring on the terrace, or in the Wemyss room. With no ballet to research, he rarely opened a book, but would move into the drawing room to watch television: the news or *Dynasty*, which Mrs Dade was instructed to watch, too, so that they could discuss the plot. His solitude was edged with loneliness, and he would talk Mrs Dade into watching him play game after game of patience to dissuade her from going home. Between ten and midnight, there would be the daily phone calls from Tony Dyson, Billy Chappell and his 'darling boy', Alexander Grant. At about 2 a.m. Ashton would go to bed.

Although Martyn Thomas was 'still blowing in and out', he had become increasingly involved with the Bazants, who had offered to set up him up in business again by opening a shop in Pimlico Road. Thomas Beaumont Antiques (Beaumont was his middle name) dealt mostly in Biedermeier furniture, but, like Thomas's first venture, it did not last long. There were disagreements over the handling of business matters, and the partnership ended acrimoniously with 'a serious falling out'.

Ashton was back to work that spring, choreographing a solo, *Die verwandelte Katze*, for a matinée given at the Staatsoper in Vienna in homage to Fanny Elssler, one of the great ballerinas of the Romantic era. Elssler had had a personal success as the cat in Jean Coralli's ballet *La Chatte metamorphosée en femme*; but, rather than attempting any kind of historical reconstruction, Ashton decided that he would send up the entire thing. Using a pot-pourri of tunes from Offenbach's operetta of the same name, he cast Merle Park as a cat-woman, in a white marabou gown (designed by Billy Chappell after the famous lithograph by Alophe), whose feline habits and arch motif of splayed claws, accompanying a snooty, *Les Biches*-style walk are, in effect, a droll corroboration of the choreographer's antipathy to cats. He despised their claws 'and that bit at the back of their necks', and suffered merciless teasing by his friends. 'All my life I've hated them and been surrounded by people who adore them. Constant used to have dialogues with stray cats in the street.' Nevertheless, Ashton claimed that he could appreciate their grace from a distance. Reflecting this, *La Chatte* combines satirical nonsense with Ashtonian lyricism. And, despite being nothing more than a bonne bouche, it has proved enduring enough to be repeated on more than one occasion as an entertaining programme filler.

Complaining bitterly about missing his garden at its best, Ashton spent the early summer of 1985 in London, improving and rehearsing *Romeo and Juliet* in its first revival, mounted by the London Festival Ballet. Acquiring the ballet was a considerable coup for director Peter Schaufuss, who had his own reasons for convincing Ashton to restage it: not only had he appeared as a small boy in the first production, but his mother and father had appeared as the original Juliet and Mercutio. Several established Festival Ballet ballerinas were rehearsing the role of Juliet, but predictably Ashton chose a sixteen-year-old newcomer to dance the first night. He found that Katherine Healy, an award-winning prodigy trained at the School of American Ballet, was alert and eager to learn, but lacked épaulement and had inexpressive arms and eyes. His coaching of Healy, which concentrated on correcting this, also gave her what she describes as an equivalent of the etiquette and deportment taught at finishing schools. ' "You are a ballerina," he would admonish me. "You must always stand like one." ' She, in turn, was struck by how such a frail-looking figure could suddenly become animated with energy as he demonstrated an effect he wanted. Ashton rechoreographed the Nursery Scene on Healy, as well as adding new passages, including a buoyant mandolin pas de trois for Romeo, Mercutio and Benvolio, and a dramatic, Ulanova-inspired run for Juliet. Hearing that Healy had once skated in John Curry's company, he encouraged her to demonstrate a 'layback spin' (a turn in attitude derrière, combined with a deep cambré back). He subsequently translated this into a movement of despair, performed by both Romeo and Juliet. Aware that his stylized, chamber version of the ballet might have been diminished by the naturalistic, epic dimensions of Kenneth MacMillan's production, Ashton made no secret of his anxiety. 'The critics are preparing to crucify me,' he remarked to Healy shortly before the première. As usual, he was devaluing his talent. The ballet was bound to be appreciated – if only as a piece of newly discovered Ashton choreography with a ceaseless flow of inventive steps. He remained unconvinced, '*cowering*' in his box at the first-night gala. For the second act, he joined Princess Margaret in the grand tier and, during the intervals, a stream of friends paid court to him, including the Marchioness of Salisbury, palely beautiful in a white tulle gown – 'like a dead deb', sniffed Billy Chappell, determined not to be impressed. By the end of the performance, the entire audience was on its feet, roaring its appreciation and calling Ashton back on stage, again and again.

Before he could unwind at Chandos Lodge, he had to brace himself for his annual stint at Sandringham, which, this year, although packed with treats, he found extremely tiring. John and Anya Sainsbury had offered to transport him to Norfolk by helicopter – 'which I quite liked because I was near the ground' – and he also took a schoolboyish delight in being The Queen's only passenger when she drove to a fête for the householders. 'Never did I think little Freddie Ashton would be driven by the *Queen*.' There had been three Holkham picnics and two concerts that week, including one by Rostropovich, with whom he always got on well. After church on Sunday 'because she knows I love carriages', The Queen Mother had arranged one carriage for Prince Charles and herself, and another for Ashton and a lady-in-waiting. 'The crowed all *peered* in. Probably wondering who the old bugger was.' Initially invited for three days, he had, as usual, been persuaded to stay on for three more, and surpassed himself in amusing the party during his ritual dance with The Queen Mother. 'Thank you for entertaining us all so splendidly,' wrote Patricia Hambleden. 'Sunday night's ballet with your hostess was simply wonderful. I've never *seen* the eldest [*sic*] daughter in such glorious fits of laughter.' For this year's birthday show, the six friends went to *42nd Street*, 'which we could all have done without'. Exhausted after nearly a week of playing courtier, Ashton postponed his departure to Eye and, when he arrived, cancelled an invitation to Sunday lunch, 'Because I couldn't face making polite conversation to my right and left.' With all but one of his remaining teeth recently removed, he had found keeping up at meals a terrible strain to begin with, and begged the head butler to serve him first as he ate so slowly. Putting in his new set of dentures was so painful it brought tears to his eyes and he grumbled that his false teeth were preventing him from enunciating properly. 'Did you hear that?' he would exclaim each time he involuntarily whistled. 'I'll have to stop saying "she" or "shut" or "shit" and have speech therapy classes.' Everything he ate now had to be either the consistency of baby food, or overcooked. 'Al dente's no good for me – I haven't *got* any dente.'

At the end of September, Ashton visited Edith in Wexford, a trip that left him in a severe depression for several weeks. The atmosphere at Clobeman Hall was like a nursing home. By this time, Harold Grenfell was seriously ill, too, and, in fact died a few months later, casting Ashton into additional gloom about whether Edith would be sufficiently provided for. 'She'll clean me out if she comes here.' Infirmity was also creeping up on him: he found it difficult to throw off a bronchial cough, he had lost weight, and was looking pinched and unwell. When he stayed at Royal Lodge in February, Ruth Fermoy chided him for not eating enough. 'Well, your Boss doesn't exactly eat either,' he protested. The spring helped to revive his spirits. At an elegant dinner given for Queen Elizabeth by Maureen, Marchioness of Dufferin and Ava, he was back on form: 'If he'd been a cat he'd have been purring.' Ashton was also enlivened by having been put to work, producing another laureate-like offering, which, although lasting only eight minutes, was touched with genius – providentially, as it turned out, because *Nursery Suite*, choreographed for The Queen's sixtieth-birthday gala at the Royal Opera House in April, was to be Ashton's swansong.

The piece is named after the suite Elgar had written in 1930 for the Duchess of York's two daughters. Ashton had stored in his mind an image of the two princesses after once spotting them in their garden off Park Lane.

> I was on the number 19 bus going home and we stopped and there they were, the two little girls playing . . . So then I came up with that idea . . . I said to Princess Margaret, 'I'll do it first and if you think it's awful when you see a rehearsal, we'll scrap the whole thing.' And then I could never get hold of her because she was busy and away and there was no time. So she didn't see it till the first night. But she helped by giving me pictures and things. 'Don't make it too whimsical,' she said.

The first movement, with the two sisters holding their skirts and skipping in counterpoint, could hardly be *more* whimsical, although it was redeemed slightly by the uncanny resemblance of the White Lodge students (Zara Deakin and Susannah Jones), with their girly frocks and stiffly coiffeured hairstyles, to well-known portraits of Lilibet and Margaret Rose. 'Queen Elizabeth thought it absolutely wonderful the way Freddie had captured something about each one of them,' said Ruth Fermoy. 'The way he had got their characters.' Princess Margaret had told Ashton what sort of games the sisters played, and Elgar's second section, entitled 'Busyness – a suggestion of tireless energy', makes use of props such as hoops, balls, and skipping ropes which the dancers convert into horses' reins, like Lise and Colas in *La Fille mal gardée*. The jaunty passage 'the wagon passing' (so popular with Elgar's first audience that the

Duchess asked for it to be repeated) also conjures up memories of *Fille* with four farm-hands who appear to be returning from a day in the fields. 'I didn't know whether to make them gardeners, or boys coming over for the day. Maybe I should have made them Eton boys in uniform.' As the quartet jig about in unison, the younger sister attempts to join in and is finally swept up by one of them into the cart and carried away. 'I wanted to suggest that she had no responsibility, that she could go off and play with the boys. "Perhaps rather apt," I said to The Queen Mother.' The passage that follows, a final example of Ashton's power to stir an audience through music and mood, left hardly a dry eye in the house.

> Dowell came to me in *tears* after the dress rehearsal because he was so moved by it. I was staggered. I wasn't moved when I was doing it and I didn't play it to be moving. It just somehow happened. I tried to give the effect of the end of childhood so to speak. Maybe she had those thoughts. Maybe she didn't. When I described it to The Queen Mother she said, 'Stop . . . You'll make me cry.'

With one arm reaching out towards her departing sister, Lillibet, left alone on stage, lets it fall and walks slowly forward. Her movements – a hand close to her cheek, a contemplative rond de jambe – are in the semi-dancing, plaintively lyrical idiom of Lady Elgar, their maturity made all the more poignant by their performance by a child. With sublime economy, each gesture says far more about the weight of responsibility with which she is burdened, the heart's ease she is denied, than the literal manifestations of gorgeous ceremony: the imaginary crown she places on her head, the black cloak her sister brings on stage for her to wear. In her solemn, upright stance, we glimpse the famous Annigoni painting of The Queen, the impact of which is heightened by the sister's carefree bustling around her. *Nursery Suite* struck a chord with every member of the Royal Family – 'They all seemed to like it, even Prince Andrew, who's not very eloquent' – and Princess Margaret wrote almost immediately to thank Ashton for his 'miraculous re-enactment' of her youth.

> How you got that child to act the last bit in the cloak, oh well you always do. It was wonderful and my mama was blubbing like anything. It was such a difficult ballet to do and it was a complete success . . . With many thanks for conceiving something so sensitive and charming. I send my love.

Princess Margaret admitted that, initially, she had had serious reservations about *Nursery Suite*: 'I thought it would make both The Queen and my mother sick, but we all ended up in floods of tears.' Letters reporting its success reached Margot Fonteyn in Panama, who wrote to congratulate him.

> Without exception they all said that it was superbly done with your touch and genius for getting things just right . . . There is really NO ONE like you. How incredibly lucky I was in my career to fall into your magic hands. Imagine where I would have been otherwise with my no elevation, no extension, no instep and feeble pirouettes! It is nice to be retired and have time to think about people one loves – especially you, you, you.

However, with most of his close friends 'either dead or ill', Ashton was in a gloomy frame of mind. William Walton and Kenneth Clark had recently died (at their memorial services, Ashton represented The Queen); Billy Chappell was suffering from bronchitis and Alexander Grant from shingles. Ashton saw an ominous portent in the fact that the willow, planted at Chandos in Sophie's memory, was dying. News of Bobby Helpmann's death a few weeks later only intensified his dejection. 'Well, who's going to be next?' he sighed to Billy Chappell. Dying itself did not unnerve Ashton, but 'where and how'. He dreaded the indignity of some fatal attack, 'Keeling over in Harrods or on the train to Diss.' He found himself living from day to day, begrudging the fact that he had lost his 'zest'. An ashram of adoring women responded to the impression of helplessness he projected, ministering to his needs – each was made to feel that he depended on her alone. The heiress Catherine Wills would post anti-flu pills through his letterbox; Joan Thring, Nureyev's ex-secretary, who was checking out nursing homes and flats for him, was one of several women positively vying with each other to find him a London housekeeper. Ruth Fermoy and Prue Penn had visited Universal Aunts on his behalf, only to be told by Camilla Cazalet, 'You don't have to worry. It's all under control.' It was felt that Camilla, who had known Ashton since she was eighteen when he had danced her off her feet at Firle, her childhood home, had rather taken Ashton over. 'She put all our noses well out of joint. I always felt that she resented any one else taking care of him.'

A housekeeper, Mrs Brown, was duly found. She woke him at ten, prepared his porridge and tea, 'then she whizzes round with a Hoover and is gone by twenty to eleven'. Occasionally, Ashton would persuade her to stay for a glass of sherry, to which she agreed only to please him, as she did not drink. These days, Ashton was surviving on a diet of little more than alcohol and cigarettes. 'I'm smoked and I'm pickled: if I stop either, I'll die.' At Billy Chappell's eightieth birthday party he ate only

two gull's eggs the entire evening, yet he could still draw on surprising reserves of energy when the occasion demanded. Invited to the wedding
ball for the Duke and Duchess of York at Claridges, Ashton cleared the
floor as he and Lord Snowdon did the twist and twirled about for a full
ten minutes.

At the end of November, Ashton received a telephone call from
Thomas's Norfolk farmer friend telling him that Martyn was dead. It had
been a foggy morning when Thomas had set out to his parents' home in
Lincolnshire for a cousin's twenty-first birthday. He had always been a
reckless driver and, overtaking a lorry, had been killed outright in a col-
lision with an oncoming car. He was forty-four years old. Ashton's immediate reaction was to ring Thomas's mother, Peggy Tuplin, but at first
he could not speak. It was unbearable, he said, and asked her to telephone him every day: 'He was in an awful state – worse than I was.' The
following week, David Cope drove him to the funeral in East Tudden-
ham, where Ashton sat holding Peggy's hand. Swathed in black, Moura
Lympany made a dramatic entrance, but even though they sat next to
each other during the service, Ashton asked David Cope not to offer her
a lift back to London: 'There was always friction between them.' So
many of Thomas's friends had packed the tiny church that the congregation, mostly young men, were spilling through the doors into the graveyard. 'Those who loved him *really* loved him. He cast such a spell.'
Afterwards, everyone went back to the farmhouse for a party – it was
what Thomas would have liked. For his parents, there was slight consolation in the fact that their son, no doubt as a result of having watched
Ashton grow old, had never wanted to go through the process himself.
Even at thirty, he had told his mother, 'If I die young, don't ever weep
about it. I've had my life.' His looks were fading, his business had fallen
apart, which inevitably prompted speculation as to whether the accident
might have been suicide. Jennifer Mellors was unconvinced. 'He was in
control. He and N— were happy. It was a less demanding relationship on
both sides.'

For Ashton, Thomas's death was a shock from which he never fully
recovered. At the funeral he had said to Peggy Tuplin, 'How am I going
to manage? I can't.' And from then on, he barely did. He appeared to be
physically diminished by the tragedy, looking permanently tired, very
small and dishevelled. He was coughing horribly, taking out his top row
of teeth to hawk into the wastepaper basket. 'Bugger old age,' he would
mutter, complaining about getting more and more rickety, and that nothing made him laugh any more. His sense of humour was now wry rather
than frivolous; his giggle, reduced to a hedgehoggy snuffle. Another grouse
was that Anthony Russell-Roberts had moved Edith to a nursing home

nearer to his house in West London, which meant that Ashton, reluctant to squander money on a taxi fare, had to change tubes twice to get there. This home, with its dusty plastic flowers and pervasive smell of urine and boiled cabbage, was even more depressing than the last. With Mrs Rochester-like cries issuing from behind closed doors and public rooms full of wheelchairs, white faces, dead eyes and gaping mouths, it was, for Ashton, a cruelly taunting indication of what might lie in store for him. As always, he would put on a great show for his sister; afterwards, he would slump into a depression from which he found it increasingly hard to surface.

Unable to face Chandos and all its memories, he spent much of the winter brooding in Walton Place. Although, in the past, he had rarely confided in anyone about his personal life, he told Prue Penn that he was filled with remorse about Martyn Thomas. 'He felt he hadn't been nice enough.' When Anne Hoellering, a Norfolk neighbour, rang from Harrods to ask if she could visit Ashton, he put his arms around her as soon as she arrived and started to cry. A gaunt, Ibsenian figure, frequently dressed in black, with her hair scraped into a bun, she was another woman to have been bewitched by Thomas. Acknowledging this, Ashton gave her as a parting gift a book of flower paintings inscribed: 'In memory of Martyn whom we both loved.'

It was an icy winter that year and Ashton suffered from the cold. He would ask visiting friends to bring some small comfort, like a thermal vest or loaf of bread. He was grateful for any company. 'I'm really awfully lonely you know. People think I'm out every night dining with duchesses but I'm not.' He would always rouse himself for a royal invitation – managing, for example, to brave the snow blanketing London to have lunch with Princess Margaret – but he had come to rely, more than ever, on the company of old chums. Billy Chappell would keep two tins of salmon in his larder, knowing that Ashton often rang at the last minute 'to cadge an invitation' for a fishcake supper. But if Chappell tried to fix a date in advance, Ashton always hedged, saying that he would let him know, 'In case he got a better offer.' Chappell was resigned to his Last-Resort role, but would occasionally lash out at Ashton's selfishness. 'It's so ingrained. He's like one of those Restoration characters, Mr Self-Absorbed.' On one occasion, he invited Ashton to his birthday party. Ashton initially accepted, then tried to back out, saying he had muddled his dates and could not cancel people [the Duchess of Devonshire] whom he had let down twice before. 'If he doesn't come,' said Chappell, 'he's lost me.' In the event, Ashton came, muttering, 'He'd drop me like a shot if Tommy [Elliott] or someone wanted to see him.' He also complained that Chappell's fuss was a sure sign of bourgeois pettiness – an aristocrat would be far too gracious to appear to be put out. With each year, the incongruity in Ashton between grand seigneur and old-age pensioner grew more pronounced. A few days after he had travelled to a memorial service in Princess Alexandra's Rolls Royce, he was pulling out his travel pass on a number 14 bus.

The spring saw him looking more spry but feeling slighted and unprized. In an attempt to create an 'authentic' version of *Swan Lake*, the Royal Ballet was eliminating recent interpolations – all of which had been choreographed by Ashton: his Act I Waltz, Act III Pas de Quatre, Spanish Dance and final act, choreographed in the style of Ivanov. Realizing that his decision was likely to cause offence, Anthony Dowell, the producer of the new version, had driven to Eye to explain it to Ashton, who seemed surprisingly reconciled to the changes. Later, however, goaded by Michael Somes, he grew so embittered at the idea of his work being 'thrown on the rubbish heap' that he would not allow Dowell to retain his Neapolitan Dance (a duet as specified in the original libretto) and refused to attend the gala première. Deploring the new trend towards scholarly reconstruction, Ashton insisted that what mattered in dance was to extract the essence of a work and to convey its poetry. 'If you're going to be authentic, then you have the original costumes and a Lilac Fairy with a 38-inch bust. Not Bryony Brind with no tits.'

Taking advantage of Ashton's dispute with the Royal Ballet, Peter Schaufuss, by presenting it virtually as a fait accompli, had managed to persuade him to let the Festival Ballet revive *Apparitions*, with Natalia Makarova in the Fonteyn role. The photographic memory of ex-dancer Jean Bedells had enabled the company to remount the bones of the ballet; Ashton, liking what he saw, agreed to supervise final rehearsals. He was fond of Makarova, who frequently supplied him with lavish amounts of caviar and shared his sense of humour. They had met soon after her defection, when Ashton immediately put her at ease by speaking a few, perfectly delivered Russian phrases. 'I was so surprised . . . he had quite a luggage of Russian words.' Makarova was charmed by his simplicity, dignity and sensitivity – 'He knew women so well, understood their weaknesses and liked them so much' – and she greatly enjoyed working with Ashton on *Apparitions*. He, however, was less enthusiastic, finding that she resisted his corrections. Watching her draw out the phrasing of a solo in her characteristic Russian way, he admonished her by remarking, 'You *must* do it to tempo, or else you'll make it boring.' When he learnt that she had reverted to performing the role her way, he refused to come to any more rehearsals as it seemed pointless. Nervousness about the reception of the ballet exacerbated his pettishness. He was confident that it had a marvellous score but worried that such an early work might look dated. As, indeed, it did. 'It was hard to recognise,' Kathrine Sorley Walker wrote some years later, 'lacking almost all the elements that once made it a captivating artistic whole.' Billy Chappell's designs, 'after Beaton', had prettified rather than retained the subtlety of colour in the originals, the Liszt score was diminished without Lambert's inspired conducting, the clarity of the action had become clouded, and the casting was ill-judged. While Makarova brought great sophistication to the role of the Woman in Ball Dress, she showed little understanding of Ashtonian style. Schaufuss was technically far more accomplished than Helpmann had ever been, but lacked the heroic authority to give credibility to the Gothic-Romantic posturings of the Poet.

The 1980s brought a profusion of royal invitations which, despite the deterioration of his health, Ashton rarely, if ever, declined, even though he was increasingly concerned about how to survive a weekend with The Queen Mother without having one of his coughing fits at table. 'They'll all be saying to each other, "Hasn't Freddie *aged*!"' Recalling how Alice had known an Infanta in Paris who was cared for by nuns during the day but free to go out to dine at night, he dreamt of ending his days in a monastery. He felt he had come close to death recently, but had not found this disturbing. 'It's time to close the book.' All the same, he was making more of an effort to improve his health, consulting an acupuncturist, Mr Siaow – 'like Miaow with an "S" to help me regain my equilibrium' – and had stopped smoking, although he still swooned for cigarettes.

> I've *not* given up, I've just not smoked for a month . . . I'm not go-
> ing to give way . . . When people say, 'Do you mind if I smoke?' I
> say, 'Of course I don't – *blow* it all over me.' My cough's much bet-
> ter I must admit, though it's not pleasant and I still have to have
> things round me to spit into. It's my faith-healer who put me on
> to . . . not homosexuality . . . homoeopathy.

To compensate for the compulsive smoking, Ashton began to drink more recklessly. By the end of an evening with friends, his elbow would be slipping off the table, his speech slurred, yet he was as entertaining as ever. Seeing Alice's daughter Romana McEwen arrive at a dinner party, he mimed an Odette-like sheltering of his face – 'Those *eyes*! Take away those eyes' – and began an unremitting flow of anecdotes about her mother. Even when inebriated, he was an endearing guest – tiny, frail and affectionate, kissing the hand of a charmless maid each time she brought him another tumbler of Martinis. Emulating The Queen Mother, he tried to restrict himself to two, but then consumed so many that he would have no memory of conversations which had taken place. After inviting Lesley Collier and her husband, Nicholas Dromgoole, for dinner at Daphne's, his favourite restaurant, he had felt obliged to telephone the maître d' the following morning to confirm that he had paid the bill.

The hurricane of October 1987, which felled about thirty trees at Chandos and damaged the crinkle-crankle wall, affected Ashton so badly that he 'took to the bottle' and, as a result, had a bad fall and cracked his shoulder. Because of a power-cut, he had been unable to listen to music, and this, together with the debris littering the garden, had so disenchanted him with the place that he returned to London, morose and anxious about the perils of living alone. 'I can't see the point of anything. I'm worried I might have a break-down.' Although Tony Dyson was as attentive as ever, letting himself into the flat bearing carrier bags of clinking bottles, Ashton sorely missed Martyn Thomas. 'If Martyn had still been around, Fred would have been a lot calmer and happier,' said Joan Thring. One night, he went to visit William Tallon, Queen Elizabeth's page, in his miniature cottage at the gates of Clarence House, where he drank so much that he had to be taken home in a taxi at three in the morning and put to bed by one of the other guests. 'He took his teeth out and I undressed him,' said Lady Carey Basset, who had met him only once before. Later that night, Ashton fell and woke to such a debilitating hangover that he was unable to face whisky – 'my poison' – for several weeks. Concerned that there was nobody else in the building at night, Tony Dyson was investigating the Distressed Gentlefolk Association's London accommodation, looking into the possibility of finding a larger, end-of-lease flat, which would enable Ashton to have a nurse or manservant on the premises. 'People keep trying to make me wear those alarms [Aid Call] but I don't want to.' A fainting spell while walking to the bank increased his fears of expiring in the street, and the discovery of dry rot at Chandos Lodge seemed a merciless reflection of his state of mind. He saw himself ending his days like Tennyson's Mariana, surrounded by dilapidation and decay.

A certain satisfaction was derived from the fact that the £5,000 it was costing him to cure the dry rot had been provided by the fee he received for allowing Makarova to include his rejected *Swan Lake* choreography in her new production. Ashton had agreed without hesitation, interpreting this as a one-finger gesture to the Royal Ballet for having snubbed him. But enough of a rapprochement existed for him to have authorized Anthony Dowell's revival of *Ondine* (although, hearing that rehearsals were a shambles and that the cast were saying it would be a miracle if it ever went on, he was regretting his decision). Ashton had chosen the young principal Maria Almeida for the first night, even though he had lit-tle faith in her ability to make the part her own. Since her schooldays, Almeida had been the sweetheart of the dancer Jonathan Cope, and Ash-ton felt that the stability of their relationship had inhibited her artistry. 'Her heart has never been made to beat or suffer pangs when he doesn't ring. And it shows.' In the event, Ashton was surprised and pleased by the success of *Ondine*, but remained sceptical about the advantages of 'disinterring' his early ballets, comparing the critics to vultures picking at old bones. His one bad notice preoccupied him obsessively; published in the *Evening Standard*, it was entitled 'A Sinking Ship', its reviewer venge-fully referred to by Ashton thereafter as 'A Stinking Shit'.

While no longer feeling the urge to create a new ballet, Ashton never-theless thought that he might have 'half an hour left' in him and admit-ted that he was drawn to one particular piece of music. 'I'm not saying what it is, just that it's short. Very short.' His memory was failing with each day and he could spend an entire morning struggling to recall the name of a favourite painter, scribbling 'Fragonard' at the bottom of a newspaper when he was cued. At The Queen Mother's birthday outing to *Lettice and Lovage*, he was in fine form, laughing and enjoying himself, and he left Ruth Fermoy's flat that night with a bag of left-over lobster. 'That will last me two days,' he told her. During his week at Sandring-ham, however, he was noticeably the frailest of the group, 'very very tot-tery indeed'. As usual, he had been solicitously indulged and allowed to drop out of any strenuous pursuits. When The Queen arrived with a troupe of corgis, she insisted that Ashton should remain sitting down during their conversation ('About horses and grass'). When he protested, she replied, 'Our grandmother taught us to stand. We're used to it.' On the Sunday evening, having been slumped in his chair, grumbling about his dry rot, Ashton got up suddenly, as if injected with new life, went over to his hostess, bowed, and, with Rostropovitch playing the piano, they per-formed an unforgettable routine, the eighty-eight-year-old Queen Elizabeth 'doing a sort of mock belly dance', using the chiffon sleeves of her dress as a yashmak, and Ashton throwing himself at her feet at the end. 'It was enchanting,' said the Countess of Gowrie. 'Grey and I were the young by-standers, and we both felt that watching them was a lesson on how life should be lived when you're very old.' But it had required superhuman effort on Ashton's part and he confessed to a friend a few days later that he would not have the stamina to go to Sandringham again. This had been his last performance. He had told Ruth Fermoy at the beginning of the week, 'If I have to dance with Queen Elizabeth, I shall die.' As it hap-pened, he did both.

He was to have spent the rest of August in Eye, his annual month in the country, but on the night of Saturday the 19th, in a perfectly choreographed coup de grâce, he 'climbed into bed and went to heaven'. It had been a wonderful day. His house guest at Chandos, Alexander Grant, had finished clipping the topiary, which had pleased Ashton. For lunch they had had his favourite combination of champagne cocktails, smoked salmon and lobster, the food brought in a hamper by Anne Hoellering. Knowing how much he disliked chewing, she had offered Ashton her lobster claws, saying, 'I'll have your body.' 'Alas, it won't be much good to you now,' he replied. Although bright and talkative at lunch, he had dwelled on the prospect of dying, again emphasizing how it was ignorance of the timing and the means that unsettled him. After some gentle gardening and a light supper, he and Alexander Grant had sat up talking until late. Very unusually, Ashton had not asked him to fetch the Chinese chequers board, the game that had always reminded him of choreography. His work was over. At nine o'clock the next morning, Mrs Dade took Ashton his breakfast as usual, but when she received no answer, she returned with the tray. When Grant came downstairs, she told him she had not been able to wake Sir Frederick and he went up to Ashton's room. 'I heard him [Grant] give a shout and say, "Mrs Dade, will you send for the doctor," but of course it was too late.' Ashton's death had been caused by a hardening of the arteries. It had been the peaceful end he had prayed for, and, as Mrs Dade said, 'He couldn't have died happier.'

His death was perfectly timed. When Alexander Grant opened the post later that day, in case there was anything that required attention, he found a letter from the Bazants giving Ashton notice to leave his London flat. Intending to move to France, the Bazants wanted to sell the property and needed vacant possession. 'Thank heavens, Freddie never knew.'

The choreographer had given no instructions about whether he wished to be buried or cremated (when asked by Anne Hoellering at lunch that day, he had looked across at Grant and replied, 'I leave that to others'). The obvious resting place was next to his mother in the churchyard of St Mary's, Yaxley, but not only could his nephew Anthony Russell-Roberts not find the headstone, he was told by the rector that there was no further space. Eventually, after strimming away nettles and bushes by the right-hand church wall, a plot was found and another next to it reserved for Edith. Brother and sister now lie side by side, some distance from the Fulcher graves at the rear of the church but in sight of pink-washed 'Ashton Cottage' across the lane.

The funeral took place on 24 August, a chilly, pre-autumnal day.

Posted along the gravel path were the chief mourners: Anthony and Anne Russell-Roberts, Michael Somes, Brian Shaw, Alexander Grant and Tony Dyson, several of whom provided new arrivals with a 'Sicilian demonstration of prolonged embraces', as Richard Buckle noted in his diary. The congregation inside was surprisingly small; close friends mingled with colleagues from the opera house, including Antoinette Sibley, Anthony Dowell and Lynn Seymour, the latter flamboyantly clad in a denim minidress, black seamed stockings and a veiled riding hat. The service was low-key – 'Very undenominational. Two obscure hymns; and Blake's (and Parry's) "Jerusalem" at the end', wrote Buckle; Michael Somes read from the pulpit in a voice clogged with tears and was among the small core encircling the coffin during the ashes-to-ashes ritual. After the funeral was over, Dame Ninette de Valois walked to the foot of the grave and stood alone for several minutes as other members of the congregation wandered among the rows of flowers. The most striking bouquet, a large wreath of pink roses and dianthus, had been sent by The Queen Mother.

In complete contrast to this very private funeral was the Service of Thanksgiving at Westminster Abbey that followed three months later on Tuesday, 29 November. For this, Ashton had made his preferences quite clear: 'It's the Abbey or nothing,' he had told Anthony Russell-Roberts after attending the service held there for William Walton. Ashton's memorial attracted the largest congregation at the Abbey for thirty years, the numbers so great that many had to be accommodated in St Margaret's next door. The wide scope of Ashton's social and professional world was represented by The Queen Mother and Princess Margaret, by members of the peerage, by Royal Ballet stars past and present and balletomanes of all ages. Mrs Dade was among the group of family and friends who sat in the choir-stalls, and so was Billy Chappell, who had not been well enough to travel to Yaxley for the funeral. Edith, brought in a wheelchair by a nurse, sat nearby holding the hand of her niece Esther Ashton, and giving a little sob each time she registered any mention of her brother's name.

The emotive combination of music and words reduced many people to tears. Extracts from six Ashton ballets, including *Enigma Variations*, were played before the service by the Royal Opera House orchestra, and towards the end Hans Werner Henze conducted the stirring Andante from Mozart's Piano Concerto K.467. Among the readings was an exceptionally apt passage from *A la recherche du temps perdu*, read by Anthony Dowell, about the profound impact on the artist of instinctive truths. But it was Margot Fonteyn, too ill to be there in person, who most movingly captured the essence of the man to whom she owed her career.

Her tribute, sent from Panama and read by Michael Somes, was remarkable for its natural eloquence, perception and lack of pretension – the very qualities that had defined her own art.

It would take a poet of equal genius to do justice to the genius of Frederick Ashton. In ordinary words I can only say that he was a rare artist, comparable in his field to Shakespeare for his extraordinary understanding of the human heart and mind and his ability to illuminate them through his own art form . . . He once said that he could not remember innocence, that he had always seen through people to their hearts, their motives and their characters, since he was a child. How he came to be able to translate that insight into movement is a mystery which must be explained only by the word genius . . .

As a man I see a paradox: on the one hand sophistication and finely developed taste in all things, yet on the other a very simple person at heart. One might expect a highly sophisticated person to make an effort to conceal some emotions. Not Ashton; like a child, if he was hurt, angry or even jealous he made no pretence. He was, above all, a very *human* human being, and for that, as much as for his extraordinary talents, he was beloved by all.

AFTERWORD

F airly early in our acquaintance, Frederick Ashton wrote in the book I had asked him to sign,

> To Julie
> Who will hold (soon) all my secrets,
> With love?
> Fred

The question mark was meant as a warning. It was a symbol of provisional trust, implying that if I betrayed his confidence in any way, I would automatically forfeit his friendship. This happened all too soon.

I had got to know Fred when I interviewed him in 1984 for *Vanity Fair*, a longish profile written to mark his eightieth birthday. We struck up an immediate rapport (owing mostly to the fact that I am married to the then Royal Ballet dancer Ross MacGibbon, whom he liked very much), and after listening to a continuous flow of witty, well-honed anecdotes about his life and his friends, I knew that I wanted to write his biography. What I didn't know was the degree of intricate fly-fishing that this was going to involve.

Ashton has always been considered a very private man – 'What he has wished to tell the world about himself is told in his ballets' – and the two books written about him to date focus entirely on his work. The main reason for his reticence was his attitude towards his homosexuality. Privately, this had never been a source of guilt or anxiety, but it was a side of his life that he did not want scrutinized. He hated the prurience and plundering of modern biography – '*Digging* into people's lives. So squalid. *Sordid*' – and although he liked nothing more than to sit reminiscing for hours, talking with surprising candour, he was unwilling, for reasons of both laziness and circumspection, to put anything in writing himself. At least a dozen letters among his papers are from publishers trying, sometimes two or three times, to persuade him to change his mind. He always declined, even when George Weidenfeld proposed sending his friend the writer Frances Donaldson to record their conversation with a tape-recorder – 'We'd have sent each other to sleep,' he said. The Queen Mother, who loved Fred's company, urged him on several occasions to write his memoirs, but his reaction was just as firm. 'I told her, "No way, Ma'am."' Consequently, when I first brought up the idea of a biography, I was quite taken aback when instead of refusing outright, he eluded the question with a tour de force of teasing. 'You're *crazy*! It's going to be the dreariest book in the world. Nobody's going to read it and nobody's going to buy it. There'll be *boxes* of it in Charing Cross Road at a quarter of the price. And [to Ross] you will go on at her and say, "Why did you waste all that time?" You should start right now.' It wasn't exactly yes, but neither was it no.

We continued to see each other sporadically throughout the summer of 1984. I would take him out to lunch, or to see a film or a play, until one day our new friendship was brought to an abrupt end. I had agreed to show Fred my *Vanity Fair* piece before sending it off to New York, and as I sat opposite him, watching him sigh his way through the pages and chain-smoke in his singular way – cigarette held between his middle fingers as he sucked in the smoke (Fred never properly inhaled), then switched to thumb and first finger as he exhaled, his hand rotating to pose close to his cheek – I noticed him suddenly blanch. I had written briefly about his closeness to The Queen Mother, a subject, he told me sternly, that I was forbidden to mention. I had quoted nothing incendiary, only a few lines about how the two of them would giggle together, talk French and do imitations ('She does American ladies very well'), but I had referred to his liking for the faded elegance of Sandringham, the fact that the carpets are threadbare in places, and this, he felt, might be misconstrued. The real issue, of course, was that I had exposed his indiscretion, showing him, however innocuously, to have broken the code of silence imposed on friends of the Royal Family. The paragraph had to go.

Fred's eightieth birthday was on 17 September, and ten days later I opened *The Times*, which had bought the British rights to my piece, and saw that his remarks about Queen Elizabeth, which I had crossed out in the text (these were pre-word-processor days), had been reinstated. With a racing heart, I immediately took a taxi to his flat to break the news, but deduced from his expression that the damage was irrevocable. The following morning I heard from my actor friend Peter Eyre, who had seen Fred at a dinner the night before, that he had brooded about it obsessively, confiding his distress to Princess Margaret and Gore Vidal, and telling Peter, 'I'll *never* talk to that woman again.' And for almost a year he didn't. It made no difference that *The Times* had written to him to apologize and exculpate me, or that, according to a courtier acquaintance, the article had caused no offence among members of the Royal Family. Fred, as one of his friends remarked, was 'a good hater', and, at any gathering at which we saw each other, I was theatrically and humiliatingly snubbed.

It was only later that I understood the full implications of what I had done. During his last few years, Fred's friendship with The Queen Mother had been one of the most important in his life. Less than a month before, she had written suggesting that it was time she abandoned the formalities and instead of addressing him as 'Sir Frederick', called him simply 'Freddie' (society knew Ashton as Freddie, the dance world as Fred). The privilege of riding by her side in a carriage or sitting beside her at table brought him immeasurable delight, not least because it seemed the ultimate acknowledgment of his achievement. 'Who would have thought this of little Freddie Ashton from Lima, Peru' was a favourite catchphrase of his, familiar to many.

For all his anxiety, however, Fred found that nothing had changed. Invitations to Sandringham and Clarence House continued to arrive, and by June 1986, when he and I saw each other at a party, he made it clear that I had been forgiven. (A few weeks later, when his remarks were quoted again in a profile of The Queen Mother, he was even able to quip wryly, 'Those threadbare carpets, they'll haunt me till I die.') Our friendship resumed and deepened over the next two years, based, I suppose, on mutual give and take. If Fred needed a lift to Chandos Lodge, and his usual roster of chums couldn't oblige, Ross and I would chauffeur him. This was a prospect to which we greatly looked forward, as he would enliven the journey with a non-stop commentary, pointing out a gruesome pink velveteen chair on the pavement in Leytonstone that looked like a commode, for instance, or a lorry that overtook us labelled 'Gayfreight' – 'Do you think there are a load of old queens inside being dumped in Suffolk?' Ross and I would spend the night in a nearby inn until he began insisting that we stay with him. In return, the deal was that we supplied the food. 'I can't cope, you see,' he'd say plaintively.

The two-day Chandos routine hardly varied. We would arrive around noon, in time for coffee prepared by his housekeeper Mrs Dade, who sat straight-backed on the edge of a stool in his Wemyss-stocked dayroom, filling Fred in on village news in her soft Suffolk burr. Then I might plant the cowslips or sweetpeas that I'd grown for him from seed, or Ross might be instructed to dig holes for a collection of new conifers accord-

ing to strict, choreographed directions. Drinks before lunch – Bloody
Marys or Bucks Fizz – lasted until late afternoon when Fred, who regarded any meal as an unwelcome distraction from drinking, smoking
and conversation, finally agreed to sit down and eat. My brief was to
cook easily chewable and digestible dishes, his favourites being consommé with a blob of sour cream followed by sole Véronique, but he
would have been just as happy with puréed nursery food. Lunch rolled
into tea, when Mrs Dade would bring a pot of PG Tips and a plate of vol-
au-vents made with the lemon curd Fred always bought at the Sandringham flower show. We learnt to devour the lot, knowing it would be our
only sustenance until ten or eleven, when he could be persuaded to have
supper. After midnight he was at his peak: springing up to imitate
Isadora's abandoned run; gripping the mantelpiece to demonstrate Nijinska's exaggerated use of the upper body at the barre; borrowing Ross as
a partner to show how an authentic South American tango should be languorous rather than jerky and angular. We were always the first to fade,
tearing ourselves away at about two and trudging upstairs to the pretty
guest room, heated in winter by nothing more than a lacy Victorian
heater that gave out as much warmth as a 40-watt bulb.

Fred complained more and more about the indignities of old age, but,
despite the physical deterioration he so resented, we never thought of him
as old. No generation gap existed between us, any more than it did between ourselves and the two friends we grew to love from his 1920s circle, Barbara Ker-Seymer and Billy Chappell, both of whom had a sense of
humour that was irreverent and sharply contemporary. All three were
wonderful company and totally unshockable. But whereas Barbara and
Billy were always the same, in Fred's case there was a marked division between the public and private persona. Countering his popular image as
the ultimate English gentleman was an uninhibitedly scatological side.
Changing-room obscenities peppered his speech, and grumbles about the
acidity of the Bucks Fizz would be accompanied by a prolonged belching
session. For all his social fastidiousness and restraint, he loved gossip and
took a novelistic interest in other people's lives. When the young Italian
dancer Alexandra Ferri left the Royal Ballet to join American Ballet Theatre at Baryshnikov's invitation, he sat with her in a corner at a party one
night and whispered, 'Fuck him if you want to, but don't fall in love with
him' (later quizzing a mutual friend, 'Well, *did* she?', meaning the former).

Fred needed a great deal of time alone, sitting for hours chain-smoking,
listening to music and staring into space, claiming that he was thinking of
absolutely nothing, but in fact semi-entranced in the state of lambent
calm that sustained his choreographic mind. He also needed an audience,
and found his biographer to be his most avid listener. In his Mrs Tiggy-

Winkle kitchen, peeling grapes for the Véronique sauce, I would hear a cry of '*Fuck* the food! Come *back*!' He enjoyed the company of women almost more than that of men, offering me advice on clothes, make-up, love affairs, and encouraging an intimate exchange of confidences. Then he would remember my journalistic role and regret his indiscretion, rounding on me with irritation. Once, when he'd asked me whether he could eat a tin of ancient anchovy paste and I'd asked him what the sell-by date was, he exploded, 'You're always asking me *dates*!' And I would overhear him complain to the coterie of friends who rang him every night, 'She's hauling my guts out, of course.'

Nevertheless, by 1987, Fred had signed a note of authorization giving me access to general archive material and told me, 'You can do it – but only when I'm dead.' Crucial characters in the story, however, were starting to appear in the obituary columns with worrying regularity, and I felt that unless Fred actively forbade it, I should press ahead with my investigations, although I also felt guiltily vulturish in doing so. To begin with, he appeared not to mind. He listened intrigued to my account of a conversation I'd had with Virgil Thomson in New York and how I'd traced the location of their original St Theresa from *Four Saints in Three Acts* to a shabby nursing home in Queens. When I announced that I was going to Peru and Ecuador to research his background, he scoffed, saying that he'd always thought I was a bit mad. Although a couple of his close friends warned me that he was not at all happy about it, the impression he gave me was not so much that he was concerned I would be excavating his past, but rather that I might stir up distant South American relatives with whom he deliberately stayed out of touch (one complained that she hadn't had a Christmas card from him for fifty years). '*Don't go*,' he pleaded. 'Because then they'll all be on to me.'

Far from having a divisive effect, the Peru trip seemed to bring us much closer; I'd come home and find a message on the answerphone saying, 'It's Fred. Old Fred. *Ring* me.' He craved company during this period and he wanted attention, making meek, heart-rending requests for soup and thermal vests. I'd grown to love him so much that, if I hadn't been married, I think I would have devoted all my free time to taking care of him. But Fred excelled at acting pathetic and I discovered there were at least half a dozen other women whom he had running round, competing to attend to his needs. He was self-absorbed by nature, never one to put himself out for anyone – Cecil Beaton used to say that he was the most ungenerous man he'd ever known – but although Fred never paid for or produced a meal in the years I knew him, he could be touchingly solicitous in his own way. I was in an advanced state of pregnancy towards the end of 1987 and he kept an avuncular eye on my progress. When I told him I was making a pilgrimage to Piero's *Madonna del Parto* in the chapel at Monterchi near Arezzo (believing, like the gullible local village girls, that she would bring me luck), he clucked with disapproval at the risk I was taking – 'With your first child and at *your* age' – even though he was every bit as superstitious as I was. He couldn't understand why I didn't just light a candle at Brompton Oratory as he always did before starting a new ballet, and he instructed me to be sure to come and see him before I left so that he could bless me, which he did with great solemnity, tracing a cross on my belly. Soon after my return, he offered to perform the Ring Test on me in order to ascertain the sex of the child. I'll always remember him struggling on to his creaky knees one night as I lay on the floor and dangling my wedding ring, tied to a single hair, over my bump, until it began to swing resolutely round and round. 'A girl [wrong]. Very determined. Just like her mother.'

He kept telling me to have my children and forget about the book, but stubbornly I persisted. By now it had become a vocation. The unspoken understanding between us was that Fred would co-operate by answering my questions way into the night. Sometimes he allowed me to tape him, sometimes not, complaining that it stopped his flow. But I noticed that he was becoming increasingly perturbed by my consultations with anyone other than himself. Although I would invariably ask his permission before contacting a new source, he began forgetting that he had agreed – 'I hear you broke my rule and went to see Edith,' he would snap, or 'How dare you *inflict* yourself on poor Rose.' He was always a touch shame-faced when I reminded him of the preparatory conversation we'd had, but he was getting so unpredictable that I decided not to tell him when I tracked down my most prized source, Guy Watson, the key not only to his Lima childhood but also to his schooldays at Dover College. One morning when I rang Fred, he burst out, 'I'm *furious* with you. Why do you want to see Guy Watson? *I* could have told you everything he can. But no. You always take no notice and do what you want. *Why* can't you wait till I'm dead?'

This was the crux. He had no real objection to my seeing Watson, a genial ex-banker, apart from the fact that he'd then been forced to resume contact with someone with whom he had nothing but his early years in common. But the book had now become synonymous with his mortality. 'It's the finality of it – knowing you're grabbing as much out of me as you can before I die.' I'd foolishly told Watson that my biography had Fred's blessing, a claim that was far too unequivocal, too presumptuous, in the light of our ambiguous understanding. During the telephone tirade he had threatened to put a notice in the newspapers disclaiming his authorization, and, as I later found out, had indeed telephoned several friends forbidding them to co-operate with me. 'If I catch you seeing anyone else I really won't speak to you again. Give me a ring one of these days when I've had a chance to cool down.'

Fred at his most imperious was quite terrifying. I didn't contact him for a month; my baby was almost due and I'd made up my mind to abandon my research for the time being, although I did surreptitiously make an appointment to see Guy Watson: at eighty-three he was too important to miss. I'd arranged to meet him on the morning of 19 March, but half an hour before I was due to leave the house, I went into sudden, advanced labour – exactly as my subject would have wished.

Fred died that summer, granted the easeful death he'd prayed for. We'd made our peace and for the past few months enjoyed the kind of friendship without strings that we should have had all along. When I rang him one evening to make a date to bring his pink sweetpeas to Chandos, he complained about being more and more rickety but sounded content enough: the phlox and daisies he loved were in flower, his beloved Alexander Grant was coming to stay and his diary for the week was full of engagements. His last words to me were, 'Send a kiss to my godson.' It was Billy Chappell who broke the news over the telephone, his statement, 'Fred's dead', having a terrible, knell-like rhyming finality about it. I found that I missed Fred dreadfully, missed not being able to tell him things and hear his cynical, witty retorts. But each Ashton ballet I saw, drenched with his presence, brought him back, and so did work on my book: his gravelly, aristocratic inflections, wonderful stories and snuffly chuckle captured on hours and hours of audio tape.

The following year I was given access to Fred's papers by his executor, Anthony Russell-Roberts, and took possession of The Box – a vast cardboard receptacle of treasures ranging from love-letters, notebooks, congratulatory telegrams and Ballets Russes programmes, to correspondence from some of the most lustrous names in twentieth-century arts and society. It even included a mouse-nibbled manuscript of a play by Gertrude Stein, annotated in her own hand. Fred had always taken pettish pleasure in telling me that any letter he received went straight into the wastepaper basket, but this turned out to be completely untrue: he had kept virtually every one.

It was liberating finally to be able to launch into research unimpeded by the old restrictions, even though one or two sources, citing Fred's edict, refused to see me. Because the English dance world had never before been exposed to biography in the conventional sense, any question straying from the path of Fred's professional career was likely to be regarded as prying. Among the 'widows', as Dickie Buckle called the ex-lovers, only the two Americans, Dick Beard and Tony Lizzul, would talk freely about their relationship with the choreographer and allow me to see his letters. Michael Somes, by contrast, was so chary of me that he wouldn't even answer a question about Fred's mother.

The usual justification made by the biographers of recalcitrant subjects is that their book will help to illuminate the work, but in Fred's case, I don't feel that I can make that claim. Does the knowledge that the Young Girl in *The Two Pigeons* is a reincarnation of the male chemistry student with whom he was infatuated really add a valuable new dimension to the ballet's achingly sweet reconciliation duet? If anything, it is a distraction, diminishing the work's power of suggestion, the raison d'être of dance. It was this – the fear that exposure of the prosaic reality of the lived life would destroy the delicate subterfuge and poetry of his art – that, I believe, fuelled Fred's resistance far more than any sense of propriety. 'Choreography is my whole being, my whole life, my reason for living,' he once told an American journalist.

For me the most important discovery of writing Ashton's biography has been the extent to which his life *generated* his work. His genius was subjective, he lived by his heart and imbued his work with the sense of yearning and suffering that he himself experienced. 'I pour into it all my love, my frustrations, and sometimes autobiographical details ... In many ways, it has more reality than the life which I live.' Fred was not a happy man; much of his adulthood was spent half-consciously seeking unrequited emotional situations that would inspire him and activate what Petrarch called the resonance of sighs. But sorrow had its beauty: from it came the ballets.

This book both is and is not an authorized life. Often while researching it, I felt akin to a date-rapist opportunistically interpreting no as yes, even though I knew that Fred realized a biography would eventually be written – his preservation of his papers is indication enough. 'I have kept your letters of appreciation,' he told Kenneth Clark in the 1960s, 'so that one day a future Mr Beaumont or Ivor Guest can find them and quote from them.' Beaumont and Guest were dance historians; the book Fred had in mind, an analytical study of the ballets such as David Vaughan produced so effectively in 1977. My book is a very different matter, almost an act of transgression, and yet, grudgingly and conditionally, Fred put his life in my hands – a privilege I have spent ten years striving to honour. The result is full of secrets, secrets about the Ashton antecedents that I kept from him, and secrets about his muses that he tried to keep from me. What I'll never know, Fred, is whether that question mark still stands.

ACKNOWLEDGEMENTS

My first thanks must go to Anthony Russell-Roberts, Ashton's executor, who authorized this biography and gave me exclusive access to his uncle's extensive archive. I am immensely grateful for his support and for the freedom he has given me throughout the writing of the book. Esther Ashton, the choreographer's niece, has been helpful from the beginning, providing me with introductions to the South American Ashtons, among whom I would like in particular to thank Arlene and Frederick Ashton Donoso, for their friendship and hospitality, and the late Elsie Ashton de Pinillos for showing me family letters that enabled me to solve the mystery of George Ashton's past. I am also grateful to Alberto MacLean for making available to me his privately printed genealogy, *Los Ashton en Londres, Ecuador, Peru y Bolivia*. Other members of the Ashton family to whom I owe thanks are: Carlos Ashton Donoso, Tita Arosema Ashton, Priscilla Ashton de Illingworth and Maria Saenz de Ashton. Ashton's sister, the late Edith Grenfell, patiently answered my questions on several occasions despite being severely debilitated by a stroke.

I owe an enormous debt of gratitude to Barbara Ker-Seymer and Billy Chappell (sadly, both now deceased), whose contribution to the book made over a number of years is inestimable. The cover illustration and many other photographs in the book are from Barbara Ker-Seymer's collection, to which she gave me unlimited access. Her generosity was overwhelming in this and many other ways. I am grateful to Barbara's and Billy's respective literary executors, Barbara Roett and Tommy Elliott, for their permission to quote from the letters, as well as for letting me use Edward Burra letters in their possession. I also owe thanks to Burra's cousin, the late Jill Brodrick, for giving me permission to quote from his correspondence.

Alice Astor's family have been untiringly helpful to me. I would like to thank her son Ivan Obolensky for answering countless questions and for giving me access to photographs and paintings in his collection. And I am also most grateful to her daughters, Sylvia Guirey, Emily Harding and, especially, Romana McEwen, for their time and valuable assistance.

Among the friends and associates of Ashton who allowed me to use his correspondence, I would like in particular to thank Dick Beard, who not only copied out by hand lengthy extracts from his collection of letters but also sent me relevant sections from his diary and a vivid account of his relationship with Ashton. I am just as indebted to Hans Werner Henze and to Tony Lizzul, who each put his cache of Ashton letters at my disposal. Cecil Beaton's unpublished diaries are a marvellously rich source from which to draw and I am most grateful to Hugo Vickers, his executor, for his permission to quote from them, as well as from the correspondence in Beaton's archive. Polly Hill, the niece of Maynard Keynes, was exceptionally generous in allowing me unlimited access to Lydia Lopokova's unpublished letters to him; and my thanks are also due to King's College, Cambridge, for permission to quote from both sides of the correspondence.

It seems unfair, however, to single out individuals when so many people have made a major contribution to this book, either by taking the time to pass on their memories of Ashton and his work, or by allowing me to use copyright material, documents and photographs. I would especially like to thank Her Majesty, Queen Elizabeth, The Queen Mother, HRH The Princess Margaret, Mark Amory, Richard Avedon, Gavin Bryars, Richard Buckle, John Craxton, Lydia Cresswell-Jones, Kathleen Dade, David Daniel, Baroness de Courcel, Julia Farron, Alastair Forbes, Countess of Gowrie, Duchess of Grafton, Alexander Grant, Janie Henniker-Major, Nicholas Jenkins, Maude Lloyd, Lady Rose McLaren, Col. Andrew Man, Fergus Mason, Pamela May, Jennifer Mellors, Pamela Mortimore, Joy Newton, Patrick O'Connor, Lady Penn, Alard Tobin, Guy and Elizabeth Watson and Gwyneth Williams.

I am also tremendously grateful to: Betty Louise Allan, Neil Alston, Lord Annan, Brooke Astor, Lady Avon, David Ball, Jean Bedells, Terence Benton, Sir Isaiah Berlin, Charles Blackburne, Neville Blackburne, Penelope Boscawen, Michael Boulton, Mark Brinkley, Rosie Camden, Leo Carey, Alan Carter, Sir Hugh and Lady Casson, Lady Elizabeth Cavendish, Camilla Cazalet, Ingrid Channon, Diana Chauvin de Précourt, Colette Clark, Pauline Clayden, Timothy Cobb, Lady Diana Cooper, David Cope, Gabrielle Crawford, Ronald Crighton, Joan Cross, Nancy Crozier, Jacques d'Amboise, Alexandra Danilova, Piers de Laszlo, Agnes de Mille, Lady Margaret Douglas-Home, Earl of Drogheda, Maureen Marchioness of Dufferin and Ava, Philip Dyer, Jane Edgeworth, Leslie Edwards, Amalia Elguera, Richard Ellis, Wendy Ellis, Violetta Elvin,

ACKNOWLEDGEMENTS

Kathleen Evison, Annabel Farjeon, Ruth, Lady Fermoy, Felix Fonteyn, Dame Margot Fonteyn, Emanuel and Gwen Galitzine, Madge Garland, Jean-Pierre Gasquet, David Gill, Sally Gilmour, Richard Glasstone, Diana Gould, Duchess of Grafton, Colin Graham, Michael Graham, Jimmy Hardwick, Pamela Lady Harlech, Lady Harrod, Lord Hastings, Anne Heaton, Anne Hoellering, Barbara Horstmann, John Houseman, Prudence Hyman, Derek Jarman, Lincoln Kirstein, John Lanchbery, Doris Langley Moore, Nicholas Lawford, Tanaquil LeClercq, Anna LeGallois, Joan and Patrick Leigh Fermor, Anya Linden, Loelia Lindsay, Sylvia Loeb, Dame Moura Lympany, Lady MacMillan, Iris March, Dame Alicia Markova, Robert Medley, Elizabeth Miller, Donald Mitchell, Ivan Moffat, Gail Monahan, Nadia Nerina, Irina Nijinska, Rudolf Nureyev, Annette Page, Sophie Pearson, John and Myfanwy Piper, Poppet Pol, David Poole, Michael Powell, Frank Raiter, Derek Rencher, Michael Rennison, Anne Renshaw, Neil Roger, Herbert Ross, Elizabeth Schooling, David Scott-Bradbury, Lynn Seymour, Moira Shearer, Dame Antoinette Sibley, Richard Smithies, Michael Somes, Doris Sonne, Humphrey Spender, Rosamund Strode, John Taras, Virgil Thomson, Joan Thring, Buster Tonge, Sir John Tooley, Peter Townsend, Wendy Toye, Antony Tudor, Peggy Tuplin, Gilbert Vernon, Gore Vidal, Patric Walker, Lady Walton, Beatrice Wayne Godfrey, Elizabeth Welch, Jean Winter, Irene Worth, Martin Wright, Francis Wyndham, Michael Zande, Franco Zeffirelli.

In addition, I would like to record my debt to the following for information, assistance, advice and many other acts of kindness: J. K. Abson, Joan Acocella, Sir Alistair Aird, John Alston, Jack Anderson, Thomas Anderson, Sir Ralph Anstruther, Fred Ashby, Constance Babington Smith, Frith Banbury, Birger Bartholin, Lady Carey Basset, Richard and Celia Beadle, Marjorie Beams, Robert Beazer, Muriel Bentley, Deanne Bergsma, Svetlana Beriosova, Lady Berkeley, Joyce Berry, Peter Blond, Sir Dirk Bogarde, Sarah Bradford, June Brae, Harry Bright de Pinillos, Dorothy Bronson, Evangeline Bruce, Terry Byrne, John Byron, Michael Caine, Simon Campion, Nicholas Capp, Elizabeth Carlisle, Humphrey Carpenter, Gillian Chanter, Miles Chapman, Gilbert Chauny, Chris Chinery, Susannah Clapp, Eileen Coley, Lady Sylvia Combe, Gerald Corcoran, Arnold Cosburn, Arlene Croce, Stewart Craggs, Betty Cuff, Jimmy Cummins, Ruth Daniel, Mary Darmandy, Kensington Davison, Derek Deane, Michael De-la-Noy, Lila de Nobili, Ralph Denne, Peter Dickinson, Christopher and Alice Dilke, Fram Dinshaw, George Dix, Zoë Dominic, Major General Sir Gerald Duke, Anne Dunhill, Leslie Durbin, George Eccleshall, Vivian Ellis, Dorothy Escolme, Tim and Lizzie Fargher, Ian Ferguson, Daphne Fielding, Elaine Fifield, Sir Edward Ford, Roy Foster, Chris France, Frederick Franklin, Brian Friel, Viscountess

Gage, Lynn Garafola, Claire Geber, Sir John Gielgud, Maina Gielgud, Keith Grant, Mona Grant, Adrian Grater, Hugh and Joanna Griffiths, Maurice Grosser, Patricia Viscountess Hambleden, Charles Harding, Colin Harding, Nicholas Haslam, John Hatt, Lady Dorothy Heber-Percy, John Hemming, David Herbert, Jane Hermann, Rosella Hightower, Sir Alan Hodgkin, Stanley Holden, Horst, Biddy Hubbard, Wallis Hunt, Ronald Hynd, Jean Innes, Robert Irving, Linda Janklow, Roman Jasinsky, Lord Jenkins of Hillhead, John Keegan, Richard Keynes, Marion King, Antonia Kirwan-Taylor, Brenda Last, Hazel Lee, Leo Lerman, Mary Edna Lockett, Bob Lockyer, Sam Lurie, P. W. Manchester, Thalia Mara, Valerie Martin, Julia Matheson, June Mayall, Angus McBean, Billy McCann, Heather McCubbin, Deirdre McMahon, Fionn Morgan, Andrew Motion, Anne Murray, The Lord Napier and Ettrick, Robert Nesbitt, William Newton Funck, Ena Norris, Chloe Obolensky, Ruth Page, Georgina Parkinson, Ann Pasternak Slater, Margaret Payton, Donna Perlmutter, David Pleydell-Bouverie, Ray Powell, Peter Quennell, Gibbs Raetz, Craig Raine, Charles Reading, Anne Reid, Peter Rice, Sir Frank Roberts, W. A. Robinson, A. M. Ross-Smith, Lord Roskill, Countess of Rosse, George Rylands, John Saumarez Smith, Chloe Sayer, Meryle Secrest, Bobby Short, Mary Shott, Lord Skidelsky, Lady Smiley, Earl of Snowdon, John Sparrow, Lady Spender, Alexandra Stancioff, Tania Stern, Marti Stevens, Lady Daphne Straight, Jane Stockwood, John Stuart, Will Sulkin, Alan Tagg, Frank Tait, William Tallon, Paul Tanqueray, Alfreda Thorogood, Marian Thorpe, Roger Trafford, Laurence Tubman, Robin Tutt, Nancy Van Norman Baer, Anatole Vilzak, John Walker, David Wall, Marie Wallace, Joan Watley, Doreen Wells, Ken White, Hugh Williams, Peter Williams, Malcolm Williamson, Michael Wishart, Geoffrey Wright, Martin P. Wright, Sir Peter Wright, Stanley Wright, Lady Zuckerman.

My analysis of many early Ashton ballets was made possible by the existence of contemporary film footage held in the Rambert Dance Company Archive, as well as by the invaluable home-movie recordings of the balletomane Edmée Wood (now owned by the Royal Ballet Company). I am extremely grateful to Jane Pritchard, Rambert's archivist, for showing me relevant material and also for her considerable help throughout my research. I am equally indebted to Robert Jude, who copied videos of the Ashton ballets and made the Royal Ballet's viewing suite available to me on many occasions.

I would like to record my thanks to the following librarians and archivists: Francesca Franchi, Royal Ballet Archives; Dr Philip Reed, The Britten-Pears Library; Jacqueline Cox, Modern Archivist, King's College, Cambridge; Caroline Cuthbert, Tate Gallery Archive; Professor Catherine Henderson and Professor Thomas F. Staley, the Humanities Research Center, University of Texas at Austin; Kendall Crilly, Yale University Music Library; Dr Howard B. Gotlieb and Sarah Truher, Special Collections, Mugar Memorial Library, Boston University; Malcolm Pratt, the Library of St John's College, Cambridge; Madeleine Nichols and Else Peck, The Dance Collection, New York Public Library at Lincoln Center; Sarah Woodcock, Theatre Museum Archives; Helen Rogers and the staff of the Upper Reading Room Reserve Desk, the Bodleian Library, Oxford; Ronald Taylor, Dover College Archives; Patricia Willis, the Beinecke Rare Book and Manuscript Library, Yale University.

I also owe thanks to: Dorset County Records Office; Library and Records Department, Foreign and Commonwealth Office; National Army Museum; Old Cliftonian Society; Post Office Archives; La Recoleta, Lima; Search Department, Kew Public Record Office; Wells Cathedral Library; Wells City Archives.

Early drafts of the work were read by several friends from whose criticisms I have greatly profited. Dickie Buckle and Dick Beard made many helpful corrections to the text, as did Peter Eyre, to whom I am indebted for his championing of my book in New York. Clement Crisp added immeasurably to my knowledge of English dance history, spared no effort to improve each chapter and gave me all the help I asked for and more. Selina Hastings, whose unerring sense of period and elegant style is a model for any novice biographer, provided unstinting editorial expertise as well as several years of moral support. Rupert Christiansen, who has been encouraging all along, alerted me to several solecisms, as did Robert Greskovic and David Vaughan. Alastair Macaulay's contribution to the accuracy of this edition has been incalculable. Although there was neither time nor space to enrich the book by drawing on well over a hundred pages of dazzlingly perceptive notes that he faxed me, his fastidious, scholarly reading and rereading of the text has saved it from a great number of errors.

I would like to give profound thanks to my editor at Faber, Christopher Reid, and acknowledge the help of other members of the Faber team who worked on the book. My thanks too to Robert McCrum for keeping an interested eye on the book over the years; to Pat Kavanagh, my agent, and to Julian Barnes, for their enthusiasm and invaluable assistance. I am enormously indebted to my New York agent Lynn Nesbit and to Cullen Stanley for their belief in the book; and no less essential has been the terrific support, patience, and friendship of Shelley Wanger, my editor at Pantheon. I also owe Bob Gottlieb special thanks for his expert help and for overseeing the layout of the photographs.

I cannot conclude without expressing my gratitude to two mentors,

Peter Conrad, my English tutor at Oxford, and Tina Brown, my editor at *The New Yorker*. Although neither was directly involved with the book, their encouragement, stimulus and generosity gave me the wherewithal to write it. *Secret Muses* is dedicated to my husband and two sons, whose patience and understanding over the years get my final and most heartfelt thanks.

SOURCE NOTES

Unless otherwise specified, the Ashton quotations in the text are from conversations I had with the choreographer over several years. As far as other sources are concerned, where no reference is given in the Notes, it is to be assumed that quotations are extracted from the many interviews I conducted with Ashton's friends and associates. (I have used the stage names of sources attributed in the Notes and the Acknowledgements.) References are given only for quotations from printed works or if the identity of a particular source is not clear in the narrative. Unless stated to the contrary, all letters to Ashton come from his archive.

Quotations from Edward Burra's letters are from *Well, dearie!*, edited by William Chappell, from the Ashton archive or from the private collections of Barbara Ker-Seymer and William Chappell. (To preserve their flavour, I have retained Burra's eccentric punctuation and misspellings.) Unless a source reference is given, all Lydia Lopokova quotations are from her letters to Maynard Keynes; quotations from Keynes, unless otherwise stated, are from his replies to her. (The Keynes/Lopokova correspondence is held in the Modern Archive at King's College, Cambridge.) The Hans Werner Henze quotations, unless a reference is given, are either from his letters to Ashton or from conversations with the author. (Ashton's letters to Henze are held in the Paul Sacher Foundation in Basle.) The Dick Beard and Tony Lizzul quotations are from their letters to Ashton or from conversations and correspondence with the author; the Tony Lizzul quotations are by permission of his executor, William Funk. Ashton quotations regarding Beard and Lizzul are extracted from his letters.

A large number of Ashton's letters are privately owned; those located in public collections are as follows: FA to Cecil Beaton, the library of St John's College, Cambridge; to Cyril Beaumont, Theatre Museum, London; to Benjamin Britten and Peter Pears, The Britten-Pears Library, The Red House, Aldeburgh; to Nora Kaye, Special Collections, Mugar Memorial Library, Boston University; to Marie Rambert, Rambert Dance Company

Archive; to Edith Sitwell, the Humanities Research Center, University of Texas at Austin; to Virgil Thomson, Yale University Music Library; to Alice B. Toklas, the Beinecke Rare Book and Manuscript Library, Yale University.

David Vaughan's pioneering *Frederick Ashton and His Ballets* was my primary published source throughout the writing of this book. It is an indispensable chronicle of the work until 1976, and will be updated and reprinted by Dance Books in 1997. Vaughan's essay 'Frederick Ashton and His Ballets: A Final Chapter' was published in *Dance Now*, The Ashton Issue, vol. 3, no. 3, Autumn 1994. Other published sources to which I am particularly indebted are listed below against the abbreviations used to identify them in the Notes. In addition to those, my main published sources include: Nancy Van Norman Baer, *Bronislava Nijinska: A Dancer's Legacy*; Cyril Beaumont, *Dancers Under My Lens*; Richard Buckle, *Adventures of a Ballet Critic*; Mary Clarke, *The Sadler's Wells Ballet* and *Dancers of Mercury: The Story of Ballet Rambert*; Violet Clifton, *The Book of Talbot*; Arlene Croce, *Afterimages* and *Going to the Dance*; Agnes de Mille, *Dance to the Piper* and *Speak to Me – Dance with Me*; Ninette de Valois, *Come Dance With Me*; Simon Fleet, *Sophie Fedorovitch: Tributes and Attributes* and *Sophie Fedorovitch: A Biographical Sketch*; Arnold Haskell, *The Ballet in England*; Dolly Pflücker's memoirs, *Don Roberto's Daughter*, by Gee Langdon; Ivan Moffat, *Raimund von Hofmannsthal: A Rosenkavalier*; Marshal and Jean Stearns, *Jazz Dance: The Story of American Vernacular Dance*; Francis Wyndham's Story 'Ursula', in *Mrs Henderson and Other Stories*.

ABBREVIATIONS

AH   Arnold Haskell
BdZ   Beryl de Zoete, 'Frederick Ashton', *Horizon*, Vol. VI, No. 31,
        31 July 1942, reprinted in *The Thunder and the Freshness*
CB   Cyril Beaumont
CC   Clement Crisp, 'A Conversation with Frederick Ashton' (BBC
        Third Programme, 21 March 1963; edited transcript in *Covent
        Garden Book*, No. 15, 1964)
D&D   *Dance and Dancers*
DMcD   Don McDonagh, 'Au Revoir?' (interview with FA), *Ballet Review*, Vol. 3, No. 4, 1970
DT   *Dancing Times*
DTJ   *Dance Theatre Journal*

DV   David Vaughan, *Frederick Ashton and His Ballets*
ED   Edwin Denby, *Dance Writings*, ed. Robert Cornfield and
            William Mackay*
JH   John Houseman, *Run-through*
LS   Lynn Seymour with Paul Gardner, *Lynn: The Autobiography of
            Lynn Seymour*
MF   Margot Fonteyn, *Autobiography*
MK   Milo Keynes, ed., *Lydia Lopokova*
Q   Marie Rambert, *Quicksilver*
SG   John Selwyn Gilbert, interview with FA in *Frederick Ashton: A
            Choreographer and His Ballets*
VT   Virgil Thomson, *Virgil Thomson*

CHAPTER 1: CHILD OF THE SUN (1863–1919)

page

3   'a kind of electrification' CB, *Pavlova*
     'Seeing her at that stage' SG
4   'the carry-on' DV
5   'If my father had lived' *Frederick Ashton: A Real Choreographer*, 1979 documentary by John Selwyn Gilbert
6   'elegant ladies' BdZ
     'I don't know why' SG
7   'He was a kind of hero' ibid
9   'He had to do what she wanted' Elsie Ashton de Pinillos interview
     'She was so well educated' John Ashton to Alec Ashton
9   'the trouble began' John Ashton to Tony Ashton
     'The answer' ibid
     'Fred had this obsession' Barbara Horstmann interview
10   'Ashton is a gentleman's name' Richard Ellmann, *Oscar Wilde*
     'His is the kind of' Agnes de Mille, *Speak to Me – Dance with Me*
     'Every ballet that I do' CC
     'I believe that if young choreographers' ibid
14   'amateur entertainment' cutting in Ashton archive
15   'She had a great zest for life' SG

*All Denby quotations in the text are from this collection.

'We girls spoke' and subsequent quotations about the Yaxley
family, Edith Bullen to FA
16 'It was really rather a question' SG
17 'She was a heroine' Elsie Ashton de Pinillos interview
18 'very soft and nice' Priscilla Ashton de Illingworth interview
'the pesthole' George Ashton to John Ashton
'so as to become hardy' and subsequent quotations from Violet
Clifton, *The Book of Talbot*
20 'Six months of it' Keith Money, *Anna Pavlova*
'the airs and graces' Arlene Croce, *The New Yorker*, 2 July 1990
'particular interweaving' BdZ
'From the songs' BdZ
21 'That was a great day' ibid
'I was disgusted' ibid
'He would have himself transported' ibid
'When I told her' Amalia Elguera interview
22 'really awfully childish' Joan Watley interview
23 'to time things' BdZ
24 'Oh I'm so sorry' Jean Innes interview
'Somehow coming' source withheld
'I remember Fred saying' Bunny Roger interview
25 'He was terribly ashamed' Barbara Hostmann interview
'such a very dear woman' Jean Winter interview
'the spitting image of Queen Mary' Guy Watson interview
26 'to calm down' Gee Langdon, *Don Roberto's Daughter*
'hell for leather' and subsequent quotations about FA's Lima
childhood, Guy Watson interview
'nuns in long trousers' BdZ
27 'displaying mahogany bodies' Langdon, op. cit.
28 'sunshine and beautiful bathing' BdZ
29 'A couple of months later' and subsequent quotations on this
page, Guy Watson interview
30 'Darling, why don't you' Jean Winter interview
31 'the free, uninhibited child' BdZ

CHAPTER 2: PLAY UP, PLAY UP (1919–1924)

32 'Because, you see' SG
'an awful old steamer' and subsequent quotations, Guy Watson
interview

33 'terribly ill-treated' SG
'the lowest form' Fergus Mason interview

34 'The whole essence of Dover' Andrew Man interview
'If you succeeded at sport' Mason interview
'We were playing' Sir Gerald Duke interview

35 'There was no teasing of him' A. M. Ross-Smith to author
'I used to write' SG

36 'as something ghastly' SG
'artsy crafty sort of chap' Duke interview

37 'Everyone in this form' and subsequent quotations about Dixon,
Andrew Man interview
'A sweetie' Gillian Chanter interview
'A C.O. can make life hell' A. S. Dixon to FA

38 'Cannot we ever meet' ibid
'a very ancient and noble place' A. M. Ross-Smith to author

40 'They were both on the arty side' ibid

41 'Give him a wig . . . obviously entertaining them' Mason interview

42 'As long as it didn't go' ibid

44 'I didn't think I'd like it' DV
'And she talked a good deal' New York Times, 26 June 1981
'You'd think, "my goodness"' DMcD
'on that one note' Victor Seroff, The Real Isadora

45 'a kind of intellectual' Peter Hall's Diaries, ed. J. Goodwin
'an expression of' Isadora Duncan, The Philosopher's Stone of
Dancing

46 'to rest the Spectator and the Eye' FA article on Petipa, first printed
in Marius Petipa Materialy, Vospominaniya Stat'l, Leningrad,
'Iskisstvo', 1971
'She was always smiling' Betty Louise Allan interview
'looked upon as a sort of' SG

47 'a joy to his teachers' Andrew Man interview
'In my philistine days' letter in Ashton archive

48 'Frankly it was more shattering . . . licking the stamps' SG
'So well do I remember' John Powley to FA
'The manager would bring me letters . . frustrated and closed
up' SG

50 'vast connections with banking' El Telegrafo, 15 January 1924

51 'owned three oilrigs' Carlos Ashton Donosa interview

52 'an encyclopedia of ballet' ED
'You looked in the' SG
'Just think of it!!!' Lynn Garafola, Diaghilev's Ballets Russes

53 'With my rigid upbringing' SG

'somewhat informally attired . . . enrolled him in the school,'
Léonide Massine, *My Life in Ballet*
'one of the most sensational feats' Richard Buckle, *Diaghilev,*
'Suddenly, the "ballet girl"' Garafola, op. cit.
'I got away with murder' SG
'I didn't know what I was doing' ibid
'the world's greatest dancer . . . I didn't like that at all' ibid

54 'When I did my first bit of business' John Selwyn Gilbert documentary, *Frederick Ashton: A Real Choroegrapher*, 1979
'terribly thin' SG
'must have been a very wise old bird' DV
'So I told him' SG

55 'He had such an individual style' DMcD

56 'So the days went by' Clement Crisp, 'The Life and Work of Walter Gore: A Tribute in Four Parts', *Dance Research*, Vol. VI, No. 1, Spring 1988

56 'just forgot' Carlos Ashton Donoso interview

CHAPTER 3: A MAD BRIGHT YOUNG THING (1924–1928)

60 'Later I realised' Q
'It was frightfully boring' *DTJ*, Vol. 2, No. 3, 1984
'Fred wouldn't have got technique' Doris Toye interview

61 'the born artist' Q
'She would haul me back' *DTJ*, Vol. 2, No. 3, 1984
'That's why I kept coming back' SG
'Margot Asquith used to steal' Agnes de Mille interview
'this shoebox' Agnes de Mille, *Dance to the Piper*
'a kind of effulgent dislike' ibid

62 'We were very close' Maude Lloyd interview
'expecting to see someone' DV
'Lifestyle modernism' Lynn Garafola, *Diaghilev's Ballets Russes*

63 'and when my mother and I' SG
'This was the fabric . . . bus tickets' Diana Menuhin, *Fiddler's Moll*
'Now and then she would stamp' Agnes de Mille interview
'Fred used to *vilify* Mim' Colette Clark interview

64 'She was the first woman' DV

65 'At midnight in her peaked cap' Simon Fleet, *Sophie Fedorovitch: Tributes and Attributes*

66   'The rhythmic spurt comes from her' Patrick O'Connor and
      Bryan Hammond, *Josephine Baker*
      'really the instigator' Barbara Ker-Seymer conversations
67   'Olivia was head girl' Bunny Roger interview
      'Two tiny rooms' Penelope Middelboe, *Edith Oliver: From Her
      Journals 1924–48*
      'She was deeply upset' Francis Wyndham, 'Ursula', in *Mrs Hen-
      derson and Other Stories*
68   'an eagerness to please' ibid
      'A magpie spectre' Cecil Beaton, *The Wandering Years*
69   'persuasively poised example' Wyndham, op. cit.
      'one of Beau Brummel's retinue' Agnes de Mille interview
70   'An intriguing survivor' Francis Wyndham, 'Ada Leverson', in
      The Theatre of Embarrassment
      'She loved popular tunes' ibid
71   'A fat little woman' Rebecca West in *Recollections of Virginia
      Woolf*
      'Together these women' ibid
72   'conjuring up the entire aura' Cecil Beaton, unpublished diaries
      'was not of Mr Baldwin' ibid
      'the sort of thing' ibid
73   'I am sure she wore fine white silk' Fleet, op. cit
      'She will successfully suggest' *Ballet Annual*, No. 2, 1948
74   'Fred became interested . . . When he heard that' *Q*
      'in a sort of lesbian-like fashion' Diana Gould conversation
75   'pearl-hung and silken' Virginia Woolf, *Diary*, Vol. III: 1925–
      1930
      'six inches taller' Clement Crisp, Anya Sainsbury and Peter
      Williams, *50 Years of Ballet Rambert 1926–1976*
      'most realistic convulsions' unattributed cutting, Rambert Ar-
      chive
76   'You can't expect it to be perfect' SG
      'a perfect expression of the spirit' undated cutting
      'I thought the offers' SG
      'I felt so inadequate' ibid
77   'We were living in one room' ibid
      'like a joke captain' Ker-Seymer conversations
78   'This, all this' *50 Years of Ballet Rambert* (op. cit.)
79   'That was the great bond' Chappell conversations
      'We spoke the same language' Ker-Seymer conversations
80   'We instinctively knew' Chappell conversations
      'sort of drawly' Agnes de Mille interview

81   'Now-a-days so many boys' Philip Hoare, *Serious Pleasures: The Life of Stephen Tennant*
     'dragging people upstairs' Ker-Seymer conversations
82   'Fred had his way with him' ibid
     'who wasn't anything' Ker-Seymer conversations
     'Fred never bothered about a costume' Chappell conversations
83   'Only one' *Evelyn Waugh: Diaries*, ed. Mark Amory (13 June 1930)
85   'something of the same inimitable brand' *Yvonne Printemps 1894–1977*, ed. Patrick O'Connor
     'I remember taking my stick of black' DV
     'Nobody noticed, and then we'd say' ibid
86   'a Greek ballet' *DT*, January 1931

CHAPTER 4: MENTORS AND MUSES (1928–1931)

88   'My very dear Mim' letter held in Rambert Dance Company Archive
90   'just like students did' SG
91   'The thing that a choreographer really needs' ibid
     'Even the Ballets Russes' Van Norman Baer, *Bronislava Nijinska*
93   'She just had to whip us' SG
     'I remember once going to her' ibid
94   'They all had square heads' Chappell conversations
99   'Her hats were like' ibid
100 'We had the feeling' Rubinstein obituary, *The Times*, 21 October 1960
     'All Diaghilev had her do' DMcD
     'the cold scrutiny . . . white-gloved and richly clad' *Times* obituary, op. cit.
101 'It is enraging to see' *Week-End Review*, Vol. 4, No 72, 25 July 1931
     'usually talking vaguely . . . sauf la virtuosité' DV
102 'We'd be dumped in a cheap hotel' Chappell conversations
     'this crazy, half-starved tour' BdZ
     'Where I was driven' ibid
105 'What a pity dramatic authors have wives' Q
     'Mr Ashton is to be warmly congratulated' *Punch*, 7 January 1931
     'You'd see everybody there' Chappell conversations
106 'a very special kind of creator' Clement Crisp, Anya Sainsbury and Peter Williams, *50 Years of Ballet Rambert 1926–1976*

107 'with her feet dangling in the air' DV
'She was relentless about pennies' de Mille, *Dance to the Piper*

109 'it was as though a spiritual effigy' Menuhin, *Fiddler's Moll*
'After that I didn't see her again' SG

110 'It functioned as a collective catalyst' Jane Pritchard and Angela Kane, 'The Camargo Society: Part 1', *Dance Research*, Vol. XII, No. 2, Autumn 1994

111 'They say you can only talk to Maynard' Robert Skidelsky, *John Maynard Keynes: The Economist as Saviour 1920–1937*

112 'a gorged seal' Virginia Woolf, *Diary*, Vol. II: 1920–1924 (22 September 1920)
'as exciting as fiction' Roy Harrod, *The Life of John Maynard Keynes*

113 'To hear that lady laugh' MK

114 'the Duse of the dance' FA in Nesta MacDonald and Francis Francis, *Tamara Karsavina*
'They were days of inspiration' ibid
'The feeling that he is introspective' AH, *The Ballet in England*
'state of profound depression' CB, *Dancers under My Lens*
'It was noticeable' *The Nation and Athenaeum*, 25 October 1930

115 'Elinor Glyn's vague "It"' AH, *DT*, April 1931
'I have always regarded Mr Dolin' CB, op. cit.
'How much was due' *DT*, February 1933

116 'We were able for half an hour' *The Nation and Athenaeum*, 25 October 1930
'We arrived on the Friday' MK

117 'the whole thing acutely embarrassing' ibid
'like a Scotch whirlwind' Frances Spalding, *Vanessa Bell*

118 'for the good reason' AH, *Balletomania*
'Today, we do not meet' MK
'Mim loved her role so much' Chappell conversations
'an exquisite Botticelli angel' Sarah Bradford, *Sacheverell Sitwell*
'Diaghilev led me to the Uffizi' Soloman Volkov, *Balanchine's Tchaikovsky*

119 'Now that I am older' unattributed lecture in Ashton archive
'an endurance of standing' Elizabeth Schooling interview

120 'He enjoyed bringing' Mary Clarke, *The Sadler's Wells Ballet*

121 'delightful little fantasia' *Punch*, 22 October 1930
'slow dreamy extension' and subsequent quotations on Markova, ED

123 'To tell you the truth' Elizabeth Salter, *The Last Years of a Rebel*

124 'one almost felt that the milk' MK
125 'The incongruity of a classically flawless' AH undated cutting
'those groups of girls' DMcD
'I'm very fond of *Façade*' CC
126 'A terrible fight' Chappell conversations
'getting nowhere fast' *Dance Research*, Vol. VI, No. 1, Spring 1988
127 'He was magnetic' ibid
'full of very interesting things' Maude Lloyd interview
'It is the Adriatic' Agnes de Mille, *Speak to Me – Dance with Me*
128 'It is a perfect interpretation' AH undated cutting
'Intended to be very modern' CB, *Dancers under My Lens*
'We used to stuff ourselves' Maude Lloyd interview
'He would dive with the children's tyre' Q
129 'a sharply radical' Val Williams, *Independent*, 22 May 1993
130 'That was because of' Anthony Powell, *Messengers of Day*
131 'like a prisoner' ibid
'They were a generation' Barbara Ker-Seymer conversations
'This glorious creature' Ker-Seymer in Marie-Jaqueline Lancaster, *Brian Howard: A Portrait of a Failure*
132 'We used to have supper' Ker-Seymer conversations
133 'the "Greek" section' DT, December 1931
'quite the best ballet' CB, *Dancers under My Lens*
134 'an orgy of sailors' ibid
135 'Because of her perfect restraint' AH, *The Ballet in England*
'dear Wally took not a great deal of notice' John Byron interview
'Once Fred got attached' Chappell conversations

CHAPTER 5: TELL ENGLAND (1931–1935)

138 'whom the poet has neglected to introduce' DT, December 1931
'giving us little bits and pieces' Elizabeth Schooling interview
139 'It was quite an interesting idea' FA in *The Times*, 7 February 1976
142 'dirty steps' Jean and Marshall Stearns, *Jazz Dance*
143 'something very like A New Art Form' Spike Hughes, *Opening Bars*
'largely last-minute affair' ibid

144 'as bright as possible' Frances Spalding, *Vanessa Bell*
'kind and terrifying' ibid
'From then on . . . snaky hips ad nauseum' CB, *Dancers under My Lens*
'naturally they lack something' AH, *The Ballet in England*
'I have never seen a European capture' ibid
'For once Ashton has kept' ibid
'beloved *Swan Lake*' Anton Dolin, *Ballet Go Round*
'It was a matter of absolute impossibility' *DT*, July 1932

145 'At every important moment' Rosie Camden interview
'things could get . . . There'd be an amazed' Bunny Roger interview

146 'the dearest little pastiche' *Observer*, 27 September 1931

147 'Once again the dimensions' DV

148 'Fred never explained anything' Maude Lloyd conversations

150 'a will power that' JH

151 'Can you imaging staging' VT
'a stunning intellect' *Drama Review*, Spring 1982
'There was no beach' Ker-Seymer conversations

152 'We ordered toasted cheese' ibid
'it practically had corks bobbing' Chappell conversations
'I could do something . . . On the credit side' Elizabeth Salter, *Helpmann: The Authorised Biography*

153 'Bobby was noisier and nastier' Neville Blackburne interview
'the ultimate instep dance' Arlene Croce, *Going to the Dance*

154 '*Les Rendezvous* is an old-world' Alastair Macaulay, 'Looking at Ballet: Ashton and Balanchine 1926–36', *Studies in Dance History*, Vol. 3, No. 2, Fall 1992
'The choreography is full of unexpected' Croce, op. cit.
'No one who saw her' P. W. Manchester, *Vic-Wells: A Ballet Progress*
'an uproarious success' ibid

155 'not only for the dance-numbers' VT
'something other than opera' ibid
'I don't really want them to act' JH
'wished in front . . . He had never directed opera' VT
'dance scenario . . . at the discretion' *Drama Review*, Spring 1982

156 'She was tiny and frail' DV

157 'so extraordinary' Wyndham, *Mrs Henderson and Other Stories*
'Harlem was a strange setting' David Herbert, *Second Son*
'If she had her way' Wyndham, op. cit.

'a kind of black ADC' DV

158 'as popular with white people' Herbert, op. cit.
'He was a rather superior type' ibid
'Sometimes it was no more' VT
'I am going to have *Four Saints*' JH
'pick out boys there' DV

159 'None of them was trained' ibid
'a kind of terpsichorean' Carl Van Vechten, *Parties*
'looking like a bank clerk' Billy Chappell conversations
'and all the things Virgil' JH

160 'One would get a whole scene set' DV
'young Freddy' Janet Hobhouse, *Everybody Who Was Anybody*
'In another scene Goya' Stark Young, *Theatre Arts Monthly*,
Vol. XVIII, No. 5, May 1934
'pug-nosed and pigeon-toed' JH

161 'They would do something' BdZ
'a kind of delicacy' DV

162 'I have worked' JH
'I was so tired by then' DV
'Thinking it over' Gertrude Stein, *Selected Letters*

163 '*Four Saints,* in our vivid theatrical parlance' ibid

164 'We felt elated by his success' Q
'I just can't take it' MF
'He was stirred up' Ker-Seymer conversations

168 'a royal scrimmage' Agnes de Mille, *Speak to Me – Dance with Me*
'Mim let go . . . although she minded' ibid
'the only thing like it' Janet Sinclair, quoted in Jane Pritchard,
'The Nostalgic Word of Fantasy', *Studies in Dance History*, Vol.
3, No. 2, Fall 1992

169 'He recognises it' FA in programme note
one of the most beautiful things Mary Clarke, *Dancers of Mercury: The Story of Ballet Rambert*
'pink and plum' ibid
'the best English ballet' *DT*, March 1935
'pot-boil with' Constant Lambert to FA
'The stage was in darkness' DV

170 'I brought her to Dulac' W. B. Yeats, *Uncollected Prose*, Vol. 2
'all the professional' ibid

172 'drunk, repressively gay' Roy Foster interview
'When she later' P. W. Manchester, *Vic-Wells: A Ballet Progress*
'It was obvious' Ninette de Valois, *Come Dance with Me*

173 'There is almost no way' MF

CHAPTER 6: TWO TERPSICHORES (1935–1936)

175 'always urging me on' MF
176 'Where I fell down' DV
178 'totally bound up' Billy Chappell conversations
181 'his opiate-induced visions' MF
'hardly one I could' ibid
'desperately afraid . . some alchemy' ibid
182 'a great collaboration' Constant Lambert to Cecil Beaton
'Ashton has made it live' AH, *DT*, June 1936
'In her Ashton has undoubtedly' ibid
184 'The key to Alice' Billy McCann interview
'impoverished Russian Prince' Serge Obolensky, *One Man in His Time*
185 'exquisite Rococo spirit' Ivan Moffat, ed., *Raimund von Hofmannsthal: A Rosenkavalier*
186 'She was always determined' Doris Langley Moore interview
188 'an off-stage rival' ibid
189 'It has a strong personality' Cecil Beaton, *The Wandering Years*
'stimulating and strangely sympathetic' ibid
'all of whom . . . forlorn sighing couples . . . who stayed for too long' Beaton, unpublished diaries
'People noticed it very much' Daphne Weymouth interview
190 'She throws a nosegay' Simon Fleet, *Ballet Annual*, No. 2, 1948
191 'first of his sophisticated ballets' AH, undated cutting
'audacious experiment' Thomas Beecham, *A Mingled Chime*
'faintly blurred edges' *New Statesman*, 24 October 1936
'everything a little misty' P. W. Manchester, *Vic-Wells: A Ballet Progress*
'one of the most successful' Mary Clarke, *The Sadler's Wells Ballet*
'I used to say' Donna Perlmutter interview
192 'dance about like lunatics' Poppet Pol interview
'He fitted in' Billy Chappell conversations

CHAPTER 7: ALICE, GERTRUDE AND ALICE (1936–1937)

195 'Everyone knew Freddie' Billa Harrod conversation
196 'her whole body talks' *Spectator*, 27 February 1937

199 'stroke of genius' P. W. Manchester, *Vic-Wells: A Ballet Progress*
200 'fluffy mixture' Beverley Nichols, *The Unforgiving Minute*
'He was very good at constructing' FA to Peter Dickinson, Radio 3, 18 September 1983
201 'I think Bobby saw her' Billy Chappell conversations
'toppled the farce' A. V. Coton, *A Prejudice for Ballet*
'You musn't tell' Cecil Beaton, unpublished diaries
203 'It is very sad' Gertrude Stein, *Everybody's Autobiography*
'absolute rubbish' Radio 3, Berners documentary, 18 September 1983.
204 'the effect is incongruous' Arlene Croce, *Going to the Dance*
'as if the last word' Stein, op. cit.
'Being one it is natural' ibid
'an inescapably English' Croce, op. cit.
205 'like a Persian' Edith Sitwell to Alberto de Lacerda, *Selected Letters*
'It's where she keeps' Parker Tyler, *The Divine Comedy of Pavel Tchelitchew*
206 'half ballet and half theatre' Gertrude Stein to FA
208 'At five in the morning' William Chappell, *Fonteyn: Impressions of a Ballerina*
210 'into something quite' John Mills, *Up in the Clouds, Gentlemen please*
'Oh dinkums and pinkums!' *Tatler*, 21 July 1937
211 'like esoteric still-lives' Cecil Beaton, *The Wandering Years*
'when a young boy in a monastery' Stein, op. cit.
213 'This will be our last . . .' Ivan Moffat, *Raimund Von Hofmannsthal: A Rosenkavalier*
'ghastly modern hotel' Billy Chappell conversations
214 'I see you're all . . . I'm not a duck . . . I never move without' David Herbert, *Second Son*
'rudely exhibiting her behind' Beaton, *The Wandering Years*

CHAPTER 8: LOVE IS NOT A BAD THING TO PUSH (1937–1939)

217 'It made him frantic' source witheld
218 'When Michael was on stage' Julia Farron
219 'He was on an intellectual level' Andrew Motion, *The Lamberts*
220 'Today . . . there is something' AH, *The Bystander*, 9 February 1938
'A fin-de-siècle Frenchman' Cecil Gray, *Musical Chairs*

221 'Grouping, characterisation' *The Bystander*, 9 February 1938
'With *Horoscope*, ballet, now truly indigenous' ibid
223 'cannot fail to become' A. V. Coton, *A Prejudice for Ballet*
224 'how to behave in public' Nicholas Lawford, unpublished diary
'They toasted each other . . . A new saga' Cecil Beaton, unpublished diaries
'extraordinarily eccentric . . . brilliant, spontaneous imitations' ibid
225 'to exchange reality' Cecil Beaton, *Ashcombe*
'It was astounding' Cecil Beaton, unpublished diaries (extracted in *The Wandering Years*)
'His sure hands . . . Her back to the public' ibid
'and those that were polite . . . a few good' Beaton, unpublished diaries
226 'Tennessee Williams was also there' Pamela Harlech interview
227 'polished, highly entertaining' A. H. Franks, *Twentieth-Century Ballet*
229 'A good deal of quiet fun' unattributed cutting, 15 April 1939
'it was difficult to get Gerald to conform' Francis Rose, *Saying Life*
'It looked as if' Julia Farron interview
'Very Fred' ibid
230 'a mixture of a courtesan' *The Bystander*, May 1939
'There were quarrels' Rose, op. cit.
'She was a Juliet' ibid

CHAPTER 9: BANG GOES THE WHOLE CONCERN (1939–1941)

234 'I am Russian' MF
'From that day on' ibid
235 'the kind of awkward' ED
236 'Look children' Alicia Markova interview
239 'Through Miss Rutherton and Mr Richardson' Richard Pleasant to FA, Charles Payne, *American Ballet Theater*
241 'gave the company' Kathrine Sorley Walker, *Ninette de Valois*
'Oh, what sore muscles' MF
243 'Gnashing of . . . when the poet' translation by Julian Barnes
'under the influence' Beryl de Zoete, *DT*, March 1940
'I felt I hadn't said nearly' SG
'some terrible unexplained' Mary Clarke, *The Sadler's Wells Ballet*

244 'How far away everything' Victoria Glendinning, *Edith Sitwell*

245 'the end of our supremacy . . . If the Sadler's Wells' G. B. Shaw, letter to *Daily Telegraph*, 6 January 1940
'a great feast of reading . . . anxious to immerse' John Lehmann, *A Nest of Tigers*

246 'neither mock-archaic' Michael Kennedy, *Portrait of Walton*
'And I tried to convey with the bodies' FA, 'The Principles of Choreography', essay in Ashton archive
'the bride's crown' *DT*, May 1940

247 'every picture told a story' Edith Sitwell to FA

250 'For all the world' MF
'Mr So and So . . . without food' undated, unattributed cutting

255 'Fred said' Pamela May interview

256 'beset by every kind' CB, in Mary Clarke, *The Sadler's Wells Ballet*
'a fantastic and highly introspective' undated, unattributed cutting
'My life being free' *Penguin New Writing*, No. 13, April–June 1942

257 'to take mobile form' Mary Clarke, *New Statesman and Nation*, 1 February 1941
'something between the Worst Woman' Dyneley Hussey, *Spectator*, 31 January 1941
'in purple rags looking like' ibid
'I always knew I'd done wrong' Graham Sutherland to FA
'a symphony of movement' de Zoete, *Penguin New Writing*, No. 13, April–June 1942

258 'with a magnificent and tingling' Audrey Williamson, *Contemporary Ballet*
'It is, one feels, Mr Ashton's wits' Hussey, op. cit.
'a triumph' de Zoete, op. cit.

CHAPTER 10: ASHTON'S WAR (1941–1944)

260 'didn't know the rudiments' SG

261 'I think I shall emerge' FA to Cecil Beaton

262 'he didn't know the front' Michael Graham interview
'this funny little man' Emanuel Galitzine interview

263 'the most amazing jitterbug' ibid

264 'I have not uttered' FA to Kenneth Clark

266 'Receipt against boredom' Mary Lutyens, *Edwin Lutyens*

267 'I am glad that you think' FA to Clark

268 'trundling round' FA to Cecil Beaton
     'the stirrings of creation' ibid
     'the Steppes [would] call again' FA to Clark
269 'I feel La is a total loss' Billy Chappell to FA
     'The person who more than any other' MF
     'shoving ballet at' Elizabeth Salter, *Helpmann: The Authorised Biography*
     'We were sensational' ibid
270 'She wanted to keep Bobby' Wendy Toye interview
     'It was an entirely original creation' John Lehmann, *I Am My Brother: Autobiography*
     'a kind of testament' CC
271 'Helpmann is an admirable dancer' Kenneth Clark to unidentified source, Tate Gallery Archives
272 'Freddy himself suggested it' collection of Selina Hastings
     'the quest . . . a search' David Mellor, ed., *A Paradise Lost: The Neo-Romantic Imagination in Britain 1935–55* (Exhibition catalogue, Barbican, London)
     'Communicating with Fred' Doris Langley Moore to Billy Chappell
273 'bribe guards on trains' Walton to John Warrack, Michael Kennedy, *Portrait of Walton*
     'distinctly forced' ' "The Quest": first impressions', in *Arabesque*, Oxford, Trinity term 1943
     'very insipid fare' CB, *Sadler's Wells Ballet*
274 'no spiritual depth' Beryl de Zoete, *Penguin New Writing*, Vol. 17, April–June 1943
     'to give any idea . . . to convey clearly' FA, undated cutting
     'dedication to anything' de Zoete, op. cit.
275 'It is better than seeing' FA to Kenneth Clark
277 'a master of evasion' Kenneth Clark, *The Other Half*
     '*Sir*, next time you drive' Rosie Camden interview

CHAPTER 11: MIDWINTER SPRING (1944–1946)

280 'This is Flying Officer' Sylvia Loeb interview
     'He hated it' ibid
281 'contemplative and almost mystical' FA to Billy Chappell
283 'I rather put myself in the hands' FA to John Percival, *The Times*, undated cutting
     'That was what the French' and subsequent Volkova quotations, from Gilbert Vernon interview and unpublished written tribute

284 'one of his posh friends' Kitty Evison interview
'I want to thank you' Mary Clarke, *The Sadler's Wells Ballet*
285 'determined to be famous' Doris Langley Moore interview
'If Bobby bought an Aubusson' Dick Beard conversations
286 'I saw that everything was becoming' DMcD
'Old Ma Gielgud' FA to Chappell
287 'Not very successfully' John Gielgud, *Shakespeare Hit or Miss?*
'One, two, three, twirl' Michael Billington, *Peggy Ashcroft*
'very bad indeed' Gielgud, op. cit.
'like Wotan' FA to Chappell
'Very Sarah Bernhardt . . . *voix d'or*' Gielgud, op. cit.
'with a posse' Barbara Ker-Seymer to Chappell
288 'To Brian épaulement' Gilbert Vernon interview
'flop-haired Cecil Beaton' Clive James, *The New Yorker*, 2 November 1992
'Fred was the first person' Alard Tobin interview
'at parties' ibid
'And yet I always felt' ibid
289 'Amor [*sic*]' Brian Shaw to FA
'It was a great theatre' Ninette de Valois, *Come Dance with Me*
290 'I visualised the possibility' ibid
'He didn't want to supplant' Gilbert Vernon interview
'the traditional two' de Valois, op. cit.
291 'Large groups of courtiers' Mary Clarke, op. cit.
'I went all over' FA, *DTJ*, Vol. 2, No. 3, Autumn 1984
'the gateway . . . the greatest artist' Arlene Croce, *Going to the Dance*
'whatever horror nudge' Ted Hughes, 'To Paint a Waterlily'
292 'Quite unbelievable' Kaleidoscope, Radio 4, 7 and 10 October 1988
293 'They were together in my mind' Simon Fleet, *Ballet Annual*, No. 2, 1948
'We came up a hill' DV
'Margot *Fon*-teyn . . . Moira *Shear*-er' Alastair Macaulay, *The New Yorker*, 25 May 1992
294 'It has that breath-taking quality' unidentifiable letter, FA archive
'Quite right' FA to Richard Buckle: extracts from Ashton's notebook and interview with Richard Buckle printed in *Ballet*, Vol. IV, No. 5, November 1947
'*Poco allegro*' ibid
295 'to whisper private and sacred things' Brian Friel, *Dancing at Lughnasa*

'I am frankly bored' FA to Audrey Williamson, *The Art of Ballet*

'simply steps, pure dancing' Moira Shearer in Barbara Newman, *Striking a Balance*

'personal fount of emotion' FA, 'The Subject Matter of Ballet: A Symposium', *Ballet Annual*, 13, 1959, ed. A.H.

'It's not abstract' Barbara Newman, *Striking a Balance*

'towards pure gladness' Vincent Indy, *César Franck*

'secret history' Paul Murray, *T. S. Eliot and Mysticism: The Secret History of Four Quartets*

296 'male and female have become' Chappell, *Studies in Ballet*

'really stretch' Alastair Macaulay conversations

'breath-taking ecstatic' *New Statesman and Nation*, 4 May 1946

'almost Greek in feeling' letter in Ashton archive

'moving alone coldly' FA to Buckle, op. cit.

'Perhaps I was afraid' ibid

297 'a cold complexity emerges' FA, 'The Subject Matter of Ballet', op. cit.

'of some acute' Helen Gardner, *The Composition of 'Four Quartets'*

'a revelation of the power' A. H. Franks, *Twentieth-Century Ballet*

'the emotional stream' *New Statesman and Nation*, 4 May 1946

'Entirely and completely of the theatre' undated, unattributed cutting

CHAPTER 12: INTERPRETERS OF LOVE (1946-1947)

300 'Fred was just like' Bunny Roger interview

'a very serious get together' Pamela May interview

'a mental reck' Brian Shaw to FA

'the sensation' *Ballet*, June 1946

301 'with a youthful zest' Richard Buckle, *Adventures of a Ballet Critic*

'The English boys' Dick Beard conversations

302 'a marvellous dame' Muriel Bentley interview

'I've been talking' Nora Kaye to FA

'great longing and nostalgia . . . stirringly sweet emotions' ibid

307 'coloured picture postcards', Jean Cocteau in Richard Buckle, *Diaghilev*

'a postcard of Lily Elsie' *Ballet Annual*, Vol 2, 1948

308 'balloon music of 1904' DT, January 1947

'While Gerald Berners worked' Cecil Beaton, *Ballet*
309 'as vulgar as humans' Beryl de Zoete, *New Statesman and Nation*, 23 November 1946
'In ballet it is the bird-like' Richard Buckle, undated cutting
'When, as the Eastern potentate' de Zoete, op. cit.
'to create an atmosphere . . . the sense of desolation . . . Lord Berners' "pop-goes-the weasel"' Beaton, op. cit.
310 'perverse and comic music' undated, unattributed cutting
'The more elaborate a joke' Buckle, op. cit.
'I think the way to keep oneself alive' CC
311 'everyone strutting about' *Ballet*, Vol. 3, No. 1, January 1947
'one of the loveliest things' ibid
'a fifty per cent success' Desmond Shaw-Taylor, *New Statesman and Nation*, 21 December 1946
312 'Only in *Manon*' Harold Rosenthal, *Opera at Covent Garden: A Short History*
314 'All the minors sang' ibid
'Massine brought something' Haltrecht Montague, *The Quiet Showman: Sir David Webster and the Royal Opera House*
316 'For the choreographer in me' FA to Dick Beard
322 'very John Fowler' Bunny Roger interview
323 'making an orgasm of it' Dick Beard account
'but must it be Tchaikowsky' Nora Kaye to FA
324 'France's day of freedom' FA to Beard
'exactly the teacher' MF
'new, exciting ballets' ibid
'the person whom' ibid
'managed to simplify' Dick Beard account
325 'very Toulouse Lautrec' ibid
'As we arrived in Cabourg' ibid

CHAPTER 13: MR A OBSESSED WITH MR B (1947–1950)

329 'suggested by actual people' FA to Richard Buckle, *Ballet*, Vol. IV, No. 5, November 1947
'Two (boys) were both attracted' ibid
330 'sensualité un peu sêche' Rollo H. Myers, *Ravel: Life and Works*
'just a party' Anne Heaten interview
'evokes a pretty' Arlene Croce, *The New Yorker*, 12 December 1988

331 'but in reverse' Moira Shearer, *Balletmaster: A Dancer's View of George Balanchine*
'neat pink scenery' Buckle, op. cit.
'It is poetic and charged' FA to Dick Beard
332 'Inactive, an inspirer' ibid
333 'associates in the journey . . . for those who troubled . . . intricate, nightmare baroque' Richard Buckle, *Adventures of a Ballet Critic*
'tiresome and superficial' FA to Beard
'Ashton was in turn' Buckle, op. cit.
334 'a railway bridge . . . rich in sadistic . . . a sort of fantastic pavilion' ibid
'*Surtout, pas de diamants!*' ibid
335 'only scenic idea . . . a black tutu . . .' Igor Stravinsky and Robert Craft, *Dialogues and a Diary*
'The French desire to astonish' FA to Beard
'a copy of *Vogue*' *Spectator*, 20 February 1948
'a mocking Parisian glitter' undated, unattributed cutting
'David and Jonathan position' Buckle, op. cit.
'I set out to display her' FA, 'The Production of a Ballet' (essay in Ashton archive)
'nothing goes on too long' ibid
336 'I used to place' CC
'anywhere could be front' FA to DV
'featherweight and sugared' Igor Stravinsky and Robert Craft, op. cit.
'shoulders and feet' Arlene Croce, *The New Yorker*, 4 August 1991
337 'a hidden beauty' FA to Beard
'come to be regarded' *New Statesman and Nation*, 21 February 1948
'AN AUSTERE NEW BALLET' *Ballet*, Vol. 5, No. 3, March 1948
'elusive . . . skeleton-like . . . devoid of warmth' *DT*, April 1948
'certaines opinions' André Beaupaire to FA
338 'Getting away from direct' Hans Werner Henze to FA
340 'not of genius' FA to Beard
'swollen images of' *Paris Review*, Vol. 24, 1959–60
'Ah! la derrière' MF
'halfway between Dali' *Ballet*, Vol. 7, No. 6, June 1949
'As a final confession' ibid
341 'physically cleansed' FA to Beard
'He does not dance' *Ballet*, Vol. 5, No. 7, July 1948
'fierce and beautiful birds' ibid
342 'If I showed the least' FA in William Chappell, ed., *Edward Burra: A Painter Remembered by His Friends*

'chi-chi ruins' Annabel Farjeon, *New Statesman and Nation*, 4 December 1948

343 'The ballet hardly touches' Audrey Williamson, *The Art of Ballet*

'This Don Juan' P. W. Manchester, *Dance News*, November 1953

'an onerous task' *Ballet*, Vol. 7, No. 1, January 1949

'what was intended' Louis Biancolli, undated cutting

'by two importunate' Cecil Beaton, *Ballet*

'really bitter blow' FA to Beard

344 'In the past, any part' MF

345 'Ballet of the' *Picture Post*, 14 January 1949

346 'English sweetness . . . Watching them' ED

'Nadia couldn't walk through' Anya Linden interview

347 'It absolutely suited her' Gilbert Vernon interview

'something of an anomaly' *Ballet*, Vol. 7, No. 2, February 1949

'a smiling threat' ED

'very well-hung' source withheld

'Brian wasn't out of the picture' source withheld

348 'Everyone loves Alexander' Anne Renshaw interview

351 'the essence of all' FA to Beard

352 'filling the house' Arlene Croce, *The New Yorker*, 25 May 1987

'a big pseudo-romantic bore' *Dance Magazine*, December 1949

'inferior Balanchine' FA to Richard Buckle

'production miracles' undated, unattributed cutting

'a terrific wallop' John Martin, *New York Times*, undated cutting

353 'the most lovely new start' Romana McEwen conversations

354 'visiting Brits' Gore Vidal interview

'I used to weep' FA to DV

355 'Kirstein and I agreed' Cecil Beaton, *Ballet*

'the Schloss up the Hudson . . . like an expensive sponge' Lincoln Kirstein to Richard Buckle

'A troupe of pierrots' Beaton, op. cit.

357 'glorious, golden, beauteous' FA to Beard

358 'too pretty, too chic' Beaton, op. cit.

'The most impressive' Walter Terry, *New York Herald Tribune*, 19 March 1950

'He went to Mr B' Jacques d'Amboise interview

360 'one of the least generous men' Lincoln Kirstein interview

'Talking over those' Tanaquil LeClercq, *The Ballet Cookbook*

'really lovely' E. M. Forster to FA

361 'anything that was not a bouquet' Richard Buckle

CHAPTER 14: ANTIPODEAN MOONSHINE (1950–1956)

362 'But as soon as' Ray Powell interview
363 'out of romantic nostalgia' Billy Chappell conversations
364 'the beautiful suspense' ED
     'Alexander was like' source withheld
     'I said to her' FA to Walter Terry, DV
     'Because M Petit's influence' Pavel Tchelitchew to FA
365 'Greek ballets with people' DV
366 'I find that often' FA to Walter Terry, DV
     'that same quality' ibid
367 'what you would call a swank yacht' Ruth Page, *Page by Page*
     'saying that he was reading' MF
368 'How do you explain' FA to Andrew Motion, *The Lamberts*
369 '[It] would hardly have won' Clive Barnes, *D&D*, September
     1951
     'fizzed up into a kind of orgasm' Pauline Clayden interview
     'still something lingering' ibid
     'Tito has made' Jane Edgeworth interview
     'pointless and vulgar . . . [an] absurd wrangle' Richard Buckle,
     Adventures of a Ballet Critic
370 'too easily reconciled' ibid
371 'the remote, the inaccessible' Richard Shead, *Constant Lambert*
     'Take the Ham' Gilbert Vernon interview
     'a sort of dwarfish' Lincoln Kirstein to Richard Buckle
     'evocative, pictorial' *Foyer*, Vol. 1
373 'Massine took charge . . . knowing which parts . . . had better
     manners' Michael Powell, *Million-Dollar Movie*
375 '*Iseult at Tintagel* must be mist-bound' Lincoln Kirstein to FA
     'very like Alexander' Jacques d'Amboise interview
     'Wagnerian [illegible] overtones' ibid
376 'a great event' Cecil Beaton to Hal Burton
     'traditional gift of narrative . . . It is primarily' Kirstein to
     Richard Buckle
377 'dull, dispirited, frustrated' FA to Cecil Beaton
     'David was the love' Frank Raiter interview
378 'That was a wonderful' ibid
     'Fred had a way' Ray Powell interview
     'Ninette adored Alexander' Derek Rencher
     'Why don't you take me' letter in Ashton archive
379 'We could talk' Alexander Grant conversations

'columns through' Susana Walton, *William Walton: Behind the Façade*

380 'Boy loves Girl' Richard Buckle, *Observer*, undated cutting
'as simple as possible' Sacheverell Sitwell to FA
'The part has everything' Clive Barnes, *D&D*, November 1952

381 'a Volinin-like solo' CB, undated cutting
'The first thing Freddie did' Alexander Grant conversations
'peculiarly French' Ivor Guest, *Ballet*, Vol. 12, No. 10, October 1952
'Hearing this 19th-century music' FA to Walter Terry, DV
'a confusion of excellence' Richard Buckle, *Observer*, undated cutting
'[Its] dance composition for Acts I and II' CB undated cutting

382 'felt cheated' Clement Crisp conversations
'She found it unusual' Peter Lethbridge, *Kathleen Ferrier*

383 'There is genius' Clive Barnes, undated, unattributed cutting
'The more trivial the subject' ED
'As the first performance went on' Simon Fleet, *Sophie Fedorovitch: A Biographical Sketch*

384 'stately dancing . . . unadulterated sublimity' Winton Dean, March 1953
'failed lamentably . . . Orpheus strolled' Mary Clarke, *Ballet Annual*, 8, 1954
'cute rather than fearsome' *D&D*, April 1953
'He was always bubbling' Derek Rencher interview

386 'among the finest' *D&D*, July 1953
'Mr Ashton has done his job' ibid
'one of the great disasters' George, Earl of Harewood, *The Tongs and the Bones*
'all the Goyas in Spain' Alexander Grant conversations
'They used to go to Schraffts's' Frank Raiter interview
'sat in melancholy silence' Grant conversations

388 'Some people drink' ibid
'Pavlova, Isadora Duncan' MF
'never be able to marry anyone' ibid
'Fred adored every moment' Leslie Edwards interview

389 'things were a little fraught' Michael Boulton interview
'adored sex' and subsequent quotations about Grant, sources withheld

390 'exeedingly feeble' Mary Clarke, *Sadler's Wells Ballet*
'a very honourable near-miss' ibid
'There is something' Richard Buckle, *Observer*, 6 June 1954

391 'didn't really spark . . . so purely set' source withheld
'great bounds, and jumps' CB, *Ballets Past and Present*
'I saw Buckle' Alexander Grant to FA

392 'She folds up' Richard Buckle, *Observer*, undated cutting
'a lovely and delicate' Clarke, op. cit.

393 'pantomiming their way' Arlene Croce, *The New Yorker*, 13 May 1985
'If I'd done it for us' DMcD

394 'Anna Magnani-size' Arlene Croce, *Sight Lines*
'Henning Kronstam was totally' Penelope Boscawen interview
'something deep in the Danish soul' ibid

396 'quite a little belly' Frank Raiter interview
'Fred was not his type' source withheld

397 'He was completely there' Annette Page interview
'The little ballet thus became' Alexander Bland, *The Royal Ballet: The First 50 Years*
'half a tribute to *Beauty*' Arlene Croce, *The New Yorker*, 2 July 1990

398 'spring-like in lemon', *DT*, June 1956
'They're all going to have to look' Frank Raiter interview

399 'pure Cat-Nip' Eileen Coley interview
'She felt something' transcript of inquest interview

CHAPTER 15: SPRING CHICKEN (1956–1963)

401 '"What is *Ondine?*"' Hans Werner Henze, *Music and Politics: Collected Writings 1953–81* (trans. Peter Labanyi)

402 'a new world of aesthetics' *Sunday Telegraph*, 6 January 1991
'In my world' Henze lecture, Berlin University, 28 January 1963

406 'brief fleeting communications' Henze, *Music and Politics*
'She consoles me a little' FA to Kenneth Clark
'the last of the' Paul Griffiths, *The New Yorker*, 18 October 1993
'a modern aqualung film' Michael Powell, *Million-Dollar Movie*

408 'whom I like & who' FA to Henze

409 'The old maestro' translation by Anne Dunhill

410 'real hellfire' Arlene Croce, *Afterimages*
'it lacked scenic action' Serge Lifar, *Serge Diaghilev: His Life, His Work, His Legend: An Intimate Biography*

'all talent . . . He glittered and suffered' Klaus Mann, *The Turning Point: An Autobiography*
'quite sympathetic' FA to Henze

411 'Freddy Ashton and Lucian Freud' Ann Fleming to Evelyn Waugh, in *The Letters of Ann Fleming*, ed. Mark Amory
'unarmigerous dancer' Waugh to Nancy Mitford, *The Letters of Evelyn Waugh*, ed. Mark Amory
'work twice as hard' Peter Quennell, *The Wanton Chase*
'Freddy was a great' Ann Fleming to Waugh, *The Letters of Evelyn Waugh* (30 June 1958)
'little Cecil Beatnik' ibid (26 January 1960)
'the pale and the placid' Frances Donaldson, *A Twentieth-Century Life*

412 'with an undergrown' Ann Fleming to Patrick Leigh Fermor, August 1959
'as pointu as her nose' Martine de Courcel interview

414 'rather a dull character' *Sunday Times*, 8 March 1959
'handsome dummy' Alexander Bland, *Observer*, 2 November 1958
'full of the true poetic' FA to Henze
'I wanted the movement' FA to Peter Brinson, undated cutting

416 'How on earth . . .' FA in *The Englishman's Garden*, ed. Alvilde Lees-Milne and Rosemary Verey
'Junk . . . extremely pretty' Cecil Beaton, unpublished diaries

417 'days of contemplation' and subsequent FA quotes on this page from his article in *La Fille mal gardée*, Famous Ballets, No 1, ed. Ivor Guest

419 'the accumulative waves . . . imposed on poor Hérold . . . musique concrete' ibid

420 'choreographically it's all' SG

421 'one of the most resonant' DV
'If you have a company' CC
'For years he has' Clive Barnes, *Spectator*, 5 February 1960

422 'The whole cast' Nerina to Barbara Newman, *Striking a Balance*

424 'Ecod! . . . his own man again' Oliver Goldsmith, *She Stoops to Conquer*

425 'carrying the applause of *Fille*' FA to Kenneth Clark

428 'Think of that passage' Clive Barnes, *D&D*, April 1961

429 'Here was something' ibid
'too stiff and English' DV
'I removed the girl's pouts' LS

'The way he grins' Richard Buckle, *Sunday Times*, 26 February 1961

430 'yearn upward' Alastair Macaulay, *Ballet Review*, Vol. 8, No. 1, 1980
'a sentimental piece' *New Statesman*, 24 February 1961
'a pot au feu of pigeons' FA to Clement Crisp

431 'We are ripe in ballet' Peter Brook, *Observer*, 17 March 1963
'He looked like' Frank Raiter interview
'Freddie's face' Cecil Beaton, unpublished diaries

432 'difficult & unsympathetic' FA to Tony Lizzul
'I hate policed states' FA to Ann Fleming
'hideous except in odd . . . dusty but beautiful' ibid

433 'one little roome' John Donne, 'The Good-Morrow'

434 'mostly written by Rudolf' Maude Lloyd interview
'The huge stage was empty' Cecil Beaton, *Self-Portrait with Friends: The Selected Diaries 1922–1974*, ed. Richard Buckle

435 'in fact, it was so charged' FA to David Daniel, November 1974
'A hymn to freedom' undated, unattributed cutting
'Tragic clutching' Richard Buckle, *Sunday Times*, 5 November 1961
'Everyone says it was' Beaton, unpublished diaries

436 'the drama of the green world' *The Anatomy of Criticism*
'doing what we thought' Billy Chappell conversations
'A veritable Russian Easter' *Persephone* record note by Robert Craft
'grande diseuse' Keith Lester to Jann Parry, introduction to a performance of *Persephone*, Radio 3, 28 May 1991

437 'really made us feel' Svetlana Beriosova, ibid
'almost like a Botticelli' Monica Mason, ibid
'a wonderful stretching out' Radio 3
'For this Stravinsky' Clive Barnes, *D&D*, January 1962
'There was great gentleness' Mason, Radio 3
'He has apparently' Barnes, op. cit.
'Nothing predominates' A. V. Coton, undated cutting
'a cross-breed' Barnes, op. cit.
'What should be stylised' ibid

440 'He's ruined it' Billy Chappell conversations
'most miraculous' and subsequent quotations on this and next page from Beaton's unpublished diaries

441 'I explained that' ibid
'tango her up and down' William Servaes interview
'for reasons of modesty' MF

'anguished choreographer' Alexander Bland, *Observer*, 19 March 1963

442 'I gave as good' MF

'the audacity of stillness' Peter Brook, *Observer*, 17 March 1963

'There's an enormous sexual impulse' FA to David Daniel

'Michael was standing with Margot' Bland, op. cit.

'one of those' MF

'electrical storm . . . Rudolf [had] burst' ibid

443 'This was before Rudi' Bland, op. cit.

'in a vein of gloom' Sacheverell Sitwell, *Liszt*

'a kind of tabloid, a pillule . . . ' Bland, op. cit.

'This seemed a marvellous thing' FA to Daniel

444 'Extraordinary actors' Brook, op. cit.

'the ballet must be . . . realistic ballet' Beaton, unpublished diaries

'little comedy scene . . . because it prevented' ibid

445 'The way they just stand' Bland, op. cit.

'It was so exciting' Maude Lloyd conversations

'This hectic choroegraphy' *D&D*, April 1963

446 'Hardly anyone knew' MF

'Rudolf's romanticism' Maude Lloyd conversations

'She was in a state' FA to Daniel

'Il m'embête' Martine de Courcel conversations

'a specimen of the personality cult' *DT*, April 1963

CHAPTER 16: THE PUPPY (1963–1970)

448 'double sourcery' *New York Herald Tribune*, 5 May 1963

'I thought that he' FA to David Daniel

'It left one with the impression' Lillian Moore, *DT*, July 1963

449 'I feel rather like' Alexander Bland, *The Royal Ballet: The First 50 Years*

'You've no right' Peter Wright, unedited transcript of *Omnibus* obituary, 'Sir Fred: A Celebration', BBC1, transmitted 30 September 1988

450 'the castigator of the inadequate' James Monahan, *DT*, November 1984

'ferocious irascibility' Michael Somes to James Monahan

'He felt that somehow' Garrett Drogheda interview

'had no organisational skills' ibid
451 'we fought like cat and dog' conversation with Alastair Macaulay
452 'He always brought' Anthony Dowell, *Omnibus* transcript
'I simply insisted' FA to Daniel
'tinkering around . . . until the whole' *D&D*, February 1964
'rather depleated' FA to Tony Lizzul
454 'a performance to remember' James Monahan, *DT*, May 1963
'That ballet is a sextet' FA to Daniel
'He thought only of himself' ibid
455 'Perhaps because she was Ninette's' source withheld
'most balletic . . . I could do something' *Ashton's Dream: Dance Masterclass*, BBC2, transmitted 9 April 1988
'a digest version' Clive Barnes, *D&D*, May 1964
'I had the play' *Masterclass*
456 'real flesh and blood' Sibley in Barbara Newman, *Striking a Balance*
'It was purely a look' Anthony Dowell, *Omnibus* transcript
457 'fetching boy god . . . throwing out . . . The extra stretch' Arlene Croce, *Afterimages*
'She's as great as he is' Barbara Newman, *Antoinette Sibley: Reflections of a Ballerina*
458 'A disappointment' Barnes, op. cit.
'mingier and mingier' *Masterclass*
'Watch how those bodies' Alastair Macaulay, *DT*, August 1986
'one of the most significant' Croce, op. cit.
'a love-match . . . ' James Monahan, *DT*, January 1965
459 'the ultimate betrayal' LS
'Kenneth always had' Lynn Seymour interview
460 'the continuity of his line' Croce, op. cit.
'athletae Dei' *D&D*, May 1965
461 'a luminous, peculiar' Croce, op. cit.
'an uncompromising experiment' ibid
'When I was younger' FA, 'Notes on Choreography', in *The Dance Has Many Faces*, ed. Walter Sorell
'Good old British' Croce, op. cit.
'a physical attraction' Peter Williams, *D&D*, June 1966
462 'is to make Number One' Monahan, *DT*, June 1966
'enormous and outrageous' and subsequent quotations on this page about Thomas, sources withheld
'He just disintegrated' Billy Chappell conversations
463 'Martyn's real father' Jennifer Mellors interview
'People were drawn' source withheld

464 'Fred didn't trust Patric' Joan Thring interview
'a kind of Svengali' David Cope interview
'He was one of those' Patric Walker interview
'polished Martyn's edges' Cope interview

465 'He'd read the biographies' David Scott-Bradbury interview
'a cheerful and extrovert' Noel Goodwin, *D&D*, April 1987

466 'an explosion . . . giant mauve' *D&D*, April 1987

467 'Quite honestly we all know' source withheld
'quite irrepressible' source withheld
'Worth a hundred' Poppet Pol interview

471 'Stop behaving like' Derek Jarman interview
'*Monotones* gone' Clement Crisp, *Spectator*, 19 January 1968
'totally unbearable' *DT*, February 1968

472 'Like the Queen Mother' Peter Williams, *D&D*, February 1968
'the balance, the measure' Martine de Courcel to FA
'Ashton Out of Date' *DT*, February 1968

473 'As a company' *Queen*, 22 June 1966
'was behind the whole thing' source withheld

474 'Fred was devoted to them' John Tooley interview
'You may have heard . . . dangerous times' source withheld

475 'part of the Ashton' Tooley interview
'That Liverpool' Colin Graham interview
'He felt sure . . . Fred used to say' source withheld

476 'From that moment' Anthony Russell-Roberts conversations
'not all the adulation' Michael Kennedy, *Portrait of Elgar*
'Elgar is in the air' Alexander Grant conversations

477 'as derived from plump' Lincoln Kirstein, 'The Composer as First Dancer', *Movement and Metaphor*
'Then I hit upon the idea' DMcD
'an accuracy which is almost psychic' Richard Buckle, *Sunday Times*, 26 October 1969

478 'An enigma, the most' *Time*, undated cutting
'It seemed wrong' DMcD
'a state of seventh-heaven' Kennedy, op. cit.

479 'galaxy of grotesques' *D&D*, September 1970
'I did several versions' DMcD
'as if we're back' Derek Rencher interview

480 'I really can't stop' Mrs Richard Powell, *Edward Elgar: Memoirs of a Variation*
'sneaks in' Stephanie Jordan, *DTJ*, Vol. II, No. 1, winter 1993/4
'Your feet are' Barbara Newman, *Antoinette Sibley*
'Fred always treated me' *Omnibus* transcript

481 'lost love still' Kennedy, op. cit.
482 'two stiff-collared' *Observer*, 27 October 1968
  'Fred wanted a peaceful life' David Cope interview
  'more a form of hand-out' Jennifer Mellors interview
  'quite apart from lover' Moura Lympany interview
  'bunch of flowers' David Cope interview
483 'If Fred sent you out' source withheld
  'like a monstrous' DV
  'the end of his love affair' *D&D*, March 1970
485 'a terrific clash . . . Martyn got into' Jean-Pierre Gasquet conversations
486 'the very type' Nicholas Boyle, *Goethe: The Poet and the Age*
487 'a ballet that makes you chuckle' John Percival, *D&D*, August 1970
  'who might have nipped over' Noel Goodwin, ibid
488 'as demonstrative an expression' *D&D*, July 1970

CHAPTER 17: EYE SOCIETY (1970–1977)

489 'frightfully bad cooking' Billy Chappell conversations
493 'The old man's gaga' Rumer Godden, *The Tale of the Tales: The Beatrix Potter Ballet*
  'It's too rhythmical' ibid
494 'just as I would for' FA to Gordon Gow, *DT*, February 1971
495 'avant-garde innocence' Kirstein to Richard Buckle
  'wearisome' James Monahan, *DT*, May 1971
497 'Anticipate with your *eyes* . . .' *Review: Ashton in Camera*, BBC2, transmitted 10 March 1972
  'Push her on on on on' ibid
498 'reality and illusion' Judith Mackrell, *Independent*, 4 November 1991
  'true to the text' *Review: Ashton in Camera*
  'Ashton never strained' Mackrell op. cit.
  'The bastard – he's done it' MF
500 'this pathetic little . . . I gave him' source withheld
  'always on and off' David Ball interview
  'certainly a contrast' Mark Brinkley to author
502 'Martyn could have' Neil Alston interview
  'Martyn was over the edge' ibid
503 'I think Fred would' Colin Graham interview
  'The next day' source withheld

504 'whipping people up' Deborah MacMillan interview
505 'like something the cat' FA to Billy Chappell
'somewhat upset' Alan Blythe, *Remembering Britten*
'frightfully excited' Prue Penn conversations
'Tadzio-orientated' Donald Mitchell in Humphrey Carpenter, *Benjamin Britten*
506 'neurasthenic queen' Peter Heyworth, *Observer*, 24 June 1973
'Aschenbach's failure' undated cutting
507 'snip out a bar' Blythe, op. cit.
508 'which can look' David Matthews, *Times Literary Supplement*, 3–9 November 1989
510 'do the character . . . usual charming . . . De Valois would *not*' Alexander Grant conversations
'little something' and subsequent quotations on this page, LS
511 'Keep your fingers' ibid
'the rose-petal' ED
512 'That's exactly' LS
'Lynn Seymour the actress' Arlene Croce, *Afterimages*
'called no less than . . . Not too easy' FA to Martine de Courcel
513 'Everywhere is the same' ibid
'negotiated these two . . . they all seemed' Jean-Pierre Gasquet interview
514 'aimed at Freddie' ibid
'why Freddie put up' ibid
'without Martyn, Chandos' David Ball interview
'He was always anxious' Jennifer Mellors interview
'She made him suffer' *Independent on Sunday*, 24 April 1994
515 'That was the least' Neil Alston interview
516 'remarkable . . . for the score' *DTJ*, Vol. 11, Nos. 1 & 2, 1978–9
'I had heard rumours' LS
517 'l'épanouissement de l'être' V. S. Pritchett, Introduction to Turgenev's *First Love*, Penguin Classics edn.
518 'That he could reach' Brian Friel to author
'a foxy little number' LS
'locked up together' Lynn Seymour interview
519 'could have been insinuated' *D&D*, April 1976
'is like some brief' V. S. Pritchett, Introduction to *First Love*
'the sole triumph' Croce, op. cit.
'Martyn had recently' David Scott-Bradbury interview
'attractive, vital' Brian Friel (after Turgenev), *A Month in the Country*
520 'almost criminally responsive' Croce, op. cit.

'In the play' ibid
'the most gentle' Friel, op. cit.
'the action resides' Brian Friel, Introduction to *A Month in the Country*

521 'In its weightless . . .' Lynn Garafola, *Diaghilev's Ballets Russes*
'new false image . . . She's becoming . . . dashes pathos' Croce, op. cit.

522 'its decline' ibid

523 'the work of a genius' Mary Clarke, *DT*, June 1971
'Ashton Could Be' undated cutting

524 'pink birthday cake' Prue Penn conversations
'like a half-closed' *The Times Saturday Review*, 4 August 1990

526 'frightfully late' Lady Hambleden
'a great enjoyer' Prue Penn conversations

528 'absolutely each other's' Camilla Cazalet interview

529 'As we rose to the skies' verses recorded for the author by Prue Penn

530 'a great theatre buff' Prue Penn conversations

CHAPTER 18: BUGGER OLD AGE (1976–1988)

532 'Old Turkish Lady' Lincoln Kirstein interview

533 'No one has done' Gelsey Kirkland, *The Shape of Love*
'Sentimental, yes' *Vandance*, May 1991

534 'All tedious to me' FA to Martine de Courcel

535 'madly conventional' Colette Clark interview

536 'They woke her up' Anthony Russell-Roberts conversations
'After a matinee of *Fille*' Mikhail Baryshnikov interview

537 'not one skid' Arlene Croce, *Going to the Dance*
'He does too much' ibid

538 'like corks bobbing' ibid
'some devised, fantastic violin' Sergei Rachmaninov, *A Lifetime of Music* by Sergei Bertensson and Jay Leyda

539 'He performs soothingly' ibid
'absolutely pea green' Frances Donaldson, *A Twentieth-Century Life*

540 'Surely if you continue' source withheld
'and just stayed' David Cope interview

541 'the usual weekend with words' Ruth Fermoy to FA
'a miracle of nature' undated, unattributed cutting

'something very detrimental' source withheld
'According to P.W.' source withheld
'not so enchanted garden' Martyn Thomas to FA
543 'the physical' Jennifer Mellors interview
544 'Who are they interested in' Alastair Macaulay, *DT*, September 1983
545 'Well, I just sat down' Barbara Newman, *Antoinette Sibley*
'a very ornate' Antoinette Sibley interview
'She is left to' Macaulay, op. cit.
546 'They seemed to give' Neil Alston interview
547 'the most delicious . . . To *think*' Princess Margaret interview
549 'a serious falling out' Alston interview
550 'You are a ballerina' Katherine Healy in *Dance Now*, Vol. 3, No. 3, Autumn 1994
'The critics are preparing' ibid
554 'She put our noses' source withheld
555 'Those who loved him' Moura Lympany interview
557 'I was so surprised . . . He knew women' Natalia Makarova, *Omnibus* transcript
558 'It was hard to recognise' *Dance Now*, Vol. 3, No. 3, Autumn 1994
560 'half an hour left' FA to Rupert Christiansen
'very very tottery' Billa Harrod conversation
'doing a sort of mock' Neiti Gowrie conversation
561 'climbed into bed' Princess Margaret interview

AFTERWORD

564 'What he has wished' James Monahan, *DT*, October 1977
566 'a good hater' Noel Annan interview
571 'Choreography is my . . . I pour into it' FA to Walter Terry, DV

ILLUSTRATION CREDITS

Following page 248:

George Ashton: Courtesy of Anthony Russell-Roberts, Ashton Archive

Georgiana Ashton in 1916: Courtesy of Maria Saenz de Ashton

Georgie Ashton with her children: Courtesy of Elsie Ashton de Pinillos

Charlie and Frederick Ashton: Courtesy of Anthony Russell-Roberts, Ashton Archive

Edith Ashton: Courtesy of Anthony Russell-Roberts, Ashton Archive

Georgie Ashton in Lima: Courtesy of Anthony Russell-Roberts, Ashton Archive

Frederick Ashton with Maud Lawson: Courtesy of Anthony Russell-Roberts, Ashton Archive

Frederick Ashton with Frances James: Courtesy of Rambert Dance Company Archives

Edith Ashton's wedding: Courtesy of Anthony Russell-Roberts, Ashton Archive

Billy Chappell by Edward Burra: Private collection

Charleston, 1932: Courtesy of Tate Gallery Archives

Les Sablettes, Toulon, 1931: Barbara Ker-Seymer Collection, Courtesy of Barbara Roett

Iris March at Buster Tonge's house: Courtesy of Buster Tonge

Sophie Fedorovitch: Courtesy of Anthony Russell-Roberts, Ashton Archive

Bronislava Nijinska with dancers: Courtesy of Anthony Russell-Roberts, Ashton Archive

Frederick Ashton as Nijinsky: Courtesy of Barbara Ker-Seymer

Frederick Ashton as Gertrude Stein: Courtesy of Anthony Russell-Roberts, Ashton Archive

Frederick Ashton as a *Vogue* model: Courtesy of Barbara Ker-Seymer

Frederick Ashton as Queen Victoria: Courtesy of Anthony Russell-Roberts, Ashton Archive

Alice Astor photographed for *Vogue*: Cecil Beaton, Courtesy of Sotheby's, London
June Brae as The Rich Girl: Cecil Beaton, Courtesy of Sotheby's, London
Frederick Ashton with cabaret singer Jimmy Daniels: Courtesy of Anthony Russell-Roberts, Ashton Archive
Michael Somes in Cambridge: Courtesy of Anthony Russell-Roberts, Ashton Archive
Frederick Ashton and Gerald Berners: Cecil Beaton, Courtesy of Sotheby's, London
Pamela May and Michael Somes: Courtesy of Anthony Russell-Roberts, Ashton Archive
Dick Beard: Courtesy of Philip Dyer
Alexander Grant: George Platt Lynes, Courtesy of Mrs. Russell Lynes
The Royal Ballet on tour: Courtesy of Anthony Russell-Roberts, Ashton Archive
Frederick Ashton with Gertrude Stein, Alice B. Toklas, Bobby Helpmann: Billy Chappell Collection, Courtesy of Tommy Elliott
Tony Lizzul: Tony Lizzul Collection, Courtesy of William Funck
Martyn Thomas: Courtesy of Anthony Russell-Roberts, Ashton Archive
Tony Dyson: Courtesy of Anthony Russell-Roberts, Ashton Archive
Brian Shaw: Courtesy of Anthony Russell-Roberts, Ashton Archive
Frederick Ashton at Chandos Lodge: Courtesy of Prudence Penn
Frederick Ashton at Sternfield: Courtesy of Prudence Penn
Frederick Ashton in the folly at Chandos Lodge: Cecil Beaton, Courtesy of Sotheby's, London
Frederick Ashton in his garden at Chandos Lodge: Courtesy of Ross MacGibbon

Following page 408:
Frederick Ashton and Marie Rambert in *A Tragedy of Fashion*: Yvonde, Courtesy of Ballet Rambert Archives
Ninette de Valois in *A Wedding Bouquet*: Courtesy of Anthony Russell-Roberts, Ashton Archive
Frederick Ashton and Margot Fonteyn in *Nocturne*: Anthony
Beatrice Appleyard and Walter Gore in *Rio Grande*: Courtesy of Anthony Russell-Roberts, Ashton Archive
Margot Fonteyn and William Chappell in *Rio Grande*: Courtesy of Anthony Russell-Roberts, Ashton Archive
Valses nobles et sentimentales: Angus McBean, Courtesy of the Harvard Theatre Collection
Margot Fonteyn and Frederick Ashton in *Façade*: Courtesy of Anthony Russell-Roberts, Ashton Archive
Grouping from *Symphonic Variations*: Baron

Margot Fonteyn and Michael Somes in *Scènes de ballet*: Courtesy of Philip Dyer

Nicholas Magallanes in *Illuminations*: George Platt Lynes

Margot Fonteyn and Michael Somes in *Sylvia*: Felix Fonteyn

Lynn Seymour and Christopher Gable in *The Two Pigeons*: Houston Rogers, Courtesy of Theatre Museum, Victoria & Albert Museum

Nadia Nerina and David Blair in *La Fille mal gardée*: Houston Rogers, Courtesy of Theatre Museum, Victoria & Albert Museum

Antoinette Sibley and Anthony Dowell in *The Dream*: Houston Rogers, Courtesy of Theatre Museum, Victoria & Albert Museum

Derek Rencher and Deanne Bergsma in *Enigma Variations*: Houston Rogers, Courtesy of Theatre Museum, Victoria & Albert Museum

Margot Fonteyn and Rudolf Nureyev in *Marguerite and Armand*: Zoë Dominic

Frederick Ashton and Robert Helpmann in *Cinderella*: Houston Rogers, Courtesy of Theatre Museum, Victoria & Albert Museum

FURTHER READING

Richard Aldington, *Death of a Hero*
Mark Amory, ed., *The Letters of Evelyn Waugh*
Thoinot Arbeau, *Orchésographie*
Brooke Astor, *Footprints*
Cecil Beaton, *My Royal Past by Baroness von Bülop as told to Cecil Beaton*
– *The Wandering Years*
– *Ballet*
– *Self-Portrait with Friends: The Selected Diaries 1922–1974* (ed. Richard Buckle)
Cyril Beaumont, *Anna Pavlova*
– *The Vic-Wells Ballet*
– *Complete Book of Ballets*
– *The Sadler's Wells Ballet*
– *Supplement to the Complete Book of Ballets*
– *Ballets of Today*
– *Ballets Past and Present*
Sergei Bertensson and Jay Leyda, *A Lifetime of Music*
Michael Billington, *Peggy Ashcroft*
Alexander Bland, *The Royal Ballet: The First 50 Years*
– *Observer of the Dance*
Alan Blythe, *Remembering Britten*
Nicholas Boyle, *Goethe: The Poet and the Age*
Sarah Bradford, *Sacheverell Sitwell*
Lionel Bradley, *Sixteen Years of Ballet Rambert*
Gyles Brandreth, *The Funniest Man on Earth: The Story of Dan Leno*
Richard Buckle, *Buckle at the Ballet*
Humphrey Carpenter, *Benjamin Britten: A Biography*
Charles Castle, *La Belle Otéro: The Last Great Courtesan*
William Chappell, *Fonteyn: Impressions of a Ballerina*
– *Edward Burra: A Painter Remembered by His Friends* (ed.)

Kenneth Clark, *The Other Half*
A. V. Coton, *A Prejudice for Ballet*
Anthony Crickmay and Clement Crisp, *Lynn Seymour*
Arlene Croce, *Sight Lines*
Ninette de Valois, *Step by Step*
Peter Dickinson, *The Music of Lord Berners*
Anton Dolin, *Markova: Her Life and Art*
– *Autobiography*
– *Last Words*
Frances Donaldson, *The Royal Opera House in the Twentieth Century –
A Twentieth-Century Life*
Lord Drogheda, *Double Harness*
Ashley Dukes, *Jew Süss: A Tragic Comedy in Five Scenes Based upon the
Romance of Lion Feuchtwanger*
Dorée Duncan, Carol Pratl and Cynthia Splatt, *Life into Art: Isadora
Duncan and Her World*
T. S. Eliot, *Four Quartets*
Maurice Emmanuel, *The Antique Greek Dance*
Winifred Ferrier, *The Life of Kathleen Ferrier*
Ann Fleming, *Letters* (ed. Mark Amory)
E. M. Fotheringham, *A Cash Concern*
Elizabeth Frank, *Margot Fonteyn*
A. H. Franks, *Twentieth-Century Ballet*
Brian Friel (after Turgenev), *A Month in the Country*
Monk Gibbon, *The Tales of Hoffmann: A Study of the Film*
John Gielgud with John Miller, *Shakespeare Hit or Miss?*
Alan M. Gillmor, *Erik Satie*
Victoria Glendinning, *Edith Sitwell: A Unicorn Among Lions*
– *Vita*
Rumer Godden, *The Tale of the Tales: The Beatrix Potter Ballet*
– *A House with Four Rooms* (Autobiography Vol. 2)
J. Goodwin, ed., *Peter Hall's Diaries: The Story of a Dramatic Battle*
Cecil Gray, *Musical Chairs*
Ivor Guest, *Adventures of a Ballet Historian*
Montague Haltrecht, *The Quiet Showman: Sir David Webster and the
Royal Opera House*
Arnold Haskell, *Balletomania*
– *The Ballet in England*
Hans Werner Henze, *Music and Politics: Collected Writings 1953–81*
David Herbert, *Second Son*
Polly Hill and Richard Keynes, ed., *Lydia and Maynard: The Letters of
Lydia Lopokova and John Maynard Keynes*

Philip Hoare, *Serious Pleasures: The Life of Stephen Tennant*

Janet Hobhouse, *Everybody Who Was Anybody: A Biography of Gertrude Stein*

Spike Hughes, *Opening Bars*

Wallis Hunt, *Heirs of Great Adventure*

Aldous Huxley, *Letters* (ed. G. Smith)

Roy Jenkins, *Charles Dilke: A Victorian Tragedy*

Stephanie Jordan and Andrée Grau, *Following Sir Fred's Steps: Ashton's Legacy*

Michael Kennedy, *Portrait of Elgar*

– *Portrait of Walton*

Gelsey Kirkland, *The Shape of Love*

Lincoln Kirstein, *Movement and Metaphor*

Constant Lambert, *Music Ho! A Study of Music in Decline*

Marie-Jaqueline Lancaster, *Brian Howard: Portrait of a Failure*

Tanaquil LeClercq, *The Ballet Cookbook*

Jane Lee, *Derain*

Alvilda Lees-Milne and Rosemary Verey, *The Englishman's Garden*

John Lehmann, *I Am My Brother*

– *A Nest of Tigers: Edith, Osbert and Sacheverell Sitwell in Their Times*

Maurice Leonard, *Markova: The Legend*

Peter Lethbridge, *Kathleen Ferrier*

Pierre Loti, *Japan (Madame Chrysanthème)* (trans. Laura Ensor)

Michael Luke, *David Tennant and the Gargoyle Years*

Ursula Powys Lybbe, *The Eye of Intelligence*

Alastair Macaulay, *Some Views and Reviews of Ashton's Choreography*

Nesta MacDonald and Francis Francis, *Tamara Karsavina*

P. W. Manchester, *Vic-Wells: A Ballet Progress*

Klaus Mann, *The Turning Point: An Autobiography*

Dame Alicia Markova, *Markova Remembers*

John Martin, *Ruth Page: An Intimate Biography*

Léonide Massine, *My Life in Ballet*

Roger McHugh, *Ah Sweet Dancer: W. B. Yeats and Margot Ruddock – A Correspondence*

Robert Medley, *Drawn from the Life: A Memoir*

Diana Menuhin, *Fiddler's Moll: Life with Yehudi*

Penelope Middelboe, *Edith Olivier: From Her Journals 1924–48*

John Mills, *Up in the Clouds, Gentlemen Please*

Donald Mitchell, *Benjamin Britten: Death in Venice*

Donald Mitchell and Philip Reed, ed., *Letters from a Life: Selected Letters and Diaries of Benjamin Britten*

Miss Anne Moberly and Miss Eleanor Jourdain, *An Adventure*

Keith Money, *Anna Pavlova: Her Life and Art*
June and Doris Langley Moore, *The Pleasure of Your Company*
Andrew Motion, *The Lamberts*
Paul Murray, *T. S. Eliot and Mysticism: The Secret History of Four Quartets*
Rollo H. Myers, *Ravel: Life and Works*
Barbara Newman, *Striking a Balance: Dancers Talk About Dancing*
– *Antoinette Sibley: Reflections of a Ballerina*
J. R. Noble, ed., *Recollections of Virginia Woolf*
Patrick O'Connor and Bryan Hammond, *Josephine Baker*
Serge Obolensky, *One Man in His Time*
George Orwell, *Such, Such Were the Joys*
Ouida, *Moths*
Ruth Page, *Page by Page*
Tim Page and Vanessa Weeks Page, *Selected Letters of Virgil Thomson*
Brenda Dean Paul, *My First Life: A Biography*
Charles Payne, *American Ballet Theater*
John Percival, *Theatre in My Blood: A Biography of John Cranko*
Donna Perlmutter, *Shadowplay: Antony Tudor's Life in Dance*
Anthony Powell, *Messengers of Day*
Mrs Richard Powell, *Edward Elgar: Memories of a Variation*
Peter Quennell, *The Wanton Chase; An Autobiography from 1939*
Francis Rose, *Saying Life: The Memoirs of Francis Rose*
Harold Rosenthal, *Opera at Covent Garden: A Short History*
Elizabeth Salter, *Helpmann: The Authorised Biography*
Joseph Sandon, *Façade and Other Early Ballets by Frederick Ashton*
Meryle Secrest, *Kenneth Clark: A Biography*
Victor Seroff, *The Real Isadora*
Richard Shead, *Constant Lambert*
Moira Shearer, *Balletmaster: A Dancer's View of George Balanchine*
Edith Sitwell, *Selected Letters*
Sacheverell Sitwell, *Liszt*
Robert Skidelsky, *John Maynard Keynes: The Economist as Saviour 1920–1937*
Walter Sorell, ed., *The Dance Has Many Faces*
Frances Spalding, *Vanessa Bell*
Gertrude Stein, *The Autobiography of Alice B. Toklas*
– *Everybody's Autobiography*
– *Selected Writings* (ed. Carl Van Vechten)
– *Selected Letters*
Igor Stravinsky and Robert Craft, *Dialogues and a Diary*
– *Memories and Commentaries*

Roy Strong, *Strong Points*
Peter Townsend, *Dual in the Dark*
Ivan Turgenev, *A Month in the Country* (trans. by Isaiah Berlin)
– *First Love* (trans. V. S. Pritchett)
Parker Tyler, *The Divine Comedy of Pavel Tchelitchew*
Carl Van Vechten, *Parties*
Hugo Vickers, *Cecil Beaton*
Gore Vidal, *Palimpsest*
Solomon Volkov, *Balanchine's Tchaikovsky*
Kathrine Sorley Walker, *Ninette de Valois*
Susanna Walton, *William Walton: Behind the Façade*
Audrey Williamson, *The Art of Ballet*
– *Contemporary Ballet*
– *Ballet Renaissance*
– *Ballet of Three Decades*
Virginia Woolf, *The Diaries* (ed. Anne Olivier Bell)
Dorothy Wordsworth, *Journals* (ed. E. de Selincourt)
Francis Wyndham, *The Theatre of Embarrassment*
W. B. Yeats, *Uncollected Prose*, vol. 2

INDEX